S0-AKP-076

THE
SPORTS
BOOK

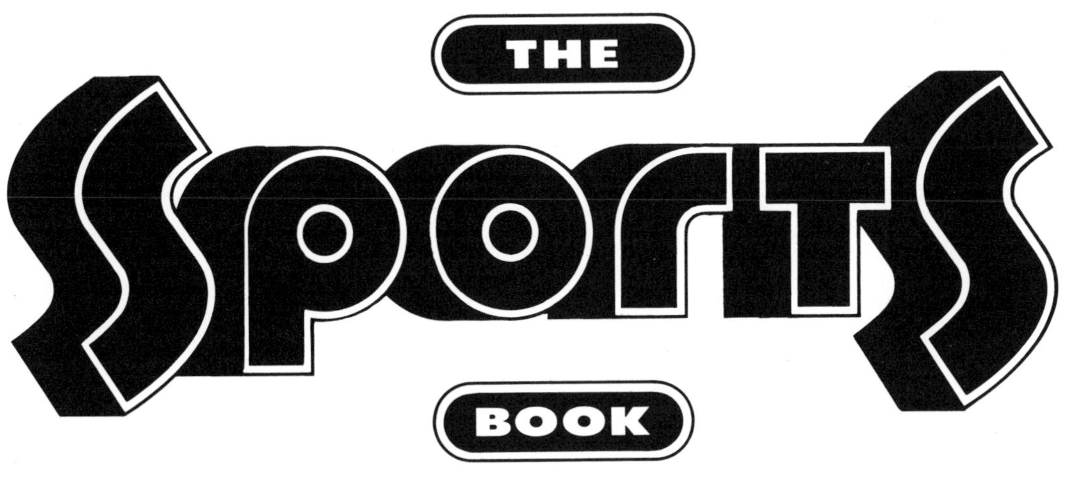

AN UNABASHED ASSEMBLAGE OF HEROES STRATEGIES RECORDS & EVENTS

Edited
by
Min S. Yee
and
Designed
by
Donald K. Wright
Illustrations
by
Sandra Forrest

Holt, Rinehart and Winston
New York

Acknowledgements

The Spitter & The Greaser from *Me and the Spitter: An Autobiographical Confession,* by Gaylord Perry with Bob Sudyk. Copyright © 1974 by Gaylord Perry and Bob Sudyk. Reprinted by permission of the publishers, Saturday Review Press/E.P. Dutton & Co., Inc.

No Cheering in the Press Box from *No Cheering in the Press Box* recorded and edited by Jerome Holtzman. Copyright © 1973, 1974 by Jerome Holtzman. Reprinted by permission of Holt, Rinehart and Winston, Publishers.

Man O' War—De Mostest Hoss Dat Ever Was from the book *The History of Thoroughbred Racing in America* by William H.P. Robertson. © 1964 by William H.P. Robertson. Published by Prentice-Hall, Inc., Englewood Cliffs, New Jersey.

Satchel Paige in His Own League, copyright, Los Angeles *Times,* reprinted with permission.

The Gallup Poll from The Gallup Poll Survey released Sunday, January 21, 1973 by George Gallup, Jr. Princeton, New Jersey.

From the Gallup Poll Survey released Sunday, January 16, 1972, by George Gallup, Jr. Princeton, New Jersey.

The Bigger They Are, The Harder They Fall from the book *In This Corner* by Peter Heller, © 1973 by Peter Heller. Reprinted by permission of Simon & Schuster, Inc.

Games People Should Play from *The Ultimate Athlete,* by George Leonard, © 1974 by George Leonard. Reprinted by permission of The Viking Press, Inc.

Published simultaneously in Canada by Holt, Rinehart and Winston of Canada, Limited.

Library of Congress Catalog Card Number: 75-5457
ISBN: 0-03-015101-5

First Edition

Printed in the United States of America

"What, then, is the right way of living?
Life must be lived as a play,
playing certain games,
making sacrifices,
singing and dancing,
and then a man will be able to
propitiate the gods, and defend
himself against his enemies, and win
in the contest."

—PLATO

For Keetja Hollowell, Tai Reed,
Min Lorentz with love.

To Jan, Steve, Sherry and Sandy
with love

Contents

TRACKS

FIELDS & GREENS

Yankee Stadium, New York

STADIUMS

Astrodome, Houston

THE SEVEN GREATEST SERIES

By Richard Pietschmann

Nine baseball writers pick the greatest World Series. Which would you pick?

With a hangover and the bases loaded, Ol' Pete Alexander fanned Tony Lazzeri.

The World Series was born in a calm New England autumn, in a time when Lowells talked only to Cabots and Cabots talked only to God, in a time when proper Bostonians strolled the Common, Brahmins walked on the water of the Charles, and the people, bless them, picnicked in the Fens.

It was a time when baseball was decidedly improper but it was also a time of young cultural sinew, of muscle-flexing and outdoor fun. It was a time for sport and competition and when the World Series was born on October 1, 1903, it was born raw, raucous and unbridled. The game was played roughly, even cruelly at times.

Broken ribs and slashed legs were as common as weeds in the outfield. A pair of sharpened spikes was required equipment. If a ball was fouled out of play, a softened replacement was ready to be sneaked into the game. Baselines were secretly banked for the home team's bunts. If a batted ball rolled too far, an outfielder was ready with another, hidden in the tall outfield grass. The lights of flashing mirrors darted wildly around the eyes of batters and outfielders. Sometimes, crowds would assault a team on the diamond or literally chase them out of town. Sometimes, an entire team would be thrown in jail.

It was a beginning, though, and the 16,242 fans loved it. After a missed year in 1904 because the two leagues were still feuding, the World Series was enshrined as America's autumnal sporting event. It became a kind of love affair and it has somehow endured time, wars, depressions, the death of God and even the onrush of new spectator sports and new modes of entertainment. The October classic still captures imaginations, flutters hearts and sometimes inspires more arguments than religion or politics. We're here to inspire one more argument: what is the greatest World Series of them all? There are 71 to think about, quite a few losers and quite a few doozers, enough to give you the warm fuzzies all over.

Here's what our nine experts think:

1926
New York Yankees
vs.
St. Louis Cardinals

Murray Olderman, West Coast Editor, Newspaper Enterprise Association

The best World Series *"because it came at a time when we were all still romantic and naive and baseball was an experience that left memories. So that even if you were too young to have been there, you knew all the details of Grover Cleveland Alexander ambling out of the bullpen in the seventh and final game to face Tony [Poosh 'Em Up] Lazzeri with the bases loaded—Ol' Pete nursing a hangover because he won the day before—and the Yankees trailing by only one run. Those were the mighty Yankees of Ruth and Gehrig and Dickey. And Lazzeri lined one toward the left field stands that barely curved foul. Then struck out! But what people don't remember is that Alexander still had to nurse that lead through two more innings to clinch the first world championship for the Cardinals. I didn't even have to look it up."*

Syndicated sportswriter Olderman has left little out of the final game, except that Babe Ruth walked in the ninth with two out and Meusel and Gehrig on deck—and incredibly was thrown out trying to steal second to end the Series. The Babe otherwise had a good Series, hitting four home runs and hitting .300, while Combs, Dugan and Gehrig all batted well over .300. Rogers Hornsby hit only .250 for St. Louis, but Alexander won two games, lost none and compiled a surprising 1.33 earned run average (at age 39) against the mighty Yankees.

1934
Detroit Tigers
vs.
St. Louis Cardinals

Jim Murray, sports columnist, *Los Angeles Times*

"Had everything. Plus the Dean Boys, the Gas House Gang, Schoolboy Rowe, Hank Greenberg, Charley Gehringer, Frankie Frisch—even Leo Durocher."

The swashbuckling Gashouse Gang came from behind to win the National League flag on the last day of the season, then went on to

Probably no team was wilder than the Gashouse Gang. Only Dizzy was daffier, dizzier, wilder and more outrageous than the rest, but he was good.

tame the Tigers in seven games. Dizzy and Paul won 49 games that season (Dizzy had 30) and split the four Series wins at two apiece. Dizzy was carried off on a stretcher in the fourth game when he subbed as a pinch runner, then came back the next day and won the fifth contest. Paul won the sixth game with a single, 4-3. In the dressing room after the game, Dizzy hugged Paul, wrestled him down to the floor, while yelping "You're the greatest pitcher the Dean family ever had." In the third inning of the final game, Dizzy got two hits and the Gang scored seven runs.

1947 New York Yankees vs. Brooklyn Dodgers

Red Barber, retired sportscaster

"1947 was Jackie Robinson's first year, and Jackie was the first black player in the World Series, which generated additional excitement. Every game was noteworthy, especially the fourth when Bill Bevens of the Yankees walked 10 Dodgers but with two out in the last of the 9th hadn't given a hit. Lavagetto pinch-hit a double, broke up the no-hitter, knocked in two runs and won the game 3-2 for Brooklyn. In the sixth game Gionfriddo took a home run away from Joe DiMaggio. Game seven was the air-tight relief job by Joe Page."

Red, for years the broadcast voice of the Dodgers and then the Yankees and now retired, highlights the first of the great Yankee-Dodger battles of the late Forties and Fifties when the cry in Brooklyn was inevitably "wait until next year." The 1947 set saw plenty of drama, as Red noted. Basically the series was a duel between two of the greatest relief pitchers in history, Joe Page and Hugh Casey. And even after 25 years, fans still debate whether Bucky Harris should have walked Pete Reiser in the ninth inning of that lost no-hitter. Going into the ninth, Bevens had a no-hitter and the Yankees were ahead 2-1. Bruce Edwards hit a spectacular fly to left but it was caught. Carl Furillo drew a walk. It was Bevens' ninth pass of the game. Spider Jorgensen fouled out to George McQuinn behind first base for the second out. The Yankees sent in Pete Reiser to bat for the pitcher, Casey. Reiser, however, could barely run because of a leg injury. Al Gionfriddo went in to run for Furillo. Gionfriddo got the signal to steal second and a good throw would have nailed him but Yogi Berra, playing his first full season, threw high and wide. With first base open, Harris ordered Reiser walked. Up to the plate stepped Cookie Lavagetto, batting for Eddie Stanky, and lined a double off the right field wall. The Yankees lost this game but went on to win the Series.

Bill Bevens had a no-hitter going with two men out in the ninth. Then, Cookie Lavagetto lined a double off the right field wall the instant this photo was taken.

1952 New York Yankees vs. Brooklyn Dodgers

Roger Kahn, author, *The Boys of Summer*
columnist, *Esquire*

"A great Dodger team, built around Jackie Robinson, played magnificent baseball in the fullness of their youth and sinew. A dollar Yankee team, with better pitching, won in seven games. The computer beat the people, but the people lost bravely."

This Series, as Kahn notes, was a seesaw affair, with first one team winning and then the other. Finally the Yankees broke the string with back-to-back victories in the sixth and seventh games, again denying Brooklyn the championship. Hitting was generally anemic, with the Yankee squad managing a combined .216 and the Dodger contingent an even worse .215. The difference was Yankee stoppers Allie Reynolds and Vic Raschi, who won two games each and allowed less than two runs each game. Johnny Mize hit .400 for the Yankees and hit three home runs; super-sophomore Mickey Mantle bombed two more and batted .345; Yogi Berra added two round-trippers and Gene Woodling batted .348. Duke Snider had the best Series for the Dodgers, matching Mize with four home runs and hitting .345, as did Pee Wee Reese. But it was a case of more Casey Stengel magic and "wait until next year" again for Brooklyn.

—The New York Yankees have won 27 of the last 55 American League pennants. They won six of eight between 1921-28, seven of eight between 1936-43 and 14 of 16 between 1949-65.

—In World Series batting, Mickey Mantle or Yogi Berra led in: home runs, walks, doubles, hits, runs, runs batted in and at bats.

—In World Series pitching, Whitey Ford leads in: wins, strikeouts, innings pitched, games pitched, walks and losses.

—Only Christy Mathewson has pitched four shutout Series games.

—The greatest sluggers in World Series history are: Babe Ruth, Lou Gehrig, Al Simmons and Lou Brock.

—Lou Brock holds the Series record for stolen bases.

—Only Don Larsen has ever pitched a perfect World Series no-hitter; the Yankees, 1956.

—Only two managers, John McGraw of the New York Giants and Casey Stengel of the New York Yankees, have won 10 pennant races.

—Roger Peckinpaugh committed more errors than anyone in Series history: eight for the 1925 Washington Senators.

—Pee Wee Reese won the losing player's share six times in seven Series, a record.

—Babe Ruth ranks second in World Series earned run average, 0.87 for his pitching in 1916 and 1918 Series. His record is 3-0.

—Babe Ruth holds the record for pitching the longest winning World Series game, 14 innings in 1916.

1955 New York Yankees vs. Brooklyn Dodgers

Bill Libby, author, *Baseball's Greatest Sluggers*, and *Star Pitchers of the Major Leagues*

"The 1955 World Series may not have been the best played of all time but it was for me the most exciting because after losing seven classics the Brooklyn Dodgers finally won one and the one they won was over their hated rival and the most dominant team of all time, the Yankees, who won 10 classics in the 16 years between 1947 and 1962. I was not a Dodger fan, but rather a Giant fan. But the Dodgers had the most devoted fans a sporting team has had and their reward after years of frustration in a Series that went the limit of seven games was thrilling to anyone who loves sports. I was not as cynical about sports as I am now. It is known as Johnny Podres' Series and he was real—imperfect but tough. Sandy Amoros made a great catch. But it is the event that I remember—Dem Bums beating the mighty Yankees at last in seven tough games and the whole world seemingly in love with them and baseball and sports."

It was Brooklyn's one and only world championship. To win it, Walt Alston's Bums broke an Old Series jinx by becoming the first team to win a seven-game Series after losing the first two games. The first two Brooklyn losses only made the final win sweeter. Sandy Amoros' incredible catch came in the sixth inning of the seventh game, with Billy Martin on second and Gil McDougald on first, and Brooklyn leading 2-0. With Berra batting, Amoros moved from left to left center since the Yankee catcher was considered a consistent right field hitter. Yogi, however, hit a high fly down the left field line, about a foot inside fair territory. Amoros ran a full 100 feet hoping to catch the ball before smashing into the barrier. He did. But McDougald, not believing the catch would be made, had rounded second. With a relay by Pee Wee Reese to Gil Hodges, Amoros doubled McDougald for a second out. The Yankees challenged again in the eighth but Podres worked himself out of the jam. At 3:43 p.m., October 4, 1955, the last putout was made and the Dodgers finally became champions. As Podres put it, "This *is* next year."

Tommy Agee, the New York Met who made this spectacular catch in the 1969 Series, was a member of the worst team in baseball history to win a World Series.

For years, the Brooklyn Dodgers suffered the ignominious line, "Wait 'til next year." In 1955, Johnny Podres, the Series pitching hero said it best: "This is *next year."*

1969 New York Mets vs. Baltimore Orioles

Pete Axthelm, sports editor, *Newsweek*

"Because it was won by the most improbable team and very possibly the worst team in baseball history. Even now, just six years afterwards, all of the stars of that series have disappeared from baseball."

It was an incredible Series. The simple fact that the Mets got to the Series at all was amazing. (Just the year before, the Shea Stadium misfits had escaped the cellar by one game.) The boroughs of New York were delirious, free beer on Flatbush Avenue, free champagne on Madison. The air in the glass-and-mortar canyons of Manhattan filled with

paper, confetti and ticker tape. After years of spectacular failure, the misfits had become gods.

Naturally, everyone (well, almost everyone) had predicted a Baltimore sweep, and after Mike Cuellar wiped out the Mets and Tom Seaver in the first game, 4-1, not many folks thought otherwise. But then came game two, and a substitute utility infielder named Al Weis, who was batting .215, cracked a single to drive home the first Mets win. The third game belonged to Tommie Agee. As the first batter, Agee poked a home run to put the Mets ahead. The New Yorkers added four more and won 5-0 but not before Agee made two fantastic catches in center field. With two on and two out, Agee raced after an Elrod Hendricks drive that would have hit the wall at the 396-foot marker. Running at full speed, he grabbed the ball backhanded on the top edge of his webbing—and held on. The second was a diving catch of a rocket liner with the bases loaded in the seventh. The next day it was Ron Swoboda's turn to make the diving save and the Mets won 2-1. In the final game, with the Orioles leading 3-2 in the seventh, Al Weis popped a homer into the left field stands to tie the game. In the eighth, Swoboda drove in the winning run and later scored himself on a Boog Powell error. Once again, Shea Stadium erupted. Only this time, it was for an entirely different reason.

1960
New York Yankees
vs.
Pittsburgh Pirates

Mel Durslag, sports columnist,
Los Angeles Herald-Examiner
Bob Prince, sportscaster, Pittsburgh Pirates
Dick Schaap, author, sportscaster and editor,
Sport Magazine

(Durslag) *"There was carbonation of some kind in every game. And, of course, the seventh [featuring Mazeroski's home run] was probably the most exciting World Series match every played. Nor have fans ever burst their moorings as the Pittsburgh following did afterward. To indicate how crazy things got, the Pittsburgh band, following Mazeroski's homer, started playing, "When Irish Eyes Are Smiling." If the game had been broken up by someone named McCarthy, the band might have played a mazurka."*

(Prince) *"I was down in the locker room at the end of the eighth inning of the seventh game to interview the Pirates. Then the Yankees tied the game 9-9. As I started out of the locker room [to go back to the broadcast booth to join Mel Allen], Bill Mazeroski hit a home run to win the game. Three minutes later, I was on television interviewing the World Champions, and I did not know how we won the game! I had not seen it, and everybody forgot to tell me how we won. Imagine how I felt an hour later when I found out that the hero of the game didn't have five seconds' air time with me."*

(Schaap) *"It was the best World Series because Lenny Bruce was appearing at a night club in Pittsburgh, and the games were played in the daytime, and I could catch Lenny's act twice a night. I took him to the seventh game—Mazeroski's home run—and he loved it...the first and last baseball game he ever saw."*

In this 57th World Series, the Yankees set a potent number of Series records—highest batting average (.338), most hits (91), most total bases (142), most runs (55), and most runs batted in (54)—and lost to the Pirates, four games to three. But let's get on to the magic. The Series was tied, three games to three. Thirty-six thousand fans gathered in cramped Forbes Field for the deciding game and coming off a 12-0 lambasting by the Yankees the day before, they were a bit shell-shocked. The Pirates jumped on Yankee pitchers Bob Turley and Bill Stafford for four runs in the first two innings, however, and the fans relaxed a bit. The game coasted along through innings three and four. Then the Yankee counterattack began. Bill Skowron homered off Vernon Law in the fifth. In the sixth, with two men on base, Yogi Berra, swinging what looked like a four-wood, golfed a high fly into the second deck in right field. It was good for three runs. A fourth run in the same inning put the Yankees ahead, 5-4. The seventh inning was quiet. With two out in the top of the eighth, Berra walked, Skowron and John Blanchard singled and Clete Boyer ripped a double down the left field line, Yanks 7, Pirates 4. The Pirates, however, came back in the bottom of the eighth, scoring five runs.

The Yankee counterattack was unabated. Bobby Richardson and Dale Long led off the top of the ninth with singles. Roger Maris flied out. Mickey Mantle hit an easy single, scoring Richardson. That made it 9-8, Pirates. With McDougald on third, pinch-running for Long, and Mantle on first, Berra smashed a vicious drive to first baseman Jim Nelson. Nelson made a heart-stopping catch but tagged first instead of throwing to second to start the double play. That enabled Mantle to get back to first, and McDougald to score the tying run, 9-9.

Bill Mazeroski was the leadoff batter in the bottom of the ninth. Ralph Terry, the fifth Yankee pitcher in the game, hummed in with a ball, low and outside. The second pitch was a fast slider, chest-high. Mazeroski swung and connected. The crowd was quiet, as it soared over the left field wall. Berra raced back to the ivy-covered wall and watched it go over. The full impact of the home run hit Mazeroski as he was nearing second base. He threw his cap in the air, jumped up and down and flailed his arms like a robot gone wild. By the time he rounded third, a screaming, running, jumping welcoming committee of fans and teammates was blocking the base path. He made it home, though, and the Pirates won, 10-9.

—Dusty Rhodes batted in seven runs his first four times at bat in the 1954 Series.

—Twice, Babe Ruth hit three home runs in a Series game, in 1926 and 1928.

—Bob Gibson holds the record for the most strikeouts in a seven-game Series, 35, 1968. Sandy Koufax fanned 23 guys in a four-game Series, 1963.

—Bob Gibson struck out the most batters in one Series game, 17, in 1968.

—Highest World Series attendance mark was established in 1959 at 420,784 when the L.A. Dodgers beat the Chicago White Sox, four games to two.

Games tied at three apiece, score tied 9-9 at the bottom of the ninth and Bill Mazeroski's blast cleared the left field wall to win the 1960 Series for the Pirates. There were so many people on the field, however, he barely made it around to home plate.

A Chronology of Baseball Eras and

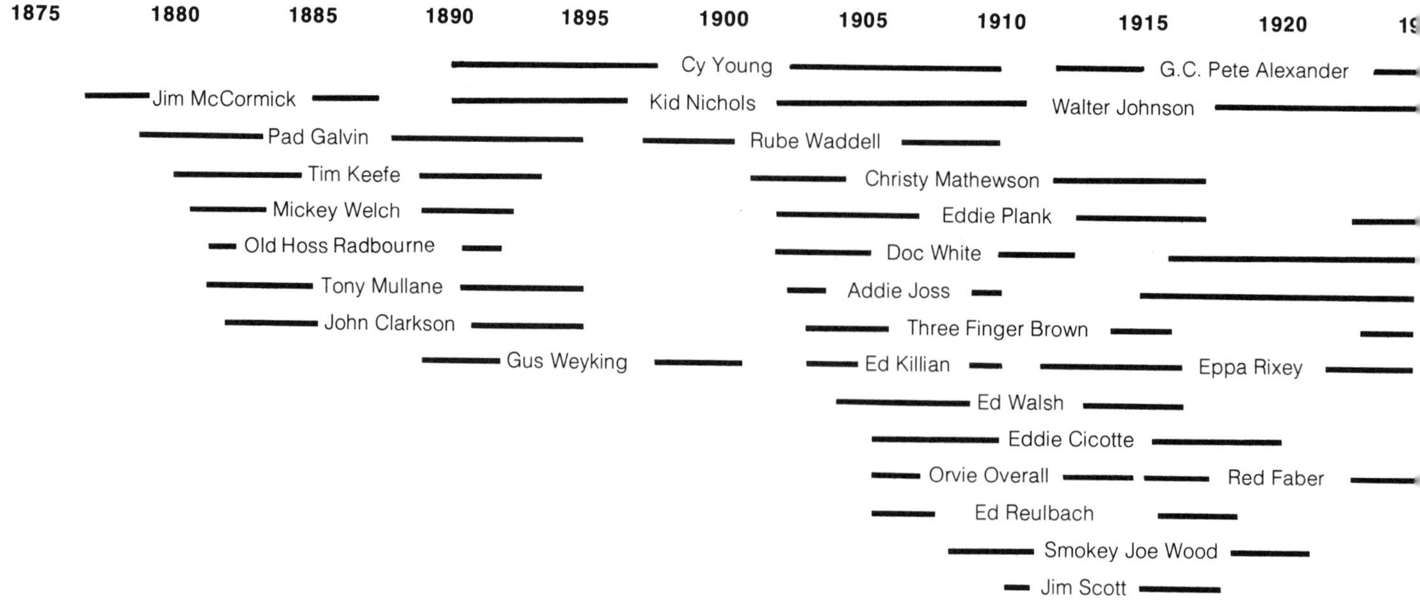

1875 1880 1885 1890 1895 1900 1905 1910 1915 1920 19

Cy Young
G.C. Pete Alexander
Jim McCormick
Kid Nichols
Walter Johnson
Pad Galvin
Rube Waddell
Tim Keefe
Christy Mathewson
Mickey Welch
Eddie Plank
Old Hoss Radbourne
Doc White
Tony Mullane
Addie Joss
John Clarkson
Three Finger Brown
Gus Weyking
Ed Killian
Eppa Rixey
Ed Walsh
Eddie Cicotte
Orvie Overall
Red Faber
Ed Reulbach
Smokey Joe Wood
Jim Scott

Greatest Pitchers - 2,000 Or More SO's - ERA 2.39 Or Lower - 250 Or More Wins

Cap Anson
Ty Cobb
Dan Brouthers
Pete Browning
Nap Lajoie
Tip O'Neill
Honus Wagner
Sam Thompson
Tris Speaker
Ed Delahanty
Eddie Collins
Billy Hamilton
Joe Jackson
Hugh Duffy
Jesse Burkett
George Sisler
Wee Willie Keeler

Greatest Hitters - Batting Average 325+ - Home Runs 350+ - Batting Average/Home Runs

The Softball Era 1845-1880
Baseball rules were first set down by Alexander Cartwright who insisted that the ball be pitched underhand, that a batter be allowed only one base even if a batted ball went into the outfield, and that a ball caught on one bounce was an out. There were no strikes or balls. A very soft, bouncy ball made of India rubber was used. But, by 1858, the pitching distance had been moved back to 45 feet, called strikes had been introduced with four strikes constituting a strikeout. Beginning in 1871, a batter could call for a high pitch or a low one. In 1880, a strikeout was three strikes and eight balls (it had been nine) entitled a batter to walk.

The Transitional Era 1881-1899
The pitcher's box was moved back to 50 feet in 1881. By 1883, a pitcher's delivery was allowable anywhere up to shoulder heighth, and a foul ball caught on the first bounce was no longer an out. More significant changes came in 1884: the pitcher could throw overhand, taking only one step before delivery; six balls made a walk. In 1887, the batter was no longer allowed to call for a high or low pitch. Walks counted as a base hit. The strike zone was set at the top of the shoulders to the bottom of the knees. In 1889, a walk was issued on four balls. Finally, in 1893, the pitching distance was lengthened to 60 feet 6 inches.

The Deadball Era 1900-1919
In 1900, the width of home plate was increased from a 12-inch square to a 17-inch wide 5-sided plate. The following year a foul became a strike. In 1903, the rules limited the height of the pitcher's mound to 15 inches above the level of home plate and the base lines. Beginning in 1908, pitchers were prohibited from scuffing, soiling or nicking any new ball being put into play. A slightly livelier ball was introduced into play in 1909 but it was essentially a "dead ball." The quality of the ball is one of the main reasons that 14 of the 15 leading pitchers in lifetime earned run average played during this era.

the Game's Greatest Players

25 1930 1935 1940 1945 1950 1955 1960 1965 1970 1975

Warren Spahn
Ferguson Jenkins
Bob Feller
Bob Gibson
Lefty Grove
Robin Roberts
Tom Seaver
Carl Hubbell
Sandy Koufax
Ted Lyons
Jim Bunning
Burleigh Grimes
Dazzy Vance
Early Wynn
Mickey Lolich
Don Drysdale
Red Ruffing
Camilo Pascual
Jim Kaat
Bobo Newsom
Juan Marichal
Sam McDowell

Ted Williams
Babe Ruth
Joe Dimaggio
Hank Aaron
Lou Gehrig
Stan Musial
Jimmy Foxx
Willie Mays
Mickey Mantle
Gil Hodges
Mel Ott
Duke Snider
Rogers Hornsby
Yogi Berra
Willie McCovey
Harry Heilmann
Ralph Kiner
Frank Robinson
Bill Terry
Ernie Banks
Riggs Stephenson
Harmon Killebrew
Heinie Manush
Eddie Mathews
Billy Williams
Al Simmons
Earle Combs
Al Kaline
Paul Waner
Rocky Colavito
Frank Howard
Orlando Cepeda
Norm Cash

The Modern Baseball Era [Daytime Play] **1920-1945**
The Modern Baseball era began with the lively "jack-rabbit" ball. Made from stronger, stouter Australian yarn, enabling the ball to be wound tighter, this new ball traveled farther when hit and bounced higher and quicker. The year this ball was introduced, Babe Ruth's home run output doubled, from 29 to 58.
A cushioned cork-center ball was introduced in 1926 and the following season the Babe poled his 60 homers During the Deadball Era, fans would see one homer every four games; in the modern era that figure would multiply eight times, to almost two per game.

The Modern Baseball Era [Nighttime Play] **1946-Present**
On August 9, 1946, for the first time in major league history, every game scheduled that day was played at night. It meant the beginning of night baseball, accomodating more fans who could come to the ball park during nonworking hours. Most important, however, was the effect on the batting eye. The introduction of night games led to a general lowering of batting averages. In 1947, the first black was allowed to play major league ball. In 1950, the strike zone was lowered to between the batter's armpits and the top of his knees, reversed in 1963 and reversed back again in 1969. In 1959, baseball stadiums were required to have a minimum distance of 325 feet to both fences along the foul lines and a 400-foot minimum to the center field fence. This rule change meant several parks, including Yankee Stadium, Fenway Park, and Cleveland and Baltimore's Memorial Stadiums, had to push their fences back, making it more difficult to hit home runs. As an experiment for three years, the American League in 1973 introduced a "designated hitter" rule. The rule states that a designated pinch hitter may bat for a pitcher without the pitcher leaving the game.

A Double Chronology of Playing Careers and Rule Changes

Year **Rule or Playing Change**

1845 Formulating the first set of playing rules, Alexander Cartwright has the game end at 21 aces (runs), insists that the ball be pitched underhand, allows only one base if batted ball goes out of the infield and has every ball (including fouls) caught on one bounce declared an out. Three outs make a hand (inning).

1848 A baserunner can be thrown out at first base.

1857 Game is set at nine innings.

1858 Pitching distance set at 45 feet. Called strikes introduced. A strikeout is four strikes.

1863 Balls and strikes called.

1871 Batter can call for a high pitch or a low one.

1872 Pitcher is allowed a snap delivery but must still pitch underhand.

Career Begun	Batter	Career Begun	Pitcher
1876	Cap Anson, .333 ba	**1877**	Will White, 227 wins
		1878	Jim McCormick, 264 wins

1879 Nine balls entitled batter to a walk.

1879	Dan Brouthers, .344 ba	**1879**	Pud Galvin, 361 wins

1880 Pitching distance moved back to 45 feet. Strikeout is three strikes. Eight balls entitled a batter to a walk.

1880	Roger Connor, .318 ba	**1880**	**Tim Keefe, 343 wins, 2,531 so**
		1880	Mickey Welch, 311 wins

1881 Pitcher's box moved back to 50 feet instead of 45.

		1881	Old Hoss Radbourn 308 wins
		1881	Tony Mullane 286 wins

1882 Seven balls make a walk.

1882	Pete Browning .341 ba	**1882**	John Clarkson 327 wins
		1882	Charlie Buffinton 230 wins

1883 Foul ball caught on first bounce no longer an out.

1883	Tip O'Neill .327 ba		

1884 Six balls make a walk. Pitcher can throw overhand. Pitcher restricted to taking only one step before delivery.

		1884	Bob Caruthers 217 wins

1885 One side of the bat allowed to be flat.

1885	Sam Thompson .332 ba		
1885	Denny Lyons .323 ba		

1886 Seven balls make a walk.

1887 Batter no longer allowed to call for a high or low pitch. Strike zone set at top of shoulders and bottom of knees. Walk issued on five balls. Walk is credited as a hit. Strikeout on four strikes.

1887	George Van Haltren .319 ba	**1887**	Gus Weyhing 266 wins

1888 Strikeout on three strikes.

1888	Ed Delahanty .346 ba		
1888	Billy Hamilton .344 ba		
1888	Hugh Duffy .329 ba		

1889 Walk issued on four balls.

1890	Jesse Burkett .342 ba	**1889**	Amos Rusie 248 wins
1891	Joe Kelley .321 ba	**1890**	Cy Young 511 wins, 2,803 so
1892	Willie Keeler .345 ba	**1890**	Kid Nichols 362 wins
		1891	Clark Griffith 235 wins

1893 Pitching distance lengthened to 60 feet 6 inches. Was supposed to have been 60 feet but field plans read 60′0″ and surveyor thought 0″ was 6″.

1894 Foul bunts become strikes.

1895 Maximum bat diameter increased to 2¾ inches, an increase of ¼ inch. Infield fly rule is adopted.

1896	Nap Lajoie .339 ba	**1897**	Rube Waddell 2.16 era, 2,316 so
1897	Honus Wagner .329 ba	**1897**	Jack Powell 248 wins
		1898	Sam Leever 247 wins
		1898	Vic Willis 243 wins
		1899	Iron Man Joe McGinnity, 248 wins

1900 Width of home plate increased from 12-inch square to a 17-inch wide 5-sided plate.

		1900	Christy Mathewson, 2.13 era, 374 wins, 2,502 so

1901 Foul becomes a strike.

		1901	Eddie Plank 2.34 era, 325 wins, 2,246 so
		1901	Doc White 2.38 era
		1902	Addie Joss 1.88 era
		1902	Bob Ewing 2.49 era
		1902	George Mullin 229 wins

1903 Pitcher's mound limited to 15 inches above the level of home plate and the base lines.

		1903	Three Finger Brown 2.06 era, 239 wins
		1903	Chief Bender 2.46 era
		1903	Ed Killian 2.38 era
		1904	Ed Walsh 1.82 era
		1904	Hooks Wiltse 2.48 era
1905	Ty Cobb .367 ba	**1905**	Eddie Cicotte 2.37 era
		1905	Orvie Overall 2.23 era

1905 Ed Reulbach 2.28 era
1905 Lefty Liefield 2.47 era
1906 Eddie Collins .333 ba
1907 Tris Speaker .344 ba
1907 Walter Johnson 2.17 era, 416 wins, 3,506 so
1907 Nap Rucker 2.42 era

1908 Pitchers prohibited from scuffing, soiling or nicking a new ball put into play.

1908 Joe Jackson .356 ba
1908 Smokey Joe Wood 2.03 era
1908 Hippo Vaughn 2.49 era

1909 Slightly livelier cork-center baseball introduced. Bunt foul on third strike is a strikeout.

1909 Jim Scott 2.32 era
1911 G.C. Pete Alexander 373 wins, 2,199 so
1912 Jeff Tesreau 2.43 era
1912 Herb Pennock 240 wins
1912 Eppa Rixey 266 wins
1912 Stan Coveleski 216 wins
1912 Hooks Dauss 221 wins
1912 Wilbur Cooper 216 wins
1913 Edd Roush .323 ba
1914 Babe Ruth .342 ba, 714 hr
Red Faber 254 wins
1914 Harry Heilmann .342 ba
1914 Sad Sam Jones 228 wins
1915 Rogers Hornsby .358 ba 301 hr
1915 Dazzy Vance 2,045 so
1915 George Sisler .340 ba
1915 Sam Rice .322 ba
1915 Ken Williams .319 ba
1916 Burleigh Grimes 270 wins
1917 Ross Youngs .322 ba
1918 Waite Hoyt 237 wins

1920 Lively "jack-rabbit" ball introduced, made from stronger, stouter Australian yarn. Enables ball to be wound tighter, travel farther when hit and bounce higher and quicker. The spitball, a favorite pitch, is abolished.

1920 Pie Traynor .320 ba
1921 Riggs Stephenson, .336 ba
1921 Kiki Cuyler .321 ba
1923 Lou Gehrig .340 ba, 493 hr
1923 Ted Lyons 260 wins
1923 Bill Terry .341 ba
1923 Earl Whitehill 218 wins
1923 Heinie Manush .330 ba
1924 Al Simmons .334 ba, 307 hr
1924 Red Ruffing 273 wins
1924 Earl Combs .325 ba
1924 Charlie Gehringer .320 ba
1924 Chick Hafey .317 ba
1925 Jimmy Foxx .325 ba, 534 hr
1925 Lefty Grove 300 wins, 2,266 so
1925 Mickey Cochrane .320 ba
Fred Fitzsimmons 217 wins

1926 Cushioned cork-center ball introduced.

1926 Paul Waner .333 ba
1926 Babe Herman .324 ba
1926 Mel Ott 511 hr
1928 Chuck Klein .320 ba, 300 hr
Carl Hubbell 253 wins
1928 Mel Harder 223 wins
1929 Earl Averill .318 ba
1929 Bobo Newsom 2,082 so
1930 Hank Greenberg 331 hr
1931 Paul Derringer 223 wins
1932 Joe Medwick .324 ba
1932 Arky Vaughn .318 ba
1933 Bob Johnson 288 hr
1934 Rudy York 277 hr

1935 Cincinnati and Pittsburgh introduced the first night baseball game.

1936 Joe DiMaggio .325 ba, 361 hr
1936 Bob Feller 266 wins, 2,581 so
1936 Johnny Mize 359 hr
1938 Joe Gordon 253 hr
1939 Ted Williams .344 ba, 521 hr
1939 Early Wynn 300 wins, 2,334 so
1941 Stan Musial .331 ba 475 hr
1941 Hank Sauer 288 hr
1942 Warren Spahn 363 wins, 2,583 so
1943 Gil Hodges 370 hr

1946 On August 9, for the first time, every game scheduled that day is a night game.

1946 Ralph Kiner 369 hr
1946 Yogi Berra 358 hr
1946 Del Ennis 288 hr
1946 Bobby Thomson 264 hr

1947 The first black, Jackie Robinson, plays for a major league team.

1947 Duke Snider 407 hr
1947 Ted Kluszewski 279 hr
1947 Vic Werty 266 hr
1947 Larry Doby 253 hr
1948 Robin Roberts 286 wins, 2,357 so
1949 Roy Sievers 318 hr

1950 Strike zone lowered to batter's armpits and top of his knees.

1950 Joe Adcock 336 hr
1950 Whitey Ford 236 wins
1951 Willie Mays 660 hr
1951 Mickey Mantle 536 hr
1951 Frank Thomas 286 hr
1952 Eddie Mathews 512 hr
1953 Ernie Banks 512 hr
1953 Al Kaline 399 hr
1954 Hank Aaron 733 hr
1954 Camilo Pascual 2,167 so
1954 Harmon Killebrew, 559 hr
1955 Roberto Clemente, .317 ba
1955 Jim Bunning 224 wins, 2,855 so
1955 Rocky Colavito 374 hr
1955 Sandy Koufax 2,396 so
1955 Ken Boyer 282 hr
1955 Brooks Robinson 258 hr
1956 Frank Robinson 574 hr
1956 Don Drysdale 2,486 so
1957 Roger Maris 275 hr
1958 Frank Howard 382 hr
1958 Orlando Cepeda 379 hr
1958 Norm Cash 377 hr
1958 Bob Allison 256 hr

1959 Baseball stadiums required to have a minimum distance of 325 feet to both fences along foul lines and 400 feet minimum to center field fence. This rule change meant several parks, including Yankee Stadium, Fenway Park, and Cleveland and Baltimore's Memorial Stadium, had to push their fences back making it more difficult to hit home runs in those parks.

1959 Willie McCovey 435 hr
1959 Bob Gibson 248 wins, 3,057 so
1959 Billy Williams 392 hr
1959 Jim Kaat 2,009 so
1960 Ron Santo 342 hr
1960 Juan Marichal 2,302 so
1961 Boog Powell 303 hr
1961 Sam McDowell 2,424 so
1961 Carl Yastrzemski 303 hr
1962 Willie Stargell 346 hr

1963 Strike zone goes back to top of the shoulders and bottom of knees.

1963 Dick Allen 319 hr
1963 Mickey Lolich 2,540 so
1965 Ferguson Jenkins 2,045 so
1967 Tom Seaver 2.38 era, 1,856 so

1969 Strike zone back down to armpits and top of knees. Pitcher's mound lowered to 10 inches above home plate and base lines.

1973 American League tries designated hitter rule for three years. Rule states that a designated pinch hitter may bat for a pitcher without the pitcher leaving the game.

The Changing Character of Baseball

Years	The Eras	Greatest Batters By BA[1]	Greatest Batters By HR[2]	Greatest Pitchers By ERA[3]	Greatest Pitchers By Wins[4]	By SO[5]
1845-1880	Softball Era	2	0	0	4	1
1881-1899	Pre-Baseball Era	10	0	1	7	2
1900-1919	Deadball Era	8	1	20	6	5
1920-1945	Modern Era—Day	11	10	0	7	5
1946-	Modern Era—Night	0	24	1	1	11
	Total Players	31	35	22	25	24

1 Lifetime batting average of .325 or higher.
2 Lifetime home run total of 300 or more.
3 Lifetime earned run average of 2.50 or less.
4 Lifetime wins of 250 or more.
5 Lifetime strikeout total of 2,000 or more.

GREAT MOMENTS IN BASEBALL

July 18-September 8, 1914 Staffed with a bunch of castoffs and misfits, the Boston Braves found themselves exactly where they might have expected to be in the National League standings after the mid-season mark had been crossed. They were dead last. Then, they began to move. Nondescript pitchers like Bill James, Dick Rudolph and Lefty Tyler started winning games. Cubs castoff Johnny Evers (of Tinkers-to-Evers-to-Chance fame) fielded tight around second base and Rabbit Maranville scooped up everything in sight at short. Although the team batted a paltry .251 by September 2, they had passed the league-leading New York Giants and by September 8, they had clinched the pennant. Then, they went to do World Series battle with the mighty Philadelphia Athletics. Connie Mack wasn't worried about the newly-dubbed Braves "Miracle Team." Behind the fearsome hitting attack of Eddie Collins, Frank "Home Run" Baker and Stuffy McInnis (who with Hack Barry made up Mack's "$100,000 Infield"), the Tall Tactician boasted of an awesome pitching staff which included three Hall-of-Famers (Chief Bender, Eddie Plank and Herb Pennock) and two other impressive starters, Bullet Joe Bush and Bob Shawkey. The Athletics expected a light outing. It's been said that all baseball fans believe in miracles; the only question is how *many* they believe in. There was one more. The Braves whomped the almighty Athletics in four straight games, 7-1, 1-0, 5-4 and 3-1. Two Boston batters, Evers and Hank Gowdy, batted .438 and .545 during the series, while the entire Philadelphia team was stunned into batting a puny .172.

October 10, 1924 For 18 years Walter Johnson had labored hard and mightily for the Washington Senators, and for 18 years the Senators never won a pennant. The Big Train, his admirers feared, just might retire from baseball without having won a World Series game, much less having appeared in one. By 1924, Johnson had won 376 games. He was 37 years old, and running out of pitching time. The Yankees had won the pennant the past three consecutive years and looked a cinch to repeat for a fourth. But something happened: the gods stepped in. The Senators won their first pennant. The old man they called The Big Train won 23 games and notched a 2.72 earned run average, leading the league in both departments. He also led in games started, shutouts, strikeouts and winning percentage. At last, the greatest pitcher of his time would play in a World Series. In the first game, Johnson was shelled for 14 hits and lost, 4-3. In game five, he was blasted for 13 hits and lost, 6-2.

On October 10, the Senators and the New York Giants were even up, three games apiece. In the last and deciding game, going into the bottom of the eighth, Washington had used up three pitchers and was behind by two runs, 3-1. But somehow they got the bases loaded, and with two men out, Bucky Harris hit a grounder down to third baseman Freddy Lindstrom which hit a pebble and bounced over his head. Two runs scored, tying the game. The Big Train came in to relieve at the top of the ninth. The gods stepped in again. In the bottom of the twelfth, with the score still tied at 3-3, the Giants' catcher Hank Gowdy tripped over his own face mask trying to catch a foul pop-up by Muddle Ruel. In his second chance, Ruel smashed a double to left. Earl McNeely came up, hit a grounder to Lindstrom and that ball *also* hit a pebble and bounced over his head. Ruel scored, winning the Series for Washington. The Big Train had won a World Series. The gods smiled: they were happy.

Raucous Boston fans break through police lines after Honus Wagner struck out in the final game of the first World Series, held in 1903.

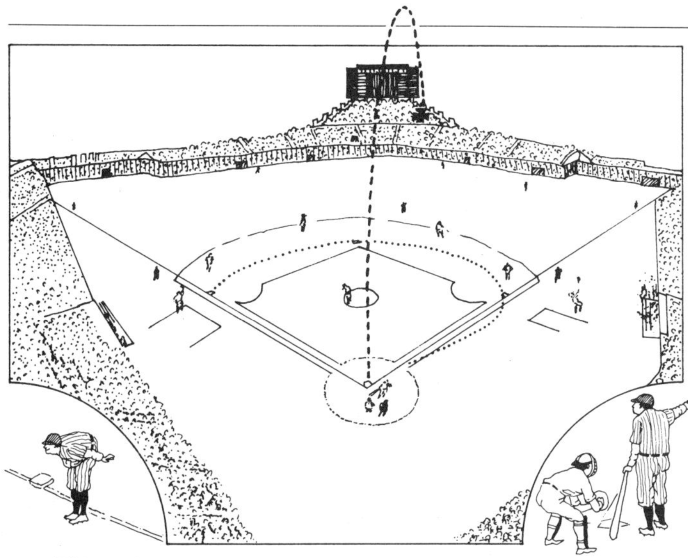

This is the famous finger-pointing shot that the Babe called.

October 1, 1932 There was a lot of bad feeling between the New York Yankees and the Chicago Cubs in the World Series of 1932. The Yanks would sweep the series, four games to zip, but not before both dugouts got off the greatest salvoes of the game in the form of oral vilification. Babe Ruth, then in the twilight of his career, was ridden mercilessly by the Chicago bench. When Chicago pitcher Charlie Root had worked a no-balls, two-strike count on Ruth, the Cubs bench went wild with its laughter and derision. Tapping the dirt from his cleats, Ruth stepped back into the batter's box and, with finger extended, pointed toward the center field stands. Or, was it Charlie Root he was pointing at? Or, did Ruth mean that he had one strike left? No one will ever know. What we'd like to think is that the Babe pointed to center field, calling his shot, because he drilled the next pitch into Wrigley Field's center field bleachers. The home run itself was real enough and, ironically, it turned out to be the Babe's last World Series homer.

October 3, 1951 The 1951 baseball season began rather drably for the New York Giants. Along with the Brooklyn Dodgers, they were favored to win the National League pennant, but the Giants lost the first 11 games they played. By August 12, as the season wound to a close, the Giants were behind the league-leading Dodgers by 13½ games. Then, the first miracle occurred: the Giants won 16 games in a row, 36 of their last 47 games, their last seven in a row. At season's end, they were tied with the Dodgers for first place, and a best-out-of-three playoff series would decide. The Giants won the first; the Dodgers the second. It all came down to nine innings of play at the Polo Grounds on October 3. It was an overcast day in New York but nothing was drearier than the hopes of Giant fans as their team went into the bottom of the ninth inning trailing the Dodgers, 4-1. Brooklyn's Don Newcombe had struck out their side in the eighth. It was time for a second miracle. Alvin Dark led off by driving a harmless single to right. Don Mueller stepped up and lashed another single to right. Monte Irvin weighed in but popped up. Newcombe was tiring now. He had asked earlier to be taken out. Whitey Lockman lined a fast ball to left, legging out two bases and scoring Dark. Mueller slid into third. The score was 4-2, one out, with runners on second and third. The Dodger manager, Chuck Dressen, waved Ralph Branca in from the bullpen. He would be facing Bobby Thomson, a tall lanky third baseman they called the Staten Island Scot because he had been born in Glasgow. The score was 4-2, one out, with runners on second and third. The tying runs were on and first base was open. Dressen could have walked Thomson, filling the bases to try for a force play, but that would have brought Willie Mays to the plate. Thomson waited. Branca drilled a fastball in for a strike, catching the inside corner. He threw another fastball. Thomson swung and connected, sending a rising line drive into the left field stands. That was the ball game. It took a second or two for the 34,320 spectators to fully realize what had happened. When they did, the Polo Grounds became a crush of mass hysteria. It was called "the miracle of Coogan's Bluff" and the "shot heard 'round the world."

August 23, 1936 The slender 17-year-old farm boy from Van Meter, Iowa, could be excused for being a little jittery. In fact, he was the only teenager in the American League. But he had a strong arm and the Cleveland Indians brought him up from high school and gave him a job working as a concessionaire just so he'd be handy if they needed him to pitch. They decided they needed him on August 23, against the St. Louis Browns. Well, the kid struck out the first eight men who faced him, then went on to strike out seven more before the game was over. That was one short of the league record. Three weeks later, he fanned 17 batters in a game, breaking the record. That farm boy, immediately nicknamed Rapid Robert, was Bob Feller and when his pitching days were over 17 years later, he had hurled more no-hitters than anyone, struck out more men in a game and in a season than anyone, and won 266 games. Had he not spent four years in military service, his lifetime totals would have been phenomenal. When his career ended, he pointed back to August 23, 1936, as his greatest moment. His reason? Because his father, who had taught him how to pitch, was there.

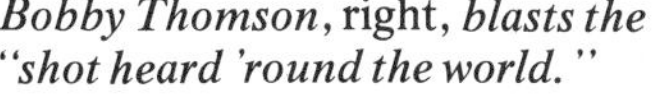

Bobby Thomson, right, *blasts the "shot heard 'round the world."*

...AND THERE IT GOES!

Highs in Hitting from your national pastime

Hits per 162-Game Schedule
(average over career)

1.	Ty Cobb	223.88	4,192
2.	George Sisler	221.59	2,812
3.	Al Simmons	214.12	2,927
4.	Nap Lajoie	212.34	3,251
5.	R. Hornsby	210.19	2,930
6.	J. DiMaggio	206.53	2,214
7.	T. Speaker	204.12	3,515
8.	Lou Gehrig	203.82	2,721
9.	H. Heilmann	200.75	2,660
10.	Paul Waner	200.38	3,152
11.	R. Clemente	199.73	3,000
12.	Rod Carew	199.37	1,266
13.	Honus Wagner	199.19	3,430
14.	Stan Musial	194.33	3,630
15.	Eddie Collins	189.79	3,311
16.	Henry Aaron	189.57	3,600
17.	Ted Williams	187.56	2,654
18.	Babe Ruth	185.95	2,873
19.	Jimmy Foxx	185.03	2,646
20.	Willie Mays	177.75	3,283
21.	Dick Allen	177.17	1,630
22.	C. Yastrzemski	173.45	2,267
23.	F. Robinson	172.52	2,900
24.	Ernie Banks	165.58	2,583
25.	Mickey Mantle	162.96	2,415

Rogers Hornsby, above right, *the* Rajah, *as they called him, was the greatest right-handed batter who ever lived, batting .402 over five seasons.*

The 1925 season, right, *was one of his last but Ty Cobb still slammed into third base like a hustling rookie.*

Nine Consecutive Batting Championships

When Ty Cobb first appeared in a minor league game in Augusta in 1904, he doubled and hit a home run. The manager kicked him off the club because Cobb homered when he was told to bunt. Three years later, with the help of an unknown minor league official named Grantland Rice, a 20-year-old Cobb won the American League batting crown with a .350 average and went on to win the batting championship for the next eight years. Then he missed one year and won the crown the following three. Twelve batting championships in 13 years. Quite a feat but that's not all the Georgia Peach accomplished in 24 years. When he retired from baseball in 1928, he left behind 90 records. Some are so spectacular they'll never be touched: highest lifetime batting average, .367; most hits, 4,191; most times hitting over .300, 23 consecutive seasons; most bases stolen, 892; most games played, 3,033; most times at bat; 11,429. Those records just can't be matched. True, Cobb never played a night game in his life. True, he never won a batting crown after the introduction of the jack-rabbit ball in 1920. And true, he averaged less than five home runs a season. But he is still considered by old timers to be the greatest hitter of all time. When baseball's Hall of Fame was completed in 1939, the very first momento to be hung in the museum was a pair of Cobb's baseball cleats with gleaming, shiny spikes. It was a most fitting gesture but the tenacious Georgia Peach would have probably spiked his way in anyway.

.402 For Five, Count 'em, Five Seasons

He was irascible as a person but there is no disputing the fact that Rogers Hornsby was the greatest right-handed batter in the history of baseball. For five seasons, between 1921 and 1925, the Rajah hit for averages of .397, .401, .384, .424 (the highest mark in modern baseball) and .403. In those five seasons, he went to bat 2,679 times and collected 1,078 hits. That is an incredible four-season mark of .404. His lifetime batting average of .358 is only surpassed by Ty Cobb, who threw right-handed but batted left. His stance at the plate was a sight to behold. With his feet close together, Hornsby stood as far back in the right-hand corner of the batter's box as regulations and white lines permitted. He was so dedicated to baseball that he refused to drink, smoke, or chase women. He wouldn't even attend movies, for fear of harming his eyesight. He led the National League in batting six years in a row, from 1920 to 1925.

59 Homers, .378 BA, 170 RBI's

It is regarded as the most outstanding set of hitting statistics amassed in one season by any batter, but even so it was not good enough to earn Babe Ruth the Triple Crown in batting. Two other batters hit for higher averages: Harry Heilmann hit .394 and his Detroit teammate Ty Cobb batted .389. It was the Sultan of Swat's second season with the New York Yankees, 1921, and for all the greatness that these statistics portended for the mighty batsman, he never would win the elusive Triple Crown. He would better his homer performance in one other season, 1927, by hitting 60. He would better his batting average in 1923, by batting .393. But in both of those his other stats slipped some, not much, but some. Never again would he drive in 170 runs. And never again would he compile an incredible slugging average of .846. (In 1920, his slugging average was .847.) No one else has ever come within 85 points of that mark.

84 Homers, Season; 1,000 Homers, Lifetime

There is a social tragedy attached to the greatest home run hitter of all time. He is in baseball's Hall of Fame, where he is credited with hitting 84 home runs in a season. And he is in the *Guinness Book of World Records,* where he is credited with smashing 800 home runs during his lifetime. (We estimate 1,000.) The tragedy is that Josh Gibson was black and could not play in the major leagues during his career. He played for the Homestead Grays of the Negro League, but that doesn't mean he didn't play in major league parks. He's the only man to have hit a fair ball over all the decks at Yankee Stadium. The round-trippers he poled over the left field wall in Washington's Griffith Stadium were of such power that old-timers still speak of them with hushed reverence. Those old-timers include Walter Johnson and Dizzy Dean.

Hitting Safely in 56 Consecutive Games

On May 15, 1941, Joe DiMaggio slashed a single in a game against the Chicago White Sox. For the next two months, the Yankee Clipper continued hitting, setting one of the most incredible records in major league baseball: hitting safely in 56 consecutive games. During that streak, he passed the American League mark of 41, set by George Sisler and the National League mark of 33, made by Rogers Hornsby. Stepping into the batters box, he faced some of the best pitchers of modern baseball: Preacher Roe, Lefty Grove, Bobo Newsom, Dutch Leonard, Bob Feller, Hal Newhouser, and Dizzy Trout.

He went to bat 223 times, collected 91 hits, including 15 home runs, four triples and 16 doubles. He batted in 55 runs, and crossed the plate 56 times himself. Baseball considered this feat so monumental, it awarded the Most Valuable Player trophy to DiMaggio despite the fact that Ted Williams batted .406 that same year. Ironically, DiMaggio only batted two points better than Williams' entire season average during his streak, and batted .321 for the other two-thirds of the season. But no one had seen a batter totally wipe out a previous record. The feat is not likely to be matched in the future, either. Night games are not conducive to good hitting. During this 56-game streak, DiMaggio played in only three night games. The streak was stopped on July 17 in Cleveland, and, yes, it was a night game.

—As far as we can determine, three men hold the distinction for hitting the least amount of home runs in their baseball careers. Ranked third on this list is Muddy Ruel, an American League catcher with a respectable .275 lifetime batting average. In 4,514 at bats, Ruel hit four home runs, one each in 1920, 1921, 1926 and 1927. Ranked second is 20-year veteran Johnny Cooney, who was an outfielder for the Dodgers and Boston Braves. In 3,364 times to the plate, he poled two out of the park, both in 1939, a very big year for him. Top of the list, though, is Floyd Baker who held the third baseman's job for the White Sox and the Washington Senators in the 1940s and 1950s. In 2,280 times at bat, he hit one home run. That was in 1949, after six full years in the major leagues. He was to play for six more seasons but no more homers came off his bat.

Above, *The* Yankee Clipper, *Joe DiMaggio, was one of the most powerful sluggers in baseball.*

Josh Gibson, upper left, *is considered one of the finest batters and catchers in the history of American baseball.*

Babe Ruth strides from home after hitting his 701st home run in Detroit in 1934, below left.

—"Joe," said Marilyn Monroe, just back from Korea, "you never heard such cheering." "Yes I have," Joe DiMaggio answered.

—"I would like to take the great DiMaggio fishing," the old man said. "They say his father was a fisherman. Maybe he was as poor as we are and would understand." *Ernest Hemingway, The Old Man and the Sea*

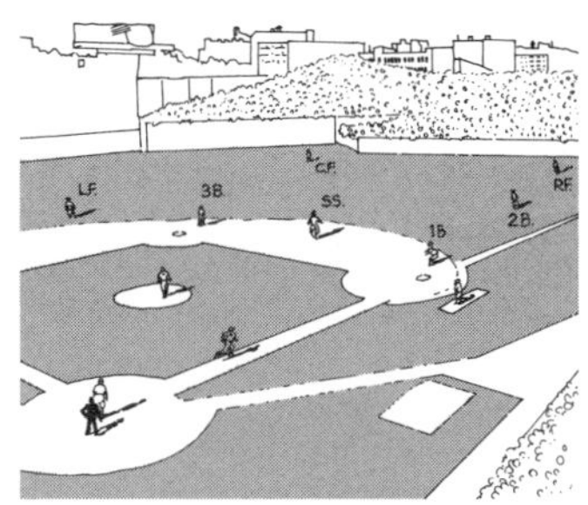

In 1946, a special defense against Ted Williams' nonstop hitting was devised by desperate American League teams. Known as the Williams Shift, it called for the third baseman to move to the right of second base, the second baseman to play deep at first and the first baseman to cover the foul line. Did it work? Well, the figures speak for themselves. That year Williams was second in the league in batting with .342 and led the league in slugging average—a whopping .667. Needless to say, the Shift was abandoned.

.406 In 1941 The number of major league ballplayers who have batted .400 or more in the 20th Century total exactly seven. The number of American Leaguers who have reached that mark can be counted on one hand, and the batters of this caliber who've played in the past 40 years is exactly one: his name is Theodore Samuel Williams.

In 1941, on the last day of the season, the Splendid Splinter (as Williams was called—and he was that) was batting exactly .39955, rounded off to an even .400. Not unselfishly, his teammates and coaches advised the 23-year-old to sit out that last day, a scheduled doubleheader, to protect his .400 mark. After all, no one had batted .400 for more than a decade. "Better sit it out, kid," his manager, Joe Cronin, advised. That advice was understandable. Not to Williams, though. He disdained a cheap record like a god disdaining mere mortality. In the first game, he laced out four hits, including a home run; in the second, he rapped out two more hits. That was six hits in eight trips to the plate, and good enough to raise his season average to .406. That feat hasn't been matched in 35 years. The closest anybody came was 16 years later. Yep, it was Williams, batting .388 at age 39.

Eight Homers in Eight Consecutive Games

Great records usually belong to great ballplayers. Dale Long was not a great ballplayer. He was a player who knew how to keep his bags packed. In 12 years, he played for 15 clubs. But in 1956 he was playing for Pittsburgh and it was with the Pirates that he flashed his comet across the major league heavens. The streak began on May 19, when he hit a home run. He hit another one in the next game, and the next, and the next, and the next. That made five. The record for homers was six in six consecutive games; it was a record held by five different batters. Long joined that company by banging number six off Curt Simmons. The suspense increased. Could he stand alone with seven in seven games? His last time up in the seventh game, with two swinging strikes against him, Long smashed the ball out of the park. After he crossed the plate, his teammates carried him into the dugout. Game eight was a night game, May 28. After striking out in the first inning, he sent a Carl Erskine curve ball into the right field seats. In those eight games, Long came to bat 28 times, got 15 hits and batted in 20 runs, with a batting average of .536. Not bad for a baseball hobo.

Match Wits with a Grandmother for $64,000

The summer of 1955 was marked by such memorable events as the summit conference at Geneva, the floods in the northeast, and the coming to television of a program called "The $64,000 Question." Two grandmothers—one an expert on the Bible, the other on baseball—won $32,000 each and quit. Here are the questions that M.C. Hal March asked septuagenarian Myrt Power. Try yourself along with the baseball grandma; the answers follow.

Questions

$64—What is the keystone base?

$128—What is meant when a player is "on deck"?

$256—What is meant by a "duster"?

$512—What is meant by a "Texas Leaguer"?

$1,000—A baseball manager dreams of a player who can hit safely every time he comes to bat. The record for batting safely—successive times at bat—stands at 12. Two men hold that record. Walt Dropo, who hit 12 successive times for Detroit in 1952, and one other man. For $1,000 name the other man who shares the record for successive hits since 1900.

$2,000—Bob Feller is the only pitcher to pitch three no-hitters,[1] but there are a number of pitchers who have pitched two no-hitters. Allie Reynolds is one. For $2,000 name a pitcher who pitched for Detroit and a pitcher who pitched for Cincinnati, both having two no-hitters to their credit.

$4,000—Babe Ruth leads all other batters in home runs hit during a season. His major league record is 60 homers in 1927. Two other major league batters are tied for second place,[2] having hit the same number of homers each, though in two different years. Now—for $4,000—I want three things—the names of the two batters—and the number of homers each hit.

$8,000—The St. Louis Cardinals have won the National League pennant at least nine times. Give me the exact dates of the last four times that the Cardinals won the pennant. You can give the four dates in any order you please.

$16,000—One of baseball's all-time highlights took place in the 1934 All-Star Game when Carl Hubbell struck out five men in a row. The brilliance of this performance can be measured by averaging the hitting record of those five American League sluggers. It comes out to .332. Now, for $16,000, name the five men struck out in succession by Carl Hubbell in the 1934 All-Star Game. You may list them in any order.

$32,000—The official record books list seven players who are credited with over three thousand hits during their careers in the major leagues. Ty Cobb heads the list with 4,191 hits garnered in his 24 years of play. Name the remaining six players who have a lifetime total of three thousand or more hits.

[1]The statement should have read "The only pitcher in modern times." After all, there were a couple of fellows named Larry Corcoran and Cy Young . . . Ed.

[2]Second place, to be fussy, belonged to a player named Babe Ruth. He hit 59 home runs in 1921 . . . Ed.

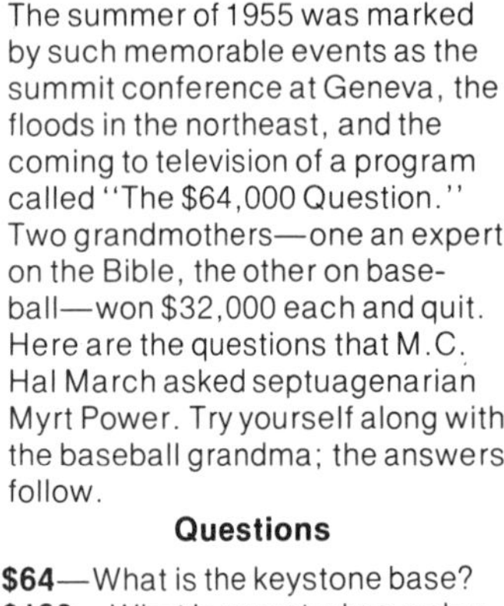

Answers

$64—Second base.

$128—He is the next batter up.

$256—A pitch thrown too close to the batter.

$512—A looping hit, too far out for the infield and too close in for the outfield.

$1,000—Frank (Pinky) Higgins for the Boston Red Sox in 1938.

$2,000—Virgil Trucks, Detroit, and Johnny Vander Meer, Cincinnati.

$4,000—Jimmy Foxx in 1932 and Hank Greenberg in 1938, 58 each.

$8,000—1946, 1944, 1943, 1942.

$16,000—Babe Ruth, Lou Gehrig, Jimmy Foxx, Al Simmons, Joe Cronin.

$32,000—Adrian (Cap) Anson, Honus Wagner, Napoleon Lajoie, Tris Speaker, Eddie Collins, Paul Waner.

61 Home Runs

For some reason, everyone seemed to hate him for it. But there was Roger Maris, slogging through the 1961 season, pounding baseballs over all the fences of the American League. Newspapers ran production charts. How many did the Babe have by this date? How close was Mantle (who ended up hitting 54 that same season)? It even seemed as if the press and the New York Yankees wanted Mantle to break the record. Writers jumped on Maris for breaking the record in 162 games instead of 154, as Ruth did.

No one mentioned the fact that major league pitching had improved significantly, that playing a night baseball schedule was much harder on batters, or even that Ruth's record came one season after the introduction of a cushioned cork-center ball that had a lot of bounce and was unperfected. And does anyone remember that in 1927, when Ruth hit 60, a ball which bounced from the field into the stands was scored as a home run? They jumped on Maris for being a .260 batter, an "unknown," and for performing well enough to better one of the most cherished records in baseball. By the time Maris had hit 50 homers, the Commissioner of Baseball decreed that, should Maris break the record, an asterisk would go by his name in the record book. The pressure was on Maris to accomplish the feat in 154 games. He didn't do it. He hit number 59 his first time up in Baltimore and had three more times at bat but struck out, flied out and grounded out. In his second time up, he smashed a prodigious foul that missed being number 60 by 10 feet.

Number 60 came a few days later in Yankee Stadium: it was a towering shot to the third deck. It came down to the final game of the season, and Maris connected with number 61 on his second turn at bat. But the normally shy Maris did not jubilantly jump around the base paths in celebration; instead, he remarked later in a slightly bitter tone: "If I never hit another home run, this is one they can never take away from me."

Roger Maris, the man with the asterisk on his name, belts one.

PICK YOUR BAT WITH THE GREATEST BATTERS

So you want to pick a bat with the greatest. But you don't know whether you can lift or even swing one like mighty Cap Anson who whipped around a hefty 44-ouncer. Or maybe you're a little fellow and feel more comfortable with something like Stan Musial's weight. The idea is to look over the chart, figure out what weight and height the great batter played at, whether he concentrated on batting average or home runs. Then after you've figured out who to emulate, pick a bat.

Batter	Years Played	Height	Weight	Lifetime B.A.	Lifetime H.R.	L of Bat	Wt. of Bat
Cap Anson	1876-1897	6′	227	.333	96	37″	44 oz.
Ed Delahanty	1888-1903	6′1″	170	.346	100	34½″	38 oz.
Honus Wagner	1897-1917	5′11″	200	.328	101	34½″	38 oz.
Ty Cobb	1905-1928	6′1″	175	.367	118	34½″	42 oz.
Eddie Collins	1906-1930	5′9″	175	.333	47	34″	34 oz.
Tris Speaker	1907-1928	5′11½″	193	.344	117	34½″	40 oz.
Babe Ruth	1914-1935	6′2″	215	.342	714	36″	42 oz.
Rogers Hornsby	1915-1937	5′11″	175	.358	301	34½″	38 oz.
Stan Musial	1941-1963	6′	175	.331	475	34½″	32 oz.
Jackie Robinson	1947-1956	5′11½″	195	.311	137	34½″	34 oz.
Mickey Mantle	1951-1968	5′11½″	195	.298	536	35″	34 oz.
Henry Aaron	1954-1975	6′	180	.311	733	35″	34 oz.
Roberto Clemente	1955-1972	5′11″	175	.317	240	36″	36 oz.
Pete Rose	1963-1975	5′11″	192	.309	117	35″	35 oz.

Four Home Runs in One Game

The 1961 season did not start out well for Willie Mays. His batting was off and he had been complaining of a persistent stomachache. In late April, when the Giants arrived in Milwaukee for a three-game series, Willie failed to make a hit in the first two games. Then, the night before the final game, he passed out in his room and had to be revived and given heavy medication. The following day, he did so poorly in batting practice that just before he came up to the plate in the first inning, he traded bats with teammate Joe Amalfitano. Amalfitano's bat was slightly heavier than the one Mays normally used. Nobody knows if that is what made the difference but his first time up Mays hit a Burdette slider 420 feet over the left center field fence. And the same thing happened the next time he came up. The Braves took out Burdette and sent in Seth Morehead but they couldn't stop Willie. His third time at bat, he hit a Morehead sinker so far out of the park, it couldn't be measured. Finally, in the eighth inning, his fifth time up, he hit his fourth and final homer of the game off relief pitcher Don McMahon. It tied the major league record for home runs in one game. Only eight others since the turn of the century had hit four home runs in a game. Mays drove in eight runs that game but more importantly broke his slump. He went on to hit 40 home runs that season, batting .308.

—Twenty-three times Lou Gehrig stepped up to the plate with the bases loaded. Yep, 23 times he hit a home run.

—In 1968, Frank Howard hit 10 home runs in six straight games.

—Johnny Burnett, remember him? In 1932 he went to bat 11 times in a game against the Cleveland Indians and collected nine hits. In a game of any length, no one else has matched that mark.

—Pinky Higgins managed the Boston Red Sox between 1955 and 1962 but he holds a more enduring baseball record. In 12 consecutive times at bat in 1938, Higgins made 12 hits.

—Ron Hunt, while playing for Montreal in 1971, suffered the unique distinction of being hit 50 times by pitched balls. That's a record.

—For years, Ty Cobb held the record for most stolen bases in a season. But that record was lost to Maury Wills of the Los Angeles Dodgers in 1962. Cobb, however, still holds the record for the most times caught stealing in a season, 38. Contrast that with the record for fewest times caught stealing in a season set by Max Carey in 1922. He was caught only twice in 53 attempts.

Others Who Have Made

Or More In Their Careers

Ty Cobb	4,192	1905-1928
Stan Musial	3,630	1941-1963
Hank Aaron	3,600	1954-1974
Tris Speaker	3,515	1907-1928
Honus Wagner	3,430	1897-1917
Eddie Collins	3,311	1906-1930
Willie Mays	3,283	1951-1973
Nap Lajoie	3,251	1896-1916
Paul Waner	3,152	1926-1945
Al Kaline	3,007	1953-1974
Cap Anson	3,022	1876-1897

Roberto Clemente, right, *swings at the pitch that became his 3000th, and last, major league hit.*

Hank Aaron watches the flight of the ball that became career homer number

breaking Babe Ruth's 40-year-old record.

Home Runs per 162-Game Schedule
(average over career)

1.	Babe Ruth	46.21	714
2.	Ralph Kiner	40.59	369
3.	H. Killebrew	38.87	572
4.	Henry Aaron	38.60	733
5.	H. Greenberg	38.49	331
6.	Jimmy Foxx	37.34	534
7.	Lou Gehrig	36.93	493
8.	Ted Williams	36.82	521
9.	Mickey Mantle	36.17	536
10.	Willie McCovey	35.77	435
11.	Willie Mays	35.73	660
12.	Eddie Mathews	34.74	512
13.	Dick Allen	34.67	319
14.	Willie Stargell	34.39	346
15.	F. Robinson	34.15	574
16.	Joe DiMaggio	33.68	361
17.	Rocky Colavito	32.92	372
18.	R. Jackson	32.88	189
19.	Ernie Banks	32.82	512
20.	Frank Howard	32.54	382
21.	Johnny Mize	30.86	359
22.	Duke Snider	30.76	407
23.	Mel Ott	30.30	511
24.	Stan Musial	25.43	475

3,000 Hits In more than 100 years of major league baseball only 12 batters have made 3,000 or more hits in their careers. For Roberto Clemente, however, number 3,000 was the last hit of his career. The hit came in the final game of the 1972 season; he was killed shortly after in an air crash while flying with relief supplies to aid the survivors of a devastating earthquake in Nicaragua.

Three Rivers Stadium was packed on September 30, 1972. Everyone had come to see Clemente try for The Hit. They had been frustrated the night before when the word "hit" flashed on the Three Rivers scoreboard but was changed to "error" when the ball bounced out of a fielder's glove. The crowd went home denied but returned the next night for Clemente's last shot of the season.

The first time he came up he flied out. Then, in the fourth inning, he slammed a rifle shot to left center. The ball took one bounce, hit the wall and Clemente had a double and his Hit. This time the entire scoreboard fired up. An umpire handed Clemente the ball while the crowd stomped and cheered. A shy man, Clemente stood smiling quietly on second base and raised his batting helmet as a gesture of thanks.

Clemente was the complete ballplayer. Possessed of running speed and a superb throwing arm, he is generally considered to be the finest right fielder to have played the game. After all, he had been known to throw strikes to home plate from 460 feet away and he had often charged in from right to field bloop bunts and throw men out at first base. Of his 3,000th hit, he said: "I give this hit to the fans of Pittsburgh and to the people of Puerto Rico." Baseball's Hall of Fame waived its five-year wait rule and voted him in the year following his death.

CHARTING THE GREATEST HITTERS

We've made our choice and it's Ted Williams, the Splendid Splinter. Disagree? then, check out our figures and make your own choice.

Batting Average

Ty Cobb	.367
Rogers Hornsby	.358
Ted Williams	.344
Babe Ruth	.342
Lou Gehrig	.340
Stan Musial	.331
Joe DiMaggio	.325
Jimmy Foxx	.325
Hank Aaron	.310
Willie Mays	.302

Slugging Average

Babe Ruth	.690
Ted Williams	.634
Lou Gehrig	.632
Jimmy Foxx	.609
Joe DiMaggio	.579
Rogers Hornsby	.577
Hank Aaron	.566
Stan Musial	.559
Willie Mays	.557
Ty Cobb	.513

At Bats Per RBI

Babe Ruth	3.79
Lou Gehrig	4.02
Ted Williams	4.19
Jimmy Foxx	4.23
Joe DiMaggio	4.44
Rogers Hornsby	5.16
Hank Aaron	5.28
Stan Musial	5.62
Willie Mays	5.72
Ty Cobb	5.83

At Bats Per Home Run

Babe Ruth	11.76
Ted Williams	14.79
Jimmy Foxx	15.23
Hank Aaron	16.15
Lou Gehrig	16.23
Willie Mays	16.49
Joe DiMaggio	18.89
Stan Musial	23.10
Rogers Hornsby	27.15
Ty Cobb	96.86

At Bats Per Walk

Ted Williams	3.82
Babe Ruth	4.09
Lou Gehrig	5.31
Jimmy Foxx	5.60
Stan Musial	6.86
Willie Mays	7.44
Rogers Hornsby	7.87
Joe DiMaggio	8.63
Hank Aaron	8.97
Ty Cobb	9.15

At Bats Per Strikeout

Ty Cobb	32.01
Joe DiMaggio	18.49
Stan Musial	15.76
Rogers Hornsby	12.04
Ted Williams	10.87
Lou Gehrig	10.14
Hank Aaron	8.92
Willie Mays	7.13
Babe Ruth	6.32
Jimmy Foxx	6.20

Composite Rankings

	Comp. Rank	B.A.	S.A.	AB/ RBI	AB/ HR	AB/ WALK	AB/ SO
Ted Williams	1	3	2	3	2	1	5
Babe Ruth	2	4	1	1	1	2	9
Lou Gehrig	3	5	3	2	5	3	6
Jimmy Foxx	4	8	4	4	3	4	10
Rogers Hornsby	5	2	6	6	9	7	4
Joe DiMaggio	5	7	5	5	7	8	2
Stan Musial	6	6	8	8	8	5	3
Ty Cobb	7	1	10	10	10	10	1
Hank Aaron	8	9	7	7	4	9	7
Willie Mays	9	10	9	9	6	6	8

It was almost baseball history but Mantle's blast was 6 feet short. Ted Williams' last homer was a dramatic finale to a great career.

Many people think Ty Cobb, far right, *was the greatest hitter of all time and Cy Young,* above, *was the greatest pitcher. Here are two charts which destroy the myth.*

The All-Time Greatest

Player*		Years Active	ERA	Difference in Winning Percentage**	Hits Allowed per 9 Innings Pitched Career	Strikeouts per 9 Innings Pitched Career	Walks issued per 9 Innings Pitched Career
1.	Tom Seaver	1967-74	2.38	139	7.1	7.7	2.4
2.	Walter Johnson	1907-27	2.17	103	7.5	5.3	2.1
3.	Sandy Koufax	1955-66	2.76	88	6.8	9.3	3.2
4.	Christy Mathewson	1900-16	2.13	79	7.9	4.7	1.6
5.	Rube Waddell	1897-10	2.16	48	7.5	7.0	2.4
6.	Bob Gibson	1959-74	2.79	78	7.4	7.3	3.0
7.	Juan Marichal	1960-74	2.84	76	8.1	5.9	1.8
8.	Smokey Joe Wood	1908-20	2.03	37	7.1	6.2	2.6
9.	G.C. Pete Alexander	1911-30	2.56	108	8.4	3.8	1.7
10.	Cy Young	1890-11	2.63	89	8.7	3.5	1.5
11.	Whitey Ford	1950-67	2.75	85	7.9	5.6	3.1
12.	Ferguson Jenkins	1965-	3.13	60	7.9	7.0	1.8
13.	Gaylord Perry	1962-	2.89	20	7.9	6.3	2.4
14.	Dizzy Dean	1930-47	3.03	84	8.8	5.3	2.1
14.	Don Drysdale	1956-69	2.95	9	8.1	6.5	2.2
15.	Catfish Hunter	1965-	3.22	61	7.6	5.6	2.5
15.	Nolan Ryan	1966-	3.04	-14	6.2	9.7	5.4
16.	Carl Hubbell	1928-43	2.97	63	8.7	4.2	1.8
17.	Steve Carlton	1965-74	3.02	45	8.1	7.1	3.2
17.	Dazzy Vance	1915-35	3.24	85	8.5	6.2	2.6
18.	Jim Bunning	1955-71	3.27	36	8.2	6.8	2.4
18.	Lefty Grove	1925-41	3.06	95	8.8	5.2	2.7
19.	Mickey Lolich	1963-	3.35	22	8.1	7.3	2.7
20.	Bob Feller	1936-56	3.25	59	7.7	6.1	4.2
21.	Warren Spahn	1942-65	3.09	54	8.3	4.4	2.5
22.	Robin Roberts	1948-66	3.41	48	8.8	4.5	1.7
23.	Red Faber	1914-33	3.15	48	9.0	2.2	1.8
24.	Jim Kaat	1959-	3.35	14	8.9	5.4	2.2
25.	Eppa Rixey	1912-33	3.15	11	9.3	2.7	2.2
26.	Ted Lyons	1923-46	3.67	72	9.7	2.3	2.4
27.	Early Wynn	1939-63	3.54	9	8.5	4.6	3.5
28.	Burleigh Grimes	1916-34	3.53	36	9.5	3.3	2.8

*Pitchers are ranked according to a composite which includes all of the categories listed on this chart: earned run average; difference in winning percentage; and hits, strikeouts and walks per nine innings pitched over their career. Currently active players are computed through the 1974 season.

**Modern day computers in major league baseball use the comparison between a pitcher's personal winning percentage and the winning percentage of his team as a gauge of the pitcher's performance. Thus, since the New York Mets had a team winning percentage of .501 while Tom Seaver (in the same years) had a winning pitching percentage of .640, Seaver's "difference in winning percentage" is 139. Conversely, the two teams Nolan Ryan pitched for had a winning percentage of .510; Ryan, however, has a winning percentage of .496. Thus, he did not win as often as his team did and his difference is a minus, -14. The implication is that Seaver greatly helped his team while Ryan did not.

1927 WHATTA YEAR!

It was the year Babe Ruth hit 60 out of the park. It was the year the Yankees won the Series in four straight. It was the year Harry Heilmann batted .398 and Paul Waner hit .380. It was the year Walter Johnson quit and the year before Ty Cobb would hang up his spikes. It was 1927 and one helluva vintage year it was.

Consider the three paragraphs at far right. In the first are a list of the major league ballplayers whose careers were predominantly between 1900 and 1926. The second paragraph lists names of men whose career began in 1928 or thereafter. In the final paragraph are the names of players who were active in the major leagues, but especially during the 1927 season. This is the total Baseball Hall of Fame list for *all* the major leaguers who spent most or all of their baseball careers in the 20th century.

If you're counting (as we do) then you'll note 23 names before 1927, 21 names after 1927, and 58 names for this vintage year. Of the major league ballplayers and officials who played in the 20th century and were eventually elected to the Hall of Fame, more than half played in 1927. It was the game's finest hour and baseball's finest crop.

The All-Time Greatest

Player*	Years Active	Lifetime Batting Average	Lifetime Slugging Average	Hits per 162-Game Schedule	Home Runs per 162-Game Schedule	RBI's per 162-Game Schedule
1. Babe Ruth	1914-35	.342	.690	186	46	144
2. Ted Williams	1939-60	.344	.634	188	37	130
3. Lou Gehrig	1923-39	.340	.632	204	37	149
4. Rogers Hornsby	1915-37	.358	.577	210	22	114
5. Jimmy Foxx	1925-45	.325	.609	185	37	134
6. Joe DiMaggio	1936-51	.325	.579	207	34	143
7. Stan Musial	1941-63	.331	.559	194	25	104
8. Ty Cobb	1905-28	.367	.513	224	6	105
9. Henry Aaron	1954-74	.310	.569	190	39	116
10. Shoeless Joe Jackson	1908-20	.356	.518	216	7	96
11. Al Simmons	1924-44	.334	.535	214	22	134
12. Harry Heilmann	1914-32	.342	.520	201	14	117
13. Willie Mays	1951-73	.302	.557	178	36	103
14. Mickey Mantle	1951-68	.298	.557	163	36	102
15. Dick Allen	1963-74	.299	.553	177	35	106
16. Tris Speaker	1907-28	.344	.500	204	7	89
17. Frank Robinson	1956-74	.295	.543	173	34	106
18. Riggs Stephenson	1921-34	.336	.473	187	8	96
19. Heinie Manush	1923-39	.330	.479	204	9	95
20. George Sisler	1915-30	.340	.467	222	8	93
21. Nap Lajoie	1896-16	.339	.467	212	5	104
22. Paul Waner	1926-45	.333	.473	200	7	83
23. Honus Wagner	1897-17	.329	.468	199	6	101
24. Roberto Clemente	1955-72	.317	.475	200	16	87
25. Earle Combs	1924-35	.325	.462	208	7	70
26. Harmon Killebrew	1954-74	.258	.521	141	39	107
27. Ernie Banks	1953-71	.274	.500	166	33	105
28. Carl Yastrzemski	1961-74	.292	.480	173	23	90
29. Reggie Jackson	1967-74	.267	.500	151	33	95
30. Eddie Collins	1906-30	.333	.428	190	3	74
31. Rod Carew	1967-74	.323	.416	199	5	62

*These hitters were ranked according to a composite of the five categories shown in the chart: lifetime batting average; slugging average; and hits, home runs and runs batted in computed according to a 162-game schedule. Currently active players are computed through and including the 1974 season.

1900-1926
Frank Baker, Chief Bender, Roger Bresnahan, Three-Finger Brown, Frank Chance, Jack Chesboro, Fred Clarke, Jimmy Collins, Stan Coveleski, Sam Crawford, Johnny Evers, Elmer Flick, Nap Lajoie, Rube Marquand, Christy Mathewson, Iron Man McGinnity, Ed Plank, Joe Tinker, Rube Waddell, Honus Wagner, Ed Walsh, Cy Young, Ross Young.

1928-1976
Luke Appling, Yogi Berra, Lou Boudreau, Roy Campanella, Roberto Clemente, Dizzy Dean, Bill Dickey, Joe DiMaggio, Bob Feller, Ford Frick, Lefty Gomez, Hank Greenberg, Carl Hubbell, Monte Irvin, Sandy Koufax, Satchel Paige, Jackie Robinson, Warren Spahn, George Weiss, Ted Williams, Early Wynn.

1927
New York Yankees: Ed Barrow, Miller Huggins, Lou Gehrig, Babe Ruth, Earle Combs, Waite Hoyt, Herb Pennock. *Philadelphia Athletics:* Connie Mack, Al Simmons, Ty Cobb, Mickey Cochrane, Eddie Collins, Zack Wheat, Jimmy Foxx, Lefty Grove. *Washington Senators:* Walter Johnson, Stan Coveleski, Sam Rice, Tris Speaker, Goose Goslin, Clark Griffith. *Detroit Tigers:* Charlie Gehringer, Harry Heilmann, Heinie Manush *Chicago White Sox:* Ray Schalk, Ted Lyons, Red Faber. *St. Louis Browns:* George Sisler. *Boston Red Sox:* Red Ruffing. *Pittsburgh Pirates:* Pie Traynor, Paul Waner, Lloyd Waner, Kiki Cuyler, Joe Cronin. *St. Louis Cardinals:* G. C. Pete Alexander, Frankie Frisch, Jesse Haines, Rabbit Maranville, Chick Hafey, Branch Rickey. *New York Giants:* Rogers Hornsby, John J. McGraw, Bill Terry, Burleigh Grimes, Edd Roush. *Chicago Cubs:* Gabby Hartnett, Joe McCarthy. *Cincinnati Reds:* George Kelly, Eppa Rixey. *Brooklyn Dodgers:* Dazzy Vance, Max Carey, Wilbert Robinson. *The League:* Judge Kenesaw Mountain Landis, Ban Johnson, Will Harridge, Billy Evans, Bill Klem, Bill McKechnie.

THE WIND-UP AND THE PITCH...

Faster than Walter Johnson's fastball come baseball's greatest pitching feats

Great Feats In Pitching

—On June 11, 1938, Johnny Vander Meer of the Cincinnati Reds pitched a no-hit, no-run game against the Boston Braves. His next scheduled mound appearance came four days later, against the Brooklyn Dodgers. Again, he pitched a no-hit, no-run game. He is the only pitcher to have hurled two consecutive no-hitters.

—There haven't been any other relief appearances like the one Ernie Shore of the Boston Red Sox made on June 23, 1917. After the starting pitcher walked the first batter, got into a violent argument with the home plate umpire and was thrown out of the game, Shore came in to relieve and threw a perfect no-hit, no-run game. It was a perfect game because the batter who walked was thrown out trying to steal second. The starting pitcher who was argumentative and was ejected from the game? Babe Ruth.

—Sure, Cy Young won 511 games, 95 more than any other pitcher living or dead. But did you know that when he started pitching the pitching distance was 50 feet and then changed to 60 feet 6 inches during his career? That the strike zone was top of the shoulders to the bottom of the knees? That it took five balls for a batter to walk? That the maximum diameter on bats was smaller than today? No one will match Young's record but comparing old-timers like him with today's pitchers is like comparing apples to oranges.

Christy Mathewson, the Big Six, above, *averaged 23 wins, that's right, averaged 23 wins a season.*

Walter Johnson, the Big Train, right, *averaged 21 wins a season over the length of his career.*

Three World Series Shutouts in Six Days

No pitcher in the history of major league baseball has had as much control as Christy Mathewson. In fact, of the fewest walks issued per nine-innings, Mathewson ranks at the top of the list. (Some experts might disagree, saying that Cy Young is ahead of Mathewson on the list, but during some of Young's career a walk was not granted until after five balls had been wide of the plate.) "Big Six," as they called him, stands on his own anyway. He won 20 or more games for 13 years, four times winning 30 or more. He ranks third on the all-time lists for wins and strikeouts and is fifth all-time for his earned run average of 2.13.

His greatest pitching feat came in the 1905 World Series when, pitching for John McGraw and the New York Giants, he hurled three shutout victories in a span of six days against Connie Mack's Philadelphia Athletics. Mathewson opened the Series with a four-hit shutout. The A's won the second game, beating Iron Man Joe McGinnity. Big Six came back with two days rest and blanked the A's with another four-hitter. McGinnity returned from his loss to shut out the A's in the fourth game. And with one day's rest, Mathewson came back to shut out the A's personally for the third time. In 70 years, that World Series feat has not been matched.

Three Shutouts in Four Days

Although Walter Johnson won three-fourths of his 416 victories during the dead ball era, he is still considered one of the greatest pitchers who ever lived. In his career, he threw 113 shutouts: no one else comes close. He fanned 3,506 batters: second place is a distant second. He pitched more innings and won more ball games in the 20th century than anyone else. His lifetime earned run average is 2.17 but for 11 years his ERA was 1.56.

His most remarkable performance came late in his sophomore season, 1908. Pitching against the New York Highlanders (later changed to Yankees), the Big Train threw a shut out game. The next day he was asked to pitch again. He did and again shut out the Highlanders. No games were scheduled for Sunday, but on Monday Johnson was once again prevailed upon to take the mound, his manager explaining that the rest of the pitching staff had sore arms. Johnson rose to the occasion and threw his third straight shutout. That record has stood for 68 years and will probably stand for a lot longer.

16 Consecutive Wins in One Season

Robert Moses "Lefty" Grove was one of the fiercest competitors who ever strode onto a major league pitching mound. Possessing a flaming temper and a scorching fastball, Grove had never touched a baseball until he was 17 and didn't make the big leagues until after he spent five long years in the minors. And yet he won 300 games, won 20 or more for eight seasons, led in earned run average for nine years, and led in strikeouts for seven consecutive seasons.

His best season was his seventh, in 1931, when he was a ripe 31 years old. He compiled a 31-4 record, with a winning percentage of .886, led in ERA with 2.06 and led in strikeouts. Most phenomenal, however, was the fact that he started the season by winning his first 10 games, lost a close one, 2-1, and then won the next 16 consecutive games. The 16 consecutive wins is a major league single season record that has stood for 44 years.

Hubbell's Strikeout Exhibition

If there is only one memorable All-Star game, it would be the one that took place on July 10, 1934. With a Murderers Row line-up, the American League was heavily favored and they would win, but not before Carl Hubbell, "The Meal Ticket," as he was affectionately called, mowed down Murderers Row.

Hubbell started for the National League and was in trouble right away. In the first inning, the first two batters got on base and coming up were five of the greatest hitters in major league history. The five with their lifetime batting average and total home runs:

Babe Ruth	*.342*	*714*	*Al Simmons*	*.334*	*307*
Lou Gehrig	*.340*	*493*	*Joe Cronin*	*.301*	*170*
Jimmy Foxx	*.325*	*534*			

The Meal Ticket threw three straight screwballs at the Babe who watched them all go by for a strikeout. Gehrig swung at a third strike. Foxx went down swinging. So did Simmons and Cronin at the top of the second. It was quite a feat and, as Hubbell later recalled, he threw nothing but screwballs (which when thrown by a left-hander, break down and away from a right-handed batter) at Ruth and Company. Carl Hubbell went on to win 253 games in his career, won 24 games in a row, pitched a no-hitter and entered the Hall of Fame. He is best remembered, though, for his performance on the mound in the 1934 All-Star game.

Perfect Game, World Series

Don Larsen never did win more games than he lost during his major league career. In 1954, while pitching for Baltimore, for example, he won 3 and lost 21. Those 21 losses led the league. But he was traded to the Yankees in 1955 and that meant he would have better batting support and a good chance at World Series money. And, in fact, the Yankees did go to the Series in 1955 but the Dodgers took it all. The fall classic for 1956 saw the same rivals take the field. Larsen appeared in the second game, along with seven other Yankee pitchers, and was belted out of the box. Yet Casey Stengel called on him to start game number five. It was a virtuoso historic performance. The tall, lanky right-hander, using the barest of windups, mowed down one batter after another. By the sixth inning, everyone knew what might happen: they just couldn't believe it was happening. By the seventh, the crowd stirred uneasily. By the eighth, every pitch drew a collective gasp that reverberated throughout Yankee Stadium. When he came up to bat in the bottom of the eighth, 64,519 spectators gave Larsen a standing ovation said to be unequaled in Yankee Stadium history. In the ninth, he would be facing Carl Furillo, Roy Campanella and Dale Mitchell. Later, Larsen told a reporter: "I was so weak in the knees out there in the ninth inning, I thought I was going to faint. I was so nervous I almost fell down. My legs were rubbery and my fingers didn't feel like they were on my hand. I said to myself, 'Please help me out, somebody.'" Furillo flied out. Campanella grounded out to short. Mixing sliders and fastballs, Larsen got Mitchell on a called strike. Then pandemonium. It was the only perfect game in World Series history.

—Back in 1912 Rube Marquand won the season opener for the New York Giants. He kept winning until he won 20 straight games. For consecutive wins in a season, he holds the record.

—Then came 1936 and 1937 when Carl Hubbell was pitching for the same Giants. He won 16 games in a row in 1936 and the first eight games he started in 1937, putting together an all-time consecutive win record of 24 games.

—The consecutive record for control belongs to Christy Mathewson who in a 30-day span in 1913 pitched 68 consecutive innings without giving up one walk. But they've been shrinking the strike zone on today's pitchers.

—If a rookie pitcher ever wins 29 games in his first major league season, he'll beat the record set by Grover Cleveland Alexander in 1911 when Ol' Pete won 28. When Alexander was 41 years old he won 21 games in a season. He was also a remarkable drinker.

—Walter Johnson can only claim to be the second winningest pitcher in major league history (414 wins to Cy Young's 511) but he is first in total strikeouts and shutout games, 3,506 and 112. Since he possessed blazing speed, "The Big Train's" biggest fear was striking the batters. He also holds the record for that, having drilled the ball into 204 batsmen during his career.

—For 31 years, Bob Feller held the strikeout record for one nine-inning game: 18. Then, in 1969, Steve Carlton struck out 19 and in 1970, Tom Seaver struck out 19. Seaver, however, fanned the last 10 San Diego Padres he faced and that bettered the previous mark of eight.

—While it's nigh on to impossible to pitch two back-to-back no-hitters, it's also tough to pitch two no-hitters in one season. Only five men have done that. They are: Johnny Vander Meer, Allie Reynolds, Virgil Trucks, Jim Maloney and Nolan Ryan.

In the history of modern baseball, there have only been eight perfect games. These were thrown by Cy Young (1904), Addie Joss (1908), Ernie Shore (1917), Charlie Robertson (1922), Don Larsen (1956), Jim Bunning (1964), Sandy Koufax (1965) and Jim "Catfish" Hunter (1968).

Seconds after Don Larsen pitched the one and only World Series perfect game, Yankee catcher Yogi Berra threw himself onto Larsen with a wrap-around hug.

Pitchers with 100 or more Saves

Hoyt Wilhelm	227
Roy Face	193
Ron Perranoski	179
Lindy McDaniel	170
Stu Miller	154
Don McMahon	153
Ted Abernathy	148
Sparky Lyle	131
Jim Brewer	123
Dick Radatz	122
Jack Aker	121
Clay Carroll	119
Frank Linzy	111
Al Worthington	110
Fred Gladding	109
Ron Kline	108
Johnny Murphy	107
Dave Giusti	103
John Wyatt	103
Ellis Kinder	102
Wayne Granger	101
Firpo Marverry	101
Darold Knowles	100

Four No-Hitters

Yeah. Count 'em. Four. The saga of Sanford Koufax—Brooklyn born, Brooklyn bred and Brooklyn (later Los Angeles) Dodger—is much more than four no-hitters. It is really an epic of triumph and tragedy, triumphant in that he was one of the greatest pitchers who ever threw a baseball, tragic in that he was forced by an arthritic elbow to retire from baseball at the age of 30 with 10, perhaps 12, or more pitching years ahead of him. Great as Koufax turned out to be, he started slow. After six seasons, he lost more games than he had won, 36-40. But those years had taught him to work the batters, psych them out and not just simply try to throw the ball right by them. On Memorial Day, 1962, he had his first no-hitter. His first inning in that game could not have been more perfect. Three strikeouts on nine pitches. By the end of the game, he had struck out 13. His second no-hitter came in mid-May, 1963, against the San Francisco Giants. He was not over-powering, recording only four strikeouts. But a second no-hitter is a second no-hitter. A year later, in June, 1964, he hurled his third and it was a gem. Only 27 men came to bat but since Richie Allen walked and was caught stealing, it was not a perfect game. 12 men were struck out. Koufax's fourth and final no-hitter came in September, 1965 against the Chicago Cubs. It turned out to be an incredible game—a perfect game for Koufax, and, ironically, a one-hitter for Chicago Cubs' pitcher Bob Hendley. Koufax did not allow one batter to reach first, struck out 14 men, and fanned the entire side in the ninth, a superb finish. He completed the season by leading both leagues in wins, winning percentage, earned run average and strikeouts.

The 1966 season was his last. He won 27 games and led in all the other departments all over again. His last major league victory, which came in the last game of the season, won the pennant for the Dodgers. His left elbow, however, was diagnosed as having traumatic arthritis. To bear the pain, he had been immersing the elbow in a bucket of ice water for an hour a day for years. He had pitched two no-hitters after that diagnosis and after hours and hours with the ice bucket but he decided that enough was enough. He quit, saying he did not want to "wind up with an arm I won't be able to use for the rest of my life." Sandy Koufax is the only pitcher to average more than one strikeout an inning during his pitching lifetime, 2,396 strikeouts in 2,325 innings. Sandy Koufax was the youngest man elected to baseball's Hall of Fame. It's simpler to say he was the greatest left-hander who ever lived.

Base On Balls Per 9-Inning Game
(average over career)

1.	Cy Young	1.49*	1890-1911
2.	Christy Mathewson	1.59	1900-1916
3.	G.C. Pete Alexander	1.65	1911-1930
4.	Robin Roberts	1.73	1948-1966
5.	Juan Marichal	1.81	1960-1974
6.	Carl Hubbell	1.82	1928-1943
7.	Ferguson Jenkins	1.83	1965-
8.	Dizzy Dean	2.10	1930-1947
9.	Walter Johnson	2.13	1907-1927
10.	Jim Kaat	2.15	1959-
11.	Don Drysdale	2.24	1956-1969
12.	Tom Seaver	2.36	1967-
13.	Gaylord Perry	2.39	1962-
14.	Jim Bunning	2.40	1955-1971
15.	Rube Waddell	2.44	1897-1910
16.	Warren Spahn	2.46	1942-1965
17.	Jim Catfish Hunter	2.52	1965-
18.	Dazzy Vance	2.55	1915-1935
19.	Smokey Joe Wood	2.64	1908-1920
20.	Lefty Grove	2.71	1925-1941
21.	Mickey Lolich	2.74	1963-
22.	Burleigh Grimes	2.79	1916-1934
23.	Bob Gibson	3.04	1959-1974
24.	Whitey Ford	3.08	1950-1967
25.	Sandy Koufax	3.16	1955-1966
26.	Steve Carlton	3.22	1965-
27.	Early Wynn	3.50	1939-1963
28.	Bob Feller	4.15	1936-1956
29.	Sam McDowell	4.73	1961-1974
30.	Nolan Ryan	5.36	1966-

*During first four years of Young's career, pitching distances were shorter (50 feet instead of current 60 feet, 6 inches) and bats were of smaller diameter.

En route to his perfect game against the Chicago Cubs in 1965, a grim Sandy Koufax prepares to unleash his patented pitch, the fast ball.

Bob Gibson, above, *scores his 17th World Series strikeout.*

17 World Series Strikeouts

Bob Gibson didn't break into the major leagues until he was 24. And he didn't start out too well: 3-5 in 1959, 3-6 in 1960. But for the next 13 years, he averaged 18 wins a season. His greatest moment in pitching came in the opening game of the 1968 World Series between his St. Louis Cardinals and the Detroit Tigers. Against him, the Tigers had not unexpectedly tapped Denny McLain, who had just finished the season with 31 wins. Gibson had only won 22 that season but had a 1.12 earned run average. The ERA was the best since the introduction of the lively ball in 1920 and second only to Walter Johnson's mark of 1.09 for pitching more than 300 innings.

Coming as a climax to what had been called "The Year of the Pitcher," the Series had been billed as a Super Duel between Gibson and McLain. McLain showed almost nothing in the entire Series but Gibson went to work beginning in the first game. By the ninth inning, he had recorded 14 strikeouts and was one away from Sandy Koufax's series record of 15. (Koufax had wiped out Carl Erskine's record of 13. Both records had been set against the New York Yankees, in 1953 and 1963.) Leading off the ninth, Gibson fanned Al Kaline for his 15th and 54,692 spectators roared. Then he got Norm Cash on three swings. The crowd roared some more. Finally, unbelievably, Willie Horton watched a third strike go by. 54,692 fans went crazy. Here is Gibson's strikeout box score, inning by inning:

1	*2*	*3*	*4*	*5*	*6*	*7*	*8*	*9*	*Total*
2	**3**	**2**	**1**	**1**	**2**	**2**	**1**	**3**	**17**

Strikeouts Per 9-Inning Game
(average over career)

1.	Nolan Ryan	9.74	1966-
2.	Sandy Koufax	9.28	1955-1966
3.	Sam McDowell	8.88	1961-1974
4.	Tom Seaver	7.71	1967-
5.	Mickey Lolich	7.32	1963-
6.	Bob Gibson	7.29	1959-1974
7.	Steve Carlton	7.07	1965-
8.	Rube Waddell	7.04	1897-1910
9.	Ferguson Jenkins	7.00	1965-
10.	Jim Bunning	6.83	1955-1971
11.	Don Drysdale	6.52	1956-1969
12.	Gaylord Perry	6.25	1962-
13.	Smokey Joe Wood	6.21	1908-1920
14.	Dazzy Vance	6.20	1915-1935
15.	Bob Feller	6.07	1936-1956
16.	Juan Marichal	5.91	1960-1974
17.	Jim Catfish Hunter	5.57	1965-
18.	Whitey Ford	5.55	1950-1967
19.	Jim Kaat	5.42	1959-
20.	Walter Johnson	5.32	1907-1927
21.	Dizzy Dean	5.29	1930-1947
22.	Lefty Grove	5.18	1925-1941
23.	Christy Mathewson	4.72	1900-1916
24.	Early Wynn	4.60	1939-1963
25.	Robin Roberts	4.52	1948-1966
26.	Warren Spahn	4.43	1942-1965
27.	Carl Hubbell	4.21	1928-1943
28.	G.C. Pete Alexander	3.81	1911-1930
29.	Cy Young	3.45	1890-1911
30.	Burleigh Grimes	3.26	1916-1934

Pitchers with 200 or more Losses

Cy Young	313
Pud Galvin	309
Walter Johnson	279
Jack Powell	255
Eppa Rixey	251
Warren Spahn	245
Robin Roberts	245
Early Wynn	244
Ted Lyons	230
Bob Friend	230
Gus Weyhing	229
Red Ruffing	225
Tim Keefe	224
Bobo Newsom	222
Jack Quinn	219
Sad Sam Jones	216
Jim McCormick	214
Tony Mullane	213
Burleigh Grimes	212
Red Faber	212
Paul Derringer	212
Pete Alexander	208
Chick Fraser	208
Mickey Welch	207
Jim Whitney	204
Kid Nichols	203
Vic Willis	203

—Baseball is a game of statistics. They even keep one-inning records. Here are five such:

Most Runs Allowed: Tony Mullane, 1894, 16 runs.
Most Hits Allowed: Merle Adkins, 1902, 12 hits.
Most Walks: Dolly Gray, 1909, 8 walks.
Most Home Runs Allowed: four round-trippers by eight different pitchers.
Most Wild Pitches: Walter Johnson, 1914, four wild ones.

—And there are a few unusual one-game records. Here are five:

Most Runs Allowed: Dave Rowe, 1892, 35 runs.
Most Hits Allowed: John Wadsworth, 1894, 36 hits.
Most Walks: four pitchers, 1887 (when five balls meant a walk), 1890, 1915, 16 walks.
Most Balks: Bob Shaw, 1963, four times.
Most Home Runs: five pitchers, 1930, 1932, 1936, 1939, 1940, 6 four-baggers.

—John Coleman, who pitched for Philadelphia in 1883, holds the record for most losses in a season, 48. With a 12-48 won-lost record, he couldn't help Philadelphia much. They finished dead last in the National League with a team record of 17 wins and 81 losses. Even at that, Coleman won more than 70 percent of their games. He was traded the following year, however.

58 2/3 Consecutive Scoreless Innings

It's not easy during three weeks of pitching to erase three ancient, almost sacrosanct pitching records; records held by Walter Johnson, Carl Hubbell and an oldie but goodie named Doc Harris. But Don Drysdale managed it in May and June, 1969. For 58 and 2/3 innings of baseball, Big D did not allow a run. He broke Harris' 1904 record of five consecutive shutouts, broke Hubbell's 1933 National League record of 46⅓ scoreless innings and, best of all, he broke Walter Johnson's 1913 Dead Ball era record of 58 scoreless innings. In setting this record, the Los Angeles Dodger pitcher faced three ninth innings with the bases loaded, left the opposition with 11 men stranded on third base and with 10 runners toeing the mark at second. It's hard enough just to finish six games in a row. Pitching six consecutive shutouts was considered impossible.

19 Strikeouts, 10 in a Row

It was early spring, Shea Stadium, 1970, New York Mets vs. San Diego Padres. Everybody knew the man on the mound. Tom Terrific, they called him. In his first three seasons, Tom Seaver had won 57 games and lost 32. The young man from Fresno, Calif., was also a fairly good strikeout artist. Seasonally, he'd been mowing down an average of 200 batters, not supergreat but great enough. But then the April 22 game got under way and the Padres batters started striking out. One after another. By the end of the sixth inning, Tom Terrific had fanned ten batters, including the last man he faced in the sixth. Seaver wasn't planning on breaking any records. He would have to strike out the next nine batters in a row to do that. Well, he did, fanned the next nine, tying Steve Carlton's strikeout record of the year before while setting a new record for most consecutive strikeouts, 10 in a row.

383 Strikeouts

In his first season with the New York Mets, Nolan Ryan won not one game and was sent back down to the minors. But in the three innings that he pitched, he struck out six batters. The then 19-year-old Texan had speed. In fact, folks called his fastball "Ryan's Express." His 1967 to 1971 record with the Mets was uninspiring; he posted a 29-37 won-loss record in four seasons. Then, just before the 1972 season, he was traded to the California Angels. In that season, Ryan began to achieve the success that his blazing fastball had heralded seven years before. He set or tied 14 Angel records, won 19 games and led both leagues in strikeouts with 329. Sometimes, he'd be fanning 16, 17 batters a game. All batting against him slumped to a measly .168 average. He even set the record for fewest number of hits allowed for nine innings, a stingy 5.26.

Things got even better in 1973. Early in the season he knocked off the Kansas City Royals with a no-hitter. Two months later, he did it again, no-hitting the Tigers, and fanning 12 of the first 14 batters he faced. It was such an awesome display of speed and pitching prowess that Norm Cash walked up to the plate with a Ping Pong paddle in the fifth inning. When the ump threw the paddle away, Cash came back in the ninth swinging a piano leg. But it didn't make any difference, Ryan still got the no-hitter. In his next appearance on the mound, four days later, he was trying to tie Johnny Vander Meer's record of two consecutive no-hitters and attempting to set the record for three no-hitters in a season. But, he lost his third no-hitter on a single in the eighth inning.

As the 1973 season rolled on toward October, Ryan was gunning for one more record, Sandy Koufax's 382 season strikeouts. He got it but not until his last appearance of the season—on the last pitch of the game.

Tom Seaver gets his 10th straight strikeout, setting a game record, and goes on to strike out nine more Padres to tie another record.

	Games	At Bats Hits	Sngls	S Game	Dbls	2 Game	Trps	3 Game	Homers	HR Game	BA SA	RBIs	RBIs Game	Leading Batters		
1901	549	38,138 10,559	8,109	14.8	1,534	2.8	688	1.25	228	.42	.277 .371	4,794	8.7	Lajoie Lajoie	.422 .635	BA SA
1905	617	40,515 9,756	7,589	12.3	1,532	2.5	479	.78	156	.25	.241 .314	3,767	6.1	Flick Flick	.306 .466	BA SA
1910	627	40,917 9,959	7,946	12.7	1,300	2.1	568	.91	145	.23	.243 .314	3,659	5.8	Cobb Cobb	.385 .554	BA SA
1915	621	40,304 10,005	7,819	12.6	1,409	2.3	617	.99	160	.26	.248 .326	4,079	6.6	Cobb Fournier	.369 .491	BA SA
1920	617	41,983 11,899	8,904	14.4	2,010	3.3	616	1.00	369	.60	.283 .387	5,140	8.3	Sisler Ruth	.407 .847	BA SA
1925	616	42,595 12,418	9,109	14.8	2,218	3.6	558	.91	533	.87	.292 .407	5,773	9.4	Heilmann Williams	.393 .613	BA SA
1930	616	42,882 12,338	8,634	14.1	2,375	3.9	656	1.10	673	1.10	.288 .421	6,157	10.0	Simmons Ruth	.381 .732	BA SA
1935	611	42,999 12,033	8,633	14.1	2,212	3.6	525	.86	663	1.09	.280 .402	5,788	9.5	Myer Foxx	.349 .636	BA SA
1940	619	43,017 11,674	8,111	13.1	2,167	3.5	513	.83	883	1.42	.271 .407	5,691	9.2	DiMaggio Greenberg	.352 .670	BA SA
1945	612	41,624 10,634	8,138	13.3	1,674	2.7	392	.64	430	.70	.255 .346	4,419	7.2	Stirnweiss Stirnweiss	.309 .476	BA SA
1950	620	42,407 11,474	8,249	13.3	1,829	3.0	423	.68	973	1.57	.271 .402	5,902	9.5	Goodman DiMaggio	.354 .585	BA SA
1955	618	41,817 10,802	7,929	12.8	1,574	2.5	338	.55	961	1.56	.258 .381	5,143	8.3	Kaline Mantle	.340 .611	BA SA
1960	617	41,838 10,689	7,609	12.3	1,720	2.8	274	.44	1,086	1.76	.255 .388	5,071	8.2	Runnels Maris	.320 .581	BA SA
1965	810	54,362 13,158	9,346	11.5	2,077	2.6	365	.45	1,370	1.69	.242 .369	5,944	7.3	Oliva Yastrzemski	.321 .536	BA SA
1970	973	65,675 16,404	11,793	12.1	2,492	2.6	373	.38	1,746	1.80	.250 .379	7,589	7.3	Johnson Yastrzemski	.329 .592	BA SA
1973	972	66,276 17,192	12,610	13.0	2,626	2.7	404	.41	1,552	1.60	.259 .381	7,766	8.0	Carew Jackson	.350 .549	BA SA

	Home Run Hitters		Leading Pitchers	Wins	Leading Pitchers	[ERA]	BOBs	BOBs Game	SOs	SOs Game	Rules Changes	Pennant Winner
1901	Lajoie	14	Young	33	Young, Cy	1.63	2,780	5.1	2,736	5.0	138 games scheduled Eight teams	Chicago
1905	Davis	8	Waddell	26	Waddell	1.48	3,008	4.9	5,107	8.3	154 games scheduled	Phil.
1910	Stahl	10	Coombs	31	Walsh	1.27	3,462	5.5	5,276	8.4		Phil.
1915	Roth	7	Johnson	27	Wood, S.	1.49	4,214	6.8	4,857	7.8		Boston
1920	Ruth	54	Bagby	31	Shawkey	2.45	3,807	6.2	3,633	5.9	Livelier ball Spitter banned	Cleveland
1925	Meusel	33	Lyons	21	S. Coveleski	2.84	4,319	7.0	3,319	5.4		Wash.
1930	Ruth	49	Grove	28	Grove	2.54	3,958	6.4	4,080	6.6		Phil.
1935	Foxx Greenberg	36 36	Farrell	25	Grove	2.70	4,546	7.4	3,942	6.5		Detroit
1940	Greenberg	41	Feller	27	Feller	2.62	4,496	7.3	4,729	7.6		Detroit
1945	Stephens	24	Newhouser	25	Newhouser	1.81	4,145	6.8	4,186	6.8	Lotsa 4-F ballplayers	Detroit
1950	Rosen	37	Lemon	23	Wynn	3.20	5,418	8.7	4,558	7.4		New York
1955	Mantle	37	Ford, Sullivan Lemon	18	Pierce	1.97	4,808	7.8	5,406	8.7		New York
1960	Mantle	40	Perry, Estrada	18	Baumann	2.68	4,447	7.2	5,993	9.7	162 games scheduled	New York
1965	Conigliaro	32	Grant	21	McDowell	2.18	5,306	6.6	9,634	11.9	10 teams	Minn.
1970	Howard	44	Cuellar, Perry & McNally	24	Segui	2.56	6,808	7.0	10,957	11.3	12 teams	Balt.
1973	Jackson	32	Wood	24	Palmer	2.40	6,647	6.8	9,854	10.1		Oak.

The best two pitches in baseball

THE SPITTER & THE GREASER

By Gaylord Perry
with Bob Sudyk

Spitball Pitchers We've Known

Bo Belinsky, 1962-70
Harry Brecheen, 1940-53
Jim Brosnan, 1954-63
Jim Bunning, 1955-71
Lew Burdette, 1950-67
Hugh Casey, 1935-49
Jack Chesboro, 1899-1909
Joe Coleman, 1965-74
Stanely Coveleski, 1912-28
Don Drysdale, 1956-69
Elroy Face, 1953-69
Whitey Ford, 1950-67
Bob Friend, 1951-66
Burleigh Grimes, 1916-34
Ron Kline, 1952-70
Cal Koonce, 1962-71
Jim Lonborg, 1965-74
Sal Maglie, 1945-58
Jim Maloney, 1960-71
Jim Merritt, 1965-74
Bob Moose, 1967-74
Orlando Pena, 1958-74
Ron Perranoski, 1961-74
Gaylord Perry, 1962-74
Pete Ramos, 1955-70
Phil Regan, 1960-72
Preacher Roe, 1938-54
Bob Shaw, 1957-67
Bill Singer, 1964-74
Don Sutton, 1966-74
Bob Turley, 1951-63
Big Ed Walsh, 1904-17
Earl Wilson, 1959-70
Whitlow Wyatt, 1929-45

"C'mon, Gaylord, tell me, where do you get it?"

That's been *the* question going on 10 years now. It's usually followed by a snicker and a couple of light jabs to my ribs. It's like people dying to know how a magician does his card tricks. Everybody always wants to know how I load up my wet one—and I mean *everybody.*

They were all after one thing: to find out where I kept whatever I was supposed to use on the ball. There was a time when those suspicions certainly had a basis in fact. But that was before I reformed, before I said goodbye to slippery elm, Vaseline, K-Y Jelly, baby oil, scuffballs—anything that would help me get out a batter.

When I came up to the big leagues in 1962, under the existing rules, spitballing was not complicated. Making the spitter behave was another thing, but loading it up was easy. Some pitchers were really careless. We true masters had little respect for them. Slobberers, we called them. Those clumsy, overenthusiastic spitballers not only showed no respect for a delicate art, they actually triggered the rule change in 1968 that ended finger-licking on the mound.

Before the new rule, the simplest form of loading the ball was merely wetting the first two fingers of the pitching hand, then faking a wipe-off. They tell me Lew Burdette of the Braves used to spit between his teeth to load his fingers. I couldn't master that. I read where Preacher Roe of the Dodgers used to spit in the palm of his hand while reaching up to wipe the sweat off his brow. He could hit it on the move. Then he'd pick up the spit with the two business fingers.

Perry's Favorite Method

My own favorite method was wetting up the back of my thumbnail area at the same time I was wetting my first two fingers with a natural and legal lick. It was undetectable by the human eye. And even by the camera eye, I might add. Then I'd wipe the two fingers dry, just in case anyone was watching. But while I was getting my sign from the catcher, I'd flick those fingers over the back of my thumb and get the ball ready for my super pitch. No one knew when I had it, not even my catcher. I always had a few special signs to let him know I was loaded up.

The Vaseline & K-Y Jelly Ball

It was during the winter before the '68 season that the rules committee decided a pitcher would no longer be allowed to touch his fingers to his mouth as long as he was anywhere near the mound. Wetting up the fingers was outlawed for all practical purposes. The spitball era was over. Today, people still talk about the spitter, but the spitter is dead. Nowadays, it's a grease ball the pitchers are throwing. The new rules ended some careers and caused others to decline, for logical reasons. Some of the spitballers couldn't adjust to the use of Vaseline, K-Y jelly, oily hair tonics and other slicky products. Actually, the rule change was a hardship on law-abiding pitchers, too—the ones who learned to pitch wetting their fingers, then truly drying them before every pitch.

I had to switch to a lubricant and learn how to apply it and hide it. Then I had to show each team I faced in 1968 that I could still get what I needed when I needed it. Once I established myself against a lead-off batter, I might never need to throw the greaser again for the rest of the game. But they'd all be watching for it. That year, I guess some of us proved that oil and water can mix.

The first time I faced the Cincinnati Reds in 1968—early May, as I recall—Pete Rose led off the bottom of the first inning. A perfect test case, I wound up and gave Charlie Hustle my slick one on the first pitch. He missed it by a foot.

"Well," he yelled, sarcastically. "It's good to see you haven't changed!"

Pete must not have been in a good mood that day because he started yapping at the plate umpire. The two of them got into it. Then I went through the usual decoy three straight times and threw Rose three straight change-ups to strike him out. He was so mad he started arguing the whereabouts of the strike zone and the umpire threw him out of the game.

Rose turned to me and yelled, "Hey, Perry, where do you keep your dip stick?"

"What do ya mean?" I said.

"How else will you know when your cap needs an oil change?"

The first couple of years, I had to use gobs of the stuff. I put it on my cap, my pants, my shirt, underneath the tongue of my shoe and on my belt. As the umpires started checking me more and more, I realized I was only safe applying the lubricants to exposed skin, like my neck, forehead, wrist, ear and my hair. I'd always have it in at least two places, in case the

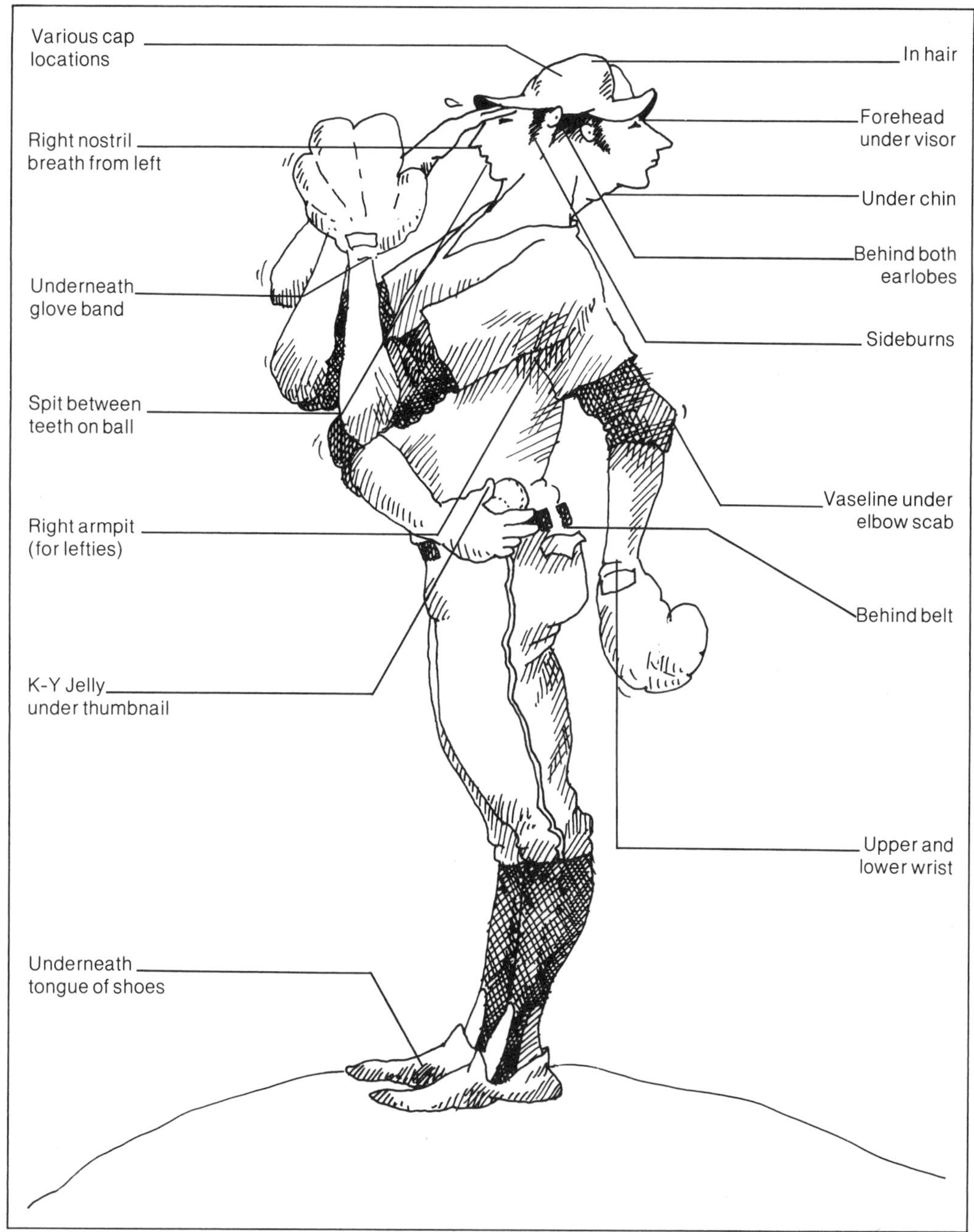

A LITTLE DAB'LL DO YA

Records Set By Pitchers Who Could Or Would Throw the Spitter and Greaser

Lifetime
Lowest earned run average
Most strikeouts (2 of top 10 on list)
Most saves (3rd on list)
Most games pitched (2 of top 10)
Most shutouts (6th on list)

Season
Most wins (top 2)
Innings pitched (4 of top 10)
Complete games (2nd on list)
Winning percentage (5th on list)
Shutouts (5th on list)

Since 1960
No-hitters (9)
Led leagues in shutouts (5)
Led leagues in saves (5)

World Series, lifetime
Lowest earned run average (1st)
Most games pitched (1st)
Most games started (1st)
Innings pitched (1st)
Most strikeouts (1st)

umpires would ask me to wipe off one. I never wanted to be caught out there without anything. It wouldn't be professional.

Just to review the process, nice and slow: first, I wet up the back of my thumb (it could stay wet for three or four pitches) while licking my first two fingers. Then I wiped real hard two or three times with my first two fingers pressed against my uniform. I wanted to make sure the batter and the bench saw me drying off. But I kept the wet backside of my thumb, by the nail, facing away from my shirt. Next I flicked my first two fingers over the thumb to get the moisture. And then I just threw my super-sinker, aiming right above the knees. Get it? The umpires never did.

The next pitch, I'd lick my fingers again. But then I'd execute a casual wipe-off that looked like a fake to the batter and his coach. They thought, "Well, here she comes again." But I wouldn't load it off my thumb that time, and, instead, I'd throw a fast ball. By then, the hitter would get a little confused. He'd be wondering, "Well, is he or isn't he wetting them up?"

The reason I didn't have to use the super-sinker too often was that I worked so hard on developing my decoy—a series of motions designed to make the batter think you're throwing a spitter even when you're not.

One of the big problems under the 1974 rule changes is that the spitter or greaser call is now a judgment call. The umpire doesn't need any evidence, just an opinion. Which means I'm going to have to cut out my decoying, or at least cut down on it, for fear I'll be faking out the wrong people—the umpires. Otherwise, they might convict an innocent man.

The Batter's Revenge: Bill Veeck's Incredible Shrinking Strike Zone

While pitchers may be wont to throw spitters and greasers, batters are inclined to have their revenge too. Take Eddie Gaedel, for example. All three feet seven of him. Eddie's revenge was his own strike zone, which pitchers could barely see, let alone throw at.

Eddie Gaedel owed his major league career to Bill Veeck. When he was hired, Gaedel's sum knowledge of baseball was "I know you're supposed to hit the white ball with the bat. And then you run somewhere." That, however was too much knowledge. All Veeck wanted Eddie to do was stand in a tight crouch and take four balls. To insure that he would, Veeck said "Eddie, I'm going to be up on the roof with a high-powered rifle watching every move you make. If you so much as look as if you're going to swing, I'm going to shoot you dead."

Eddie's debut was made in a Sunday doubleheader against the Detroit Tigers on August 19, 1951. Eddie walked out of the dugout swinging three bats and the place went wild.

Bob Swift, the Detroit catcher, went out to talk with Bobby Cain, the pitcher. Then Swift returned to the plate and kneeled to offer Cain a lower target. The first two pitches were high fast balls. On the third pitch, Cain was laughing so hard he could barely throw. Ball four was about three feet over Eddie's head.

Gaedel trotted to first, patted the Detroit first baseman on the butt like a good professional, waited for the substitute runner with one toe on the bag. After the runner arrived, he shook hands with the first base coach, waved to the cheering crowd and retired from baseball. The Browns lost, 6-2, and midgets were banned from baseball.

Developing Decoys

Every wet-ball pitcher develops his own decoys. I wanted to keep things simple. Just a tug at my cap gave me an easy decoy. I'd go to my mouth, touch my cap and deliver the ball. Actually I had to tug at my cap anyway; I was balding and I had to keep pulling at it to keep it on my head in the Candlestick Park wind tunnel. It wasn't long before some of the hitters began to figure there was some connection between my spitter and the way I tugged at my cap. That was jim-dandy with me. I used it as a decoy and kept it when I switched from spit over to Vaseline.

Hank Aaron, for one, used to really get bugged by my decoying. Once, late in the 1967 season, we were playing Atlanta. I'd get my sign, give my cap a tug and Hank would back out of the batter's box. Then he'd step in and give me a disgusted look. I'd get the sign again, tug again and Hank would step out. This happened twice more. Finally, he stepped out and yelled, "Throw that blankety-blank and I'll take it outta here."

So I tossed up a big, old, slow roundhouse curve. Hank was so geared up to go downtown with one of my sinkers that he couldn't unwind himself in time to do anything. The pitch floated lazily right though the heart of the strike zone. Hank looked down at the plate and splashed it with a wad of spit that would have lasted me three innings. He turned to umpire Doug Harvey. "Why don't you just let him carry a bucket of water out there?" Henry said. I was hurt; that pitch was as dry as a Baptist wedding.

Detecting the Greaseball

Lubricants were hard to detect. Like, you'd have some on your forehead. As you'd sweat, it'd all blend together. And no matter where you had it hid, you got a lot of time to clean off before any umpire could get out there to inspect you. The manager would come out and argue with the ump. That'd take 15 seconds. Then the two of them'd walk some 60 feet to the mound. Heck, in a few seconds, I could make myself legal. You never put it all over you. Otherwise, you'd look like you had the mad itch trying to wipe off a dozen places before the ump got to you.

Just like with the spitter, I quickly got to where I needed less and less grease to do the job right. Vaseline proved to be the best lubricant. As I became expert, I only had to rub a thin coating over my face and neck. The lubricants were blending right in with my sweat, making nothing detectable, and together, the two were more slick than spit.

The reason a lot of pitchers don't throw the greaser has nothing to do with ethics. They just can't master it. For those who can, it means victories, big money and a longer career. But it's very difficult to throw the greaser consistently well. It takes a very delicate feel to release a ball barely held with slick fingers.

Mastering the Greaseball

Normally, the baseball is gripped with the first two fingers over the top and the thumb underneath. The fingers make the last contact with the ball when it is released. The normal spin is backspin, or toward the pitcher.

But the spitter or greaser rolls in a forward rotation, toward the batter. It is released with hard pressure by the *thumb*, the slick fingers on top hardly making contact with the ball. The thumb is the last contact with the ball as it is released. I've read it described as the same action as squirting a wet watermelon seed from your fingers. It is a tricky pitch. The slick load must be in the correct place, the finger release just right, the arm motion perfectly coordinated for the pitch to sink and be controlled. It takes a long time to master. I can make that pitch break in, out, up or down. And I learned that the farther toward the end of my fingers that I held the ball, the heavier it would arrive at the plate and the more it would sink.

When I started throwing it, I didn't know exactly how much stickum to apply. When you use too much, the ball floats to the plate like a knuckle ball. It can be spotted by a batter in time for him to adjust to it. When you learn to get the same action on the ball using less spit or grease, the ball rotates more and looks like a fork ball. There are no two spitballers exactly alike. Some exert tremendous squeezing force when they throw it. Mine is a kind of snap, like the jaws on a crocodile snatching at something.

The rules committee in December, 1973, gave the umpires more power to call spitters or greasers on their own judgment. Seems to me that the umpires have enough to worry about without placing that extra burden on them. If the pitch was legal, they'd have no problems. And maybe neither would I.

SATCHEL PAIGE
IN HIS OWN LEAGUE

By Jim Murray

The grand old game of baseball and its chroniclers almost needed smelling salts not long ago when one pitcher worked in 13 straight games.

What would they say of one who pitched in 169 straight games?

Everyone gasps at the fact Hoyt Wilhelm pitched in 1,070 games lifetime.

What would they do over someone who lost track after 3,000?

So, Walter Johnson struck out 3,503 batters in his career. What about a guy who struck out that many in three years? The same guy who went around the country with a sign: "Guaranteed to strike out the first nine home town batters or your money back?"

The modern ballplayer complains about the arduousness of travel. His longest trip is four-and-a-half hours by jet. He travels in air-conditioned comfort, dines on steak and lobster. If he's a star, he makes upwards of 200 grand a year. Even if he's not, he stays at the best hotels, gets chauffeured everywhere. When he retires, his pension can reach $2,500 a month and more.

What if I told you a greater pitcher than any of them worked for less money a day than these guys get in meal money? That he went around in a three-wheeled bus, air-conditioned only when someone broke a window?

You look at the record book and it says that Leroy Paige, a right-handed pitcher, won 28 major league games, struck out 290 major league batters, and had an earned-run average of 3.2. What the record book doesn't tell you is that Paige was almost as old as baseball when he did these things. A dubious birth certificate shows he was 48 his last full season in the major leagues. I say "dubious" because there are those who remember walking to school with Satchel Paige in the year it says he was born.

There are those who say the Paige page in baseball history shouldn't count, that the big league is the standard of prowess in baseball, and the fact Satchel didn't get in one till he was at least 42 or at most 48 is unfortunate but beside the point.

The argument carried some weight in the days when ballplayers in "Negro leagues" might be said to be "unproven." In the light of what's happened since, the only thing that might be said to be unproven about them was how

JUST LOOK AT THE NUMBERS

The Record	Record Holder	Satchel Paige
Lifetime		
Years pitched	23, Early Wynn	33
Most games	1,054, J. Hoyt Wilhelm, 1952-69	2,500-3,000, 1923-68
Most shutouts	113, Walter Johnson, 1907-27	250, 1923-68
Most games won	511, Cy Young, 1890-1911	2,000-plus, 1923-68
Most games lost	313, Cy Young, 1890-1911	500-plus, 1923-68
Most strikeouts	3,503, Walter Johnson, 1907-27	30,000 minimum estimate
Most no-hit games	4, Sandy Koufax, 1955-67	45, estimate
Season		
Most wins	41-13, Jack Chesboro, 1904	54-5, 1939*
Most strikeouts	383, Nolan Ryan, 1973	600 minimum estimate
Most consecutive shutouts	6, Don Drysdale, 1968	

The Record	Record Holder	Satchel Paige
Attendance record, season game	78,672, L.A. Coliseum, 4/18/58 opening season game vs. S.F.	78,382, Cleveland Municipal Stad., 8/20/48**
Game		
Most strikeouts	19, Steve Carlton, 1969; Tom Seaver, 1970	22, 1925***
Most consecutive days pitched	3 players, 9 games in relief	29, won 28, lost 1
Most consecutive strikeouts	10, Tom Seaver, 1970	19
Oldest player, All-star game	46 or 49, Satchel Paige, 1952, St. Louis	
Oldest player, major leagues	59 or 62, Satchel Paige, 1965, Kansas City	

*While with Bismarck, N.D., team, then national semipro champions. This same team regularly defeated barnstorming major league all-star teams.

**Still a major league nighttime game attendance record.

***This record set against the Babe Ruth All-Stars.

much better they were than the whites.

Just imagine Henry Aaron, Willie Mays, Roberto Clemente, Bob Gibson, Reggie Jackson, Rod Carew and Richie Allen in one league, and we rest our case. The weight of the evidence is that Satchel Paige did what he did in a *bigger* league. Besides, every time he hooked up with a barnstorming, white big-league team he usually struck out 17 or so in a game.

I caught up with this patriarch of the pitch the other day at lunch. Satch is in Hollywood because they're going to make a movie of his life for TV. I asked the venerable right-hander what he thought of Mike Marshall pitching in 100 or so games a year. "I was in 169 straight," snorted Satchel. "Won all of them. In 1953. They had turned me loose from Cleveland and from St. Louis that year. They had took me in the big leagues when I hadn't started a game in 15 years and I pitched two shutouts. I got old but my arm stayed 19."

What did he think of today's hitters? "Josh Gibson was the greatest hitter who ever lived. He couldn't play in those ballparks with the roof on 'em. He would have hit 'em through the roof."

What about all the base-stealing? Satch looked hurt. "All that throwin' over to first base!" he snorted. "Ask anybody did I ever throw over to first base. I never did throw over there. I jes' stepped back off the mound. They had to scramble back to first base. They were the ones got tired. Let them get tired, don't you go to doin' it."

Would he like to be pitching today? "Ain't seen nothin' changed. The plate's the same. The ball's the same. You got to pitch strikes is all. They used to plant two bats six inches apart and I'd throw it between 'em. Across the label. Mr. Ted Williams wouldn't hit nothing but strikes. These players today will hit anything."

Satchel, who views the world with suspicion it might bunt on him with a man on third at any time, has a head-high fastball for anyone who expects his movie to come out "Stepin Fetchit At The Old Ballgame."

"If anyone had told me in the 1920s that coloreds would play in the big leagues, I would have said you're out your mind. They didn't want no coloreds then. Had to eat out of the back door. But I don't be mad. I jes' pity 'em. If they had it to do all over again, I don't believe they would.

"At the same time, we ain't all that far. If I get on a plane and there are four seats and I sit in one of 'em, won't nobody sit there less'n they have to. They'll circle the plane 15 times before they'll finally sit there. Shows bad a condition we're in. And I'm talking about right now. Today. 'Course, I'd be lying if I didn't say they get real different when they find out who I am."

Satch is cussed if he'll go around wearin' a sign saying, "I ain't no nigger, I'm Satchel Paige." So, he hopes the movie will show it's not only Mike Marshall, Walter Johnson and Hoyt Wilhelm who still have to catch up with him, it's all of us.

THE BLACK SPORTS HALL OF FAME*

Robinson opened the gates, and the brothers came marching in.

When Jackie Robinson first appeared in a Brooklyn Dodger uniform, there was an immediate movement among the white players to walk off the field, a move in the racial tradition of Cap Anson.

This racist movement was led not by the players from the Deep South but by players of Italian ancestry and by some sportswriters of major northern dailies. The strike failed when Ford Frick, the National League president, laid down the law in an impassioned and gutsy speech to the players in the clubhouse.

Within months, black ballplayers blossomed at every position—star performers like Larry Doby and Luke Easter, Roy Campanella and Monte Irvin, Orestes Minoso and Hank Thompson. And then came Willie Mays, who did it all.

It was a shame, however, that many of the great old-time black ballplayers were forgotten by baseball. It was only in the last few years—and after a stern blast from Ted Williams at his own Hall of Fame induction—that baseball officially began opening its eyes to black baseball history.

Baseball

Henry Aaron
Roy Campanella
Roberto Clemente
Martin Dihigo
Larry Doby
Josh Gibson
Monte Irvin
Willie Mays
Minnie Minoso
Satchel Paige
Branch Rickey
Jackie Robinson

Basketball

Elgin Baylor
Wilt Chamberlain
Chuck Cooper
Dr. E. B. Henderson
Bill Russell
Jack Twyman

Football

Jim Brown
Dr. Brud Holland
Herb McDonald
Marion Motley
Fritz Pollard
Paul Robeson
Buddy Young

Golf

Charlie Sifford

Track & Field

Cleveland Abbot
Bob Beamon
Alice Coachman
Harrison Dillard
Rafer Johnson
Ralph Metcalfe
Jesse Owens
Eulace Peacock
Wilma Rudolph
Willye White

Tennis

Althea Gibson
Dr. Robert Johnson

Boxing

Muhammad Ali
Henry Armstrong
Joe Frazier
Joe Louis
Ray Robinson
Jose Torres

Historians

Morris Levitt

* Chosen by Black Sports magazine

THE BALANCE OF POWER

It's an irresistible form of segregation. We've assembled the best white and black teams in baseball history, and compared their records. The result: see for yourself

OLD TIME ALL-STARS

Black	vs.	White
Buck Leonard	1B	Lou Gehrig
Sammy T. Hughes	2B	Roger Hornsby
John Henry Loyd	SS	Honus Wagner
Ray Dandridge	3B	Pie Traynor
Cool Papa Bell	LF	Babe Ruth
Oscar Charleston	CF	Tris Speaker
Charles "Chino" Smith	RF	Ty Cobb
Josh Gibson	C	Mickey Cochrane
Satchel Paige, Smokey Joe Williams	P	Walter Johnson, Grover Cleveland Alexander

MODERN ALL-STARS

Black	vs.	White
Dick Allen	1B	Stan Musial
Jackie Robinson	2B	Red Schoendist
Ernie Banks	SS	Phil Rizzuto
Rod Carew	3B	Eddie Mathews
Hank Aaron	RF	Mickey Mantle
Willie Mays	CF	Joe Dimaggio
Roberto Clemente	LF	Ted Williams
Roy Campanella	C	Johnny Bench
Bob Gibson, Ferguson Jenkins	P	Bob Feller, Sandy Koufax

		Batting									Pitching			
		% of At bats per yr.	Bat. Avg.	Slug. Avg.	Average per 550 At Bats: Hits	2B	3B	HRs	Stolen Bases	% of IP per yr.	Hits per 9 IP	BB per 9 IP	SO per 9 IP
1947-1960	White	88.0	.261	.393	144	24	5	13	4	93.8	8.93	3.66	4.29
	Black	7.6	.280	.455	154	22	7	20	10	2.6	8.53	3.43	5.38
	Latin	4.6	.267	.385	147	23	6	10	11	3.6	8.99	3.37	4.59
1961-1968	White	64	.251	.380	138	21	4	14	4	87.8	8.47	3.06	5.69
	Black	22	.269	.421	148	23	5	17	14	5.9	8.02	3.44	6.45
	Latin	14	.267	.380	147	22	5	10	12	6.3	8.15	2.93	6.34
1969-1973	White	58	.251	.371	138	21	3	13	5	87.7	8.55	3.35	5.49
	Black	26	.270	.422	149	23	4	17	14	7.5	7.98	3.35	6.50
	Latin	18	.265	.366	145	22	4	8	11	4.8	8.23	3.44	5.35

- Blacks have led the National League in slugging for the past 22 consecutive years. (Blacks entered the majors 27 years ago.)
- Blacks have won 17 of the past MVP awards in the NL for the past 25 years, 5 in the American League.
- Blacks led in home runs 17 of past 20 years in the NL, 4 in the AL.
- Blacks have led in batting average 7 of the past 10 years in both leagues.
- In the past five years, three black players (Willie Mays, Hank Aaron and Roberto Clemente) have reached the 3,000 hit mark. Before this, only two players (Stan Musial and Paul Waner) reached this mark in previous 40 years.
- No white player has led in stolen bases in either league in the past 20 years.
- In the past 15 years, only one white player, Johnny Bench, has led the NL in home runs.
- In the entire history of major league baseball, only three men have hit for 6,000 or more total bases: two of them (Hank Aaron and Willie Mays) are black.
- Three of the four top home run hitters of all time are black. The ranking is: Hank Aaron, Babe Ruth, Willie Mays and Frank Robinson.
- Another black star, Lou Brock, became the first man to steal 750 bases since Ty Cobb retired in 1928. No white player who started playing baseball after 1919 is among the lifetime leaders in stolen bases (350 or more); five blacks joined that list in the past five years.
- The above charted statistics clearly show that the black hitter has produced more hits, more home runs, more doubles, more triples and more stolen bases than the average white batter.
- Black pitchers have a lower earned run average than whites. Black pitchers also lead in strikeouts, less walks and less hits per inning.

FOR LOVE & MONEY MOSTLY MONEY

By Richard Pietschmann

You're a sports mogul with all the money in the world, and you want to field four superteams with only the most expensive players. How much would it cost you?

When Willie Joe Namath was interviewed about his rumoured jump to the upstart World Football League, a sportswriter asked Broadway Joe if he had ever suffered a cut in salary. "Only when I left Alabama," Joe said.

Joe wasn't kidding and no one back at the University of Alabama, including Bear Bryant was laughing. Coach Bryant might have groped for an antacid tablet but no one was really upset. That's because money and salaries have become an accepted tradition whereby our athletes can learn to love the game more.

And nowhere is this grunt-for-bucks attitude more evident than in our four major professional team sports—baseball, basketball, football and hockey. It is here that players really compete for love and money—well—mostly money.

That young fellow, above, *is Joe Namath, really and truly and he's looking at the N. Y. Jets contract which paid him $300,000 in salary, $100,000 in bonuses and $5,000 for life. Weeb Ewbank smiles.*

It's no secret that there is a lot of money in professional sports, a fact which wives knew years ago and one which even Congress recently discovered. With the coming of Big Sports it was inevitable there would be a second coming—Big Money. Major league baseball, basketball, football and hockey grossed about $400 million in 1974.

But before professional club owners had much chance to gloat over mounting gate and broadcast receipts, came the reckoning—in the form of increasing pressure from players for a bigger cut of the take. The turning point came in 1960 with the upstart American Football League bidding up the worth of rookies and veterans alike in an all-out war with the entrenched National Football League. Before 1960 only baseball players were under contract for the astronomical sum of $100,000—usually reserved for one superstar in each league.

The AFL was the first to loosen owner purse strings. A few years later the American Basketball Association began competing with the established National Basketball Association for the services of basketball players. And now the World Hockey Association has come along to challenge the National Hockey League, while the new World Football League is signing up NFL stars.

Each step since 1960 has served to increase salaries in *all* professional sports, since professional athletes (and their player associations and their business managers) tend to consider a pay raise in other sports as an increase in their worth as well. So the pro football wars increased baseball salaries and the pro basketball wars are increasing football salaries. The same is true of the newest and possibly hottest wars—the hockey and football wars.

The mechanics are the same in all cases. A new league arrives on the scene and immediately begins raiding the established league for "name" athletes to create an instant gate attraction and (almost as important) publicity for the fledgling enterprise. Often the entire league will underwrite the signing of a superstar, which happened when Bobby Hull jumped to the WHA.

The big-money signing of big-name college athletes really got rolling in 1964 when Sonny Werblin of the AFL New York Jets landed Joe Namath out of Alabama for $427,000. It was an astounding figure then, but only a start.

Of the four major professional team sports, only baseball has avoided a big-money war. But prices there have gone up, too. At least 30 players in the two baseball major leagues now make $100,000 or more.

At least 150 players make an annual wage of at least $100,000 in the four sports (American and National Baseball Leagues, National and American Basketball Associations, National Football League, National Hockey League). That doesn't include bonuses, deferred income, pensions or other goodies that often double a player's base salary.

Without doubt, money is the new love in professional sports.

The question is, can it last?

Our reason for listing the available members of what we call the $100,000 Club is to give you some idea of the relative salaries of various players in various sports at one specific point in time. It's difficult to list some salaries because they are secret. It's difficult to list others, like Catfish Hunter's multi-million salary package, because much of the money is tied up in insurance policies, loans, performance. The same holds true for Pele, the Black Pearl of soccer, who signed a presumably fantastic contract with the New York Cosmos.

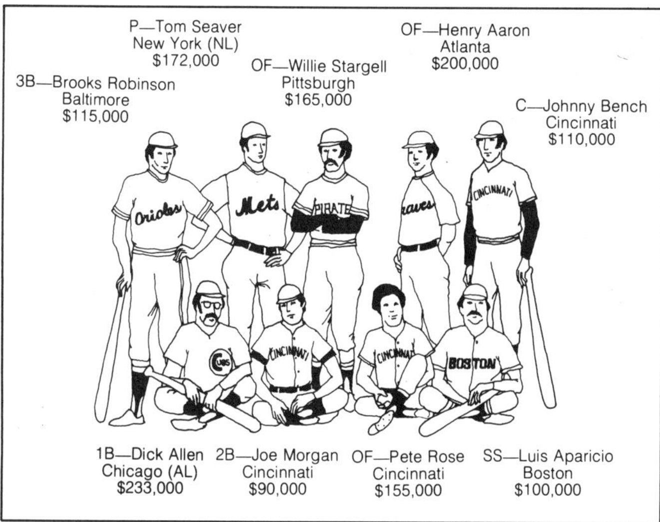

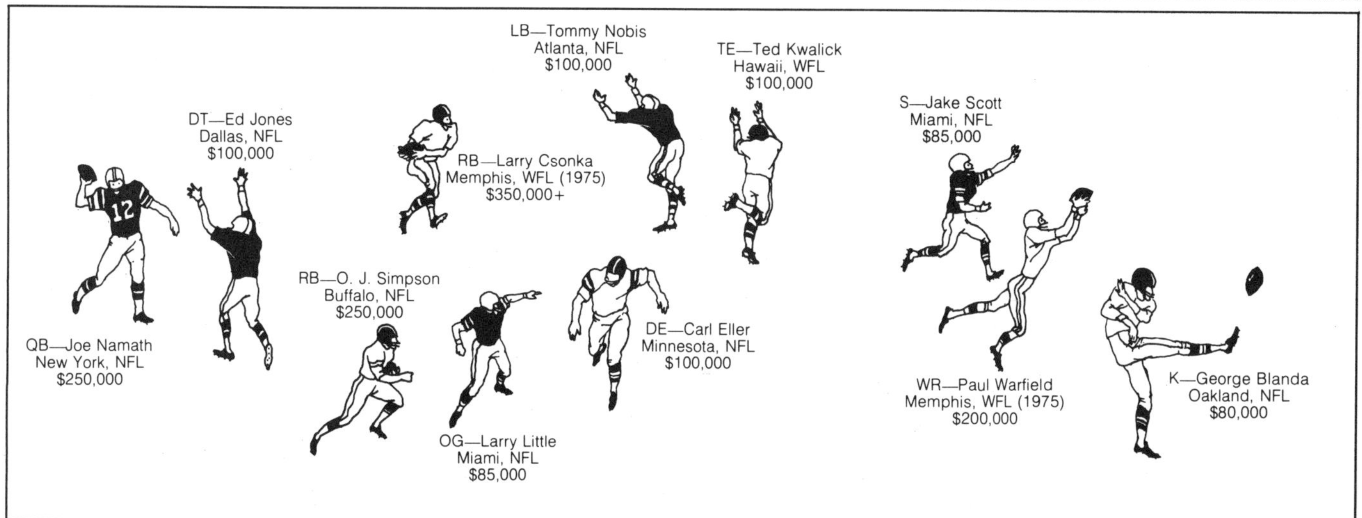

THE $100,000 CLUB

Wilt Chamberlain, basketball	$600,000
K. Abdul-Jabbar, basketball	450,000
Nate Archibald, basketball	450,000
Bill Walton, basketball	450,000
Ernie DiGregorio, basketball	400,000
Phil Chenier, basketball	400,000
Bobby Hull, hockey	400,000
Larry Csonka, football	350,000
Walt Frazier, basketball	340,000
Willis Reed, basketball	325,000
Julius Erving, basketball	325,000
Laffit Pincay, horse racing	322,583
Billy Cunningham, basketball	310,000
Marvin Barnes, basketball	310,000
Jack Nicklaus, golf	308,362
Angel Cordero, horse racing	306,483
Spencer Heywood, basketball	300,000
John Havlicek, basketball	300,000
Bob Lanier, basketball	300,000
Jim Daniels, basketball	300,000
Pete Maravich, basketball	300,000
Jerry West, basketball	300,000
Rick Barry, basketball	300,000
Gordon Johncock, auto racing	279,857
Ron Turcotte, horse racing	278,933
Bruce Crampton, golf	274,266
W. Shoemaker, horse racing	251,938
O.J. Simpson, football	250,000
Joe Namath, football	250,000
Ken Stabler, football	250,000
Gordie Howe, hockey	250,000
Brad Park, hockey	250,000
Artis Gilmore, basketball	250,000
Tom Weiskopf, golf	245,463
J Vasquez, horse racing	236,518
Dick Allen, baseball	233,000
J. Velasquez, horse racing	229,615
Illie Natase, tennis	228,750
Lee Trevino, golf	210,017
Joe Caldwell, basketball	210,000
Stan Smith, tennis	204,225
Lanny Wadkins, golf	200,455
Larry Kenon, basketball	200,000
Ted McClain, basketball	200,000
Paul Warfield, football	200,000
Hank Aaron, baseball	200,000
Stan Mikita, hockey	200,000
Phil Esposito, hockey	200,000
Henri Richard, hockey	200,000
Mickey Redmond, hockey	200,000
Derek Sanderson, hockey	200,000
Bobby Orr, hockey	200,000
Braulio Baeza, horse racing	197,691
Eddie Maple, horse racing	191,674
Miller Barber, golf	184,014
Margaret Court, tennis	180,053
Sonny Jurgensen, football	180,000
George McGinnis, basketball	180,000
Jorge Tejeira, horse racing	175,721
Bernie Parent, hockey	175,000
Bobby Clarke, hockey	175,000
Rod Gilbert, hockey	175,000
Vic Hadfield, hockey	175,000
Jean Ratelle, hockey	175,000
Don Pierce, horse racing	174,966
Tom Okker, tennis	173,500
Tom Seaver, baseball	172,000
R. McCluskey, auto racing	170,863
Enis Potvin, hockey	167,000
E. Belmonte, horse racing	166,781
Dwight Lamar, basketball	165,000
Steve Carlton, baseball	165,000
Willie Stargell, baseball	165,000
Carl Yastrzemski, baseball	165,000
Jerry Lambert, horse racing	164,303
Mike Hole, horse racing	162,782
W. Dallenbach, auto racing	160,664
Bob Gibson, baseball	160,000
Jimmy Connors, tennis	156,400
Pete Rose, baseball	155,000
Frank Robinson, baseball	150,000
Billy Williams, baseball	150,000
Jim Chones, basketball	150,000
Mel Daniels, basketball	150,000
Dan Issel, basketball	150,000
Johnny Neumann, basketball	150,000
Gary Cheevers, hockey	150,000
V. Bracciale Jr., horse racing	145,965
Chris Evert, tennis	142,949
Lou Brock, baseball	140,000
Juan Marichal, baseball	140,000
Willie McCovey, baseball	140,000
Joe Torre, baseball	140,000
Bill Vukovich, auto racing	137,023
Sandy Hawley, horse racing	136,134
Reggie Jackson, baseball	135,000
John Newcombe, tennis	133,050
A.J. Foyt, auto racing	132,892
Hale Irwin, golf	130,388
Billy Casper, golf	129,474
Carlos Barrera, horse racing	129,245
Walter Blum, horse racing	129,170
Arthur Ashe, tennis	127,850
Johnny Miller, golf	127,833
Jim Palmer, baseball	125,000
Mike Venezia, horse racing	124,939
Fernando Toro, horse racing	124,273
M. Castaneda, horse racing	122,808
R. Woodhouse, horse racing	121,344
Rod Laver, tennis	120,125
Ferguson Jenkins, baseball	120,000
Bobby Murcer, baseball	120,000
John Schlee, golf	118,017
John Rotz, horse racing	116,447
Brooks Robinson, baseball	115,000
Rusty Staub, baseball	115,000
C. Jimenez, horse racing	114,843
Hubert Green, golf	114,397
John Mahaffey, golf	112,536
Ken Rosewall, tennis	110,950
G Cusimano, horse racing	106,704
Forest Fezler, golf	106,390
J.C. Snead, golf	103,601
J. Rutherford, auto racing	103,555
Mario Andretti, auto racing	102,577
A. Agnello, horse racing	100,156

*Due to the secrecy of some player contracts, this list is not complete. Also, many player contracts have clauses whereby salaries can go upward for performance, e.g., number of home runs, pitching victories, etc.

NO CHEERING IN THE PRESS BOX

By Jerome Holtzman

Sometimes, the pen (er... ahh...) typewriter is mightier than the bat. Meet the Sultans of the Keyboard.

The average newspaper reader, surveys have shown, will usually turn to the sports pages before he reads any other part of his daily newspaper. Indeed sportswriting itself has assumed an important place in the hierarchy of sports and literature. Great sportswriters provide much more than a reporting of the straight facts. They provide (and did especially so in the pre-television age) the sights, sounds, colors, moods and clashes of the antagonists. They interpret the results of the sporting skirmishes, battles, campaigns and wars. They breathe life into our sports heroes, rogues and villains. And the best of our sportswriting has been apprenticeship and life work for some of the best writers of our generation: Ernest Hemingway, Ring Lardner, Damon Runyon, Grantland Rice, Heywood Broun, Paul Gallico, Red Smith, and Shirley Povich to name but a few. Sportswriting was at its finest in the period between the two world wars. That was the golden age of sports and, sadly enough, the golden age of sportswriting. What follows are recollections from some of the best sportswriters of that period. These recollections are from Jerome Holtzman's book, *No Cheering in the Press Box,* published by Holt, Rinehart and Winston.

Dan Daniel *wrote baseball for 50 years, covering for a variety of New York papers, and was also the national correspondent of* The Sporting News. *Elected to baseball's Hall of Fame in 1973, he was the sport's high priest, alternately reporting and editorializing, and constantly issuing encyclicals for present and future conduct. In a recent message to baseball; Mr. Daniel said: "I will never stop loving baseball. It's the national pastime, no matter what. But I do wish baseball would put on a stronger front. Please! Please! A stronger front."*

I was one of the fastest writers who ever covered baseball. If it didn't go fast, it was no good. I quit. I had to be fast. If the ideas didn't come quickly, if the response wasn't immediate and I dragged, then it meant my inward conscience was not with the idea. I just quit, that's all. I had a knack of writing fast and mostly, I did things the first time out of the box. It had to be good the first time. I couldn't afford the time to dillydally too much. I worked best in the morning, starting at nine o'clock. It never mattered where I was—home, at the ball park, in the hotel, on the trains. I could write anywhere. There were times when I got tired of writing, but I enjoyed the fun of baseball and everything about it until that damn night ball came in. That ruined the whole business.

Baseball writing started out in a very elementary way. The men who wrote baseball in the early days were far from the real experts who came later—like Ring Lardner and Grantland Rice. A lot of the early baseball writers spent too much time on the wayside, and by "the wayside" I mean with too close an association with John Barleycorn. The finest examples of that deterioration lie in the memories of the old-time baseball writers in Chicago.

The baseball writer of my heyday had something to tell. He had opinions. He was a critic as well as a historian. Now you go into the clubhouse after a game and you find baseball writers wandering around, at times even putting words into the mouths of some of the boys. That's one of the big beefs of the players—that they are made to say a lot of things either they didn't want quoted or that they didn't say in the first place. I think today's baseball writers could improve their job vastly and should offer more of their opinion, and not simply stand and quote the manager. In my time I went out myself, on my own. I was known as a digger for scoops.

Almost every argument I had with a player was a result of being the official scorer and making a call someone didn't like. I scored about twenty-one games during DiMaggio's streak. Once in a while, during the streak, I got a very deep scowl from DiMaggio, but he never, not once, complained. Scoring during his streak was a precarious life. His fans would gather behind the press box in the stadium, and they raised Cain. They felt every time he hit the ball it should be a hit. You got something like fifteen dollars a game, and it wasn't worth the trouble. The responsibility was heavy. I wouldn't have done it over again for five thousand dollars. Now Joe will tell you that my strict adherence to my notion as to what was a hit was wonderful because there wasn't a hit he wasn't entitled to. I never favored him one iota and made him get his hits as I saw them.

Shirley Povich *has been writing sports for the Washington Post for over 50 years, and is without dispute, the best known newspaperman in the nation's capital. Except during the war years, Mr. Povich has covered every World Series, Kentucky Derby, and heavyweight championship fight since the early 1930s. His column, titled "This Morning," is a treasure of literary elegance, and offers textbook examples for current and future sportswriters.*

Despite the fact that I was a precocious young sports editor, I would describe myself as a late bloomer. Maturity came late to me. I was about thirty when I discovered I wasn't a clear thinker. I was a hero worshiper, a romanticist, highly sentimental, and entirely impractical. I was constantly overwriting, often attempting to make the event and the game more exciting and dramatic than it was.

I covered the Senators, traveled with them for more than fifteen years, and when I started all the players were heroes to me. Some of them were worthless bums and shouldn't have been my heroes, though they were good ball players. I simply had to keep readjusting my values. It was a slow, evolutionary process. It began, probably when I became a father for the first time and suddenly realized there was something more important than covering baseball games; that the squeeze play and the bunt and friendship with ball players were not quite the end of the world.

I am not going to say that I was acclaiming everybody in those early years. But I was considerably less critical than I should have been. It was just that I was so excited. I simply hadn't matured. Here I was covering a big league club, and yet, in retrospect, I was somewhat the same boy I had been in Bar Harbor, the boy who had dreamed and wondered if he would ever see a big league game.

There was another thing, too, darn it! This may never have been said before, and it may be unkind, but too many young sportswriters in my era had the wrong writing heroes. Certainly, we all admired Runyon and Rice and Pegler, idolized them, but we gave up too quickly and said, "We can never write like they can." They were simply untouchable.

We made the mistake of imitating other, closer heroes—the Associated Press writers, Alan Gould and Jack Bell. Their copy was regarded as lively copy, and many of us, in our sheer stupidity, assumed that since they were the stars of the Associated Press they had to be fine writers, fine reporters. And we followed blindly.

But those wire service guys were guilty as hell. They were always writing leads such as "Gene Sarazen and his blazing putter," and "Notre Dame came roaring from behind." Evry pitcher had somebody "eating out of the palm of his hand"—all those horrid metaphors.

They made everything cataclysmal. They couldn't give you the short action word. They were overmoderated, the adjectives were endless and the same. A baseball or football team doesn't come "roaring from behind." Heavens, there is no sound. And so myself, and others like me, were constantly inserting these metaphors, or some slang. When I see it now I want to upchuck.

God, I must have been pandering to the public taste, or something. I never asserted any individuality in those days. I had to unlearn so much over so long a period that it became an educational process. As I began detaching myself from the ball players, I gained the independence and the exhilarating confidence that no matter who they were, or what happened on the ball field, I would be able to write it as it happened. This is a significant difference. The skillful writer need not fret or worry in anticipation of the event. He awaits the event—and then reports it. You say to yourself, "They're the ball players. Let them play the game. I'm a reporter." It's a necessary separation.

I don't want to sound pedantic, but for a reporter, it's more than just a game. It's a great challenge in the sense that there it is—it has happened in front of you and now you must sit down at the typewriter. It's a task.

But it doesn't come easy. I've worked with guys who come in at two in the afternoon, sit down, and bat it out in an hour. I see them and I say, "What the hell am I doing here beating my head against the steam pipes when it's so easy for him?" I can get snow-blindness looking at that white sheet of paper. And if you don't recognize how tough it is, I'd say you're hopeless, because if you think it's easy your product isn't going to be much good. But I do enjoy the sweating and I do enjoy the working, the chore of it, the challenge, the hard part. I like to attack and write.

I'm not a rewriter, but before I commit myself I like to give it some thought. I like lucidity, and I am a firm believer in getting the key—a musical key, if you will. I know nothing of music. I am not a musician. But I must have the key in the first fifty or one hundred words. I want to know what key I'm playing in. Once you hear it, it will flow. It's when you don't have the good pitch, that's when you're in trouble.

And sportswriters, above all, must realize they should not contend with the ball players for popular favor. The ball players are the heroes, and the sportswriters better know this. You just recognize it and are not affected by it. You don't try to be popular.

John Drebinger *joined the staff of the New York Times in 1923 and spent the next 37 years writing about baseball. He wrote the lead story for the Times on 203 consecutive World Series games. Inducted into the Baseball Hall of Fame in 1974, Drebinger of all the sportswriters, may have come closest to fitting the traditional image of the ideal baseball Boswell—a kindly and benevolent veteran with an endless fund of tales to fascinate the younger players, yet a man who, in times of stress, was able to offer significant counsel to veteran stars and their coaches and managers.*

The guys back in the old days used to drink

These are the saddest
of possible words:
Tinker to Evers to Chance.
Trio of Bear Cubs
and fleeter than birds,
Tinker to Evers to Chance.
Ruthlessly pricking
our gonfalon bubble,
Making a Giant hit
into a double,
Words that are weighty
with nothing but trouble—
Tinker to Evers to Chance.

—Franklin P. Adams

Cliche Kit for Budding Young Sportswriters

You too can be a sports hack. Put together the following phrases and get your own press pass to the game.

Veteran hurlers
Relief artists
Dependable redundant mainstays
Key moundsmen
Power hitters
Scrappy little whatevers
Rifle-armed outfielders
Towering first basemen
Veteran sparkplugs
Rookie sensations
Aspiring rookies
Promising freshmen
Promising rookies
Aspiring freshmen
Highly-touted rookies
Highly-touted freshmen
Youngsters who'll bear watching
Young sparkplugs
Veteran sparkplugs
Aging sparkplugs
Veteran pilots
Guiding destinies of
Using managerial strategy

Action scenes:

Win the mound duel
Lose the mound duel
Driven off the mound
Knocked out of the box
Going all the way
Curve is working
Curve isn't working
Curve is breaking
Fastball is hopping
Issues a walk
Yields a run
Yields a base on balls
Allows too many hits
Gave up a four-bagger
Gave up a three-bagger
Gave up a two-bagger
Would dust his mother
Would dust his grandmother
Batting a hefty .260, .302, 424.
Rifle the ball
Rifle the pill
Rifle the horsehide
Rifle the pellet
Banish from the game
Relegates to the showers
Takes the long walk
Swats a homer
Belts a homer
Powers one over the fence
Powers one into left
A crucial contest
A tight one
A fabulous fray
A pivotal game
Nipped in the bud
Snatched from the jaws of
Routed out of the
Drubbed into the
Crushed
Subdued
Pasted
Trounced
Downed
Smashed

a lot more than they do not, but they seemed better able to handle it. I saw Babe Ruth take down a Coca-Cola bottle full of whiskey one time. Gurgled it right down. Drinking didn't in any way handicap him. In fact, I think it helped him relax. I still contend that Mickey Mantle, if he had been able to drink the way the Babe could, he would have smashed all the home run records. When you get up to fifty home runs there's a lot of pressure. Drinking would help anybody relax. But Mantle couldn't drink. He'd take a few and get silly.

I'll tell you who could relax on the stuff. Paul Waner. He was really something. One time he tied the lifetime record of that period for hitting doubles and didn't know what the hell he was doing. It was a hot day and he'd been drinking beer all through the game. He had this fellow who brought him another cold bottle every time he'd give him the signal. And Paul won the ball game with a double that drove in the winning run. He didn't know it was a double. He told me later, "Dreb, all I remember was that I hit the ball into left center and that I hit it good. I rounded first base, just kept going, and slid into second, and that's how I tied the record."

Another guy who drank heavily and could handle it was Pete Alexander. There was the time he struck out Lazzeri. It was in the 1926 World Series, against the Yankees. Alexander had pitched and won the day before and thought that was his last appearance. So he had been out drinking the whole night. Hornsby was managing the Cardinals and found himself in a tough spot, leading by one run in the seventh. He called in Alexander, who was in the bullpen sleeping off his binge. And by God, Alexander struck out Lazzeri with the bases loaded, and then pitched the next two innings and saved the game.

Years later Hornsby and I were fanning around and he says to me, "Hey, remember when I brought in Alex? Do you remember whether he took any warm-up pitches when he got to the mound?"

I said I couldn't remember because I was too busy banging on the typewriter.

"Well," he said, "he never did. I was out there when he came in and I said, 'How are you, kid? and he said, 'Okay, but no warm-up pitches. That would be the giveaway.' "

Paul Gallico *is now best known for his fiction, in particular for his award winning story* Snow Goose *and for* The Poseidon Adventure. *But he began his career as a sportswriter, reporting for the New York Daily News from 1923-1936. He got his first byline from fighting an exhibition boxing match with Jack Dempsey. Dempsey flattened him, but it was a great story and he soon became The Daily News sports editor and was writing his own column.*

I belonged to the gee-whiz group of sportswriters. Pegler was the aw-nuts. I was impressed by athletes, by what I was seeing and also what I was trying to do. I thought I ought to impress my public, impress the people who were reading, because if I didn't make a game that I saw, and which excited me, if I didn't make that exciting to the reader, I was a lousy sportswriter.

We had an overwhelming innocence in those days. We were so naive. Not only we sportswriters but the whole country. We had fought a world war, and supposedly won, and thought that we'd saved the world for democracy. Everybody was happy. There was a big boom. There were no problems. You could let yourself go on sports. A heavyweight championship fight, the build-up, was tremendous. It was like the Israeli-Arab war, the way one approached it. Your side and their side. The goodies and the baddies. Whether it was a ball game, or a boxing title, or a tennis or golf match, there was this built-in conflict and struggle, and we were witnesses to these struggles. When the Detroit Tigers came to town we hated them. Ty Cobb was a dirty word in New York. When Helen Wills played Suzanne Lenglen, when they met for the first time, you would have thought the world was coming to an end if our fine American girl got licked by this dreadful frog, this awful Frenchwoman. That's stupid, when you look at it now, but in those days it was all played that way, for high drama. You try that today and you'd be laughed out of the newspaper office.

I contributed to this innocence, this naivete. Tremendously. I believed in it and was impressed by athletes and by what I was seeing. I've seen and heard plenty of cheering in press boxes when we sportswriters got excited about something. I remember young Jimmy Cannon, I think it was at a Billy Conn fight, getting up and yelling "Lay down, you dirty son of a bitch of a dog! Lay down!"

I was getting a hell of a big salary from the *News* at that time, between forty and fifty thousand dollars a year. At the time I quit, a syndicate offered me seventy-five thousand a year and a three-year contract as a sports columnist. I turned it down. It wasn't what I wanted to do anymore. I was fed up with sports and wanted to be a fiction writer.

Abe Kemp *began his newspaper career in 1907, at the age of 14, and continued as a sportswriter for 62 years, dividing his time almost equally between baseball and horseracing. For the final 43 of those years, Kemp was on the staff of the* San Francisco Examiner. *One of his chores there was to handicap horseraces which he did quite successfully. Over the ten-year period up to his retirement he showed an aggregate profit on a two dollar bet and several times picked the card.*

I was a lousy baseball writer and a lousy

sportswriter and a lousy newspaperman because I never believed in the concept. I went my own way, figured out my own concept of what I wanted to write about. I wasn't interested in scoops, I wasn't interested in routine stories. I was interested in the unusual, the bizarre, the esoteric. I devoted sixty-three years to pursuing that line and as a consequence came up with more God damned stories than any sportswriter who ever lived. And that's the theme of my book—the unusual. Nobody will believe what I write, and I don't give a good God damn if they do or they don't. I've entitled my book *Almost the Truth —So Help Me, Ananias*. Ninety percent of it is the truth and five percent of it is hyperbole. The rest is imagination.

What the hell, you can't be perfect. Every sportswriter has his own ideas. You take today. You know what I term these modern-day sportswriters—inspired idiots. I'll be a sonofabitch if I know what they're thinking about. They're not writing sports. They're telling the manager who to hire, who to fire, how to coach, who to play. I don't think that's the prerogative of the sportswriter. All of 'em are trying to emulate Brann The Iconoclast. Brann was the most famous iconoclast of all time, and a terrific writer. He knocked and damned everything. But the guy could write.

I started writing baseball in 1908 when I was fifteen years old, for the San Francisco *Bulletin*. I was the youngest baseball writer in the United States with a daily by-line—"Abe the Irrepressible Rooter." I was a Seals fan, and sometimes when I was rooting for the club I used to climb up the screen. Three times I was thrown out for disturbing the spectators.

In those days most writers resorted to slang, and I was trying to outdo 'em as best as I could in my feeble way. I wrote the old cliches—he "rammycackled the old tomato." He "ripped the stitches off the ball." That's the best I could do. Christ, all I graduated from was grammar school.

I was brought up under a strange philosophy that I wouldn't advise anybody to pursue today. But I pursued it and I don't regret it. I was a Pollyanna. When I broke in under Baggerly, the only advice he gave me was "Abe, I'm not telling you to do this, but if you can't write something nice about a ball player, don't mention his name."

I pursued that policy the rest of my life, and nobody could sway me. Managing editors tried, but I didn't give a shit. I hewed to the line. Now, I don't recommend it. I don't say it was good. You couldn't get away with it today, not in this critical day and age. No earthly chance. Hell, I could have written some of the most scandalous stories of all time. But I didn't. I didn't believe in it, that's all.

What the hell, when a guy dies they praise the hell out of him. But he doesn't know what the hell it's all about. I believe in Felicia Hyams's poem: "Roses to the living are better than sumptuous wreaths to the dead."

Your mind plays strange pranks when you get as old as I am. Some things I can remember vividly, and some things I can't remember at all. I can give you the batting lineups of fifty, sixty years ago, but I can't tell you what day yesterday was. Or what the hell I ate for dinner. It's events that I remember. Dates don't mean anything to me. Statistics, I detest. They're the scourge of the American sports page. The fifteenth time he wiped his ass; the sixteenth time he rubbed his nose. You're writing a story and you say he's six foot seven, he's four foot two, or his earned run average is ______ that's a lot of crap. You disturb the continuity of the story. But that's all you get today.

You know Vernon Gomez, don't you? Lefty Gomez. They just put him into the Hall of Fame. Well, he broke in with the Seals here. He had plenty of guts right from the start. Nick Williams managed the Seals, and Nick would look down the bench before the game and he'd say, "Anybody got guts enough to challenge the enemy?" and Gomez would speak up and say, "I'll challenge 'em."

Cy Slapnicka, a scout for Cleveland—he's the guy who later signed Bob Feller—was looking at Gomez. Cleveland secured a ten-day option from the San Francisco club to buy Gomez for fifty thousand dollars and three ball players. The Seals were home, and I'm sitting up in the tower talking to Charlie Graham, the vice-president of the Seals.

Slapnicka comes and he says, "Charlie, is it all right if I go down into the clubhouse where the players are dressing?"

Charlie said, "Sure."

"Well, are you sure they'll let me in?"

So Graham phoned Denny Carroll, the trainer, and he said, "Slapnicka is coming down. Let him in."

After Slapnicka left, Graham says to me, "What the hell do you suppose he wants to go in the clubhouse for?"

I said, "Charlie, I haven't any idea."

About a half-hour later Slapnicka came back and said, "Charlie, I'm going to forfeit my option on Gomez."

Graham says, "Tell me something, Cy. Why did you change your mind from the time you left here until the time you returned?"

"Well," he says. "I'll tell you, Charlie. I saw Gomez undressed in the clubhouse, and anybody who's got as big a prick as he's got can't pitch winning ball in the major leagues."

I started to laugh like hell. Meanwhile, Slapnicka ducked out and Graham says, "What the hell do you find so amusing?"

I said, "I'll tell you what I find so amusing. This is the best God damned story in my life and I can't write a word about it."

Killed
Tripped
Tripped up
Edged out
Blanked
Whitewashed
Jolted
Eked out
Bowed to the victors
Scalped by the
Mowed down by the
Mauled by the
Slaughtered by the
Halted by the
Contained by the
Foiled by the
Nicked by the
Thwarted by the
Vanquished by the
Flattened by the

Athletic types:

Lean	Huge
Tall	Big
Slim	Strapping
Rawboned	Rugged
Lanky	Powerful
Towering	Handsome
Sturdy	Quick
Chunky	Speedy
Stocky	A real speedster
Rangy	Bruiser

Advanced Sportswriting Kit Sample copy:

WALLA WALLA—Five million members of fandom clicked through the turnstiles here today to watch the opener in the fall classic, a crucial contest between the victors of the Lemon League, the Walla Walla Seeds, and the flag contenders from the Lime League, the Yakima Juices. Snatching victory from the jaws of defeat, the Seeds squeezed by the Juices 29-27 in this epic Homeric struggle.

This pivotal contest hinged on a critical mound fray between ace hurler, Les B. Squat, and that veteran sensation, Don B. Cool.

Before the thrill-packed drama began, the milling throng was rife with rumors that this heroic struggle was part of a personal feud between the two awesome moundsmen. It was sheer, tense drama, a contest packed with thrills for a baseball mad city with a great outpouring of fans who stormed through the portals to break all attendance records.

From the first pitch, the crowd released its pent-up emotions, yelling itself hoarse as it rode mercilessly the men in blue...

a Workingman's Guide to Softball

By Alan Goldfarb

Softball ain't for sissies. That ball can smart.

It must be told, once and for all, that softball is a game in which neither the ball nor the game is soft. Furthermore, it is much more than office picnics and potbellied men drunk with beer. And, for those who take this game most seriously, three kinds of national championships occur: fast pitch—a fierce game of hopping, dropping, fuzzy-fast releases from the pitching mound; the Midwestern 16-inch slow pitch version—a game played with an easy-to-hit but not-too-far muskmelon of a ball and plain ol' slow pitch that just about every working stiff manages to play during those warm summer evenings after work.

Softball has had a fascinating history. It began as an indoor version of baseball in a lakefront Chicago boathouse gym in 1887. At first everything was slow pitch. But pitchers soon learned to increase underhand speeds to the point where the ball came zooming in at speeds of 100 miles per hour.

Ironically, speed almost killed the game, along with a few less than alert hitters. Pitchers became such prize commodities that industrial firms developing championship-caliber teams used to scour the country for pitching talent. Many hurlers would hire themselves out and eventually priced themselves out of the market. And the better the pitchers became, the fewer the spectators. Afterall, who wanted to watch a 1-0 softball game? Even the batters, rather than face the humiliation of striking out three or four straight times, simply quit the game.

But in the early 1960s, this pattern began to reverse itself. Rules were initiated to neutralize the import of the pitcher. The windmill windup was ground to a halt. The pitcher was forced to deliver his toss on a high arc in order for the batter to get a bigger and fatter look at the ball. That rule change revolutionized the game. Everybody began clobbering the ball all over the lot. Fielders stopped blowing bubblegum bubbles and got busy stopping balls. And the fans started coming back.

But no matter who plays or where, all softball players must cope with the same enviornmental conditions. Dirt fields are usually poorly maintained and laced with rocks. Asphalt playgrounds provide a better surface for stopping ground balls but a slide into second base can be a painful experience. The schedule is usually crowded—when one game is over, another begins and with a minimum of warm-up.

But softball keeps getting more popular. Take Jim McBride for instance. He'd do anything to play. Jim is a radio announcer in New York but is one of the most active players among the city's numerous softball leagues. He competes in four leagues each season and still manages to squeeze in a little work. "You need a system," says Jim referring to his work and play time. "If I left a game by the sixth inning and took a cab, I could get to the station in time for the news. On some days I'd change into my uniform at the station, take a cab cross town and be there in time for the warm-up."

How To Join A League

Due to the lack of playing space in large cities, most softball fields are reserved for league play or by groups. League play, however, is usually quite varied as to the style of game and to the caliber so that if you really want to play, there probably is a team out there for you. Usually the best and most efficient way to join a league is to get a team started in the office. It's a good way to socialize with colleagues and a damned good vehicle for having fun. Depending on the city, most leagues begin play in April and keep going through October (a la major league baseball). Once you have your team you should contact an official of a league that plays the kind of ball your team is into. Because softball has evolved into such a stylized sport, you should make up your mind beforehand which game you want to play—fast pitch, slow pitch, or 16-inch slow pitch.

Fast Pitch

In all three games, most rules are the same. The differences, of course, are in the speed of the pitch, the arc of the delivery, if balls and strikes will be called or if bunting and stealing is to be allowed. One lightning-speed pitcher in the fast pitch game says, "This is really softball. Slow pitch is an atrocity. You can be a defensive hitter in slow pitch and you can wait to the last second and slap at the ball. But try until the last second and slap at the ball. But try that in this game and you're dead." Indeed. Some fast pitch players have even played minor league baseball and are generally all-around athletes. It is not an uncommon sight in the fast game to see expectant, over-anxious batters lunge at change-ups and miss. Batters often seem helpless against the blazing spheroid zooming in from a mere 46 feet out (compared to 60 feet in baseball).

Slow Pitch

34-32! No, that's not a football score. We're still talking about softball—slow pitch softball that is. And that score is not uncommon. Slow pitch is a hitter's delight. For the record, no slow pitcher has ever been known to develop arm trouble. There are no trick pitches in this game. The rules state that "a legal delivery is effected when the ball is pitched at a moderate speed and with a perceptible arch of not less than three feet." Scores have gotten so out of hand that officials have decided to use a "restricted flight ball" in national tournaments, one with eight to 10 percent less bounce. One tournament official says, "Some guys want to hit away all the time but we have to balance the game off." And many players object to the change. Theirs is an action game, they say. They sneer at fast pitch players, calling that game a two-man bore.

16-Inch Softball

"As far as I'm concerned, there is only one softball game—16-inch slow pitch," says Eddie Zolna, "Mr. 16-inch softball." Zolna, or "Z" as he's called in Chicago, where that game is very big, is a pitcher. He claims he's won more than 3,000 games and that, "I've probably struck out two guys in 25 years." Anyone can hit the over-stuffed 16-inch ball. So the amateur Softball Association took steps to standardize the game and to bring it closer to the widespread 12-inch version. In the 16-inch game, the batter and pitcher are only 38 feet apart. It makes for an interesting game where everyone hits but rarely for distance.

So which game do you want to play? In 1965 60 percent of America's softball teams played fast pitch and 40 percent slow pitch. But the fast pitch game is dying. There are very few fast pitch teams remaining, perhaps about 15 percent. An ASA official tells why: "Lots of people play slow pitch because they'd have trouble being stars in fast pitch. Anyone with a bat in their hands can be a star in slow pitch."

This is your chance to be a star!

As in baseball, the object in rounders is to hit a ball and run around a designated area to score. The score is called a "rounder" and the team that scores the most wins the match. There are nine players on each side and all nine players have tc be out before an inning is over. Only two innings are played in a match.

The game is played on a rectangular rather than a diamond-shaped field. The field in rounders is marked by posts instead of bases.

Rounders became known in this country as Town Ball. The shape of the playing field varied depending on where it was palyed. In the mid-19th century New York teams playing on a square-shaped field found that it was difficult to run around the posts when running for extra base hits. By changing the field to the diamond shape, they could almost run the bases in a circle. They also substituted flat bases for posts and the modern baseball game was born.

Which came first Rounders or Baseball?

Patriotic America has been annoyed for some time now by ruddy English assertions that our national game is a game *they* call *rounders*, a girl's game on the British Isles.

Actually, way back when the dispute began (in the late 19th century) there were two schools of thought. One, headed by A.G. Spalding, who was a fine pitcher in his day and the founder of a sporting goods company, maintained that the national game had its roots nowhere but on American soil. No shirker of his patriotic duty, Spalding vehemently shouted this belief all his life, until he died in 1915. And even with only two seasons of National League ball, 1876-1877, Spalding was voted into baseball's Hall of Fame in 1939.

The other side was the rather unpatriotic faction led by Henry Chadwick. As baseball's first writer, Chadwick had invented the box score and was an acknowledged authority of the game. He had seen it played in its most primitive form even before Spalding was born. Chadwick declared that baseball came from rounders.

Spalding would not hear of such talk. In 1905, he organized a commission (probably an American invention) to decide once and for all the *real* origin of the game. Well, the Mills Commission (headed by General A.G. Mills) decreed in 1907 that baseball did originate in the U.S. and that the first game was designed by Abner Doubleday in Cooperstown, New York.

The facts are that Doubleday was a cadet at West Point when he was supposed to have been in Cooperstown inventing baseball. And more conclusive is the fact that the name *baseball* and the diamond-shape were well-known before Doubleday was born. Doubleday never claimed he invented the game. After he retired from the Army in 1873, Doubleday spent the rest of his life writing and of the many articles that flowed from his pen, he never once mentioned baseball. And when he died his obituary in *The New York Times* on January 28, 1893, made no mention of baseball.

Who, then, did invent baseball? The answer is simple: no one. The game just grew, from rounders.

THE KING & HIS COURT

By Alan Goldfarb

"Where's the rest of your team, Eddie?" they used to bellow from the stands before they knew any better. "What's the joke?" they wanted to know. But as soon as the guy on the mound with the silver black brush cut went into his figure-eight windmill delivery with a quarter-speed outraise or his whirligig with a cross-fire in-drop at three-quarter speed, forget it. The joke was over.

Eddie Feigner is serious when he's out there on the pitcher's mound. He's an entertainer, sure. But nobody laughs when a 12-inch hard softball comes zooming in at 104 miles per hour. Nobody hits it, either. Perhaps that is why Eddie Feigner has only two fielders behind him. And in reality, he wouldn't even need them if he didn't need their bats when "The King and His Court" come to the plate.

"People always wonder why we have four men instead of two or three," Eddie says. "That's so we'll have a hitter when we get the bases loaded."

And do The King and His Court get the bases loaded. Do they ever. Feigner (pronounced Fayner) has been winning softball games all over the world since 1946, hardly ever losing a game or even allowing as much as a squibble single up the middle. They've even tried major league baseball players against Feigner, but with his assortment of 19 windups, 14 hand deliveries, five speeds and 1,300 different pitches, he has struck out and in order, Willie Mays, Willie McCovey, Brooks Robinson, Roberto Clemente, Maury Wills and Harmon Killebrew. That's pitchin'.

And the Walla Walla, Wash. native knows it. "I am the world's finest softball pitcher by at least 100 percent," The King says. "I can say this because I have never met or seen anybody who was anywhere near half as good as me. I have perfect control. I throw the best changeup there ever was. I throw other pitches nobody can. My in-drop and in-raise are superpitches and unique. Who else pitches blindfolded? Who else pitches from behind his back or between his legs? For strikes? Check Koufax. Check Feller. I'm the fastest. There have been only three or four arms like mine ever in history. I once struck out a man on one pitch; he swung and missed three times at the same changeup."*

Before he became the best pitcher in softball, Feigner drove trucks and cabs and buses and trolleys. He operated cranes, worked docks, played the saxophone, kept cost-accounting books, dug ditches, conducted streetcars, washed dishes and practiced stand-up comedy. He waited tables, hustled used cars, sold vacuum cleaners, installed furnaces, cut asparagus, picked prunes, introduced strippers, pumped gas, sang tenor at funerals, fixed air conditioners, hawked vitamin pills door-to-door, sold burlesque tickets, peddled lumber, wrote sports, hammered nails and became a gourmet cook.

Eddie Feigner The greatest softball pitcher ever

In one of The King's rare stabs at humility he exclaims, "I'll never be a big-timer because I'm not in an organized, glamorous, moneymaking operation. Just softball. Who cares about softball? I want to start a pro softball league. I want to run a softball pitching school. But would it matter? Who cares?"

The King and His Court barnstorm from town to town, city to city, and in the process they are probably saving the game of softball. They attract good crowds. "We get teams who don't care about people in the stands," Feigner laments. "They just want to beat us. They actually think the crowd came to see them."

While still in junior high school Feigner became the best pitcher for the local college team. By the time he was 16, pitching six nights a week, striking out the side almost every inning, he was banned from the Walla Walla leagues. A few years later, pitching for Kilburg's Grocery in the Green Pea League, Eddie defeated a team from Pendleton, Ore., 33-0. The Pendleton manager told Feigner he couldn't defeat them again. Feigner challenged, saying he could do it with just three players. And he did. Not one Pendleton player reached base, and Feigner's team won, 7-0. The King and His Court were born.

During the team's first 250 games, The King and His Court never lost, but played no farther east than Idaho. Then in 1950, Feigner decided to take his Court cross-country. He's been on the road ever since.

**Editor's Note: Perhaps Feigner has met his match. In 1969, a young woman by the name of Rosie Baird, calling herself the Queen and Her Maids, began challenging nine-man teams. Rosie mowed them down with blazing pitches from between her legs, from secondbase, and yes, even blindfolded.*

THE QUEEN BEE & HER BRAKETTES

By Candice Moore

After pitching 96 no-hitters, Joan Joyce concedes that Vince Lombardi was right, winning is everything. And Joyce knows about winning. In her 16 seasons as the superstar pitcher with the Raybestos Brakettes, Ms. Joyce has won 393 games and lost 27. Those are stunning statistics but in softball you get stunning statistics. Here are some more: She's struck out 4,800 batters in 3,100 innings and has allowed a mere 97 runs in 430 games. That's nearly two batters an innings for her entire career and a career earned run average of 0.23.

At 16, when most teenagers are called on to do nothing more significant than study hard and get home early, Joan Joyce was called on to relieve a tiring pitcher in the 1958 National Women's Softball Tournament. She took the call and pitched four innings of no-hit ball to win the title for the Brakettes. Since then, she has led her team to four consecutive national championships and, most recently, to the Women's World Championship in 1974. (The Brakettes were the first U.S. team to capture that title.)

The main reason she gets so many strikeouts is her pitching simply terrifies batters. She spears the ball in with incredible speed and deception. She stands sideways on the mound, swivels her hips towards the plate, shifts her weight forward, from one foot to the next. Her hand springs out, brushing her right thigh, and *snap,* the ball seems to pop out of her hand as if shot from a cannon, scorching its flight path to the plate as an inside curve, a knuckle ball, a rise or a drop. It's anybody's guess, including the batter's. Her release is so deceptive not even the first or third base coaches can help with signals to their batters.

Great hitters like Ted Williams have walked away from the plate without making contact with any of Joyce's pitches, shaking their heads. It was incidents like that, though, that have prompted many carnivalesque promoters to try to talk Joyce into staging exhibitions, pitching against all comers, something Joyce has refused to do. "I think I'm a competitive person," she says, "but I can't go out and do tricks. To do it for money is really not my bag. I like what I'm doing anyway. The thing that keeps me in the game right now is not just the pitching. It's the batting. I love to hit."

And how. Here lifetime batting average is .323, among the highest in fast-pitch national softball competition. She has won a good share of Raybesto's games, her own games, on key hits she's made herself. She learned to hit from her father, who took her and her brother out for batting and pitching practice everyday after school.

Her pitching practice came off the wall of her parents' home in Waterbury, Conn., where she grew up. She'd draw a target on the side of the house and throw at it for three or four hours a day. "That," Joyce recalls, "was driving my mother crazy." Finally, she moved her pitching target to another side of the house where there were two trees in the yard separated by the width of a home plate and batter's box. She strung chicken wire between the trees to stop the balls and "saved my mother's sanity."

Now 36, Joyce supports her pitching by coaching girl's softball, teaching and operating a travel agency in Connecticut. There isn't any money in amateur softball, even if you are one of the best in the world. Still, she digs it and looks forward to years more of competitive play. She feels good about herself. "I guess being an exceptionally good athlete gives you a naturally good feeling. In the beginning, in the early years, you have to keep going farther and farther, beyond the norm and what's expected of you, but you don't get lost. You form a good concept of yourself. And that's what life's all about."

Joan Joyce
Also the greatest softball pitcher ever

THE WORLD'S MOST TRIVIAL SPORTS QUIZ

A. Name the movie stars and you're a bona fide film freak.

B. Guess the sports stars and you're weirder still.

C. Name the movie and you're clearly insane.

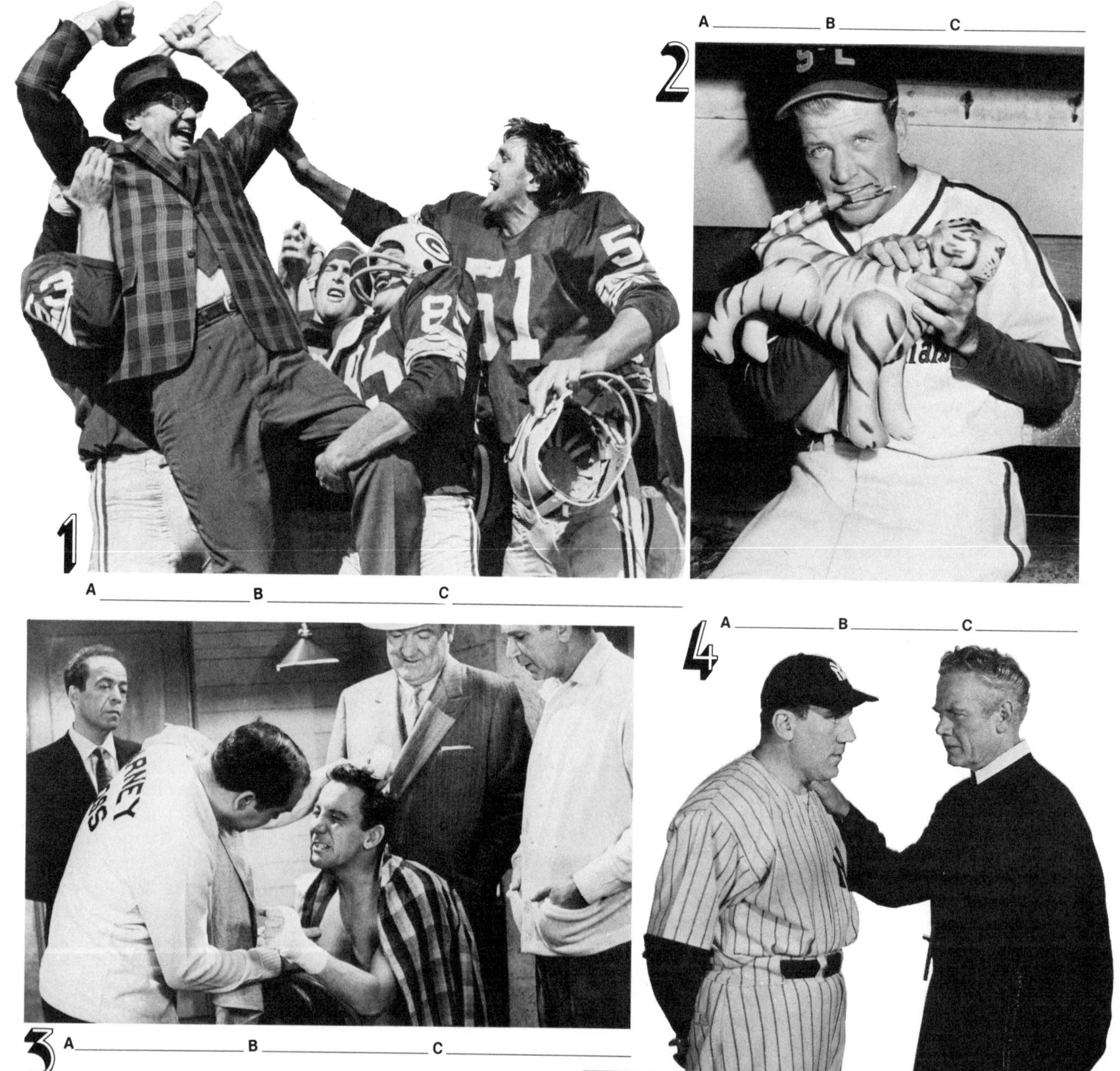

1 A ________ B ________ C ________

2 A ________ B ________ C ________

3 A ________ B ________ C ________

4 A ________ B ________ C ________

5 A__________ B__________ C__________

6 A__________ B__________ C__________

7 A__________ B__________ C__________

8 A__________ B__________ C__________

9 A__________ B__________ C__________

A. Movie Star • B. Sports Star • C. Movie
1A. Ernest Borgnine **1B.** Vince Lombardi **1C.** Portrait: Legend in Granite • **2A.** Dan Dailey **2B.** Dizzy Dean **2C.** The Pride of St. Louis • **3A.** Cameron Mitchell **3B.** Barney Ross **3C.** Monkey on My Back • **4A.** William Bendix **4B**. Babe Ruth **4C**. The Babe Ruth Story • **5A.** Tony Perkins **5B.** Jim Piersall **5C.** Fear Strikes Out • **6A.** Jimmy Stewart **6B**. Monty Stratton **6C.** The Stratton Story • **7A.** Gary Cooper **7B.** Lou Gehrig **7C.** The Pride of the Yankees • **8A.** Burt Lancaster **8B.** Jim Thorpe **8C.** Jim Thorpe—All American • **9A.** Paul Newman **9B.** Rocky Graziano **9C.** Somebody Up There Likes Me.

A HISTORY OF ORGANIZED MAYHEM

A CHRONOLOGY OF FOOTBALL STRATEGY

1823 William Webb Ellis, while playing soccer at the Rugby School in England, picked up the ball and ran with it. The new game was called Rugby in honor of the school.

1869 Princeton and Rutgers claim to have played the first intercollegiate football game. Actually, they played soccer.

1874 Harvard and McGill play the first football game, with running and tackling allowed in a rugby match.

1879 Princeton introduces blocking and running interference.

1880 One team given clear-cut posession of the ball to start play. Team set at 11 players. Two 45-minute halves.

1882 Walter Camp of Yale creates idea of downs, gaining five yards in three plays to keep possession of the ball. Signals for calling plays introduced.

1884 Princeton introduces the flying wedge.

1888 Tackling below the waist permitted.

1890 Walter Camp uses pulling guards to run interference for end runs. Uniforms begin to appear. Amos Alonzo Stagg introduces the reverse.

1893 John Heisman has center tossing ball back to begin play instead of rolling it back. First book on football, with play diagrams, written by Stagg and Dr. Henry Williams.

1894 Chicago and Stanford play first intersectional game.

1895 Camp has center snap ball directly to punter. First pro football game held in Latrobe, Pa. First forward pass, Univ of Ga. vs. Univ. of N.C.

Offensive football began as a murderous free-for-all. The idea was to grab the ball and run—whether there were a hundred men on a side or eleven—and get the ball over some kind of goal line. Played with a vengeance, the game had enough physical contact to frequently bloody noses, break bones or cause death.

This violence was a direct reflection of the rules and the game's first distinct offensive strategies. Sometimes a team would shove, push and carry a ball carrier across the goal line. Sometimes they tied a harness to the ball carrier and hauled him over. In these early days prior to the turn of the century, the runner was not counted as down until he yelled and admitted he was.

Courage or, more precisely, the refusal to yell "down" could be downright injurious to a ball carrier. Once, for example, Lawson Fiscus (who is supposed to have been the first professional football player) got very angry at a downed opponent who refused to admit that fact. Fiscus took careful aim with his heavily-shod boot and broke the man's jaw.

Nothing, however, produced as much mayhem as the flying wedge. The wedge was football's first offensive formation. Formed into a V-shaped phalanx, a team of blocking linemen would hang grimly onto suitcase handles sewed to the pants of the man in front and thunder *en masse* down the field. In the center of this group was the ball carrier. He ran in the middle of the wedge while opponents were being knocked down or bounced out of the way. In 1905, this strategem was responsible for at least 18 deaths among college and high school football players. The deaths caused a national uproar and ensuing rule changes significantly altered the game.

For American football even to get to this point, the game had evolved from a quarter century of innovations and rule changes which

began in 1874. That was the year Harvard applied rugby rules to soccer. Then Princeton introduced blocking. Rules were changed so that one team could have clear-cut possession of the ball to start play and playing time was set at two 45-minute halves. Teams were trimmed to 15 players, then 11. In 1882, Walter Camp came up with the idea of downs: a team had to advance five yards in three plays to keep the ball. The flying wedge appeared at Princeton on 1884 and tackling below the waist was permitted four years later.

By 1900, John Heisman had taught his center to snap the ball instead of rolling it backwards. The first forward pass, though illegal or unheard of, was thrown in 1895. There were huddles, even a few uniforms and one or two helmets. Amos Alonzo Stagg came up with the lateral and co-authored the first book on football strategy.

After the gridiron deaths of 1905, President Theodore Roosevelt threatened either to ban football from America's playing fields or change it. He summoned a number of football coaches to the White House in 1906 and that year marked the beginning of seven years of rule changes. The flying wedge was ruled illegal. Hurdling the line was outlawed.

Teams were given four downs to advance 10 yards. The forward pass was legalized and an end zone established for passes over the goal line. Kick-offs were moved back from midfield to the 40-yard line. Seven men were required to be on the offensive line of scrimmage but they were not allowed to interlock arms for blocking or running interference. Playing time was reset at four periods of 15 minutes each and the scoring system was finalized.

Passing rules were pretty strict. Initially, the pass was limited to five yards laterally and the field was marked with five yard squares (thus, the word "gridiron"). And it was tough to catch a ball because there was nothing to prevent a defender from knocking the receiver down and catching the ball himself. If a pass went out of bounds, the soccer rule applied: the ball went to the opposing team. Some ball carriers, like Jim Thorpe, the 1912 Olympic marvel, were charged with wearing shoulder pads made of a skin of light steel over heavy padding.

By the 1920s, football rules were considered perfect or almost perfect. The forward pass could be thrown with fewer restrictions. The dropped pass was no longer a free ball. If it was thrown out of bounds, the pass was dead. Receivers got more protection; hereafter, they would be assaulted before and after they caught the ball, not while they were in the act of trying to catch it. The quarterback could pass from anywhere five yards behind the line of scrimmage and he usually had two ends running some pass patterns, even though he did not throw very often.

One of the standard offensive formations was the very, very, tight T.

Using a low center-of-gravity crouch, the tight-T was exemplified by line play. But the linemen were so engrossed with pounding each other on the head or ramming the chest of the man across the line, he oftentimes forgot or cared little about doing anything else. The backfield lined up close behind the lineman and when the ball was snapped, it seemed the playing area quickly turned into a mass of twisting bodies, arms and legs. If a team moved the ball at all they moved it by running and they ran between the tackles. Such offenses offered so little running room that scoreless ties were not unusual and many games were decided by drop-kicked field goals. Spectators rarely saw the ball or a runner advance very far beyond the line of scrimmage.

What the runner needed was freedom, more running room, and Glenn "Pop" Warner gave it to him. What Warner designed at Pittsburgh and Stanford (he had coached Thorpe at Carlisle) was called the single wing and it became the running game of Red Grange and Johnny Blood, of Ernie Nevers and Bronko Nagurski, of Mel Hein and Sammy Baugh.

LE LT C LG RG RT RE
BB WB
FB
TB

The single wing

The single wing was conceived to exploit the weakness between the defensive tackle and the defensive end. Because the end is charged with forcing the play inside and had no help to the outside, he played wide. This left a natural gap between him and the defensive tackle. Warner developed a powerful running attack by placing his two tackles between his right guard and right end. He played his quarterback (actually a blocking back) behind and between his two offensive tackles and flanked the defensive tackle with a wingback. Thus, his teams could double team block anywhere along the interior line. For example, the offensive end and wingback would double team block the tackle, the quarterback and fullback would seal out the defensive end, and the tailback would follow a pulling guard through the hole. When passing, the wingback and ends could get downfield without much hindrance. The running pass on a fake end sweep was very potent and the backfield alignment allowed for a great deal of deception. Using what came to be called the "spinner series," the fullback could fake or give to the tailback. This offense also had the option of a direct hike to the tailback who was the key player in this formation. And from the same set, the tailback could quick kick or punt. The general tenor of single wing play was a rugged and bruising game of football. This formation remained popular until well into the 1940s.

The single wing also had its limitations, however: the ball did not reach the line of scrimmage quickly; the weak side of the unbalanced line provided very poor pass protection, limiting this attack to short passes. There was also a major personnel problem: instead of finding one player who could run, another who could pass and a third who could kick, the single wing coach had to find a triple threat tailback who could do all three.

Warner had a system which adjusted for these weaknesses in the double wingback formation. The double wingback provided excellent passing possibilities and greater deception through fakes and single and double reverses. The double wing, however, was hindered by a weak outside running attack. It required more lateral running by the ball carrier prior to reaching the line of scrimmage; this gave the defense more time to recover and arrive at the point of attack. The double wing also called for the tailback to make those runs into the interior line but not many coaches were willing to have their key player take such risks. The double wingback set reached its zenith of popularity during the 1920s: after that, it was the single wing. The next strategic development, however, revolutionized football. It would be called the T-formation.

Clark Shaughnessy had played the tight-T as early as 1908. In the years since then he had become a compulsive doodler of football diagrams. What he loved most was sitting down with a stack of graph paper, a set of sharpened pencils and about half a day to kill. He became football coach at the University of Chicago in 1933 and while there he struck up a friendship with George Halas, the owner of the Chicago Bears. In the ensuing years, Shaughnessy sent Halas a number of play suggestions but it wasn't until 1940 that the college coach and the pro owner made football history.

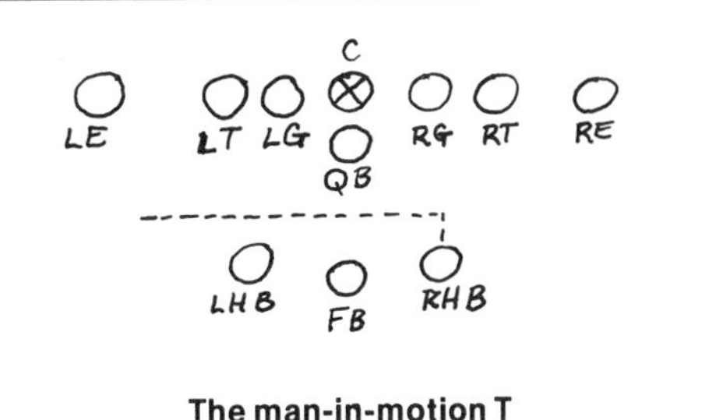

The man-in-motion T

1896 Stagg introduces the huddle and wind sprints. Helmets appear.

1897 Stagg introduces line shifts.

1898 Heisman introduces "hep" and "hike" to our vocabulary. Stagg introduces the lateral pass.

1900 Camp develops cross-blocking at the line of scrimmage. Stagg introduces the unbalanced line.

1903 Heisman suggests legalization of the forward pass.

1905 There are 18 deaths attributed to college and high school football, causing national furor. President Theodore Roosevelt summons football representatives to the White House.

1906 Beginning of seven years of rule changes: flying wedge ruled illegal. Forward pass legalized. Three downs to make 10 yards. On side kick legalized. Stagg begins awarding football letters.

1910 Play set at four periods of 15 minutes each; player taken out could not return until following period. Seven men required to be on the offensive line of scrimmage. Interlocked arms for running interference ruled illegal.

1912 Four downs to make 10 yards. End zone established. Kickoffs moved back from midfield to 40-yard line. Scoring system finalized.

1913 Forward pass popularized in Army-Notre Dame game. Gus Dorais throwing, Knute Rockne catching. Stagg numbers his players.

1925 Football is stitched and lined to hold shape throughout a game. Red Grange demonstrates broken-field running.

1930 Against Navy, Notre Dame coach Knute Rockne freely substitutes 145 players.

1934 The football is slimmed in girth for more throwing ease.

1935 Don Hutson demonstrates how to catch a pass.

1937 Sammy Baugh demonstrates how to pass.

1940 Clark Shaughnessy, George Halas, Bob Zuppke and the Chicago Bears introduce the new T-formation which revolutionizes offensive football.

1949 Clark Shaughnessy and the L.A. Rams introduce the "three-end" attack, which becomes the basic pro set of the 60s and 70s. Pro football moves into era of free substitution and specialization. No more need for 60-minute players.

1951 The Los Angeles Rams, with Norm Van Brocklin and Bob Waterfield, fill the air with footballs, rewriting record books for offensive yardage.

1957 Jim Brown demonstrates power running.

1958 As a result of the Baltimore Colts, New York Giants championship game, pro football becomes The sports spectacle of the electronic media.

1960 Red Hickey and the San Francisco 49ers briefly try out the shotgun formation.

1966 University of Houston coach Bill Yeoman introduced the triple-option, enabling the offense to adjust the point of attack *after* the ball is snapped.

1968 University of Texas Coach Darrell Royal introduces the wishbone-T, refining, the triple-option. Teams using the wishbone have decisively broken all intercollegiate records in yardage gained and points scored.

1974 Pro rules change to open up passing game and de-emphasize field goals.

That was the year the Chicago Bears introduced the new T-formation and it featured a strong passing attack and an inside running offense built around traps, when a defensive player is allowed to cross the line of scrimmage and is blocked from the side while the ball carrier runs through that vacated defensive spot.

With the quarterback over the center for a quick snap, this formation freed the center for blocking assignments. No longer did he have to look between his legs and hike the ball, except for punts. The line, which was balanced, could provide better pass protection. On running plays linemen were no longer required to charge the defensive linemen and drive or lift them backwards. Later, when linemen took wider line splits, anywhere from six inches to four feet apart in the interior line, they wouldn't have to open up holes. They would be required to brush block the defender so that a blocker and ball carrier could slip through. The lead blocker would deal with the next man in the defensive secondary. As for the quarterback, he operated up and down the line of scrimmage rather than several yards deep in the backfield. Because duties were more specialized, talented players were easier to find. The theory now was that every play was a potential touchdown.

Well, the Chicago Bears won their division championship that year and tried out their new T on Sammy Baugh and the Washington Redskins in the 1940 NFL championship game. The Eastern champs didn't have a chance. The Bears beat Baugh & Co. by a score of 73-0. Needless to say, the football world was ready to look and listen. In fact, four years later, Redskins owner George Preston Marshall hired Shaughnessy to install the T into the Washington offense. Sammy Baugh, who had been setting league passing and kicking records for seven years as a tailback, was most unhappy. "I hated it at first," Baugh is quoted as saying. "But Shaughnessy told me that [Sid] Luckman [the Bears' tailback in 1940] actually cried over the thing when they started teaching it to him." Like Luckman, Baugh went on to become a very proficient master of the new strategy and by the end of the 1940s, every pro team had converted to the new T.

In 1949, Shaughnessy came up with a new innovation. He filled the air with footballs. He was coaching the Los Angeles Rams at the time and he had a wealth of aerial specialists in Norm Van Brocklin and Bob Waterfield at quarterback and three fine receivers in Elroy Hirsch, Tom Fears and Bob Shaw. Shaughnessy placed a tight end close to the tackle, flanked one pass receiver wide right and another wide left and deployed two running backs behind the quarterback. This L.A. offense generated such a devastating and explosive attack it produced total offense, passing and scoring records that still stand. It doesn't require even careful scrutiny to see that what Shaughnessy introduced in 1949, then called the "three-end attack," is patently close to the formations of professional football today.

Red Hickey, coach of the San Francisco 49ers, engineered a brief offensive revolution in 1960 but it sputtered. It was called the shotgun and when Hickey pulled the trigger on it against the 1959 champions, the Baltimore Colts, he gunned them down, 30-22. The 49ers won four of their last five games using the shotgun. They also won their first five games of the next season, 1961. The 49er shotgun offense led the league in points, yards passing and running. Then, in the sixth game of that season, the shotgun ran into the Chicago Bears and Clark Shaughnessy. Shaughnessy, who had been on special assignment scouting the shotgun for two weeks, devised a defense forcing the shotgun to backfire and the Bears ran away with the contest, 31-0.

Some critics said the shotgun was no more than a dressed up spread formation or the Pop Warner double wing. The idea, as Hickey conceived it, was to open up the passing game. First, Hickey had his receivers draped all along the line of scrimmage so they could get downfield quickly. Second, he placed the passer (called tailback in this set) back where he could immediately see and survey the defense from the snap of the ball. Third, he built in a run-pass option. The Bears, however, saw the classic weakness. Because the center had to put his head between his legs to snap the ball, he couldn't block. Linebackers shot through on one side or the other of center all afternoon and the 49ers went on to a string of losses. Hickey later dropped the shotgun but attributed team losses to a lack of confidence after they were mauled by Chicago.

The basic formation in football today is the open, or pro, set. It consists of two wide receivers, a tight end and two running backs. It is sometimes run with one wide receiver, a tight end, a flankerback and two running backs. The open set has a number of strategic advantages over past formations: the pass is a constant threat because of the wide receivers; the line is balanced to either side; runners can hit quickly straight ahead or off tackle. The only weakness is an inability to put strong

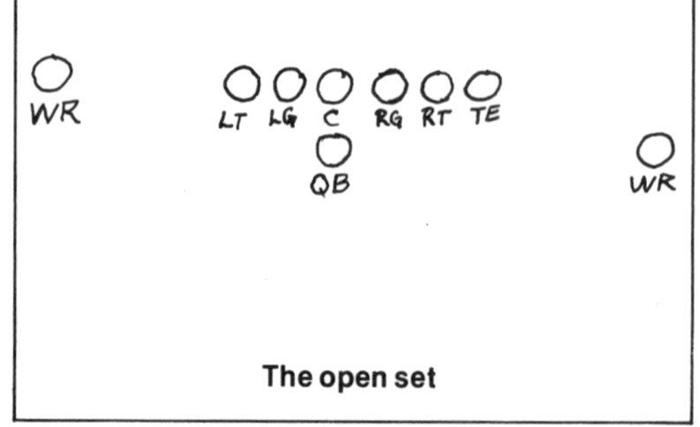

The open set

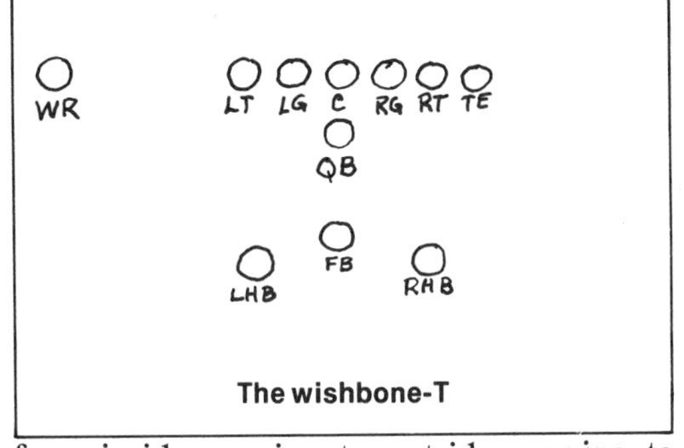

The wishbone-T

power on inside runs since you cannot hit quickly and also have a blocking back leading the attack.

Several variations can come out of this basic set. Two of them, the twin and the spread, put additional pressures on defensive secondaries. In the twin set, both wide receivers are flanked out to the same side. This means they can coordinate their pass routes and use these routes and each other to free whoever happens to be the primary receiver. Often, the twin set can be formed by a flanker in motion from the open set.

The second variation, called the spread (and looks suspiciously like a shotgun), has one or both of the running backs moved out of the backfield up toward the line of scrimmage as wingbacks. It's like screaming at the defense that you plan to pass. But then you have four or five receivers who can go at the snap of the ball. If both backs are moved up, the only real running threat is the quarterback.

A third variation off the basic set is the I-formation. It's the same except the running backs are lined up in an imaginary vertical I behind the quarterback. The running back, called the fullback in this formation, is crouched in a three-point stance directly behind the fullback. All the strategic advantages of the open set passing attack are here and the formation has the additional pressure of a powerful inside running game. The fullback can either lead block for the tailback or he can hit quickly inside.

To generate a stronger running attack, a team can adjust the I into the I-slot. The only adjustment, really is pulling the tight end back into a wingback position. Both wide receivers are flanked on the line. The I-slot enables a more flexible running game since all four backs are in a position to handle the ball. If the wingback is the ball carrier, he is usually handed the ball after a fake to the fullback or tailback.

An even stronger running attack, with some loss in passing strength, can be found in another variation of the I formation, the power-I. It is run with two tight ends or one tight end and one wide receiver (or split end) but the basic change is the flankerback becomes a halfback, lining up behind the offensive tackle. This formation has greater deception because any one of the backs can end up with the ball quickly. It also puts more power at the point of attack on a run since both the fullback and the halfback can lead block on side running plays. You will probably see the power-I when a team needs short yardage or smells goaldirt.

The most current offensive developments have come from college football. Both came out of Texas in the 1960s and both give the offense an ability to choose the point of attack *after* the ball is snapped. This choice ranges from inside running to outside running to passing. The first of these developments, the triple option, was unveiled by University of Houston coach Bill Yeoman in 1966.

It doesn't look that different from the open set but it is. It's all in the running of the play. First, one of the running backs hits off tackle. As he's doing this, the quarterback rides the ball on the runner' ship while watching the opposing defensive tackle. If the defensive tackle comes across the line of scrimmage, he gives the running back the ball. If the quarterback sees that the defensive tackle is waiting to stop the runner, he keeps the ball and moves out to try an option on the defensive end. The play now becomes the standard quarterback option. With a trailing back running behind him and five yards deeper, the quarterback runs at the defensive end. If the end moves up to tackle him, the quarterback flips the ball to the trailing back and blocks on the end. If the end commits to cut off the toss to the trailing back, the quarterback keeps the ball and heads for daylight upfield.

The Wishbone T, which has proven even more effective than the triple option, is formed by pulling one of the flankers in directly behind the quarterback as a fullback. Again, the attack is in the running of the play. The fullback runs off tackle with the quarterback looking for the commitment of the defensive tackle; he hands off or keeps as in the triple option. If he keeps, he and both running backs move forward to option the end. The same play can be run to either side since the line is balanced. The single wide receiver, or split end, is usually defensed man-to-man which means he can usually get open for a pass. Both the triple option and the wishbone are incredibly effective because it seems that anything the defense does will be wrong. That's the whole point of adjusting the point of attack *after* the center snaps the ball. In fact, teams using the wishbone have broken all intercollegiate records in yardage gained and points scored.

Right now, it seems difficult to lose under such circumstances but some coach or some doodler somewhere will eventually figure out an adequate defense. Once that happens, another tinkerer will come up with a new offense. And so it goes.

LE LG C T T RE QB LH RH FB

The double wingback

SE LT LG C RG RT TE HB FB FL QB

The shotgun

WR LT LG C RG RT WR QB HB FB RE

The I-formation

THE NFL FAMILY TREE

By Jim Campbell

The genealogy of your favorite team.

Tracing the lineage of professional football's franchises is a task akin to establishing qualifications for the D.A.R. Sometimes it just can't be done. Over the years, close to 90 teams have been in and out of the National Football League. Of the 11 teams that were given the original charters in 1920, only two exist today—neither one at their original site.

The survivors are the Chicago Bears, then as now, headed by George S. Halas, and the St. Louis Cardinals. The Bears were chartered as the "Staleys" of Decatur, Ill., and moved to Chicago a year later. The Cardinals had been in Chicago first but moved to St. Louis in 1960.

Most of the teams have moved at least once. An exception is the Green Bay Packers who were franchised in 1921 and have stayed in Wisconsin ever since. The New York Giants are another exception. Formed in 1925, they were such a strong team they gave the League true "major league" status.

But all through the 1920s and 30s teams came and went in the NFL... mostly went. Duluth, Minn.; Orange, N.J.; Louisville, Ky.; Providence, RI.; Hartford, Conn.; and Hammond, Ind. all held NFL franchises at one time. Complicated situations arose such as the geneology of the Frankford "Yellowjackets." Franchised in 1924, they became the Philadelphia Eagles and then traded franchises and players with the Pittsburgh Steelers in 1941. This means that today's Steelers are really yesterday's Eagles/Yellowjackets and that the present Eagle franchise is the one that originated in Pittsburgh in 1933. Is anybody following this?

It doesn't get any less complicated when discussing other teams in the League. For example, there is an ongoing debate over the origins of the Washington Redskins. One group claims that when the 1928 Duluth Eskimos disbanded they went to Orange, N.J. and then on to Boston via Newark, N.J. Others are sure that when the Pottsville, Pa. Marroons moved to Boston in 1929, they formed the nucleus of the team that was reactivated in 1932 and subsequently moved to Washington in 1937.

There is no question about the origins of the Detroit Lions, however. They arrived in Detroit in 1934 by way of Portsmouth, Ohio. Ohioans missed professional football and managed to get a new franchise in Cleveland in 1937. The Cleveland Rams stayed until 1946, when they took Los Angeles by storm and helped increase national interest in football.

In 1946 the All-American Football Conference was formed to compete with the NFL. Of the AAFC's original eight teams, the Cleveland Browns and the San Francisco 49ers joined the NFL in 1950, as did the Baltimore franchise, which had entered the AAFC in 1947. Baltimore played in the NFL in 1950, but disbanded in 1951. The Colts' place, loosely translated, was taken by the New York Yanks, who (again loosely translated) became the 1952 Dallas Texans. The Dallas team folded in mid-season and became a "road-team" quartered at Hershey, Penn. In 1953, Baltimore re-entered the NFL, with a nucleus of outstanding players from Dallas. The League remained stable through the 1950s, but things began to change in 1960 from within and without. In that year the American Football League was formed with the following teams: The Boston Patriots, Buffalo Bills, Houston Oilers, New York Titans, Dallas Texans, Denver Broncos, Los Angeles Chargers and Oakland Raiders. The Chargers moved to San Diego in 1961, while the Titans became the Jets in 1963. Lamar Hunt, a driving force behind the AFL's rise, moved his Texans from Dallas to Kansas City, where they play as the Chiefs. After bouncing around Boston, the New England Patriots settled in suburban Foxboro in 1971.

While the AFL was being born, the NFL expanded. Dallas got the Cowboys in 1960 and the following year the Vikings relocated in Bloomington, Minn., a suburb of Minneapolis-St. Paul. The Atlanta Falcons joined the NFL in 1966, followed by the New Orleans Saints in 1967. Meanwhile, the AFL added the Miami Dolphins in 1966, followed by the New Orleans Saints in 1967. Meanwhile, the AFL added the Miami Dolphins in 1966, and the Cincinnati Bengals in 1968.

The Leagues merged in 1966 and by 1970 all 26 teams were playing under the banner of the National Football League. To even the league, Pittsburgh, Cleveland and Baltimore joined the 10 AFL teams to give both the National Football Conference and the American Football Conference of the National Football League 13 teams. The League looks forward to 1976 when two new teams will take the field: the Tampa Bay Buccaneers and the Seattle Seahawks. Where will they go next?

The All-Time Greatest Runners

*Ranked by average gain per 14-game season.

Rank	Player	Years	Years Played	Average Gain per 14-Game Season	Average Gain per Carry	Total Attempts	Total Yards Gained	TD's	Teams
1.	Jim Brown	9	1957-65	1,461	5.22	2,359	12,312	106	Syracuse, Browns
2.	O. J. Simpson	6	1969-74	1,051	4.58	1,378	6,306	33	U.S.C., Bills
3.	John Brockington	4	1971-74	1,040	4.07	1,021	4,159	20	Ohio State, Packers
4.	Gale Sayers	7	1965-71	1,020	4.95	1,001	4,956	39	Kansas, Bears
5.	Steve Van Buren	8	1944-51	993	4.44	1,320	5,860	69	L.S.U., Eagles
6.	Cookie Gilchrist	6	1962-67	925	4.47	1,010	4,293	37	(no college), Bills, Broncos, Dolphins
7.	Jim Taylor	10	1958-67	912	4.43	1,941	8,597	83	L.S.U., Packers, Saints
8.	Larry Brown	6	1969-74	911	3.87	1,413	5,467	17	Kansas State, Redskins
9.	Larry Csonka	7	1968-74	843	4.59	1,286	5,900	41	Syracuse, Dolphins
10.	Cliff Battles	6	1932-37	841	4.19	846	3,542	27	W. Va. Wesleyan, Braves, Redskins
11.	Calvin Hill	6	1969-74	835	4.30	1,166	5,009	39	Yale, Cowboys
12.	Don Perkins	8	1961-68	777	4.14	1,500	6,217	42	New Mexico, Cowboys
13.	Joe Perry	16	1948-63	761	5.04	1,929	9,723	71	Compton J.C., 49ers
14.	Floyd Little	8	1967-74	735	3.88	1,516	5,878	41	Syracuse, Broncos
15.	John Henry Johnson	13	1954-66	666	4.33	1,571	6,803	48	Arizona State, 49ers, Lions, Steelers, Astros
16.	Leroy Kelly	11	1964-74	661	4.21	1,727	7,274	74	Morgan State, Browns
17.	Dick Bass	10	1960-69	653	4.45	1,218	5,417	34	Univ. of Pacific, Rams
18.	Ron Johnson	6	1969-74	623	3.78	990	3,738	31	Michigan, Browns, Giants
19.	Marion Motley	10	1946-55	618	5.70	828	4,720	31	Nevada, Browns
20.	Ken Willard	10	1965-74	611	3.76	1,622	6,105	45	No. Carolina, 49ers, Cardinals
21.	Mike Garrett	9	1966-74	609	4.19	1,308	5,481	35	U.S.C., Chiefs, Chargers
22.	Abner Haynes	8	1960-67	579	4.47	1,036	4,630	46	No. Texas State, Texans, Chiefs, Broncos, Jets
23.	Jim Nance	10	1965-74	540	4.03	1,341	5,401	45	Syracuse, Patriots
24.	Jim Kiick	7	1968-74	520	3.35	1,087	3,644	28	Wyoming, Dolphins
25.	Hugh McElhenny	13	1952-64	517	4.70	1,124	5,281	38	Washington, 49ers, Vikings, Giants, Lions
26.	Paul Hornung	10	1957-66	509	4.16	893	3,711	50	Notre Dame, Packers
27.	Lenny Moore	12	1956-67	507	4.84	1,069	5,174	63	Penn State, Colts
28.	Charlie Trippi	9	1947-55	491	5.10	687	3,506	22	Georgia, Cardinals
29.	Steve Owens	5	1970-74	490	3.86	635	2,451	20	Oklahoma, Lions
30.	Matt Snell	9	1964-72	476	4.05	1,057	4,285	24	Ohio State, Jets
31.	Bill Dudley	12	1942-53	475	4.00	765	3,057	15	Virginia, Steelers, Lions, Redskins
32.	Willie Ellison	8	1967-74	428	4.28	801	3,426	24	Texas Southern, Rams

From the Bowery Boy style of the 1937 Washington Redskins, running evolved to the cool efficiency of the "Juice" and his Buffalo Bills.

Running to daylight and through solid human walls

THE BEST OF THE PIGSKIN PARADE...

Single-handedly, Red Grange, the Galloping Ghost, *established pro football as a major spectator sport beginning in the 1920's.*

The Blond Block Buster, *Ernie Nevers, was a Renaissance man. Besides incredible running feats, he was also a great passer and field goal kicker.*

Red Grange

In three years of football at the University of Illinois, Red Grange scored 31 touchdowns and gained 3,637 yards rushing and returning kicks, and that, in the vernacular of the Roaring Twenties, was two miles and 117 yards. He was a consensus All-American for three years. And he put football on the American cultural landscape. What he did specifically was probably best stated by Paul Sann in *The Lawless Decade:* "Red Grange, No. 77," Sann wrote in his book, "made Jack Dempsey move over. He put college football ahead of boxing as the Golden Age picked up momentum. He also made some of the ball yards obsolete; they couldn't handle the crowds. He made people buy more radios: how could you wait until Sunday morning to find out what deeds Red Grange had performed on Saturday? He was 'The Galloping Ghost' and he made the sports historians torture their portables without mercy." How did he do it? Well, the Galloping Ghost was also the "Flying Terror." In a game against Michigan, he scored touchdowns the first four times he touched the ball, with runs of 95, 67, 56, and 44 yards—in the first 12 minutes! At Franklin Field in Philadelphia, against the University of Pennsylvania, the Ghost carried the ball 36 times for 363 yards and three touchdowns in ankle-deep mud. After his last college game, Grange signed as a professional with a Chicago promoter named C.C. "Cash-and-Carry" Pyle. Together with George Halas and the Chicago Bears, the new football marvel went on an exhibition tour. Grange packed 36,000 in Wrigley Field in a fierce snowstorm; repeated with 28,000 three days later (same blizzard, same field); crammed 40,000 into Philadelphia's Shibe Park in driving rain and pre-sold 60,000 tickets for an exhibition at the Polo Grounds during a week of rain. When it cleared on game day 73,651 paying customers sat down to watch the Ghost Gallop. In sum, Grange single-handedly established professional football.

Ernie Nevers

Ernie Nevers could do it all. When he played at Stanford he was called the Blond Block Buster. Pop Warner who coached both Jim Thorpe and Nevers stated flatly that Nevers was "the greatest football player of all time" and his opinion's good for a few points. When Stanford lost to Notre Dame and Knute Rockne's Four Horsemen in the 1925 Rose Bowl, Nevers gained 114 yards rushing and punted for a 42-yard average—while playing with two broken ankles. Rockne walked off the field, shaking his head and muttering, "What would that man have done to us with two good ankles?"

It's been 50 years but Nevers still holds the NFL records for most points scored in one game (40); most touchdowns rushing in one game (six, set against Red Grange's Chicago Bears); and most touchdowns passing or rushing (six, shared with Gale Sayers and Dub Jones). All those records were set while Nevers played 60 minutes a game and while he was, and remains, the only player-coach in NFL history. He has also completed 17 consecutive passes in a game and once kicked five consecutive field goals, at 42, 28, 26, 25 and 21 yards. In a game against the New York Giants, he intercepted a pass on his team's 45 yard line, then took it on nine consecutive running plays to score. Like they said, he could do it all.

Steve Van Buren

The record books say that Steve Van Buren played for eight years. He did, but for two of those years he ran in spite of a variety of crippling ailments and injuries. Nevertheless, he was the leading rusher for 1945, 1947, 1948 and 1949. During the last three years of those rushing stats, his team, the Philadelphia Eagles, was the powerhouse of the NFL's Eastern Division. In 1948, when the Eagles played the Chicago Cardinals for the title, Van Buren gained 98 yards to the Cardinal team's total of 96—and that was in a driving blizzard. In the title game the following year, Van Buren gained 196 yards against the Rams in slippery rain, a record that still stands. Of course, most of Van Buren's records have been surpassed in this "Age of the Running Back" but when he retired he held these career records: most yards rushing, 5,860; most touchdowns rushing, 69; most yards rushing in a season, 1,146; most years led league, rushing, four. And he set these with a significant handicap. His shoulder had been so badly injured when he was young, he could not throw a pass. He also could not bring his left arm up to stiff arm would-be tacklers. Thus, he only carried the ball in his right arm, and if he could not feint or dodge a tackler, he would simply lower his head and run right over the man.

Steve Van Buren churns around right end against the New York Bulldogs while Pete Pihos blocks two Bulldogs. Eagles won, 42-0.

Doc Blanchard and Glenn Davis

In 1944, just after Army had destroyed Notre Dame, 59-0, scoring more points than it had in the previous 15 years *combined,* an impressed Notre Dame coach, Ed McKeever wired home to South Bend: "Have just seen Superman in the flesh. He wears No. 35 and goes by the name of Blanchard." But Doc Blanchard wasn't the only one who carried the Army team—he was aided and abetted by Glenn Davis. The two were known as Mr. Inside and Mr. Outside of football in 1944, 1945 and 1946. In those three seasons, the Black Knights of West Point racked up 1,179 points to their opponents' 161. They started by rolling over North Carolina, 46-0; Brown 59-7; Pittsburgh, 69-7; Coast Guard Academy, 76-0; Duke, 27-7; Villanova, 83-0; Pennsylvania, 62-7, and Navy, 23-7, for a total of 504 points. That's 504 points, or an *average* of 56 points a game against an opponent's average of four points. The scores for 1945 and 1946 read about the same. Yet, they claim that Earl Blaik, the Army coach, held the scores *down.* In the first half against Notre Dame, for example, Davis scored three times and Blanchard twice. Then Blaik pulled them out. Flinging his helmet to the ground in disgust, Blanchard pouted, "Heck, Colonel, I want to play football and you're not giving me a chance." In their three seasons, Mr. Inside and Mr. Outside scored 89 touchdowns and averaged 8.3 yards each time one of them carried the ball. (In 1944, Davis led the nation in scoring with 20 TDs and a fantastic 12.4 yards per carry; Blanchard scored nine times and averaged 7.1 yards.) Blanchard was such a tough ol' boy from South Carolina he could smash into the line and churn up field on sheer power. ("This is the only man," said the legendary lineman Herman Hickman, "who runs his own interference.") Davis, Mr. Outside, was so fast (he was timed at 9.8 for the 100-yard dash at his California high school) that most of his touchdown runs were of 30 yards or more. Never in the history of college football has a team produced such a double-powered running threat. In three seasons of Davis-Blanchard football, the Black Knights won 27 games and tied one. They never knew defeat.

Doc Blanchard, Army's Mr. Inside, *scores against Navy in 1945. Glenn Davis trails play.*

Gale Sayers, below, *scored 22 touchdowns in his rookie season as a Bear. Here, he crosses the 1000-yard mark against 49ers.*

Gale Sayers

No one ever had a rookie year like Gale Sayers. Even though he barely played in the first three games, by the end of the season the Chicago Bears' magic runner had set NFL records for most touchdowns in a season, 22 (and, of course, most TDs as a rookie)—14 rushing, six receiving passes, one returning a punt and one returning a kickoff; most touchdowns in one game, six (tied with Ernie Nevers and Dub Jones); and most points scored in a rookie season, 132. He didn't go to the Bears unprepared. In three years at the University of Kansas he had rushed for 2,675 yards, averaging 6.5 yards per carry; gained 408 yards as a pass receiver and returned 50 punts and kickoffs for a total of 837 yards.

Wrigley Field was wet and swamped when the San Francisco 49ers trotted on the field to close out the season against the Bears. All of the fans had come to watch Sayers run a few long ones but the weather dampened their spirits at least until after the first play, in which Sayers gained 17 yards. That was his day. In the first quarter, he took a screen pass from Rudy Bukich and soared 80 yards for his first TD. In the second quarter, he ran around left end twice for scores, one a 79-yard dash, the other an easier seven-yard run. In the third, he skirted left end for 48 yards and his fourth TD, minutes later plunged one yard for his fifth. At that point, he had broken the season TD record with 21, so George Halas took him out. The fans, however, wanted Sayers to go for another, his sixth of the game. In the middle of the fourth quarter, Halas put Sayers back in to return a punt. The Kansas flash gathered the ball on his own 15 and streaked up the remaining 85 yards for his sixth and last TD. In all, he gained 336 yards in total offense that day. Sayers would have four more great seasons before all of his knee injuries caught up with him. Sadly for us, he retired young.

Marion Motley

According to two people who have good reason to know, Marion Motley was the greatest fullback ever. The two are Otto Graham, who quarterbacked the Cleveland Browns during Motley's tenure, and Paul Zimmerman, a highly respected sportswriter. Graham, of course, also played with Jim Brown, but he recalls that Brown rarely had to block while Motley consistently did. Indeed, the consensus in the rest of the football world is that Motley stands alone as the greatest pass-blocker. That's not all he did, however. He is still the all-time rushing leader for the now defunct All-America Football Conference, having gained 4,712 yards in 826 carries, which gives him an incredible 5.4 yards per carry. After the Browns joined the NFL in 1950, Motley played a few more seasons but after 1951 knee injuries hampered his powerful running gait. He still holds the NFL record for average yards gained rushing in a game, 17.09, 188 yards in 11 carries against the Pittsburgh Steelers in 1950. Zimmerman, in his book, *A Thinking Man's Guide to Pro Football,* recalls watching Motley blast through the center of the AAFC New York Yankees' line for 51 yards with Harmon Rowe of the Yanks riding his back and slugging him in the face for the last 10 yards. After the game, when a photographer asked Motley to smile, he said, "I can't. My teeth were knocked out."

Running in tennis shoes on a frozen field, Marion Motley, upper left, *gains yardage against the N. Y. Giants.*

All-Time Greatest Rushers
(ranked by avg. yds. gained)

			Avg. Yds. Gained	Total Yards
1.	Bobby Mitchell	1958-68	5.33	2,735
2.	Jim Brown	1957-65	5.22	12,312
3.	Dan Towler	1950-55	5.20	3,493
4.	Tobin Rote	1950-59	5.12	3,078
5.	Tom Wilson	1956-63	5.03	2,553
6.	Charley Trippi	1947-55	5.10	3,506
7.	Gale Sayers	1965-71	5.00	4,956
8.	Paul Lowe	1960-69	4.87	4,995
9.	Lenny Moore	1956-67	4.84	5,174
10.	Joe Perry	1950-63	4.82	8,378
11.	Ernie Green	1962-68	4.80	3,204
12.	Larry Csonka	1968-	4.77	4,148
13.	Dutch Clark	1932-38	4.75	2,757
14.	Tank Younger	1949-58	4.73	3,640
15.	Hugh McElhenny	1952-64	4.70	5,281
16.	Bronko Nagurski	1930-43	4.62	4,031
17.	Hoyle Granger	1966-72	4.54	3,653
18.	Clem Daniels	1960-68	4.48	5,138
19.	Abner Haynes	1960-67	4.47	4,630
20.	Keith Lincoln	1961-68	4.46	3,383

Jim Brown

Suggesting that Jim Brown is the greatest running back who ever lived is like suggesting that the universe is big. In nine seasons with the Cleveland Browns, Brown set almost every rushing record there was to be set. Most are still records today, a decade after he retired: most yards gained, lifetime, 12,312; most seasons led league, rushing, 8; highest average gain, lifetime, 700 attempts, 5.22; most touchdowns, lifetime, 126; most touchdowns, rushing, lifetime, 106. And the man was at his peak when he quit. Pro football started becoming a crisis in Brown's life after the 1962 season. The players were revolting against Coach Paul Brown's strict rules, signal calling and coolness. The powerful fullback told Cleveland owner Art Modell he might retire unless something was done about it. Modell fired the coach, and hired Blanton Collier. For his part, Collier redesigned the Cleveland blocking system so that linemen could option block, with the trailing runner (Brown in most cases) taking an option cut on the option block. All that did was enable Brown to average 133 yards a game, 6.4 yards per carry and complete the season with 1,863 total yards rushing, far surpassing the previous record. (The record stood until O.J. Simpson gained 2,003 yards in 1973. It should be noted, however, that Simpson gained his yardage in 332 attempts, with a 6.03 per carry average, while Brown gained his in 291 attempts, with a 6.40 per carry average.) Barring serious injury (Brown never missed a game in his playing career), Jim Brown could have easily played another seven years, perhaps 10, but by 1966 he had had enough, and he retired at his peak.

O.J. Simpson

Just as there is only one Jim Brown, there is only one O.J. Simpson. While a runningback at Southern Cal, the Heisman Trophy winner broke just about every record USC had to offer, 13 of them, including four which were held by former Trojan and 1965 Heisman winner Mike Garrett. He also set the NCAA record for yards rushing, 1,709 in 1968. He was voted college football's greatest player of the 1960s by the National College Sports Services. Then, Orenthal James Simpson was drafted by the Buffalo Bills. After he arrived at the Buffalo training camp in 1969, Simpson was disappointed to learn that he wasn't going to be the bread and butter of the Bills' offense. He discovered, for example, that his days of carrying the ball 30 or 35 times a game were behind him. His running frequency for the first three seasons was 14 carries a game. People wondered whether Simpson could run behind a nothing front line. He didn't do too badly, averaging about four yards a carry, but he didn't run to superstar form. Then came 1972 and the California marvel was handed the ball about 21 times a game: he gained 1,251 yards. Meanwhile, the Bills had been beefing up their offensive line. Simpson may be a superstar runningback but he knows he can't get far unless he has those tackles knocking down the folks in front and powerful fast-pulling guards to help get him started downfield. It all came together in 1973. With Bruce Jarvis at center, Reggie McKenzie and Joe De Lamielleure at guards and Dave Foley and Donnie Green at tackle, O.J. Simpson became the first runner in football history to rush for more than 2,000 yards—2,003 to be exact. And in the final game, after all the journalists were gathered in the Buffalo dressing room, Simpson had very little to say except to introduce the five men up front who had made that incredible season possible. He had carried 332 times, averaging 24 tries a game, and averaged six yards per try. Those are rushing records that will be very difficult for anyone to surpass—except O.J.

—The most prolific rusher of all-time is Jim Brown who gained 12,312 yards before retiring abruptly in his prime. That record is just eight yards short of seven miles.

—O.J. Simpson holds the record for most yards gained in a season and most yards gained in a single game. Both records were set in 1973 when he stepped off 250 yards against the New England Patriots on September 16. By season's end, he had gained 2,003 yards.

—The record for the highest average gain per season is held by Beattie Feathers (remember him) who averaged 9.9 yards a carry for the Chicago Bears in 1934.

—The highest average gain in a game is 17.1 yards (10 or more attempts), a record held by Marion Motley when he rushed for the Cleveland Browns against the Pittsburgh Steelers on October 29, 1950, taking 188 yards in 11 attempts.

—Six touchdowns are the most anyone made by rushing in one game and the man who holds that record is Ernie Nevers who did it for the Chicago Cardinals against the Chicago Bears on November 28, 1929. Nevers also kicked four extra points in that game, giving him a 40-point game, a record that's likely to stand for some time. With Nevers in the Cardinal backfield that day was an aging Jim Thorpe.

—The record for most touchdowns rushing in a career is held by Jim Brown who crossed the goal line 106 times for the Cleveland Browns between 1957 and 1965.

They both wear No. 32 but Jim Brown, left, *was the greatest runner in pro football history. His current challenger for that honor is O.J. Simpson shown here setting an NFL record of 250 yards rushing in 29 carries against the Patriots in 1973.*

A Chronology of the Game's Greatest

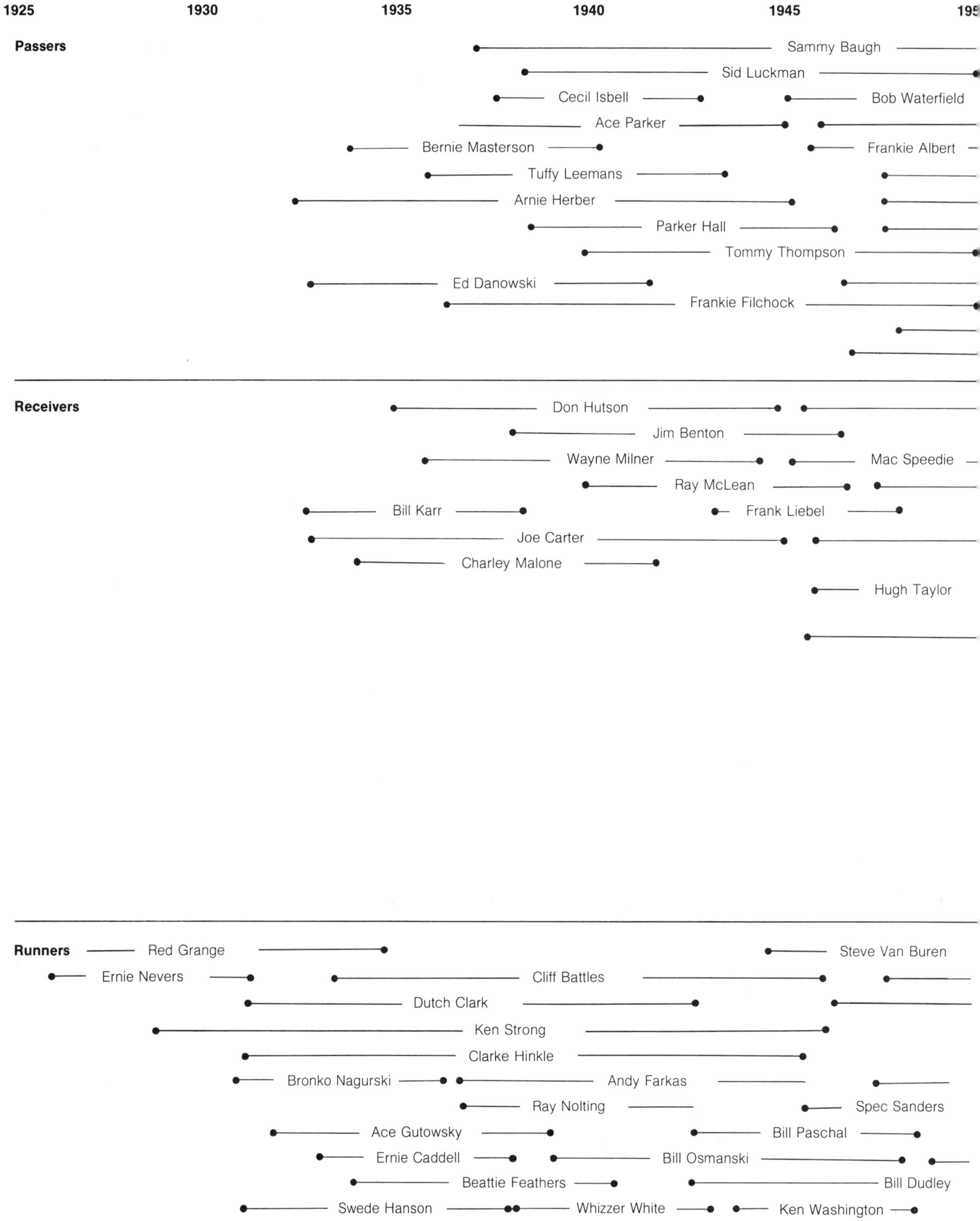

1925 1930 1935 1940 1945 195

Passers

Sammy Baugh
Sid Luckman
Cecil Isbell
Bob Waterfield
Ace Parker
Bernie Masterson
Frankie Albert
Tuffy Leemans
Arnie Herber
Parker Hall
Tommy Thompson
Ed Danowski
Frankie Filchock

Receivers

Don Hutson
Jim Benton
Wayne Milner
Mac Speedie
Ray McLean
Bill Karr
Frank Liebel
Joe Carter
Charley Malone
Hugh Taylor

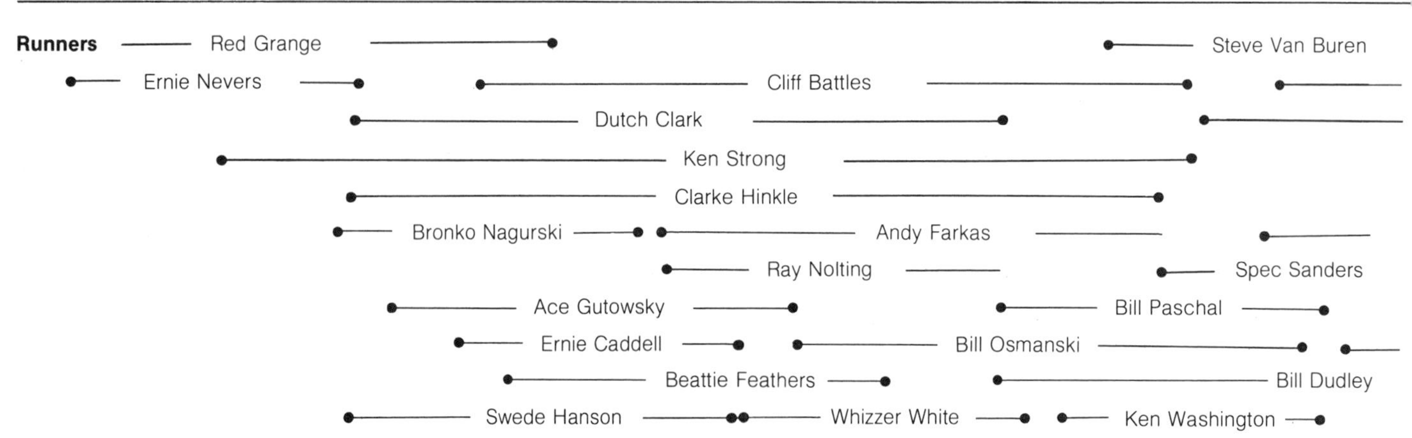

Passers, Receivers & Runners

It doesn't take much to be one of the greatest passers in football: just be a Sammy Baugh, Sid Luckman, Otto Graham or Norm Van Brocklin

...THE AERIAL CIRCUS...

Slingin' Sammy *Baugh doing what he does firstest with the mostest, throwing the football.*

All-Time Greatest Passers
(ranked by avg. yds. gained)

1.	Otto Graham	1950-55	8.63
2.	Sid Luckman	1939-50	8.42
3.	Norm Van Brocklin	1949-60	8.16
4.	Bob Berry	1965-	7.99
5.	Craig Morton	1965-	7.92
6.	Ed Brown	1954-65	7.85
7.	Bart Starr	1956-71	7.85
8.	John Unitas	1956-74	7.78
9.	Earl Morrall	1956-	7.76
10.	Len Dawson	1957-	7.75
11.	Joe Namath	1965-	7.72
12.	Sonny Jurgensen	1957-	7.63
13.	Frank Ryan	1958-70	7.52
14.	Eddie LeBaron	1952-63	7.460
15.	Fran Tarkenton	1961-	7.457
16.	Don Meredith	1960-68	7.452
17.	Bill Nelson	1963-	7.44
18.	Y. A. Tittle	1950-64	7.42
19.	Daryle Lamonica	1963-	7.41
20.	John Hadl	1962-	7.40*

*The difference between 7.50 and 7.60 is about 3½ inches. The difference between 7.41 and 7.40 is about ⅓ of an inch.

—Sammy Baugh holds the record for most seasons leading the NFL in passing, with six: 1937, 1940, 1943, 1945, 1947, 1949.

—Johnny Unitas holds the record for most passes attempted in a career with 5,186. That's an average of 288 attempts per season.

—The most enduring passing record is held by Sammy Baugh. That record is passing efficiency for one season (100 or more attempts), with a percentage completion record of 70.3 in 1945, 128 completions in 182 attempts.

—The shortest pass completion for a touchdown is two inches, an Eddie LeBaron pass in a Dallas-Washington game on October 9, 1960.

Sammy Baugh

At a time when 10 passes in a game were considered wildly extravagant, Sammy Baugh threw 30 and 40. In the mid-Thirties, while he was slinging for the Horned Frogs of Texas Christian, Baugh took to the air lanes 599 times in three seasons. The frequency of his passes, his tall, calm lanky frame standing composed just before release, and his ability to pick apart pass defenses made Baugh the talk of the nation. The Texas skies were filled with footballs and it was the greatest show on earth. In 1937, Baugh was drafted by the Washington Redskins (he was actually the second pick that year) and he immediately led them to an NFL title. His passes were as accurate as if fired through the sight of a rifle. He threw hard, he threw quick, he threw short, he threw long, and he kept throwing and throwing and throwing, sometimes eight, nine, 10 plays in a row. And he never stopped practicing. He would tie an old tire to a tree, swing it and gun the ball through the center hour after hour. He had studied throwing so thoroughly that he knew to hold the laces of the ball at his fingertips in rain and snow, but at the heel of his thumb when the weather was dry. Baugh was also the finest punter in the history of the game. His passing records have been broken but he still holds four punting records: highest average one game, punting: 59.4 yards; highest average one season, punting: 51.3 yards; highest average lifetime, punting: 45.10 yards: most punts one game: 14. When he retired he held these passing records: most attempts, most completions, most touchdown passes, most yards, highest percent completions, highest one season completion percentage (an incredible 70.3).

Baugh was always confident of his passing accuracy. Legend has it that once during a locker room session the Redskins head coach Ray Flaherty was describing a pass pattern and concluded, "The end cuts in here and when he gets here, hit him in the eye with the ball." Just as one would guess, Baugh asked, "Which eye?"

Sid Luckman

Once upon a time the Chicago Bears had three quarterbacks whose last name began with L. They were Luckman, Lujack and Layne. No one would argue, however, that of the three, Sid Luckman was the greatest, in fact he was probably the best T-formation quarterback to have taken a snap from center. One only needs to recall that it was Luckman who defeated Sammy Baugh and the Washington Redskins, 73-0, in the first outing for the man-in-motion T during an NFL title game. It was Luckman who first threw six touchdown passes in a single game. Indeed, it was Luckman who was the first T-formation quarterback. He came to that position well-prepared. At Columbia, as a triple-threat tailback for a weak team, Luckman quickly learned to dodge, duck and scramble out of the way of charging linemen, while he was simultaneously trying to pick out a receiver, hand the ball off, or run with it himself. His apprenticeship as a ball handler and peripheral-vision scrambler came in good stead. He led the Bears to four consecutive championships beginning with his rookie year in 1940, and to another in 1946, when his famous surprise run in the fourth quarter won the NFL title game from Steve Owen's New York Giants. Luckman's run was a surprise for the simple reason that George Halas had ordered his quarterback never to run. Whenever Sid did, Halas seemed to stop breathing until he knew that Luckman *was* breathing. And that was because Luckman was the whole team. (Dan Topping, when he owned the football Yankees, once offered to trade his entire team for Luckman and build a new one from scratch.) Luckman, like Baugh, played in the pre-platoon era. He was a 60-minute player. In retirement, he is modest and very realistic about the quality of today's playing personnel. "Today's players are far superior to those of my day," he recently told a writer. "They're bigger, stronger, faster, better coached and they start playing football earlier." Luckman estimates that perhaps one-third of the best players of his day could make a team today but notes that lack of size and speed would bar the rest. And Luckman himself? The consensus of the football world is that he'd make any team.

Otto Graham

They called him "Automatic Otto" and Otto Graham was just that, reaching his passing targets with a precision that was as regular as clockwork. He was so good at Northwestern (lettering in baseball, football and basketball) that he made the 1943 All-American Team in *both* football and basketball. That same year he led the College All-Stars to one of their few victories over the NFL champions (The Redskins under Baugh that year), personally scoring on a 97-yard run. He was a tailback operating under the single wing, though. The passing game which Graham found himself in the midst of when he played pro ball was different than that which had confronted a passing genius like Sammy Baugh. Graham converted to the T and worked under complex intricacies of the Paul Brown system in Cleveland. While Baugh sought out one or two primary receivers, Graham would be looking for three and four on every passing play. An end would flare out, a back would circle out of the backfield, a second back would streak a crossing pattern while the other end might be running a sideline fly pattern. The demand on Graham was that he know precisely who was "breaking" and when, so that if the primary receiver was covered (or had fallen down) then he could go to his second, third or fourth targets. Automatic Otto fulfilled that demand magnificently. Even today, more than two decades after his retirement, he ranks second on the all-time passing list with yards gained per attempt (a phenomenal 8.98 yards) and fifth in completion percentage (55.75 percent). For the 10 years that Graham played, he led the Browns to 10 consecutive division titles and seven championships. No quarterback in the history of professional football has a better record than that.

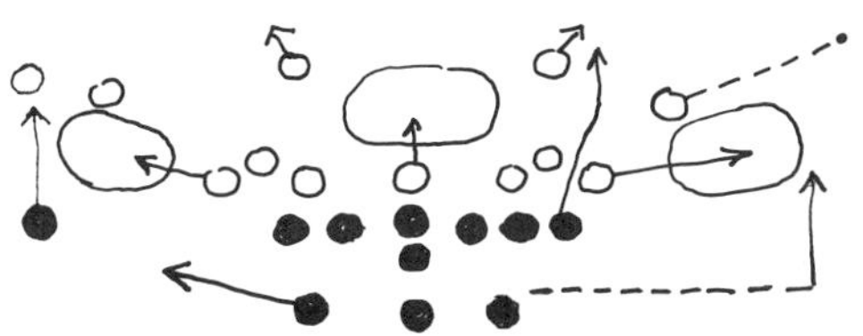

The intricacies of the Paul Brown pass pattern can be seen in the diagram at left. Remember, these were devised 30 years ago.

Norm Van Brocklin

After he had set most of the passing records in the Pacific Coast Conference, the Los Angeles Rams talked Norman Van Brocklin into finishing his college studies a semester ahead of time so they could grab him before he was drafted by another club. And with him and Bob Waterfield alternating at the passing chores, the Rams went off to three straight titles. Cool and confident, all-seeing and quick, it is generally conceded that Van Brocklin was either the best or among the best three automatic signal callers. He also brought a new dimension to the game: since he was quick enough and accurate enough to know where his receivers were supposed to be and when, he concentrated on watching the defensive backs. He wanted to know where and when a defender might leave his area open. He ranks third (to Luckman and Graham) on the all-time list for yards gained per passing attempt, and even today holds the record (set against the New York Giants in 1951) for most yards gained in one game passing, a whopping 554 yards.

—The record for most consecutive passes attempted, with none intercepted is held by Bart Starr, a string of 294 between 1964 and 1965 when he was throwing for the Green Bay Packers.

—The record for the best passing efficiency in one game is held by Kenny Stabler, who completed 25 of 29 attempts for an 86.2 completion percentage in a Raider game against the Baltimore Colts on October 28, 1973.

—The record for most yards gained in a season is tucked behind the smile of Joe Willie Namath who passed for 4,007 yards for the New York Jets in 1967.

The epitome of the passing quarterback was Norm Van Brocklin who gained 554 yds. in one game.

Sonny Jurgensen is ranked by The Sports Encyclopedia: Football *as the best passer in the pro game.*

Sonny Jurgensen

For the first four years that he played professional football Christian "Sonny" Jurgensen threw about 35 passes a season. And for the last four seasons, alternating with Billy Kilmer, he has thrown very few passes. Yet, the beloved Red Head ranks fifth on all-time career list for completions, attempts and total yards gained passing; second in completion percentage; third in touchdown passes; and fourth in fewest percent intercepted. That's because he aerial blitzed the hell out of the league from 1961 to 1969. Sammy Baugh might have thrown 350 passes a season, but Sonny was the throwingest: he whipped out more than 500, (to be exact, 508 in 1967, a record that stands, completing 288, another record that stands). But Sonny, God bless him, never seemed to be in top shape. He enjoyed playing and he enjoyed his popularity but most of all he enjoyed his indulgences. From the beginning of a season to its end, the Jurgensen trademark was a roundish gelatinous mass which both his critics and admirers could assure themselves of full view: a fine, friendly pot-belly. According to *The Sports Encyclopedia: Football* by David S. Neft and others, the definitive work in the field, Jurgensen is ranked as the best passer in pro football history. The Neft ranking was based on completion percentage, yards per attempt, percentage intercepted and touchdown passes. On our list, Sonny is ranked second. We dropped touchdown passes as a criteria because they're more a function of quarterbacking and coaching than pure passing, though admittedly, quarterbacking and coaching are also critical to passing success.

Joe Namath

The coming of Joe Willie Namath meant the coming of the American Football League. Just as Red Grange had established pro football and the Sudden Death Game had established the NFL, Joe Willie established the AFL. Only, Broadway Joe did it twice. He performed this feat first by signing with the New York Jets for an estimated bonus of $400,000. Sonny Werblin, the Jets owner, was a showman, sure, but that amount of money set the football world on its fiscal ear. It signalled that the AFL was here to stay; and within a year, both leagues agreed to a merger. The second time Joe Willie established the AFL was against the Baltimore Colts (and the NFL) in the third Super Bowl, when he brashly predicted three days before the game, "I think we'll win it. In fact, I'll guarantee it." And then went on to win it. It didn't hurt Namath's image either that he exhibited an equally brash but fun-packed lifestyle, one that raised the consternation of football's old guard but one that won the enthusiastic admiration of his young fans. Namath, however, is also a great quarterback. He is one of the best throwers that either league has seen. He reads defenses quickly and has, by consensus, the quickest release in football. In career statistics, Namath already ranks among the best quarterbacks. It is also true that no quarterback who entered the league in the same season or later is even close in any major passing category.

But the best passer in the minds of many fans is Broadway Joe *Namath,* bottom right, *who devastated the Colts in Super Bowl III in 1969.*

Johnny Unitas

At the tender young age of 25 (for quarterbacks) Johnny Unitas single-handedly turned NFL football into a mass market medium. His leadership of the Baltimore Colts to a come-from-behind sudden-death victory against the New York Giants stopped and stirred the collective hearts of this sports-minded nation as has no other single sporting event. The Sudden Death game has been called the greatest ever played. There's very little evidence to challenge that. Of course, the 1958 NFL title game occurred in Unitas' second season. He's had 14 since. And in that time Unitas has reset the benchmarks from which quarterbacks have been measured. In career marks, he holds almost everything worth throwing for: most attempts, most completions, most yards, most touchdown passes. He ranks sixth in yards per attempt and percentage intercepted, and ninth in completion percentage. For five consecutive years, in 47 straight games, he threw at least one touchdown pass per game, another record. Stooped, his arms dangling loosely, pigeon-toed, awkward in his iconoclastic high-topped black cleats, Unitas looks more like a Victorian shoe clerk than the consummate quarterback of the 1960s. Generally, he received good pass protection but when he did not, the raw physical courage of the man was undeniable. Time after time, he could be seen standing calm and still, waiting for that last moment before his release, and just as he let go, *wham!*, was knocked flat on his back or simply buried under a rush of charging linemen. "You can't intimidate him," says Merlin Olsen, the Los Angeles Rams defensive tackle. "He waits until the last possible second to release the ball, even if it means he's going to take a good lick. When he sees us coming, he knows it's going to hurt and we know it's going to hurt, but he just stands there and takes it. No other quarterback has such class. I swear that, when he sees you coming out of the corner of his eye, he holds that ball a split second longer than he really needs to—just to let you know he isn't afraid of any man. Then he throws it on the button. I weigh 270 myself, and I don't know if I could absorb the punishment he takes. I wonder if I could stand there, week after week, and say: 'Here I am. Take your best shot'." Unitas has taken best shots from all over the league, and led his team to four division titles and three championships. If he's not the best quarterback of his era, he is at least its masochistic marvel.

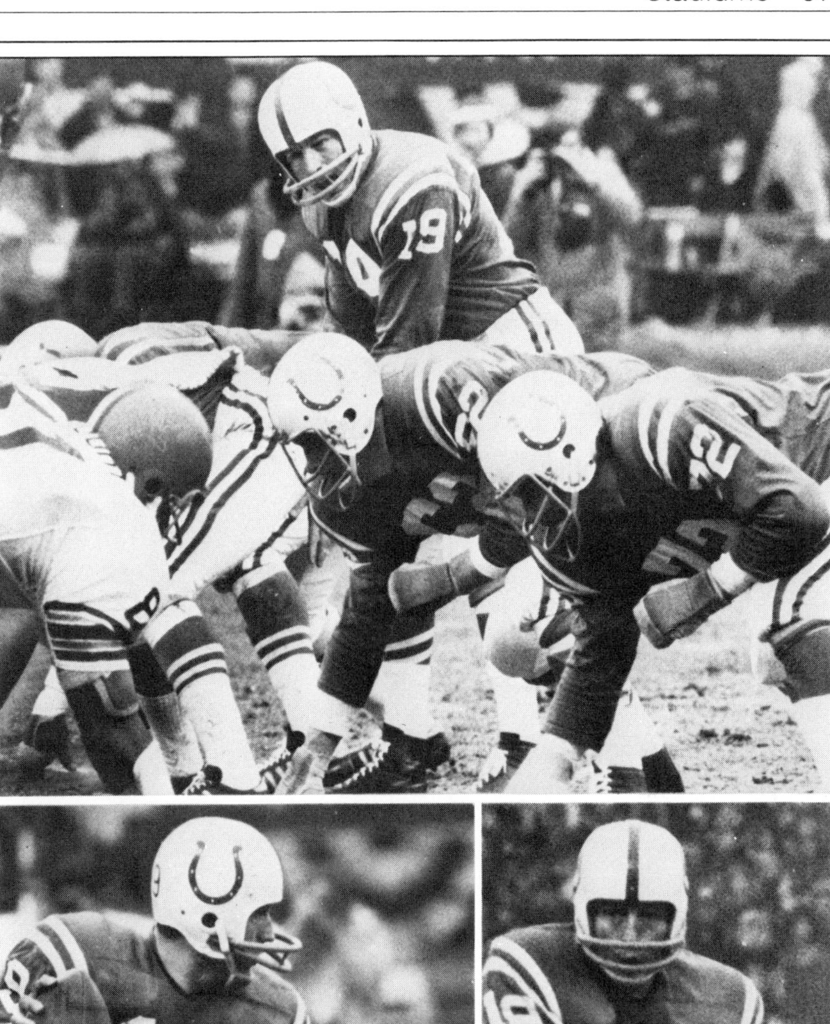

Once upon a time, Johnny Unitas played sandlot football for $25 a game. Fortunately for the NFL [and us] he was hired by the Colts. His come-from-behind victory in that incredible 1958 "Sudden Death" NFL title game established NFL football as a mass market television medium.

The All-Time Greatest Passers*

Rank	Player	Years	Years Played	Yards per Attempt	Attempts	Completions	Percntg. Cmpltn.	Total Yards	TD Passes	Teams
1.	Bart Starr	16	1956-71	7.85	3,149	1,808	57.42	24,718	152	Alabama, Packers
2.	Sonny Jurgensen	18	1957-74	7.56	4,262	2,433	57.09	32,224	255	Duke, Eagles, Redskins
3.	Len Dawson	18	1957-74	7.67	3,601	2,043	56.73	27,616	234	Purdue, Steelers, Browns, Texans, Chiefs
3.	Otto Graham	10	1946-55	8.98	2,626	1,464	55.75	23,584	174	Northwestern, Browns
5.	Fran Tarkenton	14	1961-74	7.47	4,800	2,658	55.38	35,846	266	Georgia, Vikings, Giants
6.	Johnny Unitas	19	1956-74	7.76	5,186	2,830	54.57	40,239	290	Louisville, Colts, Chargers
7.	Y. A. Tittle	17	1948-64	7.52	4,395	2,427	55.22	33,070	242	L.S.U., Colts, 49ers, Giants
8.	Milt Plum	13	1957-69	7.25	2,419	1,306	54.99	17,536	132	Penn. St., Browns, Lions, Rams, Giants
9.	Don Meredith	9	1960-68	7.45	2,308	1,170	50.69	17,199	135	S.M.U., Cowboys
10.	John Brodie	17	1957-73	7.03	4,491	2,469	54.98	31,548	214	Stanford, 49ers
10.	Billy Wade	13	1954-66	7.34	2,523	1,370	54.30	18,530	124	Vanderbilt, Rams, Bears
12.	Frank Ryan	13	1958-70	7.52	2,133	1,090	51.10	16,042	149	Rice, Rams, Browns, Redskins
13.	Earl Morrall	19	1956-74	7.78	2,620	1,343	51.26	20,388	157	Michigan State, 49ers, Steelers, Lions, Giants, Colts, Dolphins
14.	Bob Griese	8	1967-74	7.10	2,014	1,081	53.67	14,309	114	Purdue, Dolphins
14.	Norm Van Brocklin	12	1949-60	8.16	2,895	1,553	53.64	23,611	173	Oregon, Rams, Eagles
16.	Roman Gabriel	13	1962-74	6.64	4,111	2,168	52.74	27,309	186	N. Carolina State, Rams, Eagles
16.	Sid Luckman	12	1939-50	9.95	1,657	904	54.56	14,683	137	Columbia, Bears
16.	Joe Namath	10	1965-74	7.64	3,099	1,565	50.50	23,681	151	Alabama, Jets
19.	Sammy Baugh	16	1937-52	7.31	2,995	1,693	56.63	21,886	188	T.C.U., Redskins
20.	Daryle Lamonica	12	1963-74	7.36	2,601	1,288	49.52	19,154	164	Notre Dame, Bills, Raiders
21.	Charley Johnson	14	1961-74	7.20	3,250	1,672	51.45	23,389	165	New Mexico State, Cardinals, Oilers, Broncos
21.	Billy Kilmer	12	1961-62 1964, 1966-74	7.00	2,186	1,177	53.84	15,300	105	U.C.L.A., 49ers, Saints, Redskins
23.	John Hadl	13	1962-74	7.31	4,198	2,101	50.05	30,698	231	Kansas, Chargers, Rams, Packers
23.	Norm Snead	14	1961-74	7.09	4,122	2,146	52.06	29,221	187	Wake Forest, Redskins, Eagles, Vikings, Giants, 49ers
25.	Ed Brown	12	1954-65	7.85	1,987	949	47.80	15,600	102	San Francisco, Bears, Steelers, Colts
26.	Frankie Albert	7	1946-52	6.90	1,564	831	53.13	10,795	115	Stanford, 49ers
27.	Tom Flores	9	1960-61 1963-69	7.00	1,715	838	48.90	11,959	93	U.O.P., Raiders, Bills, Chiefs
28.	Eddie LeBaron	11	1952-53 1955-63	7.46	1,796	897	49.90	13,399	104	U.O.P., Redskins, Cowboys
29.	Chuck Conerly	14	1948-61	6.88	2,833	1,418	50.05	19,488	173	Mississippi, Giants
29.	Bob Waterfield	8	1945-52	7.33	1,617	813	50.28	11,849	98	U.C.L.A., Rams
31.	Bobby Layne	15	1948-62	7.24	3,700	1,814	49.00	26,768	196	Texas, Bears, Bulldogs, Lions, Steelers
32.	Jim Hart	9	1966-74	6.80	2,336	1,139	48.76	15,874	102	Southern Ill., Cardinals
32.	Jack Kemp	15	1957, 1960-67 1969-74	7.14	2,973	1,437	48.30	21,222	114	Occidental, Steelers, Chargers, Bills
34.	Babe Parilli	15	1952-53 1956-66 1968-69	6.80	3,330	1,552	46.60	22,671	178	Kentucky, Packers, Browns, Raiders, Patriots, Jets
35.	Frank Tripucka	8	1949-52	5.90	1,745	879	50.37	10,282	59	Notre Dame, Eagles, Lions, Cardinals, Dallas, Texans, Broncos

*Ranked according to total career statistics for percentage completions, yards per attempt and percentage of passes intercepted.

The All-Time Greatest Receivers*

Rank	Receiver	Years	Years Played	Receptions	Total Yards	Yards per Reception	TD's	Teams
1.	Don Maynard	16	1958, 1960-74	633	11,834	18.7	88	Texas Western, Giants, Titans, Jets
2.	Lance Alworth	11	1962-72	542	10,267	18.9	85	Arkansas, Chargers, Cowboys
3.	Billy Howton	12	1952-63	503	8,459	16.8	61	Rice, Packers, Browns, Cowboys
4.	Carroll Dale	15	1960-74	438	8,277	18.9	52	VPI, Rams, Packers
4.	Tommy McDonald	12	1957-68	495	8,830	16.9	84	Oklahoma, Eagles, Cowboys, Rams, Falcons, Browns
6.	Ray Berry	13	1955-67	631	9,275	14.7	68	SMU, Colts
7.	Art Powell	10	1959-68	479	8,046	16.8	81	San Jose State, Eagles, Titans, Raiders, Bills, Vikings
8.	Jimmy Orr	13	1958-70	400	7,914	19.8	66	Georgia, Steelers, Colts
9.	Paul Warfield	11	1964-74	371	7,701	20.8	77	Ohio State, Browns, Dolphins
10.	Don Hutson	11	1935-45	488	7,981	16.4	100	Alabama, Packers
10.	Charlie Taylor	11	1964-74	582	8,208	14.1	73	Arizona State, Redskins
12.	Bobby Mitchell	11	1958-68	521	7,954	15.3	65	Illinois, Browns, Redskins
13.	Jackie Smith	12	1963-74	459	7,601	16.6	37	N.W. Louisiana, Cardinals
14.	Bob Hayes	10	1965-74	365	7,295	20.0	71	Florida A&M, Cowboys
15.	Pete Retzlaff	11	1956-66	452	7,412	16.4	47	S. Dakota State, Eagles
16.	Otis Taylor	10	1965-74	410	7,306	17.8	57	Prairie View, Chiefs
17.	Boyd Dowler	12	1959-69 1971	474	7,270	15.3	40	Colorado, Packers, Redskins
18.	Crazy Legs Hirsch	12	1946-57	387	7,029	18.2	60	Wisconsin, Rockets, Rams
19.	Fred Biletnikoff	10	1965-74	450	7,105	15.8	60	Florida State, Raiders
19.	Lionel Taylor	10	1959-68	567	7,195	12.7	45	Highlands, Bears, Broncos, Oilers
21.	Del Shofner	11	1957-67	349	6,470	18.5	51	Baylor, Rams, Giants
22.	Dante Lavelli	11	1946-56	386	6,488	16.8	62	Ohio State, Browns
23.	Max McGee	12	1954, 1957-67	345	6,346	18.4	50	Tulane, Packers
24.	Ray Renfro	12	1952-63	281	5,508	19.6	50	N. Texas State, Browns
25.	Franke Clarke	11	1957-67	291	5,426	18.6	50	Colorado, Browns, Cowboys
26.	Buddy Dial	8	1959-66	261	5,436	20.8	44	Rice, Steelers, Cowboys
26.	Hugh Taylor	8	1947-54	272	5,233	19.2	58	Oakland City Univ., Redskins
28.	Bobby Joe Conrad	12	1958-69	422	5,902	14.0	38	Texas A&M, Cardinals, Cowboys
28.	Billy Wilson	10	1951-60	407	5,902	14.5	49	San Jose, 49ers
30.	Mike Ditka	12	1961-72	427	5,812	13.6	43	Pittsburgh, Bears, Eagles, Cowboys
31.	Pete Pihos	9	1947-55	373	5,619	15.1	61	Indiana, Eagles
31.	Mac Speedie	7	1946-52	349	5,602	16.1	33	Utah, Browns
33.	Harlon Hill	9	1954-62	233	4,717	20.2	40	Florence St.-Ala., Bears, Steelers, Lions
34.	Jim Colclough	9	1960-68	283	5,101	18.0	39	Boston College, Patriots
35.	Gene Washington	6	1969-74	262	4,834	18.5	39	Stanford, 49ers
36.	Ray McLean	8	1940-47	103	2,222	21.6	21	St. Anselm's, Bears
37.	Jim Benton	9	1938-40 1942-47	288	4,801	16.7	45	Arkansas, Rams, Bears
37.	Tom Fears	9	1948-56	400	5,397	13.5	38	UCLA, Rams
37.	Elbie Nickel	11	1947-57	329	5,131	15.6	37	Cincinnati, Steelers
40.	Gordie Soltau	9	1950-58	249	3,487	14.0	25	Minnesota, 49ers
41.	Joe Carter	12	1934-45	127	1,880	14.8	21	SMU, Eagles, Packers, Tigers, Cardinals
42.	Charlie Malone	8	1934-40 1942	137	1,922	14.0	13	Texas A&M, Redskins
43.	Wayne Millner	7	1936-41 1945	124	1,578	12.7	12	Notre Dame, Redskins

*Ranked according to total career statistics for number of receptions, total yards gained and average gain per reception. Several receivers at the end of the list were added for historical interest.

If you can run full tilt at a goal post, grab a pole, swing around in a circle and catch the ball with your other hand then you too can be a great receiver.

...AND THE TRAPEZE ARTIST

—The man who holds the record for the most pass receptions in a season is Charley Hennigan, playing for the Houston Oilers in 1964. He's the same fellow who said that just watching Lance Alworth catch passes was worth the price of admission alone.

—Most pass receptions in a game is a record owned by Tom Fears who caught 18 for the Los Angeles Rams against the Green Bay Packers on December 3, 1950, gaining 189 yards.

—The man who led the NFL most seasons in pass receptions is Don Hutson who led for eight years, 1936, 1937, 1939 and 1941-1945.

—Don Maynard has caught more passes in a career than anyone, pulling in 633 while playing with the New York Jets, the New York Giants and the St. Louis Cardinals, 1958-1973.

Don Hutson

We hardly remember that he was called the Alabama Antelope but his name, style of play and innovative development of pass patterns and fakes make Don Hutson one of the greatest ends of all-time. Some might even argue that he was the very best, but statistics and further developments in the game would argue otherwise. Nevertheless, Hutson was the first, as Red Grange was in running, and as Sammy Baugh was in passing. At Alabama, as he put it, "I just ran like the devil and Dixie Howell got the ball there." After he grabbed six passes for 165 yards and two touchdowns in the Crimson Tide victory over Stanford in the 1935 Rose Bowl, he was praised by one sportswriter as "the world's greatest pass-catching, speed-merchant end." He certainly was that then and when he joined the Green Bay Packers in 1935, he led the NFL in scoring five times, in touchdowns eight times and in total receptions eight times. All of his records (and he held every important receiving record) have been surpassed save three: 100 touchdowns, career; 17 touchdowns, season (tied with two others); eight years leading league in receptions. His catching of Cecil Isbell's passes make Isbell one of the leading passers in pro history. Hutson caught them over his head, just off the tip of the grass, at the very tip of his fingers. One of his most spectacular ploys was to dash full tilt at a goal post, grab a pole, swing himself around in a circle and catch the ball with his other free hand.

With his contact lenses firmly in place, Raymond Berry, upper right, *goes up for a TD against the Redskins in 1957.*

Raymond Berry

Without his glasses or contact lenses, Raymond Berry could barely make out the big E at the top of an eye chart. He was gangly and thin, about 180 pounds stretched over a 6'2" frame. And he was a 20th round draft pick who became, for a sizable segment of the American football populace, the greatest receiver of all time.

What made Berry so great was he devoted his young life to the obsessive study of football as if it were his personal science. While other Colt players were out carousing, Berry was running game films and designing pass patterns in his single room in an old abandoned mansion. When his teammates turned in their uniforms to be washed, Berry took his home and hand-washed them. While other players walked around camp joking and laughing, Berry walked about with a football in his hands. While other receivers enjoyed dating or a more sedate home life, Berry trained his wife, Sally, to pass. "Lead me, honey, lead me," passing strangers would hear from a vacant lot, and Sally would drill him while the all-pro end ran slants, hooks, square-outs and corners.

When Berry retired, he had caught more passes than anyone. Even today, he has been surpassed by only one other receiver, Don Maynard. Maynard, however, played three more seasons than Berry—and caught two more passes. Berry's record of an average 9.275 yards gained is still the highest lifetime total for an entire NFL career.

Greatest Receivers - First Decade Career Comparison*

Receiver	Decade	Receptions	Yards	Avg.	TD's
Don Hutson	1935-44	441	7,147	16.2	91
Raymond Berry	1955-64	506	7,583	15.0	53
Tommy McDonald	1957-66	455	8,281	18.2	79
Don Maynard	1958, 1960-68	502	9,435	18.8	78
Bobby Mitchell	1958-67	507	7,824	15.4	65
Art Powell	1959-68	479	8,046	16.8	81
Lance Alworth	1962-71	527	10,072	19.1	83
Charlie Taylor	1964-73	528	7,470	14.1	68
Paul Warfield	1964-73	344	7,165	20.8	75
Bob Hayes	1965-74	365	7,295	20.0	71
Otis Taylor	1965-74	410	7,306	17.8	57

*Listed according to year entered pro football.

Elroy "Crazylegs" Hirsch

Elroy "Crazylegs" Hirsch was the glamour player of the late Forties and early Fifties. He had wowed them at Wausau High, the University of Wisconsin, and after three fitful years with the mediocre Chicago Rockets of the AAFC, was finally unleashed as the running and receiving threat of the Los Angeles Rams. By the time he was 29, Hollywood had made a movie about his life and he starred in it.

Since passing frequencies are much higher in current football games, Hirsch no longer ranks among the most prolific receivers. Why then is he so all-fired important? Well, to put it simply: Crazylegs invented the "bomb," the long pass that increased game excitement by a considerable magnitude. In 1951, for example, Hirsch caught 17 touchdown passes in 12 games. The average yards gained on each TD was 50, yes 50, yards. Even today, in the NFL record book, Hirsch holds the record for most touchdown passes season, 17 (tied with Don Hutson) and most touchdown passes consecutive games, 11 (tied with Buddy Dial).

Of course, Hirsch was on the receiving end of passes thrown by Norm Van Brocklin and Bob Waterfield (you remember Bob, Jane Russell's husband?); he also had the good fortune of having Tom Fears running pass patterns on the other side of the field. No team could cover them both, particularly with the pinpoint accuracy of a Van Brocklin pass. Van Brocklin, as irascible as ever, worked the two men against each other. Fears made many a spectacular catch but if he ever missed one, Van Brocklin would turn to Hirsch in the huddle and ask, "What do you want, Elroy?" and Crazylegs would call his own pattern.

Emlen Tunnell

Emlen Tunnell is not a modest man. Serious yes. Modest no. "I am the greatest defensive back ever to play the game," he has averred on occasion. The serious part is that he is absolutely correct. When Tunnell retired in 1961, he held the record for the most interceptions lifetime, 79 (a record that will probably never be broken); most yards returned on interceptions, 1,282 (closest to him are Dick "Night Train" Lane and Herb Adderley, both retired); most punts returned, lifetime, 258 and most yards returned on punts, lifetime, 2,209 (the only man who can catch him is Alvin Haymond). In 1952 Tunnell gained 924 yards returning punts and pass interceptions: it was the only time in NFL history that a defensive back outgained the league's rushing leader, (Dan Towler with 894). Tunnell was the first black player signed by the New York Giants and he played 158 consecutive games for them. Elected to the Pro Football Hall of Fame in 1967, he was honored as the safety on the all-time NFL team for the league's 50th anniversary.

Crazylegs *popularized the biggest crowd pleaser in football today, the aerial bomb.*

Tom Fears

According to the Hollywood and Sunset Strip set, Tom Fears holds two records which no one in professional football can successfully challenge: they say he caught more third-down passes and more passes in the waning minutes of the fourth quarter than any end who ever lived. Now, one can't successfully challenge those stats because no statistician ever kept those kinds of records. Nevertheless, Tom Fears, running in pass-route tandem with Elroy "Crazylegs" Hirsch, was part of the best receiving combination in pro football.

Hirsch was the bomber, the deep threat, but Fears was the clutch third-down receiver. It was Fears, for example, who pulled down the late fourth-quarter Van Brocklin pass in the 1951 championship game and gallumphed 73

One of the best contemporary receivers, Paul Warfield ranks second in NFL history with an average of 20.83 yards gained per reception.

—The receiver of the shortest pass for a touchdown was Dick Bielski who caught the two-incher from Eddie LeBaron in 1960.

—Bob Shaw caught the most TD's in a game, five when he played for the Chicago Cardinals against Baltimore on October 2, 1950.

—The most consecutive games in which receivers caught touchdown passes is 11, a record shared by Elroy *Crazylegs* Hirsch of the Los Angeles Rams in 1950-1951 and Buddy Dial of the Pittsburgh Steelers, 1959-1960.

—Don Hutson caught the most touchdown passes in a career, 99 for Green Bay between 1935 and 1945.

yards for the final and winning touchdown. That pass won the team's only world championship and it has rightfully been described as the greatest play in Los Angeles Rams' history.

Fears was also not short on career stats. In 1950, he caught 84 passes in a 12-game season; it was a record that lasted until the game changed to a 14-game season. For three consecutive years, 1948-50, he led the NFL in pass receptions. He still holds the stellar record, most passes caught in a single game: 18. It's no secret that Fears put glue (or stickum) on his hands for his passes. In fact, he had a special pocket sewn in his pants near the middle of his thigh where he'd deposit the glue and pull it out as needed. He was never caught.

Bambi *Alworth's bounding leap helps him make another of his patented circus catches.*

Lance Alworth

Probably the greatest compliment paid to Lance Alworth was by Charlie Hennigan. "Once in a lifetime," said Hennigan, "a player comes along who alone is worth the price of admission; that player is Lance Alworth." Hennigan has some knowledge whereby he speaks. As an all-pro receiver for the Houston Oilers, Charlie ranks among the top 20 most prolific receivers in NFL history.

But it was Alworth who surpassed one of the most enduring pass-catching records of all time, that of catching at least one pass in 96 consecutive games, breaking Don Hutson's NFL record.

The Texan's sports career was a blaze from the start. After winning 15 letters at his high school in Mississippi, the bounding "Bambi," as he is nicknamed, startled his college coaches by stepping off a world class 9.6 100 when he was a freshman at Arkansas. A fine center-fielder as well, he passed up a bonus offer from the New York Yankees to sign a pro football contract in 1961 as the number two draft choice.

In the NFL career football record books, Alworth ranks second in most yards gained, third in most touchdowns, fourth in most receptions and 10th in average yards gained per reception. His 96-game consecutive catching record began with the first game of the season in 1962 against Houston when he caught one pass for 17 yards, and ended seven years later near the end of the 1969 season when he caught seven passes for 122 yards against the Buffalo Bills. In that eight-year span, he averaged five receptions per game.

Billie Howton

Down in Texas, they accorded young Billie Howton the "honor" of scoring the first touchdown in Rice's new stadium. That was a quarter century ago. Then, he was picked as the number two draft choice by the Green Bay Packers. As a rookie with the Packers, Howton was the sensation of the league, gaining 1,231 yards to lead all the veteran receivers in that department. And that broke a Don Hutson record as did his single-game performance in 1956 when he gained more than 270 yards in one afternoon. In NFL career stats, Howton ranks fourth in total yards gained and seventh in total receptions. By our calculations, which is a total meshing of all his receiving statistics, Howton ranks as the third most prolific receiver in NFL history.

Carroll Dale

Carroll Dale, the once familiar No. 84 in a Packers uniform, was a late bloomer. Drafted in the eighth round by the Los Angeles Rams in 1960, he was traded to Green Bay a year after Billie Howton retired. It was only after going to the Pack that Dale began churning up those 800-plus yard receiving seasons. He was one of the finest clutch receivers in the NFL, having grabbed four passes for 59 yards against Kansas City and four passes for 43 yards against Oakland in Super Bowls I and II. He also caught a 47-yard TD pass against the Cleveland Browns in a 1965 title game and a 51-yard touchdown bomb against the Dallas Cowboys in 1966, and the winning TD pass in the 1970 Pro Bowl game. In career stats, Dale ranks fifth in total yards gained, 11th in total receptions and 11th in average yards per reception.

SPORTS VIEWING ON TV

Rank	Sport or Special	Percentage of Households Watching	Million Number of Viewers	Percentage of Men, Women & Non-Adult Viewers M	W	N-A
1.	Football Super Bowl	41.6	50.7	48	30	22
2.	Baseball World Series	30.7	34.8	45	38	17
3.	Billie Jean King-Bobby Riggs Spec.	28.5	37.2	38	44	18
4.	Baseball All-Star Game	23.8	27.6	48	32	20
5.	Football-NFL on ABC	20.7	23.2	52	30	18
6.	Football College All-Stars/Bowls	18.3	26.6	47	32	21
7.	Horse Racing's Triple Crown	16.3	17.5	41	41	18
8.	Football-NFL on CBS	15.4	16.2	51	27	22
9.	Baseball Pennant Playoffs	15.0	14.7	43	41	16
10.	Football-NFL on NBC	14.6	15.0	54	27	19
11.	Football-NCAA on ABC	12.2	12.5	50	29	21
12.	Auto Racing on ABC	11.1	8.7	38	32	30
13.	Super Stars	10.9	14.3	43	25	32
14.	Wide World of Sports on ABC	10.7	12.6	44	30	26
15.	NBA Basketball	10.0	11.2	50	28	22
16.	Baseball Regular Season Games	9.3	9.0	48	33	19
17.	American Sportsman	9.1	9.8	46	29	25
18.	Bowling	8.9	9.7	39	39	22
19.	Basketball - NCAA & NIT	8.8	DNA		DNA	
20.	Golf Tournaments	7.8	8.8	48	38	14
21.	CBS Sports Spectacular	5.9	7.0	43	36	21
22.	Horse Racing on CBS	5.8	4.7	33	39	28
23.	Hockey - NHL	5.6	5.9	46	33	21
24.	Boxing - ABC	5.2	5.1	53	29	18
25.	Skiing - World Cup	5.2	DNA		DNA	
26.	Tennis Tournaments	4.5	4.0	42	38	20
27.	Tennis Classic On CBS	4.3	4.7	42	36	22
28.	Golf - CBS Golf Classic	3.8	4.1	43	33	24
29.	Basketball - ABA	3.4	3.7	38	29	33
30.	Hockey - WHA	2.1	2.5	40	31	29

GREAT MOMENTS IN PRO FOOTBALL

December 17, 1933 The nation was in the nadir of the Great Depression. People everywhere felt the powerful impact of bank panics, bread lines, soup lines, work camps and what the President called "fear itself." With the exception of horse racing, every major sport was sorely strained by the economic crisis.

Football dealt with the crisis by livening up the game with three rule changes: passing made legal from anywhere behind the scrimmage line (it had been five yards back), goal post moved up to the goal line for easier field goals, and the ball brought in at least 10 yards from the sidelines on every play. George Preston Marshall, the Redskins owner, had one other idea: creating two divisions within the league so that public interest would be focused on one championship game. It was done, and the Eastern and Western champs, the New York Giants and the Chicago Bears, met on a frozen Wrigley Field for the precursor of the Super Bowl.

The game turned out to be a razzle-dazzle tour de force, with trick plays, passes on laterals, laterals on passes and a last minute finish that left some 26,000 spectators screaming and dancing in their seats.

Running out of the single wing, New York had come with its diversified offense and a rugged defense anchored by Mel Hein. The Giants relied on Ken Strong for inside running and the quick, tricky arm of Harry Newman to carry the Eastern title. The Bears, on the other hand, ran Bronko Nagurski from his fullback position, with halfback support from Red Grange. With the closer goal posts, the Bears got off to a quick 6-0 lead. Then that was wiped out by a second period Giant touchdown, Newman to Morris Badgro. The most stunning event in the first quarter occurred when Mel Hein centered the ball with the entire team lined up to his right. That made him the center and the left end. Hein handed the ball to Newman. Newman handed it right back for what must be one of the shortest passes in history. But then Hein blew it. He was supposed to walk nonchalantly forward downfield and wait for blockers but he got excited and ran. He was nailed 15 yards short of a touchdown, and the Giants could not go in to score. The Bears hit for a third field goal in the third quarter, taking the lead 9-7 but Newman came back with his passing arm and moved the Giants 73 yards for a score. Giants 14, Bears 9. On third and long in the next series, the Bears faked a punt and the punter threw to the quarterback for a 67-yard gain. On third and six for a touchdown, the ball was hended to Nagurski who ran straight toward the line, stopped short, jumped and popped a quick pass to his right end, Bill Karr. Bears 16, Giants 14. After the kickoff, Newman completed four in a row and then set up the game's second strange play. On a reverse left, Newman handed off to Ken Strong. Strong saw he was going to be stopped so he lateraled back to Newman, who started to run wide around right end. But Newman saw he wouldn't make it either, noticed Strong waving frantically in the end zone and lofted one for the Giant's third touchdown. With just a few minutes left to play, the Bears had only three options: Nagurski, Nagurski and Nagurski. Now, with the ball on the Giants 36, Nagurski went back to what worked the last time out. He ran, jumped and popped one to left end Bill Hewitt. This time the Giants were ready and they closed fast. Hewitt, however, lateraled to Karr who took just a few steps for the final touchdown, Bears 23, Giants 21. It was an incredible finish and a helluva start—for NFL championships.

The winning play in 1st NFL title game: jump pass & lateral.

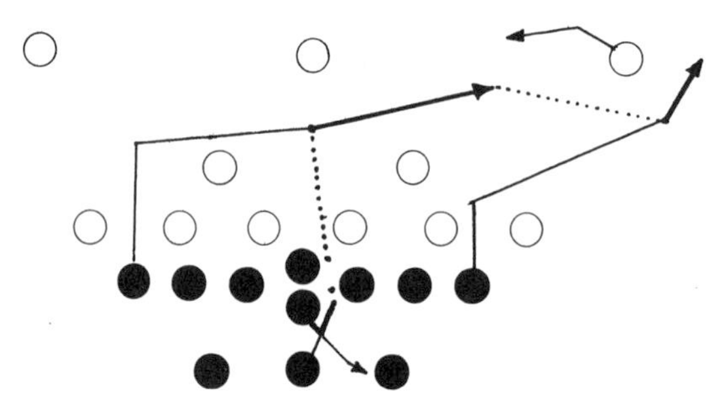

This historic photo shows Bear end Hewitt lateraling to Karr for the winning touchdown.

December 12, 1937 Lordy, lordy, they knew he could pass. After all, Sammy Baugh had completely rewritten, recharted and recast college football when he was side-arming those zingers at Texas Christian. But here he was, a rookie, whipping his slingshot arm for the Redskins, taking them to the NFL Championship. He was up against George Halas, Bronko Nagurski, Joe Stydahar, the rest of the beefy Chicago Bears and snow. Sammy Baugh had never played in snow before. But Sam also had support: halfback Cliff Battles (who led the league in rushing) and end Wayne Millner (both Hall of Famers). At the half, Chicago led 14-7, with Baugh spending most of that time getting used to the snow. But after the whistle began the second half, Baugh opened up. He hit Millner for two long touchdowns, passes of 55 and 77 yards. Then late in the fourth quarter, with the score tied at 21, Baugh ran right, stopped short and wheeled to hit his wingback Ed Justice in the deep left corner of the end zone, 35 yards away. In that game he completed 18 of 33 attempts for a then phenomenal 335 yards passing, doubling, tripling the number of passes in a game. It would take almost two decades before quarterbacks would dare to throw with the frequency (not to mention accuracy) that Slinging Sam zipped them off. He was the first, and he taught them all there was to know about passing.

For the 1937 NFL title, Ernie Pinckert catches a Baugh aerial.

December 6, 1940 Just three weeks prior to this game, the Redskins had skinned the Bears, 7-3. And no one, not even the Bears, expected the Redskins to be so cleanly scalped, especially in a championship game in which they were favored. The Bears scored three touchdowns in the first quarter, one in the second, four in the third and three in the fourth. After their ninth touchdown, the Bears were asked to pass for the extra point; you see, the officials were down to their last football after all those extra point kicks into the stands. In all, 10 different Bears scored touchdowns. When the smoke around the scoreboard had cleared, the Bears had won the NFL championship, beating Washington and Sammy Baugh, by a score of 73-0. It was the worst beating ever in the history of the NFL. When asked what he thought the score might have been if the Redskins scored first, Baugh said, "73 to 7."

Most important, this was the game which stopped the single wing dead in its tracks, ending an era of triple-threats, slow-scoring ball games, razzle-dazzles, and statue of liberties. From then on coaches and quarterbacks hunkered down to think strategy, deception and the balanced attack. It was the coming, or as some say, the second coming of the T-formation and it enriched the game of football.

Bear's Bill Osmanski in full steam to a 73-0 scalping of the Redskins.

Sammy Baugh could do it all

November 14, 1943 The sporting tradition when they stage a day for a super athlete—as they did on this date for Sid Luckman—is for the player to run on the field and provide the fans with one of the worst performances in his career. Well, until they throw more than seven touchdown passes in a single game, they won't erase Sid Luckman's name from that particular record. Because that's what the Chicago Bears quarterback did right after he thanked everyone for the $1,000 war bond and told them how honored he was. It went like this:

1st Quarter: 4-yard fourth down pass to Jim Benton; 54-yard pass to Connie Berry.

2nd Quarter: 27-yard fourth down pass to Hampton Pool.

3rd Quarter: 28-yard pass to Harry Clark; 15-yard pass to Benton.

4th Quarter: 3-yard pass to George Wilson; 37-yard pass to Pool.

After the sixth touchdown pass, the coaches decided to rest Luckman. They thought he'd done enough. But someone on the bench remembered that just two weeks before Sammy Baugh had set the record with six passes. On the Bears' next possession, Sid Luckman was sent in with orders to pass on every play. Knowing that Luckman only needed one more to set the record, the fans were screaming for the enemy quarterback to pull it off. With seconds to go, Luckman went in with the ball on his own 23-yard line. He hit Ray McLean for 40 yards, then rifled one 34 yards to Pool that the Stanford lad just barely snagged on his fingertips and staggered two steps into the end zone. Luckman had the record and, en route, he had completed 23 of 30 for 508 yards, a yardage record that would stand for eight years. The Bears won, 56-7. Going into the game, the Bears had been undefeated in 23 contests (one tie); this made it 24 but the streak ended here. Sammy Baugh and the Redskins stopped them the next week but the Bears came back to defeat the Skins for the NFL Championship.

Sid Luckman practicing.

Otto Graham and coach Paul Brown hold the French Trophy.

September 16, 1950 It was a warm Saturday night in Philadelphia's Municipal Stadium and 71,237 brotherly love partisans had pushed through the turnstiles expecting to see their Eagles claw up the Cleveland Browns in their maiden venture into the National Football League. A perfect match for the first game of the season, it brought together the 1949 NFL Champions and the 1949 All-American Football Conference Champions—Greasy Neale's Philadelphia Eagles and Paul Brown's Cleveland Browns. The Eagles had won their division title for three consecutive seasons and the NFL Championship for the last two of the three. The upstart Browns of the upstart AAFC, on the other hand, had won four consecutive AAFC Championships with a four-year record of 47 wins, 5 losses and 2 ties. Added to the NFL-AAFC drama was the fact that the Browns' popularity in Cleveland forced the NFL Champions, the Cleveland Rams to move to Los Angeles. But this was four years later, 1950, and the leagues had merged.

Greasy Neale had heard about Paul Brown. He heard from almost every other coach in the NFL, since they were sending him diagrams, photos and suggestions on how to stop Brown. But Greasy had evolved an excellent strategem of his own. It was a 5-4 defense, widely copied around the league and called the "Eagle Defense," and it had seemingly spiked the guns of the T-formation, Brown's specialty. In the Eagle Defense, the five-man line was all guards and tackles, with the defensive ends pulled off the line a few steps, aligned head to head with the offensive ends. Philadelphia had the pinpoint throwing accuracy of Tommy Thompson, the famous one-eyed passer; the sure hands of Pete Pihos; the stiff blocking and tackling of Chuck Bednarik, Cliff Patton and Alex Wojciechowicz and the powerful running of Steve Van Buren.

And Cleveland? "The game," recalls Brown, "just wasn't a sporting proposition for the Eagles. The press and the public were saying how we were going to get whipped 50 to nothing, and this would take a little doing when we had guys like quarterback Otto Graham, fullback Marion Motley and receivers Dante Lavelli, Mac Speedie and Dub Jones. Besides, this was the highest emotional game I ever coached. We had four years of constant ridicule to get us ready." As the team was leaving the locker room for the field to start the game, Brown whispered to his hushed players, "Just think, men, tonight you're going to get to touch Steve Van Buren." The Browns exploded onto the field.

But when the game got under way, it looked as if the boys from the AAFC just couldn't keep up. The Browns lost yardage on two of three first quarter runs and fumbled on two of five carries in the second. By halftime, however, the Browns were leading, 14-3, after Graham had tossed a 59-yarder to his flanker, Jones, and connected with a 26-yard touchdown pass to end Lavelli. Greasy Neale started red-dogging the Cleveland passer but Graham picked up on it after one try and popped passes to the vacated area. In the third period, Graham looped a 13-yarder to Mac Speedie for a third touchdown. And in the final period, Graham sneaked in from a yard out for a fourth touchdown and popped a two-yard pass to a back circling out of his backfield, Rex Bumgardner, for a final score. Cleveland won, 35-10.

The Eagles—well, the entire NFL, really—had never seen such pinpoint spot passing. They seemed to have the receivers covered but Graham would have the ball at a precise spot at a precise time. No one in the NFL had seen that before but Brown had been designing such plays for a decade, beginning at Massillon High School, Miami of Ohio and Ohio State. Brown's T-formation football was quick openers, traps and spot passing. So what's new? Well, it was then.

The Browns' win over the Eagles in their first NFL game gave some portent of what was to come for the next decade. They went on to win the NFL Championship that year, 1950, and either won or tied for Conference Championships in eight of their first 10 seasons in the National Football League.

December 28, 1958 The New York Giants versus the Baltimore Colts. No one questions the assertion that this was the greatest professional football game ever played. They say this was the one that turned America *en masse* onto football, making it the sports spectacle of the electronic generation with huge television contracts. This game made the NFL. All that aside, it still is the greatest game played. You can read about or hear about great games or great feats all you want: the difference in this contest was that millions of people saw it. And that was about two decades ago.

It all began with Sudden Death. Just a week before the game, the NFL commissioner, Bert Bell, had decreed that all future championship games tied after 60 minutes of regulation play would be decided by a Sudden Death overtime period. The first team scoring any points would be declared the winner.

The Giants, although they slugged hard to win the Eastern Conference, were at the height of their power. Jim Lee Howell was the coach and supporting him in strategy were Vince Lombardi, as offensive coach, and Tom Landry, as defensive coach. What can you say about a team that has Charley Conerly, Frank Gifford, Kyle Rote, Emlen Tunnell, Sam Huff, Andy Robustelli, Jim Katcavage, Roosevelt Grier, Dick Modzelewski, Harland Svare, Bill Svoboda, Rosie Brown, Mel Triplett, Don Maynard, Pat Summerall and Alex Webster. It was certainly one of the greatest defensive teams to take the field. But they were matched by a Weeb Ewbank crew that included Johnny Unitas, Alan Ameche, Raymond Berry, Big Daddy Lipscomb, Lenny Lyles, Gino Marchetti, Lenny Moore, Jim Mutscheller, Steve Myhra and Jim Parker. The rosters alone read like a couple of decades of Who's Who in Pro Football.

The first quarter didn't go well for the Colts. Unitas got off a long pass to Lenny Moore which carried to the Giants 25 yard line but Sam Huff hurdled the middle of the Colt line to block a field goal attempt. The Giants took over and on a quick Conerly pitch to Gifford, the ball was run to the Colts 31. Then Summerall toed one between the uprights for a 3-0 lead.

By the second quarter, Unitas had completed his probing and testing. After Lipscomb recovered a Giant fumble on the Giant 20, the Colt quarterback sent Ameche and Moore running up the middle for a 20-yard drive. Then Ameche slogged in from the 2 for a touchdown. The next time the Colts had possession they started on their own 14. With running plays that netted five and six yards at a clip, Unitas moved his team upfield. From 15 yards out, he zinged one to Ray Berry and the Colts were up, 14-3, at the half.

Unitas came out throwing in the third quarter. He passed and passed and when the swirling dust had cleared, the Colts were on the Giants 3-yard line with four tries at the goal. It seemed as if the game was won. A touchdown would have made it 21-3; as it was the Colts were leading by 11. But the great Giants defensive line held. It held for all four running plays. And then, for the rest of that quarter and the last, the Giants took over. They had stopped the Colts with their backs against the goal posts. Painfully, slowly, the Giants worked for a first down on their 13. Then, Conerly sent Rote out on a deep slant, left to right, and hit Rote on the Colt 40. Rote carried to the Colt 25 and fumbled. Everyone seemed frozen, watching the bounding ball, but Alex Webster, the Giant halfback who was downfield, scooped up the ball and lugged it to the one. Triplett leaped over the line for the Giant touchdown. It was now 14-10, Colts. On the next Colt series, Robustelli and Modzelewski banged through the Colt pass blockers and dumped Unitas for long losses. The Giants got the ball back as the clock ticked them into the final period. Conerly switched passing targets; he had been throwing to Rote and Gifford but now he laid two out for his left end, Bob Schnelker, on two consecutive plays, gaining 17 yards on one and 46 on the second. Then he hit Gifford on the right sidelines for a 15-yard touchdown. The Giants led, 17-14. Both teams ran off a few series and got nowhere. Then, with 1:56 remaining on the clock, the Giants punted and Baltimore took over on its 14. It was Unitas and Berry, three times, in a row for 25, 15 and 22 yards to the New York 13. There were seven seconds left. Place-kicker Steve Myhra blasted it through the goal posts from 20 yards out, and the game was tied, at 17. For the first time in pro football history, a championship game would go into Sudden Death overtime. The 64,815 spectators had not been sitting for the last 10 minutes; they would not sit for the next 10 either. After a three-minute rest, the Giants won the toss and elected to receive. But they found they could not move the ball and had to punt. The Colts took over on their own 20, with 80 yards to go. Mixing short sure passes and quick short runs, Unitas was slowly moving the Colts up field. Then, he saw an opening and sent Ameche on a quick trap for 23 yards to the Giant 20-yard line. He hit Raymond Berry for a first down on the eight. And three playes later, Ameche plunged that one final yard for the winning score. For the two teams, the thousands in Yankee Stadium and for the millions who watched on television, Raymond Berry—who caught 12 passes for 178 yards—summed it up simply: "It's the greatest thing that ever happened."

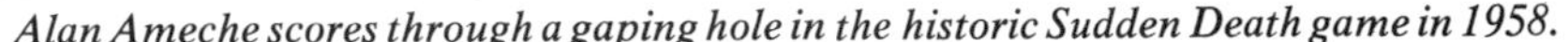

Alan Ameche scores through a gaping hole in the historic Sudden Death game in 1958.

Jets fullback Matt Snell goes around left end for the first score in the stunning Jets upset of the Baltimore Colts in Super Bowl III. Colt linebacker Dennis Gaubatz tries to stop him.

January 12, 1969 On June 8, 1966, the NFL and the AFL announced that the two warring football leagues would merge and that an inter-league football championship, soon to be called the Super Bowl, would decide the championship. Football fans could barely contain themselves. For six years, since the formation of the AFL in 1960, it had seemed that the NFL was totally oblivious to the upstart league's existence. The football draft wars raged; NFL players and writers scoffed at the bash bravura of the AFL taxi-squadders, castoffs and few genuine star draft picks. The New York Titans were a disaster. The Dallas Texans had to move. Ditto the L.A. Chargers. It was tough going for the new league. Then, along came Sonny Werblin. He bought the Titans and went out looking for talent. Werblin found Joe Willie Namath and he paid Namath a mere $400,000 to throw passes for his renamed team, the New York Jets. The Jets (like their rhymed namesake, the Mets) were losers, but suddenly found themselves on the map. More importantly, the NFL owners no doubt took a long hard look at their cash flow charts and realized it would be better to get the AFL to join them in the college draft than to start shelling out a half million to win a bidding war for an untried college star. The NFL diehards still grumbled disdainfully, however, because they *knew* the misfits and kids over in the AFL couldn't stomp people in the same cleats as their tried and true stars. And they smiled knowingly when Vince Lombardi's Packers ripped apart the Kansas City Chiefs and the Oakland Raiders, 35-10 and 33-14, in the first two Super Bowls. Even Lombardi had a dig for the AFL: he said it would take years for them to catch up. It took just one.

The team carrying the NFL banner into Super Bowl III (the Imperial Roman Numeral did not come until much later) was the Baltimore colts. And these Colts were a mean tough team. They had just completed an awesome season, 15 wins, one loss. In the playoffs, the Colts had knocked off the Vikings, 24-14, and simply shut out the Cleveland Browns, 34-0. The Jets, on the other hand, had just squeaked by the Raiders, 27-23, in the final minutes of that match. Here it was, Super Bowl III, and the Colts were conservatively rated as two or three touchdown favorites. The Colts were also armed with their terror weapon: the eight-man maximum blitz. Then Namath opened his mouth. He stated matter-of-factly, "We're gonna win it. There's no way we'll lose." Then, he added, "I guarantee it." (Oh, brazen young man.) When asked about his opposing quarterback, Earl Morrall (who led the NFL in passing that season), Namath seriously implied that Morrall was a second-rate quarterback and that there were better ones in the AFL. There were enough dares and double-dares to provoke Winnie-the-Pooh.

And there it was, Super Sunday, Orange Bowl, Miami, Fla., sun shining bright. The Colts came charging onto the field like it was a demonstration day for the local Boys Club. A light working day. They were up; they were gonna have fun, too, knocking Namath on his ass, picking off his passes. A good old-fashioned shit-stomping grudge match. Wow-wee!

We all know what happened: the Jets offensive front line moved the Colts around like they were rubber duckies; Matt Snell kept running one of the simplest plays in any playbook, the off-tackle slant, and gained 121 yards in 30 tries; George Sauer caught five Namath passes for 105 yards; and Namath, well, he completed 61 percent of his passes, 17 of 28, for a total of 206 yards, doing everything to the Colt secondary except maybe picking their teeth.

The Jet victory completely altered the face of professional football. Everybody stopped laughing at the AFL. In fact, AFL owners who were forced to pay immense "admission fees" to join the NFL wondered whether it shouldn't have been the other way around. The young league got equal space in our more crusty newspapers, bigger revenues from television. And Joe Willie Namath said he thought it'd take a few years before the NFL could catch up.

GREAT MOMENTS IN COLLEGE FOOTBALL

November 9, 1912 It was just like on the frontier, the Indians against the horse soldiers. Only this time, the scalping took place on the plains of West Point and the wielder of the blade was one Wa-tho-huck, better known to us as Jim Thorpe. The Carlisle Indian school had Jim Thorpe and he was certainly good, but he would be facing Army, the stalwart Black Knights from the New York plains country, who had been seeking and destroying almost every enemy eleven in sight. Oddly enough, Jim Thorpe and his redoubtable band of Indian school mates, led by Coach Pop Warner, overwhelmed Army by a score of 27-6, not counting the five times the Indians were stopped inside the Army 5-yard line.

The New York Times covered that game and here is part of their report: "Thorpe tore off runs of ten yards or more so often that they became common. His zigzagging and ability to hurl himself free of tacklers made his running highly spectacular. In the third period he made a run which...will go down in the Army gridiron annals as one of the greatest ever seen on the plains....[Thorpe took a punt on Army's 45.] It was a high kick, and the Cadets were already gathering around the big Indian when he clutched the falling pigskin in his arms. His catch and his start were but one motion. In and out, zigzagging first to one side and then to the other, while a flying Cadet went hurtling through space, Thorpe wormed his way through the entire Army team. Every Cadet in the game had his chance, and every one of them failed. It was not the usual spectacle of the man with the ball outdistancing his opponents by circling them. It was a dodging game in which Thorpe matched himself against an entire team and proved the master. Lines drawn parallel and fifteen feet apart would include all the ground that Thorpe covered on his triumphant dash through an entire team."

The punter was a right halfback named Dwight D. Eisenhower, a cadet who gave up football after injuring his knee a week later. He punted okay against the Nazis, though.

EIGHT DECADES OF CONSENSUS ALL-AMERICANS

1900-09

Flying Wedge outlawed, ending brutality. Field goals drop from four to three points.

E	Thomas Shevlin, Yale
E	David C. Campbell, Harvard
T	Hamilton Fish, Harvard
T	James Hogan, Yale
G	Albert Benbrook, Michigan
G	Nathan Dougherty, Tenn.
C	Germany Schulz, Michigan
B	Walter Eckersall, Chicago
B	Willie Heston, Michigan
B	Harold Weekes, Columbia
B	Ted Coy, Yale

1910-19

Seven players required on line of scrimmage. Interlocked arms for interference and flying tackles prohibited.

E	Paul L. Robeson, Rutgers
E	Bill Fincher, Georgia Tech
T	D. Belford West, Colgate
T	Josh Cody, Vanderbilt
G	Stanley Pennock, Harvard
G	Joe Alexander, Syracuse
C	Robert Peck, Pittsburgh
B	Bo McMillin, Centre
B	Jim Thorpe, Carlisle
B	George Gipp, Notre Dame
B	Chic Harley, Ohio State

October 7, 1916 This was a vintage year for sports. It was the year of the first professional golf tournament, the year of the first Rose Bowl. It was also a monumental year for sports victories in baseball and football. The Boston Braves notched the longest winning streak in modern baseball history—26 games. Pete Alexander compiled a season record of 16 shutouts. But the most phenomenal events of all were taking place on the football field. Consider these football scores: Ohio State humbled Oberlin, 128-0; Tulsa cleaned out Missouri Mines, 117-0; Oklahoma scalped the Shawnee Catholic Indians, 140-0. But surely the most marvelous slaughter of all took place on Grant Field in Atlanta when Georgia Tech magnificently, magnamiously, munificently annihilated Cumberland College by a score of 222-0. No matter which team comes along, what rule changes are made, what lay-down-and-die attitude any destitute team might take, that scoring record will never be beaten. Indeed, only the first quarter score of 63-0 was ever matched: it was matched in the second quarter. Down so far, the second half could only look up for the Cumberland eleven. The quarter by quarter scoring went like this.

GT	63	63	54	42	222
C	0	0	0	0	0

The great coach who pulled off this unique victory was none other than John Heisman, for whom the Heisman Trophy is named. Heisman was one of football's great innovators. He gave us the center snap; added "hep" and "hike" to our vocabulary; got the forward pass legalized; schemed the hidden-ball trick and invented the scoreboard. He was also an irascible eccentric: he believed that soup and hot water weakened people, so those two aqueous substances were outlawed from his training table. He also excluded whatever foods he did not like, like coffee, peanuts, apple pie. His players were treated to a lot of raw meat, however. And if his coaching philosophy could be summarized in one line of his own, it was,

Jim Thorpe, above, *boots one.*

"The coach should be masterful and commanding, even dictatorial."

It might surprise you that he had his own view about scoring and winning ball games: he was supposed to have cared little about the margin, yes margin, of victory. Legend has it that he only ran up the score on Cumberland to prove a point—his. He was reportedly incensed over newspaper articles which made much ado about comparative football scores. He said that if writers "believe in such crazy stuff we'll give them a crazy score to work with."

Georgia Tech won the toss and charitably elected to kick off. The Cumberland ball carrier was dropped on the 25, while their quarterback, Eddie Edwards, was knocked out while blocking and carried off the field. On the first play from scrimmage the substitute quarterback gained three yards over tackle and that was Cumberland's longest gain of the day. Within minutes Tech had 28 points. Cumberland switched strategy, electing to kick off when they were supposed to receive, thinking that the Yellowjackets would at least have to start far downfield. Well, Tech ran the first such return back 70 yards to the Cumberland 10-yard line. That's the way the game went: Tech scored every time it had the ball, Cumberland got nowhere. By game's end, Georgia Tech had gained 528 yards rushing, 220 yards on punt returns, 220 yards on kickoff returns, but threw not one pass. Cumberland completed two of 11 passes for 14 yards, lost 45 yards rushing, and fumbled the ball away nine times. (On one fumble, a Cumberland back exhorted a teammate to fall on the ball. "Not me," the reply came back, "I didn't drop it." Cumberland had one consolation. In a 40-year reunion, a Cumberland player observed, "Little did we realize we were playing ourselves into immortality."

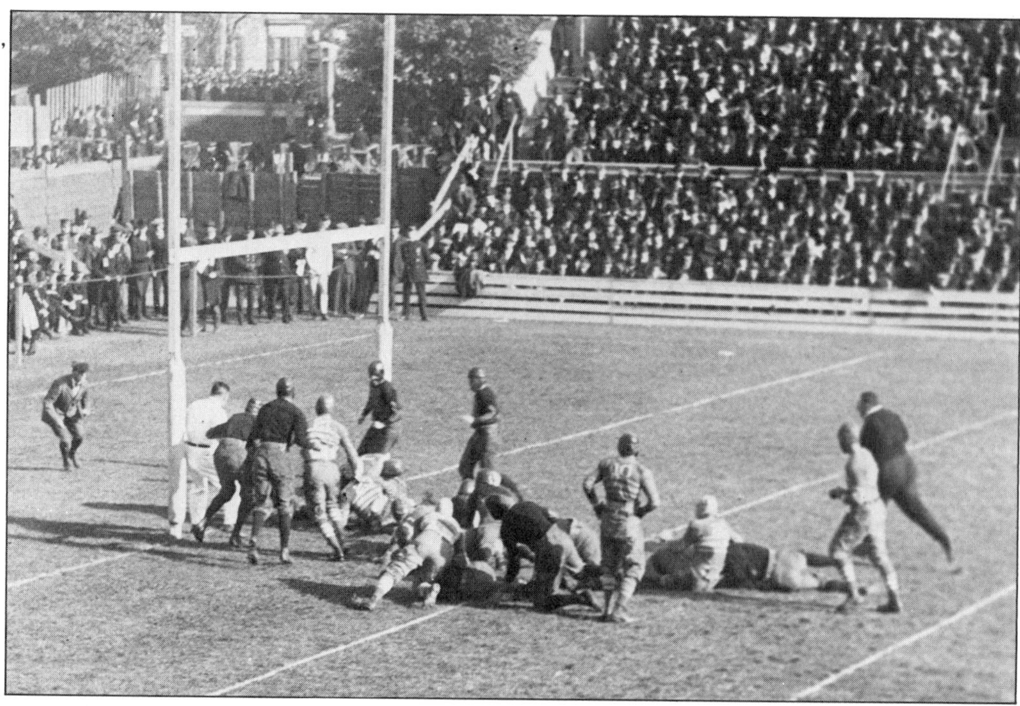

Centre College vs. Harvard, David vs. Goliath: the Praying Colonels had a stunning upset.

October 29, 1921 In 1950, when the Associated Press conducted a poll among sportswriters, asking them to name the "greatest upset of the century," they came up with a sunny October afternoon game played on the banks of the Charles River in Boston. Harvard, the Goliath of four undefeated seasons, was beaten by Centre College, the 300-student-body David from Danville, Ky.

Because they prayed in the locker room before each game, the lads from Centre were called the Praying Colonels. They had had some good seasons, too. In 1919, for example, Centre had outscored its opposition 485 to 23. So, they requested a game with Harvard and the mighty Ivy League power sent a scout down to Danville to see if Centre was a worthy opponent. He thought they were. The first game, played in 1920, resulted in a typical Harvard victory 31 to 14 but the Crimson were impressed. They decided to play again.

During the first half, both teams ran the ball in spurts, punted back and forth and missed several drop-kicked field goal attempts. At the half, neither team had scored. In the third period, however, after a punt return to the Crimson 47, a tripping penalty put the ball on the 32. Bo McMillin, later an All-American, took the Centre snap 10 yards deep, cut through right tackle and found himself in the Harvard end zone. The extra point attempt failed but the six points turned out to be enough. It was Harvard's first defeat in 40 years of intersectional competition. And Centre College became the number one team in the nation, by consensus.

October 18, 1924 The Big Game in 1924 was Illinois-Michigan. Both teams had completed the 1923 season with a perfect record. But Illinois had a sophomore that season who had gained 1,260 yards rushing and scored 12 touchdowns, a young man named Red Grange. In Champaign-Urbana, they had built a new Illinois stadium, and used it, but saved the dedication for the 1924 meeting between the two collegiate super powers. Going into the game, Michigan was riding the crest of a 20-game undefeated streak; Illinois had won 10 in a row. Michigan's coach Fielding "Hurry Up" Yost had presided over teams which had won 196 games and lost 34. Yost had 13 undefeated seasons at Michigan. Before the Big Game, he had been asked about the lean, freckle-faced Illini runner. He said, "Mr. Grange will be a carefully watched young man any time he takes the ball. There will be just about 11 clean, hard Michigan tacklers headed for him at the same time. I know he's a great runner but great runners usually have the hardest time gaining ground when they are met by special preparation."

But even special preparation couldn't stop Grange. When they lined up for the Michigan kickoff, the Michigan captain asked, "Where is this guy Grange? We want to kick to him." A member of the Illini front pointed him out.

1920~29

Goal posts moved back 10 yards behind line of scrimmage. Era of Knute Rockne, Red Grange, and Bronko Nagurski.

E Bennie Oosterbaan, Mich.
C Mel Hein, Washington State
E Brick Muller, California
T Bronko Nagurski, Minn.
T Ed Weir, Nebraska
G Charles J. Hubbard, Harvard
G Jack Cannon, Notre Dame
B Benny Friedman, Michigan
B Red Grange, Illinois
B Red Cagle, Army
B Ernie Nevers, Stanford

Michigan sent a line drive kick which Grange pulled in on his 5-yard line. The redhead started slow, gained momentum, and twisted and turned his way through a mass of Michigan tacklers. Ninety-five yards later he had scored the first TD.

Within five minutes, Illinois got the ball again on their own 33. Taking a direct snap from center, set deep in the spread formation, Grange started around right end, reversed himself, snaked his way through a half dozen tacklers and 67 yards for his second touchdown. Three minutes later, Illinois took possession again. Snap to Grange. He slanted at tackle, twisted free to the outside, turned the corner and high-tailed it 56 yards for a TD. Four minutes later, Illinois had the ball again. Grange took the snap from the Michigan 44-yard line and ran right through the middle of the Wolverine line behind one blocker for his fourth touchdown. In 12 minutes, he had taken the ball four times and scored four TD's with runs of 95, 67, 56 and 44 yards. After his fourth touchdown, Grange was leaning on the goalposts, sucking air and a substitute was sent in. But Grange came back in the second half, scored on a 15-yarder the first time he touched the ball, then passed for a sixth touchdown. In all, he gained 402 yards in 21 carries. Illinois defeated Michigan (do you really need to know?) 39-14.

The first four times Red Grange touched the ball in this game he scored four TD's, of 97, 67, 56 & 44 yards—in 1st 12 minutes.

1930-39

Football is reduced one inch in circumference. Beginning of the era of the forward pass, Sammy Baugh, Don Hutson and Tommy Harmon.

E	Don Hutson, Alabama
E	Gaynell Tinsley, La. State
T	Ed Widseth, Minnesota
T	Bruiser Kinard, Mississippi
G	Bill Corbus, Stanford
G	Aaron Rosenberg, So. Cal.
C	Alex Wojciechowicz Fordham
B	Sammy Baugh, Texas Christian
B	Jay Berwanger, Chicago
B	Tom Harmon, Michigan
B	Bobby Grayson, Stanford

1940-49

Substitution liberalized. Era of Glenn Davis and Doc Blanchard, Doak Walker and Charlie "Choo-choo" Justice.

E	Leon Hart, Notre Dame	E	Pete Pihos, Indiana
T	George Connor, Notre Dame	T	Leo Nomellini, Minnesota
G	Buddy Burris, Oklahoma	G	Bill Fischer, Notre Dame
C	Chuck Bednarik, Penn.		
B	Frank Albert, Stanford		
B	Glenn Davis, Army	B	Doak Walker, So. Methodist
B	Doc Blanchard, Army		

November 2, 1935 It's not unusual for an Ohio State eleven to be considered awesome. They certainly were in 1935. With only three defeats in four years, the Buckeyes were going into games as 30- or 40-point favorites. They were just that potent when they took the field against the Fighting Irish of Notre Dame. The Irish (then called the Ramblers) had lost much of their power and magic in the four years since Knute Rockne's death in an air crash. They had had to rebuild, practically from nothing, but by the first weekend in November, 1935, they had won eight straight games. That meant they had a chance. Although it didn't look that way at the end of the third quarter, when the Buckeyes had dragged the Irish all over the field and were leading 13-0.

That's when the miracle happened. It's unknown whether Catholics are more proficient at prayer than Protestants or Jews or Zoroastrians, but Somebody answered someone. In an age when passing and stopping the clock were considered unmanly and punk, the Fighting Irish scored three touchdowns, two of them in the last 90 seconds before 81,000 onlookers who probably went home reciting Hail Marys and the rest of the Baltimore catechism.

October 26, 1940 At the beginning of the 1940 season, Stanford was one of the nation's top picks to go absolutely nowhere. They had finished the previous fall with a 1-7-1 record, losing every Pacific Coast conference game they played. This particular season, they had one added liability, a new coach. The new coach, however, was Clark Shaughnessy and as he was unveiling the new man-in-motion T-formation for the Chicago Bears, he was also about to introduce it to college football.

Stanford began the season as a 2-to-1 underdog against the University of San Francisco and beat them 27-0. Then they knocked off Oregon 13-0, Santa Clara 7-6 and Washington State 26-14. The game against Southern Cal would be the test. Southern Cal hadn't lost a game since 1938 and they had buried the Indians three out of their last four meetings.

With 65,000 in the stands as witnesses, the game seesawed like a tedious tennis volley. First Stanford's Frankie Albert connected with Pete Kmetovic for a 60-yard touchdown, but the Trojans came back with a second-quarter interception and touchdown to tie. Then, with a tie game and a final three minutes to go, Albert stopped passing and started faking handoffs. That was the whole idea of the man-in-motion T; it was an offense in which both the spectators and the defense would have trouble locating the ball. Faking off-tackle runs, Albert stepped back and fired three completes, moving the team 76 yards to the USC 4. A run over right guard was the winning touchdown. In the last 90 seconds Albert intercepted a desperate Trojan pass and ran untouched for an added touchdown.

Stanford finished the season with ten wins and no losses and went to the Rose Bowl against

Nebraska, defeating the Cornhuskers, 21-13. A football historian has described that 1941 Rose Bowl game as the game that "revolutionized football." He meant that that was the game when a lot of "important" people first saw the man-in-motion T. On the other coast, just three weeks before that Rose Bowl, the Chicago Bears had used Shaughnessy's T-formation in the NFL title game and destroyed the Washington Redskins, 73-0.

1950-59

Two-point conversion introduced. Era of Bud Wilkinson's Oklahoma Sooners, Jim Brown, Hopalong Cassady and Paul Hornung.

- E Willie Davis, Grambling
- E Ron Kramer, Michigan
- T Dick Modzelewski, Maryland
- T Alex Karras, Iowa
- G Jim Parker, Ohio State
- G Bud McFadin, Texas
- C Bob Pellegrini, Maryland
- B Paul Hornung, Notre Dame
- B Howard Cassady, Ohio State
- B Tommy McDonald, Okla.
- B Jim Brown, Syracuse

November 16, 1957 On this date, Anwar Sadat parted the Red Sea. Chairman Mao was caught shoplifting at Macy's. Mickey Mouse married Raquel Welch. And, just as incredibly, Oklahoma lost a football game. You must remember, they had won 47 straight. The last time they lost had been almost four years earlier, in the first game of the 1953 season, and their conqueror was Notre Dame. In the years that followed that loss was almost forgotten. Oklahoma's next game was a tie, and they won their remaining eight games in 1953, ten in a row in 1954, 1955, and 1956 and their first seven games in 1957. (They also defeated Maryland in two Orange Bowls, 1954 and 1956.)

Then Notre Dame proved their nemesis again. Coming into the November 16 game, the Fighting Irish had lost to both Navy (20-6) and Michigan State (34-6). When they played Oklahoma a year earlier, they'd been annihilated by a score of 40-0. Considering that this was a home game at Norman and that the state's 50th anniversary celebration had been delayed until this game, it was surprising that Notre Dame was a mere 18-point underdog. But,

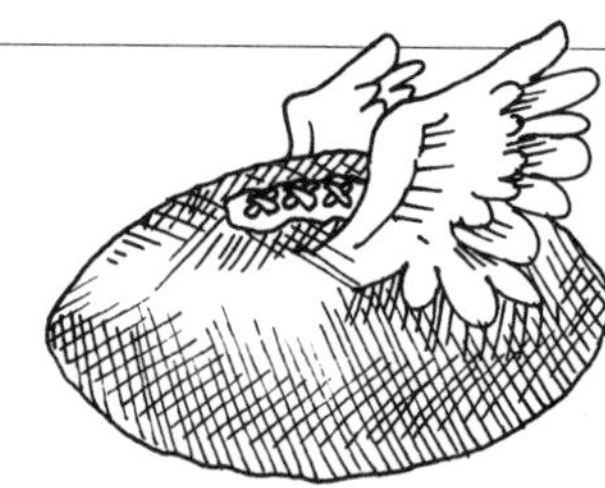

Oklahoma and South Bend rooters mostly held their breath during the game. Going into the 4th quarter, the score was tied, 0-0. Late in the 4th period, the Irish—with hard running by Nick Pietrosante—moved the ball down to the Sooner 8-yard line. Previously, Notre Dame had been stopped on the 1 and the 6. But Irish quarterback Bob Williams had noticed the Sooner linebackers keying on Pietrosante. He faked to Pietrosante, pitched out to halfback Dick Lynch, and Lynch skirted right end for the game's sole touchdown. Oklahoma had four minutes to score but their desperation passing attack failed. Nevertheless, a skein of 47 is a skein of 47—and it hasn't been matched.

In the last 42 seconds, Harvard scores two TD's and two two-point conversions to tie Yale in the Big Game of 1968.

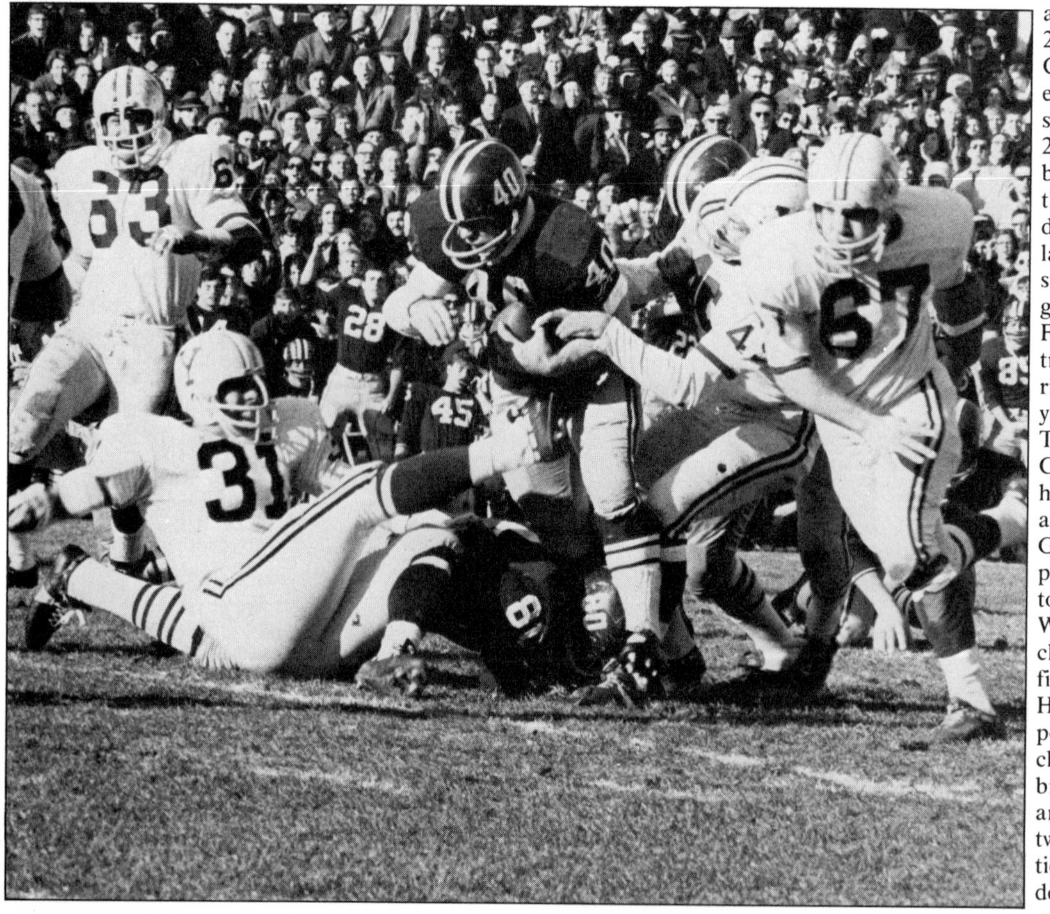

November 23, 1968 In all of college football there is probably no more historic rivalry than the annual Harvard-Yale gridiron battle. There have been numerous close contests, scores of great football players. Yet, there will probably never again be another finish the likes of which 40,280 spectators witnessed on the banks of the Charles in 1968. Harvard and Yale were vieing for the Ivy League title. Going into the game, each team had won eight and lost none. For 59 minutes and 18 seconds it was a very boring game. With 42 seconds left on the clock, Yale was leading, 29-13, and Yale partisans were proudly waving their white hankies and shouting "You're number two." Hold on folks, would you believe that the Harvard Crimson came back and scored two touchdowns and two two-point conversions to tie Yale with zero seconds showing on the clock? They did indeed.

The last touchdown was something to behold. Harvard tried an onside kick and recovered it on the Yale 49. The Crimson's substitute quarterback, Frank Champi, churned around left end for 14 yards. A face mask penalty against Yale took the ball to the 20. Thirty-two seconds left. Champi threw two incompletes, each costing six seconds. Twenty seconds left, third and 10 on the 20. Harvard's premiere running back, Vic Gatto, went back into the game, flanked right, and drew double coverage. Champi laid the ball into Gus Crim's stomach for a draw play that gained 14 yards to the Yale 6. Fourteen seconds left. Champi, trying an option pass run, ran right then left and lost three yards. He also lost 11 seconds. Three seconds remaining. Champi went back to pass, found his receivers covered and was about to lateral. Then he spotted Gatto in the left corner. A quick pass and a second Harvard touchdown. Yale still led 29-27. With no time showing on the clock, the spectators swarmed the field. But the rules state that Harvard could try for their extra points. After the field was cleared, Champi drew a deep breath, took the snap from center and rifled it to Pete Varney for the two points. The game ended in a tie and everyone went home delerious, happy or otherwise.

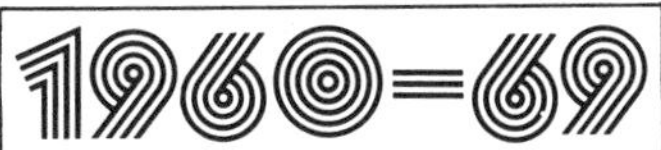

Goal post widened from 18′ 6″ to 23′ 4″, increasing field goals by 93 per cent. Era of O. J. Simpson, Dick Butkus, Joe Namath and Roger Staubach.

Offense

E	Otis Taylor, Prairie View A&M
E	Howard Twilley, Tulsa
T	Bob Lilly, Texas Christian
T	Bobby Bell, Minnesota
G	Merlin Olsen, Utah State
G	Bob Brown, Nebraska
C	Dick Butkus, Illinois
B	Joe Namath, Alabama
B	O. J. Simpson, Southern Cal.
B	Gale Sayers, Kansas
B	Ernie Davis, Syracuse

Defense

E	Bubba Smith, Michigan State
E	Ted Hendricks, Miami (Fla.)
T	Buck Buchanan, Grambling
T	Mike Reid, Penn. State
LB	Willie Lanier, Morgan State
LB	Lee Roy Jordan, Alabama
LB	Tommy Nobis, Texas
B	George Webster, Michigan State
B	Jack Tatum, Ohio State
B	Kermit Alexander, U.C.L.A.
B	Leroy Keyes, Purdue

1970-75

Defense

E	Ed Jones, Tennessee State
E	Randy White, Maryland
T	Walt Patulski, Notre Dame
T	Rich Glover, Nebraska
LB	Jeff Siemon, Stanford
LB	Robert Brazile, Jackson State
LB	Ed O'Neil, Penn. State
B	Willie Buchanon, San Diego State
B	Tommy Casanova, L.S.U.
B	Clarence Ellie, Notre Dame
B	Neal Colzie, Ohio State

Offense

WR	Elmo Wright, Houston
WR	Terry Beasley, Auburn
TE	Riley Odums, Houston
T	Jerry Sisemore, Texas
T	John Hicks, Ohio State
G	John Hannah, Alabama
G	Reggie McKenzie, Michigan
C	Dave Thompson, Clemson
RB	Johnny Rodgers, Nebraska
RB	Archie Griffin, Ohio State
RB	John Capelletti, Penn. State
QB	Jim Plunkett, Stanford

K Ray Guy, So. Mississippi

November 30, 1974 It was one of the most improbable games in American collegiate football history. It has been called the "greatest game in West Coast history" and if it's not we don't know what is. For two quarters it looked as if the Fighting Irish from South Bend, Ind., were feeding the USC Trojans to the lions on the sunny floor of the Los Angeles Memorial Coliseum. Notre Dame runners were driving through the Southern Cal line like a thunderstorm through a rainbow. When a gun sounded ending the first half, it seemed as if the Trojans were going back to their dressing room for a redressing of their wounds and a brief respite before the second half Notre Dame deluge.

As in all sports fables, something happened to the Trojans on their way to and from the Coliseum dressing room. They came out as if they were mortally-wounded rampaging bull elephants. They spewed forth such an awesome display of raw offensive football power that even a national television audience was left breathless. When the smoke had cleared, Southern Cal had scored eight touchdowns in 16 minutes and 54 seconds of playing time, all but 1.54 of that in the third quarter. And they shut out Notre Dame in the second half.

Whew. It went like this:

The stage was set when USC quarterback Pat Haden hit Anthony Davis with a swing pass good for eight yards and a touchdown just 10 seconds before the clock ran out in the first half. When Notre Dame kicked off to start the second half, Davis dropped back two yards deep in his end zone, grabbed the ball, burst out of a crowd around the USC 30 and shot down the left sideline for his third scoring kickoff return against the Irish in three years. A two-point conversion failed and that made it USC 12, Notre Dame 24.

A Fighting Irish drive fizzled early. Charles Phillips had a meager 8-yard punt return but, still, the ball was settled on the Notre Dame 38. After Haden threw 31 yards to John J. McKay (the USC coach's son), Davis broke over right tackle for six more points. USC 19, Irish 24.

Going to the air, Notre Dame QB Tom Clements completed his pass but USC cornerback Danny Reece jarred the receiver so hard, he fumbled and linebacker Kevin Bruce recovered for the Trojans on the Irish 36. After two Haden completions of 13 and 17 yards, Davis bolted over from the four, and USC led for the first time, 27-24. After another stalled drive, the Irish punted again, to safety Marvin Cobb, who danced 56 yards, setting up Haden's 18-yard bullet to McKay straight down the middle of the field for another touchdown. USC 34, Irish 24.

The Fighting Irish drove down as far as the Southern Cal 35 but Charles Phillips intercepted, and jigged 25 yards to the 50. A few plays later Haden bombed McKay with a 44-yarder which the split end carried all of one yard for the score. 41-24. Then, Bruce recovered another fumble. On first down, Haden rolled left and hit Shelton Diggs in the end zone. 48-24. And, finally, with only 1:44 gone in the fourth quarter, Phillips intercepted another Clements pass and raced 58 yards for the final touchdown. 55-24. *Whew* again.

John J. McKay, the coach's son, takes a Pat Haden TD aerial in the 1974 USC come-from-behind stinging rout of Notre Dame.

a Workingman's Guide to Touch Football

Be the Joe Namath of your vacant lot. Our primer tells you everything you need to know. A refreshingly violent way to get in shape.

Touch football is a game of guile and speed.

It's a game for vacant lot quarterbacks and backyard receivers. It's also a game of sweating torsos and aching limbs, of some frustration and much laughter. Mostly, though, touch football is what you want it to be: good healthy fun.

As in tackle, you get six points for a touchdown, two for a safety and one for a point after touchdown. The point-after can only be scored by running or passing from 20 yards out, not by kicking.

The equipment is fairly universal but the rules and strategies are not. What we've set out here are some rules most people can agree on and some formations and strategies most teams can start with.

Touch football strategy can be briefly summarized as two basic offensive tactics, which we call tortoise and hare. If a team has very fast ends and a fine passer, that team will probably run a set of hare offenses—long passes (generally against man-to-man pass defenses) where success depends on the ability of the passer and the agility of the receiver. On the other hand, a tortoise attack is a relentless five to 10 yards and a cloud of dust. This attack is most effective with stout blockers and is ideal for a team with no sandlot superstars. It would help, though, if the passer can throw accurately for 10 or 15 yards.

The Hare Offense

Hare offenses run best off the deep flanker set and the shot gun formations. If your team has poor blocking you can work out of the deep flanker set, the basic formation for hare attacks. But if you have average or good blocking ability, you can use the shot gun formation. In both formations, the passer is about 12 yards from the line of scrimmage. The passer has more time to maneuver, can more easily spot his receivers, can throw despite weak pass protection, and gives his ends more time to complete their pass patterns. In the above play, run off the deep flanker set, the ends cross to draw the defense toward the middle, and the pass goes to the flankerback shot gun, running an "up" or "fly" pattern.

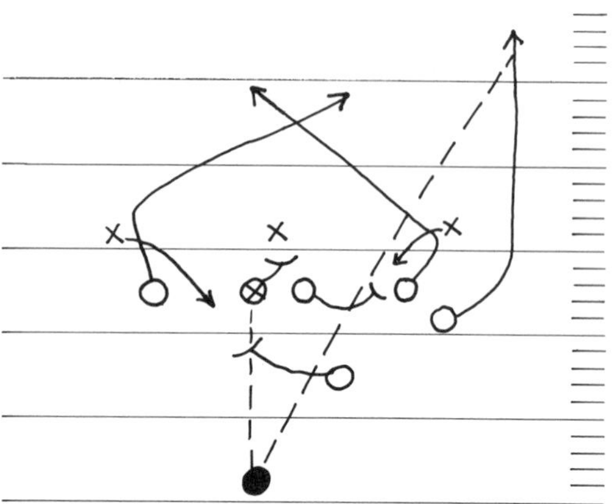

Figure 1. Deep Flanker Set. Ends cross. Flankerback up.

The same play, run off the shot gun, would look like this:

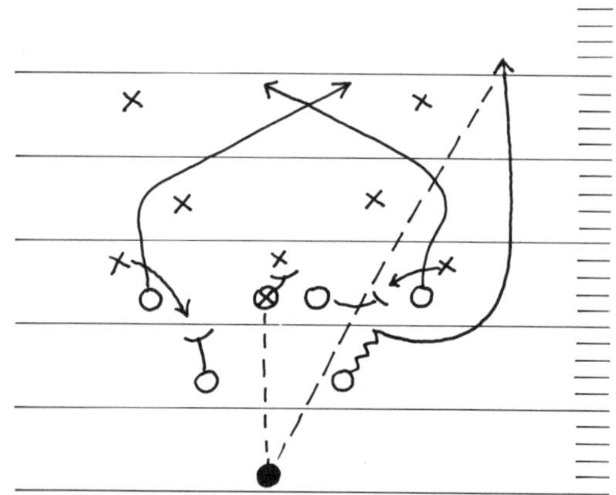

Figure 2. Shot gun. Ends cross. Flankerback up.

It should be noted that there are vast regional differences in how touch football is played in this country. In the East, where they take such matters very seriously, organized touch is a very sophisticated passing game, almost entirely (90 percent plus) a passing game. Out West, they run almost half the time. Because of the Eastern concentration on passing, the quarterback is set back even farther (in what might be called a deep shotgun) and the four linemen are running pass patterns on every play.

THE RULES OF THE GAME

Teams A touch football team consists of seven players. On offense, four persons play the line (center, guard and two ends) and three play in the backfield. All players are eligible pass receivers. On defense, the team may line up in any formation as long as other rules are not violated.

The Playing Field Because of the sometimes spontaneous nature of touch football, we recommend any of three different field dimensions. (1) 80 yards by 40 yards with 10-yard end zones, with stripes or markers at 20-yard intervals. (2) 100 yards by 80 yards with 10-yard end zones, with stripes or markers at 20-yard intervals. (3) Any dimension the teams can agree on.

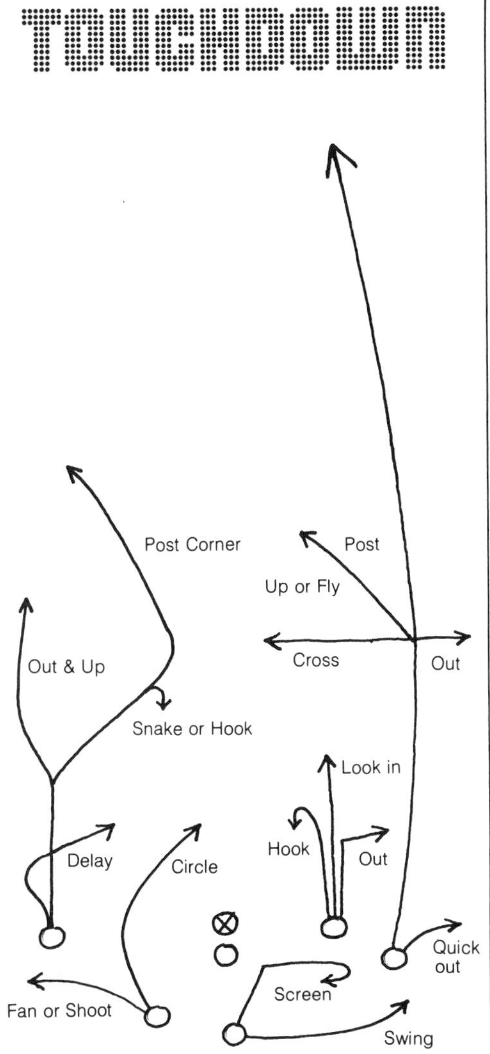

These pass patterns hook or break at 5 to 12 yards. This is the distance most receivers can cover before quarterback must release.

Playing Time If you want to time the game, we suggest playing four 10-minute quarters or four 15-minute quarters. We recommend a two-minute rest period between quarters and 10 minutes between halves. In casual timing, stop the clock only for time-outs (two per half) and emergencies (quick trips to the bushes, lost contact lens). In strict timing, stop the clock (1) when the play is ruled dead; (2) when the ball goes out of bounds; (3) when time out is called; (4) when a quarter ends.

First Downs A team has four downs to gain a first down. This is done by crossing the next 20-yard stripe. Obviously, you can't cross the same stripe twice in the same possession to get two first downs.

Passing All players are eligible to receive passes. A forward pass may be thrown from any point behind the line of scrimmage. If passer steps over the line of scrimmage and passes, the penalty is loss of one down plus five yards.

Tackling It's a foulest foul to tackle (remember this is touch), trip, push, hold, hack, straight arm or rough up another player. Penalty is 15 yards from the point of infraction. Pushing the ball carrier out of bounds is also not allowed; same penalty.

Blocking All blocks are made upright with the shoulder. Hands remain against the blocker's chest and contact must be made above the belt. You may charge block as long as the person you're blocking is in a upright position. You may also downfield block and double-team block. In no case, may a player leave his feet while making a block. The penalty is 15 yards.

The Ball Carrier The ball carrier may not run over, run into, or straight arm any defender. Penalty, at discretion of the official, is 15 yards or disqualification from the game. In charging, officials might keep in mind the charging rule as applied in basketball.

Tags A ball is tagged, or, as we say, "touched," when a defensive player places both hands simultaneously on the runner anywhere below his neck. The defensive player may leave his feet to tag as long as that person doesn't commit a penalty in doing so.

Defensive Roughness Defenders may not

tackle block push
hold trip charge into or

bump the ball carrier. The penalty is 15 yards from the point of infraction. A gross violation may mean expulsion from the game, banishment from your friends and no access to the beer bucket.

Hiding Out All ball players must go into a huddle and break from it. No loitering on or near the sidelines for sleeper plays. The play is called back and the penalty is 15 yards, down remains the same.

Safety If during a play from scrimmage the ball becomes dead in the end zone (no matter how) a safety will be called and the offensive team will have a free kick (and they may punt the ball) from their 10-yard line.

Optional Rules A game is only as fun as its rules. You can agree on any optional rules, for example, whether a player receiving a kick or punt can pass provided he does not take more than two steps after catching the ball. Of course, you can also agree to play with six on a team, or five, or four, or even with one-eyed jacks and the man with the ax.

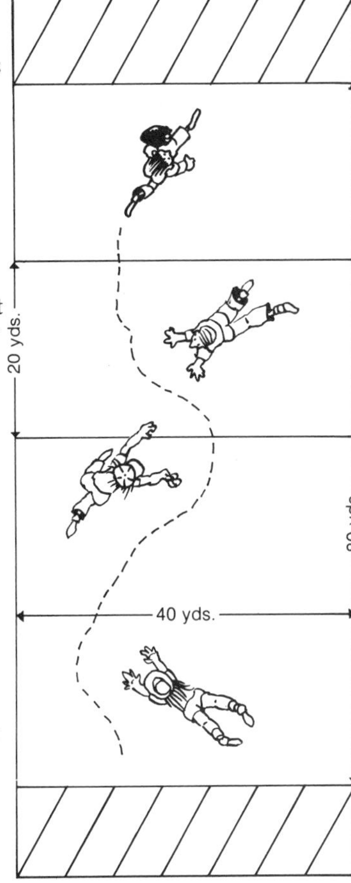

THE RULES OF THE GAME

Flag Football One fair way of determining who is "tagged" and who is not is for each player to carry "flags" tucked into their trousers, one on each side of the player. The flags, actually one- or two-inch strips of cloth, dangle down about six inches. To "tag" a ball carrier, you simply pull out the flag. It should also be noted that the ball carrier may not touch or protect his flags by guarding, hacking, or holding the flag. The ball carrier must run with arms and elbows *above* the waist when carrying the ball. If he drops either arm or elbow near the flags, the official calls a penalty for guarding the flag. The penalty is 10 yards from the line of scrimmage and loss of down.

On-side-kick There is no such thing in touch football. Penalty is five yards, kick over.
Goal Line Penalties All penalties inside the 10-yard line will be half the distance to the goal.
Punts A team must announce punts, and actually punt the ball. Four players on each team must stay on the line of scrimmage until the ball is kicked. Five yards for not doing this.
Penalties
Biggies - 15 yards for:

- tackling, holding, blocking, tripping, pushing, hurting the ball carrier.
- unsportsmanlike conduct
- ball carrier who runs over, charges or straight arms a defensive player
- flying blocks

Bantams - five yards for:

- offside
- delay of game (30 seconds for huddles)
- not centering ball between legs of center to a teammate
- blocking below the waist
- passing from beyond line of scrimmage

Fumbles A ball, when centered, is declared dead on the second bounce, at the point of the bounce. A team retains possession on all fumbles except on fourth down.
Equipment Wear tennis shoes or shoes with rubber cleats. No padding or helmets allowed. After all, you're not supposed to get rough in this game.
The Game Each of the seven players is eligible to receive a pass. Any combination of players for line or backfield may be used. If the teams are tied after four quarters of play the game is a tie. Two time-outs are allowed, by each team, in each half. Such time-outs are one minute long.
Substitutions Substitutions are unlimited. Players must, however, be recognized by the official before entering the game. If they are not, that's illegal procedure and the penalty is five yards. If there are no officials, players should be recognized by the opposing team.
Putting the Ball into Play Whichever team wins the coin toss has one of the following two choices: (1) to choose which team will kick-off or (2) to choose which goal to defend. The loser of the coin toss has second choice. Before the beginning of the second half, the loser of the coin toss makes the first designation, whether to receive or defend a particular goal.
Kick-offs All kick-offs are from the 20-yard marker and must travel 10 yards towards the opponent's goal. Receiving team must have at least three players within 15 yards of the kicking team's restraining line on all kick-offs. You may not punt on kick-offs. You may punt after a safety. In kick-offs, the ball must rest on the ground, held by a player, or on a kicking tee. Holder may not hold the ball on his foot. If the kicking team is offside, the team is penalized five yards; if the penalty is accepted, the ball is kicked over after assessment of penalty. If the kick-off goes out of bounds, the receiving team may accept placement of the ball in play at the yard marker where the ball when out. If the kick-off goes into the end zone, the ball is ruled dead and the receiving team puts the ball into play on their 20-yard line.

The Tortoise Offense
Tortoise offenses run best off the flanker set and the spread. This strategy does not count on the long touchdown pass but undermines the defense by a grind-'em-out offense, laced with good fun doses of surprise. This offense relies on steady, good blocking. Each play is part of a planned mosaic, a maneuver to set up the next play. Much deception is found in tortoise offenses run from tight formations. The option pass is a mainstay. Run to the right, from a flanker set, it looks like this:

Figure 3. Flanker Set. Option pass right.

Notice that center pulls, the weak-side end brush blocks before heading downfield and that the key block is made by the flankerback.

The following play, run off the spread, is particularly good when the defense is expecting the option run-pass to the strong, or right side. The key blocks are on the middle guard and the strong-side end.

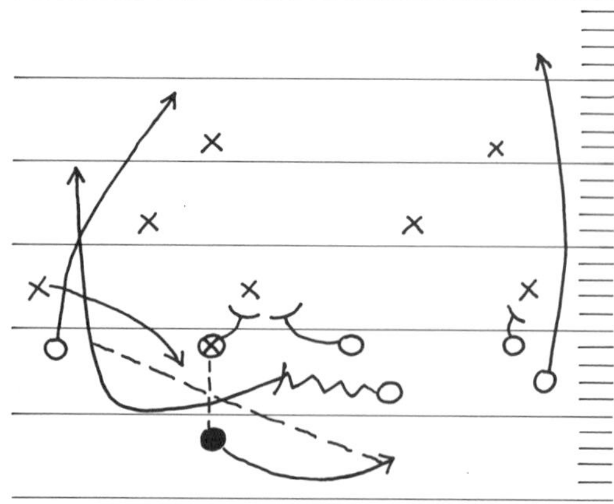

Figure 4. Spread. Left end circles. Flanker up. Halfback brushes and swings left.

The Deep Shotgun vs. The 3-1-3

This may look weird to you tackle fans but yes, Joe Willie, the Qb is 12 yards (even 15) behind the line of scrimmage. C and G split is a yard or two. Ends are split 5 to 8 yards from the linemen. Hbs are 6 yards behind the line and positioned between the ends and interior linemen. The idea, of course, is to give the Qb time, time to look, time to throw. It also gives the ends time to run their patterns, with the Hbs blocking and/or running out of the backfield for passes. Since everyone expects a pass, you might run from this with a direct snap to a Hb.

The 3-1-3, or old Diamond defense, is the best bet for stopping the Shotgun passing game. Ends play outside and pinch in for the passer. The linebacker is 2 or 3 yards behind the Middle Guard, a few steps to the strong side. He can shoot one of three gaps red-dogging but a safety should move up to cover the short center. When the linebackers shoots, deep pass coverage is sacrificed. In this formation, you can be hurt by short sideline passes.

The Flanker Set vs. The 3-2-2

The Qb is 5 to 7 yards behind the C. Ends are split 2 to 5 yards from the G and the C. C and G split is 1 to 2 yards. Hb sets 2 yards behind linemen and between the G and C. For some plays, the Hb will line up between the G and the RE. Flankerback lines up 1 yard behind the line and 1 yard to either side of the RE. Flb can also be flopped to the other side of the line. You can also form a Deep Flanker Set by moving the Qb back about 12 yards behind the C, RE and LE split 6 to 8 yards from the interior linemen, Hb is 5 or 6 yards behind the line. The Flanker Set allows a greater mixture of running plays; the Deep Flanker Set adds greater passing power.

The best defense against the Flanker Set is the 3-2-2 (what they called the "Box"). Mg is up between the C and G. Des are outside the ends to pinch the play in. Lbs are about 3 yards behind the line and a few steps toward the strong side. Two safeties are 10 to 15 yards deep.

S S
Rlb Llb
De Mg De
E C G E Flb
Hb
Qb

Figure 5
The Flanker set lined up against the 3-2-2

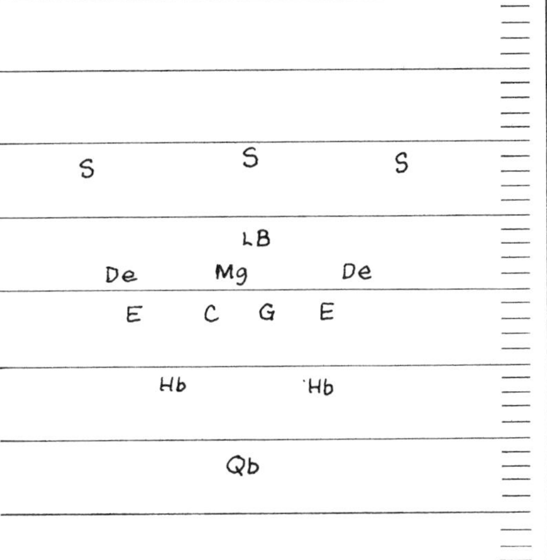

Figure 6
The Deep Shotgun lined up against the 3-1-3

Kick-offs and Kick-off Returns

To cover kick-offs expeditiously, you need to send down two waves of defenders. The first wave includes your three fastest players. The ends streak downfield to force the return inside while a third player runs full tilt down the center of the field to jam up the middle. While all that is happening, the other four linemen run straight ahead but only until they can determine how the kick-off return is developing as a play.

If a team has been returning kick-offs with specific blocking assignments, the best way to counter would be to have linemen crossover to cover the outside lanes, forcing the return inside while the two players who line up as ends are assigned to run as linemen straight ahead and slightly toward the center to watch for development of the play.

A team that intends to play "serious" touch football should have a few planned kick-off returns. The obvious are returning up one or the other sideline and shooting a flying wedge up the middle. Don't think that just because you have a plan or a play for a return that you're going to score a touchdown each time or *any* time. Generally, the results of return plays are that your team will gain an extra 10 or 20 yards, that's all. It also means everyone will have blocking assignments, which is far better than no one having any at all.

Here's the old flying wedge (remember, the wedge is not supposed to be as rough as it used to be) run against normal return coverage and a left sideline return run against ends crossing coverage.

plays, formations, pass patterns, rushing techniques. The beguiling element in touch football is that you can invent your own. And if you have a seven-foot end, there's the Alley Oop and other wonderful plays. The whole idea is to have fun—and be humane about it.

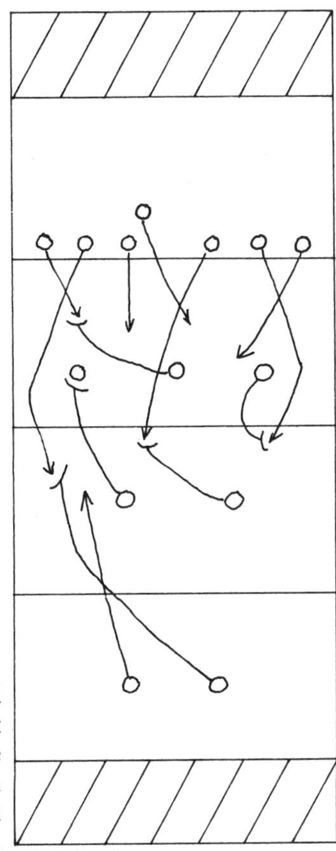

Ends cross coverage
Left sideline return

Covering team Wedge return

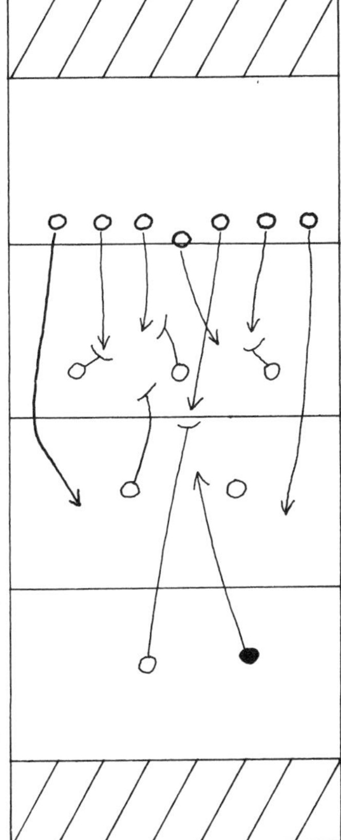

THE MOST POPULAR GAME IN THE WORLD

By Ned Riley

They pay Pele $4.7 million to play this game. Now, understand it for yourself.

To charge using one's body against an opponent; done only in pursuit of the ball. "Charging" is using your body illegally, with excessive force, and may be called by the referee.

Clear to kicking or throwing the ball well away from the attackers when they are dangerously near the goal.

Corner kick an unchallenged kick awarded to the attackers, from the defenders' corner, when the defense has put the ball out of play over the goal line.

Dribble moving the ball with light, deft touches of the feet while keeping it under one player's control.

Free kick an unchallenged kick in any direction from the ground awarded by the referee for an infringement of the rules by the other side.

Goal kick an unchallenged kick awarded to defenders when the offense has put the ball out of play over the goal line; from within six yards of a goal post.

Hands a penalty called by the referee when a player (other than the goalie) touches the ball with hands or arms; a free kick is awarded.

Holding a penalty called when a player holds an opponent with hands or arms.

To head using one's head to control the ball, pass it, or shoot at the goal.

For most Americans, Labor Day means back to school and back to football, beers in hand, cheering on the local team from the turn of the autumnal equinox to the final quarter in the Super Bowl. That's America. Everywhere else in the world, falling leaves signal the beginning of "futbol"—soccer, the most popular and most attended spectator sport in the world.

Soccer is. . .well, fanaticism. In more than 100 nations, from a United Nations roll call of Afganistan to Zambia, soccer is played in cobbled or dusty streets, outside school huts, along dank alleyways and in almost any park in the world. Kids gather, noodling with a ball, tapping it with their foreheads, cranking the ball down the field, dribbling, dribbling, dribbling, each aspiring to be the next superstar, the next Pele.

It has been played with such fervor that soccer players have been killed on the field by spectators, spectators have killed each other and nations have severed diplomatic relations and gone to war. The real excitement starts every four years when various nations select their national teams to represent them in the World Cup matches. The World Cup is considered the Olympics of professional soccer but the incredible frenzy surrounding the World Cup makes the Olympics and the Super Bowl look, in comparison, like Little League play-offs.

When West Germany met (and beat) Holland in the World Cup finals of 1974, the estimated TV audience was some 800 million people, not to mention the fanatic hundreds of thousands who came to Germany from all parts of the world to cheer and boo in person. Soccer is one of the very few cross-cultural experiences. A superstar like Hank Aaron or Kareem Abdul-Jabbar is almost a nonentity outside the U.S., but Brazil's legendary Pele, or Holland's Johan Cruyff are idolized from the sands of the Kalahari to the back alleys of Liverpool. They're paid like heroes, too: Pele in his top playing days earned at least $500,000 a year, tax-free.

Every year hundreds of the largest stadiums in the world, some holding up to a quarter million spectators, are jammed with what have to be the most frantic fans of any sport. In fact, sometimes those arenas look more like battlefields. Chauvinism is rampant, and violence is commonplace. Most fields have fences or even moats to protect the players and referees from the fans. Soccer riots happen often (though they seldom are as bloody as the one in Peru a few years back, which resulted in several hundred deaths), and specially trained and equipped police are necessary to prevent rival groups of fans from maiming each other.

Now, for better or worse, Americans have a chance to see the sport that arouses such frenzy abroad. It will be interesting to see how we react. In the past, for such an active people, Americans have preferred surprisingly ritualized sports. We've liked our play divided up into innings or downs or rounds or holes; and lots of intermissions for scorekeeping, recuperation, commentary and, of course, beer.

It makes for a slow pace—someone once took a stopwatch to a typical baseball game and discovered there was about nine minutes of actual play. All the rest was time-outs, seventh inning stretches, arguments with the ump, and the numerous ceremonies that surround the national pastime.

But in the last decade, the American taste in sports has seemed to be shifting. While the organized, ritualized mayhem of football is still box-office king, other faster, more fluid spectator sports have begun to carve out a place for themselves. First basketball, and then hockey, have been developed to meet the demand for more action, for non-stop play, for a more spread-out and discernible pattern of play, and for more speed.

Soccer's fluid, shifting, constant action and lightning-quick plays suits this developing appetite. Now for the first time American sports fans can see top-quality professional soccer. In the past the North American soccer league was plagued by too little familiarity, too much type, no native talent, poor imported players and skittering franchises. These problems have been dealt with and are being solved. Youth soccer programs are developing in the schools. (Administrators like the fact that equipment costs are so low; kids like the idea that everybody gets a piece of the action, and that you don't have to be a behemoth to play.) Some 700 colleges and many more secondary schools now offer it as a fall sport.

And the big-buck sports entrepreneurs have stopped trying to peddle the game like a new line of lingerie. They're focusing on the long run, developing native talent, educating the audience in the nuances of the game. The results are starting to show; last year's champion Philadelphia Atoms had a roster of more than half American players. And the rookie of the year was a name familiar to Americans

PELE: THE BLACK PEARL

It was in the World Cup matches of 1958 that the unknown youngster burst on the international soccer scene. Coming onto the field in the quarter-finals against Wales, he scored the only goal, boosting his lackluster team into the semifinals. There he scored three goals and went on into the finals where in front of delirious crowds he punched in two more, becoming the decisive element of Brazil's first World Cup victory.

Overnight, Pele was a sensation. He quickly became one of the highest-paid athletes in the world, receiving over a half-million dollars a year. And when it seemed likely that his Santos team would be tempted to trade him to a big continental club for an astronomical sum, the Brazilian government stepped in and declared him a "national treasure"—which meant that like other natural resources, he was to be kept at home in Brazil.

He had come into his own; but from then on the brilliant striker was a marked man. He continued to score record numbers of goals, but he also had to play with injuries much of the time. A star striker—like a good quarterback—is born, not manufactured; and they are rare. There was no one who could play like Pele, seldom anyone who could even contain him, and so the opponents' strategy too often became: lay the man out. That he returned to the game after his retirement is testimony to his guts and recuperative powers. His "retirement" came after the 1970

Pele, the Black Pearl, *makes his multi-million dollar debut in June, 1975.*

World Cup where, as it had in 1958, his presence propelled the Brazilians to an unprecedented third championship. To 130,000 weeping soccer fans he announced his retirement. Four years later, millions witnessed his return televised nationwide on CBS.

Only one player, a compact acrobatic black Brazilian nicknamed Pele, can claim the title of King of Soccer. The contract he signed in June, 1975 with the New York Cosmos proved that beyond doubt. He received an estimated \$4.7 million to play in 107 games or \$43,925 per game—the largest sum of money ever given to an athlete in any sport.

The "Black Pearl" returned to soccer after an intermittent retirement of four years. In his first 16 years of play he brought a unique electrifying sense of drama to the game.

Pacing a tight nervous circle within striking distance of the goal, stalked by two, three or more opponents, Pele would hold the attention of the crowd like a magnet. Not only could he break out of the pack to leap up for dazzling head-shots no one else could reach, or to catch a shoulder-high cross on his thigh and volley the ball into the goal with his opposite foot while high in the air; but also his mere presence insured that his teammates would come alive and play above their normal ability while the opponents went on the defensive.

Pele's background has all the drama of his presence. Born Edson Arantes do Nascimento in rural Minas Gerais, his family was so poor that when he was a boy he had to play soccer with a stocking stuffed with rags. A school dropout at 10, he was discovered by a soccer playing friend of the family playing, and beating, construction workers three times his age. After three years of tutelage he trekked to the big-league town of Sao Paulo but their team turned him down. He finally managed to persuade the team of the town of Santos to take him on, at the ripe age of 15. He soon proved his worth.

from football—Kyle Rote, Jr from the Dallas Tornado team.

Game attendance has increased yearly as the franchises begin to settle down in particular towns. Soon there will be a knowledgeable, enthusiastic audience made up of people who have played the game (or whose kids have), who appreciate top-quality soccer and who have native-born stars to cheer on the field. With that kind of support, who knows, maybe we'll have our World Cup team in the semi-finals in 1978. Then, finally, American soccer fans will have nothing to kick about.

Playing The Game

So what is it about soccer that creates this massive international appeal—such passionate partisanship?

To begin with: it's fast, it's simple, and the action is continuous. The rules are few. There are 11 players per side—who devote themselves to moving a ball that's slightly larger than a volleyball into their opponents' goal. The only major restrictions are no use of hands or arms (excepting the goal-tender), either on the ball or on other players; and no body contact except by players going for the ball.

There are no time-outs. Play stops only

To mark defending an attacker particularly closely to prevent his receiving the ball; done against the most dangerous players.

Off-side a penalty called when an attacker who doesn't have the ball is behind the defenders, having only the goalie between him and the goal; a free kick is awarded. There is no penalty if you possess the ball.

Penalty area the area close to the goal within which a rules infraction by the defenders results in a penalty kick rather than a free kick.

Penalty kick a kick at the goal awarded the attackers when the defense has broken the rules inside the penalty area. It is taken from twelve yards out and only the goalie may defend against it.

Striker the forward who acts as primary goalgetter; usually center forward. He is the man marked most heavily by two or even three defenders.

To tackle to lunge at an attacker with the ball in an attempt to force a pass or to steal the ball. It is the defenseman's act of commitment.

Throw-in an unchallenged throw from the side-lines (touch-lines) awarded at the point the ball went out to the opponents of the man who put the ball out of play.

To trap bringing a hard- or long-shot ball under control by using the feet, body, or head to absorb its momentum.

Tripping a penalty awarded for intentionally overthrowing an opponent by blocking his legs rather than the ball; a free kick is awarded.

To volley kicking the ball before it bounces.

when the ball goes out of bounds, when there's an especially blatant foul, or when someone is injured. The players remain dispersed, ready for a dash on the goal. The ball is moved mostly with the feet, although all other parts of the body come in handy (again excepting the hands and arms). The action moves swiftly from one end of the field to the other in combinations of short, flicking passes, dazzling individual foot-dribbling exhibitions, and booming 50-yard crossfield clearing kicks. The play climaxes at the goal-mouth with perhaps a lunging head-shot or an over-the-shoulder reverse kick into the corner of the net.

Although the rules are simple, the skills are not. A good soccer player can make the ball do incredible things. He can go the length of the field with the ball, never letting it touch the ground, juggling it on a dead run with just his head, feet, thighs and knees. He can kick a looping backspin pass to a teammate, or curl the ball sideways around a defender, or smash a rising cannonball shot or bounce a topspin over the goalie's hands—all when off-balance, jostled and moving.

Such individual skills are necessary since most of the action is one-on-one. The attacker tries to draw the defender into committing himself and then may pass off at the last second, or try to drive past for a shot at the goal.

But quickness and endurance are perhaps even more important. Soccer is a sport that favors the quicker, smaller man who can run all afternoon. Speed—in reflexes, in running, and in thought—is absolutely necessary. There is seldom time for a player to stop, catch his breath, map his strategy and get himself together.

The result of all this is a shifting, subtle, quicksilver game of constantly changing patterns. At first glance, it is difficult to tell which team is the better amid the swirl of play. The back-and-forth surface ripples distract from the underlying slow accumulation of momentum by the superior team. There's no yardage gains, no obvious way to tell, but gradually one team takes the initiative and remorselessly tightens the tempo; their passes are crisper, their defenders faster on the loose ball. Perhaps 20 minutes will go by without a goal being scored until the break eventually comes, the 15th shot that slips past the goalie. It may seem like a fluke if one ignores the previous accumulating pressure that shook the defenders, bewildered them, robbed them of confidence and slowed them that crucial split second.

Testimonial From An Addict

It's an absolutely beautiful game to play. Which makes it hell to watch because you get so fidgety, seeing all the green space out there, and the ball to be played, that it's hard to pay attention to the game.

Soccer is a team sport, with all the camraderie and esprit that implies. Yet it doesn't require the machine-like militaristic close-order work of football; when you have the ball, you have a multitude of choices and a whole field to move around in. Nor is there the bloody violence and expected rule-breaking of hockey. You can get laid out, easily, but it's almost always in a situation you see coming and prepare for.

The coaches, like coaches everywhere, stress the importance of conditioning, aggressiveness and drills—but they also talk about the need to cultivate "field vision," which seems to be a sort of laid-back gestalting of the pattern of play, an almost mystical sense of the rhythm of play. Perhaps because of those imponderables, I've never seen a sport where coaches were so willing to let each player develop his own style of play, where the small and devious and non-agrressive is free to play his way.

It's a very nice feeling, almost a kind of meditation, when suddenly the game begins to play *you,* when the anxieties of technique and position slip away and you go into that timeless place where all the patterns and rhythms of play manifest themselves, like a great dance. And your body senses the imperative of play and you know just where the ball *has* to go next and you slide over into that path precisely at the right moment, to intercept it and send the dance spinning off in a whole new direction...

If I were a coach, I would approach the team as a dance instructor, as an exercise in rhythm. I might even bring in Latino or Afro drummers to accustom the players to focus their senses and their intent, to listen and pace themselves, sorting out the complicated syncopation until they had penetrated to the central rhythm...and then, having caught it, I would teach them to seize, to savage it, to play out that rhythm with everything in themselves—as the dazzling, multi-paced Brazilian World Cup teams used to. They know that just plugging away is not enough. That as Zorba said, "Sometimes a man has to dance."

Soccer is also good for you. Now that all the awful research results on the effects of stress and smoking and overeating are rolling in, a good many of us sliding down the backside of the thirties are looking for a physical discipline that will wring out the respiratory and circulatory systems. But jogging's dull; tennis confining; golf slow-paced. However, put on some cleated shoes and join the local Swedes or Mexicanos in a sand-lot soccer game and you find yourself running five to 10 miles in an afternoon, straining every fiber, getting that good weary totally-spent feeling, and enjoying yourself. Strange but true, that something so good to your body can make you feel so immorally fine.

ARENAS

Old Madison Square Garden, New York

The Forum, Los Angeles

GREAT MOMENTS IN PRO BASKETBALL

Sauce For The Goose

February 19, 1948 Since their founding in 1927, nobody had taken seriously the basketball-playing abilities of the Harlem Globetrotters. Which was fine with the Trotters. They were showmen who only incidentally kept knocking off a series of inhouse opponents.

Thus, a match with them and the professional champion Minneapolis Lakers at the Chicago Stadium in 1948 was viewed with a mixture of amusement and skepticism. The Trotters would have to play basketball. And could they?

Minnesota's 6'10" center, George Mikan, regularly demolished his pro opposition. Just think what he'd do to 6'3" Trotter center Reece (Goose) Tatum. The game, nonetheless, was a promotional coup and attracted 17,853, until then the biggest crowd ever to see pro basketball in Chicago.

The barnstorming Trotters were playing their sixth game in six nights. And this one they couldn't play for laughs. By halftime, with Mikan and 6'5" Jim Pollard controlling the boards, the Lakers led by nine. So the Globetrotters began double and triple-teaming big George. He was often fouled, but he was missing his free throws. Now the Trotters were getting long set shots from Ermer Robinson and dribbling whiz Marques Haynes. Tatum—and his remarkable 84-inch reach—were drifting inside for easy baskets, one of which came after a typical Trotter gag: rolling a "pass" through the legs of an opponent.

With 90 seconds to play, the score was tied. The Trotters, zipping through their "Sweet Georgia Brown" passing routine, waited for a shot opportunity. Robinson canned a 20-footer at the buzzer, and the funny fellows had won, 61-59.

(One year later, with 20,046 sardined into the Chicago Stadium, Tatum, Haynes and newcomer Nat (Sweetwater) Clifton produced an 11-point lead over the Lakers in the fourth quarter. This gave the Trotters sufficient clowning time. They finally won 49-45. They could play, and still have their fun.)

The Globetrotters, magnificently erratic, take on the Lakers

The Indefinite Dribble

January 6, 1951 Until the 1954-55 season, pro basketball teams could move at idling speed. Or not at all if they wished. The advent of the 24-second clock not only speeded up the game by requiring a shot within the 24 seconds (no shot meant an automatic turnover), but it quashed on a very practical level any repetition of what took place on January 6, 1951, at the Edgerton Park Sports Arena in Rochester, N.Y. The attendance, including dozers, nodder-offers and cat-nappers, was some 3,000. The combination of tenseness and tedium must have prevented an actual crowd count. Said ennui ensued when the Indianapolis Olympians visited the Rochester Royals for a 78-minute National Basketball Association game.

Yes, six overtimes. Basketball's longest night.

At the end of the regulation 48 minutes, the game was tied at 65. In the first overtime period, each team scored only one basket. Period. There was no scoring at all in the next five-minute overtime period. And only two points apiece in overtime number three. The fourth overtime was scoreless.

Rochester coach Lester Harrison said that his key ball-handler, later New York Knick coach Red Holzman, "could dribble the ball indefinitely." Which he did, and did, and did. Holzman played in 76 of the 78 minutes that night.

The fifth OT awakened everyone. Each club scored four points in those five minutes. The game was now tied at 73. In the 25 minutes of overtime there had been a total of 16 points.

The players sleep-walked through most of the sixth overtime period. Then, for some reason, a Rochester player chose to shoot as the clock ran down. He missed, and Indianapolis' Alex Groza rebounded. Two passes later, the Olympians' Ralph Beard had the ball near the foul line, dribbled once and sprang for a jump shot. With one second to play, Indianapolis led 75-73. No, the Royals did not tie it. The time was midnight, four hours after the opening tipoff, and the exhausted athletes changed either into pumpkins or street clothes.

Star Light, Star Bright, The Last Star They Saw That Night

January 21, 1954 The only dressing room speech coach Joe Lapchick could make to his Eastern team at the 1954 National Basketball Association All Star game in New York's Madison Square Garden was: "Let's go fellas." They were too good to need additional coaching.

The East squad included guards Bob Cousy and Bill Sharman of Boston, top rebounder Harry Gallatin of New York, top scorer Neil Johnston of Philadelphia and rookie-of-the-year Ray Felix of Baltimore. All the greats—except for those on the West team such as Minneapolis' immaculate George Mikan and Jim Pollard, Rochester's Bob Davies and Bobby Wanzer.

Bob Pettit of the Hawks slips by Bill Russell of the Celtics to shoot and score in the first period of the first game of the NBA playoffs in Boston Garden.

In later years, NBA players would treat the All Star game with the same enthusiasm they'd extend a pre-season exhibition. Not so in 1954. The East was favored, but the West hung in, down by only four points at halftime, then ahead by two after three quarters. Much fun for the crowd of 16,478.

With only six seconds to play, the East was up by a basket. At the three-second mark, the West called a timeout to set up a Mikan last-gasp shot. The titanic Laker center didn't score, but he was fouled at the buzzer by Felix. George had two shots to take amid the tumult—and made both free throws.

Overtime now, and Cousy took over with his dribbling and shooting. In the next five minutes, the East scored 14 points, 10 coming from Cousy. And six of those 10 were free throws stemming from frustrated fouling. The East won 98-93, and in a recount Cousy won the most valuable player award. (Jim Pollard had been the press' choice just before the end of regulation time.)

Aftershock: In the NBA All-Star game three years later, Sharman whipped a halftime-ending, nearly full court pass to Cousy. Bob never touched it, for the ball went over his head and into the basket. The East didn't need an overtime to win on January 15, 1957.

Bob Cousy scores for the East in the 1954 NBA all-star game.

The Two-Second Plan

April 13, 1957 There was a deceptive imbalance in the National Basketball Association in the 1956-57 season. All four Western division teams finished under .500, all four in the East at .500 or over.

In the regular season, the Boston Celtics, with a new center named Bill Russell, were the league's best. They swept through Syracuse in three straight in the playoff semi-finals. The St. Louis Hawks, on the other hand, had to struggle through special playoff games in the West. Then in the semis, the Hawks brushed aside Minneapolis in three.

The resultant Celt-Hawk playoff title series was classic. It went the full seven games, with four of the seven decided by a single basket and two of those four going into double overtime.

The Hawks took the opener 125-123 in two overtimes on a desperation sidearm shot by Jack Coleman. Russell's defense and the backcourt work of Bob Cousy and Bill Sharman gave Boston a series-knotting 20-point win in game two.

A 30-foot jumper by brilliant Hawk center Bob Pettit swished St. Louis to a 100-98 decision in the final 45 seconds of game three. Game four was a Pettit-Cousy battle as Boston won 123-118. Then the Celts took a 3-2 series lead on the rebounding of Russell and gunning of Sharman, 124-109. In the final second of game six, Cliff Hagan tapped in a missed Pettit jumper for a 96-94 St. Louis victory, and series deadlock.

The seventh game, before a capacity 13,909 in Boston Garden, saw Hawk guards Slater Martin and Jack McMahon stifle the dangers of Cousy and Sharman. The shooting of Tommy Heinsohn kept Boston in the game. And what a game: 28 times the score was tied, 38 times the lead changed hands. The Celts were up by all of six after three quarters, then Pettit started popping from the outside. Two Pettit free throws sent the game into overtime in a 103 knot. A Coleman one-hander forced a second OT at 113 all. Jim Loscutoff's free throw gave Boston a 125-123 lead with two seconds to play. Then, as always, the Hawks would go to Pettit. Player-coach Alex Hannum banged a court-long pass off the backboard, right to his center. Pettit threw up a six-footer that teased the rim and dropped off. And Boston had the title. (One year later, with Russell injured, the Hawks beat the Celts in a six-game playoff.)

Wilt Chamberlain sinks the goal for his 100th point in Hershey.

The Hershey Hundred

March 2, 1962 Elgin Baylor, the acrobatic Los Angeles Laker, had held the single-game scoring record (71 points) before he came along with an adding machine shooting arm. On December 8, 1961, Wilt Chamberlain dropped in 78 in a triple overtime game against Baylor and the Lakers. But the world's first seven-footer of note was merely warming up.

In 46 of his team's 80 games in the 1961-62 regular season, the long fellow from Philadelphia scored 50 or more points. The "more" included an otherwise meaningless game played on March 2, 1962, in Chocolate town. The Philly Warriors had trained in Hershey, and played a few games there. This one figured to be no big deal: Only five games remained in the regular season; the Warriors had a playoff spot locked and their Hershey opponents, the New York Knickerbockers, were going nowhere.

The regular Knick center, one Phil Jordon, was out with an injury, and his backup, Darrall Imhoff, was as if trapped in a temblor as the Warriors sped to a 19-3 lead. Chamberlain had 13 of those 19 points, including seven consecutive free throws—never, never his forte. His early luck from the line had to be a harbinger. By first quarter's end, Wilt had 23 of Philly's 42 points. When Imhoff left, burdened with personals, the Knicks tried Willie Naulls and Cleveland Buckner on defense against Wilt. No matter. At halftime it was Chamberlain 41, his teammates 38, the Knicks 68.

In the third period Chamberlain was 8-for-8 from the foul line and hit 10 buckets: a 28-point quarter and 69 points in 36 minutes.

With less than two minutes gone in the final quarter, Wilt hit his 75th point—a new record for a regulation-time game. Mercifully—for him—Imhoff fouled out. With five minutes left to play, Wilt's tally stood at 89. But then he failed to score for two minutes and 15 seconds. Merely taking a breath. He quickly dropped in three free throws and two long jumpers. Up to 96.

The 4,124 fans in Hershey Arena were pleading with the Warriors to "Give It To Wilt." Which the Warriors did.

At 1:19, Wilt took a high pass from York Larese and dunked for 98 points. The Knicks had been stalling to avoid this numerical embarrassment. Coach Eddie Donovan had his lads fouling other Warriors to keep the ball away from Wilt. New York tried a collapsing defense around the big man. But there would be no deterrent this night.

Wilt stole a Knick pass but missed a jumper from the foul line. Then he missed two more shots. The last attempt was rebounded by Ted Luckenbill, who tossed outside to Joe Ruklick, who tossed back inside to Chamberlain. A stuff—and 100, with 46 seconds to play. That would be all, quite sufficient actually.

The Warriors, incidentally, won the game, 169-147, a point total that would not be matched for eight years. Wilt's records in that game would last much longer: most points (100); most field goals attempted (63); most field goals made (36); most free throws made (28 of 32, a preposterous percentage for him); and six other records for one-half and one-quarter output. After the game, Imhoff went to the nearest bar.

Being Bulletproof

1975 Championship Golden State? Oh, yes, Golden State. They were the team relegated in a preseason consensus to finish fourth in the NBA Pacific Division. But wait. They made it to the playoffs, erased Seattle in six games and squeezed Chicago in seven. But of course they had to face the Washington Bullets for the championship and everybody knew the Bullets had wiped up the NBA floors with every team in the league. So how could anyone take the Warriors seriously?

How indeed since the Bullets led by 14 points at halftime in the first game. But no sweat, said the Golden State coach, Alvin Attles. And he reached for his bench and sent in his most anonymous ballplayers, guys like Phil Smith, Charles Dudley and Derrek Dickey. Everyone thought Attles was kidding but the Bullets bit the joke, 101-95, as the Anonymous Ones out-hustled and outshot the heavily favored Washingtonians to take the first game.

The Bullets were embarrassed, but not overly concerned. They'd read the papers: this was supposed to be the greatest mismatch in NBA history. Then in the second game, behind by 13, the Warriors roared back behind a 36-point effort by Rick Barry, to win 92-91. Two days later, Barry poured in 38 points and an unheralded bench warmer named George Johnson picked off 10 rebounds and dunked in 10 points. The Bullets were starting to look bad. Even Elvin Hayes, who stood three inches taller and 45 pounds heavier than his defender Keith Wilkes, was looking bad.

But by now the Bullets realized that no team in NBA history had come back from a 3-0 deficit to win the title, and they did not.

With the win, folks explained it as a fluke, destiny. But Warrior guard, Charles Johnson disagreed. "Hey, man, this isn't a religious happening. This is us."

Golden State Warrior Rick Barry goes for two in the last quarter of that final incredible series with the Washington Bullets.

All-Time NBA Records

Individual

Single Game

Most Personal Fouls	8	Don Otten, *Tri-Cities, at Sheboygan,* Nov. 24, 1949
Most Free Throws Missed	22	Wilt Chamberlain, *Philadelphia, vs Seattle, at Boston,* Dec. 1, 1967
Most Consecutive Points	32	Larry Costello, *Syracuse, vs Boston at Boston,* Dec. 8, 1961
Most Consecutive Free Throws	19	Bob Pettit, *St. Louis, vs Boston,* Nov. 22, 1961

Season

Most Points	4,029	Wilt Chamberlain, *Philadelphia,* 1961-62
Highest Average	50.4	Wilt Chamberlain, *Philadelphia,* 1961-62
Most F.G. Attempted	3,159	Wilt Chamberlain, *Philadelphia,* 1961-62
Most F.G. Made	1,597	Wilt Chamberlain, *Philadelphia,* 1961-62
Highest F.G. Percentage	.683	Wilt Chamberlain, *Philadelphia,* 1966-67
Most F.T. Attempted	1,363	Wilt Chamberlain, *Philadelphia,* 1961-62
Most F.T. Made	840	Jerry West, *Los Angeles,* 1965-66
Highest F.T. Percentage	.932	Bill Sharman, *Boston,* 1958-59
Most Rebounds	2,149	Wilt Chamberlain, *Philadelphia,* 1960-61
Most Assists	908	Guy Rodgers, *Chicago,* 1966-67
Most Personal Fouls	366	Bill Bridges, *St. Louis,* 1967-68
Most Disqualifications	26	Don Meineke, *Fort Wayne,* 1952-53

Career

Most Points Scored	30,335	Wilt Chamberlain, *Philadelphia Warriors, San Francisco Warriors, Philadelphia 76ers* and *Los Angeles Lakers,* 1960-72
Highest Scoring Average	31.5	Wilt Chamberlain, 1960-72
Most F.G. Attempted	22,933	Wilt Chamberlain, 1960-72
Most F.G. Made	12,255	Wilt Chamberlain, 1960-72
Highest F.G. Percentage	.577	Kareem Abdul-Jabbar, *Milwaukee,* 1970-72
Most F.T. Attempted	11,403	Wilt Chamberlain, 1960-72
Most F.T. Made	7,244	Oscar Robertson, *Cincinnati* and *Milwaukee,* 1961-72
Highest F.T. Percentage	.883	Bill Sharman, *Washington* and *Boston,* 1951-61
Most Rebounds	22,298	Wilt Chamberlain, 1960-72
Most Assists	8,890	Oscar Robertson, 1961-72
Most Minutes	44,319	Wilt Chamberlain, 1960-72
Most Games	1,084	Hal Greer, *Syracuse* and *Philadelphia,* 1959-72
Most Personal Fouls	3,772	Hal Greer, 1959-72
Most Times Disqualified	127	Vern Mikkelsen, *Minneapolis,* 1950-59

Team Records

Single Game

Most Points, One Team	173	Boston vs Minneapolis at Boston, Feb. 27, 1959
Most Points, Two Teams	316	Philadelphia 169, New York 147 at Hershey, Pa., Mar. 2, 1962
	316	Cincinnati 165, San Diego 151, at Cincinnati, Mar. 12, 1970
Most F.G. Attempted, One Team	153	Philadelphia vs Los Angeles at Philadelphia, Dec. 8, 1961
Most F.G. Made, One Team	72	Boston vs Minneapolis at Boston, Feb. 27, 1959
Most F.T. Attempted, One Team	86	Syracuse vs Anderson at Syracuse (In 5 overtimes), Nov. 24, 1949
Most F.T. Made, One Team	59	Syracuse vs Anderson at Syracuse (In 5 overtimes), Nov. 24, 1949
Most Rebounds, One Team	112	Philadelphia vs Cincinnati at Philadelphia, Nov. 8, 1959
	112	Boston vs Detroit at Boston, Dec. 24, 1960
Most Assists, One Team	60	Boston at Baltimore (In 1 overtime), Nov. 15, 1952
Most Personal Fouls, One Team	66	Anderson at Syracuse (In 5 overtimes), Nov. 24, 1949
Most Disqualifications, One Team	8	Syracuse vs Baltimore at Syracuse (In 1 overtime), Nov. 15, 1952
Most Points in a Losing Game	151	San Diego, at Cincinnati, Mar. 12, 1970
Widest Point Spread	63	Los Angeles 162, Golden State 99 at Los Angeles, Mar. 19, 1972
Most Consecutive Points in a Game	24	Philadelphia vs Baltimore, Mar. 20, 1966

Season

Most Games Won	69	Los Angeles, 1971-72
Most Games Lost	67	San Diego, 1967-68
	67	Cleveland, 1970-71
Longest Winning Streak	33	Los Angeles, Nov. 5, 1971 to Jan. 7, 1972
Longest Losing Streak	17	San Francisco, Dec. 20, 1964 to Jan. 26, 1965
	17	San Diego, Jan. 17, 1968 to Feb. 18, 1968
Most Points Scored	10,143	Philadelphia, 1966-67
Most Points Allowed	10,261	Seattle, 1967-68
Highest Scoring Average	125.4	Philadelphia, 1961-62
Highest Average, Points Allowed	125.1	Seattle, 1967-68
Most F.G. Attempted	9,295	Boston, 1960-61
Most F.G. Made	3,972	Milwaukee, 1970-71
Highest F.G. Percentage	.509	Milwaukee, 1970-71
Most F.T. Attempted	3,411	Philadelphia, 1966-67
Most F.T. Made	2,434	Phoenix, 1969-70
Highest F.T. Percentage	.794	Syracuse, 1956-57
Most Rebounds	6,131	Boston, 1960-61
Most Assists	2,249	Milwaukee, 1970-71

THE GLOBETROTTERS: FROM HARLEM WITH LOVE

No gal made has got a shade on sweet Georgia SWISH!

This is the Globetrotters' Magic Circle, *the famed warmup circle in which anything can and usually does happen to a basketball.*

The Basketball Hall of Fame credits Abe Saperstein with making basketball a truly international game. Maybe. What he definitely did in nearly 30 years as entrepreneur of the Harlem Globetrotters was make basketball a truly fun game, basic family entertainment. His formula was show-biz simple: a quality clown act; a troupe that really could play the game when it wished or then turn the game into vaudeville.

Crowds everywhere could appreciate the excellence of both techniques, and what made it pleasant for the people was the nonessentialness of the final score. The Trotters won 102 percent of the time, sure, but that didn't matter.

Just how they played the game against, in the halcyon years, ersatz opposition, was the important thing. Whether they hid balls under their jerseys, dribbled into the stands, charaded other sports, tossed up baskets via giant rubber bands, tiptoed around mock-horrified defenders (who'd give them about 20 soft shots a game) for layups...whatever the piece of business it was good business; non-generational.

You would go once a year to laugh at precisely the same things you laughed at the year before. Then another dozen years would pass and you would take your children. And they would laugh.

Seeing the Trotters, noted one writer, "was part of growing up." No matter that Abe underpaid these classic showmen, no matter that some sociologists suggested the players were Uncle Toms, no matter that the halftime shows were cluttered with irrelevancies...the play was the thing, speaking a language understood everywhere—which is why Abe kept units playing all over the world. Marques Haynes' dribbling evoked the same laughter in Moscow as in Benton Harbor, Mich. Goose Tatum's mournful humor wowed 'em similarly in Luxembourg and Louisville.

The Trotters were seen in their first 45 years by some 76 million people in 89 countries and 1,300 American communities. Even when the great black basketball players were allowed a home with the straight-playing professionals, the Trotters still had their audience. And they could play it straight, too, when obvious commercial gates loomed—as against the Minneapolis Lakers in the late 1940s and College All-Star teams in the 1950s.

Saperstein might have done well with them in a league operation, but clearly not as well without the theatricality. Others (including Trotter defectors) would try to compete but lacked Abe's contacts and durability. He was short, fat and usually canny. It is surprising that Marques Haynes never tried to dribble him.

A Zany History of The Trots

They began by stompin' at the Savoy, surely did a Charleston (West Virginia), managed many a varsity drag on college campuses, were in a perpetual twist (oh, those long bus rides) and finally, somehow, even got to Harlem. Here's the way the Trotters stepped along their Sweet Georgia Brown trail (the Brother Bones' recording please, maestro):

1926 Chicago's Savoy Ballroom needed hype, and booked a team of five blacks from slum playgrounds coached by an immigrant (British) wisp (5'3") who'd played and coached a little basketball. Abe Saperstein's lads played two games a week at the Savoy, which in a short time decided that roller skating seemed more compatible to dancing than the stuff-dunk.

January 27, 1927 The Savoy Big Five became the Harlem Globetrotters (catchy, thought Abe), debuting at Hinckley, Ill. The originals: Andy Washington, Wille "Kid" Oliver, Walter "Toots" Wright, Byron "Fats" Long, Al "Runt" Pullins. (Washington may have rejected a nickname.)

Days Later Net to team after game in McGregor, Minn: $8.70.

First Season Recap Record 101-6. Saperstein names Saperstein as sixth man, also coach, chauffeur (Model T), booker of games, and everything else.

A Little Later Abe gives a bonus (bench rest, not money) for player clowning schticks. The need to cool heels overcomes pride. The Trotters find selves amusing, crowds amused.

March 21, 1940 Trotters win something called World's Championship Tournament by defeating Chicago Bruins, co-owned by pro football's George Halas.

The Dream Reemers: Goose, Marques, Meadowlark.

Reece Tatum of Eldorado, Ark., son of an itinerant preacher, was an obscure pro baseball player when Saperstein spotted him. The loose, shuffling gait, the white-toothed smile, the double-jointedness, the bizarre 84-inch reach on this 6'3" man were irresistible. Supposedly, Abe taught Goose the game and the reems (routines). Tatum took it—and how—from there, earning, according to another Trotter, as much as $13,800 in a princely season. Famed for his pendulum hook, he'd never glance at the bucket and just laze it right in with casual accuracy. Goose was a loner who hated all that travel. "Been around too much," he'd say. After he retired he was jailed on income tax evasion and died penniless in 1967. He was 45.

Marques Haynes may have invented the dribble. The ball was an extension of his hand (either hand). He's spent a quarter century, at least, as a Trotter, although he once pulled out to form his own itinerants (the Fabulous Magicians), probably because he felt Abe wasn't paying him much, which he wasn't. Goose also did a turn with the Magicians.) Described as "the spirit of the Trotters," the brilliant ad libber was from Sand Springs, Okla., and Langston University. In a game in Chihuahua, Mexico, he dribbled for an entire quarter, a sort of Krupa drum solo. Stands six feet, when he's standing. Off season he's a fashion house owner and the father of two girls.

The Harlem Globetrotters meet their kosher counterparts.

Meadowlark Lemon inherited Goose's role as The Showman starting in 1958. (Inman Jackson had been the initial funnyman.) Only 6'2" and purveyor of the half-court hook (8 for 15 once). To get the job, Lemon practiced mugging in front of mirrors, dribbling and ball handling in hotel rooms. By the 1970s he was making $85,000 a year. His teammates have called him insecure and jealous, but acknowledge that he is a great comedian. "We play to please," he said. He learned basketball at Williston High School, Wilmington, N.C., and married the drum majorette in the school band. They have five children.

The Nicknames Rock, Rookie, Chico, Sweetwater, Duke, Showboat, Tex, Piper, Deacon, Curly, Razor, Pop, Fat, Ducky, Kid, Runt, Goose, Honey, Tiny, Sonny, Toots, Geese. Meadowlark was not a nickname.

The Delightful Names Hubert Ausbie, Agis Bray, Boid Buie, Kara Coates, Alvin Clinkscales, Granville Lash, Paxton Lumpkin, Clifford Shegogg, Othello Strong, Homer Thurman, Roman Turmon, Governor Vaughn, Vertes Zeigler.

Not To Mention Nathaniel Clifton, Clifton Nathaniel.

The White Guys Abe Saperstein, Harold "Bunny" Levitt, Bob Karstens.

The Opposition Washington Generals, New York Nationals, Jersey Reds, Boston Shamrocks, Atlantic City Gulls, Chicago Demons, any team with Red Klotz on its roster, and, in the early days, any team at all.

Held For Delivery Wilt Chamberlain, Connie Hawkins.

Winning Percentage After nearly a half century—approximately 97, or 99, or thereabouts. Something like 11,500 wins in 11,900 games, or thereabouts. Why in one season (1941-42) they lost 18 and were only .882. It happens.

Appearing At The Half Cab Calloway, Peg Leg Bates, 40 Czech dancers.

The Uniforms Red, white, blue and yellow, with stars, names, numbers, vertical stripes, horizontal stripes.

Game Vocabulary A routine (piece of threatrical business) is a reem. Reems nominally begin with about six minutes remaining in each period. "Let's sell something"—time to be funny; "Let's get outta here"—a quarter-ending reem; "A trey"—three minutes left to play; likewise "A deuce" and "An ace." Names of some reems are "Clean-Up," "Connie C." and "Raise 'em Up."

April, 1946 First overseas trip—to Hawaii.

February 19, 1948 Remarkable win over the Minneapolis Lakers and George Mikan before then record Chicago Stadium crowd, 61-59. Year later—bigger crowd for rematch, with same result.

1950 First of an 11-year World Series of Basketball against College All Star teams. In opening year, Trotters are 11-7 against likes of Cousy, Arizin, Schnittker, O'Shea. In closing year (1962), it's Harlem 15-1. Overall the Trotters are 144-66 against the collegians.

Same Year National Basketball Association drafts first black (Boston's Chuck Cooper), depriving Abe of his talent-hunting exclusivity.

Same Year Still First real overseas trip—to Europe, North Africa.

1951 The "Sweet Georgia Brown" pre-game ball-handling theme used.

Aug. 22, 1951 An all-time record basketball crowd (75,000) sees them in Berlin. Nice anti-Communist P.R. move. Presumably a nice gate, too.

Around then Red Klotz joins the Opposition, plays forever.

July 5, 1959 First visit to Soviet Union, chat with premier Nikita Khrushchev, who visits Disneyland same year in retribution.

The Sixties Television exposure helps; increase in number of black NBA stars hurts.

March 3, 1966 Abe is dead, en route (four years later) to the Basketball Hall of Fame, Springfield, Mass. He had taken the Trotters to 55 million people in 87 countries. He was 63.

June, 1967 For $3.7 million, three young Chicago businessmen buy the Trotters from the Saperstein estate. Five years later their profit from the team, for a season, is $875,000. Eight years later they sell to an Arizona-based communications corporation.

1969 After 9,500 games in 42 years an appearance in Harlem—at Intermediate School 201. No score available.

March 6, 1970 Their 10,000th game, played in Miami.

Jan. 5, 1971 After 2,495 consecutive victories, Trotters beaten by New Jersey Reds, 100-99, at Martin, Tenn. Ask Red Klotz. Previous loss was in April, 1962, or thereabouts. Best season was 1963-64 with record of 420-0.

1972 Trotter talent scout at game in Iowa. Dissatisfied with players but hires halftime trampoline act, joined two years later by guts Frisbee champions, dish juggler, tumblers, ping pong players, sword balancer. Annual attendance hangs in at about two million.

Etc. Etc. Marques Haynes dribbles under but is not fouled by Red Klotz.

THE DYNASTIC SUCCESSION

By Herb Michelson

First came the old Celtics, then the Fort Wayne Zollners, Adolph Rupp's Wildcats, right up to John Wooden's Bruins.

Scattered throughout the histories of both professional and collegiate basketball are teams that were persistently effective, dependable winners. The old Celtics of the immediate post-World War I years and the Fort Wayne Zollners, of long-shooting Bobby McDermott, during World War II were two pro teams that had long winning streaks. In the college ranks, there was lingering quality in Adolph Rupp's Kentucky Wildcats and Phog Allen's Kansas Jayhawks.

The professional Minneapolis Lakers looked as if they might be champions forever in the late 1940s and early 1950s. Led by George Mikan, who would be named by one popular magazine as "basketball player of the half-century," the Lakers took six titles in three different leagues in seven years (1948-54). Two seasons after that final championship, after Mikan's retirement, the Celtics came along to begin their dissolution of the Laker legacy.

In fact there never was such as prevailing air of dynasty about any team until the Boston Celtics of the late 1950s and 1960s melded. The Celts, under Coach Red Auerbach, won the National Basketball Association playoff championship eight years in a row from 1958-59 through the 1965-66 season. Then, with center Bill Russell as coach, they picked up two more playoff titles in the springs of 1968 and 1969. The Celtics won the title 11 times in 13 years. Most of these years, they were so good they were almost too good.

The professionals, at least, could put dynasties in escrow. They had players under contract and could keep them in uniform as long as health, stamina and productivity lasted. Russell, for example, played on all 11 title teams; Sam Jones on 10.

The tempo of the pro game was more casual in the early days that Mikan, Jim Pollard, Arnie Ferrin, Vern Mikkelsen, Herm Schaefer, Slater Martin and later pro football coach Bud Grant made magic for Laker coach Johnny Kundla.

In the Celtic years, life became a matter of timing, with the advent of the twenty-four-second clock. The offense had to move much more quickly, and Boston's moved faster than any. Auerbach whipped together a nonpareil run-and-shoot team, detonated by the rebounding and quick-release passing of Russell.

Boston began its title run in the 1956-57 season. Along with Russell, Bob Cousy, Tom Heinsohn, Bill Sharman, Frank Ramsey and Jim Loscutoff formed the nucleus of the winning team. All were to become basketball figures of national import within the decade.

In their string of eight straight NBA titles, the Celts had occasional cast changes—but not many. Sam Jones and Gene Conley, later a major league baseball pitcher, turned up in 1958-59. Tom Sanders arrived two seasons later.

Sharman, a brainy guard, departed after the 1960-61 season. His replacement the following season was John Havlicek, truly a Celtic star of the future. Gaps were filled along the line as Auerback kept coming up with such productive people as Larry Siegfried, Don Nelson, and Bailey Howell. By the time he stepped up to the front office, Auerbach had left Russell with the semblance of a champion—although the dynasty was breathing its last.

To Russell, the final title in that 11-of-12 string may have been the sweetest of all. The Celtics of 1968-69 were comparatively dismal in the regular season. They finished fourth in the East with a mark of 48-34, their worst showing in 13 years. They barely made the playoffs. But they came back to take four of five from Philadelphia in the first round and four of six from the New York Knicks in the semi-finals. The final series, against the Los Angeles Lakers, went the seven-game dis-

—The great New York Yankee dynasty ended a decade ago, but while it lasted it stretched over a half-century of modern baseball. Between 1921 and 1928, the Yanks were playing the golden years of Ruth and Gehrig under Miller Huggins; they won six of eight pennants. Between 1936 and 1943, the Age of DiMaggio and Joe McCarthy, the New Yorkers took seven of eight pennants. And then, they really took off. From 1949 to 1965, mostly under Casey Stengel, they won 14 of 16 pennants. That's 27 pennants in three stretches of time. Of the 27 pennants won, 18 were good for World Championships.

DOMINANCE

is the name of the game in basketball and the man who first dominated the sport was George Mikan of the Minneapolis Lakers, shown here setting a tournament record of 40 points against the New York Rens in 1948 (far left). *Then came Bill Russell* (center) *and the dynastic succession shifted to the Kingdom of the Celts. The Boston Celtics won the title 11 times in 13 years: Russell was there for all of them. Finally, came John Wooden and Lew Alcindor [now called Kareem Abdul-Jabbar] and 10 titles for UCLA in 12 years.*

tance. In the two openers at L.A., the Lakers won by two and six points. Back in Boston, the Celts prevailed by six and one. The Lakers dominated clearly in game five and then the Celts evened it all up with a 99-90 win in the sixth game. In the finale, the Celts squeaked by to win by a basket. Sam Jones was retiring. Russell was retiring. As winners. An awfully pleasant way for a dynasty to end.

The colleges do not have that luxury of extended playing tenure. The can get, at best, four years' service from an athlete, and in many seasons freshmen are ineligible to play on varsity squads. Thus, college history's most remarkable basketball dynasty was chipped out of a constantly turning rock. Beginning in 1964, and for much of the next decade, the University of California at Los Angeles—the Bruins of UCLA—dominated its ranks awesomely.

During one long fearsome stretch, Coach John Wooden's teams won 38 consecutive games in National Collegiate Athletic Association tournaments. Not to mention 10 championships in 12 years—some of them in a row in the years 1967-73.

UCLA could have stocked an entire professional league with the players who passed through its court keyholes in that era. Wooden kept finding new stars just as the old ones were graduating. Rarely was his granary undersupplied.

Wooden's teams were not necessarily off an assembly line either. UCLA won with big centers, with small centers, often without anyone in the pivot at all. The Bruins would sometimes do it with outside shooting, occasionally with inside shooting, frequently with a nagging, pressing, pestering defense. The one consistent quality of Wooden's teams was their poise. To amass the records they did, those young men had to be controlled.

Their NCAA skein of 38 in a row tripled what Rupp's Kentucky teams of 1945-52 had compiled in tournament action. The Wildcats' record of four NCAA titles was wiped out within 17 years. John Robert Wooden, a former Purdue guard, was indeed "The Wizard of Westwood." Look at his dynasty:

1964 UCLA did not lose a game all season. Its 30th, and final, victory that year came

—There are dynasties in track and field, too, five to be exact: Harvard, Cornell, Southern California, Manhattan and Villanova. Between 1880 and 1892, Harvard was the national track and field champion in 11 of 13 years; Between 1905 and 1919, Cornell took the national title eight of the 14 (no competition in 1917, a war you know); 1925 to 1939 was the U.S.C. heyday, winning nine of 15 national crowns; for a brief five years, 1952 to 1956, Manhattan College took four; and most recently, between 1957 and 1971, Villanova has won the national championship 11 out of those 15 years.

Wooden at UCLA

Year	Won	Lost	Pct.
1948-49......	22	7	.759
1949-50..P ..	24	7	.774
1950-51......	19	10	.655
1951-52..P ..	19	12	.613
1952-53......	16	8	.667
1953-54......	18	7	.720
1954-55......	21	5	.808
1955-56..P ..	22	6	.785
1956-57......	22	4	.846
1957-58......	16	10	.615
1958-59......	16	9	.640
1959-60......	14	12	.538
1960-61......	18	8	.692
1961-62..P ..	18	11	.621
1962-63..P ..	20	9	.690
1963-64..N ..	30	0	1.000
1964-65..N ..	28	2	.933
1965-66......	18	8	.692
1966-67..N ..	30	0	1.000
1967-68..N ..	29	1	.967
1968-69..N ..	29	1	.967
1969-70..N ..	28	2	.933
1970-71..N ..	29	1	.967
1971-72..N ..	30	0	1.000
1972-73..N ..	30	0	1.000
1973-74..P ..	26	4	.804
1974-75..N ..	28	3	.903
TOTALS......	620	147	.808
Indiana St. (2 Yrs.)	47	14	.771
High School (11 Yrs.)	218	42	.839
Career Total (40 Yrs.)	885	203	.814

N-NCCA and Pacific Coast Conference Champion
P-Pacific Coast Conference Champion

in the NCAA title game, a 15-point thumping of Duke. Five players started in every UCLA game in 1963-64: Keith Erickson, Gail Goodrich, Walt Hazzard, Jack Hirsch, Walt Slaughter. The top two reserves, Doug McIntosh and Kenny Washington, were excellent. "This team came closer to realizing its full potential than any team I have ever seen," Wooden said. It was a team short on height but long on unselfishness.

1965 Of the previous year's starting lineup, only Goodrich and Erickson had returned, and the Bruins lost their season's opener. But they would lose only once more en route to an 11-point NCAA title victory over Michigan. Washington and McIntosh again contributed, along with Freddie Goss, Edgar Lacey and Mike Lynn.

1967 The era of Kareem Abdul-Jabbar (known at UCLA as Lew Alcindor) had begun. That year's Bruins possessed little experience; four sophomores and one junior started. But there was the height (7'1½" and rising) of Jabar and the leadership of Mike Warren. The season was perfect, concluding with a 15-point thrashing of Dayton.

1968 A UCLA team that had little need for vengeance managed to glean it in the NCAA semi-final game—fortuitously played in Los Angeles. Earlier in the season, Houston had ended a 47 game Bruin winning streak in the Astrodome. But in the tournament game, the Bruins destroyed Houston 101-69, then beat North Carolina by 13 for the NCAA title. Lacey and Lynn were back that year. And so, of course, was Jabbar.

1969 The big man's final Bruin year proved to be the first time that any team took three consecutive NCAA titles. UCLA defeated Purdue, 92-72, in the finale; Jabbar scored 37 points and shared 20 rebounds. Kenny Heitz, another departing senior, played immaculate defense. Others, soon to fade in the Jabbar era, were Lynn Shackelford and Bill Sweek. Several newcomers, however, showed promise that year—Sidney Wicks, Curtis Rowe and John Vallely in particular.

1970 Those last three fellows, plus high post center Steve Patterson, running guard Henry Bibby and reserves John Ecker and Kenny Booker made it four in a row for the Bruins. Wooden was using a new offense and a new defense—with an old conclusion—as UCLA knocked off upstart Jacksonville 80-69 after trailing by nine points early in the game.

1971 Patterson, never a big scorer, contributed 29 points in the championship game as loser Villanova overloaded its zone defense in hopes of stopping Wicks and Rowe, and thus the Bruins. But UCLA prevailed by six points.

1972 The front line of the three preceding years had graduated. Wood then returned to his big man offense. The new big man was named Bill Walton, a feisty redhead, a socialist All-American in the making. Bibby was the sole man with experience in that undefeated year. Still, Wooden had found other pieces. Greg Lee, Larry Farmer, baby-faced Keith Wilkes, Tommy Curtis, Larry Hollyfield. Florida State fell by 15 in the NCAA championship game, again played in Los Angeles.

1973 Title number nine, and a reprise for Walton and company—abetted by newcomer Dave Meyers. In the title win over Memphis State (after a semi-final scare against Indiana), Walton hit 21 of 22 shots from the field, ending with 44 points. Lee had 14 assists.

The ending of the seven-titles-in-a-row streak came in the semi-final NCAA game in 1974. Walton and his people fell to eventual champion North Carolina State in double overtime. Infinity, where is thy sting?

1975 Wooden's 10th, and presumably last, title at UCLA. Walton was gone but Dave Meyers, playing in his last Bruin game, and center-forward Rich Washington, a sophomore, damaged Louisville in overtime in the NCAA semifinals. Then the Wizard of Westwood announced his retirement and the boys went out and won it "for the man." As one player put it after UCLA won its 10th NCAA title, "There was just too much at stake. Coach Wooden told us his leaving should have nothing to do with the game, but...well...he's such a great person."

In his 40-year coaching career, Wooden had won 885 games and lost 203 for a phenomenal .814 win-loss percentage. In his last 12 years of coaching, the UCLA coach won 335 and lost 22 for an incredible .938 win-loss percentage.

John Wooden, right, *the* Wizard of Westwood, *shouts encouragement to his UCLA Bruins as they defeat Kentucky for Wooden's 10th national championship in 12 years.*

—As football coach of the Michigan Wolverines, "Hurry-Up" Yost had a football dynasty that was so crunching in its awesome power, folks in Ann Arbor still shake their heads. It was for the four seasons, 1902 to 1905. Here's how Yost's Wolverines outscored their opponents for those four seasons

1902	664-12
1903	564- 6
1904	567-22
1905	495- 2

And for 55 games in that string, they were undefeated.

GREAT MOMENTS IN COLLEGE BASKETBALL

A pair of peach baskets were the first baskets used in the game. Basketball was invented by Dr. James Naismith, in 1891, at the YMCA in Springfield, Mass.

First Game Between Two Colleges (with nine on a side): February 9, 1895—Minnesota State School of Mines, 9; Hamline College, 3.
First Eastern Intercollegiate Game (still a bit crowded with those 18 guys on the court): March 23, 1895—Haverford, 6; Temple, 4.
First Modern Intercollegiate Game (five on a side): March 20, 1897—Yale, 32; Penn, 10. Players that day were William Davis, Eugene Libby, John Thompson, George Weller, Wilbert Carey, Ernest Hildner, Lyman Archibald, T. Duncan Patton, Finley MacDonald, Raymond Kaighn, Genzabaro Ishikawa, Franklin Barnes, Edwin Ruggles, Frank Mahan, William Chase, Benjamin French, George Day, Henri Gelan. Genzabaro Ishikawa?
First Big, Big Crowd: 10,000 in 1920 at 22nd Regiment Armory in New York for NYU-CCNY game.
First Big, Big Twin Bill: December 29, 1934—Madison Square Garden, New York: 16,188 saw NYU beat Notre Dame, 25-18, and Westminster dispose of St. John's, 37-33.

The One And Only First One-Hander
December 30, 1936

Long Island University, the Blackbirds, had chirped to 43 straight victories when from out of the West came Stanford University and its 6'3" mystery forward, Angelo Enrico "Hank" Luisetti. The son of an immigrant chef, Luisetti possessed the strangest strategy since the dribble: a one-handed shot. Not your basic two-handed set or hook or crip. But an outside one-handed shot. A push. Oh my goodness, and 17,623 people at Madison Square Garden gushed forward to witness this phenomenon. He had scored 305 points in 18 games in the previous season, his freshman year, and was still dumping them in. One handed.

Hank Luisetti started shooting that way at Galileo High School in San Francisco because, he said, "It just seemed the natural way to get the ball in the air. I don't know how I came to think of it." His high school coach didn't tamper with the style. Stanford coach John Bunn said, "Stay with it, boy." Bye bye Blackbirds.

Stanford, with Luisetti's shooting, ball handling, passing, defense and rebounding (he could do OTHER things two-handed), broke an 11-11 tie at the 11-minute mark and won handily, 45-31. For the first time in three years, LIU had lost a game.

"Nobody but us believed we would win that night," said Luisetti.

CCNY coach Nat Holman had said—before the game—"I'll quit coaching if I have to teach one-handed shots to win." He didn't quit, and he taught one-handed shots. As did all the other stupefied coaches of the era.

"It seemed," reported the New York Times in its game coverage, "that Luisetti could do nothing wrong."

The running one-hander was officially part of basketball.

Whoops
The 1949 NIT

The box score of the championship game of the 1949 National Invitational Tournament carries an asterisk. The final score was: University of San Francisco, 48; Loyola of Chicago, 47. But Loyola's players scored only 45 points. The other two came from USF center Don Lofgran, who accidentally tapped in a bucket for the Ramblers. Lofgran also scored 20 for the Dons and was named tourney MVP. If Loyola had defeated USF, he still might have been named MVP.

NYU player drives in for a shot against Notre Dame in '34.

The Bomb
The 1946 NIT

Poor little Rhode Island was enriched in the 1945-46 season by the presence of guard Ernie Calverley, only 145 pounds but, as it would turn out, a fellow with a giant of a shot. The biggest, in fact.

In the closing seconds of Rhode Island's opening round game in the National Invitational Tournament, little Ernie bombarded from 55 feet. Yes, 55 feet. And scored. They called it the longest field goal in collegiate basketball history. A vital one, too, for Ernie's two points knotted Rhode Island with Bowling Green. Overtime, and Ernie's guys won, 82-79. Still somewhat ethereal, R.I.U. then knocked off Muhlenberg to reach the final against Kentucky. It would have been only fitting for Calverley and his companions to take the title. Drama served and all that. However...a Kentucky freshman named Ralph Beard seemed to be taking his good sweet southern time but with just seconds to go he drew a foul and hit a free throw for a 46-45 Wildcat decision. Ernie scored eight points in the finale, a good number for 1946 but, alas, none of them from 55 feet.

Those Amazing Damn Beavers
(The 1950 NIT and NCAA Titles)

A true Cinderella team, those Beavers from City College of New York in the 1949-50 season. They had only one veteran, 6'4" Irv Dambrot, and four sophomores: leaping Ed Warner, just 6'2"; 6'6" center Ed Roman, driver Floyd Lane, and two-handed popper Al Roth.

In the regular season, CCNY was unranked nationally with a won loss record 17-5. No All-Americans. Still, they had a good coach (Nat Holman) and a good club. But nothing special.

Being local, they were invited to the NIT. Their first victim was defending champ University of San Francisco, by 21. Then Kentucky, with seven-foot center Bill Spivey, by 39. Kentucky was the defending NCAA champ. So far, swell. Then Duquesne, by 10. In the final, the Beavers caught Missouri Valley Conference champion Bradley, with All-American Paul Unruh and the excellent Gene "Squeaky" Melchiorre. Bradley was the favorite with its 26-3 record. CCNY won, 69-61, and Warner, who had scored 87 points in four games, was the tourney MVP.

City College had been the last team invited to the NIT, and now was the last team invited to the NCAA tournament, in those days played on non-conflicting dates. While it was possible to compete in both tournaments, it was impossible to win both. Well, just say improbable. No school had ever done it. Yet.

The Beavers started their second tourney with a 56-55 scare over second-ranked Ohio State and All-American Dick Schnittker. Next, a 78-73 conquest of North Carolina State, ranked fifth nationally and led by Dick Dickey and Sam Ranzino.

For the championship game, a re-match with Bradley, again in New York, on March 20, 1950. Two weeks earlier, Bradley had jumped to an 11-point lead over Holman's kids. Not this time. CCNY controlled the game and won 71-68. Five Beavers scored in double figures—one of them being cool sixth man Norm Mager. Unruh was held to eight points in this game, and Melchiorre led all scorers that night with 16. CCNY's Dambrot was named the MVP of this tournament.

The Beavers had their sweep, their impossibility, their double. Less than a year later, they had their trouble.

The Beavers Damned
February 19, 1951

The CCNY team was returning home by train after beating Temple in Philadelphia. Just outside New Brunswick, N.J., a representative of the office of the District Attorney of New York told Beaver coach Holman, "I've got orders to pick up some of your boys."

Point-shaving allegations had first emanated from Manhattan College early in 1951. Two players and three gamblers were

College SCORING Records*

Career Scoring Averages

Player, Team	Last Year	Games	FG	FT	Pts.	Avg.
Pete Maravich, LSU	1970	83	1,387	893	3,667	44.2
Austin Carr, Notre Dame	1971	74	1,017	526	2,560	34.6
Oscar Robertson, Cincinnati	1960	88	1,052	869	2,973	33.8
Calvin Murphy, Niagara	1970	77	947	654	2,548	33.1
Frank Selvy, Furman	1954	78	922	694	2,538	32.5
Rick Mount, Purdue	1970	72	910	503	2,323	32.3
Darrell Floyd, Furman	1956	71	868	545	2,281	32.1
Nick Werkman, Seton Hall	1964	71	812	649	2,273	32.0
Willie Humes, Idaho St.	1971	48	565	380	1,510	31.5
Elgin Baylor, Col. Idaho-Seattle	1958	80	956	588	2,500	31.3
William Averitt, Pepperdine	1973	49	615	311	1,541	31.4
Dwight Lamar, SW Louisiana	1973	112	1,445	603	3,493	31.2
Elvin Hayes, Houston	1968	93	1,215	454	2,884	31.0
Bill Bradley, Princeton	1965	83	856	791	2,503	30.2

Season Averages

Player, Team	Year	Games	FG	FT	Pts.	Avg.
Pete Maravich, LSU	1970	31	522	337	1,381	44.5
Pete Maravich, LSU	1969	26	433	282	1,148	44.2
Pete Maravich, LSU	1968	26	432	274	1,138	43.8
Frank Selvy, Furman	1954	29	427	355	1,209	41.7
Johnny Neumann, Miss.	1971	23	366	191	923	40.1
Billy McGill, Utah	1962	26	394	221	1,009	38.8
Calvin Murphy, Niagara	1968	24	337	242	916	38.2
Austin Carr, Notre Dame	1970	29	444	218	1,106	38.1
Austin Carr, Notre Dame	1971	29	430	241	1,101	38.0
Rick Barry, Miami (Fla.)	1965	26	340	293	973	37.4
Elvin Hayes, Houston	1968	33	519	176	1,214	36.8
Howard Komives, Bowling Green	1964	23	292	260	844	36.7
Dwight Lamar, SW Louisiana	1972	29	429	196	1,054	36.3

Single-Game Scoring

Player, Team (Opponent)	Year	Pts.
Selvy, Furman (Newberry)	1954	100
Mikvy, Temple (Wilkes)	1951	73
Maravich, LSU (Alabama)	1970	69
Murphy, Niagara (Syracuse)	1969	68
Floyd, Furman (Morehead St.)	1955	67
Maravich, LSU (Tulane)	1969	66
Handlan, W. & Lee (Furman)	1951	66
Zawoluk, St. John's (St. Peter's)	1950	65

Individual Records, Season

Field Goal Percentage	Alcindor, UCLA, 1967	.667
	Martens, Ab. Christian, 1972	.667
Free Throw Percentage	Boyer, Arkansas, 1962	.933
Rebounds Per Game	Slack, Marshall, 1955	25.6
Rebounds	Dukes, Seton Hall, 1953	734
Field Goals Attempted	Maravich, LSU, 1970	1,168
Free Throws Attempted	Selvy, Furman, 1954	444

*(Restricted to games between four-year colleges.)

arrested. Now there would be more, many more names tainted by investigation. Probers said that between 1947 and 1950, 86 games had been fixed in 23 cities in 17 states by 32 players from seven colleges. The roll call: Long Island University, New York University, Manhattan College, Kentucky, Toledo, Bradley—and CCNY.

Big name players fell by the litigatory wayside. Seven from CCNY, three from Bradley, the stars of Kentucky, whose coach, Adolph Rupp, had earlier said "gamblers couldn't touch with a 10-foot pole." And three from LIU, whose coach, Clair Bee, later said, "Public confidence in college basketball is shattered, and the fault is partly mine. I was a 'win-'em-all' coach, who, by resorting to established practices, helped to create the emotional climate that led to the worst scandal in the history of sports."

Holman was suspended by CCNY, charged with laxity in supervising his players. Within three years he was re-instated, drew a standing ovation at his first game back on the job. They remembered the sweep.

Safe But Sorry
The 1963 NCAA Title

George Ireland called his pop-artist Ramblers "us peasants." It was an obvious understatement but nonetheless quite accurate considering the nature of the opposition in the 1963 NCAA championship game at Louisville, Ky. The Loyola Ramblers, the nation's highest-scoring team in the 1962-63 season (91.8 average), were facing the Bearcats from the University of Cincinnati and the Bearcats looked invincible—they had taken back-to-back NCAA titles and now seemed set, under Coach Ed Jucker, for three in a row.

Cincy had knocked off powerful Ohio State (with John Havlicek and Jerry Lucas) in 1961 and 1962, and during the regular 1963 season had put together the best defensive unit in the country (a miserly per game yield of 52.9 points). Returning from their previous title clubs were Tom Thacker, Tony Yates, Ron Bonham and George Wilson. A poised, confident, controlled club.

Loyola's big guys were Jerry Harkness, John Egan, Vic Rouse, Les Hunter and Ron Miller, and they roared through the early stages of the NCAA tourney. The Chicagoans bopped Tennessee Tech 111-42 in the opener, then stopped Mississippi State by 10 points, Illinois by 15 and Duke by 19. Cincinnati had disposed of Texas, Colorado and Oregon State to reach the final in Lousiville's gaping Freedom Hall before a record crowd of 19,153.

Classic irresistible force-immovable object matchup. And a classic result.

Behind the shooting of Bonham, Thacker and Wilson, Cincy moved to an eight-point lead at halftime. The Rambler gunners were clearly having trouble penetrating the Bearcat defense and were forcing up shots—scoring only 21 points by the half, nearly 25 under their average. Still, Cincy had been guilty of more floor mistakes than Loyola. A rout did not loom, not even after the Bearcats increased their lead to 15 points with only 14 minutes left. For at that juncture, Cincinnati decided to play it safe—passing up good shots and being victimized by steals. Furthermore, four Bearcats were in foul trouble. And so the Ramblers, starting to control the boards, chipped away.

In the final moments, Larry Shingleton, the only Bearcat starter lacking title game experience, missed a free throw that would have iced another championship for Cincinnati. The miss was to be fatal.

Down two, with only seconds to play, the Ramblers went to Harkness in the corner. His jumper was good at :06. Overtime.

The clubs traded buckets, then each lost the ball twice, then each scored another basket apiece. Loyola got the ball, and sat on it. The Bearcats let them. As the clock ran down, Harkness tried to get loose for a shot, couldn't, fed Hunter, who popped one from the outside but missed. Rouse rebounded for Loyola, however, and banked one in—with one second to play.

Ireland's "peasants" had their kingly title, 60-58. Cincy had to settle for their two in a row. Larry Shingleton, frozen on the bench, put his hands to his face and cried.

Elvin And Spain, And End Of A Reign January 20, 1968

The Alcindor era at UCLA. A 47-game victory streak, then a trip to the Astrodome, an evening with Elvin "The Big E" Hayes and his Houston playmates. Lew and the Bruins had whomped the Cougars by 15 points in the NCAA tourney semi-finals the preceding spring. But Houston appeared stronger this new season, luring a crowd of 52,693 to this rather illogical site for a basketball game, played *above* a large chunk of spectators. The event was mildly tarnished by Lew's recent incapacitation with an eye injury. He was somewhat of a surprise starter.

Yet it was staleness rather than hurt that caused Alcindor to make only two of a dozen shots from the field in the first half. In that same period of time, Hayes went bonkers with 28 points. The Cougars were up, but the Bruins nibbled back.

Houston coach Guy V. Lewis defensed the Bruins with a 1-3-1 zone. Hayes was the low man in the zone in the first half, picked up three fouls, forced a change of strategy. After the intermission, Lewis put Ken Spain low, on Alcindor. And it worked. Containment.

With 28 seconds to play and the score tied at 69, Hayes was fouled by Jim Nielsen. Elvin was not one of your great free throw shooters—carrying an approximate 60 percent average from the line. "Been improving lately, though," said Coach Lewis before the game. And Elvin sunk a pair.

UCLA's ball: Lucius Allen into Mike Warren. Pass too high. Out of bounds, touched last by the Bruins' Lynn Shackleford.

Houston's ball: Into Hayes. Dribble around, pass off to George Reynolds, who, at the buzzer, flings the ball toward the top of the Dome, no higher that night than Elvin. The U.C.L.A. 47-game streak was broken. Hayes outscored Alcindor 39-15 and had 15 rebounds, three steals and a couple of blocked shots. Spain had only one field goal. "He was the big key," said Hayes, three inches shorter than Lew at 6'9".

(Two months later UCLA buried Houston in the NCAA semis, 101-69.)

Elvin Hayes goes up for two over Lew Alcindor, now called Jabbar.

It's been called the fastest moving team sport in the world—a game of brutality, blood and beauty. A *New York Times* sportswriter once wrote of it: "For pep and speed and action, there's only one attraction, that's hockey—give me hockey any time!" Since the 1920s, the game of professional hockey has had its moments of glory, its astonishing events, its tragedies and its exalted heroes. There have been longest games anyone is willing to sit through again, fantastic sudden deaths, incredible scoring sprees. Following are some of those great moments:

Montreal Maroons vs. New York Rangers

Things didn't look good for the New York Rangers. Shut out in the first game of the Stanley Cup finals, they faced the second game without a goalie. That's when Lester Patrick performed his legendary feat. The 44-year-old Patrick, who had never before played goal, came out of retirement and turned away every Montreal shot but one. New York won the game in overtime and went on to win its first Stanley Cup. In the final game, the Rangers led, 1-0, on a goal by Frank Boucher when referee Mike Rodden called back an apparent Maroon goal. Boucher scored another goal and the Rangers won. A near riot ensued. But Rodden somehow escaped the angry Montreal fans who then took out after National Hockey League president Frank Calder blaming him for appointing the referee. Fortunately, Calder managed to lock himself inside an office while the police held them at bay. It was truly a series to remember.

The Longest Game Ever Played March 24, 1936

The Montreal Maroons and the Detroit Red Wings were considered evenly matched going into the first game of the 1936 Stanley Cup final at the Montreal Forum. And they certainly seemed so. They battled into six overtime periods and both remained scoreless. By the second overtime the crowd of 9,500 began getting restless. The players were laboring on chopped ice that didn't have the benefit of modern resurfacing machines. No matter what they tried, they couldn't seem to score. When the seventh overtime ended fruitlessly, Detroit coach Jack Adams decided it was time to do something. "The game settled into an endurance test," he said. "One o'clock came then 2 a.m. and by now the ice was a chipped, brutal mess. At 2:25 I looked along our bench for the strongest legs." Adams summoned Mud Bruneteau who had scored just two goals all season. Adams exclaimed to his team, "Let's get some sleep. It's now or never!" Hec Kilrea slid a pass across the blueline. It was cut of by Bruneteau. Maroon goalie Lorne Chabot, who had previously stopped 88 Detroit shots, suddenly fell to the ice as Bruneteau's shot went into the twine. After 116 minutes and 30 seconds, Detroit defeated Montreal, 1-0. It was the longest game in hockey history.

Sudden Death Mel Hill March-April 1939

Probably the most sensational clutch Stanley Cup performance was turned in by Mel Hill of the 1939 Boston Bruins. Hill scored only 10 goals during the regular season but in Stanley Cup play, he proved the regular season doesn't count. In the first game of the final series against the New York Rangers, the score was tied, 1-1, through the second overtime period. With only 35 seconds remaining in the third overtime, Hill raced down the right side, took a pass from center Bill Cowley and blasted the puck into the New York goal. In the second game, the score was tied in the ninth minute of the first overtime when Hill sent a 30-foot shot past Ranger goalie Bert Gardiner for another winning goal. Boston also won the following game, but the Rangers came back with three straight wins to send the series into the seventh and final game in Boston Garden. With the score tied in the third overtime period, Roy Conacher moved the puck into the New York zone and raced into the corner. Fighting off New York's Bryan Hextall, Conacher maintained possession and flicked a pass to Hill who was standing alone about 10 feet in front of the Ranger net. Hill found an open spot on Gardiner's right side and drilled the puck into the goal. It was eight minutes into the third period of overtime and it was nearing one o'clock in the morning. The capacity Boston crowd went wild. And Mel Hill, who had been a relative unknown, forever was remembered as—what else—"Sudden Death Hill."

1942 Stanley Cup Final Series Detroit Red Wings vs. Toronto Maple Leafs

The '42 Stanley Cup finals will be remembered as one of the most unique in hockey history. Why? Because the Toronto Maple Leafs lost the first three games of their final series against Detroit but won the Stanley Cup anyway. The Red Wings took the first two games in Toronto. In Detroit, the Wings won again to take what seemed like an insurmountable 3-0 lead. Facing elimination, the Leafs managed to win the fourth game. Back in Toronto, the Leafs bombed Detroit and won again. Two nights later they shut the Wings out and tied the series. In the deciding game, Syd Howe gave Detroit a 1-0 lead. But the Red Wings never scored again. Sweeney Schriner tied it for Toronto and Pete Langelle scored what proved to be the winning goal. Schriner then scored his second goal for a 3-1 Maple Leaf win and the Stanley Cup. The largest Maple Leaf Garden crowd ever saw the Leafs win in a comeback that has inspired hockey clubs ever since.

Pete Langelle scores the winning goal for the 1942 Stanley Cup.

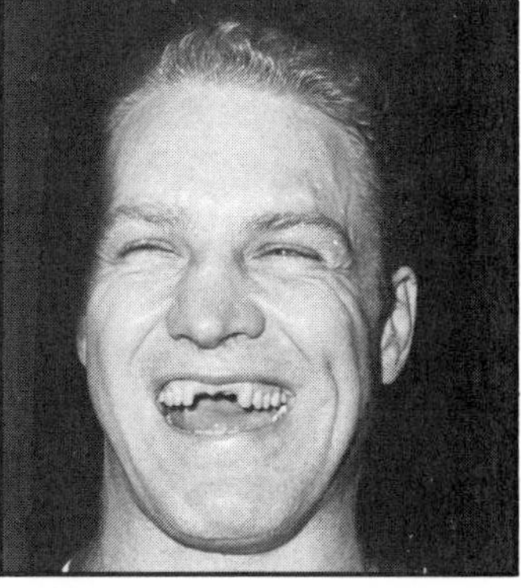

Bobby Hull grins, upper right, *after scoring his 51st goal, a 40-foot shot to the N. Y. Rangers' goal.*

The Fastest Three Goals Ever Scored
March 23, 1952

It wasn't supposed to be an exciting game the night of March 23, 1952. Madison Square Garden was half empty when the two worst teams in the NHL, the New York Rangers and the Chicago Black Hawks engaged in the final game of the season. By the fourth period the Rangers were coasting, 6-2, and the game looked boringly predictable. Then Chicago's Bill Mosienko got into the act. Three days before he had remarked to a friend, "How nice it would be to have my name in the record book with some of the hockey greats." That statement proved prophetic. With 13:51 left, Mosienko shot the puck past New York goalie Lorne Anderson. The two teams then faced off, and Mosienko took a quick pass and barreled in on Anderson. The disk flew past the Ranger and Mosienko had his second goal within 11 seconds. The Rangers and Hawks faced off again. Georgie Gee took the puck and made a perfect pass to Mosienko, who moved in on Anderson and put the puck into the top righthand corner. Time: Three goals in just 21 seconds! Mosienko got his name in the record book.

Bobby Hull's 51st Goal
March 12, 1966

Bobby Hull skated onto the Chicago Stadium ice and the standing-room-only crowd let out a thunderous roar. They were in the musty stadium to see the Golden Hawk score his 51st goal of the season. Only two others in the NHL, Maurice Richard and Boom Boom Geoffrion had ever reached the magical 50 mark. Reggie Fleming of the New York Rangers was assigned to stop Hull and stuck to him like a shadow. But nearly six minutes into the final period, Hull got his stick on the puck. He started toward the Ranger goal. Twenty-four feet out he blasted the disk past New York Ranger goalie Cesar Maniago. The crowd erupted—for seven delirious minutes. Bobby Hull broke a record that had stood for 21 years.

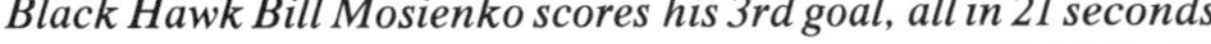

Black Hawk Bill Mosienko scores his 3rd goal, all in 21 seconds.

Canada-Russia Series
September 1972

It took Paul Henderson 10 years in the NHL to emerge a star. However, he had to travel around the world to Moscow to prove what a good hockey player he really was. And prove it he did against the Russian national team which played a group of all-stars from the NHL in the fall of 1972. It was the first time Canadian professional hockey players had ever taken on the Russians. The series opened in Canada with the Canadians the heavy favorites. However, it became clear that the Russians were greatly underrated. They won the opening contest of the eight-game series and held a 3-1-1 lead as the series continued in Moscow. But in the final three games the Canadians rallied. Henderson scored the winning goal in each carrying the Canadians to a series win of four games to three with one tie. In the next-to-last game Henderson scored the game-winner with 2:06 remaining, breaking a 3-3 tie. Henderson was flat on his rear when his shot went in high over the Russian goalie. "I was concerned when the light didn't go on," he commented later. "I looked at the ref though and he had his hand up. What a feeling!" There was even more exhiliration two nights later on September 28 when Henderson scored the decisive goal with only 34 seconds remaining in the game. "All I could think of," he said afterward, "was oh my God, we've done it, we've won." His place among Canada's greats was assured. An Ottawa journalist went so far as to write: "Even the Hon. Pierre Elliot Trudeau couldn't be too sure of his seat if it were possible to have Henderson run against him as a last minute election candidate." It was truly one of the greatest moments in Canada's history.

DYNASTIES ON ICE

By Alan Goldfarb

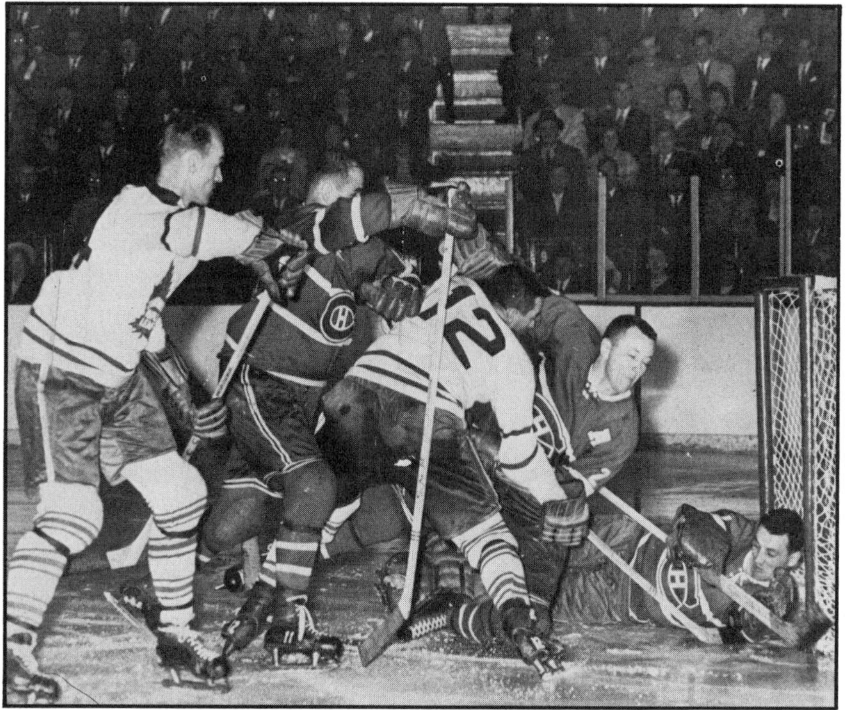

The two real dynasties on ice are the two shown above, Montreal and Toronto. And they always pile into each other.

The world has probably seen its share of dynasties: the Roman Caesars, the Tokyo Tokugawas, the Florence de' Medicis, the Peking Mings, the Moscow Romanovs, the New York Yankees, the Green Bay Packers, the Boston Celtics, and the U.C.L.A. Bruins. It's gotten so that you can't tell the dynasties without a scorecard. But in this discourse on world dynasties, we're going to be concentrating on the the ice age of the 20th Century. With the exception of perhaps the Moscow Romanovs (who were executed in 1918), there are only two dynasties on ice to discuss: the Montreal Canadiens and the Toronto Maple Leafs. That makes it easy to keep score.

Montreal Canadiens

The Canadiens grew out of the need of Montreal's French community to be represented in big league sports. In 1909 the National Hockey Association granted a franchise to *Les Canadiens.* In its first season the club finished last. But by 1916 the Canadiens were displaying the class that would eventually make them the greatest hockey team ever. They won their first Stanley Cup that year and over the next 57 years they would win hockey's highest honor 17 times. Only the Toronto Maple Leafs' 11 Stanley Cup victories come close. The man who started it all was Howie Morenz who joined the club in 1923. Along with Eddie Shore, Morenz was called the Babe Ruth of hockey (how hard metaphors are to come by). He skated on the same line with Aurel Joliat and Billy Boucher when the Canadiens won their first Cup.

As the Canadiens entered the modern era, Georges Vezina became their goaltender. He was the Lou Gehrig of the NHL playing 15 straight years without missing a game. Today the Vezina Trophy is awarded to the goalie with the lowest goals-against average.

Another colorful member during the 1920s and 30s was Sylvio Mantha. He preceded Jean Beliveau and Yvan Cournoyer, two beautiful skaters who were to anchor the team from the 1950s through the 70s. The Canadiens had the worst period in their history during the 30s but in 1942 a bellicose forward by the name of Maurice "The Rocket" Richard joined the team. From then on, until Richard retired in 1960, *Les Canadiens* failed to make the playoffs only once. After Richard there followed such stars as Elmer Lach, Bernie "Boom Boom" Geoffrion, Dickie Moore and Beliveau. The Montreal Canadiens, the finest hockey team ever.

Toronto Maple Leafs

Conn Smythe resurrected the Toronto franchise in 1926. He rechristened it the Maple Leafs and during his reign the team became not only the symbol of Canada but the symbol of hockey. The Leafs were the best team in the NHL in 1931 when they won their first of 11 Stanley Cups. But it wasn't until the 1941-42 season with Hap Day coaching, that the Maple Leafs became one of the two true hockey dynasties. Under Day, Toronto became the first team in the NHL to win three Cups in a row (1947-50). In 1944, Ted Kennedy became a Maple Leaf. He played on five Cup winners and was chosen by Smythe as the Leafs' all-time most valuable player.

The Maple Leafs performed poorly in the early 50s until Punch Imlach was brought in to coach during the 1953-54 season. Imlach, along with Sid Smith, Dick Duff, George Armstrong, Bob Pulford and finally Frank Mahovlich, made the playoffs nine straight times and won the Cup three straight times starting in 1962. Mahovlich led the Leafs in goals scored for six straight years ending in 1966 when the moody forward was traded away. It was the end of the dynasty of the Toronto Maple Leafs.

Near Dynasties

Two other clubs, the Detroit Red Wings and the Boston Bruins have won five or more Stanley Cups in the NHL, but they aren't considered true dynasties. Detroit won the Cup twice from 1935-37 with Ebbie Goodfellow and Normie Smith and again in 1942-43 with Johnny Mowers. They also were an extremely strong team from 1947 through 1956 with the great Gordie Howe skating for them. During that period they won four

Stanley Cups and finished second three other times.

The Bruins were strong in different seasons. From 1926-31 Boston won one Cup and finished second twice. Cooney Weiland and Tiny Thompson were their stars then. Their second strong period was from 1937-43 when they won two more Cups with stars like Milt Schmidt, Bill Cowley and Eddie Shore. Their last two cups were captured in the '60s with the help of hockey greats Bobby Orr and Phil Esposito.

The remaining two teams of the original NHL six, the New York Rangers and Chicago Black Hawks have won three Stanley Cups each. The Rangers, however, have not won since 1939-40 while the Black Hawks last won in 1960-61. The Philadelphia Flyers won the Cup in 1973-74 and already people have been calling the first expansion team ever to win the Cup another dynasty.

24 Stanley Cups

in 34 Seasons

	Montreal Canadiens	Toronto Maple Leafs
1941-1942	———	Won Stanley Cup
1942-1943	———	———
1943-1944	Won Stanley Cup	———
1944-1945	———	Won Stanley Cup
1945-1946	Won Stanley Cup	———
1946-1947	Lost Cup Finals	Won Stanley Cup
1947-1948	———	Won Stanley Cup
1948-1949	———	Won Stanley Cup
1949-1950	———	———
1950-1951	Lost Cup Finals	Won Stanley Cup
1951-1952	Lost Cup Finals	———
1952-1953	Won Stanley Cup	———
1953-1954	Lost Cup Finals	———
1954-1955	Lost Cup Finals	———
1955-1956	Won Stanley Cup	———
1956-1957	Won Stanley Cup	———
1957-1958	Won Stanley Cup	———
1958-1959	Won Stanley Cup	Lost Cup Finals
1959-1960	Won Stanley Cup	Lost Cup Finals
1960-1961	———	———
1961-1962	———	Won Stanley Cup
1962-1963	———	Won Stanley Cup
1963-1964	———	Won Stanley Cup
1964-1965	Won Stanley Cup	———
1965-1966	Won Stanley Cup	———
1966-1967	Lost Cup Final	Won Stanley Cup
1967-1968	Won Stanley Cup	———
1968-1969	Won Stanley Cup	———
1969-1970	———	———
1970-1971	Won Stanley Cup	———
1971-1972	———	———
1972-1973	Won Stanley Cup	———
1973-1974	———	———
1974-1975	———	———

*Note: You'll notice that there are 13 blanks in the Canadien column. In these seasons, the Montreal team lost in the semifinal round of the cup playoffs 8 times, lost in the quarterfinals 3 times and were only out of the playoffs twice. The Maple Leafs have 21 blanks. Of these seasons, they were out of the playoffs 7 times, lost in the semifinals 10 times and in the quarterfinals four times.

HEROES ON ICE

Talent is a gift but it is more than that. It is a trust which no man has a right to ignore or, worse still, abuse. Each man, whatever the degree of talent bestowed upon him, has a moral responsibility, not only to himself but to society, to develop that gift to its utmost degree...

Vince Lombardi, the great football coach, wrote that back in 1964 in a book about great athletes. Not one hockey player was included in that book. But the gifted hockey player also possesses great talent, a talent sorely needed in a game that is the fastest and perhaps bloodiest of all sports.

Although the word "superstar" is used freely, in actuality, only a handful of super-athletes manage to emerge from the quagmire of professional mediocrity. However, it is difficult to separate the great from the near-great. Trying to choose the greatest hockey players of all time is an impossible, and more importantly, a subjective task.

Therefore, in this article concerning hockey's great, only a few of the game's finest players are singled out. There just isn't enough space to include other greats such as Howie Morenz, Eddie Shore, Jacques Plante, Glenn Hall, Terry Sawchuk, Frank Mahovlich and Alex Delvecchio. We could go on, but will limit ourselves to just seven of the greatest:

Gordon Howe, from the wheat fields of Saskatchewan, is perhaps the greatest Hockey player who ever lived. The 6', 205-pound right wing started his career with the Detroit Red

—Bobby Orr of the Boston Bruins holds the record for the most assists in a season with 102 in the 1970-71 season. His 1.31 per game assist average is also a league record.

—Phil Esposito of the Boston Bruins scored 76 goals in the 1970-71 season, a record. He also holds the record for the most points scored in a season, 152 (76 goals and 76 assists) in the same season.

Gordie Howe's NHL Career Records

Most seasons: 25
Most games: 1,687
Most goals: 786
Most assists: 1,023
Most points: 1,809
These records were set between 1946 and 1971 while Howe was playing for the Detroit Red Wings.

Houston Aero's left-wing Mark Howe, right rear, *watches his dad, Gordie Howe,* center front, *go for the puck in Boston Garden.*

—The Stanley Cup, which originally cost $48.67, was first presented by Canadian Governor-General Lord Stanley in 1893.

—The most goals scored in a World Championship match was 47 when Canada beat Demark, 47-0, in 1947.

—The fastest scoring took place on March 19, 1938, when the Toronto Maple Leafs placed eight pucks in the net against the New York Americans in four minutes and 52 seconds.

—The most points scored in one NHL game was eight, scored by Maurice Richard of the Montreal Canadiens against the Detroit Red Wings on December 28, 1944, and by Bert Olmstead also of the Canadiens against the Chicago Black Hawks on January 9, 1954.

—The "hat-trick" is a term used when a player scores three goals consecutively without interruption by either an answering score by the other team or a goal by any other player on the player's own team. Bobby Hull holds the record with 28 games in which he turned hat-tricks, four of these being four-goal efforts.

—The 1972-73 Philadelphia Flyers hold the record for the most any team has been penalized in one season—1,756 minutes in the penalty box.

Although he started slowly, chunky Phil Esposito became the biggest, baddest blademan for the Boston Bruins.

Wings of the National Hockey League in 1946, when he was 18 years old. He was that League's brightest star for 25 years. He played more games (1,687), scored more goals (786), made more assists (1,023) and scored more points (1,809) than any other player in history. Howe was named to the NHL's all-star team 21 times and won the league's scoring title six times. He was also the senior circuit's most valuable player six times. But his career didn't end there. After sitting out a season in apparent retirement, Howe shocked the hockey world by jumping to the upstart World Hockey Association. The man whose name was synonymous with the NHL defected to the WHA and the Houston Aeros. In his first season with the Aeros, 1973, he quickly reestablished his superiority by scoring 100 points (the second highest of his career) and (by passing off to his two sons, Mark and Marty) making the most assists he had ever made (69). His efforts earned him the WHA's most valuable player award. As Bobby Hull once said, "He's likely the greatest hockey player that ever played."

Maurice Richard used to terrify opposing goaltenders as he swooped in on them and blasted the puck through an open corner of the net. "What I remember most about 'The Rocket' were his eyes," former goalie great Glenn Hall said. "When he came flying toward you with the puck on his stick, his eyes were all lit up, flashing and gleaming like a pinball machine. It was terrifying."

The goalies weren't the only ones who stood in fear of Richard. Opposing defensemen, coaches, fans, and anyone else who crossed his path were smart to steer clear of the cantankerous brawler. His reign of terror spanned 18 seasons in the NHL, all with the great Montreal Canadiens. He scored 544 goals, which was a record until Gordie Howe demolished it in 1963, and was also the first to score 50 goals in a season (1944-45). He holds records for scoring the most goals in a game (8), the most goals in a playoff game (5), for scoring the most goals in an entire playoff career (82), the most consecutive games with goals (8) and the most game-winning goals (18). The 5'11", 190-pound Richard was considered one of the most exciting players ever to put on a pair of skates. The NHL Hall of Fame thought so too when it waived its usual five-year rule and voted him in nine months after he retired in 1961.

Jean Beliveau, *le gros Bill* of the Montreal Canadiens became the highest scoring center in the NHL (before Phil Esposito) with 1,219 points. He finished with 507 goals when he retired in 1971 after 18 years. At 6'3", 210-pounds, Beliveau was one of the most graceful skaters in the game. He was named to the all-star team 10 times, played on 10 Stanley Cup championship clubs and twice won the Hart Trophy as the league's most valuable player. Beliveau could do everything on the ice. He could pass, he could backcheck, he was an outstanding playmaker and defender and he shot with amazing accuracy. One teammate said of him, "He does everything well and effortlessly. What he does, he does better than anyone else who does it." The late Leonard Shecter, a writer, once said of Beliveau, "Jean Beliveau in Quebec is like Mickey Mantle or Joe DiMaggio in the United States. When Jean Beliveau walks down the street in Quebec, the women smile, the men shake his hand and the little boys follow him."

Stan Mikita always had to take a back seat to the great Bobby Hull when Hull played for the Chicago Black Hawks. Nevertheless, Mikita managed to lead the NHL in scoring four times and was the only player to win the Hart Trophy (most valuable player), the Lady Byng Trophy (sportsmanship) and the Art Ross Trophy (scoring leader) in the same year (1966-67) and he did it twice in a row. And although he won the Lady Byng, Mikita was one of the more belligerent players in the league before 1966. He led NHL centers in penalty minutes six straight seasons. After that, his penalty minutes diminished. "I decided I was wearing myself out with too much brawling," the Czechoslavakian native said. "Most players won't admit they are dirty. I was and I'm still capable of being dirty, if provoked. Maybe even if I'm not provoked. I couldn't accept the fact that the other guys were bigger than me and could beat me up." The 5'9" Mikita said right after the 1966 season, "They tested me. I always had to prove myself." Mikita, however, has passed the test. He's one of the best centers the game has seen.

Bobby Orr just might be the very best defenseman in the history of hockey. At least he's the best offensive defenseman. Orr, who signed a record bonus with the Boston Bruins in 1966, became the first defenseman in NHL history to win the scoring title when he led his team to the Stanley Cup championship in 1970. It was Orr's goal in overtime which won the Cup for the Bruins and it led losing St. Louis Blues' coach Scotty Bowman to remark: "They say the Bruins started rebuilding that year (the year Orr signed). I don't believe that. I think they started rebuilding in 1948—the year Bobby Orr was born." Orr won the Norris Trophy as the best defenseman in the NHL seven straight years and became the first to win four trophies in one season. In that remarkable year, 1970, Orr won the Norris, the Art Ross Trophy for the scoring title, the Hart Trophy as the most valuable player and the Conn Smythe Trophy as the most valuable player in the playoffs. Orr also won the Hart and Smythe trophies in 1972 when he again led the Bruins to the Stanley Cup. Milt Schmidt, Boston's general manager says of Orr, "He's the greatest player there's ever been, in the past or the present. And if somebody greater ever comes along in the future, I just hope the good Lord lets me stick around to see him."

It only takes four New York Islanders to stop Bobby Orr, as he's almost lifted off the ground by Gerry Hart [2] and Bob Cook [22]. That's only because Orr is the best defenseman in hockey history.

Phil Esposito scored just three goals in 27 games in his first season in the NHL with the Chicago Black Hawks. Who would have thought he would become one of the game's highest scoring players? The Black Hawks didn't think so and dealt him away to the Boston Bruins after the 1966-67 season. It was the best thing that ever happened to the Bruins. The most goals Espo ever scored in one season in Chicago was 27 (1965-66) and the lowest he has scored in Boston is 35 (1967-68). And that was his first season in Beantown. In his first seven years with the Bruins, Espo won four NHL scoring championships and finished second three times. He was the first player to go over 100 points in a season (1968-69) and he passed the 50-goal mark four consecutive seasons. In 1970-71 he scored an all-time record 150 points which included a record 76 goals. In one season he totaled five more goals than he had totaled in four years at Chicago. The 6'1", 195-pound Esposito is a workhorse and has been known to go for six and seven minutes at a stretch, unheard of in this fast-paced game. Emile Francis of the New York Rangers tells just how strong Espo is, "He's so strong you can't get him away from the cage. All of a sudden there's a loose puck and wham, he's got another goal."

Bobby Hull, the Golden Hawk, became the Golden Jet and stunned the hockey establishment. After a glorious career with the Chicago Black Hawks of the NHL, Hull became the first superstar to jump to the WHA after the 1971-72 season. He was lured by a million dollar offer from the Winnipeg Jets after being the NHL's first $100,000 player. In 15 NHL seasons Hull scored 604 goals, won the league scoring championship three times and led the NHL in goals scored seven times, a record. He played on the NHL all-star team 10 times and became the first player ever to score more than 50 goals in a season. He did well in the new league, too. In his first season in the WHA, the Golden Boy scored 51 times and tallied 103 points, the second highest of his career. He was named the league's MVP. Hull is the fastest skater in the game, having been clocked at 28.3 m.p.h. with the puck, 29.7 without it and possesses the fastest shot. His slap shot has been timed at 118.3 m.p.h., nearly 35 m.p.h. above the league average. The 5'10", 195-pounder has been paid many compliments from rival NHL players, but the best came from Phil Esposito, who holds the most NHL scoring records: "Bobby's the best goal-scorer ever."

—The fastest player on ice is Bobby Hull who was clocked at 29.7 mph.

—Bobby Hull also holds the record for the highest puck speed, his hand-slapped shot having been measured at 118.3 mph.

—The Boston Bruins hold the record for the longest consecutive winning streak with 14 in the 1929-30 season.

—The team that went the longest undefeated is also the Boston Bruins who streaked by 23 games in 1940-41.

—It was the Bruins who, as a team, scored the most goals in a season, 399 in the 1970-71 season.

—The hapless Chicago Black Hawks of 1928-29 scored the least goals as a team in a season, 33. A quarter-century later, the Black Hawks had the distinction of scoring the fewest goals (133) and making the fewest assists (206), in 1953-54.

HOCKEY ON 900 STITCHES OR LESS

By Alan Goldfarb

Eddie Shore took 900 stitches in his body during his hockey career. But that's nothing: Gordie Howe took 500 in his face!

Between 1926 and 1940, in 15 seasons as the superstar defenseman for the Boston Bruins, Eddie Shore demonstrated a rough-and-tumble style of hockey that was unbelieveable, terrifying and wonderful to behold. He was supposed to have been such a star, they called him the "Babe Ruth of Hockey." Hell, if Yankee Stadium is the House That Ruth Built, the National Hockey League is the League That Shore Made. He made it, painfully enough, on 900 stitches. You might wonder how a guy can have 900 stitches sutured and re-sutured all over his body. You'll have to ask Shore that. Also, ask him about the 14 times he broke his nose. Or, look for the teeth that are no longer in his mouth.

Some guys have it easier. Take Gordie Howe, the all-time all-everything hockey superstar. He likes to concentrate his injuries, like taking 500 stitches in his face. How does that happen? Well, you might think, given the injury statistics, that these guys are zipping around with switchblades. That's not true; at any rate, it hasn't been proven. Simply put, it's the survival of the fittest.

Take in this scene from one, just one, game.

The penalty box had not been empty from the first minute of play and the game was now well into the third period. Three major fights had broken out, one of them a near riot. Four players had been helped off the ice and each had several stitches taken in his head. There had been no letup. Up in the stands, in a box reserved for the team's top brass, Con Smythe, head of the Toronto Maple Leafs turned to a companion and said, "If they don't put an end to this sort of thing, we're going to have to print more tickets. If you can't beat them in the alley, you will never beat them on the scoreboard."

Another hockey official once said, "Most hockey fights are more talk than action but you have to have a couple of guys who really mean it. Besides, it will help fill the building."

Indeed. And the Philadelphia Flyers, despite attempts of National Hockey League officials to curtail fighting and mayhem, have proven it pays to be violent. They loaded their lineup with maulers, bruisers and *macho* manhandlers becoming the first expansion team to win the Stanley Cup as a result of three or four of their players going through the 1973-74 season beating up on people.

The Flyers' tactics prompted a league honcho to declare, "Wait and see, next season there will be six or eight clubs fighting as much as the Flyers fought this year."

NHL president Clarence Campbell warned that the Flyers have "inaugurated an era of brawling, violence and intimidation."`

Baloney. The Flyers didn't start an era. Since its inception hockey has been known as the bloodiest of sports. So bloody that the NHL estimates that almost 5,000 stitches are taken in the hides of its players each season. Lessee, that's 55 seasons . . . hmmm, about 275,000 stitches. Ouch, that's seven stitches a game. And most of those sutures are administered by team managers, in the locker rooms, without anesthesia. After a player is sewn up, it is quite common to find him out on the ice five minutes later. Derek Sanderson, who has played for the Boston Bruins and the New York Rangers loves to tell about how his father used to keep all of his son's stitches on display in a jar.

There are two types of hockey fights. The average encounters are caused by the fact that the game is one of the fastest in the world. Players have been clocked at up to 30 miles per hour. It is a body contact sport, aided by big money. Suddenly you have a flareup in a corner and one player pulls the other's sweater over his head in order to tie up his hands and arms.

The second kind is a calculated attack. Maurice Richard was once credited with winning a Stanley Cup for Montreal when he knocked Ted Lindsay of Detroit cold with a solid right to the jaw. Another Richard fight caused a riot outside the Montreal Forum where police arrested 70 people for brawling, looting and destroying property.

Few deaths have been attributed to hockey, but the most recent occurred in a 1968 playoff game between Minnesota and Oakland. In the first period Bill Masterton moved toward the Oakland goal. As he did so he was checked by one Seal, bounced off another and went catapulting backward striking his head on the ice with such impact blood gushed from his ears and nose. He died two days later.

One of the most gruesome of fights occurred in 1969 when Wayne Maki of Vancouver sent "Terrible" Ted Green of Boston to the hospital with severe skull fracture. Maki clobbered Green with his stick. Both players were arrested but no sentences were passed. But Green wears a plastic plate in his head. However, less than a month after he returned to action, he ripped off his specially-designed helmet and went at it. "It's part of the game," he said.

THE BIGGER THEY ARE, THE HARDER THEY FALL

From the book, In This Corner!, *the best boxers tell you what it's like to lose teeth, rip off ears, and other such delicate ring memorabilia.*

By Peter Heller

Archie Moore
Light Heavyweight Champion
December 17, 1952-1962 (title recognition withdrawn)

Archie Moore fought for 17 years before he got a shot at the light heavyweight title and won it from Joey Maxim in 1952. He was 39 years old then and held on to the championship for 10 years, until it was withdrawn because the boxing commissioners said he refused to fight Harold Johnson, the top contender. Actually, Moore had fought Johnson five times and won four. In 29 years of professional boxing, Moore fought 228 bouts, won 193, 140 of them by knockout, and lost 26. Eight of the fights were a draw; one was a no contest. In other words, he averaged less than one loss a year. He retired at age 52. Here, he talks about several of his most memorable bouts including his famous fight with Rocky Marciano, when he knocked the champion down and almost put him away. Marciano was 31 years old, Moore was 42.

Then I boxed George Cochran, a Croatian boy that hated black people, spit in a man's face in the ring in public. I beat him until I almost killed him. He was calling me everything he could, and I was laying the wood to him, and I racked him up, and the people threw money and hats everywhere. All these fights had turn-away crowds.

The fight with Marciano came about through a lot of publicity, a lot of gimmickry, colorful slants. I issued a wanted poster out for Marciano. I had Marciano dressed up like a convict, and I said, "One-hundred-thousand-dollar reward for anybody who can get Marciano into a ring. Notify Sheriff Archie Moore," That started it rolling. Then I began to hit Marciano every week with newsletters to the press. They began to pick them up and it began to be a nice little thing. Al Weill [Marciano's manager] said he would never fight me until after I got forty years old, and he was doggone near right. When I fought Marciano I was near forty. He said I would have to come to the ring in a wheelchair. I didn't come in the ring in a wheelchair. But you know what happened? We drew twice as much money as Ezzard Charles or Jersey Joe Walcott, and they were bonafide contenders, and I was not supposed to be nothing but just a gimmicky guy. We drew nine hundred forty-six thousand dollars, compared to the slightly less than five hundred thousand dollars that Marciano drew with Ezzard Charles and Jersey Joe Walcott, because I was plugging that thing day and night with that publicity gimmick.

I knocked Rocky down. It was an exhilarating feeling to me, and I said, "Well, I got this title now. Here it is now. Now I can get on my platform and expound my theory about the youth." Because this is what I wanted that title for, so I could help youth. The heavyweight title was only second to the President of the United States. But I missed it just by a callous referee who had no business handling a match of this magnitude. Harry Kessler was the guy that saved Rocky Marciano. Kessler was so excited. He had no business refereeing that match because he was too excitable. He didn't know what to do. He grabbed Marciano's gloves and began to wipe Marciano's gloves and look over his shoulder and gave Marciano a count standing up. If a man is on his feet, he is automatically a target. This is what was told us at that noon, but he forgot all about it and he began to rub his gloves and then he gave him a snatch, you know, kind of to pull him to. I'll never forget it. It cost me the heavyweight title. I never take any credit from Rocky, because I think Rocky was one of the greatest

Rocky Marciano delivers a hard right to the head of Archie Moore during their heavyweight championship fight at Yankee Stadium. Marciano won in one minute, 19 seconds of the ninth round of the 15-round match.

—"The bigger they are, the harder they fall." *Attributed to Bob Fitz.-simmons, before his fight with Jim Jeffries, a much larger man, in San Francisco, July 25, 1902.*

—"I'll bet the hardest thing about prize fightin' is pickin' up yer teeth with a boxin' glove on." *Kin Hubbard*

Weight Divisions in Boxing

Division	*Pound Limit*
Heavyweight	Any Weight
Light Heavyweight	175
Middleweight	160
Welterweight	147
Lightweight	135
Featherweight	126
Bantamweight	118
Flyweight	112

The Greatest Fighters Ranked by Winning Percentage

1. Rocky Marciano	100.0	Hvywt.
2. Gene Tunney	98.2	Hvywt.
3. Tommy Ryan	96.6	Mdlwt.
4. Willie Pep	96.1	Ftrwt.
5. Muhammad Ali	96.0	Hvywt.
6. Joe Louis	95.8	Hvywt.
7. Jim Jeffries	95.2	Hvywt.
8. Freddie Welsh	95.0	Ltwt.
9. Barney Ross	94.9	Wltrwt.
10. Benny Leonard	94.6	Ltwt.
11. Joe Gans	93.7	Ltwt.
12. Terry McGovern	93.65	Ftrwt.
13. Kid Chocolate	93.55	Ftrwt.
14. Phila.	93.51	Lt.
Jack O'Brien	93.51	Hvywt.
15. Kid McCoy	93.1	Lt. Hvywt.
16. Stanley Ketchel	92.5	Mdlwt.
17. Jack Dempsey	92.2	Hvywt.
18. Jack Johnson	92.0	Hvywt.
19. Emile Griffith	91.9	Mdlwt.

The Middleweight Jinx

For some mysterious reason, the middleweight title is jinxed. Consider these facts:

—The first middleweight champion, "Nonpareil" Jack Dempsey, lost his crown and ended up penniless, forsaken by his friends, and in dismal health. He was buried in an unmarked grave.

—The greatest middleweight of all-time, Stanley Ketchel—who knocked out 21 men in a row—was murdered. And his father was murdered. His mother was murdered. His murderer was murdered. And Goldie Smith, the blonde who caused Ketchel's murder, was also murdered!

—Kid McCoy, who made boxing's Hall of Fame, went to jail for murdering his sweetheart. He had been married nine times. When he was released from prison, he committed suicide.

—Harry Greb, the powerful "Pittsburgh Windmill," died on the operating table during minor surgery.

—Mickey Walker won a million dollars in the fight game and died broke.

—Vince Dundee, the middleweight champion in 1933, died of a strange disease that turned his body to stone.

—Marcel Cerdan died in a plane crash.

The evidence will pile up as high as you please.

fighters that ever lived, and one of the nicest fellows that ever lived. But the injustice that people heap upon people... You have to be able to fight in a system! You have to fight inside the system. That's what I'm teaching young people. How to think for themselves, how to tighten up, get themselves together.

Marciano got to me by just sheer bulldogging, ruggedness, and continuously grinding. I hit Rocky Marciano some shots that would have taken the head off the average guy but he kept piling up on top of me and, finally, you understand, when he got me in a position where he could hit me, then it wasn't long before I had to crümple up because I had no legs. Probably I hadn't any legs for the past four or five years, but I had the braggadocio and the skill and the guts. But even that wasn't enough and finally Marciano beat me down. It was a fantastic fight. I enjoyed every moment of it although I was on the losing end.

Patterson was a matter of my own stupidity in trying to overdo a thing. I thought that I had been a little lax in the training with Marciano, so I said I was going to leave no stone unturned to fight Floyd Patterson and I overtrained. Not that Patterson was not a good fighter. An excellent fighter he was and did something that no other fighter has done before: won the championship twice, won it back, and I have to give him credit for that. I think that I could have beaten Patterson had I not been overtrained, the same way I think I could have beaten Marciano had I not been interfered with. But this is life. This is the way it goes.

Then the culmination of my career came, the real high point. I thought this was the real climax of my career. The real high point came in the fight with Yvon Durelle. Yvon Durelle knocked me down three times in the first round, once in the fifth round, in a sensational fight. Then I got up and knocked him down in the seventh round, knocked him down again twice in the tenth round, and knocked him out in 49 seconds of the eleventh round, and I was fresher than he was at the finish, and here I was nearly fifty years old.

They demanded that I fight Harold Johnson for the sixth time. Now, Harold couldn't draw his breath at the gate, and so why should I risk fighting Harold again when I had already fought him for the title? I had given Harold a championship match and knocked him out in the fourteenth round. They declared he was a contender and they wanted me to fight him again. This was the commission in Philadelphia's wishes. I didn't fight him so they began to peel the title away from me. First here, there, pretty soon I was only the champion of Outer Mongolia, Rumania, and places like that.

[Fighting young Cassius Clay] was a mistake because I had taught Cassius. We had eyeball-to-eyeball sessions. We had a rapport. I took him out to the ranch. I lived there with him, taught him a lot of things, then had to fight my own student. Then again, what greater thrill is it just to see the young student knock the master out and take his master's place? So I'm happy for Cassius because I know that he's one of the finest fighters that ever come down the trail. He was young enough to be my son, anyway. Beautiful, beautiful boy. He is a fighter who stands for something, and that is the mark of a fighter. He doesn't stand neutral. He's a rights fighter also, like me. The man who stands neutral stands for nothing.

Sandy Saddler
Featherweight Champion
October 29, 1948-February 11, 1949
September 8, 1950-January, 1957

Sandy Saddler, never fully given his due, fought 162 fights and won 144, 103 of them by knockout, an incredible record for his weight class. He was only knocked out once in his career, in his second bout. His most famous bouts were against Willie Pep, whom he stripped of the title in a four-round knockout. Saddler lost the title to Pep in their second match, after a 15-round decision. The two men met twice more. In both outings, Saddler knocked out Pep. Saddler was by far the harder puncher, having knocked out his opponent in 72 percent of his victories. (Pep, for example, knocked out 28 percent.) After an auto accident in which his eye was injured, Saddler retired as champion. Here, Saddler talks about his four fights with Pep.

I was number one contender and [Pep] had to fight me. I boxed in Argentina, Venezuela, Chile, Uruguay, Paraguay, I boxed in Panama, I boxed in the Philippines, I boxed in Cuba, and he just had to fight me. Archie Moore went to camp with me at the time. I figured I would go to camp and he would tell me the different movements and whatnot and get things down pat. I couldn't do it here in the city, so we went to camp and I would box Archie. He would make moves and slip and make clever moves. Archie was very clever. He taught me quite a bit. He taught me how to slip and how to get inside and how to, in case you're hurt, how to actually cover up so that all the vital spots are covered up. And that's one of my main assets in boxing. When I got hurt, how to cover up, go right in that shell, and no part is open so that a man can slip in a punch on you.

Actually, Archie Moore had a lot to do with me winning that fight. "Sandy," he said, "Pep is a very clever man and very fast mover. Being that you can punch..." He wanted me to stay on top of him, give Pep no leverage, because if you gave Pep any leverage, for crissake, you could forget it then.

You have to live a clean life. I never drank, I never smoked, and I lived boxing. I learned how to punch correctly. That gave me my punching power. Archie taught me quite a bit how to punch, punching from the ball of my feet. That was very important.

I stayed on top of Pep. Stayed on him, stayed on him, and as he relaxed I would punch. I just kept on like that until I actually knocked him out, knocked him stoned in that fourth round. Out. You could count 50, pal, I'm telling you. I remember Pep fighting Chalky Wright when he took the title from Chalky Wright. I watched Pep and, jeez, he was a clever man. The movements and the pulling and the slipping. He'd get Chalky Wright to lead, he'd pull-hand-turn him and spin him. He was really clever. I really admired Pep. I had a lot of respect for him.

I think I stopped him in the fourth round. I remember it well. I got right on top of him. [Winning the championship] just made me more anxious to continue and to hold the crown. Then came that second fight in which Pep won the 15-round decision. One of them things. He put on a very good boxing exhibition. He pulled and he slipped and he carried on. He fought a very good fight and he beat me a 15-round decision. I stayed on top of him and I cut him up and whatnot but he just got that decision over me. Then that third fight, and that third fight I stopped him in the ninth round, staying on top of him and I was punching more, doubling up on my punches. Just stayed on top of him, dug him to the body, dug him to the head, dug him to the body, didn't give him no leverage, and I stopped him in the ninth round.

The third fight, Pep knew I could punch. He knew that. When I get on top of Pep, when I started to punch him, he would grab my arm, I'm trying to pull arms away so I can punch him. Now, what was so dirty about that?* The man grabbed my arms and I pulled my arms away so I could punch, and he's holding the other one and I'm banging with one hand. I just got right on top of him, just beat him, not unmercifully, but I just beat him good. Some people say he quit, but I just banged him something terrible. The fourth fight he was in there slipping and ducking until I caught up with him.

They introduce Pep, Pep and I would be at a fight at the Garden, and they'll say, "One of the greatest featherweights, Willie Pep. Here's another retired champ, Sandy Saddler." That's why I don't care to get introduced in the ring. Instead of saying "Saddler, the undefeated Featherweight Champion of the World," instead, "Take it and like it. If you don't want it, leave it." I'm not angry at Pep at all. I'm angry at these other people who's pushing this thing. Pep and I are great friends. But one thing, though, he is white, and when you're white, you're supposed to be right. "If you're white, you're right. If you're black, get back." It's just plain ol' prejudice. Back in 1930, you know, a black man wasn't even allowed to get in the ring to second a fighter. This is just recently where a black man is able to get in the ring and second a fighter. A black man wasn't even allowed to get in the corner. Just plain ol' prejudice. This country's built up on this sort of stuff. That's all there is to it. I'll lay my cards on the table. It's just plain ol' prejudice. The black man in this country, he have to do twice as hard as the white man to gain anything, and when he get it, for chrissake, they don't give him the recognition a man should get, and that's the whole thing in a nutshell.

*All the Pep-Saddler fights were considered dirty no-holds-barred affairs. The third fight stood out above the other three for tactics that resulted in a temporary suspension for both Pep and Saddler.

Joe Louis
Heavyweight Champion
June 22, 1937-March 1, 1949

After winning his first 27 bouts in a row, 23 of them by knockout, Joe Louis went into the ring against Max Schmeling and was knocked out in the 12th round. That was in 1936 and Louis badly wanted revenge. He won the title from Braddock the following year and finally got another crack at Schmeling in 1938 as the storm clouds of World War II rolled across Europe. Everyone recognized the significance of the bout which pitted an American black against a pugilistic craftsman from the German master race. Louis knocked out Schmeling in the first round.

James J. Braddock on the Joe Louis Knock Out Punch:

"For four rounds it was all right but then he started to come on and he went to work on me. In the four rounds from the fourth to the eighth round, I got hit with more punches than I got hit with in the other 87 fights I had. Because I never got hit much, I never got cut up. But I got 23 stitches in my face. The punch he knocked me out with, he hit me with a left hook in the stomach (this was in the eighth round) and a right hand in the mouth, and I had naturally the mouthpiece in. He drove the tooth through the mouthpiece and right on through the lip. You see what power that guy had. When he knocked me down, I could have stayed there for three weeks."

Max Schmeling winces something awful from the Joe Louis punch which gave Louis a knockout in 2:04 of the first round. Hospital X rays showed Schmeling had a fractured vertebra. Schmeling claimed a kidney punch put him out.

The Greatest Boxers Ranked by *Ring* Magazine

Heavyweights

1. Joe Louis
2. Jack Dempsey
3. Jim Jeffries
4. Jack Johnson
5. Rocky Marciano
6. Gene Tunney
7. Bob Fitzsimmons
8. Jim Corbett
9. Muhammad Ali
10. Joe Frazier

Light Heavyweights

1. Philadelphia Jack O'Brien
2. Archie Moore
3. Jack Dillon
4. Bob Foster
5. Sam Langford
6. Tommy Loughran
7. Paul Berlenbach
8. Billy Conn
9. Kid McCoy
10. Jack Delaney

Middleweights

1. Stanley Ketchel
2. Sugar Ray Robinson
3. Harry Greb
4. Mickey Walker
5. Billy Papke
6. Tony Zale
7. Dick Tiger
8. Tommy Ryan
9. Emile Griffith
10. Les Darcy

Welterweights

1. Original Joe Walcott
2. Henry Armstrong
3. Barney Ross
4. Ted Kid Lewis
5. Jimmy McLarnin
6. Jack Britton
7. Kid McCoy
8. Kid Gavilan
9. Jose Napoles
10. Dixie Kid

Lightweights

1. Benny Leonard
2. Joe Gans
3. Battling Nelson
4. Tony Canzoneri
5. Jack McAuliffe
6. Freddie Welsh
7. Ad Wolgast
8. Kid Lavigne
9. Joe Brown
10. Carlos Ortiz

Featherweights

1. Terry McGovern
2. Abe Attell
3. Willy Pep
4. Jem Driscoll
5. Kid Chocolate
6. Johnny Dundee
7. Johnny Kilbane
8. Sandy Saddler
9. George Dixon
10. Younge Griffe

Against Schmeling, I don't know what happened to me, but I can tell you one thing, I got hit that night with many right hands. I'll never forget. When I got knocked down in the second round, I really didn't know what happehed the rest of the fight. I didn't know nothing. I didn't know where I was, nothing. The only thing I remember when I went out of the ring, my trainer, Manny Seamon, said, "Cover up his face," because my face, my jaw, was out like this where I had stopped so many right hands that night.

I'll never forget, when I first went with Mike Jacobs, he come to see me fight someone in Detroit. After the fight was over, he wanted to talk to me about coming to fight for him in New York. He told me then he knew there was a color line—at that time a gentlemen's agreement—that there wouldn't be another colored champ in the heavyweight division. But he said, "If you are good enough, you will be champion."

I didn't quite feel champion then because Schmeling had beaten me and Schmeling was supposed to be in my place that night instead of me. So I told the press, "I'm not champion yet. Wait till I beat Schmeling, then I'll be champion." And I got him in '38, 2 minutes and 4 seconds in the first round. On the way to the ring that night, George Raft raised his finger and said, "One round!" that he was picking one round. And I made a statement to him, said, "What's the matter? You in a hurry?"

I think that's my biggest thrill because I felt then that I was the real champion because I had beaten everybody then. The press and the radio made the Schmeling second fight somewhat a little bit more than just another fight. Country against country. At that time the Jews were taking an awful beating in Europe. I met President Roosevelt a few months before the fight. He felt my muscles and said, "These are the type of muscles we're going to need to beat Germany with." But in '38 I don't think America was thinking too much about war, at least the American public didn't know too much about it, how close we was to war. But the President must have known. That's why he made the statement.

Billy Conn
Light-Heavyweight Champion
July 13, 1939-July, 1940

A year after he won the light-heavyweight championship from Melio Bettina, Billy Conn retired his crown to fight in the heavyweight division. He went after Joe Louis. His most famous fight, his first against Louis, took place on June 18, 1941, in Madison Square Garden. For 12 rounds, Conn was the new heavyweight champion. He was tied 6-6 on one scorecard and ahead of Louis 7-5 and 7-4-1 on the other two cards. But in the 13th, the brash young boxer daringly tried to knock Louis out. Before the round was over, he himself was knocked out and Louis retained the title.

I retired undefeated to go fight the big fellows—Lee Savold, Dorazio. I put on a little weight. I just weighed about 162 pounds. So I decided to fight the heavier fellows. In the heavyweights is where all the money is. So I figured I'll try them all out.

Bob Pastor was a nice fellow. I didn't like his manager. I hit Pastor in the balls so he started beefing. I hit him low again and I said, "Now I'm really going to hit you in the balls, you big crybaby." I hit him in the balls and knocked his ass through the ropes in the thirteenth round. You're supposed to do anything you can win, see? You're not an altar boy in there. Hit 'em on the break, backhand, do all the rotten stuff to 'em. What are they going to shoot you for it?

I beat the main fellows, the contenders, so I figured we'll try Joe Louis, he's just another guy. You don't fight guys like Joe Louis unless you beat all those guys that really knew how to fight and then you learn how to fight. You're not just some mug coming in off the street corner to fight Joe Louis, because he'd knock you through the middle of next week. It's a business and it takes a long time. It's the toughest business in the world. But when you're good, you automatically know all the fine points of the game and what you're supposed to do. And the main thing is they're not supposed to hit you. That's the game. Get out of the way. I knew that you had to keep moving from side to side and keep him off balance and never let him get a good shot at you because he was a real dangerous man. Keep away from him. Just move in and out. Feint him out of position and whack him and just keep going. Left hook and a right cross, a left hook to the body and a left hook to the chin—all in the same combination, bing, bang, boom! Real fast, like a machine gun, then get the hell out of the way. There's a set that comes natural to you if you know how to fight. You look straight at the fellow and you just take the lead away from him. You try to mix him up, to befuddle him. Then you take the whole combination of shots at the same time—one, two, three, four, bing, bang, bing and you get the hell out of there real fast. Then when he goes back you get him to drop his hands, feint him out of position, then you can hit him. But every time that you lead him with one hand you have to know to keep the other one up so you don't get hit. You can't let him get set to get a clear, good shot.

I hurt him in the twelfth round so I figured I'll try and knock him out. I made a mistake. He was waiting for me. He'd have never hit me in the ass if I didn't make a mistake and try to knock him out. They told me to stay away from him, that I was beating him all the way. But when I hurt him in the twelfth round he started to hold on. I said, "I'm going to knock this son of a bitch out. Don't worry about it." Don't worry about it, and I made one mistake! I liked Joe and I knew he was a real good man. I used to be a wise guy with some of those fellows. When I hit him in the thirteenth round I said to him, "You've got a fight tonight, Joe." He said, "I knows it," and he kept on going. And that was the end of the line. He hit me about twenty-five real good shots. I tried to outpunch him, but I only weighed 169½ and he was a big fellow. He weighed 199½, a big man, and he could box, too.

He admits that I was winning. He says in the corner they told him that he can't win, that he's losing the fight and he said to them, "I can't catch him." He says, "But I knew you. You had to get fresh. I fixed your ass for you." That's exactly what happened. You only get one chance. Of all the times to be a wise guy, I had to pick it against him to be a wise guy. Serves me right. He should have killed me. What a bastard I was. He landed twenty-five punches that put me down, every goddamn one of them was on my chin, and I was up, too. Had about two seconds to go in the round and the referee stopped it or he would have killed me, which he should have done. I got up to try again. If I'd have got hit and knocked down and the bell would have rang to save my ass and they got me in the corner then I would have wised up, he'd have never hit me any-more. I'd have just kept going. He couldn't hit me, then I'd start to fight like hell in the last round. I would have beat him. I was twenty-three years old. I didn't have any sense. He was knocking everybody out, see? Here I come along, I'm a middleweight, and I almost kicked his ass for him.

I was the heavyweight champion for 12 rounds, Joe Louis says. He's real witty and one day I said to him, "Gee, what a tough break I got. I had your ass beat. I could have won the title, been the champion for six months, then I'd let you win it back." He says, "How was you gonna keep the title for six months when you couldn't keep it for 12 rounds?" Joe and I are real close friends. He never knocks any-body. He's a nice guy and he's not vicious or anything. If he had a million dollars a month, he'd give it away or he'd shoot crap. Any guy could come up to him. He had a pocket full of black chips and a pocket full of green chips one day. A bum come up to him. He gave him a black chip. I said, "Why don't you give him a green chip?" A black chip's a hundred dollars and a green chip is twenty-five. He said, "What the hell's the difference? I'm going to lose it anyway." He just don't care about

KNOCKOUTS

Records of Selected Great Fighters

	Years Active	Weight Class	Total Bouts	Wins	Losses	Won by KO	Decsn. Won	Of D. %Wns	%Wns by KO
Muhammad Ali	1960-75	Heavywt.	47	45	2	32	13	96	71.7
Henry Armstrong	1931-45	Lt.Hvywt.	175	144	22	97	47	87	67.3
Abe Attell	1900-17	Featherwt.	165	89	10	46	42	90	51.6
Paul Berlenbach	1923-31	Lt. Hvywt.	49	37	7	30	7	84	81.1
Primo Carnera	1928-37	Heavywt.	99	86	12	66	18	88	76.7
Kid Chocolate	1928-38	Featherwt.	161	145	10	64	81	94	44.1
Billy Conn	1935-48	Lt. Hvywt.	74	64	10	14	50	86	21.9
James J. Corbett	1886-03	Heavywt.	33	20	5	9	11	80	45.0
Jack Delaney	1919-32	Lt. Hvywt.	86	70	10	42	27	88	60.0
Jack Dempsey	1914-40	Heavywt.	77	59	5	49	9	92	83.1
Bob Fitzsimmons	1889-14	Heavywt.	40	28	7	23	5	80	82.1
George Foreman	1969-75	Heavywt.	41	40	1	37	3	98	92.5
Bob Foster	1961-74	Lt. Hvywt.	58	51	6	42	9	89	82.4
Joe Frazier	1965-75	Heavywt.	33	31	2	26	5	94	83.9
Joe Gans	1891-09	Lightwt.	156	119	8	54	60	94	45.4
Kid Gavilan	1943-58	Welterwt.	143	106	30	27	79	78	25.5
Emile Griffith	1958-75	Middlewt.	99	80	17	21	59	83	26.3
Jim Jeffries	1896-10	Heavywt.	23	20	1	16	4	95	80.0
Jack Johnson	1897-28	Heavywt.	114	80	7	44	32	92	55.0
Stanley Ketchel	1903-10	Middlewt.	61	49	4	46	3	92	93.9
Sam Langford	1902-24	Lt. Hvywt.	247	136	23	98	37	86	72.1
Benny Leonard	1911-32	Lightwt.	209	88	5	68	20	95	77.3
Ted Kid Lewis	1909-29	Welterwt.	250	155	24	65	87	87	41.9
Tommy Loughran	1919-37	Lt. Hvywt.	171	95	23	18	76	81	18.9
Joe Louis	1934-51	Heavywt.	71	68	3	54	13	96	79.4
Kid McCoy	1891-16	Welterwt.	105	81	6	35	45	93	43.2
Terry McGovern	1897-08	Featherwt.	77	59	4	34	24	94	57.6
Rocky Marciano	1947-55	Heavywt.	49	49	0	43	6	100	88.0
Archie Moore	1936-63	Lt. Hvywt.	225	191	25	137	54	88	71.7
Battling Nelson	1896-17	Lightwt.	132	58	19	37	20	75	63.8
Phila. Jack O'Brien	1896-09	Lt. Hvywt.	181	101	7	36	59	94	35.6
Willie Pep	1940-66	Featherwt.	230	220	9	61	159	96	27.7
Sugar Ray Robinson	1940-65	Middlewt.	202	175	9	109	66	95	62.3
Barney Ross	1929-38	Welterwt.	82	74	4	24	50	95	32.4
Tommy Ryan	1887-07	Middlewt.	109	86	3	45	40	97	52.3
Sandy Saddler	1944-56	Featherwt.	162	144	16	103	41	90	71.5
Max Schmeling	1924-48	Heavywt.	71	56	10	39	14	85	69.6
Gene Tunney	1915-28	Heavywt.	77	56	1	40	15	98	71.4
Original Joe Walcott	1890-11	Welterwt.	150	81	24	34	45	77	42.0
Mickey Walker	1919-35	Middlewt.	153	95	18	60	35	84	63.2
Freddie Welsh	1905-22	Lightwt.	166	76	4	23	50	95	30.2
Tony Zale	1934-48	Middlewt.	88	70	16	46	24	81	65.7

What Joe Louis said about Billy Conn before their title fight.

—"He can run but he can't hide."

—Joe Louis reigned as champion longer than anyone else: exactly 11 years, eight months, and nine days—from June 22, 1937 to March 1, 1949.

The oldest champion was Archie Moore who held the light heavyweight title at the age of 48 in 1962.

—The youngest champion in any class was Pedlar Palmer who won the bantamweight crown at age 19 years and six days in 1876.

—The man who held the most titles at the same time was Henry Armstrong who wore three crowns, those of the welterweight, lightweight and featherweight divisions in 1938.

—Archie Moore scored the most knockouts against his opponents in his career:136.

—More peole attended the Gene Tunney-Jack Dempsey fight for the heavyweight title in 1936 than any other fight: 120,757 spectators.

—The poor fellow who fought the most fights in a career was Abraham Hollandersky who went up against 1,309 starting bells between 1905 and 1918.

—The largest purse came out of the Muhammad Ali-Joe Frazier heavyweight championship match of 1971: $2.5 million.

—Al Couture hit Ralph Walton while Walton was adjusting a mouthpiece in his corner at Lewiston, Me., on September 29, 1946, knocking Walton out. It was the shortest fight on record, a brief 10½ seconds.

—In case you've forgotten, the first heavyweight championship fight (with gloves) was fought between John L. Sullivan and *Gentleman* James J. Corbett in New Orleans on September 7, 1892. Corbett won in 21 rounds.

—Muhammad Ali won the Olympic gold medal in the Light Heavyweight division in 1960. Joe Frazier won the gold in the heavyweight class in 1964, while George Foreman won the gold in the heavyweight division in 1968.

money, just gave it away.

I had to go in that army for four years. If I beat all those good fighters when I was so young and if I had a chance just to fight two more years, I might have been heavyweight champ, might have beat Louis or something. [After the war there was a return match with Louis.]

Gunboat Smith
Claimant of the "White Hope" Heavyweight Title
January 1, 1914-July 16, 1914

Born of Irish parents in Philadelphia in 1887, Edward J. "Gunboat" Smith spent his youth in orphanages, working on farms and sailing in the U.S. Navy. He bagan boxing while in the Navy and won the Pacific Fleet heavyweight championship. Turning professional in 1906, Smith had six years of experience behind him when he stepped into the ring against Jess Willard on May 20, 1912, in San Francisco. Smith won a 20-round decision. Two years later, Smith won the "White Hope" heavyweight championships, an artificial title created in bigoted response to the fact that the real champion, Jack Johnson, was black, controversial, arrogant and outspoken. Here, Smith talks about his defeat of Willard. Three years after that bout, Willard defeated Johnson for the heavyweight title in Havana, Cuba, in one of history's most controversial bouts.

Then I went out and I fought Jess Willard and he weighed about a hundred and one pounds more than I weighed. That was 1912. I weighed probably about 170. At 175 I was hog fat. But I had the range, I had the punch. Then I looked him over and he must have been about 6'10". I'm 6'1", and I had to look up. But he looked like a big stiff. I said, 'I'll knock him out in a round." But the dirty bum could take it. And how he could take it, and how he could hit. I found that out.

You see, where the fighters today make a mistake, they go out there and they got a good punch and they hit a fellow and they don't knock him out, and they keep punching and punching, break their hands, knocking yourself out. Some people can absorb a lot of punishment, and you can't hurt them at all. But I got wise to myself. I was pretty smart then.

With Willard, after I threw my best punch at him his hair wiggled a little bit. That's all. I said, "Holy Jesus, that was my best punch. No detours, right from the floor, right on his chin." I says, "Wait a minute, I'll have to try that again." I tried it again. Nothing happened. And he hit me with a right-hand uppercut, by God, he cracked a couple of ribs in me. Now don't forget, I've got nineteen and a half more rounds to go. Right there I said, "Wait a minute, there's only one way to do it—outbox this big bum. I'm faster than him." And that's exactly what I did. Now I figured about the tenth round I'd try it again. So in the tenth round he says, "Come on out here and fight, you big bum." Big bum? I'm hiding behind his goddamn leg! He was big, and he wasn't fat. He was rawboned like me, and weighed 260, 270 pounds. And me in there, if I weighed 169 I weighed a lot.

So in the tenth round I hit him with one of my right hands, but it was on the ear. Tore his ear right off. That hushed him up for the rest of the fight. The blood was running down, and oh, God. I, of course, had my gloves "loaded." I had insulation tape laid across my hands.*

I went 20 rounds and win the decision. But I couldn't knock him out. That's what I couldn't understand. I found out nobody was going to knock him out. He was really something, because I was a terrific hitter, and I couldn't budge him. That took a lot of steam out of me.

*This technique of taping the hands with heavy insulation tape was not prohibited in the early days of modern boxing. The insulation tape made the fighter's hands extremely hard, and his punches, therefore, much more lethal. Today this is illegal. Fighters now are only permitted to tape their hands with soft gauze and medical adhesive tape in prescribed amounts before gloving up.

Jack Dempsey
Heavyweight Champion
July 4, 1919-September 23, 1926

Born in Manassa, Colo., Jack Dempsey began fighting in Western mining towns around 1914 as "Kid Blackie." Dempsey was knocked out by Fireman Jim Flynn in one round in 1917 but was never knocked out again in 77 fights. His most famous and controversial fight was against Gene Tunney in 1927, in the fight of "The Long Count" when, after knocking Tunney down, Dempsey waited before going to a neutral corner and, under the rules, referee Dave Barry delayed starting the count on Tunney. Here, Dempsey describes it.

Tunney, I don't know if I could lick him even at my best. I'd been out about three years. You never know about fighters. There's a lot of luck in fights. I could have got my eye busted, or I could have got knocked down, or hurt my arm, so we just forget about that and go on to the next one. So long as you lost, that's it.

We had rain that night. You always think you're going to win, whether you do or not, and that's one thing a fighter must have. He must think he's going to win whether he does or not. Otherwise it isn't any use fighting.

You've got to have that desire and will to win. I felt I was losing all the way through, because he was outboxing me. I only had one chance, and that was to knock him out. If I knocked him out, then I'd have won. Otherwise I knew I'd lost. You just think you're lucky to stay up there as long as you did. I was champ from 1919 to 1926. That's seven years, and that's a long time.

We had over one hundred thousand in Chicago, one hundred twenty-five thousand. That was in '27. That was a big gate, over a million dollars. Tunney was down, and I was in the hopes he wouldn't get up. I stood there because I was anxious to get at him, see? I should have went back to the right corner but I didn't do it. If he hadn't have got up, maybe we could have had another fight. Dave Barry, the referee, said, "Go back to your corner," and I didn't go back. He grabbed me and pushed me and shoved me back. Then Tunney got up and won from then on out.

I look back on the fight, he wasn't hurt too bad. Tunney would have got up. Naturally, I was in hopes he wouldn't get up, or he'd be very weak where I could get another punch at him and knock him out. But it didn't happen. He got up. I think he knocked me down in the ninth or tenth round. I think I took a 1 or a 2 count. I think everything happens for the best. We live our lives, and we do the best we can. Maybe if I kept fighting, something may have happened to me. At least I came out of it all right. There's a lot of fighters that fight so many fights and get licked, they get punchy. At least I'm all right. We could have fought again and still make a lot of money, but Rickard didn't want it. He said that's enough.

The young lion flattens the geriatric giant in the 1965 rematch of their title bout in Maine. Muhammad Ali became the most charismatic sports figure in the world, Sonny Liston died in obscurity in Las Vegas, Nevada.

The Long Count, *as Dempsey put it, was Dempsey's own fault: "I should have went back to the right corner but I didn't do it.... Dave Barry, the referee, said, 'Go back to your corner, and I didn't go back. He grabbed me and pushed me and shoved me back. Then Tunney got up and won from then on out."*

a Workingman's Guide to Sunday Punches

Taking dead aim at the solar plexus, liver, heart and mastoid— Here's how . . .

—Sugar Ray Robinson began boxing as an amateur, and he set a phenomenal record. He fought 90 bouts and won them all, 17 by knockout. In time, he became the welterweight champion of the world. He never lost that title but he moved up in weight class to the middleweight division. He won that too. When he lost the middleweight title, he came back to win it again and again. Five times to be exact. No fighter has ever won the same crown as many times. And no fighter was ever crowned a world's champion as often as Sugar Ray Robinson.

Let's say you're on a beach and some 90-pound weakling has kicked sand in your face. Or you're in a Moroccan hashish parlor and some burly North African is trying to grab your pipe. Or you're walking through Central Park and an undercover cop is trying to lure you into mugging him. What you need, really, is a fast Sunday punch, like the Kid McCoy "Corkscrew" which leveled Philadelphia Jack, or the Joe Louis punch which knocked out five heavyweight challengers in the first round or the Sonny Liston left hook which folded up an equal number of challengers early.

Well, step right up, because what we're gonna show you here are some special instructions on *the* knockout blows.

Straight Right To Chin

You can say this is common fare, but nothing beats a good quick right to the chin. It's the best known of the knockout punches, having won more fights by stardust than any other. What happens is that the sudden jolt to the chin pushes the jaw bone back to jar the brain a bit askew.

The old boxing saying, "Never lead with your right," is true. You gotta wait, duke some with your left, stomp on your adversary's toe, knee him in the groin, whatever. Then, *wham,* send that right sailing straight to the enemy's chin. Your fist should be tightly clenched, palm inward. Remember not to swing. You're shooting your right arm out straight and fast. Simultaneously, you are stepping forward with your left foot and throwing all your body weight behind that right, with your right shoulder following through on the blow. If you can practice it, like on a tree or a pillow, try to get a snap into the punch just at the instant of impact. This puts an extra kick into it. It's the speed that counts, and hurts. Try, too, to be pushing off your toes when hitting. But not so much that you lose balance. You might have to hit him again (if you miss, if he's big, if he blocked or partially blocked the punch) so you've got to get back into position, ready to throw another.

If thrown correctly and connected, the straight right is one of the surest ways of knocking an enemy out. The two critical factors are getting an opening to throw it and then delivering it properly. Correctly done, you can walk away from that 90-pound weakling on the beach and continue building sandcastles.

Sgt. Fatso Judson [Ernest Borgnine] and Pvt. Maggio [Frank Sinatra] Sunday punch each other in From Here to Eternity.

Left Hook To Jaw

"Gentleman Jim" Corbett thought this one up. He was considered a "most scientific" pugilist and this punch's synonym, the "Corbett Hook," was what put the great John L. Sullivan away on a hot muggy day in New Orleans in 1892. Corbett had adapted the inside right hook and moved it over to the other hand, keeping his right free for the straight.

You start throwing this hummer as a straight left, aiming a bit to the side of your opponent's head. Halfway through the swing, you change its path and bring it around to the guy's jaw. While your man is still looking for a straight left that's going to miss, you connect at his jaw—*pow!*

The right hook to the jaw is also powerful pugilistic dynamite. It's not wide, but a short, swinging arced jolt that snaps on impact.

Two bloated specimens demonstrate the fine art of Sumo wrestling in Tokyo, 1965. A centuries-old tradition, early matches were often fought to the death. The practitioners of this fine art lead a regimented life of over-indulgence and spiritual piety. Eating is the beginning and end of a Sumo wrestler's concerns. Contestants often top the scales at 400 pounds.

The Solar Plexus Punch

Well, times change and this was the one that wiped out "Gentleman Jim" and gave Bob Fitzsimmons the heavyweight title in 1897. It's a paralyzing blow to the pit of the stomach and it hurts one helluva lot. It doesn't always knock a guy out but if you land one, you can follow up with anything and even have some time to think about it.

Fitz used his hand when throwing it, but the right will work as well. Again, the idea is to feint the guy into being receptive to it, like shooting a straight right but pulling it back. When his hands go up to cover his face, *kerplow!* in the gut.

Figure that while you were dusting off that right feint, your left was drawn back a ways, close to your body, elbow bent, palm up, ready. The footwork is a little different. With the left-handed throw, you're stepping forward with your left foot. Get up on your toes a bit while delivering so you get some of that leg power into the punch.

This Sunday punch is only good for serious fights. Don't mess with it among friends. It smarts an awful lot.

The Liver Punch

Another of the more sickening punches to deliver for consummate effect, is a quick hard left to the liver, one of the larger, more vital organs of the body. The blow throws the liver into a bit of shock which, in turn, causes a weak, sinking sensation. It's not knockout stuff, but it does enough damage to allow you a couple more good shots.

The liver is a bit to the right of center in the stomach area (left, as you face an opponent), and that makes it almost directly in line with your left fist. So you need to throw a left hook, straight driving left or an uppercut. Stick him just below the base of the ribs. An upward motion has a more telling effect because it drives the fist up into the liver. *Shlooosh!* and he's helpless.

The Heart Punch

Very few boxers use it these days but that doesn't mean it's not a good punch. Gene Tunney flattened Jack Dempsey with it and he was no slouch. It's a good punch because you don't have to put much power into it to have an effect. Even a medium strength blow will slow a guy up for the k.o. hummer.

Like the liver punch, a good heart-felt stinger will weaken a dude, give him that same creepy, crawly sensation and may even make it difficult for him to breathe. What you do is zap him with a straight left or right. Also effective are the hooks and uppercut. Aim straight for the heart or a bit low. Don't highside it. If you miss going low, you've still got a good crack at the solar plexus and liver.

The Uppercut

One of the great loves of boxers is the good ol' reliable uppercut: the one that Primo Carnera used on Jack Sharkey, the one that Dempsey laid on Fred Fulton. It was the best punch of one of the greatest fighters who ever lived: Jack Johnson. When Johnson hit Stanley Ketchell, the then middleweight champion, with an uppercut, Ketchell fell like he'd been hit with a steel girder. He was out for more than an hour and when he came to he found that all his front teeth were missing.

You have to be close to uppercut. With your right arm bent at the elbow, palm upward, arm close to the body, you just step forward with your left foot, knees slightly bent and, as you shoot your fist up to your opponent's chin or body, you straighten out your knees. Also, turn your waist to the left sharply and put your body and shoulders into the blow.

Naturally, with the uppercut to the body, the idea is to go for the solar plexus, the liver or the heart.

The Mastoid Punch

Another good place for a Sunday punch to roost is the mastoid bone, located just behind either ear. A good rap in the mastoid will minimally cause dizziness or maximally put out all the lights. Use the hook, left or right, standing somewhere to the side of your opponent. Now, no fair hitting the guy on the back of the neck. That's a rabbit punch and it's only useful in serious fighting.

—Probably the man who packed the most powerful punch was a Greek native of Thasos. Theogenes lived about 900 B.C. He was, by all accounts incredibly strong, skillful and meaner than a junkyard dog. He fought 1,425 opponents, and killed every one of them.

—The days when boxers put it all on the line ended in 1892 when "Gentleman" Jim Corbett knocked out John L. Sullivan in the 21st round with a scientifically executed left hook. It was a winner-take-all bout and Corbett won $25,000, leaving the great John L. dead broke, with only his bellow intact ("I can lick any man in the house!").

—Freddie Welsh, the world lightweight champ during World War I, fought three title fights in one day and won them all by knockouts! Subsequently, his manager, Harry Pollock, arranged a bout with a New York flash named Benny Leonard. Welsh went in cocky as a jaybird and came out cold, in the ninth round. After the fight, Welsh discovered that his manager had taken his purse and blown it at the race track. Welsh attacked Pollock and, it is reliably reported, bit off his ear.

—Henry Armstrong is the only boxer who ever held three boxing championships simultaneously. And he won them all in the course of one year. On October 29, 1937, he became the world featherweight champion by knocking out Petey Sarron in the sixth round. Seven months later, on May 31, 1938, he won a 15-round decision from Barney Ross and took the welterweight crown. Two and one-half months after that, on August 17, 1938, he decisioned Lou Ambers for the lightweight crown at Madison Square Garden. As Armstrong tells about it later, the whole idea of winning the three championships were conceived by his three managers, jazz singer Al Jolson, cinema badman George Raft, and Eddie Mead. "They came up with the idea," said Armstrong, "that I had to get superpopular, colossal. They had those words in Hollywood—colossal, stupendous, and all like that. I said 'Well, what do you mean colossal, stupendous? I'm that already. I've had 27 fights and 26 knockouts. What do you want me to do?' So they said, 'We want you to win three championships.'"

IT USED TO BE CALLED DIRTY FIGHTING

Yeah, it used to be called that but we cleaned up the act. Here's a pointed kick to the temple.

Now that Bruce Lee has delivered his terrifying rear thunderbolt kick to our temples, and we're all at least talented amateurs of the martial arts, (everybody knows about the backhand slash to the jaw, the eye gouge, the groin kick and so on) let's talk straight.

What they call "martial arts" in Asia, when you come right down to it, is what we've always called "dirty fighting." I mean, let's face it. If you're good at "dirty fighting" you're good at "martial arts": eye gouging, ball kicking and what have you.

There's nothing dishonorable about that at all. In fact, it explains how the famous "martial arts" systems can be kept so "secret"—in the same way that everyone in this country doesn't exactly know how to make a zip-gun, or the proper inflection of the secret mantra, "Hey, yer shoelace is untied!" As the Chinese themselves will tell you, "One does not make a prostitute out of an honest girl, nor a soldier out of an honorable man."

Nevertheless, we all know who's tougher in a contest between a "dirty fighter" and a regular guy.

But what about a contest between *two* dirty (or, as they say, "trained") fighters? That's the question all Hong Kong is asking.

Karate Karate is an adaptation of Chinese boxing to Okinawan politics. The Okinawans came under Japanese domination in the 17th century, and all weapons were banned. In the best tradition of "dirty fighting," the Okinawans invented the *te* system, which simply means "hand." *Kara-te* means "Chinese hand."

The Okinawans developed combat karate in conjunction with innocuous-looking weapons, for instance, they became masters of the *nunchaku* (the thing Bruce Lee is so expert with, when he fights off ten attackers). The *nunchaku* is actually nothing more than a rice flail, but in the hands of an expert it is one of the most deadly weapons under the gun.

The "animal" forms are not favored in karate, as they are in Chinese boxing. It is a direct, aggressive art, which does not necessitate great physical strength. Circular movements are used in stepping, turning, blocking and parrying. Those movements are practiced in formal, structured exercises, called *kata,* which follow a specific format. For instance, the *sanchin kata,* a master's style, emphasizes the correct use of the eyes, the breath and the posture. It proceeds like an elephant train from the *sanchin* stance, where the toes and knees are turned inward and the eyes never leave the opponent.

Sanchin breathing is slow and natural, as if "smelling the air." When the body rises or withdraws, one inhales; when it lowers or extends, one exhales.

The *sanchin* step is circular, protecting the groin while closing in on the adversary.

The chief feature of karate, of course, is the corkscrew punch. It's the same punch that made Kid McCoy the great middleweight champion he was. It is believed that the corkscrew motion actually creates shock waves that make the blow more penetrating. The target is literally "sucked" into the blow. However, a hardened target, such as a stomach like an oak plank, can break your wrist with this kind of punch. So, some versions of karate use the conventional "standing fist" punch, with only a half-twist, which was Jack Dempsey's punch, incidentally. What Dempsey said about boxing applies equally to karate: "The essence of boxing is *exploding body-weight.*"

Karate blocking and parrying follow the Chinese *pa-kua* principles of circular defense, which either intercept the attack or deflect it.

The famous karate kicks are generally snap kicks, delivered in a straight line. Although they pack a great deal of power, the extra time they take to be delivered can be a disadvantage —particulary the "roundhouse kick," added by the Japanese.

Judo Judo is the moral equivalent of war. It became popular in Japan in 1882, as its predecessor, *jujitsu,* began to decay. Judo is a synthetic form of jujitsu, emphasizing physical education and culture. In its modern form, frankly, you couldn't win a fight against Woody Allen.

The main feature of judo, providing its inestimable contribution to the art of warfare, is the knowledge of the correct way and time to yield. The phrase that has come down is, "use the opponent's strength to defeat him."

Sport judo, therefore, is full of break-balances, breakfalls, and push-and-pull circular throws using the hip or ankle as a fulcrum.

Modern judo also stresses pins, like the one where you crook your right arm under the bastard's neck and grab your own left wrist, so that if he makes one little move it's goodbye, grandpa.

There are also some judo holds and locks left over from the martial days of the 1880's (judo was originally *not* intended for sport), like the nice little defense against a knife attack which leaves you holding the knife and the other guy with a broken arm.

Judo was founded by a man named J. Kano who based it on what he called the "Principle of the Best Use of Energy" and the equally delightful "Principle of Mutual Welfare." He cautioned against the misuse of mental and physical energy, and against the rowdyism that had made jujitsu synonymous with wart-hogs.

Judo is governed by the Kodokan school, which is Kano's school. It has developed the famous ranking system of *kyu* and *dan,* third degree black belt.

Karate vs. judo, for my money, is like guns vs. butter. Let's get back to Bruce Lee, who was actually Jerry Lewis with muscles.

Argentine *Antonio Rocca flashes his subtle form as he kicks another villain into oblivion.*

Kung Fu *Kung fu* is actually not a fighting art. No, that would be *wu-shu,* also known as *san-shou, wu-wei* and *tzu-jan.*

But we all know what we mean by kung fu, so might as well get on with it and not worry about the accuracy of the name. We mean that amazingly effective and deadly style of fighting which is known by all Chinese, Jews and Latins, and makes them invincible, sexy and powerful. We mean, in particular, the style known as *jeet kuen do,* whose chief practitioner was the one and only Jerry Lewis-playing-the-toughest-guy-in-the-world. The Little Dragon himself, Bruce "Fists of Fury" Lee.

You *know* Bruce Lee could *pulverize* Woody Allen.

Jeet Kuen Do is the direct streetfighting style taught by Master Hu Flung Pu of Hong Kong. That's where Bruce Lee learned it. One of its most charming features is the "spear hand," where you literally use your hand like a spear, and it comes out the back between the third and fifth floating ribs.

The only fully accredited training school for *jeet kuen do* is on Hester Street, between A and B in New York, where they call it *Ringolevio.* There are no rules to speak of. One gang tries to capture all the members of the other gang. The only thing that keeps the National Guard out is the fact that each gang has a chalked-off jail, where by mutual agreement prisoners must stay unless they can (1) overpower the jailers; or, (2) get released by someone on their team.

There's also *Shaolin Kung Fu,* whose current master is the immensely tough Kao Fang-hsien of Taipei. It's more formal than *Ringolevio,* but seems quite as effective in its own way. The basic philosophy of *Shaolin,* as expressed by every immortal sage from Lao-tse on down, is summed up in the ancient Oriental dictum, "Get there firstest with the mostest."

The eight basic postures of *Shaolin Kung Fu* are as follows: the horse-riding step (which stops speeding express trains), the crouching step (which catches bullets in mid-flight), the lowering step (which can evade radar and "smart" bombs), the "Ting" step (which destroys major cities), the "four-six" step (which confounds even German scientists), the standing step (which lords it over kings), the sitting step (which wards off tigers) and the "bow" step (which pushes back nuclear flotillas).

So, in the time-honored tradition of the Jewish promoter, always remembering the words of Max Landesman ("Let's you and him fight!), I hereby challenge Muhammad Ali to duke it out with Mr. Kao Fang-hsien, anytime, anyplace, but preferably Hardesty Park at four o'clock. *Be there!*

Bradford, England

A new world record was set here yesterday when 15 karate experts demolished a house in six hours by blows with their hands, heads and feet.

"It was a well-built house but it was a worthwhile challenge," said team leader Phil Milner of the 6-room, 150-year-old house.

Milner, who is secretary of the International Judo Association, said the real obstacle was the fireplace. "We must have toppled over three tons in one go," Milner said proudly.

Two hundred spectators cheered as the team worked on the house with their bare feet and karate suits. Team members took turns as battering rams.

When the house was demolished, the team lined up and bowed towards the heap of masonry. The bow is part of the traditional Kojo ceremony in honor of a defeated opponent.

MASTERS OF THE FOIL, ÉPEÉ AND SABER

By David Saltman

Now that dueling is unfortunately banned, fencing has become a combination of athletic ability, chess and The Three Musketeers. In its sport form, it is probably more like chess than anything else, chess with muscles.

The masters of tournament fencing are the Hungarians, the Italians, the French and the Germans. The Hungarians excel with sabers, which they practically invented, or, more accurately, lifted from the Arabs after getting conquered by them and their famous scimitars. The Italians are masters of the *rapier,* in fighting and in wit.

In some parts of Europe, fencing still has high priority on the list of things every well-brought-up young man ought to know. Wherever blue blood still flows and ancestral lands are still kept, wherever the traditions of religion and patriarchy still flourish, you will find champion fencers. In Germany, for instance, they still vigorously practice the sport of *Schlager,* a vicious kind of fencing with glaives. Points are scored by scarring the opponent, and many is the German, even today, who wears his Schlager scars proudly.

Even in the United States, there is a tradition of swordfighting. For instance, it was only about 40 or 50 years ago that the cavalry sword was regulation equipment for every soldier in the U.S. Army. It was a telling weapon especially since a rifle is worthless when you're aiming from atop a moving horse. Under those circumstances, you need a saber.

But on the international fencing circuit, frankly, Americans have made little imprint. Recently, interest in the sport has been developing among collegians with the University of Pennsylvania and New York University probably being the strongest fencing schools.

Fencing is strictly an amateur sport, on all levels. Sharp promoters, en garde!

The Masters

Aldo Naldi, of Italy, is a master of the *derobement,* an advanced epee maneuver which consists of repeated "disengages" while holding the point of the epee against the opponent's wrist. In frustration, the adversary usually impales his own arm!

Count von Koenigsmarken, of Poland, the inventor of the modern fencing foil, was the finest fencer in Central Europe at the time when fencing decided all disputes of honor. He died in 1700, in an ambush of twelve master swordsmen, 10 of whom he defeated before meeting his death when a fly got into his open collar and spoiled his timing.

Christian Noel, of France, was the 1973 World's Individual Foil Champion. Scion of an old French family which traces its ancestry directly to Cardinal Richelieu, he is himself a master swordsman and strategist. (Richelieu, of course, was the man who brought two kingdoms to war because he had been humiliated into dancing a *sarabande* before the Queen.) Noel himself specializes in ripostes and counterparries.

Valentina Nikonova, of Russia is the World's Women's Individual Foil Champion. She hails from the Tambov province where skill with swords is legendary. It is said that Nikonova once defeated a master swordsman with nothing but a brush.

Aldo Mario Montano, of Italy, is the World's Saber Champion. The champion team is from Hungary, but Montano is the singles champion, mainly owing to his skill in the *fleche* and the *tempo cut.* He walks around his native village of Binaca with a saber on his hip, challenging everyone, even dogs and women.

—The first known sword belonged to Saragon, the first King of Ur. It's about 5,000 years old.

—The most treasured sword in the world is the Divine Sword of Japan. More than 2,000 years old, it is called the Rusanagino Tsurugi. A legendary sword, when it was moved in 1935 to a new shrine in Nagoya, 500,000 people took part in the procession.

—A Spanish army captain named Conzalvo de Cordova invented the hand guard which he called the *pas d'ane.* Cordova died in 1515 and his sword is in the Madrid Museum.

—The foil was used for practice, in place of the court sword, beginning in the 17th century.

—The epee became a popular weapon in the mid-1800s.

—The light saber, an invention of the Italians, became prominent in the late 1800s.

—The most individual world titles, four each, have been won by Jerzy Pawlowski of Poland and Christian d'Oriola of France. Pawlowski won with the saber, d'Oriola with the foil. D'Oriola also won two Olympic gold medals in the foil.

—Italy has won the men's foil team world championship 13 times.

—Hungary has won the saber team world championship 13 times, the Olympic gold medal nine times.

—Italy has won the epee team world championship 10 times, the Olympic gold medal six times.

—Hungary has won the women's foil team championship 11 times.

—France has won the men's foil team Olympic gold medal five times.

Galino Gorokhova of Russia and Pilar Roldan parry in the 1964 Olympic games at Tokyo. Gorokhova won the gold.

Douglas Fairbanks ripostes a dastardly villain in the classic style of, yes, Douglas Fairbanks.

A SHORT GLOSSARY OF FENCING TERMS

Disengage to shift one's blade from one side of an opponent's blade to the other.

Epee A fencing sword having a bowl-shaped guard and a rigid 35-inch blade with no cutting edge. Its fluted triangular section tapers to a small point blunted with a metal stop. Weighs no more than a foil or saber.

Fleche A method of reaching the opponent consisting of one or more rapid steps forward beginning with the rear foot.

Foil Fencing sword resembling the epee but with a flat guard and a lighter, more flexible blade of rectangular or square cross section tapering to a blunt point.

Glaive A broadsword.

Parry To ward off a weapon or blow.

Rapier A straight, two-edged sword with a narrow pointed blade.

Riposte A fencer's quick return thrust following a successful parry.

Saber Light sword with an arc-shaped guard and tapering flexible blade of fluted H section that is not more than 41 3/8 inches long and has one full cutting edge and an eight inch cutting edge on the back at the tip.

Tempo Cut Tempo cuts are generally directed at an opponent's head. They are a fast cut or thrust as the opponent prepares to attack. They succeed only if executed with lightning speed and in good tempo.

Scoring To score a hit the fencer has to strike his opponent's target area with the sword point. In saber, a cut with the edge or top third of the back edge also counts. The fencer must be on the fencing area, the *piste*, for his hit to count. Hits that land off the target in foil and saber become valid if the fencer who is hit has taken up an extreme position to avoid being hit on target.

THE FASTEST GAME IN THE WORLD

By Peter Delacorte

That damned ball comes at the rather rapid rate of 160 mph. And jai-alai players don't duck!

Part of jai-alai's visual excitement, opposite right, *is how men climb walls for shots.*

The wicker basket cesta *is a blur,* below, *as a player in the Miami* fronton *releases the ball, or* pelota, *which will slam into the front wall at a speed of about 160 mph.*

Going to jai-alai in Mexico City is a little like going to dinner in Marseilles: a good place for an elegant date, and just as good for the sleaze of the sleaze. There is betting involved, and heroism. So you get a crowd who gets off on superstars, and people just out for a little extra *plata*.

Jai-alai itself emerged from the Basque country in that mysterious mountainous land between France and Spain called Catalonia. The game still retains the curious flavor of something invented by 17th Century gypsies. It is ingrown as a royal house (the world's greatest players are all Basques, even today) and reeks with the taste of people isolated from conquering hordes and bonded by an ancient esoteric language. Jai-alai came to the Americans with the Spanish pirates and until recently was in the hands of the privateers of Miami Beach. Drawing 14,000 people a night, the Miami Fronton is right up there with dog racing.

The Fronton Mexico, the largest in the country, has the flavor of a high-class race track. There are trophies and pictures of past superstars out in the lobby, alongside displays of famous *cestas* (the wicker baskets used to catch and throw the ball) and *pelotas*, the balls.

Jai-alai is played capably by scores of Mexicans, Cubans, non-Basque Spaniards and even a few Americans. But the giants of the game have always been very short Basques, stocky men who appear hardly athletic by American standards. But after the sharp crack of the ball against the granite front wall, after the eye adjusts to the incredible speed of a front court rally, a newcomer is entranced by the lightning reflexes, the acceleration and the miraculous body control in even the squattest Basque *pelotari*. The guy may be 35-years-old and 25 pounds overweight, but he's been playing this game since he was five and his legs are hard as the *frontis*, the front wall.

The jai-alai court has three walls: the *frontis* is exactly one and a half times as wide as the front wall on a handball court but the distance from the front wall to the rear wall, at 176 feet, is four times that of the equivalent handball distance. An enormous wire net protects us spectators from the astounding kill power (and quite a few players have died) of the ball. The ball can get going to 160 miles an hour off the *cesta*, and that's fast. That's fast enough to call jai-alai the "fastest game in the world." (For comparison, Bob Feller's fast ball was timed at 98.6 m.p.h. while a golf ball has been clocked at 170 m.p.h.)

There's plenty of action on the floor, of course, with the players smashing their *rebotes, cortadas, dos paredes* and other specialized shots off one, two or three walls. The rule is that action must be continuous—you can't bobble the ball in the *cesta* or you lose the point. In fact, the ball must be caught in the *cesta* and thrown in a continuous motion to the *frontis*, and be played within the green areas on the walls.

But for me, at any fronton, and especially in Mexico City the real action is in the spectators' gallery. There are eight men down at court-side, wearing white coats and red berets. They do nothing but shout out numbers constantly (*"Mil ochenta, mil ochenta; mil noventa, mil noventa,"*) while they toss and catch tennis balls with the people in the crowd.

The red berets are the bookies. The numbers they're shouting are the odds—but they change with every point. It is possible in Mexican jai-alai to force yourself to win money. You have to be quick, incredibly quick, but you can actually back yourself to win no matter what happens by placing a bet on one player at favorable odds, and then when the odds change you can place the same bet in the other direction. The tennis balls have slits in them. The bookies toss them unerringly into the stands. The spectators put a slip of paper inside with tier bets and toss them back down. The bookies, by some legerdemain known only to them, never lose track.

Of course, it's much easier to bet jai-alai in Miami or Vegas and pretty soon you can watch and bet in Newport, R.I., or at any one of three Connecticut cities, Bridgeport, Hartford, and Milford. At least on our side of the Rio Grande, the betting will be done in English.

The Superstars

It is traditionally the flashy front court player who takes all the glory in jai-alai. The back court player's main duty is to keep the ball in play, and these are particularly lean times for back court men. Also, jai-alai superstars go by one name only. The two best back court men, Churruca and Larranaga, are unfortunately *personae non grata* in Florida, but they play elsewhere.

Churruca stands head and shoulders above the rest, but at 37 he is past his prime, as is "Chucho" Larranaga. Considered by many to have been the finest back courter ever, Chucho is still active at 45. With them out, though, that leaves Miami's Irigo and Tampa's Gorrono as the best in America.

There is no such scarcity of front court stars, however. West Palm Beach boasts a formidable tandem in Elu and Solozabal, Miami offers Asis (absurdly tall at 6'3"), Rufina and an Israeli-born American named Joey. In Las Vegas one may find the elderly but infinitely cagy Lecube.

Still, the true aristocracy are only on view in Spain: Egurbide, age 34, is perhaps on the decline, but Guisasola, now 30, is in his prime and Ondarres, when he's in the mood, plays the front court like no one before or since.

The Most Popular Shots

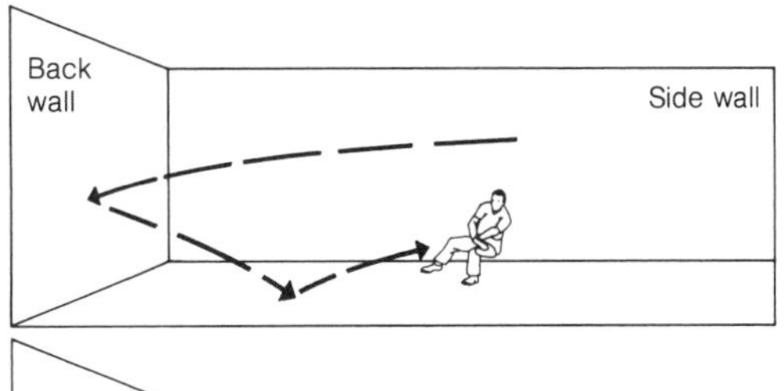

Rebote—Returning the ball from the back wall with the forehand or backhand.

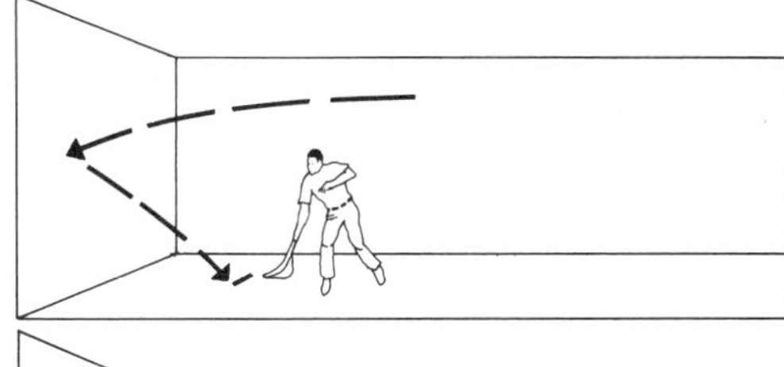

Bote Pronto—A ball that is literally picked-up underhand by the player after a very short bounce.

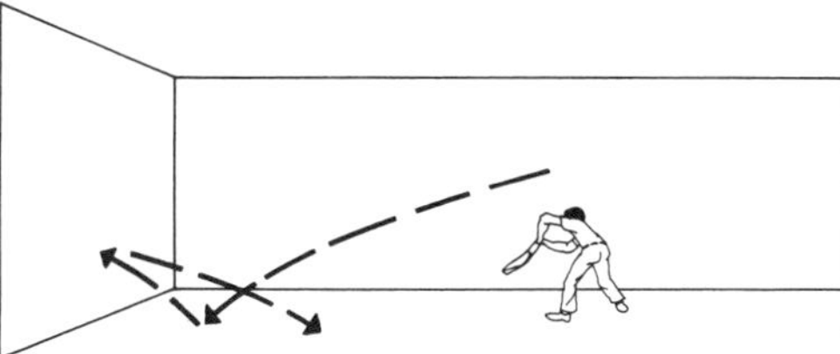

Chic Chac—A ball returned to the floor near the back wall, then to the back wall and back to the floor.

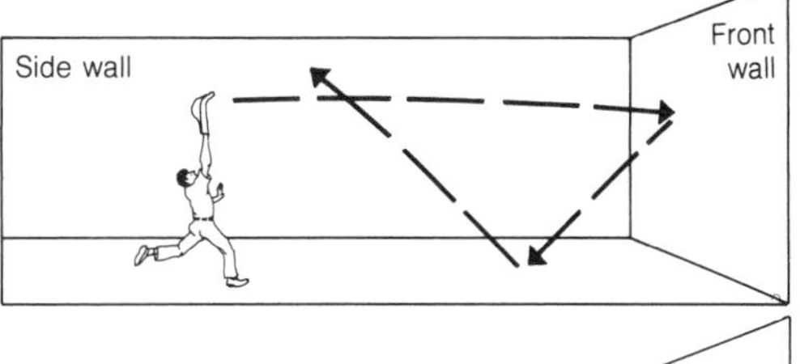

Bote Corrido—Must be thrown directly overhand with great wrist snap after first bounce goes very high.

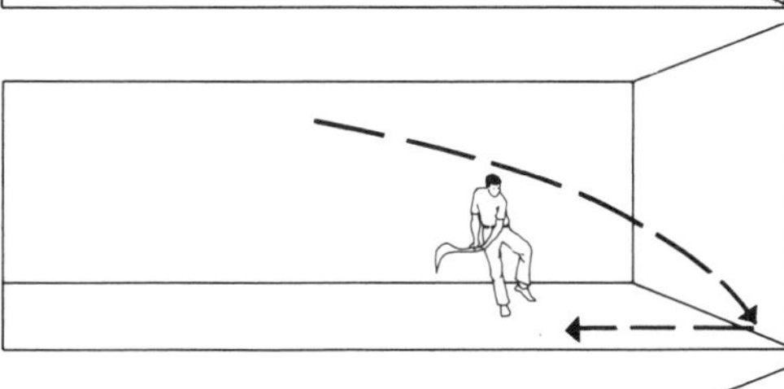

Chula—Ball hits the lower angle between the base of the back wall and the floor coming out without a bounce.

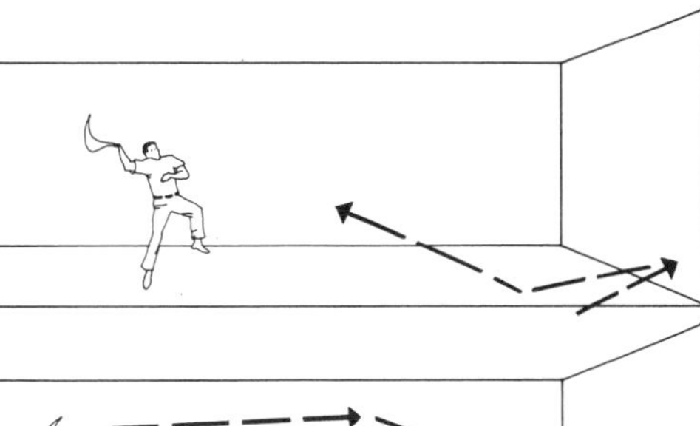

Cortada—A ball thrown from outside of the court with the forehand, hitting low on the front wall then on the floor.

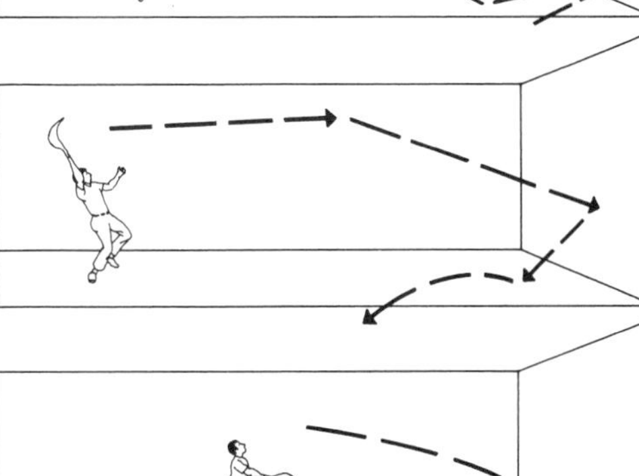

Carom—A thrown ball that hits the side wall, the front wall, the court then goes into the screen.

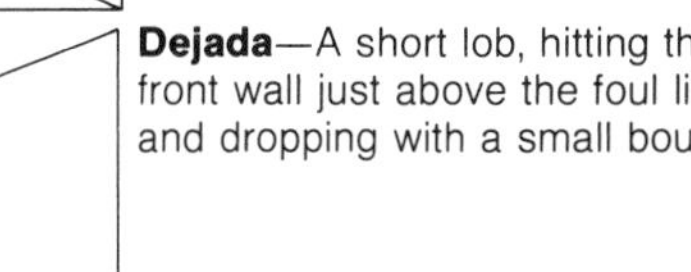

Dejada—A short lob, hitting the front wall just above the foul line and dropping with a small bounce.

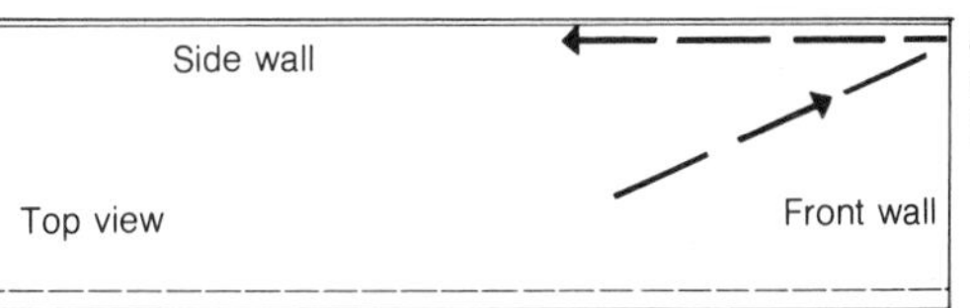

Arrimada—A ball that is returned as close to the side wall as possible, hindering the opposition's return.

Here's How You Wager At Jai-alai

Win You wager that a team (or player) will win the game. Tickets are $2 and $5.
Place You wager that team will finish first or second. Whether you team is first or second you receive the price shown alongside "Place" on the scoreboard. Tickets: $2 and $5.
Show You wager that a team will finish at least third. You receive price shown alongside "Show" on scoreboard. Tickets: $2 and $5.
Quiniela You pick two teams to finish first and second in any order. Regardless of which of your teams wins or is second, you receive the "Quiniela" price. Trickets: $2 and $5.
Quiniela Perfecta You pick two teams to finish first and second in that order, e.g.: if you pick teams 2 and 5 it means 2 must win and 5 must come in second. Tickets are $3 each and have paid well over $1,500.00.
Double You must pick the winners of two different consecutive games. Doubles are scheduled regularly throughout each performance. Tickets are $3.
Advance Wagering Both Miami and Tampa Jai-alai provide an advance wagering service. Patrons who desire to leave early can wager on all remaining games at the Advance Betting Counter located in the Main Lobby. Patrons can also wager on the following day's program at the same counter. Winning tickets may not be cashed until the following day.
How Jai-alai Differs Although betting at Jai-alai is the same as at horse and dog tracks, the *action* is far, far different! Unlike races that are over in seconds, every Jai-alai game lasts from 10 to 15 minutes or more, with no timeouts, with each player running into position as the next point begins. Even between games, the next game's players are practicing the most difficult shots, providing more continuous action for spectators than any other sport!
Quiniela Boxing You increase your chance of winning by tying up all possible combinations on a three-number box. For example, if you purchase tickets on 2-3-5, you have three numbers tied up: 2-3, 2-5 and 3-5. A win in any of these combinations gives you the quiniela price. When wagering just ask for your three numbers. This costs $6.
Perfecta Boxing To tie up all possible combinations on a three-number box, you buy six tickets. If your numbers are 2-3-5, you receive tickets on 2-3, 2-5, 3-5, 3-2, 5-2 and 5-3. When wagering ask for the perfecta box. This costs $18.
Wheeling In a quiniela wheel you tie up one team or player (post position) with all others in the game. In a six-team game you buy five tickets; seven teams, 6 tickets; eight teams, 7 tickets.

Scoring A match is played for a number of points, ranging from 6 (singles) to 40. Only the server scores. He gains a point if his opponent: [1] returns the ball after it's bounced more than once; [2] misses the ball; [3] does not return the ball on to the *frontis*; [4] plays the ball on to the floor next to the screen; [5] fails to catch the ball and throw it in one continous motion.
Officials There are three judges, standing opposite lines 4, 7, and 11. Officials traditionally wear tuxedos and carry rackets to protect themselves from the fast-moving ball.
The *Pelota* The *pelota* (ball) has a hard rubber core which is covered with one layer of linen thread and two layers of goatskin. It's two inches in diameter and weighs 4½ ounces.
Dress Players wear white trousers, a colored sash or belt, a white or colored numbered shirt, white rubber-soled shoes, and a helmet.

Betting

If you know the racetrack, you know how to bet on American jai-alai, the difference being that in jai-alai the emphasis is off simple win-place-show and on the exotic bets, like the *quiniela,* the *perfecta,* the daily double (there may be *eight* on a given night), and, God help us, the *Big Q,* which involves picking win and place teams in successive games—at odds of 783-to-1.

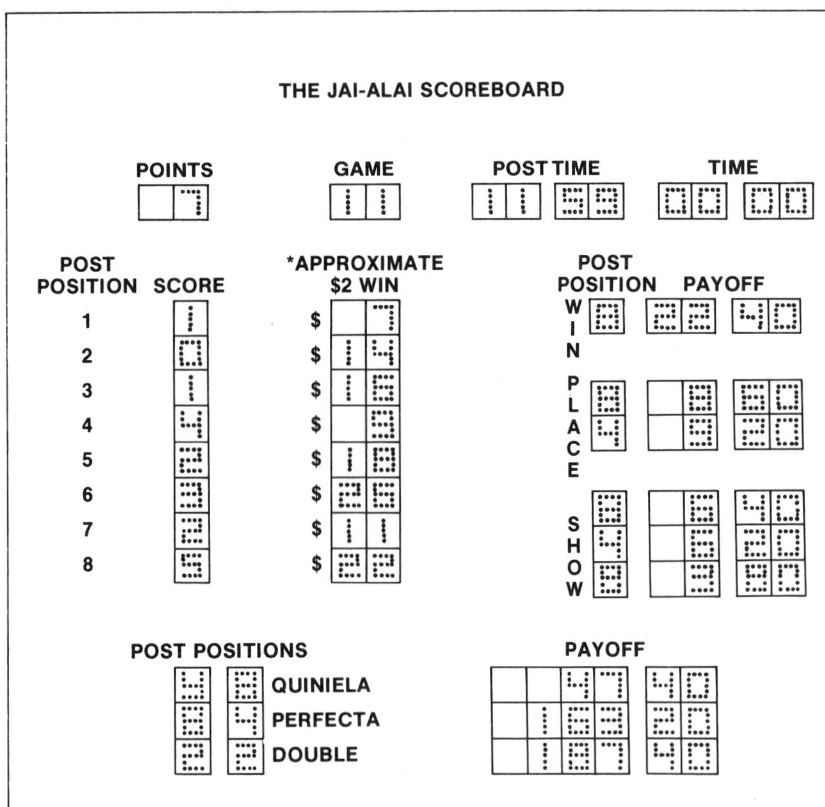

*Approximate $2 Win: represents the potential earnings for WIN ONLY on each post position. Based on final odds. (You will note that prior to start of game odds will fluctuate.) Final odds are based only on money wagered in public "win" pool and have no relation to any other prices.

Betting is heavy at all nine Florida frontons. At the Miami Fronton, for example, $500,000 is wagered nightly. At Dania's Jai-alai Palace, $26 million was bet last season. Spectators sit back in comfy theatre seats, negotiating with the runners, or they can adjourn to cocktail lounges and first class restaurants to watch the action on closed circuit television. Generally, though, the betting system is the same as at race tracks, but with a few innovations.

The Court

Imagine a gigantic squash court, 176 feet long and 40 feet wide, with walls 45 feet high. Now take away the ceiling and replace it with an arched screen, and take away one of the side walls so you can watch the game, and you've got a jai-alai court, or *cancha.* Ideally, the front wall will be made of granite and all the other surfaces of gunite, a particularly hard form of concrete.

Rules Of The Game

Following the serve, which must land in a designated service area (in Spain one fault is allowed, in America none), the squash analogy continues: the ball may hit any combination of playing surfaces but may bounce on the floor only once per exchange. Should the ball bounce twice, or strike any out-of-bounds area (a metal plate at the base of the front wall, the ceiling screen, or the wooden floor separating the *cancha* from the audience), the point is over. Unique to jai-alai is a rule which requires that every throw be a continuation of every catch; you can't catch the ball, fall down, get up, and throw the ball—rather, you must catch the ball and throw it in the act of falling down.

a Workingman's Guide to Handball

It's somewhat unfortunate, but a lot of people think that slapping a small green ball against a large wall is dumb. If that were ture there would be quite a few dumb people running around.

However, there is absolutely no connection whatever between handball and dumbness—in fact, it is one of the most exacting, demanding games in sports. Actually, handball and its variations racquetball and squash are easy games to learn. But they are also quite deceiving. It looks rather simple when someone hits a ball against a wall . . . but how about trying to hit the little bugger against that wall a second time? And that, my friends, is the simple, and sometimes complicated essence of all three games.

Handball is a game of angles, position, quick reflexes and a lot of perspiration. Unlike other games such as tennis, it does not particularly demand speed. Agility, however, is essential. Of the three variations, handball is the oldest. It originated in Ireland in the 11th or 12th century and grew into a national Irish sport by the 1800s. Handball was then known as the "game of fives" (because of the use of the five fingers). Yet even in the 1800s there were a few people who persisted in the false assumption that the sport was dumb.

One of the more eloquent refutations of this was written by British essayist William Hazlitt mourning the death of an old-time Irish "fives" champion. "It may be said," Hazlitt wrote, "that there are things of more importance than striking a ball against a wall—there are things indeed which make more noise and do as little good, such as making war and peace, making speeches and answering them, making verses and blotting them; making money and throwing it away. But the game of fives is what no one despises who has ever played it. It is the finest exercise for the body, and the best relaxation for the mind."

Handball was brought to the United States by an Irishman named Phil Casey in 1882. In fact, the first home of U.S. handball was Brooklyn, where Casey first settled. But as he soon learned, bringing *a* handball to America was far easier than bringing the entire game. When Casey arrived in Brooklyn, he professed his dissatisfaction with the New World. He couldn't find any handball players. Even worse, he couldn't find any handball courts.

That dilemma did not last long. Casey's solution was to get some quick financing and build a 65-foot long, 25-foot wide handball court. Those who wanted to play paid, and with the revenue from the new players, Casey became a handball entrepreneur.

In the following years, America began to recognize handball—not as a sport as much as a pastime. When firemen weren't putting out fires they were playing handball against the firehouse wall.

But soon, it became an established competitive sport. In 1915 the Detroit Athletic Club held an invitational tournament. By 1950, the United States Handball Association was formed. Today more than 5 million people play the game in the U.S. alone.

Up to the 1900s the game had been played with a hard ball on a court of four walls. The ball, however, proved unsatisfactory and a smaller, softer ball was introduced. And people began playing on one-wall courts as well.

Now the ball is the same for both type games, weighing about 23 ounces and measuring 1-7/8 inches in diameter. but court dimensions differ. The one-wall game has a smaller front of 16 feet and its playing surface, usually concrete or cement, is 20 feet wide by 34 feet long. The four-wall court is 23 feet wide and 23 feet high and 46 feet long with a back wall 10 feet high.

In one-wall handball a 16-foot high front wall and a floor 34 by 20 feet comprise the two playing surfaces. The contestants stand near one another and play the ball in turn off the wall. Victory in a game goes to the first side scoring 21 points, and only the serving side can score. Matches are usually awarded to the first side winning two games.

The use of the foot, or of any portion of the body excepting one hand is barred. (In the old days players could and would kick the ball, a technique still practiced in the Irish game.)

The server stands anywhere he desires in the serving zone and begins the game by dropping the ball to the floor between the short line and the service line. He strikes it with the hand on the first bounce. It must first hit the front wall and then rebound on the floor back of the front line and within or on the two sidelines and rear line. The serve may not be volleyed.

After the serve, players on both sides pay no attention to any lines except the outside ones that bound the court. The idea is to hit the ball off the wall so hard that it cannot be handled, or so low that it cannot be reached in time, or at so clever an angle the opponent cannot touch it, or in such a manner that the opponent is forced into error when trying to return it. The chief requirements are that the ball must be hit with one hand, must strike the

It's a game of angles, position, and quick reflexes. But don't forget the sweat.

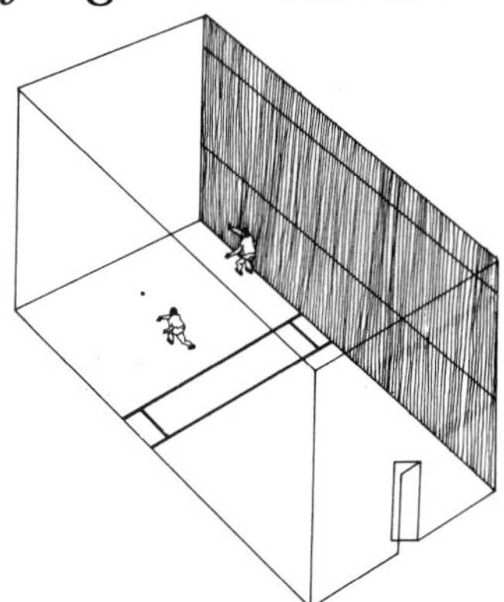

Scoring The first player or team that scores 21 points wins the game. Only the serving side winning the volley scores the point. If the non-serving side wins the volley (or rally), the serve passes to that side.

Playing rules You can hit the ball with any part of your hand, but only one hand. You cannot use any other part of the body. Although you're only allowed one touch on the ball, you may take another try on the volley if you've swung and missed completely. (Each legal return is called a volley.)

Equipment You must wear gloves. They should be light in color, made of leather or other such soft material and fit snugly on your hand. You're not allowed to slip horseshoes, steel plates or any other kind of metal under the glove. The glove cannot have webbed fingers. *Psst,* however, wrapping your poor sensitive hands with tape or gauze to prevent bruising is permissible, provided the tape remains underneath the glove. If you're playing hard and are sweating profusely, it's all right to change gloves, since you're not supposed to wet the ball.

Team Handball

Now if you really like the speed of handball, the brutality of a Karate tournament, the smashed shins of soccer, and the rib-crunching body contact of football, we have a game for you. It's called team handball.

Team handball is played by two sides of seven players and five substitutes. The object is to score the most goals. You score goals by passing and dribbling the ball with your hands down a field to throw into a net which is about one-fourth the size of a soccer net. When your team loses possession of the ball, it immediately forms a defensive formation around its goal area. The size of the field, by the way, is 44 yards long by 22 yards wide.

Well, to move the ball and get into position to take a shot, it's okay to tackle. What they mean by tackle is that you can use your arms and hands to get possession of the ball; block an opponent whether that person has the ball or not.

To move the ball around, a player can stop, catch, throw, bounce, or hit the ball in any manner and in any direction using hands, fists, arms, head, body, thighs or knees. You can run with the ball too, but you've got to stop and dribble once for every three steps you take.

Everyone gets to play for two exhausting periods of 30 minutes. A finely tuned hybrid really, combining the high-energy output of soccer with the raucous in-fighting of basketball.

front wall, and upon flying back off the front wall must land somewhere inside the playing rectangle.

There are two main kinds of handball played today. "Fourwall," the original Irish game (traced back to an ancient Irish people called Firbolgs); and one-wall, otherwise known as city handball.

Of the two games, one-wall is faster, and because no back or side walls are used, it requires more speed and stamina to be able to cover a court. But four-wall is without a doubt more scientific.

Traditionally, one-wall has been a spectator sport, since it can be watched from three sides of the court. Four-wall has been handicapped by the simple fact of its court construction. It has left no room for spectators except for a small gallery above a lowered back wall. But this is changing. In recent years, sophisticated glass-walled courts have been introduced, and four-wall handball has begun to outdistance one-wall in popularity.

Still, one-wall handball remains a big part of the urban areas, where four-wall facilities are few and far between.

There are two dangers in handball: one is that one should never play a strenuous game of handball until one learns how to play—when you play, you frequently are exercising muscles that are not even listed in the average physiology textbook. The second danger is—almost as frequently you'll get hit with a ball struck by your opponent. The novice will usually fall to the ground, grimacing in anticipated pain. The veteran handballer will nonchalantly take his beaning and will later overdose on an extra-large tube of Ben-Gay.

Besides the pain, a ball hitting a player or opponent is costly—points are lost, as well as composure. If a ball on its way back from the front wall strikes a player, it is charged against the player hit. Hitting a partner with a ball in doubles is charged against your side.

Although there are great similarities between four-wall and one-wall handball, beginning players would be well-advised to know that the differences are, well, greater. Angles, angles, and angles, dominate four-wall play. The best way to study them (and some people think even *this* is dumb) is to go into a four-wall court alone and play against yourself, trying at the same time to anticipate the angle at which the ball will fly back at you. Most handball games are lost by people unfamiliar with angles. The losers usually depart from such matches with severely bruised shoulders. And that's because they are trying to run to meet the ball from either the front or back walls. This is truly *dumb*. In the hundreds of games I've played, I'm usually beaten by little old men who take perhaps five steps in the entire game. They know the angles so well that the game has almost ceased being good exercise—it's just play.

There is also a great deal of strategic thinking involved. In a singles game, the approach is simple—keep your opponent running. Keep hitting the ball away from him—and then let him try to figure out the angles! More often than not, even a good player will be able to do little more than return your shot, thus setting you up for a kill shot. Kill shots come in a variety of sizes and disguises. And, often, each kill shot can be sometimes explained as a function of the player's age and experience. There are fast kill shots and slow put-aways. Ironically, fast kill shots *can* be returned. And, for the simple reason that they come off the wall fast enough to be handled. Older players are attracted to the slow put-aways, especially when they are pitted against younger players. The younger player will almost always be expecting a fast kill shot, so he'll play away from the front wall. When his opponent gently taps the ball against the wall, he has no other option than to helplessly watch it bounce three times before he can even get near it.

In doubles competition, the secret is once again position. Partners carve out a section of the court they want to cover, and if they are to be successful, hardly leave that area. Good doubles teams normally feature one left-handed player and a right-handed partner. With well-experienced teams, not only is position respected, but so is ball-handling. If a serve is coming down the left side of the court to a right hander, and his partner is playing close to the wall, he usually takes the shot without even letting it bounce. The odds are usually on his side that his return will be better, and stronger than his partner's. The most essential rule in doubles play is that the player with the best shot takes it.

Some serves are simply impossible to return. I once had the opportunity to play against Jimmy Jacobs, who for 10 years was undefeated and reigned as the U.S.H.A. doubles champion, with his partner, Marty Decatur. Jacobs was incredible. I was only able to return four of his serves with any degree of competency. The final score reflected my embarassment only too well: 21-3. However, handball afficionados tell me that even today, my three-point showing was respectable.

Nevertheless, it was one of the few memorable events in my lackluster handball career when I felt dumb. Because all I could do against Jacobs was slap the ball against the wall. And with each of my slaps I got to be a spectator at my own defeat. But it was worth it. I learned the angles, the corners and the tricks. I still get beaten on the courts, but now at least I know why.

A Curling Stone Gathers a Little Ice

The first time I saw a curling match was when I was a small child, and I had the distinct impression that we had arrived too late—there were men with little brooms sweeping frantically, and I was convinced that the hockey game was over and they were cleaning the rink.

But then I noticed that I was not the only person interested in this weird cleanup operation. In fact all the spectators were watching the brooms and the funny looking pucks.

Watching the sweepers, I thought that I was witnessing shuffleboard on ice for masochists. But I have subsequently been proven wrong. Curling is a deadly serious, but thoroughly enjoyable sport. In fact, it is one of the oldest sports in the world. If you can figure out some of the rather "quaint" curling terms—words like pat-lid, wicking, chipping the winner and sooping the ice—you're halfway to playing the game.

Now, if you can only stay on the ice without making a fool of yourself, you can actually participate. No one knows for sure how many centuries the game goes back, but most curling historians (yes, there are such animals) believe the game originated in Scotland. Back in the 16th century, when Mary Stuart was ruling Scotland, it is a safe historical wager that more than a few Scotsmen and their ladies were running—or sliding—on frozen lakes, pushing round boulders at each other and trying to hit a target.

The Scots, you may remember, were also fierce lawn bowlers, and there are those who describe curling as a variation of bowling on ice. Back in the "old days," the curlers used rather crude, natural boulders, drilled with a small hole in which a player was able to insert his thumb to give the rock a twist—allowing it to curl as it slid across the ice.

For such an ancient sport, curling boasts one of the youngest world championships. The first "bonspiel" (or tournament) for the world title was held in 1968. And while the Canadians won it, the Scottish curling teams have been the persistent ones.

So have the Scottish terms. Besides "bonspiel," good curlers must be intimate with their besom (the broom used for sweeping, otherwise known as sooping the ice in front of the sliding stone). A "pat-lid" is a stone lying on the tee. "Wicking" is cannoning off another stone. If you chip the winner you won't get beaten up. It simply means that you have struck a stone which is largely obscured from view.

Curling is not a fast game. It is a game of skill and sweeping. And with few exceptions (those being the winter olympiad and the traditional annual grand bonspiel played on Lake Monteith in Perthshire, Scotland) curling has earned no reputation as a spectator sport. Needless to say, there's no professional curling circuit; no curlers endorse shaving cream on TV. It's doubtful whether or not there are more than 10 curling hustlers in the world. It is a game that is almost pure—a sport that is played for the players.

Ernie Richardson, captain of the world famous Richardson Rink, releases his stone during the opening round of a championship match which he won.

But curling does have its bureaucracies. There is a supreme ruling body of the sport: the Royal Caledonian Club. It used to be called the Grand Caledonian Club, but after Queen Victoria came to watch the game, the club was obliged to change its name to "royal." The club today has chapters throughout the world.

Scotland boasts more than 50,000 curlers, and roughly one-third of them are women. It is one of the few countries where there are not only good curlers, but curling groupies. There are 16 indoor rinks in the country. At one rink in Glasgow, which is open seven days a week and 12 hours a day, there is a long wait to start sooping. More than 4,000 curlers and their friends descend on the rink each week.

In the United States, curling has enjoyed modest success. If you look hard enough, you can find curling clubs in just about every major U.S. city. Curling has especially flourished in the midwest. The United States Men's Curling Association (USMCA), in Madison, Wis., boasts 90 member-clubs, and represents American curlers in international competitions. There's even a USWCA, founded 11 years before the men's association, which carries more than 3600 women on the rolls. There are more than 65 women's affiliated clubs around the U.S.

And, if some of you are ever wondering where your doctor is, there's even an American Medical Curling Association, headquartered in Hillsboro, Ill. Apparently, there are those who look upon it as cool therapy.

The Broom

About those man with the little brooms, sweeping frantically . . . The sweepers follow the instructions of their leader, or "skip," as he directs them in sweeping frost and moisture from in front of the running stone. This helps to keep the stone straight and make it run farther. The skip also uses his own broom to give other directions.

The brooms themselves are made of brush in Scotland and in Europe. In the U.S. and Canada, the brooms are whisk and are made from nylon, horsehair, corn straw or flagged polypropylene.

VOLLEYBALL WITH SPIKE AND MALICE

By Peter Greenberg

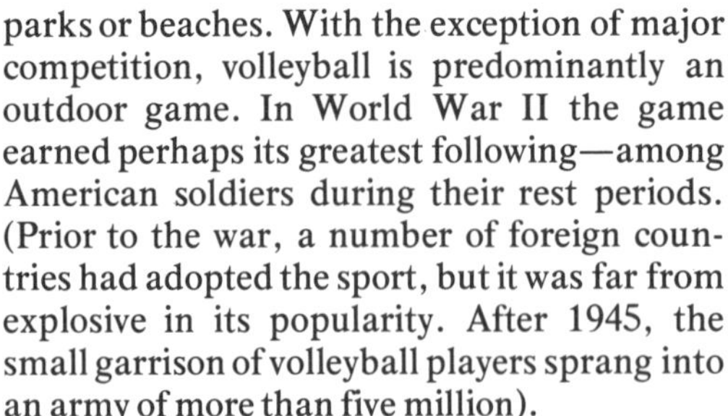

***As American as Henry Kissinger, Volleyball was imported from the Germans who called it* faustball.**

Volleyball is as American as Henry Kissinger. In 1893, the sport was introduced to Germany, where it was known as "faustball." The Germans loved "faustball," and played it with a great deal of precision and grace—bouncing a large ball over a rope. It was a slow game then, slow to play and slow to win. Since the rules allowed for two bounces of the ball, it was pretty hard to lose, unless of course you had been drinking prior to or during the volleys.

Two years after the Germans started fausting, the game was brought to America. The rope was replaced by a net, a different ball was introduced, and bouncing was severely frowned upon. YMCA's in the United States quickly adopted and promoted volleyball, and the game went from indoors to outdoors after the turn of the century. It was a time when the public playground movement was gaining momentum, so kids everywhere were out scouting for nets.

In a society fast growing with all sorts of sports paraphernalia, volleyball was a simple game. All you needed was a net and a ball, and for the most part it didn't matter where you played.

It still doesn't. Just about every YMCA in the world boasts at least one volleyball court, and you can find others in most playgrounds, parks or beaches. With the exception of major competition, volleyball is predominantly an outdoor game. In World War II the game earned perhaps its greatest following—among American soldiers during their rest periods. (Prior to the war, a number of foreign countries had adopted the sport, but it was far from explosive in its popularity. After 1945, the small garrison of volleyball players sprang into an army of more than five million).

Japan's woman volleyball team defeats Cuba 3-0 in the 1972 Munich Olympics.

Two years later the International Volleyball Federation was organized, and while Americans still viewed volleyball as a recreational activity, Europe was developing it into a big game.

It was once said by an old-school volleyball coach that volleyball "is not only a good game for all ages, but it is a sport a boy can play until he is 90 since it requires very little sprinting."

But to say volleyball is a boys' game is probably the worst assumption anyone can make. If you've ever watched the Olympics and have been lucky enough to see the women's teams from Mexico and Japan compete, then you know exactly what I'm talking about. Probably the most dedicated, determined group of players in any sport—and in virtually any country—is a girls' volleyball team in Japan. One is called the "Nichibo" team and, after sweeping more than 150 straight victories from the best women's squads in the world, they walked away with the Olympic gold medal in 1964. (Although the International Olympic Committee reorganized volleyball as an Olympic sport in 1957, it took seven years for it to be accepted in Olympic competition).

The "Nichibo" women are a fierce lot. Although smaller than their opponents, they remained undaunted by the hardwood floors, and continued to hurl themselves crazily after shots other players would concede. I was lucky enough to witness some of the most spectacular returns in the history of the game.

The women players have amazingly quick reflexes and whatever doesn't come naturally they work hard to develop. For example, the Nichibo team practices volleyball each night until midnight. "There is no success without suffering," Hirofumi Daimatsu, their coach, always says. And he should know. During the war, he trained one of Japan's only crack guerilla units in the Southwest Pacific.

Iron Curtain teams powered their way through a number of championships; South American competitors also found the going easy. The United States, however, was still very much reflecting their recreational view of the game. At the Pan American games in

1955, the Americans were humiliated. Twelve years later, at the Pan Am competitions in Winnipeg, Canada, the U.S. began to show its volleyball skills. On the college level, the NCAA became very interested in volleyball as an intercollegiate sport. Not surprisingly, UCLA was crowned the first national champion in 1970. Because of its climate, California leads the U.S. in top volleyball players, with most of the good talent gathered from the beaches of Los Angeles, San Diego and Newport.

On the west coast at least, volleyball is a year-round game. Since there is no body contact, there is little danger of injury, especially when played on the beach. (Although I must caution the regular beach player to take great care in the transition to indoor hardwood court games. If you're conditioned to dive for balls on soft sand, you'll be surprised at how easy it is to forget once indoors and get your knee—or knees—very angry with you).

Volleyball rules are simple and with minor exceptions (like the net), haven't changed much from "faustball." The court is 60 feet long by 30 feet wide and divided by a net eight feet above the floor. The ball used is small, light and round, weighing between nine and 10 ounces, and is only about half as big and heavy as a basketball.

Service is always hit by the right back, who stands in the serving area and bats the ball over the net with one hand. Volleyball is entirely an aerial game and after the serve the ball is volleyed back and forth across the net. The object of the game is never to let the ball touch the floor inside one's own court. Players cannot grasp or throw the ball (called holding) but must hit it cleanly. Points are usually scored by driving the ball to the floor of the opponents' court, or by forcing the opponents to hit it out of bounds or into or under the net. A maximum of three hits is permitted each team in returning a ball over the net and the best teams cleverly use up all three. One man may play a ball twice during a volley but not twice in succession. Bouncing the ball is still a no-no.

However, spiking is allowed, which means you can, if you are skilled, bounce the ball off your opponent's head. But volleyball is far from a violent sport.

In fact, its code of ethics is the strictest. Strange as it may seem, well-defined manners are an integral part of the game. You won't find spectators booing officials. And the players themselves are severely regulated by rules guarding their behavior. In official competition, only the team captain may talk to the official if he needs a rules interpretation. Custom has it that he whispers. Players are warned, or more frequently penalized if they display anger, or if they swear. In fact, the only time the spectators become rowdy is when someone on the court becomes unsportsmanlike.

However, being "sportsmanlike" includes jumping, diving, rolling—and a willingness to pass the ball once in awhile. It may seem like a lot of fun to have played a little one-on-one volleyball in a choose-up high school game, but in competition the key to victory is a set up shot in search of the unreturnable ball. In returning a serve, a defensive player, usually a back-line man (otherwise known as the stopper), will hit the ball—not over the net—but to one of his front line men in preparation for a spike. The front-line player makes the second pass to the spiker. If it's a good pass, the spiker will get it just above the net, allowing him to hit it at a terrific downward angle, usually with the heel of his open palm. If he's particularly skilled, he can fake a spike and gently tip the ball, thus tricking his opponents into backing up.

In official competition, the spiker is not allowed to go over the net himself—a rule often violated by amateurs—or sadists. This makes for a very exciting game—for just one player.

Nevertheless, there are a number of good defenses against a spiker. The best is to send one or two of your defensive men up against him, hands over the top of the net as a fence, and block the spiker's smashes almost before they start.

In the event that a volley actually ensues, position is important. How one handles the ball is crucial. There's the one-hand underhand pass. In tournaments it's known as the dig pass. It's one of the most difficult passes to control, since the hand is in the form of a fist during the pass. It's also known as one of the suicide passes, since it is mostly used to get under almost impossibly hard-hit balls.

The two-hand dig is about the safest pass, only exceeded by the traditional double underhand pass—a fundamental part of the game since its origin. Perhaps the surest method of handling a ball is with the head pass. It's also the way most spikes are set up.

The ultimate suicide pass—and one permitted by present rules—is the kick pass. A player is allowed to use any part of the body to keep the ball in play. This certainly allows for some incredible possibilities and variations. Historically, the kick pass has only been used by players making a desperate effort to recover a ball by using both feet, or by some disgruntled players attempting to conceal unsportsmanlike conduct with no intention of recovering the ball.

In the last two decades, dozens of books have been written on the principles of volleyball, volleyball theory and volleyball etiquette. At the same time, volleyball is being used increasingly as psychotherapy for the disturbed masses. Maybe there's hope for us yet.

Some Rules of the Game

Playing court The playing area includes the boundary lines and a ball must be completely outside of the lines to be ruled out of bounds. The distance from the playing surface to the bottom of the net is four feet, eight inches, the net itself three feet, three inches deep. The playing surface on each side is 29 feet, six inches from sideline to sideline and 29 feet, six inches from the back base line to the center line beneath the net.

Scoring A team scores a point when it is serving and the opposition fails to return the ball correctly over the net. A team wins service (gets to serve the next volley) if the opposition team was serving when it (the opposition) failed to return the ball correctly over the net. A set (or a game) is won when one team reaches 15 points with a two-point lead. For example, if the scored is tied at 14-14, the game continues until one team has a two-point edge. Remember, only the serving team can score points.

GREAT MOMENTS IN GYMNASTICS

Although gymnasts are among the world's least popularized athletes, there is probably no greater test of a person's courage, stamina, strength, control and poise than world class gymnastic competition. Gymnasts don't clout 60 home runs a season or pick their way down sidelines for 95-yard touchdown runs but that doesn't matter. Their feats require more daring, skill and strength in a single evening that most ballplayers experience in an entire season. It was only recently, after the television screens brought us the charming mass appeal of Olga Korbut in the 1972 Olympic Games, that spectators had to queue up early for a gymnastic event.

It's not surprising, then, that the world's greatest gymnasts are anything but American. And it's not surprising that most people don't understand the difference between a pommel horse and a vaulting horse or the distinction between a parallel bar and an asymmetrical bar. There is also a difference between men's and women's competition.

Men and women compete in floor exercises, the vaulting horse and combined exercises. Women compete on the asymmetrical bars and the balance beam, while men do not. Men compete on the horizontal bar, the parallel bars, the rings and the pommel horse. When competitors are working on a particular piece of apparatus, they are required to perform compulsory exercises and add optional movements. Four judges score each event, supervised by a chief judge with 10 points as the maximum score. When each of the four score cards are turned in, the highest and lowest are discarded; the middle two scores are averaged. (In world class competition, only one athlete has ever scored a "perfect" 10. That was Albert Azaryan of the USSR who received a 10.0 from each of the judges in a match against the US team at Penn State in 1962.)

For the past quarter century, 12 gymnasts have dominated world competition. They've won more than 100 Olympic medals: 60 gold, 32 silver and 14 bronze. Ten of them are Russian, one is Czech and one is Japanese.

Vera Caslavska (above) the Czechoslovakian world gymnastic champion, went into hiding in 1968 when the Russian tanks rolled into Prague to crush the Czech bid for independence. Her winning of three gold medals in 1964 in Tokyo had made her the symbol of Czech freedom—highly vulnerable to imprisonment when the Russians took over. She could not train in hiding but kept fit by lugging large sacks of coal. Somehow, she made it to Mexico City and entered all six of the gymnastic events, winning four gold medals and two silver. The golds were awarded for her stunning performances in the combined exercises, the parallel bars, the horse vault and the floor exercises; the silvers were for placing second in the balance beam and in the team combined exercises. It was the first time in the history of the summer Olympics that a woman had won four individual golds. After her last event, her competitors triumphantly tossed her in the air, and carried her from the arena. Later, in Mexico City, she married a Czech teammate, Josef Odlozil, in a wildly jubilant ceremony in the Catholic Cathedral. When she returned to Prague, she presented her gold medals to the four men who stood for that brief shining moment of Czech freedom: Alexander Dubcek, Ludvik Svoboda, Oldrich Cernik and Josef Smrkovsky.

Larissa Latynina (below), in three Olympiads—Melbourne, Rome and Tokyo—won a record total of nine gold medals, five silver medals and three bronze. She won her first gold when she was 21 and her last at the ripe old age, for gymnasts, of 29. She scored three consecutive gold medals over a period of 12 years in one of the most difficult exercises, the floor exercise, in which a gymast is asked to include her own optional exercises with a series of compulsory routines. That meant that in about 90 seconds, she had to demonstrate sureness in acrobatics, turns and balance; as well as coordination, lightness and suppleness; adding a dash of grace, variety and originality; with a sequence of exercises and musical accompaniment (one instrument) that suited her build and temperament. While all that was going on, she had to remain relaxed. No other gymnast, male or female, has ever won the same event in three consecutive Olympics. Latynina, of course, performed quite well in other events: combined exercise (two golds, one silver); balance beam (one silver, one bronze); asymmetrical bars (two silver, one bronze); vaulting horse (one gold, one silver, one bronze); team competition (three golds).

Olympic Performances: Caslavska to Korbut

	1952	1956	1960	1964	1968	1972
MEN'S						
Combined Exercise	Chukarin	Chukarin	Shakhlin	———	Kato	Kato
[all-around]	———	Ono	Ono	Shakhlin	———	———
	———	———	———	———	Nakayama	———
Floor Exercise	———	———	———	———	Kato	———
[free exercise]	———	Chukarin	———	———	Nakayama	———
	———	———	———	———	———	———
Horizontal Bar	———	Ono	Ono	Shakhlin	Nakayama	———
	———	———	———	———	———	———
	———	———	Shakhlin	———	———	———
Parallel Bars	———	Chukarin	Shakhlin	———	Nakayama	Kato
	Chukarin	———	———	———	———	
	———	Ono	Ono	———	———	
Pommel Horse	Chukarin	Shakhlin	Shakhlin	———	———	———
[side horse]	———	Ono	———	———	———	
	———	Chukarin	———	———	———	
Horse Vault	Chukarin	———	Ono/Shakhlin	———	———	———
[long horse]	———	———	[tie]	———	———	
	Ono	———	———	———	———	
Rings	———	———	———	———	Nakayama	Nakayama
	Chukarin	———	Shakhlin	———	———	
	———	———	Ono	Shakhlin	Kato	
Team: Cmb. Ex.	USSR	USSR	Japan	Japan	Japan	Japan
	———	Japan	USSR	USSR	USSR	USSR
WOMEN'S						
Combined Exercise	Gorokhovskaya	Latynina	Latynina	Caslavska	Caslavska	Turisheva
	———	Keleti	———	Latynina	———	
	———	———	Astakhova	Astakhova	———	
Beam	———	Keleti	———	Caslavska	———	Korbut
	Gorokhovskaya	———	Latynina	———	Caslavska	
	———	———	———	Latynina	———	
Asymmetrical	———	Keleti	Astakhova	Astakhova	Caslavska	———
	Gorokhovskaya	Latynina	Latynina	———	———	
	Keleti	———	———	Latynina	———	
Horse Vault	———	Latynina	———	Caslavska	Caslavska	———
	Gorokhovskaya	———	———	Latynina	———	
	———	———	Latynina	———	———	
Floor Exercise	Keleti	Latynina	Latynina	Latynina	Caslavska	Korbut
	Gorokhovskaya	Keleti	Astakhova	Astakhova	———	
	———	———	———	———	———	
Team	USSR	USSR	USSR	USSR	USSR	USSR
	Hungary	Hungary	Czech	Czech	Czech	Japan
	Czech	Rumania	Rumania	Japan	E.Germany	

Viktor Chukarin was the first of the great modern gymnasts. In two Olympiads, beginning with the first the Soviet Union ever competed in, Chukarin won seven gold medals, four silvers and one bronze. His appearance in Helsinki in 1952 completely ended the Western European dominance (Italy, France, Yugoslavia, Switzerland) of gymastics. When he had completed his exercises in Helsinki he had won four golds and two silvers. In Melbourne, he picked up three golds, two silvers and a bronze. The gymnastic range of the man was phenomenal. Of the eight Olympic gymnastic events, Chukarin entered seven and either won or placed second in all of them. He showed his all-around skill by winning the combined exercises twice; demonstrated his strength on the pommel horse and his speed, dexterity and grace on the parallel bars, vaulting horse and rings. It was a virtuoso performance. Chukarin and Boris Shakhlin brought the world team title to the Soviet Union; after they retired, Russia never won it again.

Olga Korbut was the 84-pound diminutive gymnast from the Soviet Union who captivated the American TV audience. Extremely shy, almost childlike in her young beauty, the teenage Russian girl had every spectator in the spacious Munich hall gasping and stunned when she was performing. In the end, she won two individual gold medals—the balance beam and the floor exercise—but it was her performance on the uneven parallel bars which astounded the audience, especially her flying back flip from the top bar.

Women's Events

Floor exercises

Asymmetrical bars

Horse vault

Beam

Boris Shakhlin, (*right*) of the USSR, is the only man to win 10 world championships and he won them all in one dazzling decade between 1954 and 1964. He is also the only male gymnast to win six individual gold medals in Olympic competition picking up one in 1956, four in 1960 and one in 1964. During those same three Olympics he also gathered one team gold, four silvers and two bronze. Shakhlin, who closely resembled the Russian cosmonaut Yuri Gagarin in appearance, stunned crowds into silence with the grace and intensity of his compulsory and optional routines. He helped bring three world team titles to the Soveit Union. And after his countryman, Viktor Chukarin retired, Shakhlin competed for almost 10 more years, thoroughly dominating world class gymnastics. Shakhlin's retirement marked the end of Soviet preeminence in gymnastics. Then, the Japanese took over.

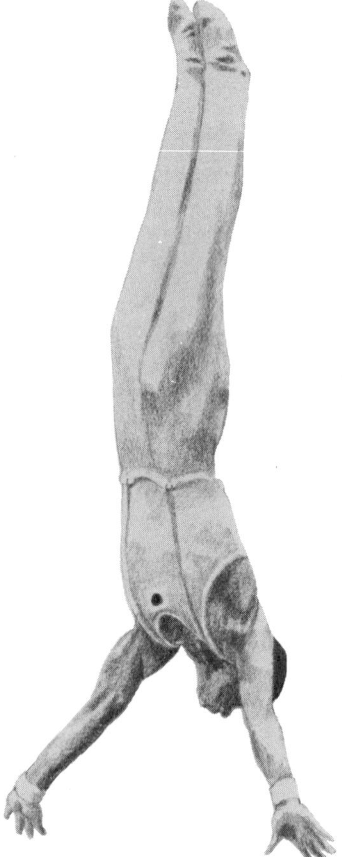

World Champion Gymnasts
[since 1952]

Men			Women		
1952	Viktor Chukarin	USSR	1952	Maria Gorokhovskaya	USSR
1954	Valentin Muratov	USSR	1954	Galina Rudjko	USSR
1956	Viktor Chukarin	USSR	1956	Larissa Latynina	USSR
1958	Boris Shakhlin	USSR	1958	Larissa Latynina	USSR
1960	Boris Shakhlin	USSR	1960	Larissa Latynina	USSR
1962	Yuriy Titov	USSR	1962	Larissa Latynina	USSR
1964	Yukio Endo	Japan	1964	Vera Caslavska	Czech.
1966	Michail Voronin	USSR	1966	Vera Caslavska	Czech.
1968	Sawao Kato	Japan	1968	Vera Caslavska	Czech.
1970	Eizo Kenmotsu	Japan	1970	Liudmila Turisheva	USSR
1972	Sawao Kato	Japan	1972	Liudmila Turisheva	USSR
1974	Shigeru Kasamatsu	Japan	1974	Liudmila Turisheva	USSR

Takashi Ono was the first of the great Asian athletes to challenge the Russian gymastic juggernaut. It was an inauspicious challenge, however, In the 1952 games, Ono entered most of the gymnastic events and came away with one bronze medal. Two Olympics later, he would hold four golds, five silvers and two more bronzes. Takashi's misfortune, if you can call it that, was that his competitive prime came'at Chukarin's full maturity and Shakhlin's first years of gymnastic conquest. Ono had arrived in Helsinki with Masao Takemoto and Tadao Uesako; Takemoto won a silver on the vaulting horse, while Uesako took a silver in floor exercises and tied with Ono for a bronze on the vaulting horse. Three other Japanese team members did not place. But the men were young, intense, courageous artists. When they returned four years later, the Japanese placed second in the world team competition. That was in 1956. Japan has placed first ever since.

Men's Events

Rings
Parallel bar
Horse vault
Horizontal bar
Pommel horse

Sawao Kato and Akinori Nakayama were the next great gymnastic stars to come out of Japan. In the 1968 Mexico City Olympics the two men so dominated gymnastics (they finished first in every event except the side horse and long horse) that the Japanese were the team victors with the largest point spread since Russia defeated Switzerland in 1952. Nakayama and Kato placed first and third in the combined exercises; they led a Japanese sweep of the floor exercises; placed first and third in the horizontal bars; Nakayama took first in the parallel bars; a countryman placed second in the horse vault; and Nakayama and Kato took first and third on the rings. The only event Japan did not place in was the side horse. Four years later, in Munich, the statistics were identical.

Gold Medalist Sawao Kato, center, *and Bronze Medalist Akinori Nakayama wave at 1968 Mexico City Olympiad.*

GREAT MOMENTS IN SWIMMING

Johnny Weissmuller, before he swung through trees as Tarzan, set 24 world swimming records. He won five gold medals during two Olympic competitions, dominating the swimming events in 1924 and 1928. What he did was swim fast, no fancy stuff, just zipping across the water in that fine stroking free-style. He won golds in the 100-meter free style twice, anchored the American team in the 800-meter free-style to two golds and won the 400-meter free-style in 1924. It is said that in 10 years of racing competition he never lost a race from 50 to 880 yards. Then he went to Hollywood and met Jane.

Johnny Weissmuller, above, *churns water. Trudy Ederle begins her Channel swim.*

Gertrude Ederle—you might not remember the name. Actually the world knew her as simply Trudy. She had learned to swim at the Woman's Swimming Association of New York, which was a small swimming club formed by a group of young businesswomen. The daughter of a delicatessen owner, she was only 14 years old when she defeated 50 other older women in a three-mile meet in New York Bay. Then, she began setting world records at distances ranging from 100 to 800 meters. Wanting to thank her swimming club by making it famous, she decided at age 18 to swim the English Channel. She failed. But, a year later, on August 6, 1926, she slipped into the choppy waters of Cap Gris Nez, France, and stroked her way to the white cliffs of Dover in 14 hours and 31 minutes. In the process, she broke the existing men's record for the swim. When she returned to New York, she was given a ticker-tape parade that still ranks as the most enthusiastic given a woman in that city.

Helene Madison, in 1932, held 15 of the 16 world free-style swimming records. Of course, all of her records have since been broken, but here is what she held:

100 yards	1:00.0
100 meters	1:06.6
220 yards	2:34.8
300 yards	3:39.0
300 meters	3:59.5
400 meters	5:28.5
440 yards	5:31.0
500 yards	6:16.4
500 meters	7:12.0
800 meters	11:41.2
880 yards	11:41.2
1,000 yards	13:23.6
1,000 meters	14:44.8
1,500 meters	23:17.2
1 mile	24:34.6

She won three gold medals in the 1932 Olympics, in the 100-meter free-style, the 400-meter free-style and as anchor person on the relay. She could easily have won more but there was nothing else to compete in.

Dawn Fraser liked to brag that she'd win swimming meets, Olympic gold medals and set world records. And when she did, and did it often, everyone recognized that between 1956 and 1964 she was the fastest woman swimmer in the world. The critical sprint test is the 100-meter free-style, something she won in Melbourne in 1956, Rome in 1960 and Tokyo in 1964. When she was 27 years old her Tokyo victory was something of a special achievement because a few months before she had been seriously injured in an automobile accident that killed her mother. Taking the water with a chipped neck vertebrae, Fraser became the first swimmer in Olympic history to win the same event in three successive games. She also won two gold and four silver medals anchoring the Australian swimming team relay events.

Mihir Sen decided to swim the English Channel in 1958. It wasn't as if it was such a major feat. After all, seven years earlier, exactly 18 people had made their way across. So, *ho-hum,* he swam the channel in 14 hours and 45 minutes, not even as good a time as Gertrude Ederle had posted 32 years earlier. But years later, Mihir Sen had a better idea. And where else to continue but off the waters of his homeland, India. On April 5, 1966, he slipped into the waters of Palk Strait and swam from India to Ceylon, taking 25 hours and 36 minutes. On August 24, he walked into the Atlantic off the rugged rock of Gibraltar and swam to Africa in 8 hours and 1 minute. The romantic swimming of the Dardanelles was next. On September 12, he waded in at Gallipoli on the European side and slowly made his way across to Asia, wading ashore at Sedulbahir, Asia Minor after 13 hours and 55 minutes. Six weeks later, on October 29-31, he took his longest plunge and crawled and kicked his way along the entire length of the Panama Canal in 34 hours and 15 minutes. No one has repeated that feat in a decade.

The map, right, *highlights the incredible long distance swims of Mihir Sen which took him around the globe.*

India to Ceylon
April 5, 1966

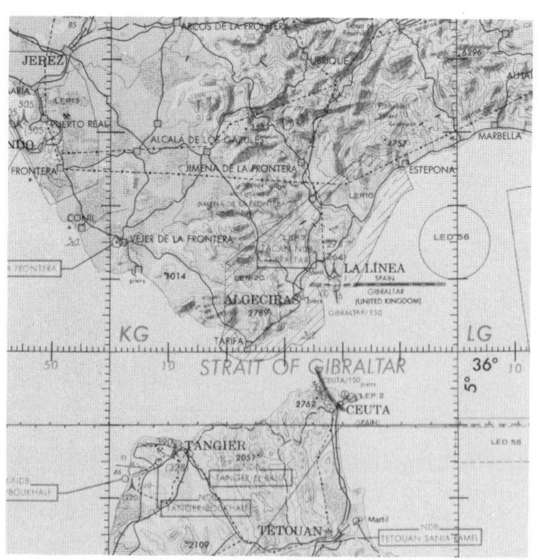

Straits of Gibraltar
August 24, 1966

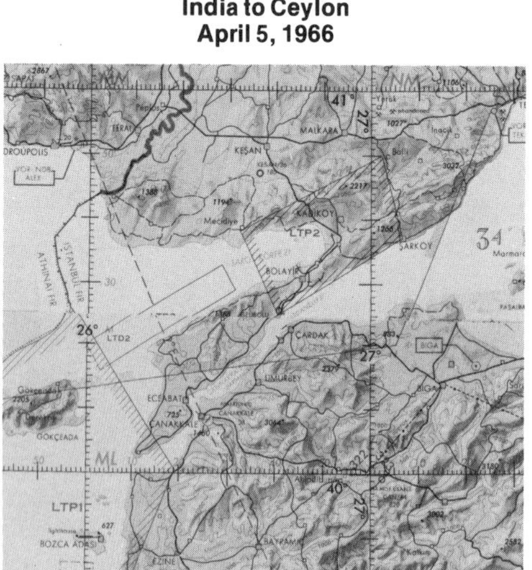

Dardanelles
September 12, 1966

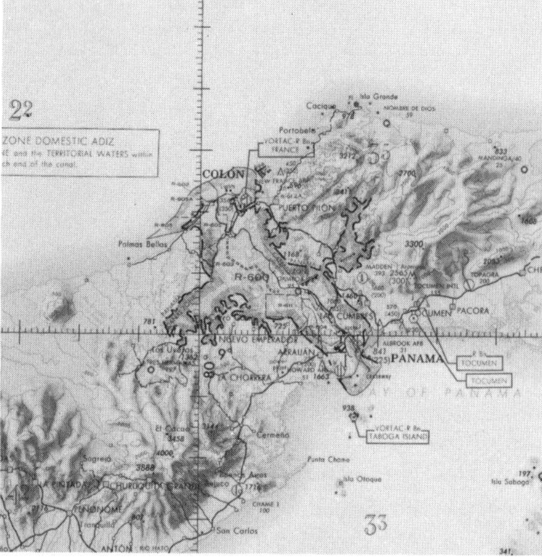

Panama Canal
October 29-31, 1966

Shane Gould was all of 15 years old when she traveled to Munich to compete in the 20th Olympiad. The Australian schoolgirl had an incredible swimming range. She could cut through the water in dashes, had enough in strength and stamina to compete in the 800-meters and four different strokes with which she could challenge in the difficult 200-meter medley.

Her first event was the 200-meter medley. Other competitors had not expected her to enter that event. In fact, the American women were so intimidated by Gould, they privately wore T-shirts with the lettering, "All That Glitters Is Not Gould." Gould won the medley in world record time. But, surprisingly, she lost the next day, in the 100-meter free-style, an event in which she already held the world record. Hampered by a slow start, Gould still managed to come away with a bronze medal. And the winner did not break her record.

She came back and broke her own record in the 400-meter free-style for a second gold, and then stunned the swimming world with a 200-meter free-style finish that lopped two seconds off her own world record. She was favored in her last race, the long, arduous 800-meter free-style but finished second behind another 15-year-old, a Californian named Karen Rothhammer. Nonetheless, when the competition ended, Shane Gould had won five medals: three golds, a silver and a bronze. That had never been done before.

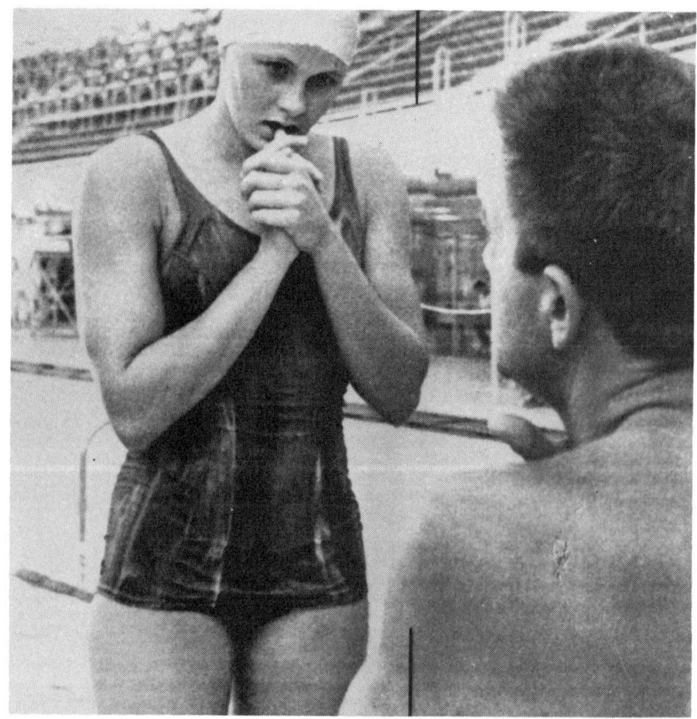

For a while, Australia's Shane Gould held every free-style record from 100 to 1,500 meters. Here, she talks with her coach.

Don Schollander was 18 years old and worried when he entered the Olympic games in Tokyo. After setting world records in both the 200 and 400-meter free-style events in U.S. championship competition, he had started to lose races, both in the Olympic tryouts and in practice. He was still fast enough to make the team, however. Yet in the Olympic village he confided to his roommate, "I can't win. I've lost my sprints." Well, he found them again. Found enough of them that he won four gold medals, something no other swimmer had accomplished in Olympic history (until Mark Spitz) and something that had not been accomplished since Jesse Owens in 1936.

Schollander won the 100-meter free-style, the 400-meter free-style and anchored the U.S. team to win gold medals in the 400-meter sprint relay and the 800-meter relay, setting world records in all events except for the 100, which was an Olympic record. "This," said U.S. swimming coach Jim Counsilman, "was the greatest moment in American swimming history." He was referring, of course, to the entire U.S. team effort, but much of that effort was supplied by a smiling young Oregonian.

Mark Spitz Does the name ring a bell? After he had predicted he would win six gold medals at the 1968 Mexico City Olympics and ended up with two (for team events), this arrogant 18 year old had four years to think about it. He thought and thought, and then, splashed into the 1972 Munich natatorium, refusing to make any predictions, emerging dripping wet with seven Olympic medals.

His first event was one of his specialties, the 200-meter butterfly, in which he had finished dead last at Mexico City. Well, he so outdistanced everyone else that by the time he won, there was a 12-foot gap between him and the second place winner. He also set a world record, a fantastic 2:00.7. Spitz scared a few supporters in the 200-meter free style when he botched up a turn, falling behind at the halfway mark but he poured it on and won in 1:52.8, another world record. He next anchored the 400-meter free-style relay, which the Americans won in world record time. Then he swam the 100-meter butterfly in the world record time of 54.3 and knocked off the final leg of the 800-meter free-style relay in 7:38.8, another world record. By the time he finished the 100-meter free-style Spitz had his sixth gold medal, and a sixth world record. Picking up that sixth medal marked the shattering of still another world record—the record for all-Olympic gold-medal record collections. The stage was set for the tenth day of competition. Spitz was assigned to the butterfly leg of the 400-meter medley relay and his American team wiped out the previous world record. That made seven gold medals and seven world records, an accomplishment that may be hard to improve on.

Mark Spitz shows the power, the style, and the intensity of a 200-meter world record effort. It added up to seven gold medals.

A Statistical History of Swimming*

	1908	1920	1924	1936	1948	1952	1956	1960	1964	1968	1972
100 Meters											
Men	1m.5.6s.	1m.0.4s.	59s.	57.6s.	57.3s.	57.4s.	55.4s.	55.2s.	53.4s.	52.2s.	51.2s.
Women**		1m.13.6s.	1m.12.4s.	1m.5.9s.	1m.6.3s.	1m.6.8s.	1m.2s.	1m.1.2s.	59.5	1m.	58.6
400 Meters											
Men	5m.36.8s.	5m.26.8s.	5m.4.2s.	4m.44.5s.	4m.41s.	4m.30.7s.	4m.27.3s.	4m.18.3s.	4m.12.2s.	4m.9s.	4m.0.27
Women***			6m.2.2s.	5m.26.4s.	5m.17.8s.	5m.12.1s.	4m.54.6s.	4m.50.6s.	4m.43.3s.	4m.31.8s.	4m.19.0
100 Meter Backstroke											
Men	1m.16.8s.	1m.21.2s.	1m.15.2s.	1m.8.6s.	1m.5.9s.	1m.6.4s.	1m.5.4s.	1m.2.2s.	1m.1.9s.	58.7s.	56.58s.
Women***			1m.23.2s.	1m.18.9s.	1m.14.4s.	1m.14.3s.	1m.12.9s.	1m.9.3s.	1m.7.7s.	1m.6.2s.	1m.5.8s.
200 Meter Breast Stroke											
Men	3m.9.2s.	3m.4.4s.	2m.56.6s.	2m.42.5s.	2m.39.3s.	2m.34.4s.	2m.34.7s.	2m.37.4s.	2m.27.8s.	2m.28.7s.	2m.21.6s.
Women***			3m.33.2s.	3m.3.6s.	2m.57.2s.	2m.51.7s.	2m.53.1s.	2m.29.5s.	2m.46.4s.	2m.44.4s.	2m.41.7s.

*Olympic results **Began in 1912 ***Began in 1924

STRIKING BETWEEN THE GUTTERS

By Peter Delacorte

Archie Bunker bowls. So did the ancient Polynesians and the team from Harvey's Exxon.

Bowling does not rank high among America's glamour sports. Who, after all, bowls? President Eisenhower was a golfer, President Kennedy was a sailor, President Johnson drove fast cars and President Ford is a skier. Archie Bunker bowls. So, of course, do millions of real Americans who are not necessarily movie stars or corporation executives or presidents of anything.

Try as it may, the bowling establishment seems to be perpetually fighting a losing battle against a pejorative image. A person plays tennis, golf and football on a court, a course and a field respectively but he or she bowls on an *alley.* And in many neighborhoods, the local bowling alley is considered the next sleaziest place to the pool hall. In fact, many bowling houses (as the establishment prefers to call them) double as pool halls or, even worse, as pinball emporia. Some offer refuge to the surliest, pimpliest adolescents to be found outside of *The Blackboard Jungle.* Most of the kids aren't dangerous, but they are frequently unsightly.

But bowling is undeniably the sport of the masses. If you can't afford to join the country club or go away for a weekend in the mountains, if you don't want to pay the greens' fees, you can usually afford $4 or so for five games at Leroy's Lanes. If you don't want to wait three hours for a tennis court, or if you can't round up 10 or 20 people for a pickup basketball or football afternoon, you can make it over to Leroy's in about 10 minutes. If you feel ridiculously uncoordinated attempting to strike small balls with larger objects, try heaving that huge rubber sphere at the fragile wooden pins 60 feet away. You'll probably still feel ridiculously uncoordinated, but every once in a while all the little bastards will fall down, and that feels good. Afterward, you can toss down a few cool ones at the bar (bowling alleys usually have absurdly low bar prices) or squeeze in among the surly adolescents for a few games of pinball.

For the reasonably coordinated but frustrated competitor, league bowling offers vistas forgotten since the moment when you were the last person cut from the high school basketball team. There is indeed pleasure in bowling a sizzling 228 against Harvey's Exxon on Thursday night, and then watching Larry Laub edge Earl Anthony 224-217 on national television Saturday afternoon, picking up $14,000 in the process. You know that you could never outplay Abdul-Jabbar, or hit even a foul ball off Nolan Ryan, or win more than three points against Jimmy Connors. But on the lanes, you can outscore the Champion. It is absolutely irrelevant that the champion has averaged 221.7 in 43 games to make the finals while your own league average is 152.

History

Bowling, or "bowls," has been around for a long time, in one form or another. While it is extremely doubtful that stone-age man possessed either bowling shoes or automatic pinsetters, numerous artifacts indicate that our prehistoric ancestors rolled rocks at pointed objects and sheep joints. Egyptologists have traced a game remarkably similar to modern tenpins as far back as 5200 B.C. and the ancient Polynesians played a game in which the object stones were shot at from 60 feet, the same distance as in modern bowling.

Bowling was a popular sport in medieval Germanic countries, and was banned in England by Edward III. The king feared that it and other "hurling" games would take precedence over archery. At the time, skilled archers were needed to keep people from taking over countries. But the game endured and in 1530 drew an endorsement from Henry VIII, who installed bowling lanes at Whitehall. (There are frightening inferences to be drawn from the near-simultaneous institution of royal bowling and divorce in early-Renaissance Britain. Henry is rumored, in fact, to have been bowling during the beheading of Anne Boleyn, and to have incurred the wrath of several subsequent wives as a result of his passion for the sport. When he was bowling he often failed to arrive in the royal chambers until 3 or 4 a.m., by which time the queen would either be asleep or angry. After one such occurrence, Ann of Cleves is said to have struck the king with a sturgeon.)

Bowling was brought to America by early Dutch settlers in the form of nine-pins (the pins forming a nine-pin diamond instead of the currently familiar 10-pin triangle.) By the early 19th century the game had become extremely popular, and by the mid-19th century it had once again become illegal—this time because gamblers had taken control of places where nine-pins was played. A large amount of money was apparently bet on the game. Around 1842 somebody realized that maybe *nine*-pins was illegal, but 10-pins was well within the letter of the law, and thus was born, or re-born (with a nod to a 7,000-year-old Egyptian) the game of bowling as we know it. In 1895 the American Congress of Bowlers (ABC) was formed to keep things clean. In 1916 the Women's International Bowling Congress (WIBC) struck an early blow for feminism. The two groups still exist, largely independent of each other, one regulating men's bowling, the other women's, and both making sure that nobody's gonna put the fix in, or put pig grease on the lanes. This is as it should be.

Ducks and Candles

It must be noted that in the eastern United States there exist two hybrid bowling forms which used to be really big in their respective domains, but of late have fallen victim to the increased mechanization and general clout of the big game. These are: Duckpins (short, fat pins shot at with a small, hand-sized ball, three balls to a frame, thus providing the possibility of shooting a (10) which is neither a strike nor a spare); and Candlepins (short, thin pins shot at with the same hand-sized ball, also with three balls to the frame, but here dead wood stays on the lane so you can pick up all sorts of strange leaves.) To the big-ball aficionado these are frustrating games—an average of 130 is roughly equivalent to a 200 average in standard bowling—but if you find yourself in Washington, D.C., or Stamford, Conn. (duckpins) or Manchester or Exeter, N.H. (candlepins) at some point before the local games become extinct, give them a try.

Stars And Legends

Bowling is one of the few popular sports in which perfection is absolutely defined: 12 strikes in a row, or a 300 game. Beyond skill and concentration, a perfect game demands a large degree of luck and an even larger degree of karma, or something like that. Many 190-to-200 average bowlers will go to their graves never having shot a 300 game; reciprocally, it isn't altogether uncommon for a 145-to-150 average bowler to find a transitory groove and roll the big one.

Among bowling's great names, there's Dick Weber with 16 300s, followed by Don Carter and Dave Soutar (13 apiece), and Ray Bluth with 12. The accomplishments of these gentlemen are dwarfed by one Elvin Mesger of Sullivan, Mo., who has 26 perfect games to his credit.

Floretta McCutcheon, a Colorado housewife, recorded 14 300 games in the 1920s and '30s, but Ms. McCutcheon's finest moment came in 1927, in a bizarre precursor to the fabled Bobby Riggs/Billie Jean King Battle of the Sexes.

Jimmy Smith was one of the reigning stars of his era (he was elected to the Bowling Hall of Fame in 1941), and when an exhibition tour brought him to Pueblo, Colo., McCutcheon challenged him to a three-game match. Smith at first refused, protesting that he would bowl only against the "best," and that he couldn't believe a woman could provide him with ample opposition. He eventually caved in to local pressure, and proved his mettle with a sizzling 686 series. Undaunted, McCutcheon bowled a 704 (for an average of 234.7) no doubt altering Smith's notion of just what was the "best."

Money

As might be imagined, there isn't nearly as much money to be made in professional bowling as in golf or tennis. But there's a lot more than there used to be. Dick Weber was bowling's top money winner in 1959 with the princely sum of $7,672; today that total would put him toward the bottom of the top 50. The winner of the Tournament of Champions, held annually in Akron, Ohio, is guaranteed $25,000, and ABC-TV gives $10,000 to anyone who bowls a 300 game in the finals of a televised tournament. This has been done only once so far, by Jim Stefanich. (But ABC has saved considerable petty cash thanks to two pins—Earl Anthony bowled a 299 on national TV, leaving the 10 pin on what seemed to be a perfect shot in the 10th frame, and Mark Roth suffered a similar fate with a recalcitrant four pin.)

The Big Statistics of the American Bowling Congress

—The high team point total is 3,858 bowled by the Budweisers of St. Louis, Mo., in 1958.

—The high team game was 1,342 points rolled by the Hook Grip Five of Lodi, N.J., in 1950.

—The high doubles total is 1,614 by Billy Walden and Nelson Burton, Jr., in 1970.

—The high doubles game is 587 points, put in the record books by Tom Dern and Ron Spohn in 1965.

—The high singles total was rolled a long time ago, in 1939, when Albert Brandt let fly with 886 points.

—The high all-events total is an older record than that, a 2,259 point effort by Frank Benkovic in 1932.

—The most 300 games is 26 by Elvin Mesger. George Billick is second with 17.

—There are 138,562 bowling lanes in the U.S. housed in 8,674 bowling centers.

—The largest bowling center is located in Tokyo, Japan, at the Tokyo World Lanes Bowling Center where there are 504 lanes.

—More than one-fourth the U.S. population bowls.

—The most strikes bowled in a row was by Ed Shay who rolled 12 off his fingertips to win an ABC Tournament title in one of the greatest finishes of all-time in 1958, scoring a perfect game.

—The most spares scored in a row was by Lt. Hazen Sweet of Battle Creek, Mich., with 23.

—The most 300's in a tournament were three, rolled by Dick Weber of St. Louis in 1966 and Roy Buckley of Columbus in 1971.

—Dick Weber holds the record for winning the most major bowling titles in a career, 23 in 14 years.

—The most 200's rolled in succession is 42 by Earl Anthony of Tacoma in 1971.

—The highest official earnings for one year was $85,065 by Johnny Petraglia of Brooklyn in 1971.

—The highest official earnings for a career is $397,228 by Dick Weber, after 14 years.

—The highest single game match on national TV took place in 1970 when Don Johnson beat Dick Ritger by a score of 299-268.

PING-PONG FOR BLOOD

By David Saltman

Get yourself a foam rubber paddle, eat lots of Chinese food, and practice, practice, practice.

It's *table tennis,* friend, and don't you forget it!

This game is played viciously and scientifically all over Asia, particularly by the Japanese, Koreans, Malaysians and Chinese. Even in this country, the champions are often Asians, like the famous Dal Joon Lee, the Korean-born American who has won the US Championship six years running.

An expert table tennis player must be in superb shape; fast, tricky and intelligent. He generally uses a foam paddle, the technical innovation which dramatically changed the game.

He must know how and when to hit at least the following repertoire of shots: chopspin, topspin, sidespin left and right, under-the-table shots, forehand and backhand slams and little drop shots. He ought to have at least two fast, tricky serves: something like the backhand topspin serve that rockets off the other end of the table like a frightened tiger.

When played for blood, and especially against the Chinese, a top player must also have *speed*—a factor which American players, in particular, have ignored until recently. The Chinese are fond of hitting their shots *just* as they come off the bounce, giving the opponent hardly any time to gather his wits. That is known in some circles as "rushing the net," and a good net-rusher is hard to beat, especially for an offensive player.

On the other hand, the best player I ever saw, a Chinese also, played so laconic a game he hardly seemed to move. His game was so undistinguished it took me a long time to recognize its one and only virtue: *he never missed a shot!* He returned every damned thing anybody hit, from drop shots to powerful smashes! And he seemed bored to death. But every once in a while, he would flash into action, dazzling everyone with a display of virtuoso table tennis that I promise you will have Chuang Tse-tung quaking in his Adidas someday.

Before the Chinese began to dominate world table tennis, the champions were usually Hungarians. They made the best paddles—pebbled rubber jobs—which were excellent for the Hungarian style—a handshake grip, using both sides of the paddle. When the Chinese came along with their penholder grip, the Europeans laughed—until they got creamed.

Most good players have now switched over to the Chinese paddles, which are made out of foam rubber with a slick rubber covering. They are the equivalent of fiberglass poles for pole-vaulters; they terrifically increase the pace and power of the game. Spin is increased at least threefold, and you can really smash the ball without losing control.

I guarantee that if you switch to a foam paddle, you can increase your normal score by at least five points after one night of practice. At two dollars a point, that's a better investment than Persian rugs.

Strategy Once when playing a man much better than I, I managed to get him off-balance by hitting shots first to one side of the table and then to the other. He finally missed one of them, and I felt a little embarrassed, even though I'd won the point fairly. He looked at me, and said,

"That's the game."

The secret is not to have the trickiest shots, but to fluster your opponent. If you can get him running while you're standing still...well, that's the game.

It can be done with an unlimited combination of shots. It's the same as the one-two in boxing, or the double-disengage in fencing. You can hit first to the left and then to the right and then to the left and then...to the left again! Or you can hit hard, then soft, then hard, then...? The choices are endless and the correct intuitive combination is what makes a champion. That's the game.

Tactics There are some pretty amazing shots in table tennis. I knew a guy who used to play sitting down. He always won, because his serve was unreturnable. It had so much backspin on it that it jumped back over the net after it had hit the opposite side of the table! Actually, in tournament play, that serve would be illegal (because it does not go off the opposite side of the table). But it's a hell of a shot.

There are few shots more serviceable than a good backhand slam. Made with the proper whip of the wrist, and by leaning into it, it can gather terrific speed and be placed easily anywhere on the table. The backhand slam is more deceptive than the forehand smash, because, unlike the latter, the angle of the paddle used does not tip off the opponent as to where the ball is headed.

Remember to hit your smashes hard, and to lean your body into them. One of the most common faults of the average-to-good player is that he leans *away* from his slams. As in a boxing punch, the power in table tennis comes from *exploding body-weight.*

On defense, learn how to hit shots from under the table. This is effective because your opponent will have a hard time telling what kind of spin you've put on the ball. In addition, you get a nice, flowing rhythm going, which can only be mastered by practicing. It is good to learn to play far back from the table, but also good to learn to play very close up.

Evidence of the world class play of the People's Republic of China is this match in which Hsu Shao-Fa, far left, *beats his Swedish opponent.*

Dell Sweeris from Grand Rapids, Mich., defeats Liang Ke-liang of China in Detroit, 1972.

Grips & Paddles Get a foam paddle and use the handshake grip. The penholder grip gives you an inherent weakness in the backhand (although the Chinese players haven't seemed to have been handicapped by it).

To use the handshake grip, lay your index finger along the bottom edge of the paddle. Move it up just a little...there. That's how to hold the paddle. It's comfortable, flexible and powerful. You can hit forehand or backhand easily and use both sides of the paddle.

Spin You must understand spin to become a good player. The conventional wisdom, back in the days of the Hungarians, was that if your opponent hit a topspin, send back a chop. The idea was to use his own spin against him—a sort of jujitsu attitude.

Foam paddles have changed this radically. If you use his spin against him, you have to hit the ball at least twice as hard as he did, because the spin is so ferocious. Now they say, just hit the ball *harder* than your opponent did, putting whatever spin you want on it, and you will neutralize his shot.

The balls, incidentally, take a terrific beating. Get the Halex ones.

Everybody Needs A Ping-Pong Hero

Take this fellow Dal Joon Lee. He gives exhibitions where he challenges anyone in the audience, and beats all comers by at least 21-4, using a *scrub brush* as a paddle! The diminutive (5'2" and 127 pounds) Lee's ultimate goal is to break the legendary Dick Miles' record of 10 U.S. championships.

Miles was the master of the backhand flick shot. He held the U.S. title from 1945-49, and won it in 1955. He played Hungarian style, both sides of the paddle, while "D.J.," (as they call Lee) used the Chinese penholder grip.

Our favorite hero, however, was the Hungarian, Victor Barna. Table tennis first became popular in the 1920s when Barna won 15 world championships. If Europe hadn't gone to war, no doubt he'd have won many more titles. From 1930 to 1935, he won the world singles title five times. Then he went on to win the world doubles championship eight times and the mixed doubles twice. He had a fantastic backhand. His forehand must have been pretty good too, since he could smash the ball at 50 mph. That's not as fast as current world class players and Barna may not have been as good as contemporary table tennis champions, but he was one of the sport's first superstars, leaving a legacy that's been hard to top.

—In a 1936 match between Austria and Rumania, Alex Ehrlich and Paneth Farcas had an opening rally that lasted two hours and 12 minutes.

—The Ehrlich-Farcas point was superseded by Nick Krajancie and Graham Lassen in Auckland, New Zealand in 1973 but that volley was staged.

—The table tennis ball weighs between 2.4 and 2.53 grams, that's 0.085 to 0.09 ounces.

—While it hasn't been measured scientifically, it has been reliably estimated that Chuang Tse-tung—the World Champion of 1961, 1963 and 1965—has smashed the ball in tournament play at speeds exceeding 60 m.p.h.

—Table tennis is a relatively new game. According to the *Guinness Book of World Records*, the earliest evidence about the game comes from the catalog of a London sporting goods company in the 1880s.

a Workingman's Guide to Shooting Pool

Pick out an ivory-inlaid cue stick about 57 inches long, weighing 19½ ounces with a 12½ millimeter tip and you're ready for Willie.

It is certainly curious to us how the grand old game of billiards can be simultaneously associated with elegant, aristocratic mansions and sleazy, grimy poolrooms. Everyone who's picked up a cue-stick knows pool is a complex, exciting game, full of strategy, heartbreakers and surprises. Just because they play it down on the docks in Marseilles doesn't mean ladies wouldn't like it, or that you should keep your children inside when the pool shark walks down the street.

For one thing, you can rest assured that if your kid knows how to shoot a good game of pool, he'll never go hungry, and might even be able to provide for you in your old age. For another, the poolish reflexes of a trained eye, steady hands and delicate touch are much in demand among brain surgeons, safecrackers and dozens of other professionals. As they tell the outgoing graduates at the Wharton School of Business, "Eighty percent of your business will be done behind the eight-ball."

Without further ado, then, we take pride in presenting this guide to pool shooting.

The Cue-stick Willie Mosconi uses an ivory-inlaid stick 57 inches long, which weighs 19-and-a-half ounces and has a 12-and-a-half millimeter tip. The tip should be rounded, like a half moon.

The Grip Find the balance point of your cue-stick. Assuming you're right-handed, slide your right hand back three to five inches from the fulcrum point. Your grip should be delicate and light, yet firm, like holding onto the handle of a teacup: only the thumb and first three fingers are involved. Gripping too tightly is the mark of a real money loser. The natural swing of the right arm will give the stick all the power it needs. Remember that pool shooting is akin to putting in golf. In fact, many golfers say they play pool to develop their putting eye, and may pool hustlers are also excellent golfers. (As well as excellent card players, dice heads and kidnappers.)

The Stance Pool expert Willie Mosconi says, "a good billiard stance puts the player into a balanced and comfortable position, and centers his head over the cue in the line of aim."

No better advice than that could be given. Keep the feet close together, about six inches apart. Begin by standing square to your shot. Then, as you bend over the table, turn both your feet to the right, just a bit. Bring your head in line with the cue-stick and the shot. (Your left knee will be bent a little more than your right, and your body will be free to move forward with the stroke.) The keys are balance, freedom to stroke smoothly, and keeping your head right above the cue.

The Bridge The bridge is the important variable in the fundamentals. If it is solid, your game will be solid. If it wobbles, you can kiss off your two-balls.

To make the bridge correctly, put your fist firmly on the table, palm down. Open the thumb and forefinger. Lay the cue along your thumb, between thumb and forefinger. Draw your forefinger down over the top of the cue, your thumb pushing it at the first joint, somewhat against the second joint of the middle finger. Then separate and extend the last three fingers, making a broad base of support. The hand turns slightly inward from the wrist.

Try it stick in hand.

The cue fits snugly, fingers are widespread but not strained. It is a rock-solid structure if executed correctly, a little piece of human architecture. It is amazing that the late J. Bronowski and similar scientists spend hours on the universe and no time at all on figuring the stress patterns of a correctly formed "bridge."

There are also "rail" bridges and "vee" bridges. You use the rail bridge when your ball is too close to the rail for the basic bridge described above. The basic bridge, according to Mosconi, should be used whenever possible. It is effective up to about 10 inches off the rail. From two to 10 inches away, the rail bridge should be employed.

You make it by tucking back your thumb and sliding the cue between your first two fingers. It is a tripodal structure, the three points being the thumb line and the two fingertips. It is also a very solid edifice from which to hustle nine-ball.

The vee bridge is used when there's a ball right in front of the cue ball, blocking your cue's path. You have to raise the cue above the intervening balls. You make a vee channel, using thumb pressure against your forefinger to keep the cue firm. The hand dances on the four fingertips, arrayed as firmly as possible on the table.

The mechanical bridge, also called the "ladies' aid," "shitstick," and other colorful names, is just what it sounds like. It's a cue-stick with a curvy metal plate on the end. You use it in one hand and your cue in the other.

The Stroke From architecture to art. Chalk up lightly now and before every stroke, it increases the friction. Remember, every leatherheaded cuetip of a hustler is working on his stroke. Use a short one, a soft one, a

—In an exhibition match against a local hotshot in Springfield, Ohio, in 1954, Willie Mosconi ran 526 balls in a row, a little better than 37 racks.

—Willie Hoppe won his first world pocket pool title in 1906 when he was only 16. Two years later, he beat Maurice Vigneaux who was the then billiard master of the world.

—He went on to win a total of 51 world title competitions between 1906 and 1952.

—Pool is probably the most scientific game played.

—Jack Carr, an Englishman who became the first "world's billiard champion," discovered "English," the spin influence a player puts on the cue ball to control the action of that ball either before or after it hits an object ball or a cushion.

smooth one. Not too hard, you are dealing with the five Platonic solids: a sphere rolling on a plane. You don't need much impact to make it go. Let no more than eight inches of cue shaft extend from your bridge to your cue ball. This means the stroke will be no more than four to six inches. Use a few warmup strokes to get ready for the money-ball.

Shotmaking in all billiard games is completely intuitive. That's what makes the game interesting. You have to simply sense and feel the correct speed and stroke control for each shot. It's the kind of feel a painter gets for colors which blend, or a writer for the sound of his sentences.

Spin This category includes draw, stop, follow, left, right, high and low English. [The reason they call it English is because you hit it at an *angle*, it says here.]

The main thing about all spinning shots is they should be hit no more than one cue-tip width away from dead center. The only shot that should be hit dead center is the stop shot, which makes the cue ball stop and not roll at all as it hits the object ball.

The Game As Cleopatra said to one of her attendants, "Let's to billiards."

Strategy in billiards develops well before one is ready to play pool. One must first grow a mustache. (Or, if female, develop a slight

Willie Mosconi demonstrates an easy beginners' shot in which the cueball orbits the room.

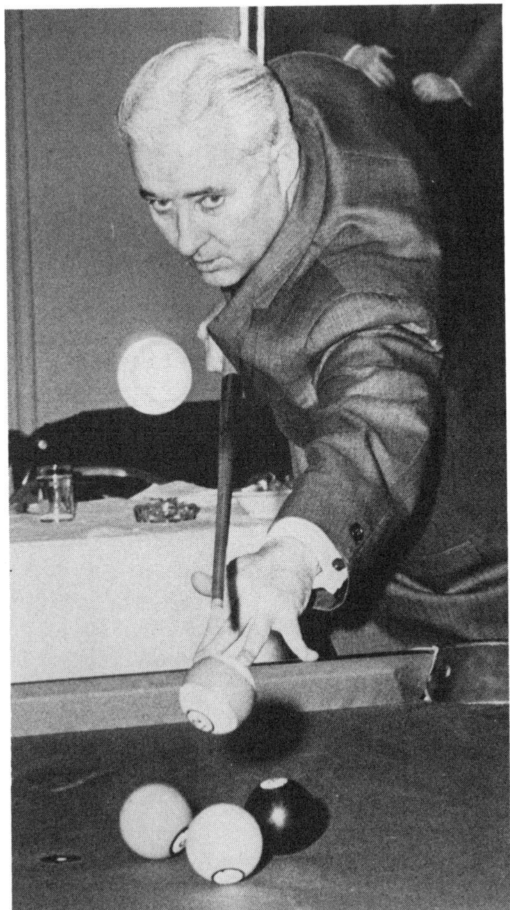

THE RULES OF THE GAME

We should point out immediately that the principal American games commonly designated as "true billiards" are balking, straight rail, and three-cushion carom. These are all played on a pocketless table. In the American game of pocket billiards, the sole objective is pocketing. In the U.S. all other varieties with pockets are usually called "pool." Thus, "billiards," used alone, means without pockets in the U.S. but it means with *pockets in England. Not to mislead you any further, we are going to talk about the pocketing kind of pool-shooting.*

Here, then, is a simple set of rules for a variety of pocket pool games. They're simple enough and brief enough to cause plenty of arguments.

Eight-ball A game played by two or four players in which the object is to sink seven balls (either the ones numbered 1 through 7 or 9 through 15) and then pocket the eight-ball, or black ball. Note that the lower numbered set is solid-colored while the higher numbered set is striped. *Options:* A "scratch" on the 8-ball forfeits the game. One team must shoot the No. 1 ball in one side pocket, while the other team must place the 15-ball in the other side pocket. First team to pocket the 1-ball or 15-ball has the option of which side; the other team must pocket in the remaining side. When shooting the eight-ball, all opponents' balls are dead, that is, they cannot be struck by your cue ball prior to its striking the eight. Hitting a dead ball first when shooting for the eight or missing the eight entirely forfeits the game.

Rotation A player must first pocket the No. 1 ball, then the No. 2, etc., in ascending order to No. 15. Additional balls pocketed on a given stroke count, provided the mandatory one is also pocketed. A game is won by the player (in a two-player game) who first sinks eight balls.

Fifteen-ball A game like rotation except that the score is decided by the actual number of a pocketed ball. The numbers of the 15 balls (numbered 1 to 15) total 120. Therefore, the player (in a two-player game) who scores 61 first is the winner.

Cut-throat A three-player game in which the winner is the last person owning an object ball on the table. One player "has" the balls numbered 1 to 5, another 6 to 10 and the third player 11 to 15. The object is to shoot the other person's balls into the pockets. Sinking one of your own balls allows another shot, although your own ball stays pocketed. If you scratch, you *must* remove a ball, your choice, from the table. If you "scratch" while sinking an opponent's ball, that ball comes back onto the table and you must remove one of your own. When all your five balls are pocketed, you may no longer shoot in that particular game.

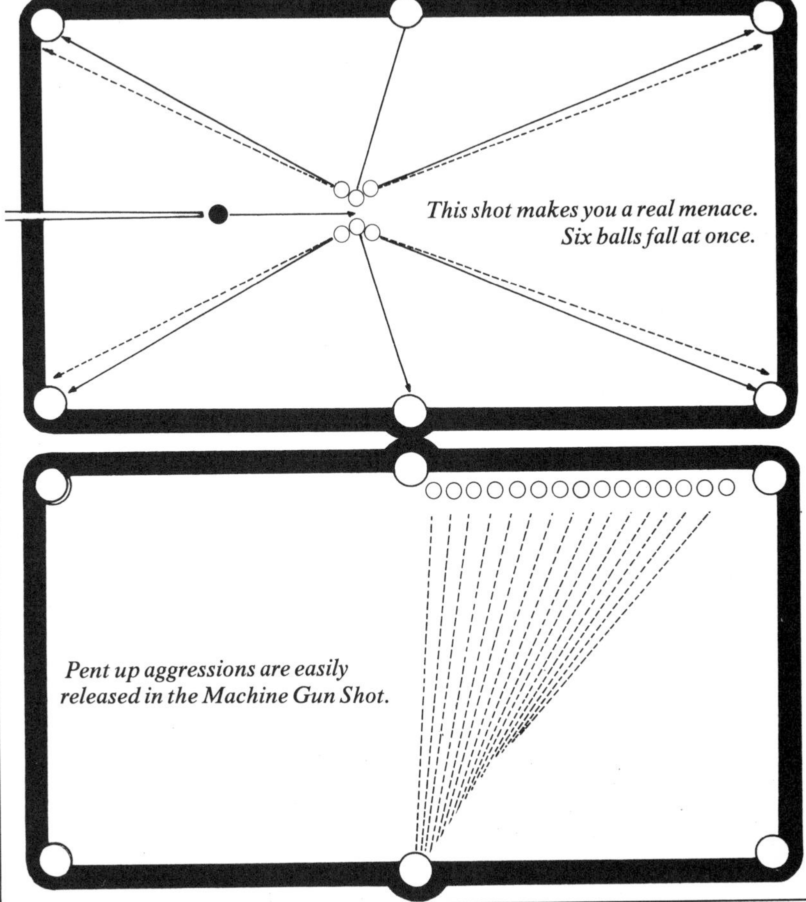

This shot makes you a real menace. Six balls fall at once.

Pent up aggressions are easily released in the Machine Gun Shot.

squint.) Pool strategy then requires the purchase of a custom-made cue-stick, the kind that breaks apart in the middle and you carry around in a leather case. You also need a nickname, such as "The Ace" or "O'Snowitz."

Then you need to decide what kind of players' market you want to get into. Are you going to frequent Anderson's Poolroom, with its green felt tables, worn in spots, and a naked hundred-watt bulb hanging by a frayed wire? Whiskey rings on the rails?

Or the Gay Nineties Billiard Parlor, with its tangerine-colored tables, snack bar and three-lane bowling alley, where the proprietor doesn't know a shitstick from a stick-in-the-mud?

These things are important, because, more than anything, pool shooting is a war of nerves. You have to be in your proper atmosphere.

The next thing is to talk about your previous high runs. Only don't claim that you've gotten any higher than 526, because that's the record, held by Willie Mosconi.

The way to run the table, as all good pool players know, is to play position on the cue ball, and avoid long shots. It helps to break apart object ball clusters, and to plan all your shots at the first shot.

The only thing left is poolhall jargon. Practice these:

"That son of a bitch left me snookered!"

"Oh, man, you're cancered!"

"Wanna make it dollar a ball?"

"The Ace?! You mean that little blond shit that throws his cue-stick...!?"

Let's see, a few other tidbits I've gathered: don't play nine-ball unless you're really good at it—it's not like straight pool, it has special strategy that can cost you bucks if you don't know it.

When playing straight pool, play safe on the break, and play safeties until the rack has been sufficiently broken. In other words, don't break them up yourself, make your opponent do it. (A safety is a shot where either an object ball hits one cushion, or the cue ball hits a cushion after hitting an object ball. A safe break shot cuts the corner ball thinly.)

Finally, watch out for poolsharks and don't bet more than you can afford. Have fun.

Bank A *bank* is the same as a *cushion*. When a player drives a cue ball into a cushion before it strikes an object ball, that is known as *banking*.

Bank Shot What happens when a player banks the cue ball. Also, if an object ball is driven against a *cushion* (banked) and then into a pocket from that *cushion*, that's a *bank shot*.

Break The first shot of the game, driving the cue ball into the *pyramid*.

Bridge A bridge is formed when the left hand is placed on the table to hold and guide the tip-end of the cue-stick in stroking. Can also be mechanical—a cue-like stick with a notched plate at the tip end used in shooting over a ball or in making a shot otherwise inaccessible.

Calling A Shot When the player designates the ball he intends to shoot and the pocket he is aiming for, this is *calling a shot*. If he hits any other ball or drives the ball into a different pocket, it is a miss.

Called Ball The ball designated in calling a shot.

Called Pocket The pocket designated in calling a shot.

Carom When the cue ball bounces off one object ball into another.

Cue Ball in Hand Putting the ball into play wherever one chooses within the head string. The opportunity occurs when an opponent commits a foul or error.

Cushion The felt-covered resilient ridge bordering the inside of the table rails. Also, objects such as cushion caroms and 3-cushion, requiring cushion contact for legal scores.

Draw A method of stroking enabling the player to draw the cue ball away from an object ball, *draw* is achieved by striking the cue ball below center with a sharp, firm stroke.

Draw Shot Applying draw to the stroked cue ball.

English Also known as *spin*, *English* is the stroking influence used on a cue ball to control its action either before or after it hits an object ball. Striking the cue ball on the left side is called "left" *English*, on the right side is called "right" *English*. Use of excessive *English* is not recommended.

Follow Making the cue ball "follow" in the same general direction as the object ball just struck. The opposite of *draw*, *follow* is achieved by striking the cue ball slightly above center.

Follow Shot: Applying *follow* to the stroked cue ball.

Follow-through When stroking the cue ball, a continuous movement of the cue following in the path of the cue ball just struck (instead of checking or jerking the cue back after it strikes the cue ball).

Force Amount applied to the cue ball should vary according to the shot. Around-the-table or cross-table shots may require more force than "close-up" shots. wooden *triangle* that encompasses the object balls for the opening shot of the game and to the grouping of those balls after the wooden *triangle* has been removed. On the opening shot the player drives the cue ball into the rack.

Rail The flat exterior of the table, above the table bed, from which the cushions slope. There are two end rails: the head rail—marked with the manufacturer's name plate, and the foot rail—the unmarked short rail, and two side rails (the right rail—the rail to the right of the table as you stand at the head facing the foot, and the left rail).

Safety If a player does not wish to attempt a difficult shot he may call a *safety*. He then loses his turn (as well as an opportunity to score) in order to leave a more difficult shot for his opponent.

Scratch When a player's stroke causes an unanticipated development such as "scratching" the cue ball into a pocket or "scratching" a point as the result of a kiss (which point would not otherwise have been made). Sometimes a scratch may be a foul depending on the situation and rules of the game.

Snookered When the player is unable to shoot the cue ball in a direct line at the object ball due to the placement of the balls on the table, he is said to be snookered.

Triangle Wooden *rack* used to pyramid the balls on the foot spot at the beginning of the game.

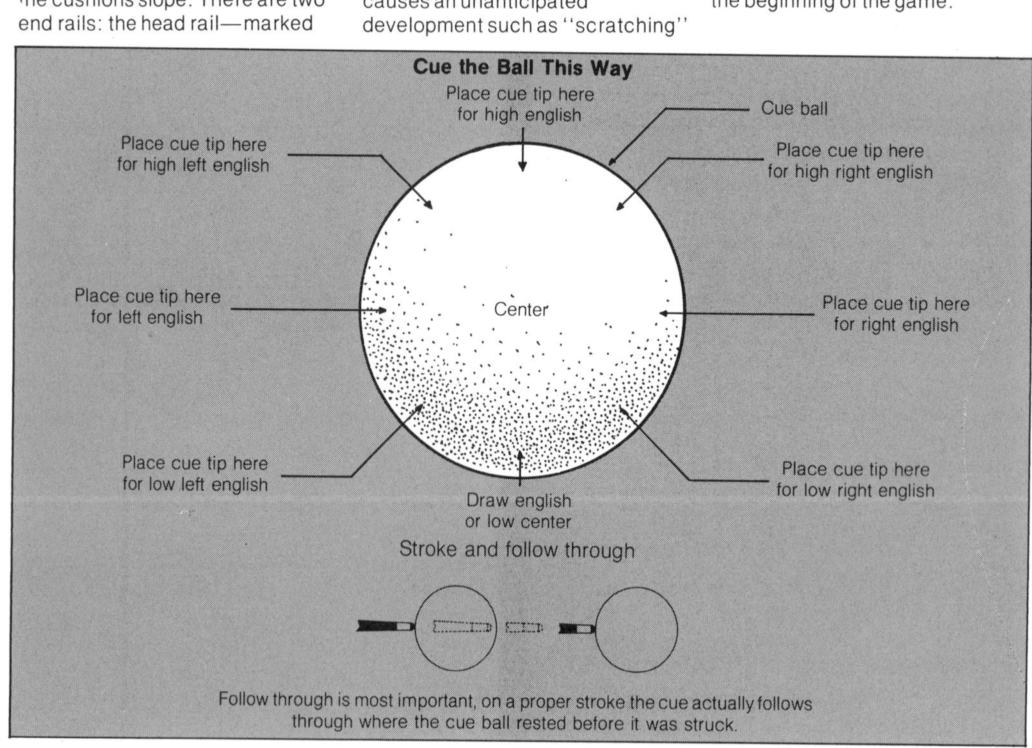

Churchill Downs, Louisville

TRACKS

Indianapolis Speedway, Indianapolis

A GUIDE TO THE WORLD'S GREAT AUTO RACING CIRCUITS

The ins and outs, ups and downs of the most challenging tracks in the world.

Nurburgring

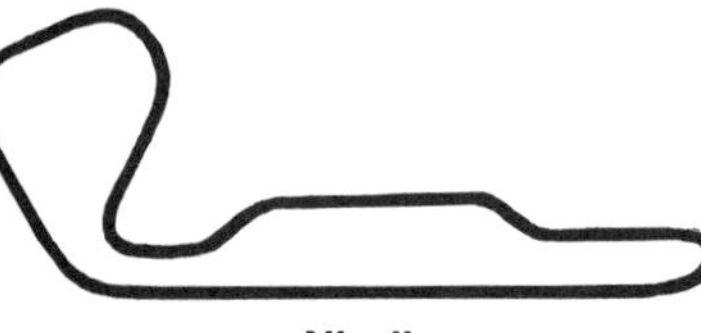
Nivelles

Oesterreichring

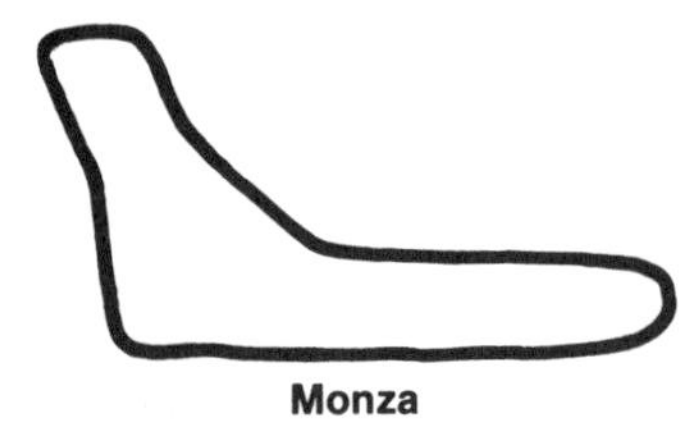
Monza

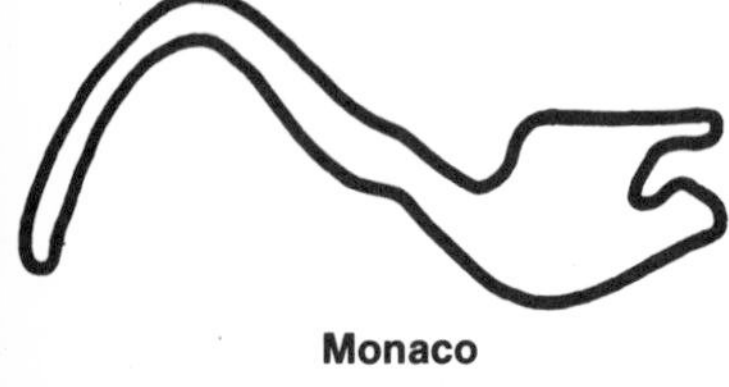
Monaco

Nurburgring

The Nurburgring is a merciless beast with 178 curves packed into 14.1 miles of tortuous roadbed that winds through a pine forest in the Eifel mountains of West Germany. It's still one of the most exciting race tracks in the world and dangerous due to the proximity of trees and ditches. More than 200,000 regularly turn out on a racing day—almost all of whom are able to see numerous combinations of curves and short straights. One of the most spectacular is the Sudkehre, or South Curve, which is followed by the North Curve and then goes into a series of fast downhill twists and turns. Hatzenbach, Flugplatz and Schwedenkreus are good for campers/spectators. And if you're a photographer and want the super shot, get near the Brunnchen where the cars still spectacularly leap up in the air over the rise. It was on the Karussel curve that the legendary Juan Manuel Fangio passed two Ferraris and won his fifth and last world driving championship. The lap record is 117.55 mph set by Jacky Ickx in a Ferrari 312B. For his performance at the Nurburgring, Ickx is called the "King of the Ring." Other drivers who have driven well on this most difficult course have been given the title "Ring Master;" with that bestowal goes an ugly-looking ring which the recipients wear with pride.

Nivelles

Even though it looks like an upside-down revolver, it's generally considered safe and dull. Located within a triangle formed by roads linking Brussels, Mons and Namur, the Nivelles course is the site of the Belgian Grand Prix. It's not the fastest track on the GP circuit but the longest straight, leading past the start/finish and main spectator sections, is a super-fast run leading into a very quick right bend (the curves here are yet unnamed). A much slower right-hand turn follows as if it were a wide circle, leading to a left, left, right, right which all drivers take in third gear. The real excitement, according to afficionados of this circuit is to watch someone like Emerson Fittipaldi roar, with exquisite position, through the fast right, fast left leading to the straightaway and into the hairpin. The course record is 115.12 mph, set by Chris Amon in a Matra-Simca MS120B.

Osterreichring

Osterreichring, the Austrian Ring, is among the safest courses on the Grand Prix circuit. It is also the fastest, with a record lap speed of 134.21 mph set by Denis Hulme in a McLaren-Ford M19 V8. A track of careful, precise maneuvering, this Ring is nestled along the north wall of the Mur Valley and offers much more than Grand Prix auto racing. Whenever there's a race, there's a regional folk festival complete with blaring bands, steins and steins of beer, quaint but potent dodgem cars, boxing matches, concerts, bratwurst, knockwurst or wurst. The circuit itself is a wide and smoothly banked track spread out over an up-and-down-hill meadow. Many spectators prefer the ease and visual range of the Zeltweg arena but the subtle right-hand downhill Bosch Curve, leading to the Schikane radius, offers more challenge to the drivers and more appreciation to racing enthusiasts.

Monza

Among the most famous circuits in racing, the Monza Grand Prix track is situated in a beautiful northern Italian royal park on the outskirts of Milan. It is a high-speed 3.51-mile course. Its lap record of 133.85 mph, set by Jacky Ickx, is only 0.36 mph slower than the fastest lap record on the Grand Prix circuit (Osterreichring). The track itself is flat and uninteresting. Of all the circuits, the late Jim Clark disliked it most. "It isn't much of a driver's circuit," he said just before he died in a Lotus Formula 2 in Germany. "It's a straight speed track and the turns are either very fast or very slow." It could have been faster but the safety-conscious Italians added two *chicanes* (quick tight reverse curves): the first, a controversial one, which comes some 300 yards after the start, the second after the final Curve di Lesmo as a precaution for entering the Curva del Vialone. The *chicanes* wiped out two areas where the drivers played back and forth in slip-stream duels which the spectators loved. The Lesmo calls for third and fourth gear down-shifting while the *chicane* which comes after the final Lesmo curve calls for a drop from fifth to second. The most difficult part of the course is the run into the Curvetta which requires a very delicate application of brakes and a fine eye for the line on the curve. Historically, it should be noted that this course was built in exactly 100 days in 1922, was destroyed during World War II, then rebuilt in exactly 100 days after the war.

Monaco

Yes, it's completely out of date with today's modern racing circuits. Yes, it is the slowest track on the Grand Prix racing circuit. And yes, modern racing cars are too fast for the streets of Monte Carlo and it's difficult to keep count of all the cars who drop out from accidents or transmission trouble. But, what a magnificent course, what countless gear changes, what multitudinous brushes with guard rails and road edges, what marble buildings, glass store fronts and what a harbor to drive by! As Stirling Moss said: "Driving through a corner at the absolute maximum on most courses was one thing. There was a stretch of grass beside the track to skid on if you lost control. But when you're flat out in a turn at Monaco and you lose it, you bang a wall. Well, that's something else completely." The start goes right into the fast right hand curve at Ste. Devote, straight to the climb to Casino bend and there, between the Casino and Mirabeau, is where they separate the men from the boys. Because it is there that the drivers can pass but only if they have left the Casino curve in the best possible combination

Ronnie Petterson of Sweden, below left, *leads Fittipaldi in the 1972 Grand Prix of Italy. Petterson went on to win.* Below, *Regazonni leads Fittapaldi, Ickx, Hulme, and Cevert in the 1972 Grand Prix of Belgium. Fittipaldi won.*

Emerson Fittipaldi, driving a Lotus-John Player Special, leads Andrea de Adammich around a turn at Monaco, above.

of gearing and speed. It is an exhilarating battle to watch. Later, comes the uphill La Gare hairpin and the tunnel by the sea. The tunnel is no longer there but circuit organizers have put in a *chicane* to ease the dangers of left-right combination, and making the Tobacco Curve a bit easier to take. The lap record, 85.40 mph, was set by Jackie Stewart in a Tyrrell-Ford V8.

Watkins Glen

Formula I drivers are not very fond of the American Grand Prix track. It's a bit dull. It's generally dirty, what with the fact that racing officials allow spectators to walk on the course before the race, scattering debris all over. And the spectators don't much like the new higher crash barriers which they say block views which were formerly exciting. And yet, it is the richest purse on the Grand Prix tour, four times better in prize money than whatever circuit is second. And it is the only Grand Prix the U.S. has. Located at the foot of Lake Seneca, near Ithaca, N.Y., the American Grand Prix is the last on the tour.

Watkins Glen

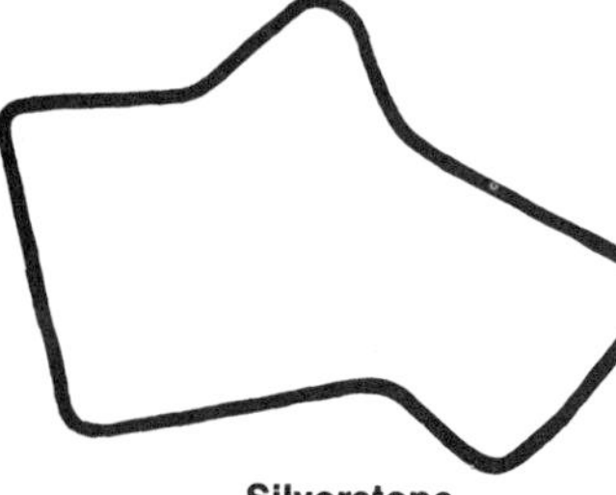

Silverstone

Brands Hatch

Kyalami

Silverstone

Called the "airfield circuit" because the rather flat course lies on an abandoned World War II airstrip, Silverstone is an unusually wide track marked off by earthen walls and wooden stakes. It is fast corners and short straights. The most exciting part of a race can generally be seen near Woodcote Corner where some of the most thrilling finishes in Grand Prix history have taken place. There have been occasions in which a driver, turning it on for the line, has crossed it sideways and backwards! The race also starts at the Woodcote Corner, shoots down a straight for a right-angle turn on Copse Corner, eases into the left-hand Maggotts bend to a sharp right, the slowest curve, at Becketts Corner. After Becketts, the machines really blast into the easy Chapel Curve and the incredibly wide Hangar Straight, roar on into the famous Stowe Corner (one of the best vantage points), downhill to Club Corner, and then make an uphill curve left around Abbey bend for a straight short run to the Woodcote bend.

Brands Hatch

Brands Hatch alternates annually with Silverstone as the racing circuit for the British Grand Prix. A humps and bumps course, set in rolling countryside, the Kent circuit is steeply banked in places and is a twisting snake of bends, hairpins, bends, and more hairpins. The most startling curve is the Druids hairpin which is both tight and narrow. The course itself is 76 laps around 2.63 miles, with most of the track about four or five cars wide. Pile-ups usually occur at Paddock Hill Bend and at the Druids Hill. The lap record was set by Emerson Fittipaldi in a John Player Special at 113.56 mph.

Kyalami

Kyalami is without question the Grand Prix racing drivers' favorite circuit for testing their tires and their machines. Set in the South African Transvaal between Johannesburg and Pretoria, Kyalami is a fine combination of fast, moderate and slow curves with an impressive straight that runs from The Kink to Crowthorne Corner. Racing enthusiasts aver that the grandstand at Crowthorne Corner is among the most spectacular in Grand Prix racing. One reason why the track is such a favorite for racing teams and journalists is the breathtakingly beautiful Kyalami Ranch which is very near the course. The lap record for the 2.5-mile course is 116.12 mph, set by Mike Hailwood in a Surtees-Ford TS9A V8.

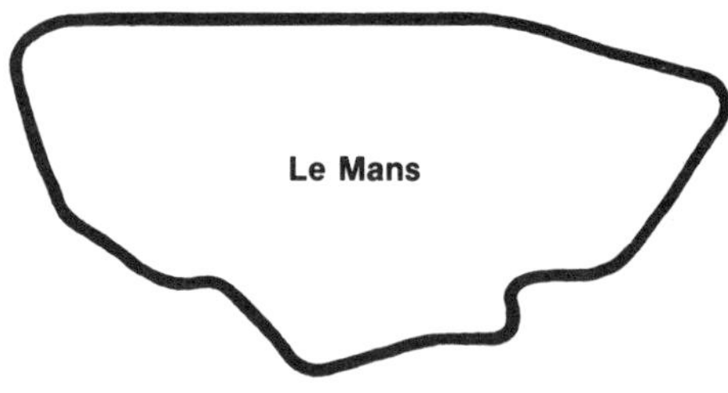

Le Mans

Le Mans is a grueling, 24-hour endurance race over an 8.3-mile course of public roads in the placid farming country of mid-western France. In the Le Mans, the prize goes to the winning car and the manufacturer, not to the winning driver. Run on the Sarthe circuit, the *Grand Prix d'Endurance* is measured by miles traveled in 24 hours. The greatest winning distance was 3,315.210 miles, with an average speed of 138.134 mph, set by Jonkheer Gijs van Lennep and Dr. Helmut Marko in a 4,907-c.c. flat-12 Porsche 917K Group 5 sports car in 1971. The actual lap record is 151.632, set by Pedro Rodriguez in a Porsche 917 L in the same year. Le Mans has been monopolized by Ferrari, whose cars have won this endurance race nine times: 1949, 1954, 1958, 1960-1965.

Interlagos

Interlagos is considered the best Grand Prix course for spectators. Situated in the suburbs of Sao Paolo, Brazil, the course is 4.95 miles long with 18 twisting bends and curves. At least 80 percent of the circuit is in view from the grandstands above the straight leading to the finish and along the stands lining the Retao. Not only that but the designers have included every imaginable kind of curve, from sharp precise hairpins to fully-banked high-speed curves. The greatest challenge for the drivers is to find the correct gear ratios for each curve. Not surprisingly, the fastest lap record (114.45 in a John Player Special) is held by Emerson Fittipaldi, the Grand Prix champion who was born in Sao Paolo and whose father is the administrator of Interlagos.

Indianapolis Motor Speedway

The Indianapolis track is an asphalt surface with two 3,301-foot straightaways, two 660-foot straightaways, each at 50 feet wide, four 1,320-foot curves, each at 60 feet wide and banked nine degrees, 12 minutes. The initial idea, when the Indianapolis began on Memorial Day, 1911, was that 500 miles was the longest possible race for a crowd to watch during the daylight of an entire day. The Brickyard has never been a slow track. As early as 1914, the one-lap mark was 99.85 mph, set by Georges Boillot in a Peugeot. In 1927, Peter DePaolo raised it to 120.546 in a Perfect Circle. Driving a rear-engine Lotus-Ford, Jim Clark upped the mark to 160.973 in 1965. Currently, Johnny Rutherford owns the lap record with 199.071, set in 1973 in a Gulf-McLaren.

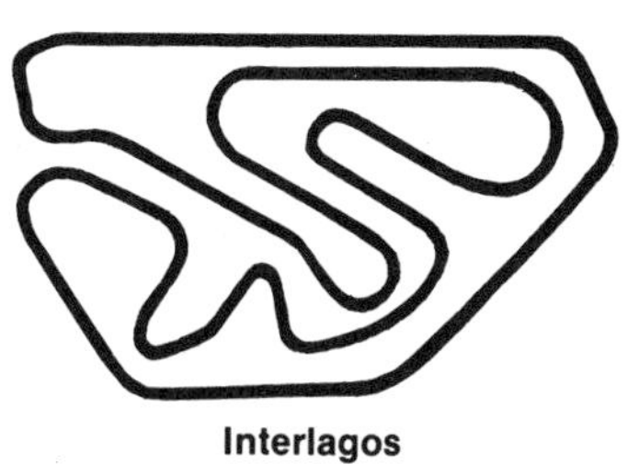

Interlagos

Tires were popping in the air and cars were piling up on the ground in this prize-winning photo from the 1966 Indy 500, left.

Drivers race across the track, far left, *in a traditional Le Mans start. Moments after this photo was taken, British driver J. Woolfe was killed when his Porsche slammed into the side of another car.*

Indianapolis Motor Speedway

Grand Prix Track Records

Course	Distance	Lap Record, Record Holder and Racing Car
Le Mans, France	24 hours on 8 mi., 650 yd. circuit	151.632 mph by Pedro Rodriquez in a Porsche 917L
Oesterreichring, Aus.	54 laps, 3.7 mi. = 198 mi.	134.21 mph by Denis Hulme in a McLaren-Ford M19 V8
Monza, Italy	55 laps, 3.51 mi. = 196 mi.	133.85 mph by Jacky Ickx in a Ferrari 312B2
Watkins Glen, U.S.	59 laps, 3.37 mi. = 199 mi.	119.32 mph by Jackie Stewart in a Tyrrell-Ford 005 V8
Nurburgring, W. Ger.	14 laps, 14.1 mi. = 197.4 mi.	117.55 mph by Jacky Ickx in a Ferrari 312B
Mosport, Canada	80 laps, 2.45 mi. = 196 mi.	116.64 mph by Jackie Stewart in a Tyrrell-Ford 005 V8
Kyalami, S. Africa	79 laps, 2.5 mi. = 200 mi.	116.12 mph by Mike Hailwood in a Surtees-Ford TS9A V8
Nivelles, Belgium	85 laps, 2.316 mi. = 196.96 mi.	115.12 mph by Chris Amon in a Matra-Simca MS120B
Interlagos, Brazil	37 laps, 4.95 mi. = 183.15 mi.	114.45 mph by Emerson Fittipaldi in a John Player Special
Brands Hatch, G.B.	76 laps, 2.63 mi. = 200 mi.	113.56 mph by Emerson Fittipaldi in a John Player Special
Clermont-Ferrand, Fr.	35 laps, 5 mi. = 190 mi.	103.39 mph by Chris Amon in a Matra-Simca MS120C
Autodromo, Argentine	95 laps, 2.121 mi. = 201.5 mi.	101.35 mph by Jackie Stewart in a Tyrrell-Ford 003 V8
Jarama, Spain	90 laps, 2.117 mi. = 190.53 mi.	93.80 mph by Jacky Ickx in a Ferrari 312B2
Monaco	80 laps, 1.95 mi. = 156 mi.	85.40 mph by Jackie Stewart in a Tyrrell-Ford V8

MASTERS AT THE WHEEL

Four events which changed the course of auto racing history.

Last Year At Nurburgring

Nurburgring is like a beautiful woman: lovely and treacherous, full of falls, turns and curves, impossible to memorize or second guess.

It stretches 14 miles through the Eifel mountains of Germany, near Bonn. Grand Prix drivers consider it the supreme challenge.

In 1957, at Nurburgring, Juan Manuel Fangio drove his last championship race. Stirling Moss said of Fangio: "The best classroom of all time for a driver, I'm convinced, was a spot about two car lengths behind Juan Fangio."

Standing on the starting grid, Fangio said, "I'm a minute behind before the race even starts." He was driving a Maserati against Ferraris, which meant he required a pit stop for fuel and tires, while the Ferraris could go the distance (310 miles) with no stops at all. Because of the pit stop, he started with his tanks only half full. That gave him an advantage out of the blocks. He pushed his big red Maserati harder than anyone ever had, and by the time he made his pit stop he was out in front by 28 seconds.

But when he returned to the track he was nearly a minute behind, and he had the additional handicap of full tanks. The 46-year-old Argentinian didn't seem to have a chance.

Some people say Fangio held back on purpose when he came out of the pit, to lull the Ferrari team into a false security. The Ferrari timers flashed the "slow down" signal to their drivers, when they saw Fangio wasn't gaining much. But when Fangio came past his pit, behind the Ferraris, his crew gave him the high sign, and he peeled out. Two laps were run before the Ferrari timers could frantically tell their crew that Fangio was gaining fast.

On 10 laps in a row, Fangio broke the course record. One man in the pits said, "Fangio is possessed by the Devil."

He was gaining at the rate of six seconds per lap. Going through the treacherous Karussel turn, on the 21st lap, through a foggy pine glen, the wily South American slipped ahead of the second place Collins by going low on the inside. As he sped by, his Maserati's back wheel kicked up a stone that broke Collins' goggles. Before the lap was over, Fangio had blasted his way to the front of the pack.

He crossed the finish line four seconds ahead of Mike Hawthorn, who could do nothing but tip his hat. When he climbed out of his car, Fangio was trembling all over.

"I'll never do that again as long as I live," he said, and retired from Grand Prix competition a stunning five-time champion.

Foyt, Ford & Ferrari At Le Mans

As a tortuous 8.3 mile run over the public roads of France, Le Mans is to road racing what the Indianapolis 500 is to track racing. It's not the easiest or most difficult, nor the safest or most dangerous, nor even the fastest or oldest. It is the Grand Prix d'Endurance—the summit in a series of endurance races for the World Manufacturers' Championship. The prize goes to the car, not the driver.

It's quite a prize for an auto company. Enzo Ferrari knew that. His Ferraris had won it in 1949, 1954, 1958, 1960, 1961, 1962, 1963, 1964 and 1965. Ferrari loved to build finely crafted cars. A man who built racing cars and raced them for the love of the sport, his emphasis was on excellence rather than profit. Then, along came the Ford Motor Company. Ford builds cars to sell them. The company wanted to win the Le Mans with their Mark IV because an endurance victory at Le Mans might help sell more cars. It was as simple as that. By 1965, Ford had reportedly invested $8 million in the Mark IV and was gunning for the Ferrari teams at Le Mans. They lost that year when all the Fords failed mechanically. And, although they finally won in 1966 it was a controversial victory. 1967 would be the decisive year.

After losing to Ferrari at Daytona and then winning (but not against Ferrari) at Sebring, Ford placed their hopes on the endurance stage at Le Mans. For that race, the American company had contracted with 18 drivers, among them A.J. Foyt, Mario Andretti, Mark Donohue, Dan Gurney, Bruce McLaren and Lucien Bianchi. Enzo Ferrari wasn't impressed. He knew that Ford's "track" drivers had very little road-racing experience and, as one of his drivers observed, road-racing was different. A driver had to know the entire course, not one single oval.

It wasn't long after the race began that the racing strategy became clear. The powerful Mark IV's surged to the lead, claiming four of the first five spots. The Ferarri strategy was to hang on, staying in a position to challenge but making certain their machines could finish the race. They were gambling on the Fords not being able to finish. It didn't seem like they were far from wrong. Within an hour, three of the seven Fords were in pits with mechanical difficulties.

Driving a bright red Mark IV with a big red 1 on the side. A.J. Foyt shot past his teammates into the lead. Before he had traveled to France for that 24-hour endurance test, A.J. Foyt had never seen the Le Mans circuit. Indeed, he had had very little experience on any road courses. His driving partner Dan Gurney, however, had. (In the Le Mans, as in other such races, one member of the driving team stays in the pits while the other drives the machine.)

By nightfall, the lineup was Foyt-Gurney in first place, with the Ford team of McLaren and Donohue in second, Phil Hill and Mike Spence in a Chaparral in third, closely followed by two Ferrari teams, Ludovico Scarfiotti and Mike Parkes and Chris Amon and Nino Vaccarella. There were three other Fords running strong.

By 3 a.m., Andretti and Bianchi had moved up to second place but then Biachi veered into the pits for a new set of brake pads and fuel. Andretti roared out moments later but when he lightly tapped the brakes on the first turn, the right front wheel grabbed and the Ford began spinning all over the road. It hit the wall, bounced off, spun across the road, slammed into a dirt embankment and finally came to rest in the middle of the road. Andretti jumped out of the Ford and ran off the track. It was a good thing, too, because Roger McCluskey, coming right behind Andretti in another Ford, saw the Andretti car and swerved into the wall to avoid hitting it. McCluskey said later that he had to plow his car into the wall because if he'd hit the other Ford with Andretti inside, he would have killed him for sure. Then along came Jo Schlesser in yet another Ford and he, too, slammed into the wall to avoid the Andretti car. By then, there were only three Fords left in the race, of which only two were running well.

By mid-morning, the rear body section of the Donohue-McLaren Ford had dropped off. McLaren drove around the course slowly, picking up the pieces, but by the time they could get going again, they were running about 132 miles behind the third place Ferrari. Another Ferrari was in second place, a mere five laps behind the first place Ford, driven by Foyt and Gurney. Like birds of prey, the Ferraris waited. They knew that any pit stop, any malfunction, would mean a Ferrari victory. They nursed their position, waited and hoped.

But A.J. Foyt was nursing his car, too, and it didn't fail him. As he blazed across the finish line, Gurney jumped on the right front fender and the two jubilant drivers made their traditional victory lap. Foyt, a quick-tempered Texan, smiled easily in the winner's circle. "That's some ol' car," he said. The Ford Motor Company thought so too. They placed it in the Ford museum. But 1967 was the last great year of endurance competition.

Fittipaldi Shoots The Gap

Emerson Fittipaldi, the Brazilian whizkid, was 1974's world champion Formula One driver. He began the Fittipaldi era in 1972, at the Brands Hatch course in England, driving a John Player Lotus-Ford. He was the man to

After the classic drivers sprint, the grueling 24-hour Le Mans race gets under way in a cloud of smoke and a screaming wail.

Jacky Ickx in car No. 5 roars into an early lead at Brands Hatch in 1972, followed closely by Emerson Fittipaldi in a John Player Lotus Ford.

beat for Jackie Stewart, racing's first millionaire. Stewart was trailing the relatively unknown Brazilian flash by 13 international points.

Jacky Ickx had the pole position, with Fittipaldi beside him. Peter Revson, the Revlon heir, was in the second row.

Ickx took the lead in the first turn, and by the end of four laps Stewart was third. Fittipaldi's black-and-gold Lotus was holding close to Ickx, with Stewart maneuvering like mad to try to steal the lead. It was a classic: three-way perfect driving, each waiting for the other's slightest mistake in judgment. If ever a duel was fought in the minds of three men, it was at the 1972 British Grand Prix.

On lap 25, Fittipaldi had to swing wide to avoid a collision with a slow car, and Stewart sneaked like a whippet into second place. The three cars were nose-to-tailpipe for 20 more laps, with only one second separating them.

Suddenly, Stewart's visor was splattered with oil; a loose hose in Ickx' Ferrari was spraying it into his opponent's face. Fittipaldi stayed in third place, calmly waiting to make his move. At Druid's Corner, Stewart slipped sideways on some pebbles, and Fittipaldi snookered his way into second.

At lap 49, Ickx had to give up—his car had lost too much oil. Fittipaldi moved into the lead, five seconds in front. Stewart made his charge, driving the two fastest laps of the whole race, but he couldn't close the gap. Fittipaldi maneuvered his Lotus with incredible precision over the pebbly and bumpy track.

Fittipaldi kept his five second lead for the rest of the race, which he called the most competitive of the season, and won his first world championship.

Rear Engines On The Red Brick Road

In 1963, a "funny-looking little racer" appeared on the Indy 500 track. It was light, a bit "flimsy," and it had an engine at the wrong end, the rear end. Well, lots of folks laughed, but after all, the great Scottish driver Jim Clark was behind the wheel. And while Parnelli Jones eventually won the race, the "Flying Scot" was not far behind.

Some people would even admit that the rear-engine machine was the racecar of the future. By 1964, 12 of the 33 entrants drove rear-engine machines even though the big name Indy drivers, winners like A.J. Foyt, Parnelli

They cracked the 150 mph barrier at Indy, as the chart, below, *shows. Can 200 be far behind?*

Gentlemen, Start Your Engines!

'You've come a long way baby.' The pace car at extreme right is being hand-cranked in preparation for the start of the 1st Indianapolis 500 race.

Jones, Troy Ruttman, Jim Hurtubise and Johnny Rutherford stayed with the Offenhauser dinosaurs. That year the dinosaurs took nine of the first 10 places, with Rodger Ward finishing second in a rear-engine Ford.

By 1965, however, the drama was building. Everyone knew that that was the challenge year. More and more rear-engine spidery critters were being built for the challenge. And a funny thing happened. In some respects, the rear-engine machines had won before the race started, because of the 33-car starting lineup, only six qualifiers were driving front-engine machines.

For the second year in a row, Jim Clark broke the qualifying record. But after midway through the race there weren't that many surprises. A.J. Foyt's transmission expired at that point and Clark's only real competition was scratched. Toward the end of the race, the Scot slowed down some to conserve his car but even then he set an Indy 500 record at 151.388 miles per hour.

The revolution, however, was complete. By the start of the Indy 500 the following year, only one front-engine racer qualified to start the race.

1911 Ray Harroun, in a Marmon Wasp, top right, *wins the first Indianapolis 500. His average speed was 74.59 mph.*

1923 Bedecked in his white driving suit, Indy winner Tommy Milton poses in a pasture in his H.C.S. Special, which averaged 90.95 mph.

1955 Bob Sweikert won the Indy with his No. 6 John Zink Special, averaging 128.209 mph.

1975 Bobby Unser, the 1975 winner, waves from his Jorgensen Eagle.

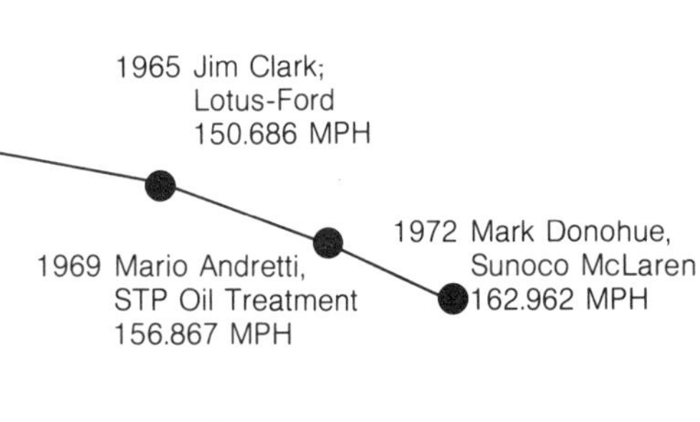

GREAT MOMENTS IN AUTO RACING

Death taps these men on the shoulder at literally every turn. In the sportsworld full of superheroes, there are only about 10 or 20 racing car drivers you can truly call world class. They are the ones who give Death their best Bronx cheer, which is drowned out by the sound of superbly tuned engines.

In a way, the race car driver is the ultimate human hero: he is totally dependent on regular folks, men and women who are flabby, wear glasses and get off on the smooth bore of a piston. They are the ones who design his ever-faster racing engines. He is also dependent on his own astounding reflexes, intelligence and dancing ability—Stirling Moss once said the only thing comparable to driving was dancing.

The racing world is more full of ghosts and references to the supernatural than any other sport. Oftener than any other, its grim aspect raises its gray head. It is not considered a good year unless someone is spectacularly wiped out. And yet, it is also a good year when the wipeout is turned into a legend, like the year Juan Manuel Fangio survived a broken neck to become the greatest Grand Prix driver of his time.

More than in other sports, race car driving is a duel between individuals, more than an attempt to win. For instance, the May, 1961, race at Zandvoort, in New Zealand, where from the beginning it was clear that Wolfgang von Trips was the winner. The real excitement was in the fight for second place, between Jim Clark and Phil Hill. They dueled, wheel to wheel, for three laps, first Clark snatching the lead and then losing it moments later to Hill. The racing experts say it was only when Clark's Lotus fuel tanks became light, and the handling got more erratic, that he had to concede to Hill. It was, however, the first time Clark had ever come to the general public's attention—particularly in view of the fact that Stirling Moss finished fourth.

That same year, at Monza in Italy, Clark dueled with von Trips himself. That time, it was the lady or the tiger, and even today, Clark is accused of causing the German aristocrat's sudden death in the Curvetta, an accident which also killed 12 spectators. Clark went on to become undisputed world champion of the Grand Prix—until *his* final flag fell in "an insignificant race at Hockenheim" in 1968.

Racing drivers are a lot like gunfighters. When one dies a natural death, it is, in reality, testimony to his incredible skill. But one detects, in the fans, a feeling of disappointment. In the sport of speed freaks, speed must kill to be fast enough.

Juan Manuel Fangio was five times Champion Driver of the World, and one of the only drivers to retire alive. He had the reputation of never losing a race (not true, but almost). A true man of the people, he was originally backed by the peasants of his hometown of Balcarce, Argentina. The name Alfa Romeo became famous because he drove their cars. Although he broke his neck on the Seraglio in 1952, by the end of the next year he was again winning everything in sight.

After racing for over 20 years, he retired in 1958. He had been brushed by death too many times—not his own, but the death of his friends Felice Bonetto (1953 Carrera Panamericana) and Onofre Marimon, his protege. In his career, he only lost one Grand Prix—to Stirling Moss, at Aintree, in 1955. Fangio made headlines even in retirement when he was abducted by Cuban revolutionaries to draw world attention to Castro's takeover. When they let him go he became a public relations man for Mercedes in South America, assured of a place in motor racing history for all time.

Jackie Stewart is the most successful Grand Prix driver in history. When he retired in 1973 with 27 victories, he had won well over a million dollars on the racing tour, and become one of the most famous sportsmen in the world. And he was only 34 years old. He had cheated death, but he would never cheat the income tax: he lives in Switzerland, where racing drivers are tax-free heroes.

In the tropical forest of race drivers, he was the fire-tree: flamboyant, fortunate and good-humored.

He was also the driver most devoted to safety—to the disappointment, it must be said, of some of his fans. He took the attitude that he was not paid to risk his life—just to drive a car very fast.

But some people, secretly, wanted him to risk his life. Incredible as it seems, he has been accused of being chicken-shit.

It was 1949 and Fangio leans into a turn at Monza, above, *while Jackie Stewart takes the winner's flag at Watkins Glen in 1972*

Graham Hill is known as "the cabaret star." He didn't even begin racing until he was 29, being perhaps wiser than his colleagues, and is still alive and more or less kicking. The world was impressed by his guts and determination when he returned to championship competition only four months after injuring his legs in the American Grand Prix at Watkins Glen, New York. They'd said he'd never race again.

A master of understatement, Hill said, "You have to learn to cope with fear. . . I get afraid and everybody gets afraid. I think every normal person gets afraid. If you don't then you won't last very long. . ."

His ambitions are to win still another Grand Prix (he is the oldest champion, having won a Grand Prix at age 39) and to live to be 100. He's 44 now.

Hill won the Indy 500 the first time he raced in it, in 1966, and then two straight victories in Monaco in 1968 and 1969.

On British television, he explained how he could even want to flaunt the terrific odds in motor racing: "I think there is a very basic instinct in man that we *have* to find danger somewhere. To know where it is and just experience it occasionally. . . ."

Graham Hill, above, *smiles as he is congratulated for winning the 1968 World Driving Championships. Earlier that year, Jim Clark,* below, *was killed.*

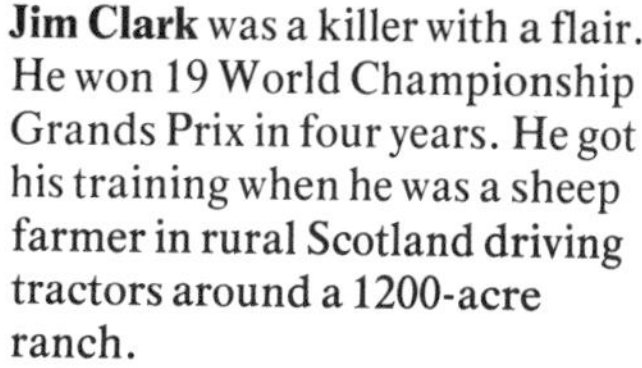

Jim Clark was a killer with a flair. He won 19 World Championship Grands Prix in four years. He got his training when he was a sheep farmer in rural Scotland driving tractors around a 1200-acre ranch.

His philosophy of Grand Prix racing was "Kill them from the start." And his style was just that—to get the lead immediately and maintain it to the end. His reflexes were regarded, even by other drivers, as uncanny.

After the "von Trips incident" at Monza, in 1961, Clark was threatened with imprisonment. For the next two years, he continually dodged reporters and police interrogations whenever possible. Nevertheless, the adverse publicity helped to establish him as the best driver in the world.

Clark was regarded as the supreme tactician of Grand Prix drivers: in 1962, he took the pole position in six of nine Grands Prix, using his electrifying last-minute dash in the final half hour of the Grande Epreuve. Graham Hill said of Clark: "He changed completely when he stepped into a car. He had an aggressive, almost killer instinct in his tactics. He was scrupulously fair. . .but he used to just storm away—." He was killed in a race April, 1968.

Stirling Moss has been classed the "Winston Churchill of motor racing." Stubbornly patriotic, he would only drive British cars, despite lavish offers from Enzo Ferrari himself.

In 1962, he miraculously survived a 120-mph crash which drove him out of racing for good. Notwithstanding, he is still regarded as the greatest all-round Grand Prix ace of all time. He placed in more than 65 percent of all his races.

His make-weight, Denis Jenkinson of Motor Sport, called him a "superman," with mental and physical faculties far beyond even the normal professional athlete. Reputed to be a true speed freak, Moss has never been known to relax for even five minutes.

Of the dangers inherent in racing he said, "No, to my mind, the greatest hazard in racing is the man behind the wheel. Very few accidents are caused by mechanical failures."

Moss's racing philosophy was summed up by him in a single sentence, "I'd rather lose a race driving fast enough to win, than win a race driving slow enough to lose."

Jochen Rindt died when he was 28; he had planned to retire from racing at 30. He said of his life: "Time is the most valuable thing you can have. . . . But I have taken out from 28 years more than you can usually gain. Isn't that simple to understand?"

It is simpler, perhaps, if one takes into account Jochen's description of one of his earlier crashes (the Barcelona Grand Prix, where his winged car actually took off and hit the guardrail): "I always wanted to know how Jimmy [Clark] felt, I think I know it now: nothing, absolutely nothing. You watch what is going on from a neutral position, as if somebody else is going to crash. . . ."

Grand Prix drivers seem to have an uncanny faculty (along with all their other uncanny faculties) for blocking out the memories of crashes. They do not refer to someone's death, only to his "accident."

Rindt was an Austrian, the first German-speaking champion, and the first posthumous champion. He left behind a wife and one child.

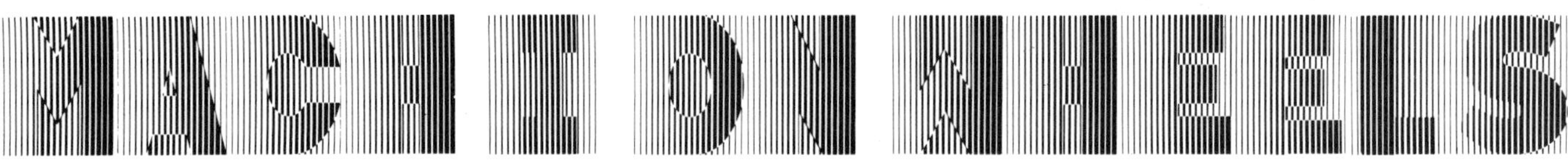

Since the turn of the century, men have sought the World Land Speed Record.

Malcolm Campbell, above, *went 301 m.p.h. in 1935. Gary Gabelich,* right, *went 622 m.p.h. in 1970.*

The Evolution of Speed on Land

- 1898 Chassenloup-Laubat in a Jeantaud 39.24 mph
- 1899 Jenatzy in a Jenatzy 65.79 mph
- 1902 Augieres in a Mars 77.13 mph
- 1903 Duray in a Gabron-Brille 84.73 mph
- 1904 Barras in a Darracq 109.65 mph
- 1905 Bowden in a Mercedes 109.75 mph
- 1906 Marriott in a Stanley (Steam) 127.659 mph
- 1910 Oldfield in a Benz 131.724 mph
- 1911 Burman in a Benz 141.732 mph
- 1919 DePalma in a Packard 149.875 mph
- 1920 Milton in a Dusenberg 155.046 mph
- 1926 Parry-Thomas in a Thomas Spl. 170.624 mph
- 1927 Seagrave in a Sunbeam 203.790 mph
- 1928 Keech in a White Triplex 207.552 mph
- 1929 Seagrave in an Irving-Napier 231.446 mph
- 1931 Campbell in a Napier-Campbell 246.086 mph
- 1932 Campbell in a Napier-Campbell 253.96 mph
- 1933 Campbell in a Napier-Campbell 272.109 mph
- 1935 Campbell in a Bluebird Spl. 301.13 mph
- 1937 Eyston in a Thunderbolt #1 311.42 mph

0 **50 mph** **100** **150** **200** **250** **300**

OVALS: THE FASTEST PASS

American Auto Racing Records

Track and Race	**Average Speed Record Holder, Racing Car and Year**
Firecracker 400, Daytona I.S.	167.247 mph by Cale Yarborough in a '68 Mercury, 1968
Indy 500, Indianapolis Speedway	162.962 mph by Mark Donohue in a Sunoco McLaren M16B-Offenhauser, 1972
Daytona 500, Daytona International Speedway	161.550 mph by A. J. Foyt in a '71 Mercury, 1972
Motor State 400, International Speedway	153.485 mph by David Pearson in a '71 Mercury, 1973
Yankee 400, Michigan International Speedway	149.862 mph by Bobby Allison in a '69 Mercury, 1971
Texas 500, Texas World Speedway	147.059 mph by Buddy Baker in a '71 Dodge, 1972
National 500, Charlotte Motor Speedway	145.240 mph by Cale Yarborough in a '73 Chevrolet, 1973
Alamo 500, Texas World Speedway	145.114 mph by Richard Petty in a '73 Dodge, 1973
Dixie 500, Atlanta International Speedway	142.712 mph by Richard Petty in a '70 Plymouth, 1970
World 600, Charlotte Motor Speedway	142.255 mph by Buddy Baker in a '72 Dodge, 1972
Atlanta 500, Atlanta International Raceway	139.554 mph by Bobby Allison in a '69 Dodge, 1970
Miller 500, Ontario Motor Speedway	134.168 mph by A. J. Foyt in a '71 Mercury, 1971
Southern 500, Darlington International Raceway	134.033 mph by Cale Yarborough in a '73 Chevrolet, 1973
Rebel 500, Darlington International Raceway	122.655 mph by David Pearson in a '71 Mercury, 1973
Carolina 500, N. Carolina M.S.	121.622 mph by Richard Petty in a '74 Dodge, 1974
American 500, N. Carolina Motor Speedway	119.811 mph by Cale Yarborough in a '69 Mercury, 1970
Riverside 500, Riverside International Speedway	105.516 mph by Richard Petty in a '69 Ford, 1969
Golden State 400, Riverside I.S.	101.120 mph by Richard Petty in a '70 Plymouth, 1970

The 1973 Atlanta 500 finds Richard Petty riding the guard-rail after hitting Buddy Baker.

The wealthiest man in stock car racing, Richard Petty awaits the start of the Purolator 500.

● 1938 Eyston in a Thunderbolt #2 357.5 mph

● 1939 Cobb in a Railton 368.9 mph

● 1947 Cobb in a Railton-Mobil 394.2 mph

● 1963 Breedlove in a Spirit of America 407.45 mph

● 1964 Arfons in a Green Monster 536.71 mph

● 1965 Breedlove in a Spirit of America 600.601 mph

● 1970 Gary Gabelich in a Blue Fame 622.407mph

350 **400** **450** **500** **550** **600 mph**

A QUARTER MILE IN 5 1/2 SECONDS

By Herb Michelson

From the back-roads of Los Angeles, drag racing has exploded into the big time.

The Record-Holder

—Donald Glenn "Big Daddy" Garlits is our man. He holds the record for the highest speed recorded by a piston-engined dragster, 247.25 mph, with an elapsed time of 5.8 seconds. To set the record, Garlits drove a rear-engined AA-F dragster, powered by a 7,948-c.c. super-charged Dodge V8 engine at the National Hot Rod Association's All-Pro Supernationals at the Ontario Motor Speedway near Los Angeles on November 23, 1973. Garlits also holds the record for the lowest elapsed time recorded, 5.78 seconds (with a terminal velocity of 244.56 mph) set at the same meet. In February, 1974, he equaled both of these records in one run during the American Hot Rod Association's Grand American No. 1 at the Beeline Raceway in Phoenix, Ariz.

Sociological implications aside (man meets car, man marries car, man races car), the automotive age has furnished historians with a remarkable object lesson in gamesmanship, a unique toy. If the car beat walking, it also beat horseshoes and world class whittling. In the hands of the right people—and who was to say anyone was unfit for the task—the automobile could be reminted for pleasure without purpose, for a non-function, for a frantic 1,320-foot spin that would dazzle. A sport off the streets, a test of fibrous manhood, a dread badge of courage to those lacking a heavy foot. And very American. Drag racing was a gift from our children; why one day it would even provide its own Christmas tree.

You Wanna Drag?

Southern California in the 1930s. Not yet two cars in every garage, but enough old Model A and Model T Fords around for tinkering, for souping up, for playing. Some sped into the Mojave Desert. Most simply sped out the driveway and up your block—at high speed, side-by-side to the end of the block, or any convenient wasteland strip. A game, a race, a quick thrill—two young men stopped at an intersection waiting for the light to change, then blasting off. Police were aghast at the trend—enforcement did not lead to containment. Often, in fact, they had trouble catching up with the cars they were chasing. The only civic solution, and a wise one it was, was to take the dragsters off the busy streets and organize them in safer, saner venues. Hello, drag strip. And hello, in 1951, the National Hot Rod Association. Within the next quarter century it would guide drag racing into a lucrative, tumultously attended, impressively organized national sport with a 100-page list of guidelines and sufficient participants to launch a new republic. In not many years drag racing has become one of America's most popular misunderstood sports. Blue collar pride, and passion, with a perhaps surprising emphasis on safety. The NHRA works closely with the Specialty Equipment Manufacturers Association, and often the wisdom of the dragster is applied to safety features in your everyday car.

The Event.

You can drag in almost any kind of car (well, at least a hundred anyway), and even on a motorcycle. Depending on the dragster you drive, you can use pure gasoline or an exotic fuel blend. The car, the pure dragster, is a 45-foot long, three-foot wide, one-to-three foot high monument to mechanism—not artistic design—for most of the pure dragster's 1,500 pounds is in the engine. The lightweight metal frame is supported by two thin bike-type wheels up front and two squat plane-type tires in back. This skeletal design supports a lofty, high-powered, mid-car engine and the driver's cockpit (behind the engine, between rear wheels). The car must meet a variety of stringent standards; its driver must be licensed by the NHRA. All this for a short quarter mile (some strips are one eighth mile) spin that, depending on the class of vehicle, will be covered in between 5½ and 17 seconds.

The dragster is built for this distance, this time. Purely, and expensively.

The start is the key to the race. Two cars pull up side by side to the starting line. Some 20 feet downcourse is the "Christmas Tree," a standardized system of vertical lighting that triggers each start. Lights flash on and off in descending order. When the green glows, the drivers go from a standing start (racing either the clock or each other, depending on the event; the big shots drag head-to-head). If a driver jumps the light, he's disqualified. If he drifts from his driving lane, he's disqualified. Instant acceleration is all that matters in the end—to reach the finish line first. However, records are kept in a "peak speed" area, the 66 feet on each side of the finish line. At the finish, drivers pop braking chutes, hit the brakes and hope for a smooth slowdown. There's a net or cushioned wall waiting to catch them. Hours of waiting, hours of elimination heats, all for a few flashing seconds at speeds exceeding 200 miles per hour--and first prize money that occasionally reaches $30,000.

The Action

As the driver is enveloped by his dragster ("like a pebble in a slingshot," wrote one fellow), the vehicle itself is cloaked in smoke at the start. At getaway, all the power is transmitted to the rear wheels. The front end rises; the takeoff is accompanied by a maelstrom of sound, flames, dust—much less than in early dragging days, but still mildly spectacular. Yet the fan seems at least as enthralled by the atmosphere as by the quick-as-a-wink race itself. The drag buff is permitted a glimpse at pre-race activities, a visit into the pits. The hours of racing are relieved by the sniffing of cars, drivers, crews. There is nothing impersonal about "watching" drag races. One may not partake, but one can certainly get the feel. Thus the inaction can be of greater moment to the spectator than the fitful start-chute-break heats.

The Heroes

One Wally Parks saw dragsters through their formative years, as multi-termed president of the NHRA. His work spawned, by the mid-1970s, more than 600 strip arenas with as many as 5,000 meets annually, including nine major national events drawing the sport's biggest names. And none was bigger than dragdom's initial superstar, Don "Big Daddy" Garlits, raised by a horticulturist mother in Tampa, Fla., but early a lad more interested in hotrodding than hothousing. He called dragging a "dangerous, cockeyed thing," but for many years was better than anyone else in the field. Garlits was the first drag racer to hit 170 m.p.h., the first to exceed 200 m.p.h. "A lot of guys thought those speeds were unreachable," he once said, "so they started inviting me to their tracks to prove it." Expense money, appearance money: a drag racing professional. (The preponderance of drag racers are "sportsmen," folks who earn their living at non-racing trades, yet if they defeat a professional in a race they, too, receive cash prizes.) Garlits is a scarred success. He broke his back and charred much of his body in a variety of engine blowups and end-of-runway crashes. He survived; another early idol, John "The Zookeeper" Mulligan, a one-time street racer from Garden Grove, Ca., didn't. Mulligan had a clutch explode in his face at the 1969 Nationals.

Garlits' long-time rival was Don "The Snake" Prudhomme, whose mid-1960s Plymouth-powered dragster, called "The Hawaiian," was the fans' most beloved vehicle. Drag racing's cars and people are nickname prone —for the fans' sake. Tom "The Mongoose" McEwan prospered as a wrestling-like villain by popping off, engendering rivalries. He won his share of arguments, and races—although not as many as Gordon Collett, the sport's first "grand slam" winner. Collett, an Ohioan nicknamed "Collecting," chose to compete in the gas-powered events and dominated them all. Infrequently, a drag racer would try his hand in the longer, road racing events. But as one veteran drag racer pointed out: "Dragging is more precise. There are too many mechanical variables in road racing. The fastest car doesn't always win the road race. But every drag race proves who's fastest." Prudence is also essential. As Garlits once said, "I honestly think if you had a drag strip running up to a cliff with a 2,000-foot drop at the end of it, the top 10 [drag racers] would pass it up. But there'd be a hundred others almost as good who want to crack the top 10 who would go out there and race right off the end of the cliff, thinking the other guy would chicken out and shut off before they would."

Chris Karamesines, far left, *pulls ahead of Lyle Fisher in a 1963 fuel eliminaton run. In this World Series of Drag Racing, Karamesines bettered 200 mph.*

Drag Racing Records

Date	¼ Mile Elapsed Time	MPH***	Driver	Site
7-3-60	9.06	168.85	Joe Tucci	Atco, N.J.
5-20-61	8.97	175.09	Jack Chrisman	Emporia, Va.
5-19-62	8.63	176.12	Jim Nelson	Memphis, Tenn.
2-16-63	8.24	———	Don Garlits	Pomona, Calif.
2-16-63	———	187.86	Steve Porter	Pomona, Calif.
5-16-64	7.96	———	Bobby Vodnik	Cecil County, Md.
8-1-64	7.78	201.34	Don Garlits	Island Dragway, N.Y.
5-16-65	7.54	———	Buddy Cortines	Dallas, Texas
9-24-66	7.38	———	James Warren	Irwindale, Calif.
9-24-66	———	213.76	Tommy Allen	Irwindale, Calif.
5-7-67	6.97	———	Tom McEwan	Carlsbad, Calif.
5-7-67	———	226.12	Bobby Edmunds	Carlsbad, Calif.
9-14-68	———	229.59	John Mulligan	Orange County, Calif.
9-13-69	6.64	———	Tom Raley	Atco, N.J.
10-25-70	6.53	———	Tom Raley	Dallas, Texas
9-18-71	6.26	———	Don Garlits	Gainesville, Fla.
7-7-72	6.15	———	Clayton Harris	Long Beach, Calif.
11-17-73	5.78	247.25	Don Garlits	Ontario, Calif.

The Records

The National Hot Rod Association gleans its major records from the National World Championship Series races, the National Open or other specially designed record meets. The NHRA, with great frequency, and competency, tallies the records for national distribution via its allied publications in these classes: Top Fuel Eliminator, Funny Car Eliminator, Pro Stock Eliminator, Pro Comp Eliminator, Competition Eliminator, Modified Eliminator, Super Stock Eliminator (both standard shift and automatic transmissions), Stock Eliminator (standard and automatic) and 1/8 Mile. The immense growth of the sport and sophisticated development of the hardware has resulted in an almost monthly turnover in records since the NHRA began its bookkeeping of official marks in 1960. A look at the records in just one of the classes—the prestigious Top Fuel Eliminator—is illustrative of the rapid speed turnover.

TWO HUNDRED MPH BETWEEN YOUR LEGS

The most macho sport of all or a form of zen? Choose your style.

Those efficient, industrious Germans started it in 1885—Karl Benz with his three-wheeler (wooden wheels yet), Gottlieb Daimler with his two-wheel boneshaker. The cycle was originally a European passion, both in terms of use and sporting prominence. Americans were simply too much in love with those machines on four wheels.

Cycle racing began in isolated fashion, on an island in fact, the Isle of Man off Scotland in 1907. Everyone with a bike, whatever the engine size, wished to enter. And so, classes of competition. And speed. Just after the turn of the century, some bikes (22 horsepower) were zipping at 80 mph. To think England had had a road speed limit of four mph . . . .

In America, meanwhile, the original bikes were literally bicycles with motors attached. Their first use was to pace bicycle races. Then, bolstered by manufacturers' prodding and cooperation (Indian, Harley Davidson), board track and hillclimbing events took hold in the days just after World War I. There followed "The Gypsy Tour" weekend road race-like events throughout the country, drawing as many as 75,000 spectators by 1922. The American Motorcycle Association, organized to minimize manufacturers' control of the sport, came along in 1924 and truly put the cycle onto the American sporting scene. By its 50th anniversary, the A.M.A. had a membership of 140,000 individual motorcyclists, 1,500 chartered clubs, 7,000 sanctioned amateur events and control of all major professional competition in the United States.

Mike Kessler hangs on tight after losing control during a 1975 motocross at the Daytona International Speedway. Kessler was not hurt in this fall.

Still, not until 1974 did a non-industry sponsor delve into cycle racing. The first was R. J. Reynolds Tobacco Company with its $15,000 Camel Pro Series. Cycle purists in Europe deigned generally to ignore the U.S. competition until 1970, when the Federation Internationale Motorcycliste finally embraced the A.M.A. as an affiliated organization. Previously, an American could race in Europe only by purchasing an international license. Women began racing actively, although not abundantly, in 1940, but none turned pro until Kerry Kleid was licensed by the A.M.A. in 1971. A year later, the pits were opened to licensed female mechanics. Slowly, motorcycle racing matured in the U.S. Once a spectator could sort out the multiplicity of events (which even included dragsters), the sport began making sense, bolting with justification from its dust-leather-macho milieu that retarded early acceptance.

Motocross Some call it the most physically demanding of any machine racing event. It is certainly the fastest growing of all motorcycle events. One writer's description: "The world's first two-wheeled, two-stroke, gasoline-burning mystical experience, complete with levitation...."

The name comes from the French slang for motorcycle (moto) and the cross in cross-country. Europeans had so much fun scrambling on their bikes over bomb-bruised roads after World War II that they gave the riding form and substance. The first official motocross race came in Holland in 1947, and within a few years the event was clasped to the bosom of riders and fans alike. Americans became enamored beginning in the early 1970s. They saw motocross as a combined marathon-steeplechase, with great commercial impact.

Most motocrosses consist of three short heats, or motos, over an obstacle-cluttered dirt track between a half mile and a mile and a half long. The heats can run between 15 and 45 minutes—over jumps, bumps, mud, sand, hills, ruts, gullies, water. With so many obstacles over so contained a course, the bikes are actually airborne much of the time. Riders must hang in there for all the heats, with no breathing time in between. Thus, the competitors are tougher than in other cycle racing events. Endurance is the key. Points go to the cyclists who complete the most laps in each moto; the winner is the bruised fellow with the highest combined point total.

Hillclimbing Although an early favorite, interest in hillclimbing has declined; but it will never face extinction. There are too many hills, too much bumpy fun. Organized climbs range from 200 to 400 steep yards. The starting line's 30 feet from the hill's base, the finish 20 feet from the top. Time is the winning factor, yet if a rider goes too fast his rear tire spins, preventing mobility. Lack of speed puts the bike in his lap. Fuel over 100 octane permissible.

Enduro An outgrowth of road runs, the enduro is not really a race. The key is precision —maintaining an average speed and arriving at predetermined, secret checkpoints on time. Most courses are from 50 to 250 miles long, over every conceivable kind of terrain. The desert, though, offered an appealing enduro test—seemingly for everyone who could beg, borrow or, *uh,* acquire a bike. In 1973, for example, some 3,000 riders filled the 170 miles between Barstow, Calif., and Las Vegas, Nev., with the scent of enduro. Only 1,700 of them endured. Six classes of cycles (engine sizes) are eligible. Pack a lunch, and don't be late. Or early either. Both ways you lose points.

Flat Track The most consistently appealing cycle competition category is flat track. The racing is counter-clockwise on dirt, asphalt or boards. The oval tracks, no wider than 30 feet, can vary in distance from a quarter mile to mile. (A one-tenth mile track proved handy in winter months: bad weather, arena-warmed hearts.) There are usually three events—elimination heats of five laps, semis of 10, finals of 15 to 50. Riders wear a steel-bottom left boot for braking and cornering; the lexicon is "broadsliding." With high speeds (up to 125 mph) and tight company, crashes tend to have a domino effect. The oval track boom was necessitated by lack of outdoorsy road racing venues, although road racing was more favored, and accessible, in Europe. The paved pursuit is smoother obviously than the dirt scrambling, yet few dirt track drivers are able to make the transition. Cycle buffs consider road racing a true test of a racer's versatility—thus the Grand National Series of 21 races in America, culminating in the classic at Daytona, Fla. It was at first (1937) a full-speed blast along five miles of beach and blacktop road, then moved to the 190 mph straightaways of Daytona International Speedway. The biggie: 200 miles.

Desert Racing

In vast areas of desolate and arid land in the southwestern states, thousands of avid motorcyclists engage in their favorite pastime: desert racing. Like motocross, this sport pits men and machines against each other and against nature; here nature includes rocks, dirt, gullies, washes, uphills, downhills, unending whoop-de-doos and immense stretches of soft sand and fine, powdery silt. Races are held almost every Sunday throughout the year and are sponsored by motorcycle clubs belonging to the American Motorcycle Association or by organizations like the Desert Racing Association (DRA) or the Sportsman Racing Association (SRA). There are two major types of desert races—they're called Hare Scrambles and Hare-and-Hound.

In the Hare Scrambles the course consists of two or three 30- to 45-mile loops through the desert marked off with lime and colored ribbons; the loops start and finish in the same place. Hare-and-Hounds races, on the other hand, run from one starting point to a different finishing point over a distance of 100 miles

Wide-eyed with apprehension, Hal Rooks quickly contemplates the fact that he didn't quite make it as his bike topples in the Canadian hillclimbing championships.

The Heroes

Ken Roberts was not yet 23 years old when he won his second straight Grand National Championship—and more than $200,000—in 1974. He picked up points in every event in the Grand National Series. A road racer and dirt tracker, the young man from Modesto is the brightest light in the Yamaha stable.

Gary Nixon has long been recognized as one of America's finest pavement racers after a notable beginning on dirt tracks. Often injured, he came back from a near-career ending accident in 1969 to win three straight 1973 road races and finish third in National standings. He's from Cockeysville, Md.

Mike Hailwood is a jet-setting British bachelor who became a road racing terror at 18 on a variety of bikes and in several classes of competition. Known as "Mike the Bike" when he ruled the roads for Honda in the mid-1960s, he's done well in U.S. competition also.

Roger DeCoster is the main man of Motocross. The Belgian three-time World titlist picked up his first American championship in 1974. He leads the Suzuki pack.

Ken Roberts gives the photographer a thumbs up signal on his last lap en route to a win in the 100-Mile Expert-Junior 250cc Combined Road Race at Daytona in 1975. Roberts is twice AMA Camel Pro Series champ.

World Land Speed Records

Date	Rider	Site	Machine	MPH
4-14-20	Ed Walker	Daytona	Indian	103.5
4-27-24	Bert LeVack	Arpajon, France	Brough Superior	113.5
9-5-26	Claude Temple	Arpajon	OEC Temple	121.5
9-19-29	Ernst Henne	Munich	BMW	134.5
11-6-30	Joe Wright	Arpajon	OEC Temple JAP	150.5
10-12-36	Ernst Henne	Frankfurt	BMW	169
10-21-37	Piero Taruffi	Brescia-Bergamo Italy	Gilera	170.5
4-12-51	Wilhelm Herz	Munich	NSU	180
8-4-56	Wilhelm Herz	Bonneville	NSU.	210
9-5-62	Bill Johnson	Bonneville	Triumph	224.5
8-25-66	Bob Leppan	Bonneville	Triumph	245.6
9-17-70	Don Vesco	Bonneville	Yamaha	251.9
10-16-70	Cal Rayborn	Bonneville	Harley-Davidson	265.4
*10-1-74	Don Vesco	Bonneville	Yamaha	281.7

*(Recognized by A.M.A. but not internationally.)

The Number One Plate In the first two decades plus of Grand National racing, only 11 men gleaned the Number One Plate of the A.M.A.—the shield on their bike designating their pre-eminence in the Grand National Series for a give year:

1954-56-57: Joe Leonard
1955: Brad Andres
1958-59-60-61: Carroll Resweber
1962-65-66: Bart Markel
1963-71: Dick Mann
1964: Roger Reiman
1967-68: Gary Nixon
1969: Mert Lawwill
1970: Gene Romero
1972: Mark Brelsford
1973-74: Ken Roberts

or more. The longest Hare-and-Hound race held annually is the Check Chase, a 250-mile contest through the desert from Lucerne Valley, Calif. to Parker, Ariz.; it's run every October. The *largest* Hare-and-Hound race held annually is the Barstow-to-Vegas classic, a 170-mile event that attracts upwards of 3,700 riders. (The average number of entrants in an ordinary Southern California desert race is between 800 and 1,000.)

Further information on desert racing can be obtained from your local bike shop, from the American Motorcycle Association or from *Cycle News*, an excellent weekly newspaper on motorcycling that's sold in most bike shops.

Cow-Trailing

Cow-trailing is the Midwestern and Eastern counterpart of desert riding; the rocks, sand and parched wilderness of the Southwest are replaced by trees, mud, streams, narrow logging roads and mountainous trails. The motocross and desert model bikes can be used for cow-trailing, but most play-riders prefer the "enduro" models that have instruments, lights and universal tires with a semi-knobby tread pattern.

Observed Trials

Motocross and desert racing are distinguished by their speed and fury; trials riding is just the opposite. Trials is a contest of skill, maneuverability and balance—riders try to take their motorcycles at very slow speeds over exceptionally treacherous sections of terrain. The sections may be anywhere from 10 yards to 100 yards in length; riders must traverse the section without falling off their bikes and without putting a foot down for balance. Each time the foot is put down (this is called a dab), the rider receives points and the winner, of course, is the rider with the fewest dabs and the fewest points. Trials bikes must have certain operating characteristics: the engines must be capable of running without stalling at ridiculously low speeds, yet they must have a sufficient torque (pulling power) to climb a 60° banking or hurdle a log or rock 15 inches in diameter. Trials bikes are very narrow (so they fit between closely-spaced trees), very light, usually have no lights or instruments and have only token seats—most trials riding is done while standing on the pegs.

Watching a good trials rider at work is like watching a skilled artist or musician; these sportsmen can do things with a motorcycle that most people consider impossible. (On a flat road a good trials rider can pick up the front wheel and balance the bike on its back wheel and then ride it down the road for miles if he so desires.) The courses selected for trials competition are chosen for their degree of difficulty and will include rocks, fallen logs, gullies, sheer uphill and downhill embankments, water crossings and soft sand. About the only thing a trials rider doesn't have to do is climb up the side of a tree, but many of them could probably do it anyway.

Side-Hacks

Three-wheeled motorcycle and sidecar combinations, commonly referred to as "side-hacks," are generally used for leisurely touring, but they also participate in motorcycle races. In races, the sidecar is replaced by a simple but effective platform arrangement which holds another rider. The platform rider

Sidecar action goes back as far as 1928. Here, in a race for the Bristol Cup, F. R. Blackpeel looks warily while his side-hack rider leans low to the turf.

spends most of his time moving around to transfer his weight to the place where it will do the most good and hanging on for dear life to the myriad of tubes that support the platform and provide handholds. Because of his wild motions and weird hanging-over-the-edge positions the platform rider is called the "monkey."

Information on hacks is hard to come by, except from hack racers themselves. Some people think you have to be crazy to drive a hack. . . and even crazier to be a monkey.

Cafe Racing

"Cafe Racing" is for those who like to stay loose. Motorcycle enthusiasts convert their street bikes into highly-modified machines much like the road racing cycles and then race or just ride for the fun of it along twisty, challenging backroads—and they get the thrills of road racing with none of its rules or contraints.

The sport originated in England where it was called pub racing or TT (tavern-to-tavern) racing, and in Europe where it was called cafe racing. Riders emulating road racing heroes would race each other from cafe to cafe or from pub to pub, and then relax at each watering hole behind a tall cool one. Admittedly, the racing got a little ragged by the end of the day, but it was still fun for those who wished to compete. Though the name is still used in this country, the actual cafe-to-cafe jaunts are much rarer—the phrase is simply used to describe enthusiasts who have personalized their machines and enjoy riding them fast over difficult, out-of-the-way sections.

Cafe racing bikes usually feature fairings, clip-on handlebars, racing seats and gas tanks, modified engines, top-dollar paint jobs and even racing tires and lightweight magnesium wheels. Cafe racing is a form of personal expression first and a high-speed sport second.

Speedway Racing

Speedway racing can best be described as motorcycle pandemonium. A night of speedway racing consists of several short heats in each division or class that qualify the riders for the longer Main and Consolation events at the end of the evening. Speedway tracks are small dirt ovals averaging anywhere from 200 to 300 yards around. Rules require that the bikes be single-cylinder machines no larger than 500cc. Because of these limitations, almost all speedway bikes are either the Czechoslovakian Jawa or the English JAP—these are manufactured specifically for the sport.

Speedway is a sport that has to be seen to be believed. It's a symphony of colorful racing attire, the sound of big-bore motorcycles and the smell of all sorts of exotic fuels. The bikes have no brakes—riders stop by straightening up the bike and turning off the throttle or by falling off, whichever is easier.

The race consists of a combination of short bursts of speed down the straightaways followed by full-bore sideways slides through the corners. From the standing start the racers charge for the first turn with the throttle full-on; then suddenly they fling the rear end of the bike around sideways and plant the steel-plated left boot onto the track for balance and stability while pointing the front wheel in the direction of travel—the result is that they slide wildly through the corner with the spinning rear tire flinging dirt everywhere.

All you need to race is a bike, an entry fee and the proper safety equipment. Information on this growing sport can be obtained at your local Jawa or JAP motorcycle dealer.

Street Touring

Street touring enthusiasts are people with no desire to race or challenge the elements of nature—they simply enjoy the sense of freedom and relaxation that only riding a motorcycle can instill. If you've never felt the wind in your face at 65 m.p.h. or even looked out at the world through goggles or a face shield, then you have no idea of the immensely pleasurable sensation that you get from simply finding a quiet backcountry or mountain road and going for a ride on your bike. The grass is greener, the air smells cleaner and the troubles of the urban world seem to disappear—whether you're just going to the grocery store on a 250cc street bike or you're going cross-country on a 750cc tourer fitted with fairings, saddlebags and floorboards. Street touring is a sport for everyone, the young and old, rich and poor, male and female.

Different strokes for different folks, even in the world of motorcycling!

In the not too distant future, say our Hollywood futurists, wars will no longer exist. There will, however be Rollerball, a macabre game of killing and maiming which involves anything from roller skates to motorcycles.

The Unabashed Cannonball

E. G. "Cannonball" Baker became an early bike behemoth by motorcycling from Los Angeles to New York in 1914 in 11 days, 12 hours, and 10 minutes. In 1922, his time was six days, 22 hours, and 52 minutes. By 1935, "Cannonball" had crossed the country 106 times in gas-propelled vehicles. His last major run came in 1941, when he was 60, and he shaved his time to six days, six hours, and 25 minutes, "without," he said, "breaking any laws."

Daytona 200-Miler One Lap (3.84 mile course)

It was set at 111.009 mph by Ken Roberts of Modesto, Calif., on March 6, 1975, but Roberts didn't finish the race. It was won in record time, 106.451 mph, by Gene Romero of San Luis Obispo, Calif.

AMERICA'S HOME TEAM

By David Saltman

You forget your troubles in a hurry when you go to rollerderby.

—HELEN MURLEY, A FAN

The Effect of TV
Roller Derby is unique in American sports in its use of television.

The Derby jams America with videotapes, with the idea of softening up the crowds for the road tour. During the season, the teams travel the old vaudeville circuits, taking their track with them, sending the "24-hour men" out in scouting parties with armfuls of handbills and a pot of paste. It is like the circus coming to town, and the crowds come out in packs. (The largest crowd was 50,000 in Chicago.)

The Track
The Roller Derby track is a portable, banked affair that would just about fit between first and second base on a regular ball diamond. The angle of bank is 38-and-a-half degrees; it used to be 45, but the television cameras had a hard time shooting the Derby stars' carefully-wrought hairdos.

During the roadie days, the players themselves set up and strike down the track, changing into workman's clothes so as not to disturb the creases in their snappy black-and-orange uniforms.

The Crowd
More than 50,000 excitable Roller Derby fans jam Chicago's White Sox Park for a stimulating evening of mayhem in September of 1972.

Hooray for Roller Derby and how can you knock it? Impossible—it's cut from the same block as carnivals, wrestling, dime museums and freak shows, designed on a tablecloth in 1935 and raking in the nickels now like crazy. It is as popular as football and basketball, and much more so than *Meet the Press.* "Every week," says a Derby expert, "at least 3 million persons in the United States see a Derby game on television." Slightly more than half these people are women, the expert says with a sly grin.

The soul and spittle of Roller Derby is the Bay Bombers. They're home team for every Derby fan in the country, the Harlem Globetrotters of the banked track, always playing some villainous opponents and sending the videotapes out to the silver mines of Coeur d'Alene and the glass factories of Steubenville. Wherever the Derby is shown, says our expert, it forces the opposition TV to "take a Brodie!"

The Derby was born of a father who had dabbled in everything from agriculture to six-day bicycle races: the infamous Leo Seltzer.

"One night I was in Ricketts, in Chicago," Seltzer reminisces, "and I bet the boys—sportswriters, they were, too—I bet 'em they couldn't guess what was the greatest participant sport in the United States. Of course, they said baseball or basketball, and when I proved to them it was roller skating they were surprised as hell!"

He can jabber 50 hours straight about Roller Derby, but he sums it all up in one sentence: "I see now that using women was the big thing.

"What we've got going now," Seltzer says, "is a game whose success, in part, is built on the cynicism of the men because they can't believe it's a real sport. . . . But the women, thank God, bring them along and at the games these men go wild!"

Yes, there is a titillating undertone of those nude lady mud wrestlers in Hamburg, or the Zona Rosa in Cuernavaca (wasn't Raquel Welch the star in the Derby movie "Kansas City Bombers"?), but basically The Derby is *clean*—clean as an American laundromat. It's a 20th-century American sport classic, with

The 1950 Roller Derby World Series was witnessed by 16,000 fans at Madison Square Garden.

Commissioners, rules and everything.

Even villainesses like Ann Calvello are basically clean: "They're paying my salary and they can call me anything they want. . .as long as they don't touch or throw things."

Part of its specially American mixture of sex, violence, melodrama, fun and showbiz are the superstars, like Charlie O'Connell (invariably referred to as "Bomber Great Charlie O'Connell, A Living Legend in The Whirlwind World Of Skating..."): "I was the spotlight kid on that track. You could tell that this kid was gonna be a skater. . . ."

And there are the Golden Girls, like Joanie Weston, who says this about skating: "There's a certain amount of childishness in every Roller Derby skater. You stay this way. You stay young."

"Skaters are a mishmash of different backgrounds," she continues. "It's naturally going to attract people that are interested in sports, or they wouldn't be there in the first place. It's going to attract a man skater of the caliber of somebody, let's say, who wanted to play football and maybe just couldn't make it in that sport but wanted to be in some sport. So they come to Roller Derby. And the girls are people who love skating, travel, independence. Derby looks like fun."

Right. Roller Derby looks like fun. That's the fat and thin of it. I believe it was Cicero who said "the things most congenial to man are those things simple, true and sincere." What could be more simple and sincere than a bunch of roller skaters beating each others' brains out? As the Turks say, "there's no hokeypokey about it!"

Or, shall we say (shifting our cigar to the other side of the mouth), your only hokeypokey is right in your front office, where it belongs. Leo Seltzer, the brains, tells the story of his encounter with Damon Runyon, the great sportswriter who, for a time, was Roller Derby's leading luminary:

"A chauffeured car drove up to the tents and a man wearing a porkpie hat got out. . . . He introduced himself as Damon Runyon and asked if we could talk a little. . . . I was very impressed.

" 'Whaddya gonna do with it?' he said.

"So I told him we hoped to make a national sport out of it, with rules and team games and everything. And he said, 'Do you want my help'?' I said, 'Naturally.' And he said, 'All right, I can get all the big people all over the country to get behind you. . . .' "

Yes, friends, step right up—it's the old flummola again, the American Dream, Yankee knowhow and little droodles on a tablecloth: it's the story of success.

Postscript: Roller Derby is dormant for the moment, pending moneylending. There's another league, based in Los Angeles, that's muscling in on the action, but the players are the same and so is the atmosphere.

Charlie O'Connell
Bomber Great Charlie O'Connell, A Living Legend in The Whirlwind World Of Skating, is the perfect example of the bad-ass kid who becomes a superstar.

He's been described as "38 and surly," and he is definitely the top male draw in the game.

He started serious rollerskating at 13, down at the Gay Blades roller rink on the Lower East Side. He beat everyone in sight, and Roller Derby picked him up then and there. Now he lives in the East Bay suburbs of San Francisco, glad to be away from New York, and he can see all the bay bridges from his swimming pool.

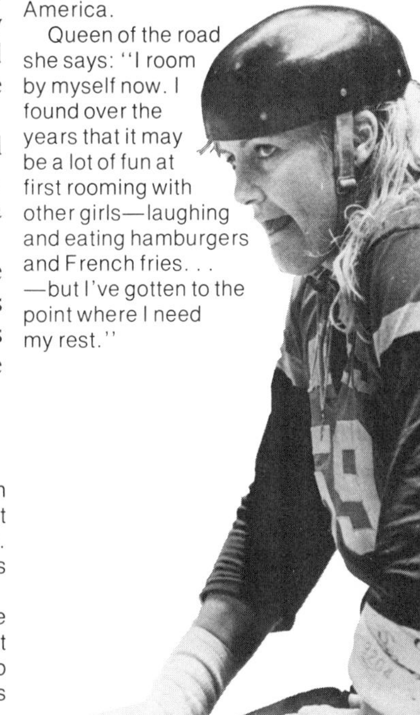

Joanie Weston
Golden Girl Joanie Weston, 38, the top female draw. She told her mother it was a waste of time to go to college, because she just wanted to skate. A lovely blonde, close to her mother like all well-brought-up American women, and a terror on the track. All elbows and dizzying speed, she likes to cuddle up with her dog and has driven 11 Chevvies into the ground. She is reputed to have said she's washed her clothes at every laundromat in America.

Queen of the road she says: "I room by myself now. I found over the years that it may be a lot of fun at first rooming with other girls—laughing and eating hamburgers and French fries. . . —but I've gotten to the point where I need my rest."

THE FAVORITES ARE AT THE POST

Place and show were all but unknown to the 12 greatest winners of all time.

"It has always amazed people," Sherlock Holmes once observed, "that one horse can run faster than another."

Even though that remark was made in the Victorian Age, it is unquestionably the observation of a town-dweller. People who live in the country know the value of good horseflesh, and know that without the horse and his sterling qualities—like speed—the towns would never have gotten built in the first place.

America, in particular, was built by the horse, and even the wonderful technical innovations which replaced him were honored with his name: the iron horse, the horseless carriage, horsepower and so on and so forth.

And so, after driving our Mustangs to work, parking behind the Pintos and Mavericks and peering at the folks who work in the buggy whip company down the hall, let's tip our Stetsons to that fine beast that got us here. Here's our guide to America's greatest horses and their greatest moments.

Hindoo	Count Fleet
Kingston	Citation
Exterminator	Tom Fool
Man o' War	Native Dancer
Gallant Fox	Kelso
War Admiral	Secretariat

Secretariat, with Ron Turcotte up, wins the Belmont Stakes—and the Triple Crown—by 31 lengths. His time of 2:24 shattered the previous mark of 2:26 3/5 held by Gallant Man.

Hindoo The first great champion in modern racing history was Hindoo, owned by Philip J. Dwyer who was president of the Brooklyn Jockey Club. He won his first seven starts in 1880, lost in his eighth (but finished in the money) then went on to win his next 18 starts as a three-year-old. One of those victories was the 1881 Kentucky Derby which he won with ease. Hindoo went on to win five of six as a four-year-old and then retired with 31 victories, three seconds and two thirds in 36 starts.

Hindoo ran his last race in June, 1882, competing for the Coney Island Cup at Sheepshead Bay. He easily defeated Fred Gebhart's Eole but Gebhart took the loss angrily. Turning to Hindoo's owner, Dwyer, Gebhart declared, "If you will come to the Union Club I will match Eole against Hindoo for $5,000 a side to run the race over." "If you will come to our butcher shop," Dwyer replied, "we will match Hindoo against Eole for $10,000 a side." Hindoo never raced again because, say the experts, the 2¼-mile distance for the Coney Island Cup ruined him.

Kingston There never was and there probably never will be another horse like Kingston. The son of Spendthrift and the foal of Kapanga won 89 races, a number unmatched in American thoroughbred racing history. Not only that, Kingston, in nine years of racing, made 138 starts and finished out of the money exactly four times. In 80 starts between 1888 and 1892, Kingston never finished out of the money and only placed third three times. That means he either won or placed second in the other 77 starts.

His amazing record looked like this:

Age	Starts	Won	2nd	3rd	Un-placed
2	6	2	4	—	—
3	18	13	2	2	1
4	14	10	3	1	—
5	15	14	1	—	—
6	10	9	1	—	—
7	21	15	5	1	—
8	20	13	6	1	—
9	25	9	8	5	3
10	9	4	3	2	—
	138	89	33	12	4

Exterminator Because he was such an ugly gelding, Exterminator bore the rather disdainful sobriquet, "Old Bones." But Old Bones could move, and he had a rather auspicious beginning. His first race was the Kentucky Derby which was run on a field of mud. Starting good but slow, Exterminator began to really move after going three-quarters of the mile-and-a-quarter, then slipped through on the inner rail and outran everything in sight. He paid, by the way, $61.20, not a bad return at the $2 windows.

The unprepossessing gelding would eventually make believers of everybody. In 100 starts, a phenomenal number, Exterminator finished first 50 times, second 17 times and third 17 times. Not only that, but he won at 16 different race tracks in three different countries at distances from 5½ furlongs to 18 furlongs (2¼ miles). He also raced under the guidance of nine different trainers.

No doubt about it, at distances over 1½ miles, Exterminator was the greatest race horse that ever was.

Gallant Fox The only time Gallant Fox finished out of the money, the bay colt was left at the post, busy gazing at an airplane which flew overhead. Other than that, he was the first American thoroughbred to lead the world in earnings and is the only Triple Crown winner to sire a Triple Crown winner, Omaha. (Omaha's victories, by the way, began the journalistic sobriquet, "Triple Crown," which Daily Racing Form columnist Charlie Hatton recalls "kind of fell out of my typewriter.")

Gallant Fox initiated many "firsts." He was the first of a line of champions trained by Sunny Jim Fitzsimmons. His 1930 Derby was the first in which a stall machine was used at the starting gate. And he was the first horse Earl Sande would ride to come out of retirement. His Derby victory, with the great Sande astride, prompted this verse from Damon Runyon:

So have they turned the pages
Back to the past once more,
Back to the racin' ages?
An' Derby out of the yore?
Say, don't tell me I'm daffy!
Ain't that the same ol' grin?
Why, it's that handy
Guy named Sande
Bootin' a winner in.

"The Fox of Belair," as Gallant Fox came to be called, went on to win the Belmont and set attendance records wherever he ran. A New York Governor named Franklin D. Roosevelt motored to Saratoga to watch the bay colt; the crowds were so packed that automobiles had to be abandoned some two miles away. But society walked only to see the Fox of Belair lose to a 100-to-1 shot, a horse named Jim Dandy.

War Admiral This small brown colt, the most famous offspring of Man o' War, often had problems getting started. He held up both the Kentucky Derby and the Belmont for almost 10 minutes because he kept breaking through the stall gates. Once he got started, however, he would bolt quickly into the lead and very few horses could keep up. And he always seemed to win with power in reserve. In 26 races, he finished out of the money just once.

But that was War Admiral's most important race. For some time, racing enthusiasts had been clamoring for a match race between him and Seabiscuit. In fact, the two were related; Seabiscuit's father, Hard Tack, was sired by Man o' War. Seabiscuit, who resembled a chunky cow horse, made 18 starts before he won his first race. But, by the time he was a four-year-old, he had won 11 of the 15 starts, placing second twice and third once. The folks at Belmont Park put up $100,000 for a match between War Admiral, the pride of the East, and Seabiscuit, the hero of the West —the four-year old son of Man o' War against the five-year-old grandson. But, the cow horse had knee trouble and the match was called off. Finally the much anticipated race was held at Pimlico on November 1, 1938. FDR interrupted a White House conference to listen to Clem McCarthy broadcast the match. War Admiral was heavily favored at 1-to-4; Seabiscuit gave odds of 11-to-5.

The distance was 1 3/16 miles, a good distance for Seabiscuit but a bad one for War Admiral. Still, Seabiscuit's owners agreed to a walking start instead of using the stall gates, conceding War Admiral's problem with stall starts. After two false starts, the race was on. Seabiscuit shot to the lead like a howitzer, whipped by his jockey from the start. By the first quarter pole the cow horse was two lengths in front. The Admiral surged forward with his long strides. By the half mile mark, they were running head to head. Seabiscuit ran tenaciously, refusing to let the brown colt pass. At the mile, both jockeys were whipping furiously. But with one furlong to go, the crowd quieted and gasped for breath. Inch by inch, Seabiscuit pulled ahead. The champion's son ran out of reserve while the grandson ran harder, pulling away by the yard. War Admiral surrendered in mid-stretch and Seabiscuit won by four lengths. The time, 1:56 3/5 was a new track record.

Count Fleet As a two-year-old juvenile, Count Fleet seemed to be setting new track and world records every other time out. It was an auspicious beginning for the gangly little brown colt and he did not disappoint anyone when he continued running as a three-year-old and retired having never finished out of the money.

He was a Triple Crown winner and of the 21 starts in his career, he won 16, placed second

Horse Racing's Hall of Fame, National Museum of Racing Saratoga Springs, New York

Horses

Armed, foaled 1941
Artiful, 1902
Beldame, 1901
Ben Brush, 1893
Blue Larkspur, 1926
Boston, 1833
Broomstick, 1901
Buckpasser, 1963
Bushranger, 1930
Cicada, 1959
Citation, 1945
Colin, 1905
Commando, 1898
Count Fleet, 1940
Discovery, 1933
Domino, 1891
Dr. Fager, 1964
Eclipse, 1888
Elkridge, 1938
Equipoise, 1928
Exterminator, 1915
Fair Play, 1905
Gallant Fox, 1927
Gallorette, 1942
Good and Plenty, 1900
Grey Lag, 1918
Hanover, 1884
Hindoo, 1878
Imp, 1894
Jay Trump, 1957
Kelso, 1957
Jolly Roger, 1922
Kingston, 1884
Lexington, 1850
Longfellow, 1867
Luke Blackburn, 1877
Man o' War, 1917
Miss Woodford, 1880
Nashua, 1952
Native Dancer, 1950
Neji, 1950
Old Rosebud, 1911
Omaha, 1932
Peter Pan, 1904
Regret, 1912
Roseben, 1909
Salvator, 1886
Sarazen, 1921
Seabiscuit, 1933
Sir Archy, 1805
Sir Barton, 1916
Swaps, 1952
Sysonby, 1902
Tom Fool, 1949
Top Flight, 1929
Twenty Grand, 1928
Twilight Tear, 1941
War Admiral, 1934
Whirlaway, 1938

MY KINGDOM FOR A HORSE

four times and third once. The brown colt came from and produced a good family line. His father, Reigh Count, had won the 1928 Kentucky Derby and his son, Count Turf, would win in 1951.

The "Count of Stoner Creek" rolled over his opposition, winning every race as a three-year-old by three or more lengths. He capped the Belmont by winning by 25 lengths but he injured his right front ankle at the same time and was retired to stud. In his last starts, he was 1-to-20, the minimum legal odds.

Johnny Longden, the only man to ride Count Fleet in a race (and second only to Willie Shoemaker in most wins), declared that "The Count" was the best horse he had ever seen.

Citation The Calumet Farm Triple Crown Winner was the first millionaire in American thoroughbred racing history. As one of the greatest colts to bound out of the stall gates, Citation won in mud, on sloppy tracks and on fast ground. He won from up front, from running just a bit off the pace and coming up fast from way behind. He won in the warmth of Florida, the blue grass of Kentucky, the free soil of Maryland and on other tracks ranging from New York to Illinois to California. And he won with three different jockeys.

As his trainer, the late Ben Jones, was fond of saying, "Citation beat the best sprinters sprinting, beat the best mudders in the mud, beat the best milers at a mile and beat the best distance horses going a distance." In 45 starts, he finished out of the money only once, and placed third twice. He won 32 races and came in second 10 times.

Not only did Citation easily trot through the Triple Crown, winning the Kentucky Derby by three lengths, the Preakness by five and the Belmont Stakes by eight, he got there by breaking two strong jinxes in American racing: no horse had won the Futurity at age two and gone on to win the Derby; just so, no horse had won the Derby Trial and gone on to win the Derby. Citation won the Futurity by three lengths and then, at one-to-10 odds, easily turned back all challengers in the Derby Trial.

Many people like to compare Citation with Man o'War but it's nigh onto impossible. They raced almost three decades apart. Man o' War raced on slower and fewer tracks. Citation ran on aluminum shoes while Man o' War ran on steel. Man o' War carried six and a half more pounds, on the average, as a two-year-old, and five more as a three-year-old. Finally, 17 horses beat Citation in his career: only one, a horse named Upset, beat Man o' War, and that when Big Red was caught in a pocket. Even so, Man o' War came back a number of times to trounce Upset.

Tom Fool "While they have not been numerous, a leading two-year-old money winner who goes through a season undefeated scarcely can be classified as a rarity. Undefeated three-year-old financial leaders since World War I can be counted on one hand, and handicap horses of this caliber can be counted on one finger: his name was Tom Fool." That's how thoroughbred racing expert William Robertson described this handsome bay horse and not much more need be said.

Tom Fool never won the Triple Crown but some folks will remember that he came down with a bad virus and cough which kept him out of racing for two months, *the* two months during which the Triple Crown Classics are held. He did win another, more difficult Triple Crown—the Handicappers' Triple Crown: the Metropolitan, the Suburban and the Brooklyn Handicaps. In 40 years of racing, only one other horse had earned that laurel, a six-year-old marvel named Whisk Broom II. Tom Fool won it by charging from behind. Eight years later, that crown would be worn by Kelso.

The end of Tom Fool's racing career did not mean the end of the reddish bay colt's imprint on American horse racing. He sired Buckpas-

Career Records of the Greatest Thoroughbreds

Year Foaled	Horse	Starts	Finishes 1	2	3	Unpl.
1814	American Eclipse	8	8	—	—	—
1855	Planet	31	27	4	—	—
1878	Hindoo	35	30	3	2	—
1880	Miss Woodford	48	37	7	2	2
1884	Kingston	138	89	33	12	4
1884	Hanover	50	32	13	3	2
1915	Exterminator	100	50	17	17	16
1917	Man o'War[1]	21	20	1	—	—
1917	Sir Barton*	31	13	6	5	7
1928	Gallant Fox*	17	11	3	2	1
1928	Equipoise	51	29	10	4	8
1932	Omaha*	22	9	7	2	4
1933	Sea Biscuit	89	33	15	13	28
1934	War Admiral*	26	21	3	1	1
1938	Whirlaway*	60	32	15	9	4
1940	Count Fleet*	21	16	4	1	—
1943	Assault*	42	18	6	7	11
1945	Citation*	45	32	10	2	1
1949	Tom Fool[2]	30	21	7	1	1
1950	Native Dancer[3]	22	21	1	—	—
1952	Swaps	25	19	2	2	2
1952	Nashua	30	22	4	1	3
1953	Needles	21	11	3	3	4
1954	Round Table	66	43	8	5	10
1957	Kelso	63	39	12	2	10
1963	Buckpasser	31	25	2	—	4
1964	Northern Dancer	18	14	2	2	—
1965	Dr. Fager	22	18	2	1	1
1966	Majestic Prince	10	9	1	—	—
1970	Secretariat*	21	16	3	1	1

*Triple Crown Winner.
[1]Held back from Kentucky Derby or would have won.
[2]Virus kept him out for two months, *the* two months for the Triple Crown.
[3]Bumped and ridden all over the track.

ser, who won 25 of 31 starts. Buckpasser, like his father, missed the Triple Crown events. Buckpasser was out with an injured hoof. Coming off the injury, however, Tom Fool's son set the record for the world's fastest mile by a three-year-old colt. Then, Tom Fool sired Tim Tam. Tim Tam took the Kentucky Derby from Silky Sullivan, won the Preakness and, in the final big one for the Triple Crown, fractured a sesamoid bone in his right front leg as he passed near the quarter pole. Even so, he finished second in the Belmont.

Native Dancer The racing record of this mighty steel-gray colt is better than Man o' War's. He won more races, earned more money, and sired prodigious progeny. And yet somehow his name is not whispered in the same breath as Big Red's. Possibly it's because "The Grey Ghost of Sagamore," as he was called, lost the big one, the Kentucky Derby, while Man o' War did not make the run for the roses.

Native Dancer won 21 of 22 starts and came in second once. That's quite a career record. There have been a number of reasons advanced as to why he did not win the 1953 Derby. Some experts say he was fouled, deliberately or otherwise by Money Broker with jockey Al Popara astride. But others just as emphatically blamed Native Dancer's jockey, Eric Guerin, for a bad ride. Said one member of the Churchill Downs' board of directors about Guerin's ride: "He took that colt everywhere on the track except the ladies room."

With aristocratic poise, Mrs. Dupont reassures Kelso and Arcaro after winning Aqueduct, 1961.

Horse Racing's Hall of Fame

Trainers

Guy Bedwell
P. M. Burch
W. P. Burch
J. Dallett Byers
William Duke
Frank E. Childs
James E. Fitzsimmons
John M. Gaver
T. J. Healey
Sam Hildreth
Max Hirsch
John Hyland
Hirsch Jacobs
B. A. Jones
H. A. Jones
A. J. Joyner
Henry McDaniel
William Molter
W. F. Mulholland
John Rogers
James Rowe, Sr.
D. M. Smithwick
H. J. Thompson
M. H. VanBerg
Robert W. Walden
William Winfrey

Jockeys

Frank D. Adams
John H. Adams
Edward Arcaro
Ted Atkinson
Steve Brooks
Frank Coltiletti
Buddy Ensor
Laverne Fator
Mack Garner
Edward Garrison
Henry Griffin
William Hartack
Charles Kurtsinger
William Knapp
John Loftus
John Longden
Danny Maher
Linus McAtee
James McLaughlin
Walter Miller
Isaac Murphy
Ralph Neves
Joseph Notter
Winnie O'Connor
George Odom
Frank O'Neill
Gil Patrick
Sam Purdy
John Reiff
Alfred Robertson
Earl Sande
Carroll Schilling
Bill Shoemaker
James Stout
Todhunter Sloan
Fred Taral
Nash Turner
George Woolf
Raymond Workman

The Match

In racing history there have been a number of ultimate match races. In these matches, only two horses are running. No other horse is on the track. Which horse won these five great match races?

Seabiscuit vs. War Admiral at Pimlico in 1938?

Whirlaway vs. Alsab at Narragansett Park in 1942?

Assault vs. Armed at Belmont Park in 1947?

Coaltown vs. Capot at Pimlico in 1949?

Nashua vs. Swaps at Washington Park in 1955?

Why, of course, it was Seabiscuit, Alsab, Armed, Capot, and Nashua.

The Jockey Club

There has, of course, been horse racing in this country since colonial times, but it is only during the past 50 years or so, dating to the closing of the past century, that the sport has had uniformity of rules and administration. These grew out of the feelings of the aristocratic horsemen themselves, who wanted some semblance of racing regularity no matter on what track or in what state they were racing.

And so, in 1893, the owners and trainers got together in a meeting and created the Jockey Club. It is the most powerful institution in American horse racing today.

Most of its work involves the registration of the race horses. The name, breeding and pertinent facts about every thoroughbred horse now racing in the country are filed and cross-indexed at the Club's registration bureau offices at 250 Park Avenue in New York City. All this work is part of the chore of maintaining the American Stud Book. The Jockey Club took over custody of that responsibility from the *American Turf Register* and *Sport Magazine* in 1896, and the Club is responsible for assuring the purity of breeding to the owners.

The Club also maintains color files. From these files, they can tell a new owner whether the colors he wants are already in use or whether they are acceptable.

The Club also maintains a record of all leases of horses between owners, partnership agreements and the assumed names under which horses are raced. Breeders can try out a new name on them and they'll tell the owner whether that name has been used, when used and whether it is available for use. You might not get approval on a name like "Man o' War" but try "Clementine."

Of course, the grey colt went on to win the Preakness and the Belmont Stakes, the other two races for the Triple Crown. Indeed, he went on to win every subsequent race he entered. Native Dancer began a career as a four-year-old but was retired to stud after he re-injured his forefoot.

Since his racing days, the "Grey Ghost of Sagamore Farm" has sired some of the best racing colts American racing enthusiasts have seen. First came Raise A Native, who won four out of four starts but was forced into retirement by an injury. What was so promising about Raise A Native was that on three of those four starts, he set three track records. Next, Native Dancer sired Majestic Prince, who won the Derby and nine out of 10 starts with one second. Injury also sent Majestic Prince into early retirement.

Native Dancer also sired Dancer's Image, the beautiful iron-grey horse who won the Derby in 1968 but was disqualified after a urinalysis showed traces of phenybutazone, a pain-killer. But Native Dancer continued producing champions, among them Northern Dancer and Kauai King. Kauai King won the Derby in 1966 and Northern Dancer won the Derby in 1964, won 14 of 18 starts, finishing second twice and third twice and never out of the money. That means that Native Dancer, who tragically lost the Derby in 1953, sired the Derby winners of 1964, 1966, 1968 and 1969. Then his son, Northern Dancer sired Nijinsky, who won his first 11 races and became the first horse in 35 years to win the British Triple Crown.

Native Dancer died young, following an emergency operation, but his legacy is an impressive one. His career coincided with the birth and growth of television and he left behind a vivid image, his silvery head leaning forward, his dark tail streaming behind, the cerise and white diamond Vanderbilt racing silks flashing in an afternoon sun, his majestic steel-grey body pounding down the homestretch.

Kelso For a thoroughbred who was voted Horse of the Year for five consecutive years, Kelso certainly started slowly. He only raced three times as a two-year-old, winning but once, and did not start his three-year-old career until June, 1960, which was after all three Triple Crown events had been run. And yet, he went on to win the Handicapper's Triple Crown, a feat accomplished only two other times in the past 45 years. He won $1,977,896—the most ever by any race horse—in 63 starts, with 39 wins, 12 seconds and two thirds. He won the Jockey Club Gold Cup five times which was three more victories than Nashua's two, and Kelso twice beat Nashua's two-mile course record for the event. "Old Kelly" or "King Kelly," as he was affectionately called, equaled or broke 15 speed records, and set two American records, much of this while carrying great handicapped weights. He was never beaten at distances over two miles. And during eight years of competition, he defeated the best of some 75,000 thoroughbreds.

There was magic in Kelso. His owners dearly loved him; his trainers and handlers were devoted to him; he was deluged with letters and gifts from racing enthusiasts. When he finally won the Washington International (after being runner-up for three consecutive years), the ovation in the stands was the greatest ever heard on an American race track. Such was America's love for this horse.

Secretariat Sure, he was the first Triple Crown winner in a quarter-century. Sure, he set the course record for the Kentucky Derby and the Belmont Stakes with phenomenal times. And sure, he won 16 of 21 starts and only finished out of the money once. "Big Red," as they called him (repeating Man o' War's nickname) was considered a superhorse even before he stepped on a track as a three-year-old. Everybody knew because 32 investors had paid more than $6 million to syndicate the colt. It was and is, by far, the highest-priced syndication agreement in American racing history.

Twenty million viewers watched the big chestnut colt roar from behind to win the 99th run for the roses and a spectacular victory it was. Secretariat left the gate last, and in a long, steady drive surged from 11th (of 13 starters) at the quarter mile pole to sixth at the half mile, to fifth at the three-quarter, to second at the mile, and—in a devastating finish—roared past his opposition, Sham, in the stretch to set a new, and very impressive, Kentucky Derby Record.

Secretariat's trainer, Lucien Laurin, always worried about Big Red's late start, and even pointedly asked the chestnut colt's regular jockey, Ron Turcotte about it. "I don't know if you're putting on a show, or what," he said to the jockey, "but why do you have to be so far out of it?"

"There's nothing anybody can do," Turcotte replied, shaking his head, "to make him run before he hits the half-mile pole. Nothing. But once he gets there, all you got to do is steer him where nobody will get in his way, and then hang on."

Charlie Hatton, who is a columnist for the *Daily Racing Form*, has an expert eye. He decribes Secretariat succinctly: "He runs in front, comes from behind, handles classic weight, and runs up a tin roof and over broken bottles." So far he's never been asked to go over a tin roof and roar down a home stretch over broken bottles but, yes, not much doubt about it. He could.

MAN o' WAR De Mostest Hoss Dat Ever Was

By William Robertson

In the history of thoroughbred racing no other horse has captured the heartbeat of generation after generation of American racing enthusiasts like Man o' War. Not Secretariat. Not Kelso. Not Native Dancer. Not Tom Fool. Not Citation. The big red chestnut colt foaled in 1917 holds that honor. Although he never raced in the Kentucky Derby, he won every race he entered but one, running easily, setting track records, American records, world records. One of America's foremost thoroughbred racing authorities, William Robertson, writes about "de mostest hoss dat ever was:" Man o' War.

Except for his single defeat, the huge chestnut won all of his races by open daylight. He set all of his eight time records—three world records, two American records and three track records effortlessly. Normally it requires two horses to break a record, one to force the other to run faster than usual. "Big Red" was under no pressure to set his records; he ran fast for the sheer joy of it, and he didn't shave or clip existing records—he shattered them.

In the Lawrence Realization, which he won by 100 lengths, he lowered the previous world record by 6 4/5 seconds; in the Kenilworth Cup he lowered the track record by 6 2/5 seconds and in the Belmont Stakes his time was 3 1/5 seconds faster than the former world record. He was never in a drive at the finish of any of his 20 victorious races; he was running easily at the end, according to the official charts, except for his furious but futile charge in the Sanford.

This loss to Upset, to whom he was conceding 15 pounds, is the most discussed race of Man o' War's career, although it wasn't such a shock at the time. Golden Broom, for example, coming off an impressive win in the Saratoga Special, was conceded a reasonable chance (5-to-2) before the race, and preoccupation with Mrs. Jeffords' colt undoubtedly was a factor in the result. Regular starter Mars Cassidy was not in the stand that day, and substitute C.H. Pettingill sent two of his fields away in what were officially described as "poor" starts; the Sanford was one of them. Finally, Man o' War got caught in a pocket.

The chart description of the race reads, "Start, poor and slow... Upset followed the leader closely from the start, moved up with a rush in the last eighth and, taking the lead, held on gamely when challenged and just lasted long enough to withstand Man o' War's challenge. The latter began slowly, moved up steadily to the stretch turn, where he got into close quarters, and came to the outside in the final eighth, and, responding gamely to punishment, was gaining in the closing strides. Golden Broom showed great speed in pacemaking, but tired when challenged..." (The four other horses in the race never figured in the running.)

Man o' War had beaten Upset before in the U.S. Hotel Stakes, and he beat him again three times afterwards. That no one took the champion's defeat seriously is illustrated by the fact that 10 days later Man o' War met Upset again in the Grand Union Hotel Stakes. Although he had to concede 5 pounds to the colt which had just defeated him, Man o' War met Upset again in the Grand Union Hotel Stakes.

Although he had to concede 5 pounds to the colt which had just defeated him, Man o' War was an odds-on favorite, while Upset went off at 6-to-1.

On the other hand, in August of 1913 the Sanford Stakes was merely another race in which a high-flying two-year-old had been trapped and had his wings clipped, a commonplace occurence. Man o' War had not yet become a legend, his great record-breaking feats still lay in the future, and it is significant that

The Jockeys

—The most successful jockey of all time is Willie Shoemaker. The "Shoe," after 23 years in the saddle, finally beat Johnny Longden's lifetime record of 6,032 winners on September 7, 1970. By March 31, 1974, he had ridden 6,624 winning mounts and his purses have totaled more than $50 million. Shoemaker, who is four feet 11½ inches tall, weighed into this world at 2½ pounds. These days, he weighs 98 pounds.

—Shoemaker once held the most wins in a season but that record fell to Sandy Hawley, a Canadian, who passed the "Shoe" 485 mark and went on to saddling 515 winning mounts by the end of 1973.

—For one card on one racing day, the greatest number of wins was recorded by Hubert S. Jones at Caliente, Calif., where he finished first eight times on June 11, 1944. Five of those wins were decided by photo-finishes.

—Trainers can set records too. The greatest amount ever won by a trainer in one year is $ 2,456,250, the amount won by Eddie Neloy in 1966 when his horses won 93 races.

—Laffit Pincay, Jr., holds the record for the greatest amount of purse money won by a jockey in any one year. His vintage year was 1971 when he won $ 3,784,377 by riding 1,627 winning mounts.

Man O'War's Complete Racing Record

As a two-year old, 1919

Date	Track	Event	Weight	Distance	Track Condition	Time	Finish
June 6	Belmont Park	Purse race	115	5 fur. (s)	Fast	:59	Won by 6
June 9	Belmont Park	Keene Memorial Stakes	115	5 1/2 fur. (s)	Slow	1:05 3/5	Won by 3
June 21	Jamaica	Youthful Stakes	120	5 1/2 fur.	Good	1:06 3/5	Won by 2 1/2
June 23	Aqueduct	Hudson Stakes	130	5 fur.	Fast	1:01 3/5	Won by 1 1/2
July 5	Aqueduct	Tremont Stakes	130	6 fur.	Fast	1:13	Won by 1
Aug. 2	Saratoga	U.S. Hotel Stakes	130	6 fur.	Fast	1:12 2/5	Won by 2
Aug. 13	Saratoga	Sanford Memorial Stakes	130	6 fur.	Fast	1:11 1/5	2nd by 1/2
Aug. 23	Saratoga	Grand Union Hotel Stakes	130	6 fur.	Fast	1:12	Won by 1
Aug. 30	Saratoga	Hopeful Stakes	130	6 fur.	Slow	1:13	Won by 4
Sep. 13	Belmont	Futurity Stakes	127	6 fur. (s)	Fast	1:11 3/5	Won by 2 1/2
		As a three-year-old, 1920					
May 18	Pimlico	Preakness Stakes	126	1 1/2 mi.	Fast	1:51 3/5	Won by 1 1/2
May 29	Belmont Park	Withers Stakes	118	1 mi.	Fast	#1:35 4/5	Won by 2
June 12	Belmont Park	Belmont Stakes	126	1 3/8 mi.	Fast	#2:14 1/5	Won by 20
June 22	Jamaica	Stuyvesant Handicap	135	1 mi.	Good	1:41 3/5	Won by 8
July 10	Aqueduct	Dwyer Stakes	126	1 1/8 mi.	Fast	#1:49 1/5	Won by 1 1/2
Aug. 7	Saratoga	Miller Stakes	131	1 3/16 mi.	Fast	1:56 3/5	Won by 6
Aug. 21	Saratoga	Travers Stakes	129	1 1/4 mi.	Fast	#2:01 4/5	Won by 2 1/2
Sep. 4	Belmont Park	Lawrence Realization Stakes	126	1 5/8 mi.	Fast	#2:40 4/5	Won by 100
Sep. 11	Belmont Park	Jockey Club Stakes	118	1 1/2 mi.	Fast	#2:28 4/5	Won by 15
Sep. 18	Havre de Grace	Potomac Handicap	138	1 1/16 mi.	Fast	#1:44 4/5	Won by 1 1/2
Oct. 12	Kenilworth Park	Kenilworth Park Gold Cup	120	1 1/4 mi.	Fast	#2:03	Won by 7

#Time Records, as follows:

Equaled track record, Travers Stakes, 1 1/4 miles.

New track record, Potomac Handicap, 1 1/16 miles.

New track record, Kenilworth Cup, 1 1/4 miles.

New (competitive) American record, Withers Stakes, 1 mile.

New (competitive) American record, Jockey Club Stakes, 1 1/2 miles.

New World Record, Dwyer Stakes, 1 1/8 miles.

New World Record, Belmont Stakes, 1 3/8 miles.

New World Record, Lawrence Realization, 1 5/8 miles.

In all his starts as a two-year old, Man o'War was ridden by John Loftus; Clarence Kummer was his jockey in all his starts at three, except the Miller Stakes (Earl Sande) and Travers Stakes (Andy Schuttinger).

***Because an elapsed time record has been set in given race does not necessarily mean a miles per hour mark is also established. The elapsed time is measured from start to finish line. The m.p.h. record is measured at the "peak speed" stretch of 66 feet on each side of the finish line. Thus the loser of a race can claim a new m.p.h. record. Rather nice consolation prize.

at the end of the season he was being compared to exceptional two-year-olds of the past, no more.

According to Man o' War's owner, the colt's greatest race was in the Potomac Handicap as a three-year-old when he carried 138 pounds, highest weight of his career. When the barrier rose, Man o' War was being held by an assistant starter and he broke to the right, losing about three lengths, but despite his heavy burden he overcame the deficit to win easily by one and a half lengths going away, breaking the track record on a surface officially fast, but cuppy.

If Man o' War's weight was impressive, the concessions he was making were more so. To runner-up Wildair, winner of that year's Metropolitan, he conceded 30 pounds; to Blazes, who finished fifteen lengths behind Wildair in third place, and who later was to beat John P. Grier in the Maryland Handicap and to win the Laurel Stakes from The Porter and Sir Barton, he conceded 33½ pounds; and to last-place Paul Jones, winner of that season's Kentucky Derby and Suburban Handicap, he conceded 24 pounds.

Man o' War's final start, in a special match race against Sir Barton for an $80,000 purse at Kenilworth Park, Canada, was such a cakewalk it is generally conceded that Sir Barton was off form. Nevertheless, the Ross colt was coming off a string of four straight victories—in the Rennert Handicap under 132 pounds; the Saratoga Handicap under 129 (in track record time beating Exterminator, Wildair, The Porter and Mad Hatter); the Dominion Handicap under 134 pounds; and the Merchants' and Citizens' Handicap under 133 pounds, in new American record time of 1:55 3/5 for 1 3/16 miles. Sir Barton never won another race after his match with Man o' War, but he raced creditably enough in the Maryland fall handicaps.

As had been done in the case of American Eclipse, various details concerning Man o' War were faithfully recorded for posterity. The high-spirited, muscular colt had been a terror to break to saddle, but once he learned that the human beings who intruded upon his majestic presence wanted only that he should run—which is what he intended doing on his own account—he became tractable enough.

In training, his day began at 3:30 a.m., when he was given his first meal, 2½ quarts of clipped oats mixed with a little cut hay. Because of his voracious appetite, he was fed with a bit in his mouth. At 7:30 he was brushed and massaged; the bandages he wore at all times except in action were removed, and his feet washed; his face, eyes and nostrils were sponged and he was rubbed with a soft cloth.

During this activity, he was docile, yet playful. He was very fond of his caretaker, Frank Loftus, and sometimes showed off for visitors by fetching his hat and carrying it around. Like all horses, Man o' War loved sugar and he begged for it; he also was fond of oranges.

At 8:30, morning exercise began. On Mondays, Wednesdays and Fridays, ridden by Clyde Gordon, Man o' War would be jogged half a mile and cantered a mile and a half. Tuesdays, Thursdays and Saturdays were work days—at distances and speeds specified by trainer Feustel, depending upon coming races.

After work, on warm days, he was washed with a mixture of alcohol, arnica and witch hazel; then he was rubbed thoroughly, his feet were picked clean, his hooves washed and he was left to rest in his stall.

On work days, the colt was given walking exercise from 4:00 to 4:30 p.m. and at 5:15 received his final ration of feed, 5 quarts, making a daily total of 12 quarts. On alternate days, the evening meal was varied, and a mash consisting of crushed oats and bran substituted. Thrice a week, at intervals of 10 days, he was given a tonic of equal parts oil meal, cream of tartar and sulphur. At 8:30 p.m., he was left alone for the night.

Racetrackers have four classic standards to evaluate a horse: how fast could he run, how far could he go, how much did he carry, and who did he beat?

That Man o' War could run fast and far, under heavy weight, is obvious. In all his starts he either carried or shared highest weight on the scale, except his second race, when the assignments were even but Ralco's jockey was 1½ pounds over weight.

As to whom he beat, the answer is simple: every horse that ever took the track against him. The quality of his opposition might look somewhat pale in Man o' War's presence, and the quantity admittedly was sparse. In his 21 races, "Big Red" faced only 48 individual opponents; although some of them tackled him more than once, most of them did not, and a lot of others avoided him entirely.

Apart from the Sir Barton match, which was scheduled as such, there were five other occasions when only one horse could be found to oppose Man o' War. In the Stuyvesant Handicap, all his opposition was scratched, and R.T. Wilson threw in Yellow Hand as an added starter just to provide a race. (This colt was an ex-claimer who later developed into a good handicap runner, and Wilson sold him for a nice price to Charles Stoneham, owner of the New York Giants.)

Man o' War answered all the questions of greatness that can be put to a race horse, with the possible exception of one: the ability to beat his elders in open competition. Sir Barton was the only older horse "Big Red" met.

In the fall of 1920 the Kentucky Jockey Club offered to put up $50,000 for a match between Exterminator and Man o' War, but Riddle refused it. This caused some sniping, but the owner of Old Bones had everything to gain and nothing to lose, while Riddle was tinkering with destiny: he already had decided to retire Man o' War.

The story goes that Riddle had asked Jockey Club handicapper Walter Vosburgh how much weight his colt would be expected to carry in handicap racing if he remained in training as a four-year-old. Vosburgh could not provide a specific answer, since that depended upon the caliber of the opposition, but he assured Riddle that he would assign Man o' War more than he ever had put on any horse before. As the horse already had carried 138 pounds as a three-year-old, to proceed further would have been to tempt fate.

Physically Man o' War was a glowing chestnut, almost red, standing 16 hands 1 5/8 inches. He girthed 71¾ inches and weighed 1,100 pounds in training (at the end of his three-year-old season he was up to 1,150 and as a stallion his weight reached 1,370 pounds). He had a straight profile, large nostrils, stout neck and a broad chest. His barrel was unusually long, his hind legs straight and his gaskins exceptionally powerful looking. He stood over a lot of ground and strode over considerably more; estimates of his stride varied between 25 and 28 feet although, oddly, it never was officially measured.

Measurements, however, cannot convey the picture of this colt who inspired such expressions as "look of eagles" and "living flame." Neither tape nor scale could capture the tremendous vitality that he exuded. As the late Joe Palmer expressed it, "Even when he was standing motionless in his stall, with his ears pricked forward and his eyes focused on something slightly above the horizon which mere people never see, energy still poured from him. He could get in no position which suggested actual repose, and his very stillness was that of the coiled spring, of the crouched tiger...."

Talented writers and eloquent speakers did their best to find phrases to express adequately the glory of this great horse. It fell to a groom, Will Harburt, who did not become associated with Man o' War until some years after his retirement, but who digested thoroughly every iota of his greatness, and was his constant companion thereafter, to devise the description which fit best. Man o' War, as Will never tired of telling the thousands who came to see him, was "de mostest hoss dat ever was...."

A number of fabulous offers, reportedly in the million-dollar range, were made for Man o' War, but the most staggering one came from Texas. Fort Worth cattle baron and oilman W.T. Waggoner handed Riddle a blank check to be filled in with whatever amount he desired, but that, too, was turned down.

Will Harburt, who had quite a way with words as well as with horses, said, "Lots of folks can have a million dollars, but only one man can own Man o' War. Stand still, Red."

One Man, One Horse

In American racing history, there has always been the magic of matching the special qualties of an outstanding jockey with that of a finely trained thoroughbred. If you were the trainer or owner [or how's your old nostalgia quotient?], can you match these jockeys with their winning mounts in the Triple Crown events.

1. Eddie Arcaro
2. Johnny Sellers
3. Bill Shoemaker
4. Ron Turcotte
5. Manny Ycaza
6. Braulio Baeza
7. Bill Hartack
8. Johnny Longden
9. Earl Sande
10. Gustavo Avila
11. Ishmael Valenzuela
12. Dave Erb
13. Ted Atkinson
14. Don Brumfield
15. Conn McCreary

a. Cannonero
b. Tim Tam
c. Citation
d. Count Fleet
e. Chateaugay
f. Pensive
g. Secretariat
h. Needles
i. Capot
j. Count Fleet
k. Kauai King
l. Carry Back
m. Quadrangle
n. Northern Dancer
o. Swaps

The envelope, please. . . Ah, yes, here they are: 1-c, 2-l, 3-o, 4-g, 4-m, 6-e, 7-n, 8-d, 9-j, 10-a, 11-b, 12-h, 13-i, 14-k, 15-f.

THE MOST EXCITING TWO MINUTES IN SPORTS

By David Saltman

On the first Saturday in May, elegant folk and dirt farmers alike sip Mint Juleps and watch the greatest race of all.

—The Kentucky Derby is a triumph of the promotional genius of the late Colonel Matt J. Winn, who knew how to put it all together. As he told a Louisville reporter, "My first love was the Kentucky Derby, and I saw to it that the owners of the three-year-olds with box office appeal flirted with no other stake but the Derby when Derbytime came around. And we played one society queen against another until we steam-rollered Louisville into a one-day capital of celebrities."

—Only one filly ever won the Derby. That was Harry Payne Whitney's Regret in 1915. Said Whitney after the race: "She has won the greatest race in America, and I am satisified."

—The first Triple Crown winner was Sir Barton. But that honor came retroactively since the concept of "Triple Crown" was not dreamed up and instilled into racing lore until well after 1919 when Sir Barton won the Derby. In any event, you should know that Man o' War, who did not compete in the Derby (if he had run, Big Red would have entered the 1920 Derby), was matched against Sir Barton in a two-horse match race at Kenilworth Park in Windsor, Canada. The race was the last race of Big Red's career, and the young colt defeated Sir Barton by seven lengths.

Irvin S. Cobb, the philosopher of Paducah, was once asked by Grantland Rice what made the Kentucky Derby so special. No one since has provided a better answer. Said Cobb:

"If I could do that, I'd have a larynx of spun silver and the tongue of an angel. But if you can imagine a track that's like a bracelet of molten gold encircling a greensward that's like a patch of emerald velvet...All the pretty girls in the state turning the grandstand into a brocaded terrace of beauty and color such as the hanging gardens of Babylon never equaled...All the assembled sports of the nation going crazy at once down in the paddock... And just yonder in the yellow dust, the gallant kings and noble queens of the kingdom, the princesses royal, and their heirs apparent to the throne, fighting it out.... Each a vision of courage and heart and speed.... Each topped as though with some bobbing gay blossoms by a silken-clad jockey.... But what's the use? Until you go to Kentucky and with your own eyes behold the Derby, you ain't never been nowheres and you ain't never seen nothin!"

As Mark Twain said about swindles, the Kentucky Derby is without compeer among races. It is perfect, it is rounded, symmetrical, complete, colossal. It is, in its way, a human achievement, even though the principal actors are horses, because, also in Twain's words, "it were not best that we should all think alike; it is difference of opinion that makes horse races."

The Derby's now been run 102 times, and is one of America's prime repositories for lore, color and family feuds. The mint julep, Kentucky Fried Chicken, the Mississippi Riverboat gamblers and the rambling bluegrass ranches...all make up what a Louisville newspaper called "the nation's most prominent celebration of avarice."

America is a horsey country, of course, and horsey people always intercourse with rich ones. Take August Belmont, for instance — the man who bred Man o' War and owned Whirlaway. He was the American top banana for the Rothschild banking empire. The word "Derby" itself came from the 12th Earl of Derby in England, who, it is said, conceived the whole idea in a drunken fit at a wild orgy among the elms. "Seldom has a carouse had a more permanent effect," commented Lord Rosebery, his upper lip stiff as a stallion's pecker.

In Louisville, the approach of Derby day, the first Saturday in May, brings out the Texas gamblers and the spring flowers in equal profusion. As the slush burns off the Gateway to the South, one is more and more aware of a vee of cigar-chawing, homburg-hatted fat-wallets, with occasional conspicuous bulges under the proverbial left armpit. Sidling up to these Texans can be seen furtive, overdressed, swarthy types, resembling Chico Marx, wearing diamond stickpins and full of the most believable lore that ever came out of the mouth of a Southern gentleman. They are the touts, of course, and all of them said Broker's Tip was a helluva bet in 1933, and that they were the only ones who gave Dark Star a chance against Native Dancer, and that they remember Whirlaway..."Now listen, boss, I tell ya it's Sham in this one. No way he can lose; Secretariat's a Bold Ruler, remember, and no Bold Ruler yet has been able to go the distance. I tell ya, boss, it's Sham. And I can get a bet down for ya right now, at the big odds...."

The Derby is a focus for all America's spring hope, whether it's for nice weather, great riches or just the exhilaration of seeing good horses run. It was first run in the age when racecourses were swarming with pickpockets, cardsharps, touts and freaks of all kinds. In the early days of racing, the most common sight at the track was the partnership of the man who could eat razor blades and his assistant who drank ink and other poisonous substances. It is no wonder opium balls have found their wicked way into various horses' gullets. As they're fond of saying down there in Louisville, "when there's no Indians to be chased, there's arguments to be settled, and in Kentucky it usually takes a horse race to settle an argument."

There is counterpoint to this view. Johnny Nerud, the trainer of Tartan Farms, has said, "the Derby is a great publicity gimmick, but it has ruined more good young horses than any other two races put together." It is a fact that the Derby focuses tempers and secret Swiss bank accounts. You wonder, when you see all America's money tied up (I mean big money, like Standard Oil and the Whitney family), and when you read the list of horses rendered *hors de combat* after the Derby run: Calvacade, Bold Venture, Pensive, Hoop, Jr., Jet Pilot, Count Turf, Hill Gail, Tim Tam, Dark Star, and many others.

Nevertheless, the prize is so great, in money and prestige both, that trainers and owners are usually willing to risk an unprepared horse rather than no horse at all. You only get one shot for the roses.

Citation and Eddie Arcaro romp home to the winner's circle, ahead of Coaltown in the 1948 Kentucky Derby.

What causes the toll on the horses is that the universal birthday for thoroughbreds is considered to be January 1, no matter when they were actually born. Riva Ridge, for instance, was officially three years old on January 1, 1972. But in fact, Riva Ridge was born on April 13, which would make his third calendar bithday come just three weeks before the Derby, scheduled for May 6. A Derby writer says, "At a time when thoroughbreds are still growing fast and their bones are still soft, they are asked for the first time to run one-and-a-quarter miles with 126 pounds on their backs against the best available horses in the nation."

That makes it very hard on a horse. It was the only reason Man o' War's owner, Sam Riddle, held "Big Red" out of the 1920 Derby.

But there have been some great, well, super great Derbies, and immortal (if you believe in statues and records) winners: the most romantic win of a favorite; the roughest, toughest Derby; the greatest owners and the greatest upset.

The largest field in history breaks for the rail in the 100th Kentucky Derby.

—Hill Gail, like Whirlaway, inherited a crazy streak from Blenheim II. And Hill Gail, like Whirlaway, could run. In the paddock just before the running of the 1952 Derby, Hill Gail was acting up in his paddock and his trainer Ben Jones told the groom to hold the horse's head still. The groom did, whereupon Jones punched Hill Gail right on the nose. That calmed the colt some. The race started. As the field was flying around the first turn, Hill Gail's jockey, Eddie Arcaro, thought his horse was going to duck through the gap into the stable area and not finish the race. The jockey reached back and slashed the colt with his whip, and Hill Gail almost ran off from under Arcaro, opening up a six-length lead on the backstretch to win in a driving finish.

—The 1957 Derby has come to be called "The Bad Dream Derby" because Gallant Man's owner, Ralph G. Lowe, dreamed a few nights before the Derby that his jockey, Willie Shoemaker, would misjudge the finish and lose the race. Lowe told Johnny Nerud, his trainer, about the dream. And Nerud told Shoemaker. Nevertheless, coming into the sixteenth pole on Derby day, with Gallant Man running head-to-head with Iron Liege, Shoemaker stood up for a moment, misjudged the finish line, and lost the Derby by a nose to Iron Liege.

—The best paying winner in Derby history was Donerail who paid $184.90 in 1913. He was such a long shot, however, his owner-breeder-trainer, T. P. Hayes, did not bet on him.

—The first great Derby track record was set by Old Rosebud with Johnny McCabe up. The game little gelding won the 1914 Derby in 2:05 2/5, a record that stood until Twenty Grand covered the distance in 2:01 4/5 in 1914. Old Rosebud was the first of five Derby winners bred by that master horse-trader John E. Madden.

—In one of the great come-from-behind finishes, Ben Brush stumbled at the start of the 1896 Derby and almost tossed his rider, Willie Simms, to the ground. Simms gamely hung on and the horse rallied to win by a nose. By the time the colt was cantered back to be unsaddled, his flanks were dripping blood from Simms' spurs, and the jockey apologized for punishing the colt so.

—The jockey with the best winning percentage in mounts at the Derby—two wins, one second and one third in four starts—was a black man named Jimmy "Wink" Winkfield. Wink, however, moved to Europe in 1905 and lived there racing and training horses until well into his nineties. He rode in numerous continental races and won most of the major internationals like the Moscow Derby, the Prix du President de la Republique, and the Grosser Prix von Baden. Still, his American riding record has been unassailable. In 1,412 races between 1875 and 1895, Winkfield rode 628 winners, a 44 winning percentage. No rider has yet come close to that.

1924 The first of these was the fiftieth running of the Derby in 1924. It was the most romanticized of them all and Black Gold, "the Indian Horse," was the overwhelming crowd favorite. He was owned by Rosa Hoots, an Osage woman from the new state of Oklahoma. She named him for the Indian phrase which described the crude petroleum that oozed from his home soil of Oklahoma: Black Gold. At the start of the race the black colt was slammed into the rail so hard, you could hear the crowd moan as if with a single voice. Then he was boxed in for a quarter mile. Going into the clubhouse turn, he was sixth. Into the five-furlong backstretch there was a brief opening, he seized it but was still running a poor sixth. At the half-mile pole Bracadale, with Earle Sande up, was leading, and Black Gold was starting to weave his way forward. Galloping into the far turn, the Indian horse was third. In the turn for home, Chilhowee was making his move and was almost head to head with Bracadale but the Sande horse would not give an inch more. Meanwhile, Black Gold was running like the wind, closing from the outside when suddenly some photographers rushed the track and the great black colt lost stride. His jockey, J.D. Mooney, damned near club-bed him and he came on once more. As the wire drew near, Black Gold got a nose in front, then his head, his neck and he won by a half-length. They say the ovation was one of the greatest in Derby history.

1933 The roughest, toughest, meanest Derby of them all was the "Rodeo Derby" of 1933. It was the Derby of the "Fighting Finish." It was won by Brokers Tip in a close driving finish against Head Play, in a finish in which both jockeys shoved, slashed and grabbed at each other for the entire stretch drive. Coming into the homestretch in front of the pack, Herb Fisher, on Head Play, swung wide. Don Meade, up on Brokers Tip, took advantage of that and flew inside along the rail. Suddenly, Fisher angled in toward Meade and the two jockeys and horses were running neck and neck, and closer and closer. Meade shot out a hand "to keep him off. I wasn't going to have him put me through the fence," he said later. Just as suddenly, Fisher shot an arm out, trying to grap Meade's saddlecloth to slow him up. With his right leg completely out of the stirrup, Fisher tried to maintain his balance and grab equipment on Brokers Tip. Meade kept trying to shove him away. When they crossed the finish line, no one could tell which horse won. Nevertheless, Fisher started slashing Meade with his whip while the two jockeys were standing on their stirrups. After Brokers Tip was declared the winner, the fight continued in the jockey room; Fisher jumped Meade as soon as he entered. It was an unusual race, one that prompted the saying that "anything goes in the Derby." There was one other unsual aspect: Brokers Tip never won a race before the Derby; he never won one afterward.

1941-1968 In Derby history, no other stable comes close to the record and heritage established by Calumet Farm. Beginning with Triple Crown Winner Whirlaway in 1941, Calumet has produced eight derby winners, three seconds, one third and two fourths in 17 starts. The list: Pensive, 1944; Triple Crown Winner Citation, 1948; Ponder, 1949; Hill Gail, 1952; Iron Liege, 1957; Tim Tam, 1958; and Forward Pass, 1968. The magic of Calumet is generally ascribed to Benjamin Allyn Jones ("Plain Ben" or "B.A.") and his son Horace Allyn Jones ("Jimmy"). They joined Calumet in 1939 and it was mostly their eye for horses and their training that booted home the winners. Ben Jones had trained six winners; double the number Sunny Jim Fitz-simmons has produced.

1940 Second to Calumet Farm was the stable of the stylish gambler, Colonel E.R. Bradley. He owned four winners: Behave Yourself, 1921; Bubbling Over, 1926; Burgoo King, 1932; and Brokers Tip, from the Rodeo Derby of 1933. In 1940, however, he went to the post at Churchill Downs with Bimelech.

The All-time Winners Race on the Same Track

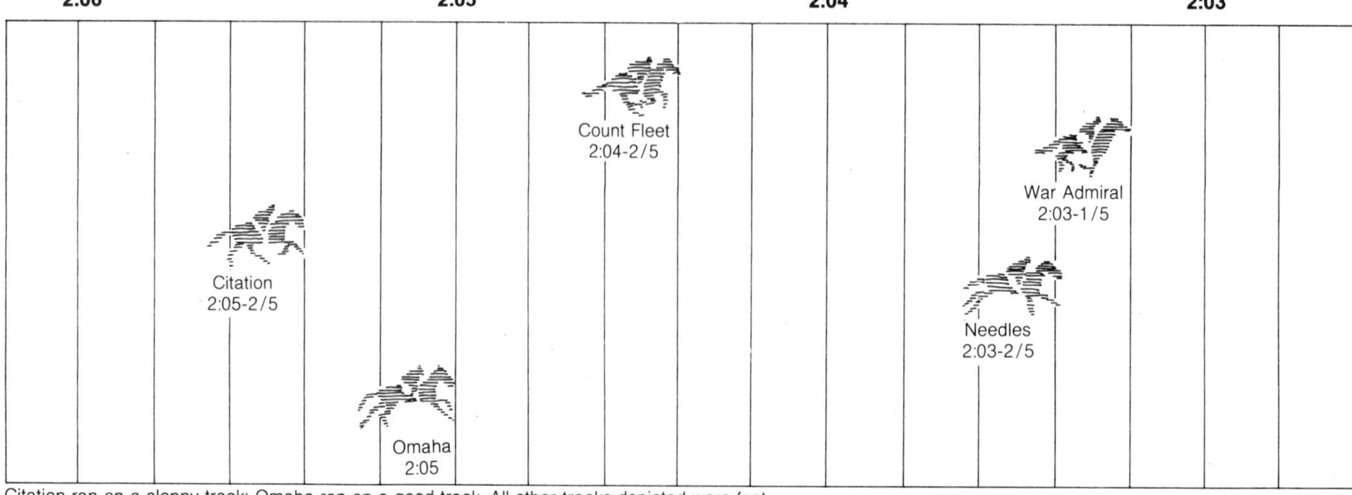

Citation ran on a sloppy track; Omaha ran on a good track. All other tracks depicted were fast.

Bimelech, or "Bimmie" as he was called, became the heaviest favored horse on the winter book in the history of the Derby. Going into the Derby, Bimelech had just clicked off nine straight victories. He seemed unbeatable but he was tired. The Colonel liked his horses run, often. Bimmie lost on the home stretch but went on to win the Preakness and Belmont Stakes. Colonel Bradley died in 1946 but he had spoken his own epitaph 12 years earlier when he was attacked in a Senate hearing by the Louisiana Kingfish, Huey Long. Long disliked Bradley because the Kentuckian had supported some anti-Long politicians in New Orleans. "What is your occupation?" the Kingfish asked. "I'm a speculator, racehorse breeder and gambler," Colonel Bradley answered. "What do you gamble in?" asked Long. "Almost anything," the Kentuckian answered softly.

Don Meade and Herb Fisher fight for the roses in the 1933 Kentucky Derby.

Career Records of the Greatest Derby Winners

Year	Winner	Years Raced	Starts	Finishes 1	2	3	Earnings
1881	Hindoo	3	36	31	3	2	$ 71,875
1918	Exterminator	8	100	50	17	17	252,996
1919	Sir Barton*	3	31	13	6	5	116,857
1930	Gallant Fox*	2	17	11	3	2	328,165
1935	Omaha*	3	22	9	7	2	154,755
1937	War Admiral*	4	26	21	3	1	273,240
1941	Whirlaway*	4	60	32	15	9	561,161
1943	Count Fleet*	2	21	16	4	1	250,300
1946	Assault*	6	42	18	6	7	675,470
1948	Citation*	4	45	32	10	2	1,085,760
1955	Swaps	3	25	19	2	2	848,900
1956	Needles	3	21	11	3	3	600,355
1964	Northern Dancer	2	18	14	2	2	580,806
1969	Majestic Prince	2	10	9	1	0	414,200
1973	Secretariat*	2	21	16	3	1	1,316,808

*Triple Crown Winner

Derby Times

Fastest Winners

1973	Secretariat	1:59 2/5
1964	Northern Dancer	2:00
1962	Decidedly	2:00 2/5
1967	Proud Clarion	2:00 3/5
1965	Lucky Debonair	2:01 1/5
1941	Whirlaway	2:01 2/5

Final Quarter-Miles

1973	Secretariat	shaded:23 1/5
1941	Whirlaway	shaded:23 3/5
1949	Ponder	shaded:23 4/5
1967	Proud Clarion	shaded:24
1964	Northern Dancer	:24
1969	Majestic Prince	shaded:24 1/5

Final Half-Miles

1973	Secretariat	:46 2/5
1967	Proud Clarion	shaded:47 4/5
1941	Whirlaway	shaded:48
1971	Canonero II	shaded:48 1/5
1962	Decidedly	shaded:48 3/5
1956	Needles	shaded:48 4/5

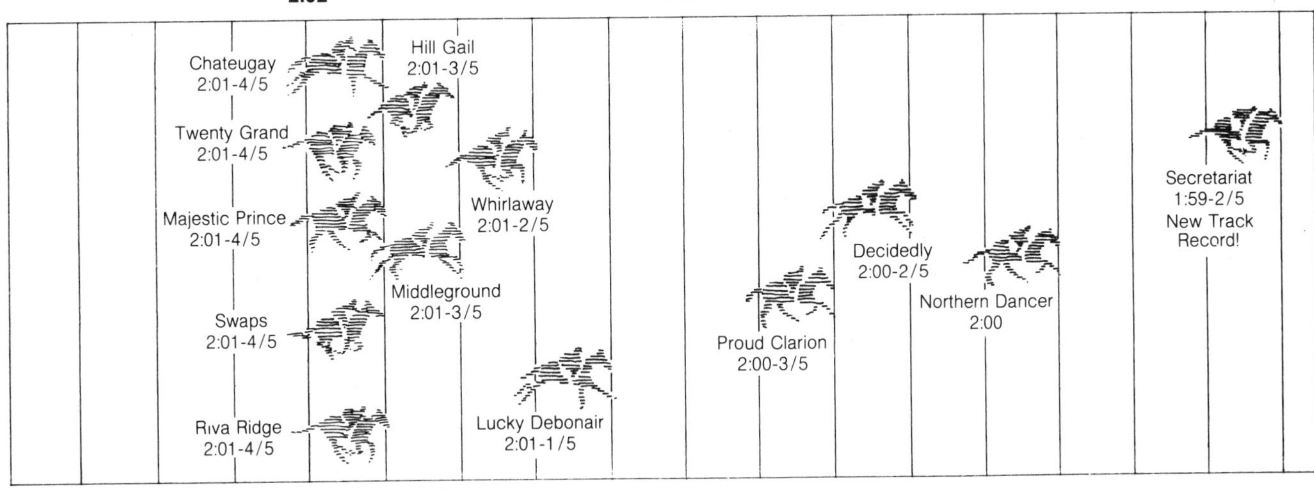

a Workingman's Guide to Betting the Horses

Getting the odds in your favor is a sure bet but keep your life savings in the bank.

By Nick Sanabria

As millions of Americans know, going to the racetrack and betting on the horses is *fun*—even if you don't win a cent. If you've never done it before, you should, and here are some pointers on what to do when you go to the races for the first time.

The first rule in betting on the horses is the hardest to learn, for it is the easiest to forget. It says that betting on thoroughbreds is an entertainment and not a way to get rich quick. If you approach your day at the races with this in mind, you should have a fine time at the track.

Betting on horse races is simple. The track brings together a field of horses to race a set distance; the horses in each race are the same age and of similar ability. All you have to do is decide which horse is going to prove best. You then back your opinion at the pari-mutuel windows, which are plainly marked as to cost and classification—win, place and show (that is, first, second or third.) You wager with the aid of the official program, which lists the horses by number—you will mention you horse's number when betting. The program also has explanations of other forms of betting, but simplicity should be the keynote, so stick with the easiest approach—bet on your horse to win, place or show.

In addition to the official program, racing fans use the *Daily Racing Form*, which tells about the past performances of the horses. The information in this publication is the most complete available to racing fans anywhere in the world. There are graded handicaps, selections and instructions on how to read the past performances. (There are also graded handicaps and selections in most local newspapers.) All this is yours for the buying. Included in these publications and the program are lists of the top trainers and jockeys, which will help you frame your estimate of the probability of a particular horse's winning.

In addition to the program and the racing form, a pair of binoculars is a piece of equipment that is indispensable at the race track. Buy or rent them.

Your serious handicapping begins when the horses come on the track. (Going to the paddock is for the advanced bettor only.) One thing to look for in the post parade is a horse that is "broken out"—sweating profusely. This is a sign that the horse may be too upset to run his best. And look for bandages on the legs—not the small ones, but the ones that run up the shins of the front legs. These could be a sign of problems.

When the horses gallop off, bring your glasses into play. Watch for a horse with his neck bowed under the restraint of his jockey. Watch the horses' strides—a smooth, seemingly effortless stride is good and a choppy gait is bad. A smooth strider who acts as if he were "crying to run" could be a good bet. Remember to allow yourself enough time to get to the betting windows. Sometimes the lines are quite long.

A few other hints: race track design being what it is—something like Ming Dynasty—the novice racing fan should put some effort into seeking out a good vantage point from which to watch the races. Don't even think of watching them on TV—too much is lost, for the camera, of necessity, must concentrate on the front runners. To watch a race develop, you must watch *all* the horses—here, again, use your glasses. Do not indulge in just staring at your horse to the exclusion of the others. Scan the field. You know your horse by the colors his jockey is wearing (it's in the program).

If you've combined your own observations with the expert opinions in the program and racing form, your horse should give a good account of himself, even if you don't win any money. (After all, even the favorite wins only 33 percent of the time.) The great sport at the track is in picking your horse yourself—reveling in your own cleverness if you do win is just part of the fun.

A Guide to the Daily Racing Form

Betting Systems

There is no successful system for betting every race, every day. If you think you've found one, forget it; in any case, you'll learn that lesson soon enough.

Here are some thoughts to keep in mind, though:

—The closing favorite (the favorite at the time betting ceases) wins about 30 percent of the races.

—The closing favorite finishes either first or second about 50 percent of the time.

—The state and the track manage to take out about one out of every five dollars wagered, and you know they won't let you steal from them, so forget about getting rich and concentrate on having fun.

Horse Racing Classification (by age)

Foal — birth
Suckling — feeding mare's milk
Weanling — withdrawn from mare's milk
Yearling — first year to second year
Colt — male under five years
Filly — female under five years
Horse — male over five years
Mare — female over five years
Sire — male parent
Stallion — full male horse
Gelding — castrated male horse
Stud Horse — male used for breeding
Maiden — non-winner of flat race
Dam — female parent
Foal — newborn, male or female

Horse Racing Terminology

Track Conditions	Colors
Fast	Bay
Good	Brown
Slow	Black
Heavy	Chestnut
Muddy	Gray
Sloppy	Roan

Distance poles on a standard one-mile racetrack.

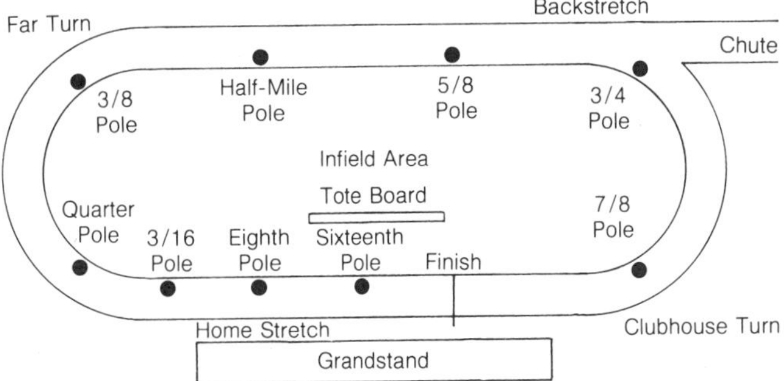

How To Look Over A Thoroughbred

Neck should be full. Too short or long causes an imbalance while running.

Face should be sharp, alert and bright, eyes not too close together, ears straight with quick reactions to all sounds.

Withers should be clearly defined and appear strong.

Coat should be shiny.

Back should have a slight indentation. A deep indentation or a sway back could mean weakness.

Croup should be long and sloping, not flat or appear to fall off abruptly.

Buttocks should be rounded, full and muscular. Narrow buttocks tend to indicate weakness and/or lack of muscular development.

Shoulder should be long and slightly sloping.

Chest should be broad, not narrow.

Forearm should appear very muscular and be longer than the cannon bone.

Hind Legs provide the go power and should appear very strong.

Forelegs should neither be too narrow nor too wide spread into the chest.

Hocks should be perpendicular to buttocks on line to the ground.

Knees should blend into the leg. Watch out if the knees curve in or out.

Cannon Bone should have well-defined tendons and not be too narrow.

Hind Pastern should have a greater angle than the front.

Feet should not be small, irregular or too narrow.

Fetlock should not be overly large or puffy.

Pastern should angle down at 45 degrees, should not be too long or too short.

TROTTING AROUND AMERICA

From near extinction, harness racing has emerged as a favorite sport of gamblers.

Harness racing was born and grew up with America. It evolved out of our rural past, off the village greens of the East, the red clay tracks of Midwestern country fairs and the lush dirt ovals of California's Central Valley. It grew and was loved by a populace who thrilled to the swaying gait of Dan Patch, Greyhound, Adios Butler, Bret Hanover and Nevele Pride. (And it didn't hurt a President's image to be stopped three times in one day for speeding on a trotter: Ulysses S. Grant loved it.)

"The trotting horse," said Harry Devereux, who was president of the harness racing Grand Circuit during the gaslit era, "is as distinctive of North America as the bald eagle. He is the only horse that has been able to do what all other horses combined can accomplish. He can out-hackney the hackney, he can beat any horse in the world on the trot or pace, he can work on the farm, on the delivery wagon, under saddle, and is the only ideal gentleman's horse." For most of his life, Devereux fancied himself as a sort of spokesman for America, but he can be forgiven for that: he's best known to us as the drummer boy in that classic Americana painting, "The Spirit of '76." And he helped harness racing through its most difficult days, the early onslaught of the automobile. Today, however, some 30 million people annually pass through the turnstiles at the harness tracks and wager some $2 billion at the pari-mutuel windows.

The fastest trotter in the history of harness racing, Nevele Pride, with driver-trainer Stanley Dancer, churns around the track at Monticello Raceway.

Harness racing is an acquired art. Harness horses are driven from a light, two-wheeled "sulky" around a track for a distance of one mile and must "trot" (a high-stepping diagonal gait, in which the right front and left hind legs are thrust forward in unison, followed by the left front and right hind legs) or "pace" (a lateral, swaying gait, in which the legs on one side are thrust forward in unison followed by the other side).

Pacers

Pacers are more popular than trotters these days, but after the Civil War harness racing experts were predicting that pacing would disappear from America's harness racing circuits. The problem was that pacers were thought of as "poor men's trotters." Pacers looked like they had just been unharnessed from a plow and brought over for an afternoon's run; they were ungainly, heavy, coarse creatures. "No gentleman drives a pacer," declared Robert Bonner, who owned the first great trotters, Maud S. and Sunol.

Well, pacers might have been ugly but they were quick—faster than trotters. And folks loved them. Every county fair from DuQuoin to Stockton had 'em and they were burning up the tracks. By 1875 they were popular enough to be allowed to race the Grand Circuit beginning at Boston's Mystic Park, but they were a bust. The Easterners booed.

Then came the first great popular pacer, Sleepy Tom, who was touted as "the world's toughest piece of horseflesh." Stephen C. Phillips bought Sleepy Tom for a bottle of whiskey, a broken watch and a three-year-old colt. He talked to that horse all race day long, before, during and after the race. He had to: Sleepy Tom was blind, and Phillips was his eyes. Knocking almost three seconds off the mile record, Sleepy Tom became the world champion pacer in 1879, and pacing was off to a rousing start.

Since Sleepy Tom, there have been a number of other great pacers.

Here is a gallery of the great world champions:

Dan Patch Probably the most popular standardbred to have paced the tracks of

Mile Records by the World Champion Pacers and Trotters

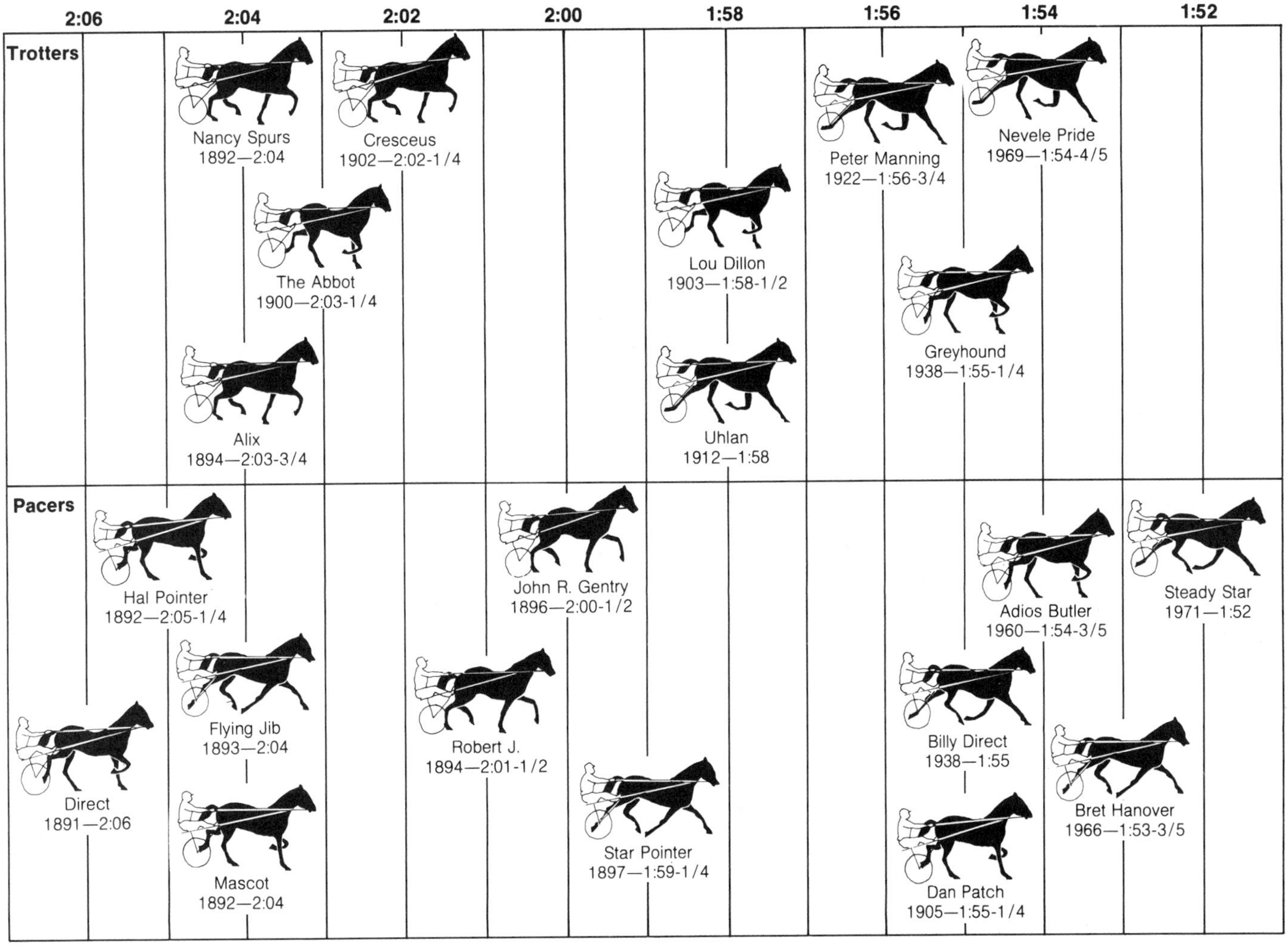

2:06 2:04 2:02 2:00 1:58 1:56 1:54 1:52

Trotters

Nancy Spurs
1892—2:04

Cresceus
1902—2:02-1/4

The Abbot
1900—2:03-1/4

Alix
1894—2:03-3/4

Lou Dillon
1903—1:58-1/2

Uhlan
1912—1:58

Peter Manning
1922—1:56-3/4

Greyhound
1938—1:55-1/4

Nevele Pride
1969—1:54-4/5

Pacers

Hal Pointer
1892—2:05-1/4

Direct
1891—2:06

Flying Jib
1893—2:04

Mascot
1892—2:04

John R. Gentry
1896—2:00-1/2

Robert J.
1894—2:01-1/2

Star Pointer
1897—1:59-1/4

Adios Butler
1960—1:54-3/5

Billy Direct
1938—1:55

Dan Patch
1905—1:55-1/4

Steady Star
1971—1:52

Bret Hanover
1966—1:53-3/5

American harness racing, Dan Patch was the only world champion never to have lost a race. When Dan Patch was running, crowds lined the streets to the track, hoping just to touch that magnificent animal. He knew he was a star. He loved the crowds, perked up at the band music and smoothly, effortlessly, knocked off the competition. He began traveling in a private railroad car and wherever he went, it was Dan Patch Day. Eventually, America would have Dan Patch chewing tobacco, Dan Patch cigars, Dan Patch washing machines, pillows, even the Dan Patch two-step. His estimated earnings in races and exhibitions were in excess of $3 million. In 1905, more than 70,000 people watched him lower the Allentown, Pa. track record for the mile from 2:03 to 2:01. Seventy years later, that record still stands. Then he clicked off a 1:55¼-mile at Lexington and the harness world was stunned. No horse had come close to that before. When Dan Patch retired in 1909, he retired undefeated, holding nine world records. He died seven years later on July 11, 1916; and his owner, Marion Willis Savage, died the next day.

Billy Direct In 1938, four-year-old Billy Direct beat Dan Patch's mile record by ¼ second to become the world's fastest harness horse, until Adios Butler lowered the mile record a split second more in 1961. In fact, his 1:55 pacing record for the mile was set at Lexington, on Sept. 28, 1938, just a day before Greyhound set the trotting record on the same track. Both records lasted until the 1960s.

Adios No matter which harness track you visit in this country on any given day, you'll probably find at least one starter on the racing card whose name begins with "Adios." Except for Hambletonian, no other standardbred has produced so many great progeny. Adios was foaled in 1940, and although he never surpassed Dan Patch's record for the mile, he did set five world pacing records and is best known for siring Adios Butler and Bret Hanover, two of the greatest pacers the harness world has ever seen. He also sired Bullet Hanover, Dancer Hanover, Henry T, Adios and Adios Vic. In 18 crops of foals, he left behind 537 registered horses who have won about 6,000 races and earned well over $15 million. At least 77 of his sons have paced the mile in less than two minutes, holding nine percent of all the two-minute-or-less marks on record.

Adios Butler In 1959, Adios Butler became the first horse to win the Pacing Triple

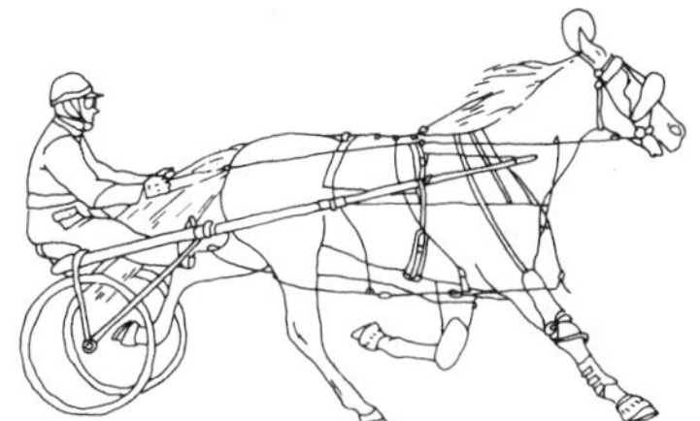

A pacer has a side-swaying motion caused by parallel legs moving forward at the same time

Trotters run kitty-corner style with opposite front and rear legs moving together.

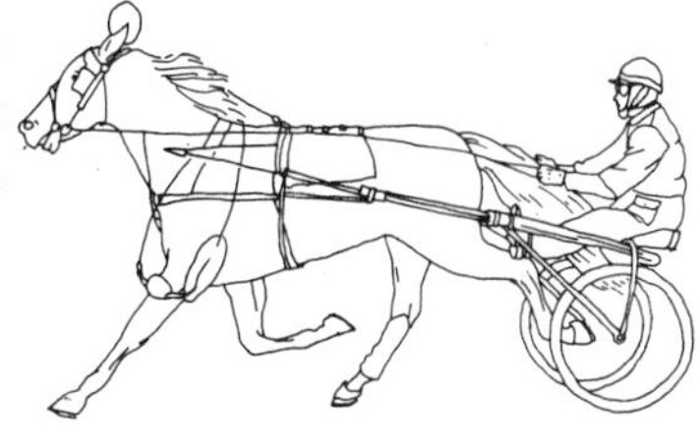

A Guide To Betting The Pacers And Trotters

There's one small advantage to betting on harness races: trotters and pacers run truer to form than do thoroughbreds. That means that while a closing favorite in a horse race will win about 30 percent of the time, the closing favorite in a harness race will win about 37 percent of his starts.

When betting your trotter or pacer you should look for the following:

1. the horse's best performance
2. how well he's done, in actual time, in recent races
3. the condition of the track
4. the speed rating of that track compared to other tracks
5. the driver's record and ability
6. the opposition in that race
7. the post position (harness horses in the first post position win three times as often as the number eight horse, two out of three races are won by horses in positions one to four)
8. a horse runs three to four seconds faster for a mile on a mile track as opposed to a half-mile track
9. a horse that was "parked out" (running on the outside with one or more horses between him and the rail) can run one second faster for each time he was parked in a race
10. whether the horse "broke," from its required gait and had to be pulled to the outside
11. the odds

Crown. Within a year, he held the world record for the mile, at 1:54 3/5—a record which stood until Albatross broke it in 1972. Half-mile tracks are more difficult because of the tighter turns but Adios Butler was the master of the curve. On such tracks he paced in under 1:59 five times in races and twice in time trials. That's only been done 12 times in harness history and never more than once by an individual horse. Adios Butler pulled it off seven times.

Bret Hanover The son of Adios and a blue-blooded mare named Brenna Hanover, this world champion bred in 1962 was named after Bret Maverick, a Western television hero played by James Garner. He was anything but a maverick, though. Out of 68 starts in three years, he won 62, finished second five times, third once, and never ran out of the money. In the course of competition, he set nine world records, matched two others, and broke literally dozens of track and stake records. He paced more sub-two-minute miles than any horse in history, breaking Dan Patch's record for that feat, a record that stood for 57 years. In 1965, he became the second horse to win the Pacing Triple Crown.

Albatross As the all-time money winner, with $1.2 million, Albatross was voted Harness Horse of the Year in 1971 even though another pacer, Steady Star, clocked off a phenomenal 1:52 mile. That doesn't mean Albatross was slow. He still holds four world pacing records: fastest time on a 5/8-mile track for all ages at 1:54.3; fastest time on a half-mile track for all ages at 1:55.3 and ditto for that record as a four-year-old. Albatross still holds the world record for the mile paced in a race. He also holds the world record for the highest price paid for a pacer, $2.5 million and is still the fastest racing standardbred in harness racing history.

Trotters

In today's harness racing, pacing dominates over trotting by a wide margin. One of the reasons is that the trotting gait, while a natural one, is an easier gait to break. And when a favored trotter breaks his gait and loses a race, that's tough on the fans. The trotting gait was first witnessed in England in 1750, enjoyed immense popularity in the U.S. in the 19th century, but began losing favor a few decades ago.

There have been a number of great trotting champions, beginning with Goldsmith Maid, Rarus, St. Julien and Jay-Eye-See. Maud S. and Sunol were the last two champions to have raced with the old high-wheeled sulkies. A year later, in 1892, Nancy Hanks appeared in a bicycle-wheeled sulky, and lowered the world record for the mile three times that season, clipping more than four seconds off the world record. Then came Alix, The Abbot, Cresceus and Lou Dillon, world champion trotters who even then trotted off incredible times. But with the coming of the automobile at the turn of the century, harness racing declined in this country. Uhlan held the world record for a decade, until 1922, when Peter Manning lowered the mile mark three times in a year. Manning was considered the "Trotting King of the Twenties," but harness racing did not really catch fire again until after the Depression. The new era began with the arrival of the greatest horse to run in harness: Greyhound.

Greyhound From 1934 until he retired in 1940, this gray gelding set no less than 25 world records, many of which are still on the books. He was the quintessential trotter, and his mile mark of 1:55¼ was assailed by at least 100,000 trotters and unbeaten until 1969 by Nevele Pride. He won 71 of 82 starts, finishing second five times and third twice. All but one of his losses occurred when he was an inexperienced two-year-old. He could never win the Triple Crown because, as a gelding, he was disqualified from the Kentucky Futurity. By 1939, there were no other records for him to break. So, popular demand pushed him toward trying a double harness record with the then trotting queen Rosalind, taking a shot at a 27-year-old record set by Uhlan and Lewis Forest. The pair broke the record twice. On their second try, they ran the mile in 1:54¼ at Indianapolis and that record is still unbroken. There was only one last record to try for: the mile for trotters under saddle. Ridden by Mrs. Frances Dodge Johnson (a daughter of the auto manufacturer), Greyhound shattered that world record by nearly four seconds. It was his farewell appearance and he retired, as one writer put it, "staggering under his laurels."

Nevele Pride As "eleven" spelled backwards and pronounced like "reveille," Nevele Pride was foaled in 1965 and became the first trotter to break Greyhound's mile record. He won the Triple Crown for Trotters in 1968, the second trotter ever to win it at age three. By the end of his career, he had trotted a mile in less than two minutes 19 times, a mark surpassed only by Greyhound. Of 67 starts, he won 57, with four seconds and three thirds. His earnings of $873,000 rank him among the top five money-winning trotters of all-time. And he currently holds the world records for the fastest times for a mile: on a mile track, all ages, 1:54.8; on a mile track by a two-year-old, 1:58.2; on a mile track by a four-year-old, 1:54:8; on a 5/8-mile track, all ages, 1:58; on a 5/8-mile track by a three-year-old, 1:59; and on a 5/8-mile track by a four-year-old, 1:58. Nevele Pride is the fastest trotter in history and while his records may be beaten, it will take the next wonder trotter of our age to do so. He resides near Lexington, Ky. at the stallion barn at Stoner Creek Stud. His current owners paid $3 million for him—the highest price ever paid for a trotter.

Wimbledon Center Court, Wimbledon

FIELDS & GREENS

Olympic Stadium, Munich

DECATHLON: THE ULTIMATE TEST

Run, jump, vault, leap, heave and hurl with the champions.

Bill Toomey wins the long jump on his way to victory in the 1968 Olympic decathlon.

The quintessential American hero is always incredibly versatile: he can run, rope and shoot from the hip, and of course he knows no fear. He can fly a plane when necessary and it wouldn't surprise us if he also knew how to trepan a skull. (This is the attraction of all those quarterbacks with Ph.D.'s.)

In that symbolic battleground of the sports arena, the closest equivalent to the "World War I Flying Ace" is the Decathlon man; he can dash, broad jump, put the shot, high jump, run the quarter mile, run the high hurdles, throw the discus, pole vault, fling the javelin and run a mile—all of these in championship style, and one right after the other.

Not only that, but he has only two days to do it in. The events are held in the order listed in the previous paragraph and a competitor is considered to have withdrawn from any further competition if he misses any event. Who goes first is determined by draw. A competitor is allowed three tries for field events and three false starts in track events. If he fails on all three, he's eliminated from that particular event. Scoring is done according to performance tables set by the International Amateur Athletic Federation.

In decathlon contests it seemed too restrained to give such great symbolic heroes just one point, or a few points, for winning an event; instead, up to 1,000 points can be awarded for each event. If an athlete ties or beats an established record, he gets 1,000 points. So the star he's shooting for is 10,000. The record number of points in the decathlon is 8,454, set by Nikolay Avilov in Munich in 1972.

100-Meter Dash The world record for the 100-meters is held by several people at 9.9 seconds. A world class decathlonist would run this distance between 10.4 and 11.0 seconds. Avilov, the world champion, raced it in 11.0, which is considerably slower than top American high schoolers.

Long Jump No one does very well in the long jump. Avilov's 25-plus feet was more than seven inches short of Bill Toomey's distance in the 1968 Games at Mexico but, again, both are behind the best individual high schoolers in this event. In fact, some decathlonists have recorded 18-feet leaps which would be about junior high level.

Shot Put Decathlon champions seem to follow definite patterns. A man who'll do very well in the shot put, for example, will also do well in the discus and the javelin. Bob Mathias and Rafer Johnson were essentially throwing champions. More recent champions have not yet surpassed their throwing marks, set in the 1952 and 1960 Olympics. Avilov, the current champ, is among the worst throwers in the shot. Still, he scored well enough, 47 feet-plus, for a respectable average. The world record is 71 feet 7 inches.

High Jump Avilov, however, is one hell of a high jumper. His leap of 6 feet, 11½ inches would have been a world record in 1956. Most competitors in this event fall between 5'6" and 6'2". No one has come close to Avilov in decathlon high jumping. The world and high school records, respectively, are 7 feet 6½ inches and 7 feet 3 inches.

400-Meters Bill Toomey, the 1968 Decathlon champion, could burn up the tracks. His mark of 45.6 seconds for the 400-Meters has been untouched in decathlon competition and it's almost world class for that event alone. Avilov's pace was 48.5, considerably slower than the world record 43.8 or the high school 45.8.

110-Meter Hurdles Toomey and another former decathlon champion, Milt Campbell, hold the best times for the hurdles at 14 seconds and 14.09. Again, in terms of world class competition, those times are very respectable. The hurdles begin the second day of decathlon competition. In fact, Avilov was quoted after he won the Munich event that he'd prefer to have all the events run off in one day, that is, if they'd drop the 400-Meters and the 1,500-Meters.

Discus If anywhere, the decathletes fall shortest of world marks when they compete in strength-throwing events. They may be a few seconds or fractions off from world running marks but when it comes to throwing, they're way behind. The main difficulty, of course, is that they have to prepare themselves to be fast, agile, and strong, with a maximum endurance effort. The best decathlon mark for the discus was set by Rafer Johnson in the 1960 games but his 159 feet was far short of the world record 224 feet. His throw would have been good enough for a world record in 1931, however.

Pole Vault Decathletes don't have much of a problem with the pole vault, once they get the hang of it. That's about what it takes. Mathias, the 1948 champion, took his first jump about six weeks before competing in the Olympics. Their best marks (Avilov's 14 feet 11¼ inches is among them) would have been world records in the mid-1950s.

Javelin Rafer Johnson, a throwing decathlete, set a champion's mark of 228 feet

10½ inches in the Rome games way back in 1960. No other champions have come close but the Johnson's toss is nowhere near the world mark of more than 308 feet, or the American high school best of 260 feet.

1,500-Meter Run Most decathlon purists agree that the contest should really come down to this final long distance running event. When it came down to this event in Munich in 1972, Avilov had pretty well clinched the

Yan Chan Kwang, right, *the perennial bride's maid wins the 100 but loses the decathlon.*

Russian star Nikolai Avilov, below, *unleashes his javelin on the way to a record-breaking victory in the 1972 Olympic decathlon.*

American Milton Campbell, bottom, *clears the last obstacle in the 110 meter hurdle decathlon event in the 1956 Olympics.*

Rafer Johnson, below, *out-heaves the field in shotput event of the 1960 Olympic decathlon.*

championship. What he had to gun for was the decathlon point record held by Bill Toomey. To get the record, Avilov had to run the 1,500-Meters in 4:28.0. He had run under that time only three times in his life in dozens of tries. This time, he clicked it off in 4:22.8, his own personal best, and with it took the decathlon championship and set a new world record of 8,454 points.

The most important intangible in the decathlon is the mental chess match among the competitors. In the 1948 Olympics, for example, the Argentine competitor informed 17-year-old Mathias that he would do better in any and all events the California kid tried. As it turned out, the Argentine's needling just inspired Mathias to really push himself so that by the time of the last event, the 1,500-Meters, all he needed to do to win was jog around the track. He could have even fallen down a few times. The Argentine, on the other hand, went home without a medal.

It should be noted that in the 1960 Rome Olympics, C.K. Yang defeated Rafer Johnson in seven out of the 10 events and still lost the championship to Johnson. How that could happen was that Johnson beat Yang badly on the three events he won, (shot, discus, javelin) and placed very close to the Taiwanese on the seven he lost. The final point difference was 8,392 to 8,334. Going into the final event, the 1,500, Yang had to beat Johnson by 10 seconds. Yang's best time had been 4:36.9 for the distance, Johnson's best was 4:54.2. It seemed like Yang would win. But Johnson, a consummate strategist, knew he had to finish within 10 seconds of Yang. He dogged Yang all over the track, finishing 1.2 seconds behind the Taiwanese and winning his decathlon gold.

Such close matches are not uncommon in the decathlon. In the Tokyo decathlon of 1964, Willi Holdorf, the eventual gold medalist, knew that any one of five men could beat him out for the championship, depending on how they finished. He knew that the Russian, Rein Aun would win if the Russian outran him by 18 seconds; that his German countryman Hans-Joachim Walde would win the gold if Walde outran him by 8.5 seconds; that the American, Paul Herman, would win if the time difference was 23 seconds; that the Russian, Vassily Kouznetsov, needed 21.5 seconds and that C.K. Yang needed a 21-second edge. And they're going to run in the same race, right? Well, it gets complicated. As it turned out, Holdorf ran the best 1,500 of his life and won.

A Statistical History of the

MODERN DECATHLON

Performer	100-M	Long Jump	Shot Put	High Jump	400-M	110-M H	Discus	Pole Vault	Javelin	1,500-M	Score
Nikolay Avilov, 1972 Olympic Champion	11.0	25-2½	47-1½	6-11½	48.5	14.31	154-1½	14-11¼	202-3½	4:22.8	8,454
Bill Toomey, 1968 Olympic Champion	10.4	25-9¾	45-1¼	6-4¾	45.6	14.09	143-5½	13-9½	206-½	4:57.1	8,193
Willi Holdorf, 1964 Olympic Champion	10.7	22-11½	49-½	6-½	48.2	15.0	151-1	13-9½	188-2½	4:34.3	7,887
Rafer Johnson, 1960 Olympic Champion	10.9	24-1¼	51-10¾	6-¾	48.3	15.3	159-1	13-5¼	228-10½	4:49.7	8,392
C. K. Yang, 1960 Olympic Silver Medalist	10.7	24-5¾	43-8¾	6-2¾	48.1	14.6	130-8	14-1¼	223-9½	4:48.5	8,334
Milt Campbell, 1956 Olympic Champion	10.8	24-⅝	48-5⅛	6-2⅜	48.8	14.0	147-6⅞	11-1⅞	187-3¼	4:50.6	7,937
Bob Mathias, 1952	10.9	22-10¾	50-2⅜	6-2¾	50.2	14.7	153-10	13-1½	194-3⅛	4:50.8	8,450
Olympic 1948 Champion	11.2	21-8⅓	42-9¼	6-1¼	51.7	15.7	144-4	11-5¾	165-1	5:11	7,139
Worst complete performance, 1972 Olymp.	11.95	18-7¾	40-3	5-5	52.7	18.54	127-4½	10-10	233-10	4:37.4	6,227
World Record for each event	9.9	29-2½	71-7	7-6½	43.8	13.1	224-5	18-5¾	308-8	3:32.2	———
U.S. High School record for each event	10.1	26-2¼	61-6¼	7-3	45.8	13.9	177-4	17-4¾	259-9	3:39.0	———

GREAT MOMENTS IN THE FIELD

Jim Thorpe could be modestly described as the greatest athlete who ever lived. Although he later went on to excel in professional football and baseball, the proud Sac and Fox Indian from central Oklahoma first stunned the athletic world as a track and field star.

Thorpe became interested in athletics while studying to become a tailor at the Carlisle Indian School in Pennsylvania. There, he received the coaching which led to his entry in the 1912 Olympics at Stockholm, where he won the pentathlon (a total of five events) and the decathlon (a total of 10 events). It was an exhibition of all-around athletic prowess that has never been equaled and we can probably rest pretty easily knowing it won't be.

In the pentathlon, he won four of the five events—the 200-meter dash, the 1,500 meter run, the long jump and the discus—and placed third in the javelin throw. His score for the pentathlon was double that of his nearest competitor.

He went on to win the decathlon with victories in four events, placed third in four others and fourth in another two. He won the shot put, the high jump, the high hurdles and the 1,500-meter run. He placed third in the 100-meter dash, the pole vault, the discus and the long jump. He placed fourth in the javelin and 400-meter run.

Not surprisingly, when King Gustav V presented the two trophies to Thorpe, the Swedish monarch was moved to comment: "You, sir, are the greatest athlete in the world."

Thorpe grinned and said simply, "Thanks, King."

Months after the games, a Boston newspaper published a story charging that Thorpe had been paid some money to play minor league baseball in North Carolina. The International Olympic Committee investigated the claims and when Thorpe admitted they were true, asked him to return his medals. Thorpe did and his name and his accomplishments were struck from the record book.

It should be noted that Avery Brundage (who would rule the I.O.C. for more than 20 years) competed against Thorpe in the pentathlon and the decathlon in that same Olympiad. Years later, as president, Brundage would be deluged with requests that Thorpe's medals be restored to the Oklahoma Indian. To those, Brundage would reply, "Jim Thorpe was the greatest athlete of our time. Why does he need medals to prove it?"

Ray Ewry contracted polio as a small boy. In fact, he was in such frail health his family physician had lost hope that the youngster would ever walk or run properly. He advised the boy to build up his legs by jumping. Well, Ewry jumped and kept on jumping. By the time he was 27 years old, he could really jump. That's a late age to enter an Olympics but the New York Athletic Club agreed to sponsor him, and sporting the club's winged-foot emblem on his chest, Ewry traveled to Paris for the 1900 games. There he picked up three gold medals. Four years later, in St. Louis, he earned three more. He won two more at the 1906 Olympics in Athens (the "unofficial Olympics") and a final two in London in 1908. Let's see, well, that's 10 gold medals.

Ewry captured his gold medals in three events which are no longer held: the standing high jump, the standing long jump and the standing hop, step and jump. The last of the three was dropped from the 1906 and 1908 Olympics; otherwise, he'd have probably ended up with 12. Even so, Ewry's record of 10 individual golds in track and field has never been equaled.

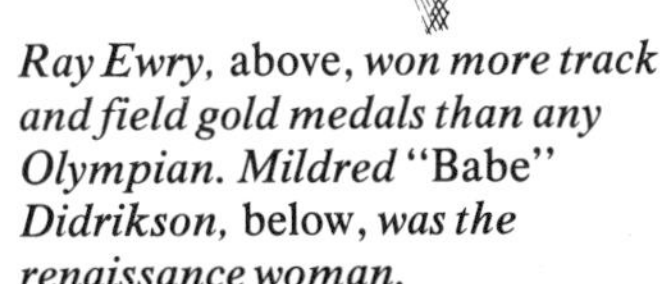

Ray Ewry, above, *won more track and field gold medals than any Olympian. Mildred* "Babe" *Didrikson,* below, *was the renaissance woman.*

Babe Didrikson was the greatest female athlete of our age. No doubt about it. The Babe from Beaumont, Tex., (her given name was Mildred) was a one-person track team, an Olympic champion, All-American in basketball, a skilled semi-pro baseball player (playing with men), and the winner of every major golf title. In her spare time she gave billiards exhibitions.

She began her career as a clerk at the Employers Casualty Company of Dallas. The firm sponsored athletic teams and they hired Babe because she was all-state in basketball. In 1930, she took the team to the national tournament and was named All-American. That was repeated in 1931 and 1932.

Babe's greatest moment in the field came in the spring of 1932 when she entered the combined Amateur Athletic Union championships and the Olympic tryouts as the lone competitor representing her Dallas insurance company. There were 10 individual events in track and field that afternoon and Babe entered eight of them against 200 other contestants. She won five events outright: the javelin throw, broad jump, 80-meter hurdles, baseball throw and shotput (which she had never tried before). She tied for first in the high jump and she placed fourth in the discuss (another event that was new to her). When they totted up the score, Mildred Didrikson had 30 points. In second place for the entire meet was the Illinois Women's Athletic Club which had sent 22 contestants.

A greater moment might have come in the Olympics but women were only allowed to enter three events. (There were only six track and field events for women then.) Ms. Didrikson chose the javelin, the 80-meter hurdles and the high jump. She set a world record in the javelin with a throw of 143 feet 4 inches and cleared the hurdles in a world record time of 11.7 seconds. Babe had a close rival in the high jump; she and her competitor both cleared 5 feet 5 inches, an improvement over the then world record by two inches. After both women had cleared the bar at another quarter-inch, the judges ruled that Babe had dived over head first and not feet first as the rules then required (and have since been changed). Babe was given second place.

Bob Mathias was a powerfully built California schoolboy of 17 when his high school track coach suggested he compete in the decathlon at the U.S. Olympic team tryouts. At that point, the kid had never pole-vaulted, never broad-jumped, never touched a javelin and knew next to nothing about the 400-meter run or the 1,500-meter distance race. But, with only three weeks preparation, Mathias won a regional decathlon meet and a month later won the U.S. decathlon championship, assuring himself a place on the 1948 Olympic team.

The decathlon, according to Olympic rules, must be completed in two days. The events are run in this order: Day One: 100-meter dash, broad jump, shot put, high jump, 400-meter run. Day Two: 110-meter high hurdles, discus, pole vault, javelin and 1,500-meter run.

When he first stepped onto the wet turf of London's Wembley Stadium, Mathias had competed in only two decathlon meets and had less than three months of coaching and practice in half the events. The first day wasn't bad. He tied for first in the high jump and did well enough in the other four events to place third among the 28 contestants at day's end. That night he was so tense he couldn't sleep.

The next day, Wembley was awash with rain and fog. Mathias pole-vaulted with a wet and slippery pole. When it came his turn to throw the javelin, the light was so poor the officials had to illuminate the take-off line with flashlights. In spite of all that, by the time he got to the final event, the 1,500-meter run, Mathias was far in front of the other competitors. If he could just finish the race in half-way decent time he'd be the youngest gold medalist in Olympic track and field history and he would have had that victory in the most demanding contest of all.

He won, of course. He had run the 100-meters in 11.2 seconds, run the 400 in 51.7, the long-distance 1,500 meters in 5 minutes and 11 seconds, cleared the 110-meter hurdles in 15.7 seconds, broad-jumped 21 feet 8 inches, high-jumped 6 feet 1¼ inches, pole-vaulted 11 feet 5½ inches, hurled the javelin 165 feet 1 inch, tossed the shot 42 feet 9 inches; and threw the discus 144

Bob Mathias whirled all the way to Congress with his 1948 Olympic performance.

A Statistical History of Field Events*

	1896	1900	1904	1906	1908	1912	1920	1924	1928
Long Jump									
Men	20-9¾	23-6⅞	24-1	23-7½	24-6½	24-11¼	23-5½	24-5⅛	25-4¾
Women**									
High Jump									
Men	5-11¼	6-2 4/5	5-11	5-9⅞	6-3	6-4	6-4¼	6-6	6-4⅜
Women									5-3
Shot Put									
Men	36-9¾	46-3⅛	48-7	40-4 4/5	46-7½	50-4	48-7⅛	49-2½	52-¾
Women***									
Discus Throw									
Men	95-7	118-2	128-10	136	134-2	148-3	146-7	151-5	155-3
Women****									129-11⅞
Hammer Throw									
Men*****	———	167-4	168-1	———	170-4	179-7	173-5	174-10	176-7
Women									
Javelin Throw									
Men	———	———	———	175-6	179-10	198-11	215-9	206-6	218-6
Women									
Pole Vault									
Men*****	10-9¾	10-10	11-6	11-6	12-2	12-11½	13-5	12-11½	13-9⅜
Women									

*Olympic results. **Women's events began in 1928. ***Women's shot weighs 8 lb. 13 4/5 oz. Men's shot weighs 16 lb.

feet 4 inches. He actually won only one event, the discus throw, and tied for first in two others, the high jump and pole vault, but he placed so well in the other seven, he earned 7,139 points. No other competitor reached the 7,000-point mark. His margin of victory for the decathlon gold was even greater at Helsinki, in 1952, but his greatest moment came in London in 1948.

Tamara and Irina Press, the two heavy-duty Russian sisters, won five Olympic gold medals between them. Tamara, the older (and bigger) sister, tossed the shot and the discus, winning gold medals in 1960 and 1964, while Irina won golds in the 80-meter hurdles and the pentathlon in the same two Olympics. People wondered, given Tamara's weight and strength whether she might be a man in disguise. This gave much impetus to the controversial "sex test," but even at 220 pounds, Tamara could not (as some observers suggested) have made the Chicago Bears' front line that year.

The pentathlon, (not to be confused with the "modern pentathlon," which consists of riding, fencing, shooting, swimming and cross-country running), is a modified decathlon for women. It consists of 100-meter hurdles, the shot put, the high jump, long jump and 200-meter dash. The pentathlon Irina won was the first scheduled in Olympic history.

Tamara Press makes a manful throw in the 1964 Olympics.

Al Oerter likes to throw the discus and he has done it more often and far farther than most anybody else. Consider the simple fact that Al Oerter has won four, *four* Olympic gold medals in the discus. That's being number one in the world over a span of 12 years. The first time he won, in Melbourne in 1956, he was scared to death. "I just went to pieces," he said afterward. The second time was at Rome and it was sort of uneventful—although he would break an Olympic record each time (his own), and no one since has broken his. The third time he almost didn't start. It was the 1964 Games in Tokyo and Oerter had ripped the cartilages off his rib cage in a practice throw. Team physicians encased him in ice packs to ease the pain and stop the hemorrhaging and would allow him no other form of exercise than walking. He was up against the Czechoslovakian world record holder Ludvik Danek and had four throws zing out too low: his awkward strait-jacket hampered his style. But the big aircraft computer analyst from West Babylon, Long Island, gritted his teeth, reminded himself, "This is the Olympics, boy," and sent his 4-pound, 6½ ounce platter soaring out to a new Olympic record. After watching Danek get off an insignificant, almost feeble toss, Oerter called it a day. He flipped his discus to the ground and declined his final toss. He figured he had it won and he was right. The fourth time was not unlike the rest. Oerter was up against the world record holder, he was not favored to win and yet he did. How did he do it? "I get fired up," he said.

1932	1936	1948	1952	1956	1960	1964	1968	1972	
									Long Jump
25-¾	26-5¼	25-8	24-10	25-8¼	26-7¾	26-5¾	29-2½	27-½	Men
		18-8¼	20-5⅝	20-9¾	20-10¾	22-2¼	22-4½	22-3	Women
									High Jump
6-5⅝	6-7⅞	6-6	6-8¾	6-11¼	7-1	7-1¾	7-4¼	7-3¾	Men
5-5¼	5-3	5-6¼	5-5¾	5-9¼	6-¾	6-2¾	5-11¾	6-3½	Women
									Shot Put
52-6	53-1¾	56-2	57-1½	60-11	64-6¾	66-8½	67-4¾	69-6	Men
		45-1½***	50-1½	54-5	56-9⅞	59-6	64-4	69	Women***
									Discus Throw
162-4	165-7	173-2	180-6	184-11	194-2	200-1	212-6	211-3	Men
133-2	156-3	137-6½	168-9	176-2	180-8	187-11	191-3	218-7	Women****
									Hammer Throw
176-1	185-4	183-11	197-11	207-3	220-1	228-9	240-8	247-8	Men
									Women
									Javelin Throw
238-7	235-8	228-10	242	281-2	277-8	271-2	295-7	296-10	Men
143-4	148-3	149-6	165-7	176-8	183-8	198-8	198-1	209-7	Women
									Pole Vault
14-1⅞	14-3¼	14-1¼	14-11.14	14-11½	15-5⅛	16-8¾	17-8½	18-½	Men
									Women

****Women's discus. *****No Women's events.

GREAT MOMENTS IN TRACK

Jesse Owens, they say, was the hero of the 1936 Olympics. And rightly so, because what the black race did to the master race in that Berlin extravaganza still shakes a few Aryan heads.

Owens' greatest moments, however, came on a warm spring day in 1935. That was when he set or equaled four world records in 45 minutes. In this century, no other runner has set more than one world record in a day. Owens' records were in the 100-yard dash, the long jump, the 220-yard dash and the 220-yard low hurdles.

The date was May 25, 1935. The place was Ann Arbor, Mich., and Owens was running for Ohio State in the Big Ten Conference Championships. His afternoon went like this:
3:15 p.m.—100-yard dash. Owens ran a 9.4 dash, equaling the world mark.
3:25 p.m.—long jump. Owens took only one jump, arching 26 feet 8¼ inches, surpassing the record by half a foot.
3:34 p.m.—220-yard low hurdles. Scissoring the hurdles in 22.6 seconds, Owens erased an 11-year-old world record.
4:00 p.m.—220-yard-dash. He won in 20.3 to better the previous mark by three-tenths of a second.

Jesse Owens' records stood for a long time, the 220 dash and hurdles stood until 1960 and 1966, the long jump until 1960. But we ought to ponder one other fact: when Owens ran, there were no starting blocks, no rubberized jumping runways in the long jump, no all-weather fast tracks. You ran on cinder or you ran on clay. In Ann Arbor, Owens ran on cinder.

Paavo Nurmi is remembered as running with one arm across his chest, holding his stopwatch and glancing at it periodically. On his last lap, he would gently toss the watch on the grass and sprint off to an impressive kick finish. Few people appreciated the significance of this at the time, but Nurmi's legs and stopwatch enabled him to set 22 world records from 1920 to 1931. He set world marks in everything from the 1,500 meters to the 20,000 meters, from one mile to 13 miles.

Nurmi's greatest moments came in the 1924 Olympics, with an incredible week of running on July 8 and 9 he won heats in the 1,500 and 5,000 meters. The next day he won the 1,500 finals, running the first 500 meters faster than Jim Ryun when he set his world record in 1967. Within minutes, he lined up for the 5,000 meter finals and won that. On July 11, he and the Finnish team won the 3,000 meter team race heats. On July 12, Nurmi won the 10,000 meter crosscountry in 100-degree heat. On July 13, Nurmi won his fifth gold, the 3,000-meter team final. Nurmi went on to win a total of 10 gold medals, seven individual golds and three team medals.

SEX, TAPE AND TIMES AT THE OLYMPICS

Event	Athens, 1896 Men	Munich, 1972 Men	Munich, 1972 Women
Long Jump	20′10″	27′½″	22′4½″
100-meter run	12.0	10.1	11.0
400-meter run	54.2	44.7	51.0
800-meter run	2:11.0	1:45.9	1:58.6
1,500-meter run	4:33.2	3:34.9	4:01.4

Fanny Blankers-Koen liked to say that she was just a 30-year-old Dutch housewife with two young children. Everybody else said she was the greatest female athlete of her day. Her day was the 1948 Olympics and she ran off with four gold medals in a driving rain in London's Wembley Stadium. She won the 100-meter dash, the 200-meter dash, the 80-meter hurdles and anchored the 400-meter Netherlands relay team. Something else to consider: in the 1948 Olympics, women were limited to entering three individual events. When she won her four golds, she also held the world record for the long jump and the high jump.

Emil Zatopek trained in army boots and ran with a clumsy gait and a grimacing face. Although he did not begin running competitively until he was 18, the Czech army officer won the 5,000-meters in the 1948 Olympics and the 5,000- and 10,000-meters and marathon in the 1952 Olympiad.

The marathon was his greatest moment. Having never run a marathon before, Zatopek went up to Britain's Jim Peters, at that time the world's best marathon runner, and asked for advice. Peters suggested Zatopek carefully pace himself and the Czech did just that, running alongside Peters for mile after mile. After 16 miles, Zatopek turned to Peters and said a bit plaintively, "We go a little faster, yes?" Yes, Peters went faster but there was Zatopek at his elbow, grinning, "Don't we go faster?" It was too much for Peters: he didn't finish the race. Zatopek won, setting an Olympic record.

Zatopek's long distance triple—the 5,000- and 10,000-meters and marathon victories—has never been matched, before or since.

Wilma Rudolph could not walk when she was seven years old because she had polio. By the time she got to the 1960 Olympics in Rome, she could run so fast she was called the Black Gazelle. She won three gold medals, the 100- and 200-meter dashes and put on a tremendous drive as the anchor leg of the 400-meter relay.

From W. C. Gibbs to Filbert Bayi— 100 years of nonstop running.

ASSAULT ON THE MILE

4:24.5
Walter Slade, G.B., 1875

4:15.6
Thomas Conneff, U.S., 1895

4:10.4
Paavo Nurmi, Fin., 1923

4:18.4
Walter George, G.B., 1884

4:12.6
Norman Taber, U.S., 1915

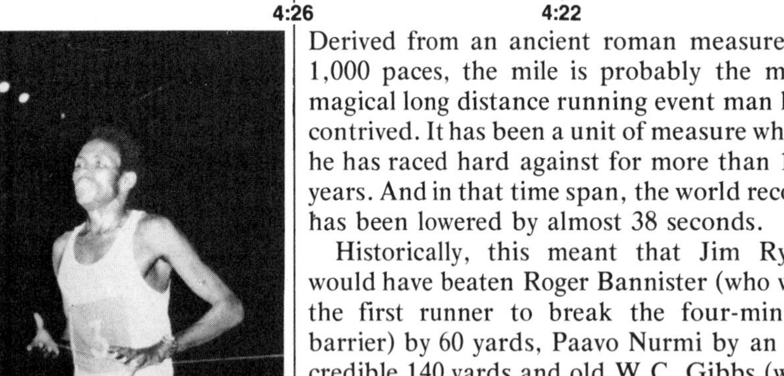

4:26 4:22 4:18 4:14 4:10

Filbert Bayi of Tanzania clocks a 3:51 mile, May 17, 1975.

Derived from an ancient roman measure of 1,000 paces, the mile is probably the most magical long distance running event man has contrived. It has been a unit of measure which he has raced hard against for more than 100 years. And in that time span, the world record has been lowered by almost 38 seconds.

Historically, this meant that Jim Ryun would have beaten Roger Bannister (who was the first runner to break the four-minute barrier) by 60 yards, Paavo Nurmi by an incredible 140 yards and old W.C. Gibbs (who held the record in 1868) by 275 yards.

Not to say that Ryun necessarily could have beaten those fellows. The great milers of history and antiquity were probably just as strong, just as fast and just as dedicated to the fine art of running. What Ryun and other current runners have to their advantage is strenuous but extremely effective training plus that most critical factor of all—a record to aim for.

When Walter George set his mile mark at 4:18.4 in 1884, thereby breaking the 4:20 barrier, he was hailed throughout the sports world as one of its super-heroes. And yet George ran a race in which he set out with a blazing start, slowed down some, slowed down some more and then hung on grimly until the end.

Nothing much happened in the mile for 40 years. Then, along came Paavo Nurmi who revolutionized the distance event. Nurmi introduced the concept of "level-paced" running. Runners train for endurance in Finland and the "Flying Finn," as the media called him, level-paced himself by running behind a suburban trolley. When the track world first saw him run, it was astonished. The Finn ran with superb ease and an amazing grace. He clicked off his paces with a flowing movement that more resembled a smooth running machine than the teeth-gritting milers who kept up but only for awhile. And running with his stopwatch in his hand (he was also the first to do that), Nurmi raced against time rather than against any specific runner. That doesn't always work but it worked for Nurmi.

The next big slice off the mile was taken by Glenn Cunningham, "The Kansas Flash," who dueled through the 1930's against Gene Venzke and Bill Bonthron. Venzke's career peaked early but the Cunningham-Bonthron battle led to numerous sub-4:10 miles. In seven years of racing, Cunningham ran the mile more than 20 times under 4:10. That was more than all of his rivals combined. The Kansas Flash brought his own unorthodoxy to the mile. He turned in a faster second half-mile than a first. His best time was 4:06.7. The four-minute mile seemed within reach.

A Swede named Gunder Haegg came close in 1945 with a world record 4:01.4. Haegg trained by plowing his legs through the snows of his native Sweden. But nothing further happened for nine years. Then, on May 6, 1954, more than 85 years after an Englishman had set the world record at less than 4:30, an Oxford medical student named Roger Bannister crossed the threshold into sports immortality by running the mile in 3:59.4 seconds.

In more than 20 years since, the sub-four minute mile has been run so often, it's not even useful to list here. Assaulted by John Landy, Ron Delaney, Herb Elliott, Peter Snell, Michel Jazy and Jim Ryun, the mile record has fallen, fallen, fallen until 1975 when Filbert Bayi lowered the mark to 3:51 flat, besting Ryun by .1 second.

The assault on the mile is not an easy task. Most world class milers practice by running 120, 140, even 160 miles a week. And it's up hills and down, not level jogging. And that's in addition to swimming and weightlifting exercises during cross-country season. The mileage drops to 80 to 100 miles a week during indoor track season and goes up to about 90 to 110 miles during the outdoor season. If a miler is preparing for a special meet, he'll probably drop the weekly practice distance to about 50

miles. One month a year, he'll rest.

The essence of the mile run has never been more eloquently stated than by Paul O'Neil when he reported for the first issue of *Sports Illustrated* on the "Mile of the Century," the Vancouver duel between John Landy and Roger Bannister which took place three months after Bannister broke the barrier:

"The art of running the mile consists, in essence, of reaching the threshold of unconsciousness at the instant of breasting the tape. It is not an easy process, even in a setpiece race against time, for the body rebels against such agonizing usage and must be disciplined by the spirit and the mind. It is infinitely more difficult in the amphitheater of competition, for then the runner must remain alert and cunning despite the fogs of fatigue and the pain, his instinctive calculation of pace must encompass maneuver for position, and he must harbor strength to answer the moves of other men before expending his last reserves in the war of the home stretch. Few events in sport offer so ultimate a test of human courage and human will and human ability to dare and endure for the simple sake of struggle."

Bannister does the impossible as he cracks the four-minute barrier in 1954.

The "mile of the century" finds Roger Bannister beating John Landy in 1954.

a Workingman's Guide to The Sprints

If you want to be the world's fastest human, here's how.

So you want to run hard and fast, swig beer out of your track trophies, pawn your Olympic gold medals or do milk commercials on TV. That means you want to break nine seconds in the 100-yard dash, do the 220 in less than 19 or leg out the 440 in 44. Something crazy like that, right?

Well, before you continue reading, check yourself out. Can you sprint four and a half steps a second? If you can't, forget about becoming a world class sprinter. If you can, read on. If you can do five steps a second, lean back, relax, and fantasize about where you want your free college education, being surrounded by track groupies and reading your name in newspapers like *The New York Times* and the *Yakima Eagle.*

You'll have to work at it, of course. Ho-hum stuff like rigid training schedules for every day of every year you plan to compete. Little things like that.

The 100-Yard Dash

The 100-Meters

The Start

It was the kangaroo that taught us how to start these races. When the late Charles Sherill, running for Yale in 1888, introduced the crouch start in a Harvard-Yale track meet (and won), the technique revolutionized sprinting. People got right down to it, even digging holes in the track to get more push. Well, we have starting blocks these days but the idea is the same. The idea is to get to full sprinting stride as quickly as possible. Let's start with the blocks. The leg you would use to kick a ball goes into the rear starting block. Place the front block 15 to 18 inches behind the starting line, the rear block 16 to 20 inches behind the front one. When the man says, "On your marks," get into the starting blocks, rest your weight on the rear knee, keep your eyes on a spot about three feet in front of the starting line. Relax. When the dude says, "Get set," get tight. This is the Moment of Truth. You're waiting for the starter's gun. Don't think about the gun and don't concentrate on the sound. Instead, concentrate on what you're going to *do* when you hear the sound. Concentrate on jerking forward the arm nearest the front leg block and throwing back the arm near the rear block. Just that. It'll get you going quicker than anything else track coaches have figured out. This piece of advice comes from James O. Dunaway who happens to have written the best how-to book for running events. The book is called *Track and Field: Running Events.* He'll tell you such things as reaction time to concentration on a *sound* is 0.225 seconds, while reaction time to concentration on an *action* to be taken is 0.120 seconds.

Acceleration

You'll reach your top speed after five or six seconds, about 50 to 60 yards down the track. You'll tool along for 25 yards at top speed. Then, at the 80- to 85-yard mark, you'll start to lose speed. It's teeth-gritting time.

The Fastest Humans In Stop Action

The past masters of the 100-yard dash run on the same track.

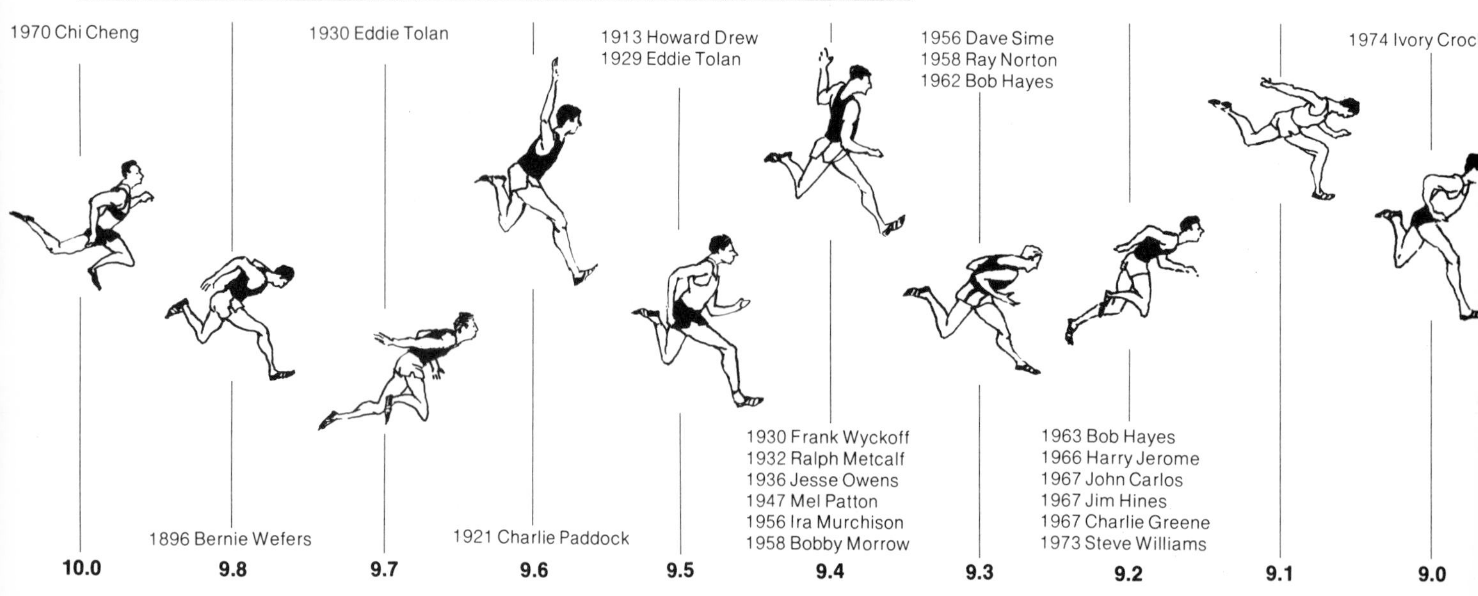

A Statistical History of the Sprints*

	1896	1900	1904	1906	1908	1912	1920	1924	1928	1932	1936	1948	1952	1956	1960	1964	1968	1972
100 METERS																		
Men	12.0	10.8	11.0	11.2	10.8	10.8	10.8	10.6	10.8	10.6	10.6	10.6	10.4	10.5	10.2	10.0	9.9	10.1
Women**									12.2	11.9	11.5	11.9	11.5	11.5	11.0	11.4	11.0	11.1
200 METERS																		
Men	None	22.2	21.6	None	22.4	21.7	22.0	21.6	21.8	22.2	20.7	21.1	20.7	20.6	20.5	20.3	19.8	20.0
Women***												24.4	23.7	23.4	24.0	23.0	22.5	22.4
400 METERS																		
Men	54.2	49.4	49.2	53.2	50.0	48.2	49.6	47.6	47.8	46.2	46.5	46.2	45.9	46.7	44.9	45.1	43.8	44.7
Women****																52.0	52.0	51.1

*Olympic results. **Women's event began in 1928. ***Women's event began in 1948. ****Women's event began in 1964.

Finish

Well, you can't go any faster. You've got to hang in there. Pump those arms harder. Push harder off your toes. Pick those knees up higher. And concentrate on running at least five more yards beyond the finish line.

Improvement

For the 100-yard dash, you should be knocking off 2/10 of a second for each year you're running competitively. If you don't improve that much, forget it.

Germany's Armin Hary wins the 1960 Olympic 100-meter dash in a photo finish.

The 220-Yard Dash

The 200 Meters

The Start

Get to top speed as in the 100-yard dash. This will get you about 60 yards down the track, and there is where you shift gears.

The Float

The idea is to maintain your top speed, or as much as you can of it, with the least amount of effort and tension. What you're supposed to do is run your ass off and relax. That may sound a bit flaky but it's sort of like an engine pulling a train. Once that train gains momentum, it's a lot easier to haul across the ties. You can't slow down but you've got to save yourself for the finish. Figure that you'll be relaxing for about 100 to 120 yards. That leaves only 40 to 60 yards to go.

The Finish

It's nitty-gritty time again. Push on those toes; up with the knees, higher; piston those arms. You'll be happy to know that most world class sprinters in this category don't float much: they can go flat out for the distance.

Improvement

Knock off two-tenths of a second a year for yourself and hang in there. Otherwise, butt out.

The 440

The Start

Again, get to top speed as in the 100-yard dash. You're 60 yards down the track with a lot more to go.

The Float

It's time to shift gears and float as in the 220. Only this time, you've got to hang in there for three times as long, for a total of about 300 yards. The idea is to run the first 220 yards of the 440 about two seconds slower than your fastest time for the 220-yard dash itself. Try to breathe naturally in this one, taking in a breath whenever you feel it's needed. During practice, inhale through the nose and exhale through the mouth. In competition, open up everything.

The Finish

By now, you'll really be feeling the strain. But this is where they separate the gold from the silver and the silver from the bronze. Hit it. Accelerate easily, don't get too tense. You can win many a 440 during these last 80 yards—if you've got the reserve, if you've got the training, if you've got the will.

Improvement

You should figure on improving your time by 3/10-4/10 of a second each year. Worry some if it's three; feel good if it's four.

Speed and Stamina Requirements

The Distance	% of Speed Needed	% of Stamina Needed
100-yard dash	95	5
220-yard dash	90	10
440-yard dash	80	20
half mile (880)	65	35
mile	50	50
two miles	40	60
three miles	20	80
six miles	10	90
marathon (26 miles)	5	95

GREAT MOMENTS IN GOLF

September 20, 1913 As in England and Scotland, golf in America began among people of wealth who wanted pleasurable outlets for their money. It came with the country clubs of Newport, Southampton, Brookline and Shinnecock Hills. It was the sport of Kings—American kings of finance and industry. Then, on September 20, 1913, came a sporting bombshell that made golf middle class. It came in the U.S. Open. Either of two great British professionals, Harry Vardon or Ted Ray, was supposed to win it. Vardon had won the British Open five times. Ray had won the U.S. Open the previous year and when the tournament opened at The Country Club in Brookline, Mass. the outcome was supposed to have been predictable. Twenty-year-old Francis Ouimet lived across the street from the Club and he caddied there. At the urging of friends he borrowed $25 to enter the Open. In the qualifying round, Ouimet shot a rather mundane 151. (Another unknown named Walter Hagen, also in his first national tournament, shot a 157.) Then came 72 holes of medal play. After 54 holes, Vardon, Ray and Ouimet were tied at 225. Everyone was sure the pressure would get to the kid on the last 18. Ouimet, however, shot a 79 (they had high scores then) and scorched through the last six holes in the rain with two birdies to tie Vardon and Ray again. Young Ouimet was carried off the 18th green on the shoulders of the crowd. But he still had to confront the playoff. The next day, as the three men completed one hole after another, it became clear to the crowd of 8,000 that they were witnessing magnificent golf history. Since the U.S. Open began in 1894 only one American had won it and he was a pro. As the unperturbable amateur Ouimet sauntered from hole to hole the crowd shouted itself hoarse. Coming into the 17th, Ouimet was ahead of Vardon by one stroke, ahead of Ray by five. On the 360-yard dogleg, Vardon risked a chancy drive, hooked into a bunker and took a five. Ouimet shot a three and teed off the 18th with a three-stroke lead. He never let up. He parred the final 18th in four and won the match. The American press called Ouimet's win "The Shots Heard Round the World." And no wonder. Golf was henceforth a game that almost any American could play. When Ouimet defeated Vardon and Ray, there were about a quarter of a million golfers in the United States. Within a decade there'd be 10 times that number.

Jones drives the third tee en route to his Grand Slam

September 29, 1923 When Walter Hagen arrived in Deal, England, for his first try at the British Open, the very proper organizers of the tournament told him that the club house was closed to him and that he would have to dress in the pro shop. The "facilities" in the pro shop turned out to be a peg on the wall and a pile of shoes in the corner. Hagen, bristling with indignation, chose to change in his hired limousine. Although he won it later, he did not win it that year. The next week, he arrived in Paris to play in the French Open. French tournament officials were as snobby as their British cousins across the Channel. Only this time, Hagen threatened to withdraw unless he was allowed full clubhouse privileges. The French gave in, and that confrontation went a long way toward giving golf professionals equal status with whatever pompous gentry there was around. Sir Walter, or The Haig, as he was affectionately called, was the kind of man who could make his demands stick. He was without question the most flamboyant, most colorful professional to stroll a link. The public loved him. He was fond of saying that he was the first golfer to make a million dollars and spend two. His greatest moment came in 1923. He had won the PGA championship in 1921, decided not to compete in the 1922 tournament (won by Gene Sarazen), then on September 29, 1923, he was beaten in match play by Sarazen, one up on the 38th hole. On that date he made a vow to himself and he kept it: he won the next four consecutive PGA championships (1924-1927) making a total of five PGA titles, a figure yet unmatched. His eleven major tournament victories (including two U.S. Opens and four British Opens) rank third (to Jack Nicklaus and Bobby Jones). But The Haig was more than one of the best golfers of all time. He singlehandedly broke the social barrier between amateurs and professionals. He refused to go second class, demanded greater prize money, threw all-night parties just before a crucial match, toured in splendor with his chauffeurs and suitcases full of money. He was the roaring golf king of the Roaring Twenties. He met Bobby Jones in an unofficial "world championship" match in Florida in 1926 and gave Jones the beating of his life, 12 and 11. Sir Walter, unlike Jones, hated to practice. "Why waste good shots in practice when you might need them in a match?" he'd ask. And when his game began to deteriorate in the middle Thirties, he attributed it to the bad Scotch he was drinking.

September 27, 1930 Completing his unmatched Grand Slam, Robert Tyre Jones, Jr., defeated Gene Homans by eight and seven strokes for the U.S. Amateur championship at Merion, Pa. Earlier in the year, he had won the U.S. Open, the British Open and the British Amateur. The amazing thing about his slam was that Bobby Jones was, and remained, an amateur. Thus, unlike pros, he only competed in a few tournaments a year. Just those few, however, were enough for him to win 13 major championships (four U.S. Opens, five U.S. Amateurs, three British Opens and one British Amateur) and then retire from competition at the rather tender age of 28. How he dominated when he played can be seen in his U.S. Open finishes from 1922 to

1930: four firsts, four seconds, and an 11th in 1927. Shortly after his retirement, Jones and Clifford Roberts founded the Augusta National Golf Club, designed the course (now considered the best in the world) and established the Masters Tournament (the most prestigious championship in golf) there in 1934. After Jones won his 13 major titles, his biographer, the noted golf historian O.B. Keeler, said, "I'll let you in on this much: it will never happen again." Keeler was wrong: Master Jack, nee Nicklaus was yet to come along.

April 7, 1935 It was the second Masters Tournament and Craig Wood, who had finished second in the inaugural Masters one stroke behind Horton Smith, was again playing brilliantly, completing the last round with a 282, careening through the last eight holes in four under par. The tournament officials, the press, and the movie stars on hand were offering their congratulations and the tournament committee was about to hand him the first prize check. But wait. Gene Sarazen was still out on the course and he had just banged in a double eagle 220-yard four-wood shot for a two on a par five on the 485-yard 15th hole. Sarazen finished the next three holes in par, tied Wood for the title, then beat him in a playoff the following day by five strokes. His double eagle spoon shot has come to be admired as the most famous shot in golf. Sarazen has another claim to a more secure niche in golf history. Puttering around in his Florida garage in 1930, he invented the sand wedge. His total record includes two U.S. Opens, three PGAs, a Masters and a British Open. And, to go back a bit further, he and the late Ed Sullivan were caddies in the 1913 U.S. Open Tournament won by Francis Ouimet.

June 7, 1939 It could be argued that Sam Snead has won more tournaments of any kind than any other male golfer. It all depends on how and what you count. He burned up the courses from 1937 to the mid-1950s, winning three PGAs, three Masters, three Canadian Opens, a British Open and opens in such places as Panama, South Africa, Brazil and Argentina. If they were playing, you could count on the "West Virginia Hillbilly" (aka "Slammin' Sam") to be puttering around the course. The Achillean problem he encountered was he could never win the U.S. Open. He came closest on June 7, 1939. Coming into the last hole, a par four, he needed a five to win the Open, a six to tie. Snead shot an eight, and placed fifth. He tied Lew Worsham in 1947 for the Open but lost the playoff. He finished second in 1949 and 1953. He never won it. If Snead had his way, all tournaments would be played barefoot. "If the rules said that everybody had to play barefoot, I'd hardly ever lose a tournament." Then, in the 1942 Masters tournament, he shot two consecutive birdies before surprised officials noticed his bare feet and ordered him to put his shoes back on. Known as a good ol' boy with a vast storehouse of colorful and off-colorful jokes, Snead most liked the stories about how he kept all his money buried in tin cans around his home in West Virginia. Some folks are still digging around those parts.

Sarazen putts out in his come-from-behind playoff victory over Craig Wood at the 1935 Masters.

Doughty Ben Hogan chips to the green in the 1950 L.A. open.

1953 Ben Hogan was at the peak of his career in 1949. He had won the Vardon Trophy five times for the lowest annual scoring average (1940-42, 1946, 1948). He had won the PGA championship once and the U.S. Open twice. But then, in 1949, while he and his wife were driving to a golf tournament, Hogan was injured in an automobile accident which left him with a broken pelvis, a broken collar bone, fractured ribs and a broken ankle. For days, it was questionable whether he would either live or walk again. Playing golf was considered impossible. But the doughty little Texan gritted his teeth, mustered his spirit and literally forced himself back out on the golf course. The following year he won the U.S. Open a second time, and again in 1951, along with a Masters title. Then, in 1953, he almost won it all. In sizzling rounds of tournament play, Hogan took the Masters, the U.S. Open and the British Open. Unfortunately, he lost the PGA, but it was still a great triumph: he had won six of his nine major titles after his near-death accident. Spectators who watched the Bantam Ben in the 1952 and 1953 tournaments remember the many times he came down to the closing holes limping with pain and visibly exhausted. In skill, he is ranked among the five golfers of all time. In guts and determination, no one else comes close.

June 16, 1945 The question people always ask about Byron Nelson is: was he the greatest golfer who ever lived or did he simply win because everyone was off to war and he had no competition? (For example, during these years he did not compete against Ben Hogan, the Vardon Trophy winner for three consecutive years—1940-42 and the professional with the best tournament record for those three years. Hogan went off to war.) Nelson had been rejected by the Army because he had hemophilia. So he stuck to golf. In 1944, he won seven tournaments, was the nation's leading money winner and averaged 69.67 strokes in 85 rounds of tournament play. Good? Guess what happened in 1945? He won 11 tournaments in succession, 19 in all, was again the leading money winner, and shot an incredible average of 68.33 strokes for 120 tournament rounds. During his prime, Nelson played in 113 consecutive tournaments and *never* finished out of the money. And if his competition wasn't strong enough, his strokes were. In Seattle in 1945, he shot a scorching 62, tying an 18-hole tournament record and set a 72-hole record with a stunning 259, averaging 64.75 per round.

Babe Didrickson, below, *and Byron Nelson,* right, *demonstrate their champion swings.*

Arnie's English fails him.

July 3, 1954 Babe Didrikson has won more titles in more sports than any other athlete, male or female. From Olympic gold medals, to All-American basketball and softball honors, world track and field records, she did it all. Mostly, though, she loved golf. In 1947, she was the first American to win the British Women's Amateur championship. Following that title, she came back to the U.S. to take 16 straight golf victories in tournament play. In 1950, she was unanimously voted the Woman Athlete of the Half Century by the Associated Press (she had been voted Woman Athlete of the Year in 1932, 1945, 1946, 1947 and 1950). In 1953, she was told she had cancer. After the surgeons operated, they said she would not be able to compete again. She didn't believe them and on July 3, 1954, she fired a 291 to win the U.S. Open by a record of 12 strokes. It was a week after her 40th birthday. She won four more tournaments that year and two in 1955. She died in the fall of 1956.

August 10, 1945 Chick Evans, the grand old man of amateur golf, won his share of national tournaments. He was the first man to win the U.S. Open and the U.S. Amateur in the same year, 1916. In the decades that followed, he won the Amateur again in 1920, won five Western Amateurs and was on five Walker Cup teams. His first great tournament win, however, came in 1907, when at the tender age of 17 he won the Chicago Amateur. Then, he won it again in 1908, 1911, and, get this, 1944. And would you believe he repeated that victory in 1945? Yes, he did. More recently, he has been known as the gent who established the Evans Caddie Scholarships, grants which have financed the college education of more than 3,000 caddies.

April 7, 1957 Doug Ford had not won a major tournament in 1956. And he had not won the Masters, ever. But there he was, bragging at the New York Golf Show on March 24, telling everyone how he was going to win the Masters that year and win it with a score of 283. Then came the Masters. Beginning the final round on April 7, Ford had shot 217. He was three strokes behind the leader, Sam Snead (and Snead had won the Masters title three times). Ford won by three strokes, shooting a 66, to hit both predictions on the button. To make his 283, however, Ford had to hole out and sink a shot from a bunker on the 18th. He did, of course, for a birdie, got his Masters title, and got his 283.

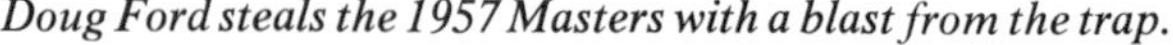

Doug Ford steals the 1957 Masters with a blast from the trap.

April 6, 1964 When Arnold Palmer strolled onto the lush greensward of the Augusta National Golf course in the spring of 1964, he was one of three men who had won the Masters tournament three times. Jimmy Demaret had won the coveted titles in 1940, 1947 and 1950; Sam Snead had won in 1949, 1952 and 1954. Palmer, himself, had won in consecutive even-numbered years, 1958, 1960, 1962. In 1964 he didn't even have to put on his famous charge. When the final round was over, it was Palmer by six strokes, and he was the first golfer to win four Masters championships. Arnold Daniel Palmer of Latrobe, Pa., made golf big-time in this country. Just as the flamboyant Walter Hagen made professional golf popular, Arnie and his Army turned a genteel sport into one complete with the jarring tensions of football and the quiet suspense of a baseball no-hitter. Palmer visibly agonized over a missed putt, smiled jubilantly over a well-placed drive, shared his good humor and boldly attacked every course he played on. His Army loved it, even when he was not in contention. No matter where or when he played, his galleries were the largest and they greeted every birdie with an exhultant "Charge!" And he was a go-for-broke charger. That was firmly established in 1960 when he birdied the last two holes of the Masters to win by a stroke and followed that victory with a front nine 30 and a back nine 35 to come back from impossible last round odds to win the U.S. Open at Cherry Hills the same year. One dedicated volunteer in his Army well recalled the charge in the Open: "He's down one stroke on the 15th, and he needs a birdie to tie. So, instead of playing it safe from the green, he misses, chips past the hole and he's down in par. Well, he comes up to the 16th, and he's in the same spot again. And damned if he doesn't try the same shot again, knock the ball in the cup this time, and went on to win the match." "How did you have the nerve," a reporter asked, "to try that shot again?" "Well," said Palmer, with the same confidence with which he stroked the balls, "I figured the course owed me one."

June 16, 1968 If there was ever any doubt that Mary Kathryn (Mickey) Wright is the best woman golfer of all time, it must have disappeared on this date at Indianapolis when Wright won her 80th professional tournament, the "500" Womens Open. The tall, long-hitting blonde from San Diego had already won the U.S. Women's Open and the LPGA four times, a feat unmatched by any other female golfer, and she was the only person to win both titles in the same year, twice, 1958 and 1961. She also once shot a 62 in tournament play: it was the finest round of golf ever played by a woman. In 1963, she won 13 tournaments, another record, and won 10 tournaments in two other years. In the late 50s and early 60s, Wright's domination of women's golf was nearly total.

April 13, 1975 The greatest golfer who ever lived is Jack Nicklaus. Bobby Jones might be a close second, Walter Hagen a more distant third. Then maybe Arnold Palmer and Ben Hogan, or Ben Hogan and Arnold Palmer. But Nicklaus is the only one to have won 15 major tournaments. No one else has won five Masters Tournaments. No one else has won all four major golf tournaments—the U.S. Open, the British Open, the Masters and the PGA—at least *twice.* And no one else shares or holds the scoring records for both the Masters (271 in 1965) and the U.S. Open (275 in 1967). The 1975 Masters has already been called the "finest finish in the history of golf," and that by none other than golf's premier writer, Herbert Warren Wind. When the 39th Masters Tournament started, Nicklaus was the favorite even though he had only won once at Augusta in the last eight years. Nicklaus was confident although going into the tournament he told reporters he thought Johnny Miller (who had won eight tournaments going into this one) and Tom Weiskopf had "more ability than anyone out here." Except for Miller, the field stroked true to form. Halfway through the tournament, it looked as if Nicklaus was going to stroll off easily with the title. The Golden Jack shot a 68 and a 67 for a 135 and led by five strokes. One stroke back was Arnold Palmer, two back was Tom Weiskopf, and Johnny Miller, who shot a 75 and a 71, was 11 strokes off the lead. But on the third round, Nicklaus limped in with a 73. Palmer limped out with a 75 and Weiskopf and Miller shot scorching rounds of 66 and 65. Weiskopf led by a stroke going into the final round. Going into the 16th hole on the final round, Weiskopf still had a one-stroke lead. But Weiskopf's luck must have slipped into the azalea bushes, flown through the magnolia trees or trickled down Rae's Creek. The 16th is a 190-yard par-three over a huge lake with a green that has more breaks than a dropped mirror. Nicklaus was playing in a twosome just in front of Weiskopf and Miller. He had driven the green but the Golden Bear had a 40-foot putt that looked more like 4,000 feet. Nicklaus stroked it strongly and damned if the ball didn't roll and snake and dance and find its way into the hole. The usually serious and calm Nicklaus did a war dance. Weiskopf and Miller were watching. It's not known what imprint that putt made on Weiskopf's mind. Johnny Miller said Nicklaus "left Bear prints." Said Nicklaus: "I knew Tommy was standing on the 16th tee watching me. I knew he was going to have a hard time playing the hole." He did. Weiskopf hit the ground a half-inch behind the ball with his five-iron and smacked it about 85 feet short of the pin—could have looked 8,500—made a bad chip, missed an 18-foot putt for a bogey. That put Nicklaus one up. both Miller and Weiskopf had a chance to even the tournament on the last hole, but Miller's 20-foot putt broke too much and Weiskopf, watching that break, stroked an eight-footer that broke not enough. Johnny Miller had set the records in the second half of the tournament, low for the final two rounds (131) and low for the final three rounds (202). Nicklaus, however, set the most important record: a fifth Masters victory. "Winning," said Jack, "is the only thing that matters."

En route to his fifth Masters win, Jack Nicklaus erupts in joy as his serpentine 40-foot putt snakes its way into the difficult 16th hole.

a Workingman's Guide to Tennis

Rod Laver

Billy Jean King

The Serve—Laver

With your opposite shoulder pointing to where you want to hit the ball, your feet about 18 inches apart, your racket pointing towards the service court, lift (don't toss) the ball into the air. As you release the ball, the racket hand goes back simultaneously, as far back as possible as if you were going to scratch your back. You're weight is shifting to your racket foot (right foot, if right-handed) on the back-swing. Then, you whip the racket forward and up, with the weight shifting to the opposite foot, hitting the ball while it is at the top of its flight. This is one smooth flow, like a pendulum, with no pauses, a smooth arc back and an explosive one forward.

The Serve—King

If you can, take an old racket and actually hurl it into the opposite court. You are really "throwing" the tennis ball off the racket as an extension of your arm. When the racket is back in the full back-scratcher position, you are fully coiled, ready to explode your energy. Back is straight or arched backward slightly. Hit the ball slightly outside the racket side of your body. (If you let the toss drop, it should fall to that side and about two feet in front of you.) When you come forward, everything moves at once. The follow-through ends up on the opposite side of the body.

The Service Return—Laver

Just get the ball back over the net. If it's a superfast serve, just block it back over. If it's moderately fast, stroke it back easily. Prepare for your return by getting your racket back as quickly as possible.

The Service Return—King

Hold racket at waist level, pointed directly at the net. Grip racket for the shot you would least like to hit, making your weaker shot less difficult.

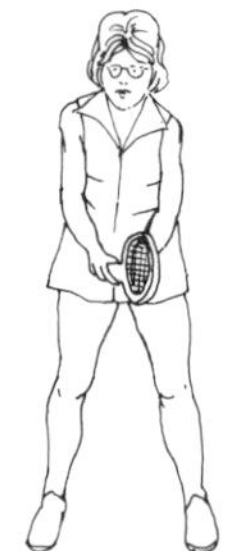

The Forehand—Laver

Swing level, connecting with the ball almost at arm's length from your body. Your opposite shoulder is toward the net; opposite foot steps forward on hit. Grip stays firm. Squeeze the handle on impact.

The Forehand—King

Turn opposite shoulder towards the flight of the ball, get your racket back quickly, with weight on racket foot, wrist firm, arm steady, head down, eyes on ball, step first with your opposite foot, stroking to hit the ball when its just even with your forward foot, with your arm fully extended.

The Backhand—Laver

Racket shoulder points toward the net. Pull racket back with your opposite hand. Opposite foot pivots while body swings. Racket foot steps forward on hit, with racket almost at arm's length from body. Swing level and hit solid.

The Backhand—King

Moving sideways and into the ball, bring racket back, with shoulders and feet perpendicular to the net, racket elbow tucked against racket hip, pull racket straight back, opposite hand lightly holding throat of the racket, fully outstretching racket arm. Hit the ball when it is 12 to 18 inches in front of your racket foot, swinging level and hitting ball on the rise at waist level for maximum power.

The next time someone asks "Tennis, anyone?", use these tips and blow them off the court.

Tony Trabert

Pancho Gonzales

The Serve—Trabert

Use your wrist to guide your serve. Never telegraph your aim by looking at a spot or by placement of your legs. With the weight on the back leg, toss the ball up on the racket side of the body. Hit it with a good wrist snap. Remember to adjust for the service curve: if you are serving to the deuce court (the right-hand court or the forehand court or the first court served into) and want to hit the ball near the center service line, start the serve to the right of the center service line, allowing for the curve; do the opposite if you're left-handed. It's best to aim the serve straight at your opponent.

The Serve—Gonzales

Take an old racket, walk out about 200 feet, mark the spot, and throw the racket that far. Proper service is very similar to that throw. Don't think "toss" but think of "placing" the ball over your head. Place the ball about three inches above your highest racket reach. If you let the ball drop, it should hit about a foot to the outside of your opposite (non-racket) foot. Hit the ball on its upward flight. Power comes from snapping the wrist and turning the body into the serve just at the moment of contact. Snap the index and middle fingers in a chain reaction after the wrist snap for even more power.

The Service Return—Trabert

Point your toes at the server, feet a shoulder's width apart, with weight on the balls of your feet, knees bent and torso tilted slightly forward, racket held waist high, parallel to ground and pointed at server. Return the ball low and deep.

The Service Return—Gonzales

Try to return low, limiting server's offense. The best percentage shot is to return low without trying to do too much with it.

The Forehand—Trabert

As the ball approaches, get the racket in ready position, with the weight on the back leg, shoulders perpendicular to the net, step into the swing, hips and shoulders face the net on the follow-through, knees are slightly bent.

The Forehand—Gonzales

Turning body sideways as soon as possible, knees bent, draw racket back, head down, eyes focused on the ball. Cradling racket neck with left hand can help snap racket into position. Hit ball waist high just in front of your belt buckle, hitting up and through, stepping forward as you swing.

The Backhand—Trabert

As the ball approaches, the racket is in the ready position, the weight shifts to the front leg, step into the ball with the front leg. In making contact, the arm straightens out at impact, with a high follow-through. Your hips and shoulders will have rotated on the shot.

The Backhand—Gonzales

The most natural stroke for right-handers. Turn your body to get the racket back, swing level, shifting weight from opposite foot to racket foot, hitting the ball off your right hip. Advanced plaqyers hit the ball at a point a little farther forward. Follow through with the racket at shoulder height.

The Attack Lob—Laver

Hit a low trajectory, just over opponent's head at last moment of his rushing the net, placing, if possible, to his backhand side.

The Attack Lob—King

Hit from inside the baseline on a low trajectory to your opponent's backhand side, just a bit higher than your opponent can reach with a slight jump.

The Attack Lob—Trabert

Use a full stroke without much backhand but good follow-through. Hit from inside the baseline, on a low trajectory, just high enough so your opponents can't jump and reach it.

The Attack Lob—Gonzales

Fake a ground stroke by delaying your shot. Make a smooth swing, hitting through and over the ball so it literally climbs straight up and loses its forward momentum and drops quickly into the court.

The Defensive Lob—Laver

Since this is supposed to give you time, knock it 50 or 60 feet into the air, hitting it with your racket face almost parallel to the court.

The Defensive Lob—King

Hit the defensive lob as close as possible to your opponent's baseline, lobbing across court because that gives you more playing area to keep the ball in bounds.

The Defensive Lob—Trabert

Take a full swing, hitting the ball as high as you can while still making it come down as deep as possible to the opponent's baseline. Beware of any existing wind—cross, follow or facing—and adjust for it.

The Defensive Lob—Gonzales

Draw the racket back and give it a full stroke with a firm wrist. The follow-through gives it the distance. Use this lob from behind your baseline or from an out-of-court position to gain time and position.

The Smash—Laver

It's like smashing a nail into the wall, with the nail at the highest point you can reach. Smash with a hard, downward stroke. Best to be next to the ball, jump into the air to get your body into it and hit the ball out of the air before it bounces.

The Smash—King

Turn sideways to flight of the ball, get your racket back into the back-scratching position, then hit the ball as you would hit a serve: up and out, not down. Don't think down. Aim it down the center of the court, since a smash is difficult enough to control without trying for angles.

The Smash—Trabert

With your racket flat behind the ball as if you were going to hit your palm against a wall, smash the ball with the face of the racket flat like a flat serve. Always snap your wrist, as in serving. Remember to hit the ball on the racket side of your body, the right if you're right-handed.

The Smash—Gonzales

Have your racket behind your back in a comfortable position, and think of it as the trigger of a gun. Your head is up, eyes focused on the ball. When the ball is a few feet over your head, pull the trigger, remembering that placement is more important than how hard you can swing the racket.

Tactics—Laver

Make the fewest mistakes and you'll win. The safe shot is the best shot and you should strive to keep the ball in the court and let your opponent make the mistakes. If you haven't played your opponent before, probe for his weaknesses and concentrate on hitting to that weakness whenever possible, keeping a few surprise shots and placements to keep him guessing. Go to the net only after preparing for it with a good approach shot. Do your best to win the first point in every game. Make the pace of the game work for you: if your opponent is playing slow, speed things up, and vice versa. Never get discouraged because your opponent will only get encouraged.

Tactics—King

Hit your forehands well enough and deep enough down the line; follow them to the net. Concentrate on winning your serve. Serve deep and follow to the net. Try to return serves steadily. Always, always watch the ball, even to the point of contact. Don't overhit but concentrate on hitting every shot with the center of your racket. Hit the ball on the rise. When playing the baseline, think of hitting the ball so far in front of your body that your racket will follow through to the far service line. Go to the net whenever possible.

Tactics—Trabert

Get to the net as quickly as possible. Never stay in no-man's land. Hit the ball low. Make your opponent hit up. Always hustle into a good volleying position. Make the percentage play by hitting your own best type of strokes, thus, giving yourself the best chance for success. Hit a spin serve instead of a flat serve: there's more percentage of it getting in. Volley up the center, because you're more apt to get the ball into the court. Aim at the lowest part of the net, the center, because you have six inches less to clear. Maintain a positive attitude. Know your own game and know your opponent's.

Tactics—Gonzales

Matches are won by opponents' errors. Play the percentages. Don't go for the big shot when you don't need it. Put your total concentration on the ball, and what you intend to do with it. Be respectful and cordial but pay as little attention to your opponent as possible. The moment you give your opponent an identity (to yourself) or sneak a peek at him, you lose your concentration. If you know the strengths and weaknesses of your opponent, practice shots that will capitalize on those weaknesses. Don't change a winning game, if you're winning from the baseline, stay there.

GREAT MOMENTS IN TENNIS

August 3, 1914 Americans had generally sneered at the sissy game called tennis. After all, there were all these men and women running around, patting a ball across a net, shouting "15-love," "30-love," serving up a spongy ball underhanded and volleying with easy lobs while moneyed straw-hatters and lace-bustled folk watched under the cool of lawn umbrellas at places called Nahant, Newport and Southampton. It was one hell of an atmosphere for a national championship. In 1914, however, Maurice M. "Red" McLoughlin, the California Comet, came East with a dazzling game of power serves, rushes to the net, passing shots and hard, smashing volleys. No one had seen that kind of play before. But the California Comet had a great competitor in Norman Brookes, an Australian who had beaten the U.S. in the Davis Cup in 1908, 1909 and 1911. Before more than 12,000 spectators at Forest Hills, the two played one of the greatest sets of tennis in Davis Cup history. It was a clash of titans, a battle of youth and power against guile and experience. When the first set got to 9-8, in favor of the wily Brookes, it was McLoughlin's service. If Brookes could break service, he would win the set, 10-8. Brookes got the first three points, love-40, one point to go. But the California Comet served three straight aces and tied the game up. Then McLoughlin rammed home two more cannonball serves which the Australian got his racket on but could not return. The match was even up, 9-9. The battle of the services went on and on. It finally came down to the 31st and 32nd game. In the 31st, Brookes reached 40-15 on his service and got ad after deuce had been reached. But McLoughlin brought it back to deuce, his advantage, then drove a Brooke's serve back hard at the Australian's feet, and won the game, leading the set, 16-15. The final game was another bitter contest, again reached deuce, and again McLoughlin rifled two aces past the Australian, finally winning the set.

1920-1929 Of all the major sports and sports heroes of the Golden Twenties—baseball's Ruth, boxing's Tunney, football's Grange—none dominated a game and a decade like William Tatem Tilden II. His great moment *was* the decade. He was the first American to win at Wimbledon. He won it three out of five tries. In that decade he was the U.S. Champion seven times, for six consecutive years (1920-1925) and in 1929. He was a member of 11 Davis Cup teams (a record in itself) and it was mainly due to him that the Cup remained in this country for seven straight years. By the time he quit active tournament competition, he had won more than 70 American and international titles. His greatest strengths were his booming cannonball serve and his low sizzling forehand. He preferred to stay near the baseline and disdained rushing the net, although he could cover the court in three long strides if he needed to. The only remaining controversy is: *was* he the greatest player ever? No. He was, indeed, the King of the Nets, as they called him then, but most contemporary experts would acknowledge that at least a dozen players since World War II would have rushed Bill Tilden off the court. It wouldn't be easy, mind you, but he's dead and long live the King and all that but there are new, more powerful, more exciting monarchs on the courts.

Big Bill Tilden creases the net with another blazing forehand return. William II was the King of Tennis during the 1920s.

February 17, 1926 "Never was any amateur sporting event the world over staged under such atrocious conditions." That, in sum, was what one writer observed while he sat in Cannes, France, waiting for the only confrontation between the two greatest women tennis players of all time: Helen Wills and Suzanne Lenglen. What prompted the remark, made just five minutes before the match began, were the workmen hammering and pounding on the stands, the mob yelling and screaming in an alleyway, the people climbing all over the fences and trees around the court, the saw mill angrily buzzing away nearby, and the 17-by-11-foot clubhouse which had no electricity, no towels, no toilet. Suzanne Lenglen was the reigning queen of Wimbledon. She had won the women's singles and women's doubles there for five consecutive years (1919-1923), then won them both again in 1925. Helen Wills, "Little Miss Poker Face" from California, had not yet won at Wimbledon but she was a three-time U.S. champion in singles (1923-1925) and doubles (1922, 1924-25). But Wills could hit a ball harder than any woman who ever played. Her ground strokes were so potent and steady that she rarely came to the net Her game was called tedious and boring but it brought her seven American championships and eight Wimbledon championships in 16 years, and that is a record untouched by anyone. So Cannes was quite a setting for this, the greatest match of the time. The match started. The workmen were persuaded to stop. Lenglen took the first set, Wills the second, and the Frenchwoman was surprised. When Lenglen moved ahead in the fifth game, the noise of the French crowd was impossible to control. Lenglen won the set. The second set started out differently. After Wills had taken a 3-1 lead, Mlle. Lenglen paused, went over to the side of the court and sipped a brandy. The games went to 5-5. Finally, Lenglen got to match point. A Wills cannonball slammed into Lenglen's forehand corner, and thinking it was out, Mlle. Lenglen rushed to the net to congratulate the valiant American loser. But wait, the ball was not out. In a moment, the California girl evened the score, and that was where Lenglen summoned up all her courage. She was the then woman champion of the world, she had though she had won it, and she had not. She was tired, exhausted, the wan smiles and the strained lines in her face showed all that. But after deuce, after deuce, after deuce the Frenchwoman won. She *was* the greatest woman player that day. The young Californian, however, went on to be the greatest woman player ever. She went on to win eight Wimbledon singles titles and nine U.S. women's singles titles.

Suzanne Lenglen, above left, *and Helen Wills,* right, *ruled tennis in the 1920s. Maureen Connolly,* opposite page, above, *gained the throne in the 1950s.*

Don Budge flashes his winning form at the 1937 Wimbledon. Twenty years later, Althea Gibson, opposite page, *wins on the same courts.*

1937 There used to be sedate courtside arguments over whether Bill Tilden or Don Budge was the greatest tennis player of all time. It's a moot question these days but there's no doubt that Budge, the carrot-topped redhead from California was among the greatest. He had the most explosive backhand in pre-Rod Laver court history. Wimbledon, 1937, the match between Budge and the German, Baron Gottfried von Cramm, has been described by many tennis historians as "undoubtedly the greatest match ever played." It was perfect tennis, with each competitor scoring more winning points than error points. Von Cramm, who had finished second to Fred Perry the previous two Wimbledons, was in superb form. He won the first two sets but Budge took the third and fourth. In the final set, even though the Baron rocketed to a 4-1 lead Budge never lost his courage or his cool. After a sip of water, he leaned over to the American team captain, Walter Pate and whispered, "Don't worry, Cap. I'll make it." And Budge pulled even to 5-all. They carried the match to 6-all. In the 13th game, Budge broke service and led 7-6. In the 14th game, match point came and went, came and went, six times. Budge delivered a rocket serve to von Cramm's forehand. Amazingly, the German returned it, and later blasted a liner behind Budge and to his left. Turning instantly, Budge raced to his left, whipped around with his best shot, the backhand, and the ball passed von Cramm like a flashing meteor. The match was won, and Budge went on that year to win the French, U.S. and Australian championships, scoring the first simultaneous Grand Slam in tennis history.

1953 Little Maureen Connolly came out of the blue skies and loam hills of San Diego at the tender age of 16 and won the 1951 National Women's Singles Championship at Forest Hills. When she was 17, she won her first title at Wimbledon. But 1953 was her big year. At age 18, she became the first woman to win the Grand Slam: the Australian, the French, the Wimbledon and the U.S. The following year, Little Mo repeated her victories in the French and the Wimbledon, but just before the U.S. she was seriously injured in a riding accident. She died in 1969 when she was 34.

August, 1957 They called her Big Al and she had a booming serve and a fine volley. Her problem was that she had learned tennis on the streets of Harlem and she was black. They didn't allow black folks to play at lily-white Forest Hills. Althea Gibson was the first black player to make it. She was invited to compete in 1950 and she was eliminated in the second round. That didn't deter her though. Beginning in 1947 she won a string of 10 ATA National Women's Singles titles. But her development was hampered by the fact that she had very little access to top-flight competition. She could only play in a few select white tournaments because the other clubs would not invite her. It took her seven years to reach the top. In 1956, she won the French championship. In 1957, she won the best: the Wimbledon and the U.S. Championship. She repeated that double victory in 1958. She was 30 and 31 at the time, her peak competitive years passed. But she was a stunning black meteor who opened up those pearly white tennis gates.

January 27, 1969 The greatest living tennis player in the world is Rodney George Laver. If there was any doubt about that, it was dispelled on the grass at Forest Hills in September, 1969, when he won the Grand Slam of tennis for the second time. Laver first won the Grand Slam seven years earlier, in 1962, as an amateur. He and Don Budge are the only men who have ever won the Big Four, but Laver is the only double winner. He beat Andres Gimeno in January on tricky resodded Australian grass. Playing in one of his finest clay matches, he breezed over Ken Rosewall in May on a very slow French clay court. In June, he overcame the powerful John Newcombe on the grass at Wimbledon. And, finally, on the grass at Forest Hills, he overpowered Tony Roche for the last sweet win. For Laver, however, the toughest match en route to his second Slam was none of the final round matches, nor even Wimbledon or Forest Hills. His greatest victory leading to his greatest moment came in the semi-final round of the Australian, when he eked out a win from Tony Roche—7-5, 22-20, 9-11, 1-6 and 6-3—under a blistering Brisbane sun, 105° heat, and three sunhats which he thoroughly soaked. The second set, which Laver won 22-20, was the longest he ever played, and the eighth longest on record anywhere. By the end of the third set, which Roche won, Laver was absolutely groggy. A merciful intermission allowed the two men to shower but Roche came back and won the fourth set, 6-1, to tie the match at two sets each. But even though Roche won, the fourth set was the critical one. They had gone to deuce in the sixth game of the fourth set. Roche was up 5-0 but Laver realized that he had to win that particular game, even though both players knew that Roche had the set sewed up. Winning that game, then losing the next, would make Roche a 6-1 victor of the fourth set—to even the match—but it would also mean that Laver would serve first on the fifth final and decisive set. As Laver explained later, "that's why I tried so hard for a seemingly meaningless game when I was down 0-5 in the fourth. I wanted to serve that leadoff game." And serve he did. Laver also knew that every time he held service, it would pile more pressure on Roche. Each held service and the set went to 3-all. Laver served to 4-3 and the two men changed courts. Laver wrung out his third, and last, sunhat which he later said was "like squeezing out a sponge." (He has been known to put a piece of wet cabbage inside his hat, but he had none that day.) "It was his turn to serve," Laver wrote later, "and I screwed my mind into working for every point as though it were the last. If

you do that when you come down the stretch in a tight match you'll be surprised how often a superhuman effort will come out of you.... 'I'm going to hack and grub,' I told myself. 'Just do anything to get the ball over the net. It doesn't matter how you look. Form won't win this one.'" Winning that game meant Laver would be serving for the match with a 5-3 advantage. Roche had to be tight for it. After two volleys, it was 15-all. Roche missed a volley and was behind, 15-30, a big point under those circumstances. Laver returned the next serve with a crosscourt chip shot. Roche seemed relieved because he thought the ball was out. "15-40," the umpire called. A debatable call but what the hell: what the ump calls stands forever. On the next point, Roche served and volleyed to Laver's backhand, the best backhand the world has seen. Laver drove that ball with all the wristsnap he could muster, loading the ball with topspin. It was a passing winner—and Laver went on to win his service game, on to beat Gimeno in the final, on to the French title, the Wimbledon crown and the American finale.

Lunging for a shot at the 1969 U.S. Open, Rod Laver demonstrates the unbeatable style that won him two tennis Grand Slams.

Although nursing an injured left ankle, Margaret Court Smith still managed to capture the 1970 Wimbledon.

1970 Margaret Court Smith had won them all and she just plain quit. In seven years of major competition, she had won the Australian title exactly seven times, the Italian championship three times, the French twice, the U.S. twice and Wimbledon twice. She was the epitome of the mighty serve, the powerful volley and the heavy groundstroke. Going back to her native Perth to open a sportswear boutique seemed about the only thing left to do. Or was it? She couldn't get the racket out of her hand. She played squash to keep it. She got married and was drawn back to the championship trail. She won the Grand Slam: the Australian, the French, the U.S. and the Wimbledon.

Wimbledon Winners — The Last 15 Years

Men		Women
Neale Fraser	**1960**	Maria Bueno
Rod Laver	**1961**	Angela Mortimer
Rod Laver	**1962**	Karen Hantze-Susman
Chuck McKinley	**1963**	Margaret Smith
Roy Emerson	**1964**	Maria Bueno
Roy Emerson	**1965**	Margaret Smith
Manuel Santana	**1966**	Billy Jean King
John Newcombe	**1967**	Billy Jean King
Rod Laver	**1968**	Billy Jean King
Rod Laver	**1969**	Ann Hayden-Jones
John Newcombe	**1970**	Margaret Court
John Newcombe	**1971**	Evonne Goolagong
Stan Smith	**1972**	Billy Jean King
Jan Kodes	**1973**	Billy Jean King
Jimmy Connors	**1974**	Chris Evert
Arthur Ashe	**1975**	Billy Jean King

Forest Hills Winners — The Last 15 Years

Neale Fraser	**1960**	Darlene Hard
Roy Emerson	**1961**	Darlene Hard
Rod Laver	**1962**	Margaret Smith
Rafael Osuna	**1963**	Maria Bueno
Roy Emerson	**1964**	Maria Bueno
Manuel Santana	**1965**	Margaret Smith
Fred Stolle	**1966**	Maria Bueno
John Newcombe	**1967**	Billy Jean King
Arthur Ashe	**1968**	Margaret Court
Rod Laver	**1969**	Margaret Court
Ken Rosewall	**1970**	Margaret Court
Stan Smith	**1971**	Billy Jean King
Ilie Nastase	**1972**	Billy Jean King
John Newcombe	**1973**	Margaret Court
Jimmy Connors	**1974**	Billy Jean King

Billie Jean King, below and left, *muscles her way to victory over the* Happy Hustler.

September 20, 1973 Billie Jean Moffitt King has won more major tennis championships than any woman ever, but her greatest moment surely came before the largest crowd ever assembled for a tennis match. It was billed as the "Tennis Match of the Century" and she soundly whipped Bobby Riggs in straight sets at the Houston Astrodome. Riggs, you remember, had hustled Margaret Court Smith, the best woman tennis player in the world, right off the court, 6-2 and 6-1, at Ramona, Calif., four months earlier. Then he went after Billie Jean. "She's a great player," the 55-year-old Riggs would sneer, "for a gal. But no woman can beat a male player who knows what he's doing. I'm not only interested in glory for my sex, but I also want to set Women's Lib back 20 years, to get women back into the home where they belong." Ms. King had only one comment: "I'd break my bozzonga to beat that guy." The fans, the curious, the feminists and the chauvinists jammed the Astrodome that night. Along with millions of Americans, residents of 36 foreign nations were tuned in live via television. Frequently rushing the net, playing to Riggs' weak backhand, Ms. King trounced the middle-aged former male tennis great, 6-4, 6-3 and 6-3. He leaped the net to congratulate her. She put her arms around him. "Good try, Bobby," she said.

May 3, 1975 They called it the Heavyweight Championship of Tennis. In this corner, the contentious champion of the 1974 Wimbledon and Forest Hills—22-year-old Jimmy Connors. Seeded number one in world rankings, tennis' Bad Boy faced mustachioed Australian star John Newcombe in a winner-take-all match at Caesars Palace in Las Vegas. There, two months earlier, Connors had leveled Rod Laver in a challenge match, netting himself over $100,000 and more enemies. The crowd cheered for the enormously popular Newcombe, in the hopes that he would humiliate the arrogant "Tennis Brat."

In the first set Connors broke the Australian's heralded serve with the finest service return in the game, and went on to win 6-3. The second set went to Newcombe 6-4 but then Connors took command, blitzing through the last two sets 6-2 and 6-4. Although Arthur Ashe later humbled him at Wimbledon, Connors had proved himself the hottest young head in tennis.

a Workingman's Guide to Cross-Country Skiing

By Brian Vachon

A pair of skis and a bag lunch is all you need to join America's fastest growing winter sport.

There's a black figure gliding on snow, inside the white bowl of mountains and the green cirque of pines, slowly, silently, at a proper pace for the god of the woods and the gods of men.

The silence of winter and the overpowering quiet of woods demand something more from the sportsman than ski lodges. If a man loves the winter he will lean (knees bent) in the direction of cross-country skiing, the only real rival to dogsledding and snowshoeing in the class of events called "getting across snows without turning them brown."

They say it's "the fastest-growing winter pastime in America," which in this case means it's still small and homespun, not a cancer. In any case, it's got a lot to offer us sporting types, especially the exclusive ones like me (no diphtheria cases allowed):

It's cheap (far cheaper than downhill skiing); it's exciting but not dangerous; you can do it anywhere there's any kind of snow; it's superb exercise which strengthens nearly every muscle; and it takes about five minutes to learn the basics.

Purists make ado about the differences between "cross-country skiing," "ski touring," "ski jogging" and "ski running" but essentially they all refer to the same activity: moving over snow on skis using a gliding motion.

Generally, cross-country skiing refers to the more leisurely aspects of the sport. (For the competitive, there are plenty of races—from short distances to overnight treks. But ski racing is an entirely different breed, requiring very specific technique and equipment. Cross-country skiing requires neither.)

Above all else, cross-country skiing is a sport with unlimited options. Skiers can ski alone or in a group. They can ski in a forest or down a sidewalk. They can take lessons or teach themselves. They can rent equipment or buy their own. Finally, skiers can worry about technique, or totally forget that such a concept could intrude upon the sport. Is there anything else to ask for?

Only snow.

Getting Started

The average semi-coordinated, middle-aged, overweight American person who has never been on skis before can learn to ski tour in a matter of a few hours. And anyone who likes to walk will love ski touring, because the emphasis is on the touring, rather than the skiing, even though there is a great sense of grace and speed in the splendid, gliding strides.

The touring technique is the oldest in skiing (Norwegians were doing it 4,000 years ago)—it is a sort of sliding walk on those long light skis. You plant the pole into the snow, shift your weight to the opposite foot and push ahead (this is on level land). To climb hills, a simple herringbone walk—ski tips pointed outward, edges dug in—or a sidestep will suffice nicely. In going downhill, a novice must learn—first —how to stop. The classic, ancient and honorable snow plow—ski-points pigeon-toed inward—is the most common way of stopping. But John Caldwell, former U.S. Olympic skier and lately American team coach, points out that the most foolproof way to halt a downhill plunge is to fall down. "It never fails," he says, "and the chances are you won't get hurt even a little bit if you do it *soon* enough!"

Other instructors also advise beginners to slow themselves down by reaching out and grabbing brush or branches—a blatantly graceless technique, but very effective.

You can ski tour anywhere—even in city parks or suburban back yards. Golf courses

are perfect, and the unmanicured countryside always beckons. And, consider this—in almost every case, the agitated farmer who habitually refuses access to snarling, air-fouling cavalcades of snowmobiles will smile and welcome the gentle cross-country skier to his woods and pastures.

In cross-country skiing there is none of the maddening standing in line, shifting from ski to ski, waiting for the next lift to the top. Cross-country skiing is *safer* than downhill skiing because the boot is a pliable thing. And cross-country skiing is *friendly.* There is almost instant equality, and thus togetherness, because it is almost impossible *not* to master the art immediately. There is no pecking order in ski touring, either. At the typical alpine ski resort, no one is more derided than the "brown baggers," people who bring their own lunches—they often wind up miserably munching their sandwiches in some corner or cellar of the lodge, humiliated by their lack of big-spender wherewithal. But the cross-country skier finds it both natural and comfortable to carry his own lunch in a bag and his own wine in a bottle and to grab his nourishment somewhere sitting on a log.

State recreation departments in all skiing states, including those in the Midwest, have brochures on, or at least lists of, cross-country ski groups or resorts that are particularly good. Another good source of information on the sport is:

Ski Touring Council, Inc.
342 Madison Ave., Room 727
New York, N.Y. 10017

The Council has a guide to trails in the United States and Canada for $1, and can give you information on where to get lessons and on good places to go cross-country skiing.

Equipment and Costs

The uniform for the sport can be anything that provides warmth and protection from wind and moisture. Parka and sweater on top, knickers and knee socks below are common but not mandatory. Cotton thermal-knit long underwear is in vogue, but red long johns get the job done. Clothing should be loose for flexibility, breathable—because you'll perspire while cross-countrying, no matter what the temperature—and water resistant. Other than that, just be comfortable.

Skis, should be narrow and flexible, and about as high as your wrist when your arm is extended—$50 to $85.

Bindings, those which grip only the toe of the boot are the most popular and practical—$5 to $8.

Boots, should be comfortable, durable, and mated to the bindings—$20 to $40.

Poles, light-weight, slightly curved at the tip with an adjustable hand strap, should be as tall as your arm pit—$6 to $10.

Best Places in the U.S.

While cross-country skiing only requires snow to be enjoyed, it is best at ski facilities where trails have been cut and are maintained. (The only major exceptions are old logging roads — cut in forests throughout the country — which are very often perfect cross-country ski runs.) Most ski resorts have cross-country trails and their worth can generally be measured by the rating of the resort itself.

The *Trapp Family Lodge* in Stowe, Vt. is very successful and very large. There are many miles of well-marked trails, offering plenty of opportunity for isolation. The same can be said for the *Scandinavian Lodge and Mount Werner Traning Center* in Steamboat Springs, Col. That is the home base of Sven Wiik, the high priest of cross-country skiing and a former Olympian. Other cross-country centers—with qualified instructors—can be found throughout the Northern United States as well as Canada and Europe. The Adirondacks, in upstate New York, is a perfect cross-country ski area, with excellent trails in the forests (13 million acres of wilderness) and several good, medium-sized ski slopes, like Whiteface Mountain in Wilmington, N.Y.

Every lodge that has a ski touring trail is likely to have a professional to offer lessons. Beginners should probably try an hour or so alone to see if lessons seem necessary. (They usually will seem very much so.) The first time out, skiers should also call ahead and find out if rentals are available. Many resorts have extensive equipment for rent and at least for the first time on skis, the $100 investment should be postponed. You might hate it (you won't, but you might).

Where to Get Started

AMC Cross-Country Ski Program
AMC Northern New England
Reg. Office
Pinkham Notch Camp
Gorham, N.H. 03581

Copper Cross Country
P.O. Box 397
Frisco, Col. 80443

Royal Gorge Ski Touring School
c/o The Ski Hut
1615 University Avenue
Berkeley, Ca. 94703

Silent Tours
c/o Mountaincraft Shop
810 Lincoln Avenue
Steamboat Springs, Col. 80477

Sugar House
P.O. Box 5436
South Lake Tahoe, Ca. 95795

Wilderness Alliance
Route 2, Box 12D
Conifer, Col.

Wilderness Experience
P.O. Box 1042
Canoga Park, Ca. 91304

Waxing

The rules for waxing cross-country skis are not complicated. Skis don't go without wax—the right wax for the right atmospheric and snow condition. The right wax—spread evenly over a base along the length of the skis, underside—allows the skier to glide uphill and down with no difficulty. The wrong wax can cause extensive slipping, or so much hold that forward progress is all but impossible. Because conditions calling for one way or another vary to a significant extent, it is best to refer to our chart. (Or skiers can refer to instructions on the label of the wax.) There are also cross-country skis with fur or fishscale surfaces that eschew wax of any kind, and skiers who swear by them.

New Snow	Old Snow Corn Snow	Rough Corn Snow, Ice
Special **Green** 18°F and colder	Special **Green** 10°F and colder	**Blue** Klister Below freezing ice and crust
Green 18°F to 27°F	**Green** 10°F to 21°F	**Violet** Klister Crust and wet snow from 25°F to 37°F
Blue 27°F to 32°F	**Blue** 21°F to 30°F	**Red** Klister Wet or soaking wet snow
Violet Freezing to thawing 32°F	**Violet** Freezing to thawing 32°F	
Yellow Klister Soggy snow, slipping tracks, wet snow	**Red** Soggy snow	
	Red Klister wet or soaking wet snow	

THE MACHO-SIDEWINDER COMES TO FRISBEE

By Scot Morris

The story, the stars, the secrets of success.

A few years ago I hired a Mexican woman to clean up my apartment. She spoke no English so I just pointed to the things that needed cleaning and went out for the day. When I came back I was dazzled by how clean everything was, then I had a taste of culture shock. In the dishrack next to the sink my plates were all stacked in a neat row, and there, in between the brown stoneware and the flowery Safeway dishes, was my Frisbee.

Last spring, after Richard Nixon gave the commencement address at Annapolis, the midshipmen gave him the customary gag gifts. He got a stuffed alligator, which amused him, and a Frisbee, which seemed to baffle him. He looked at it as if he wasn't sure whether to wear it, hang it on the wall, or take it home and eat off it. Then something must have clicked in his preconscious, for he suddenly flipped it toward the audience and showed the world how out-of-touch he was. The Frisbee only went three or four yards: he had thrown it upside down.

There *are* people who still don't know what a Frisbee is, but they are dwindling to a small group of isolated people like our ex-President and a few Mexican cleaning women.

As for me, I'm a Frisbee Freak and I'll admit it. I've been hooked since about 1960, and I'm ready to go Toss the Friz on a moment's notice. There's something about the way those things fly that just draws me—graceful, unearthly, a "kinetic air-sculpture" as Bob May calls it. I keep one in my car at all times, for emergencies. You never know when you'll need one.

"Play Catch—Invent Games"

Mostly I just play catch. The only game I ever play is called Limits. The object is to make the person you're playing with press himself to his maximum limits. If your throw is too easy for him to catch, that's a bad throw; if it's clearly beyond his reach, that's a bad throw too. But a throw that makes your partner run, leap, reach, and just *barely* miss it off the tip of his fingers—that's a perfect Limits throw. You throw to the imaginary hemisphere of your partner's outer capacity—a hemisphere that varies according to how skilled or exhausted he is. As for catching, you judge yourself on whether you gave maximum effort. I'm told that Limits Frisbee originated at Esalen and I don't doubt it: it's the kind of noncompetitive self-improvement game that might make excellent therapy.

Once you have mastered the basic backhand throw you move on to the exotic variations. You make it skip off the pavement or arc around a telephone pole, or you throw it forehand or behind your back or between your legs. I've seen guys on the beach who can throw it accurately upside down in a long barrel-roll that loops out gracefully for 50 yards or more—a throw that might be called the Modified Milhous. There's a guy in L.A. who can even throw with his toes.

For many, Frisbee is a lot more than a game of catch. It's contemporary culture, a phenomenon, a way of life, with its own traditions, heroes, and history. It all began in the early Fifties, they say, when Yale students started playing catch with the pie-tins put out by the Frisbie Baking Co. (that's how they spelled it), of Bridgeport, Conn. The baker went out of business in 1957, but some of those original tins are still around, hoarded reverently in private collections.

"Flat Flip Flies Straight," it says on the back of every Frisbee, but it isn't precisely true—though it's truer now than it was with those old pie-tins. The fact is, a perfectly flat backhand throw by a right-hander invariably fades off to the right somewhat, because of its clockwise spin. A great deal of air whooshes by on its left side—relative to its line of flight—increasing the air pressure on the left; whereas much less air passes by its right side, producing a relative vacuum there, and the Frisbee gets sucked off to the right. It's the same aerodynamic principle that causes a clockwise-spinning golfball to slice into the right rough, and the design of Frisbees has been improved through the years to cut down on this tendency. Someone, somewhere, has been taking this thing very seriously. There are different weights and sizes now, designed for short-range speed and accuracy, for distance, or for extra stability on windy days. And the model names—the Master, the Tournament, the Professional—are serious and self-inflated to the point of parody. The *Professional Frisbee,* 108 grams: as if *this* were the model used by the guys on the circuit—the people who make their living with these things. Some Frisbees bear their own individual serial numbers, and they're all stamped "IFA Approved."

IFA? The International Frisbee Association, of course, and they're deadly serious. I sent in 50 cents for their membership package once, just to see how far they had taken this thing. (Actually, I went in halvies with a friend named Candy Bates. We registered under the combined name, Candy Scot.) Here's what we got:

1. A wallet card and a registration certificate ("suitable for framing") identifying Candy Scot as a lifetime IFA member.
2. Assurance that the serial number we had sent in had been recorded in an IFA file somewhere, so that—God forbid—if my Frisbee were ever lost or stolen and turned in, it would eventually find its way back to its rightful owner.
3. An Official IFA Proficiency Manual, which told exactly what throws and catches you have to perform in order to achieve the grade of Frisbee Amateur, Expert, or Master.
4. The latest issue of the IFA *Newsletter,* which told about the Frisbee Tournament held every year at the Rose Bowl in Pasadena.

The Run For The Roses

When I read about the World Frisbee Championships, I decided to truck up to Pasadena to see just how far Frisbee had come from the days of "Play Catch—Invent Games."

There they were: the greatest collection of Frisbee talent ever assembled, flown in from all over the country for a three-day meet, all expenses paid. They have known each other for many years, this inner circle of Frisbeedom: they have read about each other in the IFA Newsletter and have competed in previous tournaments, though never in a meet as big as this. They have acquired colorful nicknames over the years. Victor Malafronte of Berkeley is called "Mighty Mouse" because of his size (though he hates the name), and he's dwarfed by Dan "The Stork" Roddick. Physics professor Jay Shelton is known as "The All American Boy," and Paul Richardson is called "Sky King" because he's a pilot for Eastern Airlines. Then there's John "The Great Pretender" Kirkland, from Allston, Mass., who was given the nickname after a *Christian Science Monitor* article erroneously printed that John was last year's World Frisbee Champion.

Behind everything was the hand of "Steady Ed" Headrick, Executive Vice President of Wham-O, in charge of everything have to do with Frisbees. Steady Ed has devoted his life to Frisbee—he is the father of three Frisbee Masters, and his IFA membership number is 001.

A Company Outing

The Wham-O company, despite some expectations, remains unobtrusive and unspoken—through a constant background force. The IFA is an independent organization; guided not by Wham-O people but by sincere Frisbee freaks—people who just love the way those damn things fly. The whole Rose Bowl outing was financed by Wham-O (admission was free), and one *could* say that it was all a giant corporate publicity stunt. It was, of course, but no one I spoke to felt exploited, and some felt just the reverse, that it was about time Wham-O started paying as much promotional attention to Frisbee as it does to, say, Silly String.

Guinness Challenged

For me, the individual performances were the most interesting—distance and accuracy, flash and style. The women's distance throw was won easily by Monika Lou of Berkeley, She chucked one 78 yards—a long, floating field-goal that nestled through the uprights at the North end of the field.

The men's distance throw brought out the first intense individual match-up of the day. The *Guinness Book of World Records* lists the longest distance throw in official competition as a 95-yarder by Bob May. The key word is "official": that record has already been broken 30 or 40 times by May and others, I was told, but never "officially." Just the day before, Victor Malafronte had thrown one 98 yards, but that was in the qualification rounds and not "official."

Today's distance throw promised not only to

A FRISBEE CHRONOLOGY

1948 First plastic flying disk invented. Inventor unknown, reputed to be one Fred Morrison.

1949 First "sky pie" spotted in Los Angeles.

1952 First intramural Guts game at Dartmouth College, Hanover, N.H.

1956 Dr. Julius T. Nachazel creates the first Frisbee trophy out of tomato cans.

1957 Frisbie Baking Co. goes out of business in New Haven, Conn. Namesake of pie tins thrown from Yale rooftops.

1964 First Wham-O Professional model, also known as "Olympic Ring #1," rolls off production line.

National Satellite Association formed, predecessor of today's International Frisbee Association.

1968 Frisbee thrown in Rose Bowl, Pasadena, Calif.

1969 American astronauts take first Frisbee to the moon.

1974 Macho-sidewinder throw debuts at world championship in Rose Bowl.

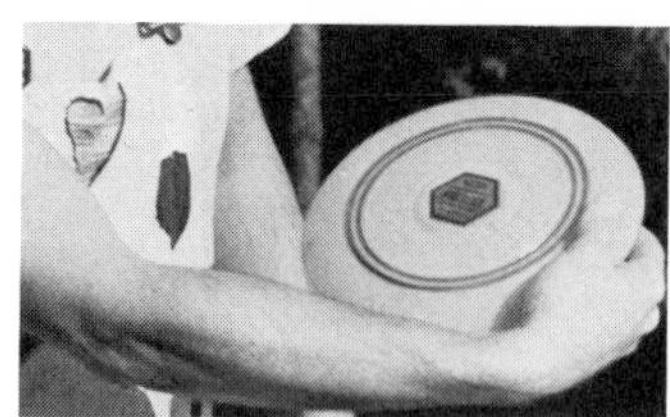

The basic Frisbee throw is the **backhand** (top). The grip is thumb on top, four fingers on the bottom. Wrist snap just before release is essential in all throws, because this produces the stabilizing spin. It's good for right and left curves and skips. It's also good for Guts, the best throw for MTA and is unbeaten in distance competition.

The sidearm or **two-finger shot** (below) can be thrown behind the back, between the legs or while running. Keep the elbow close to the body and the forearm just a bit lower than level when throwing. The short, snappy stroke for this shot is forward and angled slightly to the left. To get it off behind the back, bend the knees and arch the back slightly, using the same short, snappy stroke.

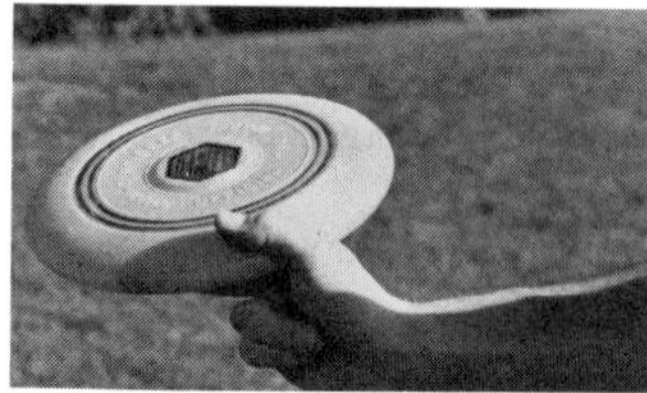

The **overhand wrist flip** (below) is held with thumb pressed against the inner rim, index finger extended and pressed against the outer rim, middle, ring and little fingers extended on top of the Frisbee toward the center. The arm is fully extended, the elbow stiff. Start the stroke with the arm extended to the rear, wrist cocked. The swing forward is almost level with your shoulder, with a slight upward angle from back to front.

be something of a showdown between May and Malafronte—longtime friends from the Berkeley Frisbee Group—but also a confrontation in styles. May throws the traditional backhand, the throw that has never been beaten in distance competition, but Malafronte uses the forehand "sidewinder." A forehand is potentially more powerful because it uses the stronger biceps muscle—like the forearm smash in tennis—but most people can't give it enough spin for a stable flight. Malafronte can, however, and when he wings it from a running start—"the *macho*-sidewinder"—it is a spectacular slingshot of a throw. He claims a personal best of 140 yards: "unofficial, of course."

As the several entrants stepped to the line, I was watching May and Malafronte, the never-been-beat backhand vs. the upstart *macho*-sidewinder. Bob May took three throws, but the best he could do today was in the mid-80s. Bob was disappointed in the way the distance throw was being run: "The wind makes such a tremendous difference," he told me. "A little gust can make a throw go 20 or 30 extra yards. The only fair way to run a distance competition is to have everyone throw at once, or at least go in heats, like three at a time. That way you cancel out the wind's effect and you can really see who throws the farthest. This way, throwing one at a time, it doesn't mean anything."

A teammate, John Kirkland, agreed with Bob May, but most of the others seemed to prefer the one-at-a-time format. When Kirkland was through with his three throws he led the distance event with a throw of 91¾ yards. "It's just luck gonna win today," he said to Bob May, and then walked over to Victor Malafronte. "Jeez, Vic," he said, "if you don't hit your throws I'm going to have to hang up that 'Great Pretender' nickname."

Malafronte stepped up and hurled three *macho*-sidewinders but they weren't working today, and none went far enough to beat 91¾ yards. Kirkland was the 1974 Distance Champ with the old standby throw—the backhand. I asked him whether he thought the backhand could be beaten.

"Sure," he said. "It's the traditional power throw, the easiest throw, but the *macho*-sidewinder is the throw of the future."

And if anyone should know about Frisbee-throwing it's John Kirkland, the Meadowlark Lemon of Frisbee, who claims he can throw 26 different ways with either hand. I have to take his word on this—I didn't count them all—but after watching him do unheard-of things with Frisbees all afternoon, I'd say 26 is a good conservative estimate.

Kirkland is a Frisbee showboater, always "on stage," whether competing or just fooling around. It got to be a familiar sight: I'd be watching some official event and then I'd look up and see John Kirkland doing something I'd never seen before. At one time he would be juggling three Frisbees, sending them in precise parabolas above his head; at another time he would be standing off to the side, casually twirling a Frisbee upside down, transferring it from his left index finger to his right index finger and back. When he wasn't soloing, he was practicing catches with Victor Malafronte. One throw was heading straight for Kirkland's chest: instead of reaching out and grabbing it like anyone else would, he placed the backs of his hands against his butt, ducked his head down, reared up—and caught it *that* way. When a low throw came in he would wait until it was between his legs and then his hand would sweep down and back, catching the Frisbee by overtaking it from behind.

The two of them, Kirkland and Malafronte, are undoubtedly the flashiest Frisbeers I have ever seen, and when they throw it back and forth it is more like a dance than a game of catch. Malafronte has a way of leaping, catching and throwing in one continuous, graceful movement, that brings Frisbee to the level of art: you've seen him do this already if you have caught that incredible TV commercial Wham-O has been running: "The new Super-Pro Frisbee from Wham-O. It flies like a dream." Though his sidewinder wasn't working for distance today, it couldn't be faulted for accuracy. After the individual competitions were over—a series of prescribed throws and catches under the eye of the judges—Malafronte was the Men's Individual World Frisbee Champion. It was appropriate that he and Kirkland were the two major individual winners, because last Fall the two of them turned professional, doing a hot-dog halftime show for the Harlem Globetrotters.

There were other events too, but I missed a lot toward the end of the day. Seeing all those flying Frisbees was just too frustrating, so I walked down to the north end zone, set my camera down by the goal post, and got into an exhausting but inspiring game of Limits. For me, it's still the only way to fly.

Like the two-finger shot, the **thumb throw** stroke is short, snappy and forward, with the elbow again held close to the body and the forearm close to level. A slight bow forward from the waist facilitates the throw.

The thumb-shot grip is also used for the **upside-down shot.** The stroke is like that of a ball thrown overhand; the Frisbee is close to horizontal, but upside down, when released.

NO EASY PITCHES, PLEASE

Hold on to your straps—Here come the new jocks.

By Susan Jacoby

One of the oldest and most widely accepted rules of the Great American Femininity Game used to decree that it was all right for girls to be good sports, but never to be good *at* sports. OK to be a good sport, because being a good sport meant losing gracefully. And, as every girl learned early on, losing was the only way to win the Femininity Game.

I was a slow learner. In fourth grade, in the 1950s, in Lansing, Mich., we still played coed baseball at recess. There were only 30 kids in the class, and there weren't 18 boys, so it was impossible to field two full teams without letting some girls play. My shining moment in sports came one day in the bottom of the ninth when I stepped up to the plate with our team a run behind, two men (boys, to be precise) on and two out. I was in love with the opposing pitcher, Lewis McCairn. We had established the fragile beginnings of a relationship, an exchange of one of his Hostess twinkies for one of my chocolate creme-filled cupcakes at lunch. He lobbed me a slow, high, easy pitch—maybe because he was a lousy pitcher, maybe because he didn't think I could hit anything. In the split second before I swung, it crossed my mind that Lewis might not like it if I knocked in a tying or winning run. But the ball was so beautiful, so slow, so easy to clobber. I hit a home run. Lewis, who hadn't learned how to be a graceful loser, stamped his foot and threw his glove on the ground. The other boys teased him because he had lost the game to a girl. We never exchanged another cupcake. It was my first lesson in the bitter fruits of beating a boy at anything.

That was the whole point of why girls were supposed to be bad at sports: to be good at athletics, whether in mixed competition or all-girl games, meant being competent at something that was supposed to be the province of boys. The lesson was driven home most strongly in high school, where the only outlet for an energetic, coordinated girl was cheerleading. Regardless of how athletically inclined they might be, girls did not become cheerleaders for the thrill of leaping, twirling or doing the splits. Cheerleaders were popular; high school homecoming queens were nearly always cheerleaders; cheerleaders had the best chance of dating the stars of the basketball and football teams.

Before the 1970s, most high schools had only the most limited intramural sports programs for girls—occasional volleyball tournaments sponsored by the Girls Athletic Association (GAA). Interscholastic competition for girls was nonexistent in most sports; in many areas of the country, local and state regulations actually banned interscholastic athletics for girls. Girls who were interested in sports could join the GAA, but they were usually regarded as musclebound freaks.

Women physical education teachers were frequently rumored to be lesbians unless they were married and had half a dozen children. Teachers who refused to excuse girls from P.E. during their menstrual periods were the targets of especially vicious attacks from teenagers and their mothers. At the high school I attended, the P.E. teacher was severely reprimanded by a counselor for telling a girl that a little exercise would help reduce the pain of first-day cramps. Who knew what might happen to the reproductive organs if volleyball instead of Midol was used to chase away cramps?

The main significance of such negative attitudes toward athletic girls was not that few girls grew up to be the female equivalents of Babe Ruth or Red Grange (although those attitudes are directly responsible for the lack of public attention and money that, until recently, has been the lot of nearly every outstanding woman athlete). After all, most boys who played in the Little League did not grow up to be Babe Ruths either. No, the broader significance was lodged deep in the mind of every girl; we grew up believing there was a contradiction between being a woman and being coordinated, capable, able to make our bodies do what we wanted them to do. (Would there be as many rapes if both men and women knew that little girls, like most little boys, have grown up learning how to run, jump, catch, throw, kick and punch if necessary?)

The stigma of being a girl jock in high school had a good deal in common with the stigma of being a "brain," but there was one important difference. Schools were required by law to provide the basic tools for girls who wanted to use their brains, even if society was delivering contradictory messages. We were taught to read but we were not taught how to throw a ball or climb a rope. A girl could develop a quick mind from an American education, circa 1950 to 1970, but she could not learn how to be quick on her feet.

The attitudes about sports that most girls grew up with until the late 1960s have under-

Sonja Henie displays the right form to use in capitalizing on a sports career.

Robyn Smith waits in the paddock for her next mount.

gone dramatic changes during the past five years. And some of the most noticeable changes are taking place where it counts the most—in the elementary and high schools. These changes can be attributed partly to the feminist movement and to the efforts of top athletes like Billie Jean King to obtain a fairer share of money and publicity for women's sports. But they are also coming from the grass roots level; it is impossible to travel around the country without realizing that today's girls' attitudes about their bodies are different from those of most women over 25. The difference is related to feminism, but is also closely connected with the changes in fashion and sexual mores that took shape in the 1960s. Girls don't torture themselves by wearing uncomfortable clothes any more—at least not during the daytime. Tight skirts, cinch belts, girdles—all of the equipment that remained standard until the mid-60s—seem as ridiculous to today's teenagers as bustles and corsets did to previous generations. Little girls who go to school in blue jeans don't need to worry about displaying their underpants or cutting their knees as they slide into a base. In cities as diverse as New York, Los Angeles and Peoria, Ill., girls tell me their teachers no longer accept menstrual periods as an excuse to get out of gym class. If a girl really is suffering from cramps, her teacher is more likely to pack her off to a doctor to find out what's wrong than to let her think that monthly physical disability is an inevitable part of becoming a woman.

"My mother thought it was really freaky that I wanted to play on a softball team," said

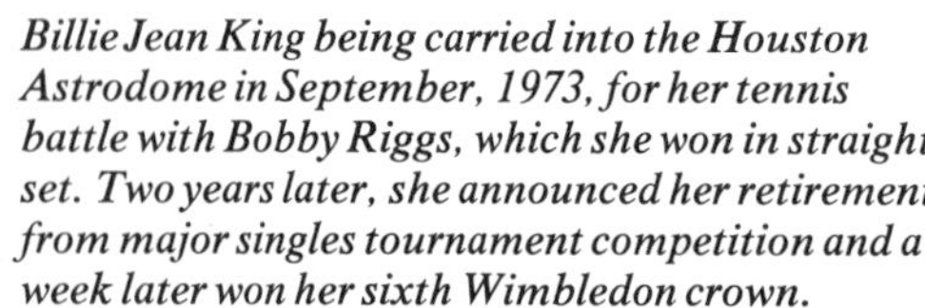

Billie Jean King being carried into the Houston Astrodome in September, 1973, for her tennis battle with Bobby Riggs, which she won in straight set. Two years later, she announced her retirement from major singles tournament competition and a week later won her sixth Wimbledon crown.

Thirteen-year-old Yvonne Burch stepped up to the plate and slammed the first pitch for a triple. She is the first girl among 300,000 boys who play in the Babe Ruth Baseball League.

a 16-year-old at Peoria Central High School. "None of my own friends, boys or girls, think anything of it. It's like swimming in summer, something you do to keep in shape. No big women's lib issue."

Although she said girls' softball was "no big women's lib issue," the same student complained bitterly because scheduled girls' games were always delayed if the boys needed the field for practice. This is a common rule in high schools and small colleges throughout the country; boys' teams are given priority over girls' teams not only in regularly scheduled games, but even in practice sessions. Last year in Cincinnati, for example, a closely fought women's intercollegiate basketball game between Miami of Ohio and the University of Cincinnati was halted with 4:50 remaining to allow the men's teams their full 35-minute warmup time.

Although the going is slow, women are fighting such practices—and fighting them successfully—in many sports and many areas of the country. The great furor over letting girls play Little League ball began in 1972 in New Jersey, when 12-year-old Maria Pepe was accepted by the Hoboken Little League team. The boys on the team said they didn't object to Maria's presence, but national League officials announced they would expel the Hoboken local if it kept a girl on the team. In the spring of 1974, after several court cases—most of them decided in favor of the girls—Little League President Creighton Hale announced that the League would "defer to the changing social climate" and let girls play. But the Babe Ruth League, for boys above age 13, is still fighting the admission of girls.

In high schools, participation of girls in both interscholastic and intramural sports has increased significantly since 1970. According to a survey released by the National Federation of State High School Associations, participation by girls in interscholastic sports increased 175 percent between 1971 and 1973, while participation by boys only increased 3 percent. That growth is due partly to the fact that most schools never bothered to provide any money for girls' interscholastic sports before Congress passed the Education Amendments Act of 1972. Title IX of the act bans sex discrimination in athletic programs sponsored by schools receiving Federal funds.

The High School Association reported that the number of girls participating in indoor and outdoor track and field events increased from 62,000 to 186,000 during the same two-year period, while participation in gymnastics doubled, from 17,000 to 35,000. Softball attracted a larger percentage of new teenage participants than any other sport; the number of girls playing on intramural and interscholastic teams rose from 9,800 to 81,000. Faced with lawsuits, many state education departments abolished rules prohibiting interscholastic competition by girls. For many years, the official rationale for such restrictions was the idea that athletics would harm the reproductive organs of teenage girls.

Collegiate athletics are already being affected by the changing attitudes of women students who acquired an interest in sports during their high school years. All large universities have active women's groups pushing for a bigger share of the athletic budget, and they are backed up by the Title IX ruling against sex discrimination in sports programs. No one knows whether the Federal government will actually require football-bloated budgets to be distributed equally among sports that attract female participation, but all of the universities have received notice that they must significantly increase the amount of money devoted to women's athletics. The government will no longer tolerate imbalances like the one at Ohio State University, which spent more than $6 million on men's athletics in 1974 and less than $43,000 on women's programs.

It will be several years before the new generation of sports-minded young women emerges into the limelight of professional athletics, but one thing is certain: like their female counterparts in every other profession, they will expect to be regarded as normal people doing a job and not as curiosities.

For the vast majority of young women who—like the majority of men—don't intend to become professional athletes, the changing attitudes toward sports simply mean that the female of the species will be stronger, fitter and better coordinated. She will not limit her activities on the basis of stereotypes that found women strong enough for childbearing but too weak for anything else. She may still know how to lose gracefully but she'll know just as much about how to win. No easy pitches, please.

Twelve-year-old Felicia Lee of Teaneck, N.J., was interviewed by *Ms* magazine after she earned a place on her local Little League team. Said Ms. Lee: "After I made the team, I read in *The New York Times* that my manager said he didn't want me on the team. I just laughed.

"In my second game, I hit a 200-foot home run. Now, my batting average is about .300.

"I'm the only girl on my team, but the boys treat me just like one of them. Pitchers on opponents' teams sometimes hit me on a pitch. Them hardballs don't tickle. I don't think they're doing it on purpose, but I got ways of finding that out. If they are doing it, I can bat that hardball right back into their faces if I have to."

"Baseball Diamonds Are a Girl's Best Friend,"
by Letty Cotton Pogrebin,
Ms Magazine, Sept., 1974

"One advantage of having girls in the [Little] league is that when candy-sales time rolls around, girls usually do a better job at bringing in money to help the program," said one league official. "Our highest candy sales were made by a girl."

WomenSports, April, 1975

My doctor (an athlete himself) said, "If it's a good egg, nothing will knock it out; if it's bad, it will abort even if you lie in bed."

From a letter to
WomenSports, April, 1975
by Mary Nickerson,
on the advantages of
exercise during pregnancy

★ SPORTS QUIZ REVEALS ALL! ★

By Scot Morris

If you'll take the time to pick the 30 sports you'd most like to try, we'll tell you what your choices reveal about the kind of person you are.

If you wouldn't mind laying down your glove, ball, club, racquet or bat for a few minutes, we'd like you to take our sports questionnaire. Assuming that you have the time, money and ability to do well in any of the 75 sports listed below, please pick the 30 you would most enjoy participating in. Which would be the most fun? (In some cases you may need a little imagination, since you probably haven't tried some of the sports. Imagine yourself as a skipper or crewperson on a racing yacht, or fantasize that you're behind the wheel of a Grand Prix racer or that you're a karate black belt or hang-gliding enthusiast.)

We'd like you to score your preferences this way: mark "10" in the space next to your first three choices; mark "9" next to the next three; "8" by the *next* three—and so on 10 times, until you've marked "1" next to the last three of your chosen 30.

Don't worry about being super precise. It might make it easier, incidentally, if you go through and check your favorite 30 without thinking about ranking at all, and then go back to rank your choices.

Disregard the numbers and letters in front of the spaces. They'll be explained to you later.

★ ★

1d___Archery
3c___Arm Wrestling
1a___Badminton
3A___Baseball
3A___Basketball
4e___Bicycle Racing
2b___Bicycling
5D___Bobsled, 4-man
1d___Bowling
5c___Boxing
1A___Bridge
3B___Canoeing
1a___Chess
1d___Darts
3c___Demolition Derby

4d___Diving (10 meters)
2c___Fencing
3D___Fig. skating (cpls)
3d___Fig. skating (indv)
1b___Fishing
4C___Football (tackle)
1d___Golf
5e___Grand Prix Racing
4d___Gymnastics
2a___Handball
5b___Hang-Gliding
3e___Harness Racing
3d___High Jump
4b___Hiking
3e___Horse Racing

3e___Hurdles
4C___Ice Hockey
3b___Ice Skating
1b___Jogging
4c___Judo
5c___Karate
4C___Lacrosse
2d___Long Jump
3e___Marathon
5e___Motorcycle Racing
5B___Mountain Climbing
1a___Ping-Pong
1a___Poker
4A___Polo
1a___Pool (billiards)

5e___Powerboat Racing
2E___Relay Racing
2D___Road Rally
3C___Roller Derby
2E___Rowing (crew)
4C___Rugby
2E___Sailing (crew racing)
3b___Sailing
2d___Shot Put
5d___Ski Jumping
3b___Skiing
4b___Skin Diving
5b___Sky Diving
3d___Slalom
3C___Soccer

3E___Sled Dog Racing
3A___Softball
3e___Speed Skating
5e___Stock Car Racing
4b___Surfing
2b___Swimming
2e___Swimming (100M freestyle)
2A___Tennis (doubles)
2a___Tennis (singles)
3C___Touch Football
2A___Tug-of-War
2A___Volleyball
3C___Water Polo
4b___Water Skiing
4c___Wrestling

Risk Factor ____ Aa___ Bb___ Cc___ Dd___ Ee___

★ ★

Now for the scoring. What we've tried to score with this quiz are two traits associated with sports: competitiveness (which is related to agressiveness), and the attraction to physical danger.

You total up your scores this way: first, add up all the *code* numbers (not the rank numbers you wrote in) next to the 30 sports you chose. Divide the total by 30 and write the result in the blank next to "risk factor score." This is your "risk quotient."

Then, add up your scores for each of the five capital and small letters, using the rank numbers you wrote in. You will have totals for five different letters, all written in the space provided.

It's impossible to say with certainty what personality traits are common to those who prefer one class of sport over another. Still, there are enough transparent differences between the sports to allow one to make some general observations. You should judge for yourself whether the statements accurately fit your character or not.

The risk-factor score is fairly easy to analyze. The average score is three; so any score much above or below that means you have a more-than-average attraction to—or aversion to—physical danger.

Now for your one-to-10 rankings: if you were absolutely evenhanded in your preferences, you would end up with 33 points in each of the five categories (you had 165 points to distribute altogether). In looking over your scores, then, you should note any marked deviation from that average—either above or below it—and pay special attention to the discussion of the sports in that particular category.

First, the 25 capital-letter sports on the list are *team* sports; the 50 small-letters designate *individual* sports. If you checked more than 10 capital letters your preference for playing on a team, rather than by yourself, is above average, and less than five is below average. There's an element of sociability in team sports: you have to be able to cooperate and get along with others to pilot a yacht or a baseball team to victory. A high small-letter score may mean that you're shy in social situations; that you're asocial or independent, or that you're so competitive you'd rather not share the glory with anyone else if you win; of course if you lose, you have to be big enough to take the loss alone—you can't blame an inept teammate if you lose a footrace. It may be that for you victories are more exciting and defeats less crushing when both can be shared with others.

The sports have been divided into five classes according to the *type of competition* involved: that is, how important it is to beat the opponent, to win, or to avoid losing.

The five categories are: active contact (Cc); active competition (Aa); passive competition (Ee); delayed competition (Dd); and no competition (Bb). The five classes are roughly in the order of decreasing competitiveness. If your score in any category is very much greater, proportionally, than your score in others, then you tend toward that competitive type, described below.

Cc: contact sports. There are 15 physical contact sports on the list, including eight team sports (touch and tackle football, ice hockey, lacrosse, roller derby, rugby, soccer, and water polo) and seven individual sports (arm wrestling, boxing, demolition derby, fencing, karate, judo, wrestling). Physical contact is the most immediate, personal form of competition. It's head-to-head, "I'm stronger, you're weaker, and I'm not afraid to put my body on the line to prove it." If your score was more than 40, you like the feeling of physical striving against other bodies, and may like to see your opponents beaten by your own hands. You may feel there is virtue in physical strength, and you may enjoy venting your hostilities by direct physical force. (A low Cc score, on the other hand, doesn't mean you're not hostile—you may have learned more subtle ways to express it.)

Aa: active competition. There are 15 Aa sports listed, eight team efforts (baseball, basketball, bridge, polo, softball, tennis—doubles, tug-of-war and volleyball) and seven individual competitions (badminton, chess, handball, Ping Pong, poker, pool and tennis—singles.) The only difference between Cc and Aa sports is that the former involve physical contact, and so are more personally, immediately competitive. Both types involve direct, active competition: you win by making your opponent lose. To play these games you must try to prevent your opponent from doing well—trick him, outsmart him, get in his way, defend your goal, block his shots, return his serve, capture his pawn, or otherwise cause him to make a poor showing, while at the same time prevailing over his efforts to do the same to you. More than 75 points here is above average and indicates your preference for direct, personal confrontation, short of physical contact.

Ee: passive competition. Three team sports of the passive-competitive sort are listed (relay racing, rowing and sailing—crew racing), and 11 individual sports (bicycle racing, Grand Prix racing, harness racing, hurdles, marathon, motorcycle racing, powerboat racing, sled dog racing, speed skating, stock car racing and swimming), making 14 in all. Participants in these sports aren't necessarily passive people, but their competition is based on winning through their own individual efforts and merits rather than by directly confronting an opponent. Those partial to this type of sport may be shying away from the personal confrontations of A and C sports: they would rather win by outshining their opponents than by "beating" them as such. When they do play an A or C sport, they'd rather play offense than defense. Opponents may see each other, but generally don't interfere; Mark Spitz and Eddie Arcaro may wish for their opponents to lose, but there is not much they can do to affect it directly. It's "You do your best, I'll do my best, and we'll see who crosses the finish line first."

If C sports are head-to-head and A sports are face-to-face, E sports are side-by-side. The competition is still simultaneous: the winner can look back and see those he has beaten; the loser knows he has lost as soon as he crosses the finish line. In the next sport category, passive competition is made even more passive, through delay:

Dd: delayed competition. Fifteen delayed competition sports are listed, including three team sports (four-man bobsled, figure skating—couples and road rally, and 12 individual (archery, bowling, darts, diving, skiing, figure skating—individual, golf, gymnastics, high jump, long jump, shot put and ski jumping). In these sports, the competition may be intense, but it is impersonal: it's not so much me against you, as both of us against some agreed-upon standard: a stopwatch, a measuring tape, par or a judge's decision. The competition is not simultaneous: "I'll take my best shot, then you take yours, and then we'll measure to see who won." The joy of winning is still there, but it is a matter of individual pride in achievement rather than in beating someone else; and the pain of losing is tempered by the fact that one may never have to face the person who has beaten him.

Bb: no competition. Sixteen are listed, including two team sports (canoeing and mountain climbing), and 14 individual sports (bicycling, darts, fishing, hang-gliding, ice skating, jogging, mountain climbing, sailing, skiing, skin diving, sky diving, surfing, swimming and water skiing). These are the activities usually played "for the fun of it," with little or no competitiveness involved. There may be winners and losers (e.g., darts) and any of them *can* be performed competitively, but the emphasis, for most people, is on sociability, amusement, and self-improvement. If you have a high Bb score then competing with others doesn't interest you much: you'd rather be a friend than a hero, and you probably don't get much kick out of seeing others proven inferior to you. You reject the competition-ethic for some reason: perhaps it's insecurity and a fear of losing; perhaps it's excessive compassion and a fear of winning, or seeing others beaten. At any rate, you'd rather cooperate than compete, and avoid classifying people—including yourself—as superior and inferior, better and worse; and prefer to enhance yourself by expanding your experiences rather than your victories.

THE SPORTING OF AMERICA

Mr. Gallup asks a nation at play about their favorite sports.

One of the most remarkable trends of the last decade and a half—a trend which appears to be gaining momentum—is the growth in interest in sports, in terms of both participation and attendance at sports events.

The sharpest increases in terms of participation since the 1959 survey have been recorded for swimming, bowling, tennis and baseball (including softball). But considerable growth in the percentage of participants has also been noted for volleyball, golf, horseback riding, skiing and ice skating.

At the same time, however, participation in the traditional outdoor activities of hunting and fishing appears to have levelled off or declined.

Following is the question asked to measure sports participation, and the comparison showing the trend:

"Which of these sports and activities have you, yourself, participated in within the past 12 months?"

Participated In At Least Once During Last 12 Months

	1959	Latest	Point Change
Swimming	33%	42%	+ 9
Fishing	32	24	- 8
Bowling	18	28	+10
Hunting	16	14	- 2
Baseball/softball	11	19	+ 8
Golf	8	14	+ 6
Ice skating	6	9	+ 3
Horseback riding	5	10	+ 5
Roller skating	4	5	+ 1
Tennis	4	12	+ 8
Volleyball	4	11	+ 7
Skiing	3	5	+ 2

Several factors can be cited for the sharp growth in sports participation, including growing affluence, increased leisure time, the desire to escape crowded living conditions and the continued stress on the importance of exercise for health.

Sports Attendance Also up Since '59

The growth in sports participation has been paralleled by an increase in sports attendance, particularly in the case of soccer, football, boxing, hockey and basketball.

Here is the question asked and the table showing the comparison between the 1959 and latest surveys:

"Which of the sports on this card have you, yourself, attended in person within the last 12 months—that is, since this time last year?"

Sports Attended At Least Once During Last 12 Months

	1959	Latest	Point Change
Baseball	28%	30%	+ 2
Football	23	33	+10
Basketball	18	23	+ 5
Stock car racing	9	2	- 7
Horse racing	9	10	+ 1
Wrestling	6	7	+ 1
Boxing	4	14	+10
Hockey (ice)	4	7	+ 3
Dog racing	2	4	+ 2
Tennis	2	2	——
Track & field	2	6	+ 4
Soccer	1	13	+12

It is important to bear in mind that the above figures include attendance at high school and college as well as professional games.

Football is currently America's No. 1 spectator sport.

The latest results show 32 per cent of all American adults naming football as their favorite sport to watch, compared to 24 per cent who named baseball. Next is basketball, named by nine per cent.

In 1937, in the first sports poll ever taken, baseball was named as the favorite sport by 36 per cent of people interviewed, while football was named by 26 per cent. Basketball was third, named by 11 per cent.

By 1948 baseball was even more entrenched as the nation's favorite spectator sport. However, from that point on football started to gain in appeal, while baseball declined in appeal.

The latest survey shows a slight drop-off in football's appeal and a gain for baseball since an early 1972 survey. Seasonal differences, however, may account for this slight change in preferences, since this year's survey was conducted shortly after the end of the baseball season, while the previous measurement was taken just prior to the 1972 Super Bowl.

The latest Gallup sports audit is based on in-person interviews with 1,616 adults, 18 and older, interviewed in more than 300 scientifically selected localities during October and November.

Favorite Sport To Watch

	Latest	'72	'61	'48	'37
Football	32%	36%	21%	17%	26%
Baseball	24	21	34	39	36
Basketball	9	8	9	10	11

A Nation of Spectators — Americans name the one sport they enjoy watching most.

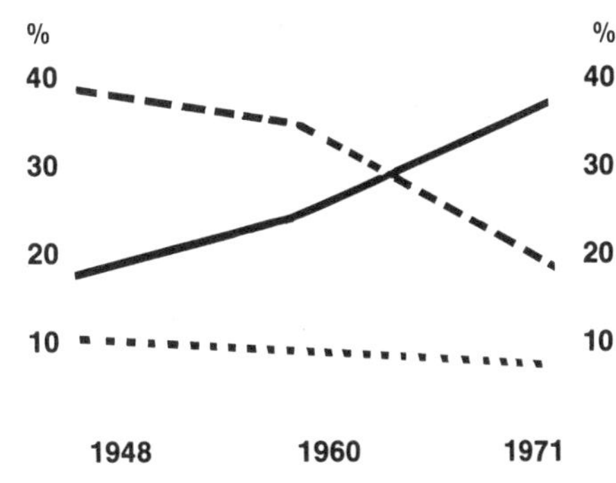

Football, named by 36 per cent of all Americans, now outranks baseball as the country's most popular spectator sport. Basketball finishes third.

Favorite Sport To Watch

	1972 %	1961 %	1948 %
Football	36	21	17
Baseball	21	34	39
Basketball	8	9	10
Bowling	4	5	1
Wrestling	3	5	1
Hockey	3	3	2
Skiing	2	1	*
Boxing	1	3	3
Golf	1	1	*
Swimming	*	1	2
Horse Racing	1	*	4
Other	10	4	9
Don't know	10	13	12

Less than one per cent

Here are the results from a recent survey broken down by men and women:

	Men	Women
Football	44%	28%
Baseball	24	17
Basketball	6	10
Bowling	2	6

Past Gallup International surveys have shown that skiing is the most popular spectator sport in the Scandinavian Countries, while soccer captures the top rating throughout other parts of Europe.

Umpteen million people file into modern pleasure palaces like this to pursue their sporting pleasures.

GAMES PEOPLE SHOULD PLAY

The wave of the future? Jimmy Connors playing Yogi Tag, Billie Jean King, Mating.

The seasons are subtle and often mischievous in my part of California. Spring is early but undependable; languorous January days may precede slashing winter storms. To know the change of seasons, I depend not on calendar or temperature but the ten-year-old next door. A day comes (never mind the weather) when he marches from his house carrying a baseball and glove rather than a football and helmet, and I am satisfied that a seasonal milestone has passed.

My amber-eyed, honey-haired neighbor is slight of build but large of heart. He has a voice for driving mules. During football season that voice takes on the clipped authority of a quarterback directing a two-minute drill. When the baseball is flying that same voice achieves a Middle Eastern drone. Pepper talk. "Put-it-there-baby-now-let's-hear-it-attaboy-baby-come-on-come-on-let's-have-it-right-here-baby-at's-the-way." My neighbor plays flag football (tight end) and Little League baseball (pitcher). After the games, he returns to our neighborhood, his face flushed with the heat of victory or salt-encrusted with the tears of defeat. Still, he has not had enough. On those afternoons, the ball flies up and falls back into his hands until it is a pale shadow against the trees. We have no way of knowing his particular dreams as he plays with gravity and darkness, but we do know that he has a tried-and-true portfolio from which to choose: the tie-breaking home run, locker-room jubilation, his name on bubble-gum wrappers.

The games he has taken for his own are rich ones, reaching wide and deep into the culture and the psyche. They have well-established heroes and traditions, a reliable vocabulary, thoroughly documented norms, and satisfying complex strategies. They connect with the larger world in a thousand known and unknown ways, yet they are worlds in themselves, complete with relationship, redundancy, difference—the pattern of certainty upon which men with confusing lives can practice making fine distinctions. No wonder disagreements concerning three points out of a thousand in a batting average can start a fight in a bar. And if all this were not enough, there are hidden dimensions, worlds within worlds, in even the most traditional games.

And yet the moment finally comes in every culture when the larger world itself begins to change in ways that confound the old games and the old rules. Our most cherished sports begin to parody themselves. One time too many the announcer reaches down into that bottomless bag of statistics to tell us that a new record for triples in one game by left-handed batters against left-handed pitchers on cloudy days has just been set. One time too many we leave the television set dispirited and dyspeptic after nine straight hours of pro action and God knows how much beer and peanuts. At last (the moment finally comes) we are sick of being pummeled and twisted and squeezed dry by every promoter who can sell another ticket, put together another league or push another underarm deodorant.

It all started back in school, when we began learning precisely those sports that are least likely to become lifelong pursuits. My ten-year-old neighbor may have vivid dreams, but the cold odds are long against his playing baseball or football into his thirties. Those and the other team sports taught in the typical high-school athletic program practically demand that we turn into adult spectators and gulls. They call for specialized, standardized players, officials, coaches, equipment salesmen. They are exclusive, hierarchical. They travel poorly and age not well at all. For the run-of-the-mill householder, a gridiron, diamond or court is a place to practice sitting down.

And what if we *could* play football, basketball, baseball all of our lives? Would we really *want* to? Anthropologists, after decades of neglect, are beginning to study the significance of play. their basic conclusion is obvious if overdue: a culture's sports and games mirror the culture's structure and values. That being the case and the world being as it is today, let's ask how much more we need to encourage aggression and territorial war (football), relentless fakery (basketball) and obsession with records and categories (baseball). It's a fundamental law of evolution that the final period in any line of development is marked by grotesqueries and extremes. The widespread glorification of winning at all costs reached its height during a war this nation did not win. Hyped-up sports metaphor—"game plans," "enemy lists" and the like—came to preoccupy a national Administration just before that game was up. Even tennis, once a relatively gentle and somewhat stuffy game, began to go crazy as it went public. Net play more and more resembled World War II, with red-faced, tense-muscled, middle-aged men crouching at the front lines every Sunday, itching to fire their nylon howitzers down their opponent's throats. And golfers by the millions still idolize Arnold Palmer, even though he is past his prime, simply because he found a way to liken this game of contemplative strolls and shimmering distances to a calvary charge. No wonder I began to find the sports section of my newspaper particularly unsatisfactory. The new games of a new culture should have their physical equivalents, but here were the same old pictures, the same old cliches, year after year. By the mid-sixties the World Series had lost its charm for me. I watched the Super Bowl on television, but each year I swore I wouldn't watch it the next. The football I kept in the trunk of my car went flat. I turned to the more complex and aerodynamically pleasing flight of the Frisbee. I took up aikido, a martial art that completely dismantles the game of attack and defense as we know it.

I began to have my own dreams of sports glory. I envisaged a Super Bowl of the new culture. A mythic valley, sunstruck at noon, shrouded by mist in the setting sun. Tents and domes and multicolored banners. Thousands of people glowing with their own radiance—all players, no spectators. Men, women and children playing together, flowing in and out of games which themselves flow and change. The air filled with Frisbees, balls, kites and laughter. A scene both medieval and surreal. A picture by Brueghel, Salvador Dali and Hieronymus Bosch. A tournament of new games!

The dream did not wholly possess me; it seemed too unlikely. But I managed to get a piece of it into my 1968 book, *Education and Ecstasy*. I thought I was describing a playfield of the year 2001, where futuristic children could glide gracefully past the limiting boundaries of our present-day sports. But futurists are always wrong. The first New Games Tournament took place not in the twenty-first century, but in October, 1973. Over five thousand people attended, and it was held, yes, in a mythic valley in the Marin County headlands near the edge of the Pacific. In many ways, the event surpassed my dreams.

Early in September, 1973, [Stewart] Brand phoned to tell me that his own POINT Foundation, originally endowed with about a million dollars left over from the *Whole Earth Catalog*, was giving $12,500 for a New Games Tournament of large dimensions. They had their hands on a fabulous piece of land, 2200 acres of wild valley and rolling hills. The Tournament would be held as soon as possible, to beat the winter rains. He asked me to be there.

A month later, at noon on Friday, October 19, the first New Games Tournament officially opened. At that hour, some of the pavilions and winglike tensile structures were not quite completed; our aikido mat, a canvas tarp stretched out over straw, was still "on the way"; and there seemed to be more media people than game-players in attendance. But by the next afternoon there were some two thousand people playing Earth Ball, Le Mans Tug-O-War, Infinity Volleyball, Yogi Tag, New Frisbee, Boffing, Slaughter and other games too numerous or obscure to mention. The rains came that night, so the Sunday session was canceled and the Games were repeated the next weekend, on two gorgeous Indian summer days.

During that first Tournament, something about the nature of New Games began to come clear. We learned that the team games adapt themselves easily to groups of varying size. Earth Ball, for example, can be played by two people or by two hundred, the object of the most common version being simply to push the six-foot ball over one goal line or another. Players can wander in and out of the game at the end of each segment of play. A majority of the games require no specialized equipment whatever. No game is played against time as are football, soccer, basketball and the like; a leisured sense of informality generally prevails. And all the games are subject to further evolution. They are, in physical-education jargon, "low-organization games."

Regular teams, standings and statistics would be impossible in this setting. Sharp competition adds spice to the proceedings, but there is simply no way to build up the rigid machinery that supports the overblown, institutionalized, codified worship of winning that currently defaces our national sports scene.

Slaughter was played, with more laughter than strategy, at the Tournament, and there were other games offering hard physical contact for those who wanted it. But there were also gentle games and games of cooperation. In Infinity Volleyball, for instance, the object is to see how long the ball can be kep in the air. Just as in regular volleylball, no team must hit the ball more than three times before sending it over the net. Both teams chant the number of times the ball has been hit, and both share the final score. This game was among the Tournament's most popular.

New Frisbee

The day passes swiftly. The sun drops behind a hill and a pennant of afternoon fog slips in to take its place. Deliciously exhausted, I return home.

That night I phone a friend who had turned down my invitation to come to the Tournament since he had tickets to a pro football game.

"How was the game?" I ask.

"Terrible. The Forty-niners lost."

"How was the traffic?"

"Terrible. It was awful."

I can't resist another question. "Did your children enjoy it?"

"Oh, they didn't go. I only had two tickets."

He asks about the Tournament and I begin telling him. But it's hard to explain. And anyway he's not very interested. So we talk about the 49ers. It's not a very good year. There are some injuries at key positions. But maybe next week. The game will be on TV.

For people who would like to try new games, here are the rules for seven:

1. New Frisbee

New Frisbee is based on the principles of maximum performance, human potential and impeccable personal morality. There are in this game no officials and no lined areas—and there must be none.

Before beginning play, both players declare with which hand they will throw and catch. They may throw and catch with different hands or with the same hand; they must, however, throw and catch with the declared hand throughout the game. (A player may throw right and catch left if he or she wishes.) Players take turns throwing and catching.

Thrower launches the Frisbee in any direction. Catcher makes an all-out attempt to reach it and catch it.

If catcher cannot possibly reach and touch the Frisbee at any time during its flight, *catcher takes one point.* To establish all-out effort of maximum performance, catcher must follow a direct course toward the best possible position to catch the Frisbee and, if close enough to reach it by diving, must dive.

If the Frisbee comes within catcher's potential limits and yet catcher fails to reach and touch it—that is, if catcher fails to make an all-out effort or misjudges the Frisbee's flight —*catcher gives one point to thrower.*

If catcher touches the Frisbee, then drops it, *catcher gives thrower two points.* Catcher must give thrower two points if the Frisbee touches any part of catcher's body, then falls, or if the catcher catches the Frisbee with the wrong hand, or if the Frisbee is caught by cradling against the body or other arm.

If the Frisbee should tilt more than forty-five degrees from the horizontal at any time during its flight, catcher may call aloud "Forty five!" In this case, *catcher takes one point.* The call must be made while the Frisbee is still in flight.

If catcher makes a clean catch with the declared hand, *no points are received by either player.* Perfection is expected and thus not extrinsically rewarded.

If catcher is in danger of running into a physical obstacle, catcher or thrower should call, "Obstacle!" loudly. The point is then replayed. If at this point there is another obstacle, *catcher takes one point.*

Catcher calls all points. Upon hearing the call, thrower must make no outcry or gesture of disapproval. A *casual game* consists of eleven points. Players change sides when one player reaches six points. The first player to reach eleven points wins.

A *match game* consists of twenty-one points. Players change sides when one player reaches eleven points. The first player to reach twenty-one points wins. At least one knowledgeable observer must be present at match games. Observers are encouraged to applaud good plays and good calls. Though they cannot change catcher's calls, observers' signs of approval or disapproval may be helpful in catcher's efforts to evaluate his or her physical physical limits.

2. Infinity Volleyball

The object of this game of cooperation is to keep the ball on the volley indefinitely. In general, the normal rules of volleyball apply, except that no specified number of players is required. As in regular volleyball, one team may hit the ball no more than three times before sending it over the net. Players of both teams chant aloud the number of times the ball has been volleyed. Both teams share the final score. For average players, any score over fifty is very good; one hundred or more is phenomenal.

3. Yogi Tag (or Dho-dho-dho)

Yogi Tag, a game of speed, agility and breath control, is played on a relatively flat area that can be divided into two equal parts by a center line. In this game of reflexes and balance, the surface should be soft enough to cushion a fall. Typical play areas are a gym mat, beach or grassy area. Any number can play, depending upon the size of the play area.

Players divide themselves, half on each side of the center line, thus forming two ad hoc teams. The two teams take turns sending one player across the center line. A flip of a coin may decide which team sends a player first.

Before crossing the line into opposing territory, the player takes a deep breath. From the moment player crosses the line, he or she must say aloud, "Dho-dho-dho," in a continuous flow, without taking a breath. If at any time in opponents' territory player stops making this sound, player is out of the game. The purpose is to touch one or more players of the opposing team and return safely to home territory, all in

Standoff

one breath. If the player can make it back across the line with any part of the body, even a fingertip, before running out of breath, all the opponents the player touched must leave the game.

The opposing team members, however, attempt to catch the invading player and to hold him or her in their territory until the invader is out of breath, in which case the invading player must leave the game, and those the invading player may have touched can remain in the game.

As soon as one interaction is completed and all players who have been eliminated have left the play area, the other team may immediately send one of their players across the center line. Play continues alternately until all the players of one of the teams have been eliminated.

In capturing and detaining an invading player, *team members must use no unnecessary force.* No running tackles are allowed, and no one can be grasped below the waist. Anyone using unnecessary force must leave the game. Either a referee or the honor system may be used to enforce the rules.

4. Environmental Tag

Any number may play this game of speed and ecological knowledge. The game-planner lays out a course about a quarter of a mile long. Starting at home base, players are taken on a nature walk along the course, during which they are told the names of ten to fifteen flowers, trees or other plants. At the far end of the course, certain players are appointed as "it." There should be an "it" for every five to ten players. The object of the game is to get back to home base without being tagged by "it." Players are safe whenever they are touching one of the identified plants. "It" may challenge players to name the plant they are touching. If they fail to do so, they are considered to be tagged and thus out of the game. "It" also may tag players in the normal manner when they are not touching identified plants. All those who reach home base win.

5. Standoff

In this game of reflexes and balance, two players stand facing one another so that the fingertips of the shorter player can reach the shoulders of the other. Each player must stand with feet together at heel and toe. Players place hands in front of them chest high, palms toward opponent's palms. The object is to strike opponent's palms in such a way as to make opponent lose balance. The first player to move either foot, or to fall into the other player, loses. If a player strikes the other player anywhere except on the palms, he or she loses. The first player to make the other lose balance five times is the match winner.

6. Mating

For this acting game, you must provide cards bearing the names and/or pictures of mammals, birds, fish and reptiles. Endangered species are preferred—golden eagle, Rocky Mountain wolf, brown pelican, etc. There must be the same number of cards as there are players, and two cards for each species. The cards are shuffled the the players draw. All the players enter a circle. On their hands and knees and without using words, they act out the part of their species in an attempt to locate their mate. Once mating has occurred, signified by holding hands or embracing, that couple may leave the circle. The last two players in the circle have the honor of planning the next game.

7. Circle Football

This tricky and particularly exciting game offers the New Games strategist almost unlimited possibilities. It is played in a circle of from thirty to fifty yards in diameter, depending upon the number of players. (Thirty yards is good for two teams of five players each.) There is another concentric circle five yards outside the first circle, creating a peripheral *goal zone,* analogous to the end zone in ordinary football. In the center of these circles, there is an *inner circle* two yards in diameter. A *corridor* two yards wide extends from the inner circle to the goal zone.

After a huddle, one member of the offense, the *passer,* stands with the ball in the inner circle. Other members of the offense, as well as the entire defensive team, may position themselves anywhere between the inner circle and the goal zone. The passer begins play by counting aloud, at one-second intervals.

When the count begins, all players may move. Before the count reaches fifteen, passer must either pass the ball or run down the corridor toward the goal zone. While in the inner circle, passer is safe. In the corridor, passer may be tagged or tackled, depending upon the mode of play agreed upon. Passer may start down corridor then return to inner circle, but can pass only from inner circle.

Passer may pass to any member of offensive team. Offensive player who catches ball may either attempt to run to goal and thus score one point, or may pass to another team member. Unlimited passing is allowed. If pass is not completed or if offensive player is tagged or tackled before scoring, ball comes back to passer for a new down. Three downs are allowed before ball goes over to other team.

If defensive team intercepts a pass, it may attempt to score immediately. If defense intercepts and fails to score, it gains possession of the ball for three downs.

Rules not covered here are guided by the rules of ordinary football.

Warning. Players new to this game may encounter unexpected collisions. Since Circle Football is a game of 360-degrees, all-around alertness is required as never before. Hard body-blocking is not recommended.

Environmental Tag

photo credits

Baseball Hall of Fame	16, 28
Edmund's Book Store	50, 51, 118, 123, 120
Gulf Photo	219
Harlem Globetrotters	96
Indianapolis Motor Speedway	153
Loew's Inc.	51
Kate May	212
Pro Football Hall of Fame	16, 74
Rand McNally	136
Milt Roth	124, 125
20th Century Fox	50
United Artists	50, 163
UPI	10, 12, 13, 49, 59, 66, 72, 80, 100, 101, 103, 104, 105, 106, 107, 109, 113, 127, 137, 147, 148, 149, 151, 154, 155, 158, 165, 166, 180, 196, 203, 204, 214
USC	83
Wide World Photos	10, 11, 12, 13, 18, 19, 20, 21, 23, 24, 25, 26, 27, 29, 30, 31, 32, 36, 37, 40, 48, 57, 59, 60, 61, 64, 66, 67, 70, 71, 75, 76, 77, 78, 79, 81, 82, 89, 91, 92, 93, 94, 97, 98, 99, 105, 108, 111, 117, 119, 121, 122, 124, 130, 134, 135, 136, 141, 143, 147, 151, 152, 156, 157, 160, 161, 162, 164, 165, 169, 175, 177, 184, 185, 187, 188, 189, 190, 191, 192, 193, 195, 197, 198, 200, 201, 202, 204, 205, 206, 207, 213, 214, 215

How to Keep Young By Leroy Satchel Paige

1. Avoid fried meats which angry up the blood.

2. If your stomach disputes you, lie down and pacify it with cool thoughts.

3. Keep the juices flowing by jangling around gently as you move.

4. Go very lightly on the vices, such as carrying on in society. The social ramble ain't restful.

5. Avoid running at all times.

6. Don't look back. Something might be gaining on you.